PAST
IMPERFECT

*History According
to the Movies*

GENERAL EDITOR: MARK C. CARNES

*Edited by
Ted Mico, John Miller-Monzon, and David Rubel*

A Society of American Historians Book
To Encourage Literary Distinction in the Writing of History and Biography

An Owl Book
HENRY HOLT AND COMPANY
NEW YORK

Henry Holt and Company, Inc.
Publishers since 1866
115 West 18th Street
New York, New York 10011

Henry Holt® is a registered trademark
of Henry Holt and Company, Inc.

Library of Congress Cataloging-in-Publication Data
Past imperfect: history according to the movies/general editor,
Mark C. Carnes.—1st ed.
p. cm.
"A Society of American Historians book."
Includes index.
1. Historical films—History and criticism. 2. Motion pictures
and history. I. Carnes, Mark C. (Mark Christopher). II. Series.
PN1995.9.H5P37   1995   95-354
791.43'658—dc20   CIP

ISBN 0-8050-3759-4
ISBN 0-8050-3760-8 (An Owl Book: pbk.)

Henry Holt books are available for special promotions and
premiums. For details contact: Director, Special Markets.

First published in hardcover in 1995 by Henry Holt and Company.

First Owl Book Edition—1996

An Agincourt Press Book

President: David Rubel
Art Director: Tilman Reitzle

Design: Sherry Williams
Photo Research: Khara Nemitz
Maps: Alan Irikura
**Portraits of John Sayles & Eric Foner
    and Mark Carnes & Oliver Stone:** David Plakke
Editorial: Mary Elin Korchinsky, Julia Banks Rubel
Research: Lisa Aschkenasy, Susanne Pichler
Copy Editor: Ron Boudreau
Proofreader: Paul Lipari

We would like to acknowledge the assistance of Tom Benton and Ed Benton of Video Cave, Hudson, New York;
Geri Fallo; Deborah Goodsite of The Bettmann Archive; Kiggundu Michael Mukasa; Jerry Ohlinger and John
Garzillo of Jerry Ohlinger's Movie Material Store; Sal Principato; and George Vogel.

For text permissions and photo credits, see page 320.

Printed in the United States of America
All first editions are printed on acid-free paper. ∞

10 9 8 7 6 5 4 3 2 1
10 9 8 7 6 5 4 3 2 1 (pbk.)

CONTENTS

65,000,000 B.C.
The species *Velociraptor* becomes extinct along with the rest of the dinosaurs.

c.1250 B.C.E.
Moses defies Pharaoh Ramses II and leads the Hebrews out of slavery in Egypt.

73-71 B.C.
Spartacus leads a slave rebellion against the Romans.

March 15, 44 B.C.
Brutus, Cassius, and other republican-minded senators assassinate Roman dictator Julius Caesar.

October 25, 1415
Henry V and his English army defeat the French at Agincourt.

May 30, 1431
At Rouen, Joan of Arc is burned at the stake as a heretic.

1492
Christopher Columbus makes his first voyage to the New World.

January 25, 1533
Henry VIII of England secretly marries second wife Anne Boleyn.

July 6, 1535
Thomas More is beheaded for refusing to support Henry VIII in his Great Matter.

July 4, 1561
Lope de Aguirre and the remnants of the Ursúa expedition reach the mouth of the Amazon.

1632
French Jesuits in Canada begin annual publication of the *Relations*.

1757
A French and Indian army besieges Fort William Henry on the New York State frontier.

June 28, 1762
Catherine the Great becomes empress of Russia after a military coup.

July 4, 1776
The Second Continental Congress adopts the Declaration of Independence.

August 2, 1777
Col. Barry St. Leger besieges American militiamen at Fort Stanwix in the Mohawk Valley.

1903
Abraham Cahan begins editing the *Jewish Daily Forward*.

April 25, 1915
Australian and New Zealand troops invade Turkey's Gallipoli peninsula.

July 1, 1916
The first battle of the Somme begins when eleven British divisions attack across a fifteen-mile front.

October 26, 1917
V.I. Lenin's Bolshevik party establishes a revolutionary government in Russia.

January 15, 1919
During the Spartacist Revolt, Rosa Luxemburg is arrested and executed by Berlin police.

May 5, 1920
Anarchists Nicola Sacco and Bartolomeo Vanzetti are arrested for the murder of a factory paymaster.

1920
A bitter coal-mine strike in southern West Virginia culminates in the Matewan Massacre.

May 1923
Chinese bandits seize a train bound for Tientsin and hold twenty-six Western passengers for ransom.

October 31, 1926
Harry Houdini dies of peritonitis in a Detroit hospital.

May 29, 1932
The Bonus Army of World War I veterans arrives in Washington, D.C.

May 23, 1934
Bonnie Parker and Clyde Barrow are ambushed and killed outside Arcadia, Louisiana.

May 1934
Dust storms blow the topsoil off more than fifty million acres of farmland in the Midwest.

December 7, 1941
A Japanese surprise attack on Pearl Harbor devastates the U.S. Pacific Fleet.

August 2, 1943
A Japanese destroyer rams PT 109, commanded by Lt. John F. Kennedy.

June 6, 1944
The D-Day invasion begins with Allied landings at five beaches in Normandy.

March 28, 1945
The U.S. Third Army under Gen. George S. Patton, Jr., begins crossing the Rhine in force.

July 16, 1945
Scientists from the Los Alamos laboratory detonate the first atomic bomb at Alamogordo, New Mexico.

August 9, 1945
Soviet tanks invade Manchuria, which has been a Japanese puppet state since 1932.

August 15, 1947
India becomes independent after nearly two centuries of British colonial rule.

September 30, 1953
Robert Anderson's *Tea and Sympathy* premieres on Broadway.

December 5, 1955
Blacks in Montgomery, Alabama, begin a year-long boycott of that city's segregated buses.

1962
Herman Kahn publishes *Thinking About the Unthinkable*.

November 22, 1963
President John F. Kennedy is assassinated in Dallas.

June 21, 1964
Three civil rights workers disappear in Neshoba County, Mississippi.

February 21, 1965
Members of the Nation of Islam murder Malcolm X at the Audubon Ballroom in New York City.

April 13, 1970
Fifty-five hours after liftoff, an oxygen tank in the Apollo 13 service module explodes.

April 30, 1970
President Richard Nixon reveals that U.S. troops in Vietnam have crossed into Cambodia.

June 17, 1972
Police arrest five men for breaking into the Democratic party offices at the Watergate.

August 8, 1974
During a nationally televised speech, Richard Nixon announces that he will resign the presidency.

INTRODUCTION

Historians love movies about the past, and this book proves it. All of its three score authors gleefully leapt vast chasms of commitments, raced to their VCRs, crafted their essays, and returned them by next-day mail. Well, perhaps not. Like all renderings of the past, this one fails to encompass a multitude of thoughts and actions—a multitude, in any case, of phone calls and faxes.

But even if all imagined pasts are imperfect, their imperfections are distinctive. Professional historians, for example, pluck from the muck of the historical record the most solid bits of evidence, mold them into meanings, and usually serve them up as books that, though encrusted with footnotes and redolent of musty archives, can be held and cherished, pondered and disputed.

Hollywood History is different. It fills irritating gaps in the historical record and polishes dulling ambiguities and complexities. The final product gleams, and it sears the imagination. Who can forget Marlene Dietrich as Catherine the Great, George C. Scott as Patton, or Ben Kingsley as Gandhi? Even Malcolm X, whose meteoric career blazed through our own times, becomes hard to distinguish from Denzel Washington's electrifying portrayal of him. Hollywood History sparkles because it is so morally unambiguous, so devoid of tedious complexity, so *perfect*.

Books, Gore Vidal has observed, have had their day—or rather, millennium. Much as the printed word superseded oral traditions, movies and television have eclipsed Gutenberg's cumbersome invention. Vidal suggests that we concede the inevitable, scrap the existing educational system, and introduce the young to the past through film. The idea is not that farfetched, nor even that farsighted. Many history teachers of TV-besotted students have committed a fair proportion of instructional time to films such as *1492*, *Gandhi*, and *Malcolm X*. Video distribution companies target schools as a major market. And television's continuous old movies function as night school, a great repository of historical consciousness in these United States of Amnesia. For many, Hollywood History is the only history.

They could do worse. Many of the authors of these essays acknowledge that movies were what attracted them to history as youngsters: Yul Brynner's sword-wielding bravado in *The Buccaneer*; Ingrid Bergman's fearless innocence as Joan of Arc; John Wayne's single-handed defense of Civilization against the onslaught of (at times indistinguishable) Mexicans, Indians, and Commies. The purpose of this book is not to censure, much less censor, the filmmakers to whom we are indebted. (I suspect they will be neither chastened by our criticisms, nor heartened by our praise.) In any case, a movie script is (mercifully) not a dissertation; a feature film is not a documentary. Shakespeare, by omitting the fact that Henry V slaughtered hundreds of French prisoners at Agincourt, perhaps failed as a historian; yet we do not propose that *Henry V* be stricken from the literary canon, or that some committee of earnest historians undertake its revision.

Like drama and fiction, movies inspire and entertain. They often teach important truths about the human condition. They do not provide a substitute for history that has been painstakingly assembled from the best available evidence and analysis. But sometimes filmmakers, wholly smitten by their creations, proclaim them to be historically "accurate" or "truthful," and many viewers presume them to be so. Viewers should neither accept such claims nor dismiss them out of hand, but regard them as an invitation for further exploration.

Past Imperfect opens with Eric Foner's conversation with director John Sayles; and it concludes, through the spiritualist medium of Simon Schama, with an interview of Napoleon Bonaparte. In between, we examine nearly one hundred films, proceeding in chronological fashion according to the subject of the movie, from Stephen Jay Gould's discussion of dinosaurs (as revivified by Steven Spielberg in *Jurassic Park*) to William Leuchtenburg's essay on *All the President's Men* about Watergate.

We have attempted to encompass as many times and places as possible. Though most of the films were made by Hollywood, we have also included Australian, Japanese, German, French, Canadian, British, and independent American films. Even in these cases we have occasionally used "Hollywood" in the generic sense to distinguish film from historical fact.

Some of the movies we discuss were not regarded as historical when they were made, but have since become important historical documents: For example, *Tea and Sympathy* explored tensions over homosexuality in the 1950s, and *Dr. Strangelove*, fears of nuclear deterrence in the 1960s. Even some explicitly "historical" films are chiefly important for what they say about the era in which they were made. Cecil B. DeMille's lavish depiction of ancient Egypt in his *The Ten Commandments* (1956) served as a dusty mirror to the soulless materialism he perceived in 1950s America. Similarly, *Bonnie and Clyde* (1967) revealed more about gender in the Sixties than gangsters in the Thirties.

Because movies have powerfully affected the way we visualize the past, we have juxtaposed film stills with paintings or photographs of the historical subjects. (Warner Brothers, which encourages popular magazines and tabloids to make free use of its film stills, denied us permission to do so on a paying basis.) We have devoted the second page of each essay to these juxtapositions, provocatively labeled "History" and "Hollywood." Hans Holbein's sixteenth-century painting of Thomas More was not the historical More. As Plato pointed out, a representation of a thing is not the thing itself; yet a comparison of renderings is instructive.

Filmmakers have had their say about the past. They have spoken both eloquently and foolishly. Sometimes their fabrications have gone unnoticed, sometimes their truths unappreciated. But they have spoken, nearly always, in ways we find fascinating. We acknowledge from the outset movies' unique capacity for stimulating dialogue about the past. This book serves not as a rebuttal, but as a reply— one of many, we hope. We think of *Past Imperfect* in the grammatical sense of continuing action: This book is our contribution to the ongoing conversation between past and present.

Mark C. Carnes
Barnard College, Columbia University

John Sayles: Why do people make movies about history? That's a question with a lot of different answers, and the answer depends on who the muscle behind the movie is. Sometimes historical movies get made because they're just good stories, and it's easier to begin with a story that already exists than to pick one up out of your head. Somebody's already done the living and the plot. Very often, if the story is fairly old history, if it's more than fifty years old, there's been some shaping over the years—the story has become legend—so a lot of the details that aren't necessarily dramatic have fallen away. A lot of the work has already been done for you

Very often, though, historical films get made because the muscle is a star actor who wants to play a particular character. "I always wanted to be Davy Crockett," "I always wanted to be Wyatt Earp," whatever. There's something about the character, historically or mythically, that attracts the actor, and the line between the two of them can get pretty dim. If a very popular actor says he wants to play a historical part, it's not very hard to get the movie made.

Eric Foner: But your movies aren't star vehicles in the way that many historical films are. One of the strengths of your films, from a historian's point of view, is that you focus on ensemble situations, whether it's the team in *Eight Men Out* or an entire community in *Matewan*. Your films aren't like *Hoffa*, which concentrates on one guy, with a star playing him, and his name is the name of the picture. Presumably that's a conscious choice on your part.

Sayles: I've often had the experience of seeing a historical movie and then reading some history—and thinking that the history is a better story, a more interesting story, and certainly a more complex story. I feel that history, especially the stories we like to believe or know about ourselves, is part of the ammunition we take with us into the everyday battle of how we define ourselves and how we act toward other people. History is something that is useful to us and that people feel we need. I'm

always interested in getting something new into the conversation that may have been overlooked, that may have been forgotten, and so sometimes I may err in not including something obvious that everybody knows about and instead going toward the stuff that people have forgotten or that was tilted in a totally different way when it was first put on the screen.

Foner: Now maybe I'm wrong about this, but my impression is that until rather recently most films about American history have been basically celebratory, whether they're *Gone with the Wind* or westerns of the traditional kind. I think you wrote in your book about *Matewan* [*Thinking in Pictures*] about the gap between American myth and American reality. I know you're not a Hollywood filmmaker, but do you think people in Hollywood are driven to make films that cheer audiences and make them feel good just because they've got to make back their fifty-million- or hundred-million-dollar investments?

Sayles: I would say so. Certainly there was no idea at the beginning of the movie industry that it was anything other than an industry. The stories that were filmed were supposed to be popular; they were the equivalent of stage shows, which were celebratory as well. Popular history was just more grist for the mill. But you have to remember that things tend to show up in movies about third: First, historians start working on something and take a look at the record. Their work usually stimulates novelists, and the novelists often stimulate movie people. Finally, things end up on television. Now we're getting Ted Turner making all these revisionist Indian stories. Sometimes the white people are a little one-dimensional, but the Indians at least get to be three-dimensional characters.

Historians started doing that during the 1940s and 1950s. Then Thomas Berger wrote *Little Big Man* in 1964, and when the countercultural thing hit the movie screen—when they stopped making *The Sound of Music* and started making *Easy Rider*—that revisionism crept into historical movies, too, and you got Dustin Hoffman as Little Big Man. Now it's reached television. What was done in *Little Big Man* may have been very broad and one-dimensional, but it was one of the first times those ideas were presented to a film audience.

I think there's actually a kind of time curve after a major war during which the enemy becomes more and more human. It was a good fifteen years after World War II before you started seeing Japanese in films who were not just spectacled, buck-toothed, evil-empire kind of guys. The same thing has happened with Vietnam: Oliver Stone's *Heaven and Earth* came along fifteen or twenty years after the fact, and people may not have been quite ready for that film because it had some problems, but they *were* at least ready to entertain the possibility that a Vietcong could be a three-dimensional person.

Foner: On the subject of things going into novels first, it's probably worth mentioning that you are a writer and were a writer before you became a filmmaker, which I assume is unusual among filmmakers. Although my own connection with the film industry is much less intense, of course, I have been an adviser for a number of historical docudramas, documentary projects, etc., and I always tell the filmmakers I work with that a word is worth a thousand pictures. What I mean is that you can put so much more information into a book than into a film. That doesn't mean film can't teach in a very effective way, but I'm just wondering whether as a writer you feel constrained when you make a film. Film presents things in dramatic, visual, and direct ways, but doesn't the medium also force omissions and oversimplification because you can't put as much into a film as you can into a five-hundred-page book?

Sayles: That's why I choose different formats for different projects. When I wrote *Los Gusanos*, I was dealing with 120 years of Cuban and U.S. history through this one family. Because it was a novel, it could be complex. Each chapter in the book was told from a different character's point of view. In a two-hour movie, though, it's very, very difficult for an audience to accept or follow more than three points of view. You have the omniscient point of view; then there's the protagonist's point of view—he's the one in the closet waiting for the chain saw to rip through the door; and finally there's the antagonist's point of view—he's on the other side of the chain saw. With those three viewpoints, you can do a lot, but for an audience that's used to making an emotional connection with a film, it's very, very alienating to have too many points of view—and that fact mitigates against complexity.

One of the things that you have to do is say, "Okay, am I going to re-create this entire historical world, or am I going to take one episode that stands for it?" In making *Matewan*, I chose to focus on the Matewan Massacre because it seemed to me that this episode epitomized a fifteen-year period of American labor history. To make it even more representative, I incorporated things that weren't literally true of the Matewan Massacre—such as the percentage of miners who were black—but *were* true of that general fifteen-year period. I wanted to be true to the larger picture, so I crammed a certain amount of related but not strictly factual stuff into that particular story. That was a simplification.

Foner: Okay, it was a simplification, but *Matewan* has more than three points of view, and that's one of its strengths.

Sayles: It's a more complex story than you usually get in a strike movie, but I'm always aware that I'm simplifying certain things.

Foner: In *Matewan* and your other films, if I'm not mistaken, you abjure not only Hollywood money and Hollywood control but also Hollywood techniques of, you might say, melodrama—I mean, the usual ways in which films hook people. There's no sex in *Matewan*, no affair between Joe Kenehan and some woman in the town—

Sayles: Nothing tacked on.

Foner: You know that if *Matewan* had been made in Hollywood, there would have been. It's also a fairly slow moving film, and it's not entertaining in the Hollywood sense. Why is that? How could you afford to make those decisions?

Sayles: The decision to make a film and the ability to make it put you on very thin ice, which is why filmmakers have more freedom when they work with low budgets. You're not carrying the responsibility of having to make money for a large corporation and the three people in that corporation who just gave you the license to spend fifty million dollars of their money, not to mention another fifteen million dollars they're going to use to advertise the film. If you make a movie in a country as big as this one, with as many people in it who watch movies as this one has, and you're spending only three and a half million dollars, which is what *Matewan* cost, then you feel the people who invested in your film have a decent chance to make their money back—and that's all you really can tell anybody who's investing in a film. On the other hand, if you have to make back fifty million dollars, you know so many people have to see the film that you have to reach the mainstream of people who go to the movies to look for who's the good guy and who's the bad guy and to see the good guy win. If your movie isn't that kind of story, those people are going to be disappointed, the word of mouth is going to be bad, and you're going to fall short of the audience you need to pay back your budget.

Foner: I imagine you've had opportunities to make studio films, but you don't. Can you imagine any circumstances under which you might make a big-budget Hollywood film?

Sayles: I've actually made a couple of movies for studios. I made *Baby, It's You* for Paramount, which was a bad situation at the end of the day. I finally got the cut that I wanted, but there was a lot of me getting kicked out of the editing room, put back in, and all that kind of thing. And *Eight Men Out* about the 1919 Black Sox scandal was made for Orion. The interesting thing about that one is that I got to make it eleven years after I wrote the first draft of the script, which was based on Eliot Asinof's book.

One of the reasons it took eleven years—not just because I was a new filmmaker and it was a period movie that would cost a certain amount of money to make—was that I wanted to tell that story, *Eight Men Out*. Not *One Man Out* or *Three Men Out and a Baby*—different versions, as the studio would say. The history said these eight guys threw the World Series, and I wasn't going to have a scene at the end where I froze the frame on somebody going, "We're number one!" These guys didn't win—unlike *The Natural*, which wasn't history but was a book. In the book, you know, Bernard Malamud has the guy strike out at the end. But in the movie, not only does he hit a home run, he hits lights that probably didn't

even exist in that era, and there's a shower of sparks. I think the filmmaker said he wanted to be more in tune with the Eighties. Or he may have meant, "I want to make more money, and that's what we're doing."

I don't think Bernard Malamud was too thrilled with the new ending. You know, there's a story that Elmore Leonard called him up and said, "So how did you feel after *The Natural* came out?" And Malamud said, "I stayed in my apartment for a week." And Elmore Leonard said, "Well, I just saw the movie they made of my last book, and I'm leaving the country for a year." So you don't have to be a historian to feel the record has been distorted.

But *Eight Men Out* was interesting in that all I had to pay—if you think you have to pay something for the price of admission, to get the budget for the film—was some casting. The studio that finally made it had turned the script down three times before, and they still weren't that crazy about the story. But at that particular time, there were a lot of young actors around. So how do you get more than two or three young actors into the same movie? It's got to be either a war picture or a sports movie. And the studio said, "Well, who do you want to cast in this?" And we made up parallel lists, and I said, "Here are all the people I would like to have in this movie. Write down your list of the people you would like to have." It turned out that there were a number of people on both lists, and we actually got three or four of them to do the film. So I was happy and they were happy, and I didn't have to sacrifice the story in order to—I didn't have to burn the town in order to save it.

Usually what happens when somebody falls in love with a historical story of some sort is that a struggle develops, and you start giving away pieces of it. Your take on it may not be accurate to begin with, but you feel as though it's your story, and you resent having to make compromises to make it more dramatic and get it financed. The lie of the movie may be only the casting. Everything else might be totally historically accurate, but the person you are forced to cast just doesn't have it in him to do historical justice to the role. I read William Manchester's very psychological review of *Young Winston*, and he comes to that conclusion. The facts may have been accurate, but they missed the point of the man.

Foner: To get more into the mechanics of historical filmmaking, what sort of things did you do to re-create the period of *Eight Men Out*?

Sayles: You do the things that you think are going to strike people. For instance, I got hold of the rules of baseball from that era and the records of that World Series. We knew what happened on every play of every game because they kept those kind of line scores then. If somebody hit a ground ball to the shortstop in the third inning of the fourth game, that was the way it was shown on the screen. We had a lot of arguments, though, about the number of games. For three years beginning in 1919, major-league baseball went to a nine-game World Series, instead of a seven-game Series, to make extra money. Because the movie was run-

ning long, the studio said, "Couldn't we just have a seven-game World Series?" But I said no. I told them it was an interesting thing and that I'd make it work for the story.

Foner: Is the portrayal of White Sox owner Charles Comiskey in *Eight Men Out* accurate, or was it just Comiskey as the players saw him, if you know what I mean? I'm prepared to believe that Comiskey was a totally selfish man—

Sayles: Actually, what I tend to do is make these guys a little bit more appealing than they really were so that people will believe them. The stuff that's in the movie, he pulled all that and a lot worse. After *Matewan*, for instance, I was criticized a little for the two guys who were Baldwin-Felts agents—

Foner: I thought you made them much more appealing than they probably deserved to be.

Sayles: I made that attempt. I mean, these were guys who used to stop Red Cross milk wagons, put kerosene in the milk, and send them off so the kids would drink the kerosene. It was hard not to dehumanize these guys.

Foner: This might seem like a leading question, but do you and other filmmakers care what historians think of your films or is it of no particular concern one way or another?

Sayles: I think it's generally of very little concern. I like to think of it more as—Let me compare it to what happened in the 1960s with the New Journalism. Tom Wolfe was one of the first guys to do it at *Esquire*; Gay Talese was another. The idea they had was that if you were true to the spirit of the story, you didn't have to get all the facts exactly right. Their work led to a lot of what I consider creative writing. When it's bad, of course, you start reading it and say, "Wait a minute, this isn't about this guy, this horseshit is just here so the writer can do some moves." Take Albert Goldman's books: All of a sudden when you're reading them you realize, "Wait a minute, he wasn't there. How does he know this conversation happened?" He's making it up, but he feels he's being true to the spirit of it. I think most filmmakers feel the same way about history.

Foner: It's a resource.

Sayles: It's a story bin to be plundered, and depending on who you are and what your agenda is, it's either useful or not. You may read six books about the story you're filming. Maybe you find some of what you read useful, and you get rid of the rest: characters, ideas, countries—

Foner: I'm sure that's absolutely right, but why not just present a historical fiction? Why did Spike Lee make a film called *Malcolm X*? Why didn't he create a fictional black leader and call him Joe Something Else? A film like *She Wore a Yellow Ribbon* doesn't claim to be an accurate presentation of a particular event in history—it's a generalized picture of what happened in the West—but to name a film *Malcolm X* after a real person is a claim of some kind of truth. So is calling a movie *Matewan*, because there really was a Matewan Massacre. Why not just create a fictional town and entirely fictional characters?

Sayles: There's a certain power that comes from history. I mean, I've heard producers say many, many times that the only way a movie is going to work is if the ad says "Based on a true story." Audiences appreciate the fact that something really happened. Whether it did or didn't, they're thinking that it did or knowing that it did. That gives the story a certain legitimacy in the audience's mind and sometimes in the filmmaker's mind, whereas if you make something up out of whole cloth, it's not the same. William Goldman, the screenwriter, once said that it's not important what is true, it's important what the audience will accept as true. Barbara Kopple, who made *Harlan County U.S.A.* and *American Dream*, also made a wonderful documentary about Mike Tyson for network television. If you took that documentary and fictionalized everything word for word, nobody would believe it. Nobody would believe Mike Tyson; nobody would believe Don King; nobody would believe Tyson's mentor who's the gay handball champion of the world and also the greatest curator of fight films who's ever lived. Even *I* don't buy it; it doesn't make any sense. But if you call it a documentary, people will believe it and say it's amazing, amazing stuff.

Foner: When the film *Glory* came out, the producers called and asked me to come to a screening, which I did, and then they asked me to write a statement about the film. I wrote one saying that the film revealed a little-known feature of the American past and blah-blah-blah.... They called me back and said, "Well, this statement is of no use to us." And I said, "Well, what do you want?" They said, "We want a statement that says the film is accurate from a historian's point of view." And I said I couldn't do that because what *I* mean by accurate is not exactly the same thing as what *they* mean by accurate. I thought the film was accurate in a general way, but there were many historical inaccuracies in it. I didn't necessarily want to criticize all of them, but I wasn't going to give the film my Good Housekeeping Seal of Approval.

Sayles: So they found someone else.

Foner: So they found someone else. I guess "This is true" has a really big appeal. Have you ever been attracted to making a documentary to get around that question? Or maybe you don't want to get around it.

Sayles: The minute someone sits down in an editing room, even for a documentary, choices are made. Some footage is kept; other footage is not. I've seen some extremely biased documentaries—some well made, some not—so making a film a documentary doesn't really solve the problem, and documentaries are a lot more work. Barbara Kopple spent seven years on *American Dream*. I think Fred Wiseman comes as close to the ideal of accuracy as you can—he just turns on his camera and sees what people will do—but even he uses only some of his footage.

There's also that principle of physics—the Heisenberg Uncertainty Principle—which says that just by your presence you change the reality. Some filmmakers love that, and they actually start talking to the people: "Say, why don't you do this, and why don't you do that? Will you come and repeat that thing you did yesterday or you said yesterday?" And others really hate it. I think Wiseman hangs around for a while without pulling the trigger on the camera so people can get used to him. He figures, "They're not good enough actors, and I'm going to be here forever. They're going to get tired of me, and they're going to start acting like themselves sooner or later." That's pretty much what happens in most of his films.

Foner: Have you ever used historical consultants on your films? I mean, when historians go to see a film, we always complain, "Oh, damn, if that guy had just spoken to me or had shown me the script, I could have pointed out seventy-five errors." I know that when Richard Attenborough did the film *Gandhi*, he sent the script to Ainslie Embree, who used to teach the history of India at Columbia. It was full of little historical errors that were of no importance to the drama—you know, the years Gandhi was actually in South Africa, or did he actually meet this guy, little things. Embree wrote them all down and sent them to Attenborough—and, of course, not a single one of them got changed. Not even the date. Now correcting some of them might have altered the film, but fixing others wouldn't have changed the film at all. Attenborough didn't care what the historical—

Sayles: Or it got in the way of his storytelling.

Foner: Or it got in the way of his storytelling. You know, you can read books about history and distill their essence, but that still doesn't make you a professional historian. Do you ever feel the desire or the need to talk to a historian, or do historians just get in the way?

Sayles: I would say that I probably use historians the way most directors use them: I tend to use people who are well versed in historical details, very specifically in the details, but not in the big picture.

Foner: People who know what kind of uniform a particular guy wore in the Civil War?

Sayles: That's right. You call up people who know about trains and say, "Do you have any pictures of what a sleeper car looked like in 1920?" Or you call the telephone company and say, "Were there phone booths in 1920? Did people dial first?" I wasn't around then, but amazingly there are people who know that stuff.

Foner: But they're not so easy to find.

Sayles: What you find is that people who work in your art department have sources, because they've worked on historical films before and these problems have come up. There are also some researchers who work on films just as historical fact checkers.

Foner: I know. They're always calling me and asking me for all this information. If it's one or two questions, I say sure, that's fine. After half an hour, though—

Sayles: They think you're the public library.

Foner: And then they say they don't have any budget for this.

Sayles: We had a tent guy for *Matewan*. He told us that the miners would still be using white tents because the tents would probably be war surplus from the Spanish-American War. Back then, troops didn't have to worry about balloons or airplane attacks, so their tents could be white. The tent guy wore the right clothes and put the pegs in and everything. We also had coal miners working with us who had mined with the kinds of equipment they used in 1920.

Foner: But you didn't consult with a labor historian or someone who might have written about the history of the mine workers' unions?

Sayles: I would have read their books but not necessarily brought them on for that particular story. I think part of the fear and resistance to hiring historians is the same thing I encounter when I rewrite other people's movies. I can always sniff out a movie that's the writer's own story. You know, very often it's about his divorce. It might even be a little more interesting than that, but there are things about the story that don't work dramatically, and the author is sitting on them because that's what happened to him. It doesn't make a good story, so you have to say to the guy, "Unless this is a documentary about you, and nobody knows who you are, we have to change the story."

I was just working on this film about Apollo 13, and the producers were being very, very technically accurate. I got to talk to astronauts, and my job was to translate what they were saying into language that nonscientists could understand. I had to find ways to get in the technical information without simplifying it to the point where it wasn't true anymore.

But I had to make it simple enough so that nontechnicians could understand. The problem is, you can't have the head of NASA saying, "Oh, by the way, we don't point the rocket at the moon. We point it where the moon is going to be." So you find ways to do that: You create characters who didn't exist but who are commentators. You combine some characters. With the Apollo 13 script, there was quite a bit of fudging around to make it a better story, which the astronauts resisted at first. Then they started calling up with ideas. What was interesting about their ideas was that sometimes they were very melodramatic but they usually did help you solve the story point without being untrue to the spirit of the people, because our astronauts knew those people.

On other pictures, I tend to work a lot with the Chicago Historical Society. One thing about Chicago is that sociology was kind of born there, so there are records in Chicago about poor people that are older than records from almost any other part of the country. I've written two or three gangster movies, and they've been very helpful with the details. But that's just the letter of the law. Preserving the spirit of what happened is really up to the filmmaker's abilities and intentions, though his work can be changed enormously by the studio and later by the test audience. If the test audience doesn't like the way the Civil War came out, maybe the studio will release another version for Alabama.

Foner: Do you think we as historians ought to be concerned when we see the "truth" altered somewhat for dramatic purposes? Should we be concerned about that as historians? I mean, after all, many more people learn their history from watching the film *Malcolm X* than from reading some academic tome about Malcolm X. And *JFK*—God knows how many people now think Jim Garrison had the assassination all figured out. Or *Glory*, which is a very good film in many ways but still makes some very striking historical errors—like the idea that this unit was largely made up of former slaves. In fact, they were all free people from the North. It may be good dramatically to have a guy take off his shirt and show his lashes, but it's not who those people really were.

Sayles: There were other units that had former slaves, but that one—

Foner: That was a specific unit with a specific commander, Robert Gould Shaw, and it was made up of free Negroes from the North.

Sayles: Which is an interesting choice, I think, in that it reminds me of those guys who went to the Spanish Civil War to fight in the International Brigades. They didn't have to; they were already free. But they put their asses on the line for somebody else—which is almost more of a risk.

Foner: Absolutely. It's a dramatic story, but maybe the filmmaker didn't think it was dramatic enough.

Sayles: Once again, he probably felt that to bring the bigger story into his specific story, he need to create things.

Foner: So should we protest? Should we send letters to the producers saying, "Look here, you are distorting history by showing this—"

Sayles: I think sending a letter to the producer is the wrong thing to do. The letter should go to *The New York Times*. The letter should go to—I just saw a nice documentary about the civil rights movement, *Freedom on My Mind*, and part of the reason it was made was because of *Mississippi Burning*. The people who made the documentary wanted to set the record straight. If people know more about a story, then it's their responsibility to keep putting what they know into the conversation.

Foner: Does the movie industry as a whole have any responsibility to get the story right?

Sayles: I think using *responsibility* in the same sentence as *the movie industry*—it just doesn't fit. It's not high on their list of things to think about. You know, one of the things that's been happening in the industry lately is that the way politicians have been marketing themselves has affected the way movies are made, not just the way they're sold. There have always been famous cases of endings being changed because test audiences didn't like them, but now, more and more often, people are saying, "Why should we wait until the movie is made? Why don't we do the test marketing when we're writing the script, or when we're planning on the movie, just like they do with political campaigns?"

Foner: Let's just take a poll, see what moviegoers want to see, and then make it for them.

Sayles: Exactly. You remember what one of Reagan's press people used to say? "You don't tell us how to stage the news, and we won't tell you how to report it." Those people always talked about "scenarios." You know, "This is the scenario." And one of Bill Clinton's problems is that he doesn't stay with his scenarios.

Foner: Or he doesn't have the right scenario.

Sayles: And he starts one, then backs off it instead of saying, "Well, I'm going to take a stand here and play it out." Franklin Roosevelt had a lot of scenarios, and he thought this one would fly and that one wouldn't. He didn't get us involved in the Spanish Civil War because he didn't think it would play out. He thought he would lose the Catholics and that would be worse. But he had the right scenario for getting us into World War II, and it included some pretty high-handed stuff. But once he had

made the decision, he stayed with it. Sometimes he lost and sometimes he won, but he won more often than he lost.

Foner: So what you're saying is, the way the movie industry is going now we're not likely to hear a lot of concern about historical accuracy.

Sayles: No, because coming up with the scenario that sells is the same thing as staying in office. You know, it's the difference between a leader and a politician.

Foner: And the stakes are so much higher now. You stand to lose a hundred million bucks instead of five million.

Sayles: I think the stakes were always the same, personally, for those guys: "Don't make a movie like this. It doesn't make money." If historical accuracy were the thing people went to the movies for, historians would be the vice presidents of studios. Every studio would have two or three historians.

Foner: Fortunately, or unfortunately, that doesn't seem likely to happen.

Sayles: You were asking before about the difference between fiction and movies. The one thing I feel that I can do in movies that I can't do in fiction is—I can do anything in a movie, and it doesn't have to go through your head first. When you're in a movie theater, you experience the film viscerally. It goes straight to your gut. If it's a true story— if it says, "This is a true story"—that adds a lot of weight, too.

Foner: But in your films you keep that much more under control than most directors. You don't go for the cheap shot. You don't go for the cheap emotional high.

Sayles: I tend to pull you in and push you away, pull you in and push you away. In *Matewan*, there's that really awful scene in which you see the kid's throat being cut. Now if that movie were just about pulling you in, the answer—what everybody would want—would be the *Walking Tall* answer: We're going to kill all those guys, and we know the audience will feel good when we do. The Clint Eastwood film *Unforgiven*—it's just one example—is predicated on the audience knowing that the lead character may be called something else but he's really Clint Eastwood. It's funny when he falls off a horse because it's Clint Eastwood falling off a horse. The foreboding of the movie, what everybody knows, is that at the end Clint Eastwood is going to kick ass, which is a fairly simplistic revenge sort of thing. I think a lot of movies like that added up to why people were ready for the Persian Gulf War—that and a certain amount of Arab-bashing, especially since the Arab-American community isn't large enough to put up much of a fuss.

Foner: They did complain about *Aladdin* a little bit, but—

Sayles: That was a mild, mild version. I'm talking about characters like those on "Mission: Impossible"—the slimy, rich Arab guys, the bad guys. But getting back to that scene in *Matewan* of the kid's throat being cut, the point was to push you back a little.

And that's one of the things that the Joe Kenehan character did when he spoke out against more violence. He said, "Well, number one, just tactically it's a bad idea, because we're going to get creamed—maybe not tomorrow, but eventually we're going to get creamed. Also, morally, this strike isn't about killing people, it's about getting what we want. It's about not living in a world where you have to have eye an for an eye." He's pushing away the Hatfields and the McCoys, whereas many movies use a feud as their emotional release, and that's often what the filmmaker is going for: getting people so worked up that when they leave the theater, they want sign up. Bertolt Brecht even talked about that. He said that he wanted people to leave the theater and join the revolution. As alienating as he made most things, that was one thing he wanted people to get viscerally involved in.

Look at any World War II film made between 1940 and 1948 or 1949. The movie industry worked very much hand and glove with the government to the point that, when John Huston made a documentary showing very, very accurately what fighting was like, he couldn't screen it because people felt it was a little too raw. That's a consequence of using film as an element to keep people mentally in a war.

Every filmmaker, like every historian, has an agenda. The difference is that historians read one another, and, because of the academic world in which they live, there's a little bit more checking up on the facts. There's a little bit more of, "Okay, this is your agenda, but where's your documentation? Where did you get this? What have you ignored? What have you overemphasized? What have you underemphasized?"

Foner: Well, we're trained to do that, and so are most readers of history. But most moviegoers don't go to a film thinking how—They think *JFK* is true; they think *Matewan* is true. They basically think whatever they see is true.

Sayles: While the movie is happening. And I think that's an important point about movies: They exist during those two hours. If you make them, you hope that they have some echo, but the only thing you really have to do for the audience to buy in is to be true to the world you create for those two hours. If it's a world in which people have superhuman powers and can jump higher and run faster—if you set that up early and stay true to it—then people will buy it. But if you create a world in which there are only six shots in a six-shooter and somebody fires seven shots without having to reload, then people will get upset. In *JFK*, for example, one of the things Oliver Stone did was hit you with so many images so quickly—some of them familiar, some of them new information—in such a barrage of documentary styles that he was able to pass off stuff that was fairly speculative. Sometimes even he must have thought, "Well, I don't have any way to back this up, but it makes a great story, and I think it might be true."

Foner: I thought that film was a brilliant example of manipulation of the highest order.

Sayles: Sure.

Foner: And the way—You're right, he created new footage that looked exactly like the original documentary footage, and you couldn't really figure out where the "real" documentary footage left off and the "new" documentary footage began.

Sayles: Unless you came to that film with a very strong sense of history, having done a lot of research and knowing the Kennedy years very well. Otherwise, you get swept up, and at least for the world of that film, for those three hours, you buy it. You buy that Kevin Costner is Jim Garrison, even though it's bad casting. I don't know whether you've ever seen Jim Garrison, but he looked around six-foot seven.

Foner: Is there any film you'd like to mention that you think was particularly successful in its treatment of history? And I guess we should narrow our definition of *history*. Most movies are set in history in one form or another—except *Star Trek* or some other futuristic film—but some are more insistent than others in claiming to be history.

Sayles: I think the more successful historical films tend to be smaller stories because of that complexity thing we talked about earlier. When you tell a wider story, it becomes either a lot of production value without much to hold you emotionally in the story or so simplified that it doesn't seem real. Sometimes people have taken a historical story about the Rosenbergs or whatever—you know, a very, very, very small piece of history—but time after time I see them crap out. What was the one about—*Guilty by Suspicion*—the blacklisting film. It seemed as though they had a good idea there, but finally they weren't comfortable enough with the period to really deal with the story, so it became just another Hollywood movie.

Foner: What about *The Front*?

Sayles: *The Front* was an interesting movie in that it fictionalized a real case, so it was able to play things both ways. It kind of captured one little aspect of the blacklisting, which is that some guys who were somewhat sympathetic became fronts and managed to keep their hands clean enough not to get blacklisted themselves. There's an interesting moral ambiguity there—of not really fighting against the blacklist; in fact, profiting from it, which was what an awful lot of the friends of blacklisted people did.

Now I happen to see the world in a fairly complex way—I see complexity everywhere—but that's not the direction that movies were going during the 1980s. Think of the big stars of the Eighties, like Arnold Schwarzenegger and Sylvester Stallone. They played Ur characters—you know, mythic characters. It was this simplistic and even heightened good-guys-and-bad-guys thing—*The Terminator*—as opposed to the moral ambiguity of the 1960s and 1970s. I was definitely swimming against the current during the Eighties, and it was a conscious choice. Now, getting back to that idea of filmmaking as a conversation: One of the things that I feel is useful about making a small movie is that film can provide a voice for people who are not being heard and not being seen on the big screen. Let's try to get them up there, even if it's in a stunted non-Hollywood movie. Don't historians feel that way, too? Aren't you trying to broaden the debate?

Foner: Most of us want to be relevant. We want to feel that the history we're writing has some impact on the way people think about America. I write a lot about black history, about the Civil War, Reconstruction, the history of American radicalism. Why do I choose those subjects instead of other ones? It's because I think they have relevance and they relate to the way I grew up. But there are a lot of pressures now from many directions: There are people who feel they've been left out of history, and they want a new version that may not be any more accurate. There are even some people who think that history's gone too far in the other direction; they think it's too critical now, and they're demanding a more celebratory history. Lynn Cheney, the former head of the National Endowment for the Humanities, was complaining recently that historians are too negative, that we're too depressing. Why don't we write about the greatness of America and not dwell upon all these—

Sayles: Which was the 1950s version that I got in—

Foner: A lot of people want to go back to that. As you well know, the public presentation of history is a tremendous battleground right now, whether it's the Smithsonian exhibition on the A-bomb, which you may have read about, or—

Sayles: Columbus.

Foner: Columbus. How are we going to present Columbus? I'd say there's more public pressure on historians today than there probably ever has been. There's more scrutiny on what historians are doing from political, social, and other angles than ever before. So filmmakers are not alone in having people watching very carefully what they're doing. It's a new thing for many of us and I welcome it. It would be worse if everyone thought we should just be ignored.

Sayles: Put it in a book and put it away.

Foner: You know, the hardest thing for people who don't think much about history to realize is that there may be more than one accurate version of history. In other words, there may not be just one "correct" view of something, with all other views incorrect. There are often many legitimate interpretations of the same historical event or the same historical process, so none of us can claim that we are writing history as objective fact, in the only way that it can be legitimately presented. I hope we can all accept what you said earlier, that we all have agendas, we all have points of view. My history is a point of view. On the other hand, there are limits. If my point of view was completely divorced from the evidence, other historians would know that my views were implausible, and they would point that out because the evidence is there and there are standards.

Sayles: Like "The Holocaust didn't happen."

Foner: Exactly. There are standards of historical proof and presentation—there are outer limits—but within those outer limits are many possible ways of looking at things, all of which may be plausible.

Sayles: Among the biggest difficulties in making a historical film is presenting just that: the idea that there may be more than one reasonable version of events. It's one of the reasons that my book *Los Gusanos* is told from about twenty-six different points of view. When I was down in Miami kicking it off, I told the Cuban community, "You are going to find your best friend in one chapter and your worst enemy in the next, but they may both be right." If you take what happened historically on a personal level, it's

like a pool break: One guy went into the pocket, and that was the worst thing that ever happened in his life, while for another guy it was the best thing that ever happened to him. And they're both right from their own points of view. If either of them were to write a history of the original event, it would be difficult to recognize the shot that started the whole thing—the Cuban Revolution. Understanding that is a very, very difficult thing for most Americans, who have been trained by popular entertainment to want an answer in half an hour, an hour, or two hours, depending on whether it's television or the movies. And they want an unambiguous answer.

Another thing that is very, very difficult to do in a movie—and only a little more possible to do in a book—is to remember that people's thought processes were different at different times. For example, being a socialist in America in 1920 was a very different thing than being one in 1970 or 1990. Being religious in Rome in 1722 was different than being religious today in very secular New York City. When you see a historical movie and it doesn't quite jibe, it's usually because the mindset is wrong. Maybe you go with it if it's *Butch Cassidy and the Sundance Kid*. The sensibility of that film was very 1970s, and it was meant to be. The filmmakers got away with it because the movie was an entertainment and you kind of bought these guys as—well, they're not much different than the guys in *Easy Rider*. They're a couple of revolutionary devil-may-care guys who happen to be outlaws. But there really were historical figures named Butch Cassidy and the Sundance Kid, and real things happened to them.

When I'm making a historical film, I often spend maybe the first twenty minutes trying as subtly as possible to get the audience into the heads of the people living at that time. Maybe there wasn't sexual freedom. Or if there was, maybe it was limited to a small group. There were certain givens as far as what people believed. When James Earl Jones came to be in *Matewan*, the first thing we talked about, and he brought it up, was that we didn't want his character to be a revisionist black man. "This is 1920 and he's a black man from Alabama behind enemy lines. If he talks back, he knows that the next thing to happen may be a noose around his neck." So big powerful James Earl Jones really put a tether on his voice and on his body language, because we were trying to get people into the mindset of where these black guys were coming from. You know, there was no "up against the wall" back then. It was "yes, sir" and "no, sir."

Foner: That was another problem with *Glory*. In *Glory*, the soldiers talked as though they were on the streets of Harlem in 1990, with all this slang.

Sayles: When they were around white people.

Foner: And even by themselves. You know they weren't saying, "Hey, brother, give me five" during the Civil War. *Glory* had no sense, as you say, of language, of thought processes, of the way people related to one another. Life was very different back then.

Sayles: And who even knows exactly what the slang was? Most black vernacular from that time was written by white guys who were lampooning it. You know, one of the things that I often do—for instance, when I wrote *Eight Men Out*—is read a lot of the period writers, especially guys who were known to have had an ear for dialogue—Ring Lardner, James T. Farrell, Nelson Algren. I also showed the actors Jimmy Cagney films because there was a speed of delivery affected by urban guys then that Jimmy Cagney used. Actors today, since they've been through the "method revolution," take these incredibly long pauses. I showed them a movie called *City for Conquest* in which a hundred different things happen in an eighty-minute movie because everybody talks really fast. I told the actors—except the one who played Joe Jackson, because he was supposed to be from Georgia—"This is your rhythm. Spit it out." That made a statement back then, spitting it out.

It's interesting now what you see in sports. There's a certain modesty that has come in, especially with the white players—I think it comes from John Wooden, who coached all those championship basketball teams at UCLA—whereas the black players are still on that "I'm the greatest," Muhammad Ali kind of thing. Back in 1919, though, the white athletes were poor kids, and they were in your face. "We're going to kill those guys tomorrow. They don't have a fuckin' chance." They didn't say "fuckin'," but there was the same kind of cockiness that you see among black players today. You've got to be aware of that stuff when you're making a historical movie. There wasn't any of that "Well, geez, I'm just going to hope the Lord Jesus Christ helps me out tomorrow when I do my job." There's been a lot of that in the Eighties and Nineties with white athletes, but it didn't exist in the Teens and Twenties.

Foner: On another point, one of the major trends in the writing of history nowadays—and it may take years for this to get into film—is the tremendous interest in women's history. With a few exceptions, not many historical films are really that interested in women. Most of these films are male worlds. *Matewan* is basically a male world. In fact, *Eight Men Out* is a completely male world. Why can't filmmakers make films about women's history? Is it the same reason people are always complaining that there aren't enough good roles for serious actresses?

Sayles: You know, if you look at the five hundred films that were released this year, you're going to find that about ninety-five percent of them were directed by men. The decision-makers who finance the big films are also ninety to ninety-five percent men. So part of it is just a lack of interest in women's stories. Another part is that audiences go to movies with certain expectations that have been raised by all the other films they've ever seen. Even something like *Reds*, which tried to work a woman's story into a larger historical picture, became in the second half just a romance, just a woman trudging across the tundra looking for her guy, instead of really saying, "Okay, let's drop John Reed and really see what Louise Bryant is doing."

There is this feeling in the industry that if people see a woman on the screen, she has to be involved in a romance—that to get women into the audience, there has to be some kind of romantic payoff for them. That can change, though, the same way that the treatment of blacks and Indians has changed. Before the 1950s, there were certain things you could do that were accepted because a large number of the moviegoing public didn't feel these people were totally human. You could demonize these people, stereotype them, and present them in one-dimensional ways. But then the consciousness changed—partly because of movies, partly because of life, partly because of history and the efforts of the people who were in the civil rights movement—and once that changed, all of a sudden you couldn't present people in the same bad way anymore. I'm sure there are things that we accept in movies right now that, twenty years from now, people will say, "I can't believe they made a movie like that."

Foner: I suppose you can never quite predict how an audience will react to a film. I was once at a conference on all this and I heard a man speak who had made a documentary about Caryl Chessman, a guy whose execution in 1960 aroused a lot of protest against capital punishment. Anyway, the man who had made the documentary said that he had made the film as a powerful statement against capital punishment. But a lot of people saw the film and said, "Great, they fried the guy at the end—and, boy, he really deserved it." They thought the film had a happy ending because the guy was executed. So there's a limit to the degree to which you can control how an audience will react to your work.

Sayles: You load the dice, more or less, but one thing I definitely do in my movies is allow people to draw their own conclusions, which means that some of them are going to draw conclusions I don't necessarily want them to draw—or come down on a side I think is the wrong one. It's better in the long run, though, to have people question things rather than just react without any thought, without any kind of analysis. The struggle that you often see in the making of a historical film is the struggle between how much of a viscerally page-turning, emotionally stirring story you want and how much you want people to think about what's going on.

Foner: What about changing the facts to make a point? Especially when the audience isn't aware of the changes, which is usually the case?

Sayles: You know, I ask a lot of the people in the audience. I try not to condescend to them, and implicit in that is a presumption that they will take some responsibility not to believe everything they see and also to see more than one thing. If you're not going to condescend to people, you do have to ask that. Because if you are going to condescend and spoon-feed them everything and simplify everything, then you're saying the people aren't capable of complexity, they're not capable of reading two versions and making up their own minds about which one to believe. That can be a very dangerous point of view.

PAST
IMPERFECT

JURASSIC PARK

Stephen Jay Gould

THE DEEPEST MESSAGES OFTEN LIE IN APPARENT TRIVIALITIES—FOR EXAMPLE, IN DIALOGUE regarded as too insignificant to scrutinize for error or inconsistency. For me, the most revealing moment in *Jurassic Park* occurs early in the film, as paleontologist Alan Grant, at his western field site, discourses to his assistants on the genealogical relationships of dinosaurs and birds, as illustrated by a skeleton, just unearthed, of the small dinosaur *Velociraptor*. Grant correctly points to several anatomical features that suggest a link—hollow bones and a birdlike pelvis, for example. He then ends his discourse with the supposed clincher: "Even the word *raptor* means 'bird of prey.'"

Consider the absurdity of this last pronouncement. First, Grant is flat wrong. *Raptor*, from the Latin *rapere* ("to seize," or "to take by force"), is an old English word, traced by the *Oxford English Dictionary* to the early seventeenth century and first applied to humans, not birds, in its literal meaning. (The word *rape*, now restricted to sexual assault, has the same root and originally referred to abduction by force. Titian's *The Rape of Europa* records Jupiter's seizure and transport of a woman, not whatever happened afterward.) Later zoologists borrowed *raptor* as a technical name for large carnivorous birds (just as *primates*—defined as the category for monkeys, apes, and humans—postdates usage of the same word—meaning "first," in the sense of preeminent—for church leaders).

More important, Grant's error lies in confusing a human construction—and an arbitrary one at that—with an empirical reality. The word is not the thing; the representation not the reality (though we can view only through representation—and there's the rub). The bones of *Velociraptor* speak of relationships with birds; the name that we bestowed on the creature is only our fabrication.

Do we not grasp, through this example, the essence of what troubles us so much about the representation of history in film, the raison d'être for this book? All records of history must present biases, yet factual reality remains our partially attainable goal. (You will never get practicing scientists like me to espouse postmodernist relativism in pure form; we spend too much time engaged in the daily and excruciatingly tedious tasks of cage cleaning and sample preparation to believe that knowledge is nothing but social construction.) Eyewitness testimony has its biases; written text embodies more severe prejudices. But films intended for popular audiences include more fact-distorting conventions (often quite honorable and necessary) than any other medium. Sean O'Casey said that the stage must be larger than life and the needs of drama must distort the complexities (and the boredoms) of history. If we could keep the two personas separate— Ingrid Bergman as Joan of Arc vs. the enigmatic and probably schizophrenic Maid of Orléans—then cinematic distortion would not be problematical. However, when a movie image, with all the conventions that falsify history, becomes our primary representation of a person—as has happened again and again and again—then we face a troubling situation, for *Velociraptor*'s arbitrary name then supersedes the creature's own bones in establishing a public image.

This article, by chronology of its subject, appears first in the book, and I do not wish to set our collective effort on a wrong course with carping criticism and cheap shots in the "nyah-nyah" mode. I assume that most of the authors, as children of our time, adore the movies and can only be engaged in a lover's quarrel about the representation of history. So let me say that, in my view, *Jurassic Park* deserved all its substantial success.

The special effects of living dinosaurs, in particular, are spectacular and represent— in a point that should interest historians of technology—the cusp of an epochal transition between the new frontier of computer-generated images and older methods that relied on manipulation of objects (humans inside *Velociraptor* costumes, robotics based on hydraulic machinery, and, above all, the granddaddy of monster movie techniques, pioneered by Willis O'Brien in *King Kong*, stop-motion photography on small-scale models). Only three major scenes use computer animation, and even these represent a late decision, for usable techniques of adequate realism did not exist when Steven Spielberg began filming and became available only as the movie neared completion. Nonetheless, I was awestruck when I learned that actor Sam Neill (as Alan Grant) and the two children reacted to nothing on the film's set and that the stunning herd of charging *Gallimimus* dinosaurs were computer images added later!

I could list a compendium of factual errors from a professional paleontologist's viewpoint, starting with the observation that most dinosaurs depicted in *Jurassic Park* date from the later Cretaceous period. I once asked Michael Crichton why he had placed *Tyrannosaurus*, a Cretaceous dinosaur, on the cover of the book version. He replied, with absolutely honorable candor: "Ohmigod, I never thought of that; we were just fooling around with images, and that one looked good."

Instead, I would rather concentrate on the film's two "great" errors, for these faults share two properties that motivate this book and operate on sufficiently grand scale to preclude pettiness: They pervade the movie and constitute a flawed core of its being (and of so many others in the genre). These errors belong to the juicy and informative class of faults so well characterized by the economist Pareto as expansive and informative: "Give me a fruitful error any time, full of seeds, bursting with its own corrections. You can keep your sterile truths for yourself."

1. Insufficient recognition of nature's complexity. If anyone on this planet remains unaware of *Jurassic Park*'s plot line, let me epitomize: Entrepreneur sets up theme park of living dinosaurs. He extracts dinosaur DNA from blood preserved inside mosquitoes trapped and fossilized in amber (and thus shielded from decay over a minimum of sixty-five million years, since the extinction of dinosaurs). His scientists amplify the DNA, put together complete sequences, inject the code into eggs, and induce embryological development. Dinosaurs of many species are thus revivified (females only, as a protection against uncontrolled breeding). The park's defenses do not work for various reasons rooted in human scheming and technical malfeasance, and mayhem of all sorts results.

The scenario is clever (it had been discussed as fantasy by several scientists before Crichton wrote his book and constitutes a marvelous and legitimate device for science fiction). However, we should understand why such revivification is impossible—for nonacknowledgment of this reason promotes one of the worst stereotypes about science and its role in our culture.

We should distinguish between two very different claims for "impossibility" often made by scientists. The first (impossible to reach the moon, impossible to split the atom) records lack of imagination and only embarrasses those prognosticators who spoke too definitely. But another species of impossibility—the true and permanent disappearance of historical records—seems ineluctable because the only conceivable data have not survived. If, for some reason, I wanted a list of every rebel crucified with Spartacus along the Appian Way (wasn't Kirk Douglas great in that scene?), I could not acquire such a record because it doesn't now exist (and probably never did). Historical items are not formed predictably under laws of nature; they are contingent configurations that, if lost, cannot be reconstituted.

Dinosaur DNA falls into the category of Spartacus's list, not into the domain of predictably reconstructible consequences of nature's laws. Someday we may (one dubious report says we already have) recover short fragments of dinosaur DNA. (One complete gene, for example, has been recovered from a twenty-million-year-old magnolia leaf.) But remember that an entire organism contains thousands of different genes all necessary for revivification. DNA is a very fragile and decomposable compound; coding sequences can survive for geological ages only in the most favorable circumstances, and I see little prospect that anything close to a complete set of dinosaur genes could be preserved under any conditions. Moreover, the situation is even more hopeless—even if a complete set of genes could be reconstituted, an embryo still could not form, for development requires the proper environment in a maternal egg. Embryology cannot proceed without a complex set of maternal gene products already in place within the egg. So the scientists of Jurassic Park would not only require the complete dinosaur code but also have to know the maternal genes needed to produce proper proteins and enzymes within the egg—thus heaping impossibility upon impossibility.

Michael Crichton understood these limitations perfectly well. John Hammond, the godfather of Jurassic Park, admits that his scientists couldn't reconstitute an entire dinosaur code, so they patched in some frog DNA to supply the missing pieces. This lame solution (to a real problem) embodies the worst stereotype of science as a reductionist enterprise. Double, double, toil and trouble—just mix the right ingredients (or the best surrogates) and the desired entity will emerge. But organisms are discrete and indissoluble entities, not simple sums of (imperfect) parts. You cannot dump in eighty percent of the required pieces, then add twenty percent of things close enough, and emerge with a functioning totality (frogs aren't even genealogically near dinosaurs—why not use birds?). Such a mixture would be a cauldron of undevelopable glop.

History is the tale of unique and contingent items functioning as emergent wholes. We must debunk the silly idea that scientists are wizards who break totalities into little bits of chemistry and physics and then know the essence of the thing itself, thereby gaining the power to build it anew from basic constituents—shades of Hollywood's Frankenstein myth. This stereotype both misstates the nature of historical science and drives a wedge of misunderstanding between science (which seems arcane, all powerful, and dangerously manipulative) and the arts. Complex, whole organisms have emergent properties that arise nonadditively (to use the technical term) from interactions among their parts and cannot be predicted or built by simply stringing the bits together. We cannot decompose intelligence (or anything else) into percentages of nature and nurture; we must study organisms at their own level, in all their multifariousness and interactive complexity. I make no mystical plea for ineffable unknowability; I am a natural historian committed to understanding organisms and the reasons for their being. But I do assert that much of this comprehension must engage contingent history in all its uniqueness and emergent complexity.

2. Stereotypes of science and history. Hollywood seems to know only one theme in treating the power of science—hubris, otherwise rendered (in old-style language) as "man must not go where God (or nature's laws) did not intend." The movies, throughout scores of versions, have distorted Mary Shelley's moral tale about the responsibility of creators toward their "offspring" into a story of technology transgressing the boundaries of its legitimate operation (not a word can be found in Shelley about the

dangers of science or technology; nor did she or her atheistical husband discourse on what God did or did not license us to do).

Given the weight of such an overbearing tradition, the film of *Jurassic Park* inevitably took this same hackneyed course: The theme-park proprietors shouldn't have remade the dinosaurs (even though the technology to do so had been developed) because such a project violates nature's intended course—and human malefactors must therefore pay the price. In the film, mathematician Ian Malcolm plays the role of conscience for the canonical Hollywood posture. When John Hammond, the park's creator, explains his method for revivifying dinosaurs, Malcolm chides him: "The lack of humility before nature that's being displayed here staggers me." When Hammond asks whether Malcolm would oppose revivification of the California condor from preserved DNA should humans drive this great bird to extinction, Malcolm makes no objection because we would then only be reversing an unnatural act of human depredation. Why, then, object to dinosaurs, Hammond asks. Malcolm gives the pap answer: "Dinosaurs had their shot, and nature selected them for extinction." In other words, don't mess with the natural and intended order of evolutionary succession and progress (an inconsistent point, I hasten to add, because the revivified dinosaurs can beat any mammal in the park, including *Homo sapiens*).

Crichton's book takes a more subtle and opposite position, more consistent with history as historians understand the enterprise—but quite unusual for film and therefore capable of striking a blow for genuine understanding, if only Hollywood had found the courage to try something new and more accurate. The book's Malcolm is a specialist in chaos theory (the film's Malcolm makes a similar claim but then stakes out a position opposite to the theory's implications). Book Malcolm argues from chaos theory that Jurassic Park must fail, spectacularly and unpredictably, because the failsafe systems are far too complex and too interdependent to function properly—for one bit must inevitably fail and bring the whole system down. In so arguing for unpredictability, rapid transitions from apparent stability, and strong contingency in the power of individual events (and persons) to make radical alterations in historical pathways, book Malcolm expresses the key aspect of history's fascination and complexity, while film Malcolm promotes a theory of evolutionary inevitability and touts the tired theme of penalties for transgressing an intended natural order.

Film will always use history (and prehistory) as its major subjects, for many of the best dramas ever devised by human artistry are rooted in the actual lives and struggles of individuals and nations. We are all used to the claim, so prominent in postmodern criticism, that history (or any knowledge) cannot be fully objective but must be socially constructed. We recognize the preeminent source of these biases in political preferences, social conventions, and the psychological hopes of individuals and communities. History—whether presented in books, on the stage, or in films—is subject to yet another distinct and profound form of bias in representation—literary bias, based on dramatic conventions about story plots that work to move our souls and pique our fascination. If the actual history of life (both prehistoric and human) contains the strong elements of contingency and unpredictability (not to mention stability and tedium) that most historians regard as intrinsic to our reality (and that chaos theory, in book Malcolm's formulation, strongly implies), then the conventional plots of literary bias convey many wrong messages, especially about purpose and directionality as motivating and predictable forces of history. (Such literary bias is particularly prominent in paleonto-logical studies of human evolution where, whatever the limited evidence of fossils, we tailor our interpretations, usually unknowingly, to the conventions of epic tales in great mythologies, particularly in themes of heroes sallying forth to overcome great obstacles.)

We cannot hope for even a vaguely accurate portrayal of the nub of history in film so long as movies must obey the literary conventions of ordinary plotting. But must film be so unimaginative? Why couldn't a movie about genuine historical characters treat contingency as seriously as science fiction always has (where contingency is the classical theme in treatments of time travel, as in the *Back to the Future* trilogy)? What would history look like on film if presented with the themes that most historians regard as dominant? Could we stand such a presentation as drama? (*Gettysburg* showed Pickett's charge in real time, and I found the sequence riveting—though I admit that most of history's half hours are not nearly so interesting.)

Could we, following my opening theme in this essay, find a way to uncover the bones of history and not rely upon human conventions about the names? God showed Ezekiel "the valley which was full of bones . . . and lo, they were very dry." He asked the prophet: "Can these bones live?" and Ezekiel replied: "O Lord God, thou knowest." Since Jehovah seems uncommunicative about our filmmaking, we shall simply have to answer that question for ourselves. This form of revivification might well reward the effort.

1993/USA/Color
DIRECTOR: Steven Spielberg; PRODUCER: Kathleen Kennedy, Gerald R. Molen; SCREENPLAY: David Koepp, Michael Crichton, Malia Scotch Marmo; STUDIO: Universal; VIDEO: MCA; RUNNING TIME: 127 min.

CAST

Moses   *(Charlton Heston)*
Ramses   *(Yul Brynner)*
Nefretiri   *(Anne Baxter)*

THE TEN COMMANDMENTS

Alan F. Segal

MOST SCREENWRITERS WHO TURN BOOKS into movies do a great deal of editing to transform even a short novel into a tight film narrative. The authors of the *Ten Commandments* screenplay found themselves in the converse position. Rather than providing too much detail and too many subplots, the Bible does not supply enough material even for a film. It tells us nothing, for instance, of Moses' youth between his entrance into the pharaoh's household and his later career as Israel's lawgiver.

In a personal prologue to the film (and also in the opening credits), producer/director Cecil B. DeMille declares his intention to use Philo, Josephus, Eusebius, and the rabbinic commentaries of the midrash to complete the biblical picture. What DeMille fails to mention is that, because all these sources were written more than a millennium after the Exodus, scholars consider them irrelevant to the task of assessing the historical accuracy of biblical events. However much scholars may enjoy reading them and however relevant they may be to the time of Jesus (during which many of them were written), they have little to offer when it comes to ascertaining the truth of biblical history. (DeMille actually relied just as much on modern romances—including Dorothy Clarke Wilson's *Prince of Egypt*, J.H. Ingraham's *Pillar of Fire*, and A.E. Southon's *On Eagle's Wings*.)

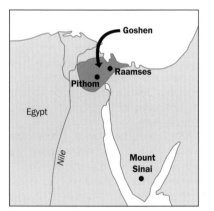

For this undertaking, we are left primarily with the Bible, which contains three types of material: myth, legend, and historical tradition. The first eleven chapters of Genesis are myth—everything from the Creation to the Tower of Babel and the dispersion of the peoples. The history of the Hebrews that follows, beginning with Abraham (Genesis 12) and ending with the arrival of the Hebrews in Israel (Judges), is mostly legend. This section includes the story of the Exodus, in which Moses leads the Hebrews out of slavery in Egypt.

According to the Bible, the Israelites served in "hard bondage" in Egypt, building the "treasure cities, Pithom and Raamses" for the pharaoh. But there is little external verification of this story. Egypt is silent about the deliverance of the Israelites (although Egyptian chronicles are notoriously unreliable when it comes to describing events uncomplimentary to their pharaoh's dignity). Apart from the Bible, there is no direct evidence that any of the Hebrew personages existed or that the events of Exodus ever took place.

The oldest known reference to Israel outside the Bible appears on a stone tablet from the reign of Merneptah, the son of Ramses II. Its hieroglyphs suggest that by around 1215 B.C.E. the people of Israel had taken

HISTORY

Michelangelo's statue of Moses

As is typical of biblical movie spectaculars, the screenplay for *The Ten Commandments* treats each textual event literally, whether or not scholars have much confidence in it today. Notable in this category is the story of Moses in the bulrushes. This tale employs a common folkloric motif, that of the abandoned infant hero, found in numerous ancient traditions—among them the Greek (Oedipus, Herakles), the Roman (Romulus and Remus), and the Persian (Cyrus, founder of the Achaemenid empire during the sixth century B.C.E.). The most relevant parallel to the story of Moses may be that of Sargon of Akkad, the great twenty-third-century B.C.E. unifier of Mesopotamia, who claimed he was abandoned in the Euphrates in a basket of rushes and raised by the god Akki, the water-drawer, before becoming the consort of Ishtar.

HOLLYWOOD

Charlton Heston as Moses

In this, his last work as director, Cecil B. DeMille spared little expense, filming the story of the Exodus on a grander scale than many people imagined possible. He made particularly effective use of his well-publicized "cast of thousands" in the Exodus sequence, which employed twelve thousand people and fifteen thousand animals. Because they were stretched out over three miles, DeMille had to stand atop a crane and deliver orders through a public-address system.

DeMille chose Charlton Heston for the role of Moses because of his resemblance to Michelangelo's famous statue. "My choice was strikingly affirmed," DeMille recalled, "when I had a sketch of Chuck in a white beard and compared it to . . . [the] statue. The resemblance was amazing."

The Midrash

The Hebrew word *midrash*, meaning "exposition" or "investigation," refers to a collection of textual interpretations of the Bible. Although DeMille occasionally uses motifs found in later Jewish literature (not in the Bible), he generally takes a free hand in inventing stories intended mostly to further the plot and galvanize the interest of the moviegoer. In this respect, one might make the case that he is following the method of the rabbis who created the midrash.

These rabbis and their followers invented stories wholesale but always for a specific holy purpose: to explain a textual problem or to answer any number of questions that arose in later ages concerning the moral motivations of the biblical characters or the outcome of the story. The rabbis faced the same problem as DeMille's screenwriters: The Bible itself was entirely too enigmatic, refractory, and terse to answer adequately the questions of later generations. Of course, the screenwriters' additions were intended to pique the interest of moviegoers, while DeMille himself wanted to portray the tension between rule by God's law and rule by a dictator, as well as the conflict between totalitarian states and free souls.

up residence near Canaan. Their arrival might have been recent, because the Stela of Merneptah refers to Israel with the hieroglyphic symbol for a people, not a country, suggesting that they had not yet taken possession of the land. Following this analysis, Ramses II (reigned 1290–1224 B.C.E.) becomes the most likely candidate for the pharaoh of Exodus, which could plausibly have occurred sometime within half a century of 1250 B.C.E.

DeMille's *Ten Commandments* amplifies the biblical account by asserting that the Exodus indeed took place during the reign of Ramses II—consonant not only with the Stela of Merneptah but also with other evidence uncovered by modern scholars who have shown that Ramses II's father, Seti I (reigned 1305–1290 B.C.E.), moved the capital of Egypt from Thebes to the desolate city of Avaris, west of Lake Timsah in the land of Goshen. Remembered as a master builder, Seti made extensive use of forced labor. An egotistical Ramses later renamed the refurbished capital Pi-Ramses ("house of Ramses") and built Pr-Itm. These names suggest "the treasure cities, Pithom and Raamses" mentioned in the Book of Exodus, and they are located in Goshen, where Joseph's brothers were said to have settled (Genesis 47:27). Egyptian records note that a people known as 'Apiru (the word *Hebrew* in Hebrew is *'ivri*) were used to construct these cities. However, scholars still debate whether these words are related.

Less convincingly, DeMille also makes use of a theme found only in the later commentaries, including those of Josephus: the prophecy that the Hebrews will produce a redeemer whose presence will be signaled by a star. (This folk motif is clearly more relevant to the time of Jesus and the infancy stories found in the Gospels.) The film's touching Passover celebration suffers from similar anachronisms, largely ignoring the lamb sacrifice of the ancient Passover celebration described in Exodus and instead concentrating on later rabbinic seder liturgy. The seder shown in *The Ten Commandments* was not part of First Temple Judaism, nor can we demonstrate that it was the custom of the Hebrews at the time of the Exodus; the practices depicted are, in fact, Hellenistic innovations that were possibly the basis for the Last Supper and continue today as much-cherished Jewish practices.

A final anachronism that creeps into the film from these later commentaries is Moses' final gift to his supporters: At the end of *The Ten Commandments*, as Moses climbs Mount Nebo to his final resting place, he hands over to Joshua the five scrolls of the Pentateuch. This scene confirms the notion, which arose much later and now has become widely accepted throughout the West by Jews and Christians alike, that Moses wrote the entire Pentateuch. In fact, the Bible itself makes no such claim.

Even more interesting than these matters of provenance, however, is the characterization of gender roles in *The Ten Commandments*, especially the romance between Moses and the Egyptian princess Nefretiri, good for the box office but entirely absent from the biblical account. Nefretiri is captivated by the young Moses and much less impressed by Ramses.

When Moses is banished, she marries Ramses and ascends the throne but still longs for Moses. The torch of romance burns even after Moses returns with his Midianite wife, Sephora, though it slowly turns to hate as Moses ignores her. (The movie makes clear that Moses ignores both women in favor of his vocation, as would any good American tending to his business during the 1950s.) In a very real sense, the most terrible of the plagues—the slaying of the firstborn—symbolizes God's reprisal for the manipulating and underhanded cruelty of a scheming woman scorned, because it is Nefretiri who hardens Ramses' heart.

The cliché of the woman scorned as the source of all evil may offend modern gender sensibilities, but it also makes Nefretiri the only really interesting character in the film. Everyone else, Moses especially, is imprisoned by the language of the Bible—or worse, by biblical-sounding dialogue. But Nefretiri, historically a wife of Ramses but otherwise fabricated from the gender conventions of the 1950s, is free to be evil—and tragic.

What is so hard for modern readers of the Book of Exodus to appreciate is the extent to which the biblical story is written as a contest between the true God of Israel and the pharaoh, or false god, of Egypt. That is why the usually terse biblical text goes on at length about the plagues and how the pharaoh is only very slowly convinced to allow the Israelites to leave. Each time he does so, God hardens his heart, and the pharaoh's recantations bring terrible, punishing reprisals. That is also why the biblical text takes such glee in exaggerating the details of God's strength: turning the most powerful man on earth into a puppet, robbed by a ragtag group of pastoralists who purloin vast quantities of gold and silver as spoils from the wealthiest nation in the Ancient World and then escape punishment because God drowns the world's most feared military machine in the Reed (not Red) Sea.

The legend of the Exodus is a tale of wish fulfillment of the sort that inevitably arises when a small people with limited power suffer for a long period and then escape political domination. Theirs being an ancient wish, it is a difficult one to depict understandably on the modern screen. Yet the subplot of the vengeful Egyptian princess Nefretiri at least allows DeMille to make the biblical contest meaningful to modern audiences.

Background Reading

Judah Goldin, *The Song at the Sea: Being a Commentary on a Commentary in Two Parts* (Yale University Press, 1971)

Werner Keller, *The Bible As History* (Morrow, 1981)

Nahum M. Sarna, *Exploring Exodus: The Heritage of Biblical Israel* (Schocken, 1966)

1956/USA/Color
DIRECTOR: Cecil B. DeMille; PRODUCER: Cecil B. DeMille; SCREENPLAY: Aeneas MacKenzie; Jesse L. Lasky, Jr.; Jack Gariss; Frederic M. Frank; STUDIO: Paramount; VIDEO: Paramount; RUNNING TIME: 219 min.

Engraving from a fifteenth-century Bible

Later...

In DeMille's epic, created by and for a modern age, the contest between Moses and the pharaoh evokes the many conflicts between faith and science. Into Ramses' mouth DeMille places the same sort of pseudo-rational scientific explanations of the plagues that became so popular in technologically sophisticated America after World War II: red soil washed into the Nile caused fish to die, leading to a proliferation of insects, which caused skin infections, and so on. These and other explanations (an earthquake caused the sea to part) were offered in vain attempts to shore up the credibility of the biblical text, mostly by well-meaning apologists who wanted to bring science and the Bible into harmony.

On the other hand, the screen Moses champions the more sympathetic position (in the context of the film): that the miracles are produced directly by the power of God. As it does in the Bible, this emphasis on faith helps explain God's dogged pursuit of the pharaoh, followed by His otherwise incomprehensible hardening of the pharaoh's heart. God wanted to make an example of the pharaoh to demonstrate the power of faith—not only over reason but over might as well.

This victory of faith, however, troubled the rabbis, who perceived and tried to explain a different moral problem, one omitted entirely by DeMille in his film's blockbuster ending. The midrash invents a dialogue at the sea between God and the angels, who have joined Moses and Miriam's song of triumph after the drowning of the Egyptians. God silences the angels and says: "How can you sing when my creatures are drowning?"

SPARTACUS

W.V. Harris

Spartacus and the Rebels

Spartacus's achievement in holding his rebel force together was a remarkable feat, all the more so because the rebels came from many different lands and they had to be armed as well as fed and sheltered. The film makes the rebel leadership rather more harmonious than it probably was. Their cause was always doomed: The slave rebels could expect no ultimate escape from Roman power, especially once their move to northern Italy had failed. They knew very well that Roman punishments for rebellious slaves were draconian. The entire horizon was dominated by Rome. Yet the escaped slaves remained a cohesive fighting force.

SPARTACUS IS, BY HOLLYWOOD STANDARDS, a highly political movie. Its chief scriptwriter, Dalton Trumbo, had been on the Hollywood blacklist during the 1950s as a supposed subversive (*Spartacus* was his first screen credit in more than ten years), and he sympathized strongly with Spartacus's slave rebellion. So did Howard Fast, whose 1954 novel *Spartacus* was Trumbo's main source. The script makes the Roman senator Crassus echo Sen. Joseph McCarthy: "Lists of the disloyal have been compiled!" Yet the populist political messages of the film are so muffled by the immense remoteness of ancient Rome that they could hardly have aroused revolutionary passions. In the climate of 1961, with McCarthyism discredited, it no longer took much courage for President Kennedy to give the movie an endorsement, over the opposition of the American Legion, as he did shortly after taking office.

The slave rebellion led by the historical Spartacus, which lasted a little less than two years (73–71 B.C.), shook Rome more than any other in the long history of Roman slavery. Although surviving sources leave many important questions unanswered (that tends to be the way with slave rebellions), we know that Spartacus, with about seventy other slave gladiators, did break out of the training school of Lentulus Batiatus at Capua and set up a base on the slopes of Mount Vesuvius.

There the rebels attracted so many other supporters that their army was able to defeat a series of Roman military expeditions. The rebellion spread to many parts of southern Italy, and in 72 B.C. the rebels overcame (or at least stood up to) both of the Roman consuls of that year, who probably had at their disposal no fewer than forty thousand well-armed soldiers. In the end, an army commanded by M. Licinius Crassus killed Spartacus in a decisive battle and later crucified some six thousand survivors along the 132 miles of the Via Appia between Capua and Rome.

Much of this, and a great deal else that really happened, appears in *Spartacus*. The brutality of the Roman slave system, the facts of gladiatorial life and death, and the Mediterranean-wide power of Rome are conveyed well enough. The gladiatorial training school of Batiatus is also convincingly reconstructed. We are made to realize that the Roman Empire was indeed a slave society and that slave rebellions were certain to be suppressed. In short, the film gets a remarkable number of things right, and the critic who described it as a "travesty of historical truth," apparently because Spartacus's victories occur mostly off camera, was badly mistaken. Even the scene in which Crassus (played by Laurence Olivier) attempts to seduce his slave Antoninus (Tony Curtis)—which

HISTORY

A nineteenth-century French representation

Gladiators (from the Latin *gladius*, meaning "sword") were professional combatants in ancient Rome. Their exhibitions originated at Roman funerals, where the contestants usually fought to the death. (It was believed that those who perished would serve the dead man in the afterlife as armed attendants.) After the first known gladiatorial competition in Rome in 264 B.C., the shows became extremely popular. The earliest competitions featured three pairs of gladiators; by the time of Julius Caesar, however, competitions showcased three hundred pairs. During the reign of Emperor Titus (A.D. 79–81), a single gladiatorial festival lasted one hundred days. With the spread of Christianity, though, gladiatorial combat fell into disfavor. It was abolished twice, first by Emperor Constantine I in 325 (with little success) and again by Emperor Honorius a century later.

HOLLYWOOD

Kirk Douglas in the arena

A splendid cast virtually guaranteed that Universal would recoup the twelve million dollars it spent on *Spartacus*—the most expensive Hollywood production to that date. Laurence Olivier (Crassus), Charles Laughton (Gracchus), and Peter Ustinov (Batiatus) all gave performances that demonstrated a strong British affinity for evil. (Ustinov even won an Oscar.) However, studio censors cut the Turkish bath scene in which Olivier attempts to seduce Tony Curtis because studio executives felt that its blatant homoeroticism was too depraved. Director Stanley Kubrick had the opportunity to restore the scene in 1989 when a "director's cut" of *Spartacus* was released. An exhaustive search of studio archives uncovered most of the missing footage, but the soundtrack had decayed. Kubrick therefore re-recorded the dialogue. Convincing Tony Curtis was easy, but Olivier was dead; instead, Anthony Hopkins impersonated the peerless actor.

The death of Spartacus

Appian's Account

The best source on Spartacus and the slave rebellion is Appian of Alexandria, a second-century Greek historian. This is his account of the final battle between the armies of Spartacus and Crassus:

> Spartacus tried to break through and make an incursion into Samnite country, but Crassus slew about six thousand of his men in the morning and as many more towards evening. Only three of the Roman army were killed and seven wounded, so great was the improvement in their morale inspired by the recent punishment. Spartacus, who was expecting a reinforcement of horses from somewhere, no longer went into battle with his whole army, but harassed the besiegers by frequent sallies here and there. He fell upon them unexpectedly and continually, threw bundles of faggots into the ditch and set them on fire and made their labor difficult. He also crucified a Roman prisoner in the space between the two armies to show his men what fate awaited them if they did not conquer. But when the Romans in the city heard of the siege they thought it would be disgraceful if this war against gladiators should be prolonged. . . .
>
> The battle was long and bloody, as might have been expected with so many thousands of desperate men. Spartacus was wounded in the thigh with a spear and sank upon his knee, holding his shield in front of him and contending in this way against his assailants until he and the great mass of those with him were surrounded and slain. The remainder of the army was thrown into confusion and butchered in crowds. So great was the slaughter that it was impossible to count them. The Roman loss was about one thousand. The body of Spartacus was not found. A large number of his men fled from the battlefield to the mountains and Crassus followed them thither. They divided themselves into four parts and continued to fight until they all perished except six thousand, who were captured and crucified along the road from Capua to Rome.

was, in 1960, an attempt to show that the rulers of Rome were unspeakably decadent—we now see as consistent with the bisexual nature of many upper-class Roman men.

The historical critic, in any case, risks absurdity. Spartacus's rebellion was already the subject of mythmaking in the first century B.C., and today some of the most militantly radical students are still called Spartacists. It would be utterly unreasonable to expect a movie to present a demythologized Jesus or Napoleon—or Spartacus.

There are innumerable misrepresentations and "mistakes" in *Spartacus*, yet the responsibility for such errors belongs not to Hollywood alone but also to the entire nonacademic (or popular) culture, which has its peculiar ways of thinking about the past. This film was put together by Kirk Douglas, Dalton Trumbo, and director Stanley Kubrick (who replaced Anthony Mann). However, they were responding to the American mass imagination of the 1950s (itself, in good part, a Hollywood creation). In a more direct sense, they were responding to Fast's novel, which contributed its own share of distortions, some of them ideological. Trumbo, in fact, eliminated some of the book's absurdities (such as the claim that the Romans converted many of the defeated slaves into sausage meat) and produced a script vastly superior to Fast's novel.

The filmmakers showed some desire to know what actually happened, but they had no notion how to find it out. For them, historical research was a question of trying to make sense out of Howard Fast's book and out of Arthur Koestler's much more grown-up novel *The Gladiators*. These works were viewed through the lens of ideological probability. Meanwhile, a research assistant could have gathered all the ancient textual evidence (from Appian, Plutarch, and others) in ten pages. A hundred pages would have given a wealth of historical background. Such a procedure seems unimaginable; yet a vast effort was devoted to creating realistic physical details.

The historical Spartacus was not born into slavery (he was a prisoner of war from Thrace, where modern Bulgaria is now situated). He did not survive to be crucified outside the gates of Rome, and he certainly had no opportunity to exchange a heartrending farewell with the now miraculously free Varinia (played by Jean Simmons) and their infant son. A mass audience required such sentimental scenes with the slave Varinia, a fictional character. Also, neither Gracchus nor Julius Caesar had anything to do with Spartacus; the last Gracchus to lead the Roman *plebs* had been killed fifty years earlier. The motive here was evidently to put as many famous Romans as possible into the same film.

Another tendency of the filmmakers is to divide the human race into good and evil. Everything seems a little too harmonious on the side of the rebels (there was probably some understandable confusion of purpose among Spartacus's followers). The real Spartacus was brutal enough to put to death some three hundred Roman prisoners in honor of Crixus, his slain comrade-in-arms (unless this is atrocity propaganda). The unrelieved viciousness required of the Romans compels the movie to keep the ordinary Roman citizens out of the story, with the result that some of the audience must wonder what the legionaries who defeated Spartacus were fighting for.

There is also a degree of political distortion in *Spartacus*. We are led to believe that the crisis precipitated by Spartacus led to Crassus's becoming a dictator. It is true that the Romans had suffered briefly from a dictator, Sulla, between 82 and 80—and would soon suffer from another, Julius Caesar, from 49 B.C. onward—but during the 70s the Romans still had the form, and even the reality, of a republican system of government. (The job that the film gives successively to Glabrus and to Caesar, namely prefect of the city, did not yet exist.) When Crassus was sent against Spartacus, he was simply an ex-praetor (although an unusually rich one); his success helped him gain election as one of the consuls for the year 70 B.C., but a dictator he never was.

The reason for this distortion was evidently to suggest that Spartacus's rebellion began or at least foreshadowed the breakup of the slave system. Similarly, the narrator at the beginning of the film tells us that Christianity was soon to create "a new society"—without slavery, so it is implied. In reality, as the script itself says at another point, slavery survived just fine for another two thousand years or so.

Roman Slavery

In the first century B.C., many Roman slaves were, like the historical Spartacus, prisoners of war; others were the children of slaves and thus slaves from birth. Most slaves worked on the land or as domestic servants, although some, like Kirk Douglas's Spartacus, labored in quarries or mines. For most slaves, the physical conditions of life were extremely harsh, and even household slaves were subject to sexual exploitation (the movie's Antoninus escapes this abuse only by running away). For the favored few, there was the possibility of freedom (a custom called manumission). Those lucky enough to receive manumission from their owners became full Roman citizens.

Later...

During the many centuries of Roman history after Spartacus, there was never again a slave rebellion of such dimensions—partly because of the brutality of Roman repression, partly because the Romans were intelligent enough to understand the advantages of rewarding a few slaves with privileges, including their freedom. Sometimes slaves did rebel, but they were quickly defeated. The changes that came over slavery during late antiquity and the early Middle Ages are a matter of dispute among historians, but slavery certainly survived and on a substantial scale. The changing economy of the later Roman Empire altered the role of slavery, but the institution itself was never challenged by Christianity. The Christians of antiquity, like other ancient peoples, accepted the existence of slavery without a qualm. However, the Christian emperors did finally, after delaying for many decades, put an end to gladiatorial combat.

Background Reading

Keith R. Bradley, *Slavery and Rebellion in the Roman World, 140 B.C.–70 B.C.* (Indiana University Press, 1989)
Keith Hopkins, *Conquerors and Slaves* (Cambridge University Press, 1978)

1960/USA/Color
DIRECTOR: Stanley Kubrick; PRODUCER: Edward Lewis; SCREENPLAY: Dalton Trumbo; STUDIO: Universal; VIDEO: MCA; RUNNING TIME: 196 min.

W. V. HARRIS

JULIUS CAESAR

Michael Grant

Caged birds were used to determine the future.

Soothsayers and Portents

Ancient history can be understood only by those modern readers who appreciate that in the Greco-Roman world there was a widespread, if not almost universal, belief in portents and prodigies. The Romans in Caesar's time were convinced that these indications foretold the future. Thus, it was extensively believed that a soothsayer had warned Caesar in advance of his assassination. It is quite possible that Caesar was indeed warned of the danger posed by his political conduct.

The Romans also believed that dreams could foretell the future. In Shakespeare's play, Caesar's wife, Calpurnia, dreams of her husband's murder, warns him not to visit the Senate that morning, and pleads with him to feign illness. Such events may well have preceded Caesar's death that day, but there is no firm historical evidence to support this scenario.

AS HAS BEEN WELL KNOWN FOR CENTURIES, Shakespeare's *Julius Caesar* is a wonderful play. Of course, it is fabulously well written, extremely dramatic, and very complex in its portrayal of people and emotions. All this can sometimes be obscured by the well-known and hackneyed quotations commonly drawn from the play: "Beware the Ides of March," "He doth bestride the narrow world like a Colossus," "Friends, Romans, countrymen, lend me your ears," and so forth. Yet in spite of these saws, eternally repeated out of context, one must say again that this is a wonderful, unforgettable drama.

The first inevitable question concerning any film version, such as this one made in 1953, is: How well does the movie live up to Shakespeare's play? The answer is, on the whole, rather well. Such a statement, of course, requires qualifications. One obvious qualification is that a good many lines were cut. But the main part of the play remains intact. Or does it? The film utilizes a good many famous actors who cannot possibly be expected to submerge their own personalities entirely into the machinery of the plot. I am thinking particularly of John Gielgud and James Mason, who bring Cassius and Brutus to life even more than Shakespeare did—but in their own ways. My other complaints are minor ones: There seems to be a mix-up about the location of Caesar's murder, and I was sorry to see portrait busts that look suspiciously like Hadrian, who was not born for a very long time to come. I also thought, for a moment, that I saw Nero, but never mind.

The second inevitable question is: How well do the play and the film live up to the historical Caesar? In this regard, I am afraid that far graver reservations are required. This should not be entirely surprising, as Shakespeare himself relied on very precarious historical material. He based his play almost wholly on a popular work of his time, *Plutarch's Lives of the Noble Grecians and Romans*, published in 1579 in an English translation by Sir Thomas North. North, in turn, founded his work not on Plutarch's original but on Jacques Amyot's French translation, which had been published in 1559. Although North's work powerfully affected English literature and style, Shakespeare certainly went a good deal beyond him, particularly in his delineation of character and his creation of an exciting, well-proportioned plot. Yet in regard to history, Shakespeare relies on North's (on the whole not too bad) interpretation of Plutarch. On the values and disadvantages of doing this, may I quote myself from *Readings in the Classical Historians* (Scribners, 1992):

HISTORY

Marcus Junius Brutus was probably born in 85 B.C. When the Civil War broke out, he sided with Pompey, but Caesar pardoned him after Pharsalus. In 46 B.C., Caesar appointed Brutus governor of Cisalpine Gaul, then two years later made him praetor of the city (*praetor urbanus*).

Brutus joined the conspiracy against Caesar for patriotic, idealistic reasons. He yearned for the restoration of republican rule, and he prided himself on his alleged descent from Lucius Junius Brutus, the traditional founder of the Roman Republic. After the second battle of Philippi in 42 B.C., realizing that the republican cause was now surely lost, Brutus committed suicide, at the age of forty-three.

HOLLYWOOD

James Mason as Brutus

Producer John Houseman and director Joseph L. Mankiewicz surprised no one when they cast the distinguished British actors James Mason and John Gielgud as Brutus and Cassius, respectively. However, they shocked everyone when they chose Marlon Brando for the part of Mark Antony. At the time, Brando was still known as The Mumbler for his garbled performance two years earlier as Stanley Kowalski in *A Streetcar Named Desire*. After being offered the role by Mankiewicz, Brando spent a month studying records of Laurence Olivier and his idol, John Barrymore, performing speeches from Shakespeare. Then Brando recorded his own versions of the speeches and played the tape for Mankiewicz. "You sound exactly like June Allyson," Mankiewicz said.

Julius Caesar

Gaius Julius Caesar was born in 100 B.C., the scion of a patrician Roman family that traced its lineage back to the goddess Venus. Yet the Julii Caesares were not rich, influential, or even very distinguished. In 84 B.C., Caesar committed himself to political radicalism when he married Cornelia, a daughter of Lucius Cornelius Cinna, who along with Gaius Marius had led a revolution in 87 B.C. (Horrible massacres followed their election as consuls for 86 B.C.)

After activity as a lawyer, Caesar left for Rhodes to study oratory under the famous professor Molon. En route, he was captured by pirates, who held him for ransom. (At the time, the inept Roman nobility had allowed the Mediterranean to become a dreadfully lawless and disordered place.) Caesar successfully raised his ransom—then raised a private army, which he used to capture and crucify the pirates. After returning to Rome, he supported the surviving followers of Marius (Caesar's uncle by virtue of Marius's marriage to Caesar's aunt). However, Caesar's first wife died in 69 B.C., and he subsequently married Pompeia, a distant relative of his political ally Pompey (and the granddaughter of Marius's enemy Sulla).

In 63 B.C., Caesar was elected chief priest (*pontifex maximus*), and three years later, he formed the First Triumvirate with Pompey and Crassus, becoming consul in 59 B.C. (in the same year he married his third wife, Calpurnia). For the next nine years, Caesar fought the Gallic Wars, invading Britain in 55 B.C. and again in 54 B.C. In 49 B.C., he broke with Pompey, whose supporters now controlled the Senate. In early January, he crossed the river Rubicon separating Cisalpine Gaul (then a separate province) from Italy and began the Civil War (which continued until 45 B.C.).

In 48 B.C., with Mark Antony commanding his left wing, Caesar defeated Pompey at Pharsalus in Greece. In 46 B.C., he crushed the last of the Pompeiians at Thapsus in North Africa. Returning to Rome, he had his tenure as dictator (since 49 B.C.) extended to ten years. In 44 B.C., he became dictator for life. Then, while preparing for war against Parthia and Dacia to restore order to the Greco-Roman world, Caesar was murdered.

Plutarch was, and is, regarded as the greatest of all biographers. His special gift lies in his choice of intimate anecdotes, calculated to catch the attention of his readers and to bring out the moral character of his subjects. He sees their deeds as huge theatrical performances and gives us the illusion of entering into their hearts and their thoughts. Nevertheless, his historical sense invites criticism. Unfounded conjectures, imaginary conversational tableaux, and shaky personal judgments abound, as do distortions of the truth, when virtue or vice is exemplified.

Plutarch was also rather keen on dreams and portents and soothsayings—which are, after all, part of history because people believed in them and acted on them. Nevertheless, one must not expect marvelously accurate history from Shakespeare's play, as I am sure he himself was perfectly aware.

The views of Shakespeare and Plutarch are rather too simple, or perhaps it is merely that modern research has moved beyond them. Certainly, they were right to suggest, or insist, that Caesar was indeed something of a megalomaniac. Caesar himself was, apparently, well aware of this reputation, which is why he publicly and ostentatiously refused the kingship that was offered him early in 44 B.C. Its acceptance (if this was ever seriously in the cards) would have been a very serious matter because it would have been a formal declaration that the Republic was at an end. All the same, Caesar took an almost equally grave constitutional step, as his coins made clear. Not only did his portrait appear on them, so that he became the first Roman ever to be thus portrayed in his lifetime, but also he allowed himself to be appointed dictator *perpetuu*.

From the point of view of the Roman nobles, this was a really serious step to take, for the conversion of Caesar's essentially emergency post into a permanent autocracy meant that they could never again compete for real control of the state, and all the pickings that went with it, no matter how many consulships they might acquire.

In other words, the Republic truly was at an end. And this condition forms the basis for all the anguished discussions that follow among Brutus, Cassius, and their friends, which Shakespeare and the film record. Surely what brought their conspiracy up to the boil, about which we are told far too little, was Caesar's decision to depart for the East, as early as March 18, 44 B.C., in order to emulate Alexander the Great, far away from critical, carping Roman nobles.

This decision was indeed an ominous one for republican-minded senators. It was bad enough to be under a perpetual dictator at home. In Caesar's absence, they would be governed by Caesar's henchmen, the financial expert Oppius and the wealthy Balbus, who were not even senators (and Balbus was a foreigner, a Spaniard who had been adopted by a

46

JULIUS CAESAR

Mytilenaean). As this prospect was absolutely intolerable, the matter came to a head on the Ides of March.

If, as I suppose, there was a sense of urgency, it may provide the explanation for a problem that has always worried me, though whether it worried Shakespeare I do not know. How could intelligent men such as Brutus and Cassius really believe that the assassination of Caesar could lead to the restoration of the Republic? Even if they had won the battle of Philippi in 42 B.C., instead of losing it (and thus their lives), could they seriously have believed that the Republic would simply revive?

One has only to read the most elementary history book to see that the Republic had hopelessly, and irreparably, fallen apart. As it was, Octavian and Antony won at Philippi, and soon Octavian became Augustus, and the Roman principate began. But what would have happened if the battle had gone the other way? And would it, in fact, have been better for the Roman world, and for the world in general, had Julius Caesar lived? These are vital questions to which no answer can be obtained from Shakespeare or Plutarch.

Caesar's career came at a critical turning point of history. Indeed, it constituted that turning point itself. Some writers interpret Caesar as the founder of the new era, while others prefer to cast him as the terminator of an old one. That he completed the destruction of the old, collapsing Republic cannot be denied; on the other hand, to credit Caesar with the foundation of the new imperial age is scarcely correct. Throughout the ages historians have disagreed on these points, and no doubt they will continue to do so. But such is the background of the wonderful discussions between Brutus and Cassius that make Shakespeare's play so eternally fascinating.

Cassius

Although Brutus's participation in the plot against Caesar convinced several dozen senators to join the cabal, he was not the chief conspirator. That was Gaius Cassius Longinus. A somewhat violent, sarcastic, and ruthless man, Cassius survived the 53 B.C. battle of Carrhae, in which Crassus lost his life to the victorious Parthians. Between 53 B.C. and 51 B.C., with a regrouped Roman army, he repelled a Parthian invasion of Syria.

As tribune in 49 B.C., Cassius supported Pompey in the Civil War, and, like Brutus, he was pardoned by Caesar after Pharsalus. Although Cassius obtained a praetorship in 44 B.C., he nevertheless played a leading role in the plot against Caesar. After Mark Antony defeated him in the first battle of Philippi, Cassius ordered his freedman to kill him. Brutus subsequently mourned Cassius as "the last of the Romans."

Later...

Five months after the assassination, popular resentment of the conspirators—stirred up by Caesar's chief lieutenant, Mark Antony—forced Brutus and Cassius to quit Rome. Cassius returned to Syria, the scene of his previous military triumphs, where he raised an army. Brutus raised one of his own. Meanwhile, in 43 B.C., Antony formed the Second Triumvirate with Marcus Aemilius Lepidus and Octavian (later the emperor Augustus). By a will dated September 13, 45 B.C., Caesar had adopted his eighteen-year-old grand-nephew, Octavian, as his chief personal heir in the event that he produced no son of his own.

In 42 B.C., the armies of Octavian and Antony crossed the Adriatic and engaged the armies of Cassius and Brutus near Philippi in Macedonia. Although Brutus defeated the Caesarians under Octavian during the first battle of Philippi, Cassius could not withstand the Caesarians under Antony. Three weeks later—on October 23, 42 B.C.—with Cassius gone, the combined armies of Octavian and Antony crushed Brutus and the remaining republicans.

Background Reading

Michael Grant, *Julius Caesar* (McGraw-Hill, 1969)
Zvi Yavetz, *Julius Caesar and the Public Image* (Cornell University Press, 1983)

1953/USA/B&W
DIRECTOR: Joseph L. Mankiewicz; PRODUCER: John Houseman; SCREENPLAY: Joseph L. Mankiewicz; STUDIO: MGM; VIDEO: MGM/UA; RUNNING TIME: 120 min.

HENRY V

Two Films

Anthony Lewis

THE BATTLE OF AGINCOURT WAS FOUGHT ON a field not far from Calais on October 25, 1415. Some six thousand English archers and men-at-arms, led by Henry V, defeated a French force perhaps five times their number, inflicting wildly disproportionate casualties: six to ten thousand French dead to one hundred English, most of them wounded. The battle was described by contemporary chroniclers on both the French and the English sides. They say that when the English saw the enormous French forces, Sir Walter Hungerford said: "I would that we had ten thousand more good English archers, who would gladly be here with us today." To which King Henry replied: "Thou speakest as a fool! By the God of Heaven on whose grace I lean, I would not have one more even if I could. This people is God's people, He has entrusted them to me today and He can bring down the pride of these Frenchmen who so boast of their numbers and their strength."

That inelegant exchange was transmuted by Shakespeare into one of the great moments in all English drama. He has the earl of Westmoreland say: "O that we now had here but one ten thousand of those men in England that do no work today!" The king's reply is the St. Crispin's Day speech, fifty lines that would rouse the most inert audience to passion.

The historical question raised by Laurence Olivier's *Henry V* (1944) and Kenneth Branagh's 1989 remake is a double one: How faithfully do they reproduce Shakespeare's play? And how faithfully did Shakespeare himself represent history? That Shakespeare took liberties with history should not be a surprise. He glorified English kings in general and the Tudor monarchy in particular. King Henry, as a young Prince Hal in *Henry IV, Part One*, proves he is more than a scapegrace by killing Hotspur in single combat at the battle of Shrewsbury. In real history, Hotspur was killed by an arrow at Shrewsbury. Shakespeare's Henry, as king, is noble, decisive, tough, generous, witty, forgiving, and so troubled by his father's seizure of the crown from Richard II that before the battle he tells God he has built chantries where priests "sing still for Richard's soul."

In reality, a recent biographer, Margaret Wade Labarge, writes, "Henry had none of the more attractive virtues—he had little charm, although a real concern for his soldiers; no sense of humor, and a truly terrifying conviction of his own position as the instrument of God." Princess Catherine of France would hardly have been teased and charmed into a kiss by such a one. Labarge adds that, though his usurpa-

The Globe Theatre

The first part of Laurence Olivier's 1944 *Henry V* shows a performance of the play at the Globe Theatre in Shakespeare's time, complete with boys playing the female parts and orange sellers in the audience. How accurate is that picture of theatrical craft in the year 1600? I was a student at Harvard when I first (and many times) saw the Olivier, and my English tutor was the great and demanding Prof. Harry Levin. He regretted what he saw as the film's demeaning of the Elizabethan theater: some hammy acting by Olivier in the tennis-balls scene with the French ambassador, missed cues, and catcalls from the audience.

The original Globe Theatre, in which Shakespeare's plays were performed after 1599, was built by brothers Richard and Cuthbert Burbage, who owned its forerunner, aptly named The Theatre. After The Theatre closed in 1597, the Burbages had it dismantled and hauled to Bankside, a district west of the London Bridge on the south side of the Thames, where they used the old timbers to build a new theater. The original Globe burned to the ground in 1613 when a cannon shot, used as a stage effect, set its thatched roof on fire. The rebuilt Globe (this time with a tiled roof) was torn down in 1644, two years after the Puritans closed all theaters.

HISTORY

Henry V was born at Monmouth in 1387, the eldest son of Henry Bolingbroke (later Henry IV). Bolingbroke was himself the eldest surviving son of John of Gaunt, the duke of Lancaster. During the early years of young Richard II's reign (1377–1399), John of Gaunt ran the English government, but his son came to oppose the king. In 1398, Richard II banished Bolingbroke, and in February 1399, when John of Gaunt died, Richard seized the Lancastrian estates, depriving Bolingbroke of his inheritance and providing him with an excuse to invade England as champion of the nobility. After Richard's surrender on September 30, 1399, Bolingbroke became Henry IV and founded the Lancastrian dynasty.

Raised by his uncle, Henry Beaufort, the bishop of Winchester, young Hal learned to read and write with ease in the English vernacular. (He would be the first English monarch to do so.) On October 15, 1399, he was created Prince of Wales, and in 1403 he took over personal command of the war against the Welsh rebels.

HOLLYWOOD

Laurence Olivier was the dominant figure on the English stage in the postwar years, a status symbolized by his becoming Sir Laurence in 1947 and Lord Olivier in 1970. No one who saw him in the Old Vic productions of *Henry IV*—as Hotspur in *Part One*, then as Justice Shallow in *Part Two*—will ever forget the bravura of the contrasting parts. Olivier was a highly physical actor, handsome, with a heroic voice for Henry: perfect for a production whose subliminal message was to celebrate heroic Britain standing against the Nazis. In his film of *Hamlet*, playing a more reflective ruler, Olivier was, I found, mannered and unconvincing.

Kenneth Branagh is not handsome in the usual sense. He was twenty-seven when he made *Henry V*, the same age as the king at Agincourt, and he looked callow and pasty—more of a Brecht antihero than a symbol of British valor. By then the idea of British exceptionalism was as dead, for English intellectuals, as the idea of noble wars. It was after not only Vietnam but also Margaret Thatcher's adventure in the Falklands. Whether or not Branagh ever achieves the stature of Olivier—which may well be the aim of his phenomenal energy—he did create a King Henry for his time.

ANTHONY LEWIS

The Crispin's Day Speech

This day is called the feast of Crispian.
He that outlives this day and comes safe home
Will stand a-tiptoe when this day is named
And rouse him at the name of Crispian.
He that shall live this day and see old age
Will yearly on the vigil feast his neighbors
And say, "Tomorrow is Saint Crispian."
Then will he strip his sleeve and show his scars,
And say "These wounds I had on Crispin's Day."
Old men forget, yet all shall be forgot,
But he'll remember with advantages
What feats he did that day. Then shall our names,
Familiar in his mouth as household words,
Harry the King, Bedford and Exeter,
Warwick and Talbot, Salisbury and Gloucester,
Be in their flowing cups freshly remembered.
This story shall the good man teach his son,
And Crispin Crispian shall ne'er go by,
From this day to the ending of the world,
But we in it shall be remembered—
We few, we happy few, we band of brothers.
For he today that sheds his blood with me
Shall be my brother. Be he ne'er so vile,
This day shall gentle his condition.
And gentlemen in England now abed
Shall think themselves accursed they were not
  here,
And hold their manhoods cheap whiles any speaks
That fought with us upon St. Crispin's Day.

Henry V, 4.3.40–67

tion of the crown worried Henry IV at times, "no shadow of such a doubt ever appeared to have crossed his son's mind."

Shakespeare's audience was familiar with the history of the monarchy and of England to a degree that Americans, an ahistorical people, can hardly imagine. They knew the context of the episodes that he dramatized in his history plays: the context, especially, of the Hundred Years' War between England and France. To us, the idea of an English king claiming the throne of France by right and title seems absurd, a thin cover for a military conquest that seems just as unlikely to succeed. But at the time it was not so fantastic. The line of the English crown went back to William I, the Norman who conquered England in 1066 and ruled on both sides of the Channel. In 1337 Edward III declared himself king of France and began what became a war lasting more than one hundred years. He won great victories at Crécy in 1346 and Poitiers in 1356, but thereafter the French regained what they had lost. That was the situation when Henry V set sail from Portsmouth with a great fleet on August 11, 1415.

The ships carried eight thousand English archers, two thousand men-at-arms—the knights and nobles who wore armor in battle—and an unknown number of cooks and boys and helpers. They landed at the mouth of the Seine, where Le Havre is now, and lay siege to the fortified town of Harfleur. It fell after five weeks: an English victory that is painted in glorious terms by Shakespeare. ("Once more unto the breach, dear friends, once more, Or close the wall up with our English dead. . . . Cry, 'God for Harry! England and Saint George!'") However, in the play we next see the English soldiers as a weak, dispirited band the day before Agincourt. What happened?

History tells us what the play does not. Dysentery had ravaged the English, leaving some dead and many ill. A force had to be left at Harfleur to hold the city. The remainder—about nine hundred men-at-arms and five thousand archers—set out for Calais, which was in English hands. They marched 260 miles in seventeen days, often in the rain, with little to eat toward the end but dried meat and walnuts. Shakespeare no doubt romanticized the French herald, Montjoy, who called on Henry to give himself up for ransom rather than fight; his army was in such poor shape that Montjoy's comment in the play when Henry rejects the offer, "Thou never shalt hear herald any more," just might have been made. What brought the English troops to this point of seemingly inevitable defeat is accurately indicated in Branagh's *Henry V*, which has scenes of bedraggled, exhausted soldiers marching in the rain.

The battle at Agincourt is the centerpiece of the play and both film versions, as it was of Henry's short life (1387–1422). How did the weary English not merely defeat but crush the fresher and far more numerous French? Shakespeare attributes the victory to French decadence, English mettle, and the inspiration of King Henry. I was ready to volunteer myself when Olivier finished the St. Crispin's Day speech on a rising cadence. Military historians would not discount the role of an inspirational com-

HISTORY

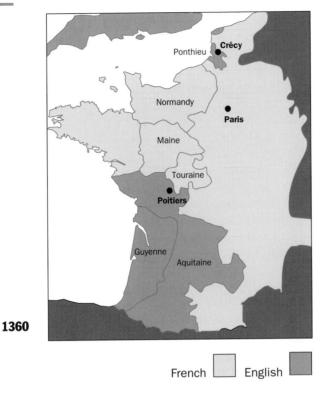

1360

French ☐ English ▨

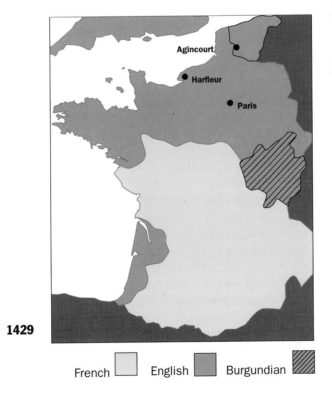

1429

French ☐ English ▨ Burgundian ▨

English Land Claims

The Hundred Years' War began in 1337 when French king Philippe VI confiscated Guyenne, an English-held duchy in the south, prompting Edward III to mount an invasion. Important English victories at Crécy in 1346 and Poitiers in 1356 produced the Treaty of Calais (1360), which ceded Aquitaine and several northern territories to the English king, with no homage required. The treaty was soon breached, however, and the war resumed. Sporadic fighting continued until 1389, when Richard II concluded the Truce of Leulinghen. Desiring peace, he agreed to evacuate Brest and Cherbourg and do homage to Charles VI for Aquitaine, thus waiving his rights under the Treaty of Calais. To bind this relationship, Richard married Charles VI's daughter, Isabella, in 1396.

Many English nobles objected to Richard's peace. They had become quite fond of frequent expeditions into France and feared the loss of profits associated with them. Accordingly, when Bolingbroke returned from exile in 1399, the nobility rallied around him and helped depose Richard. The French nobility, meanwhile, had its own objections to a peace that ceded land to the English. In 1405, while Henry IV was preoccupied with the consolidation of his throne, the dukes of Orléans and Burgundy began the reconquest of Aquitaine. A year later, though, a disagreement between them widened into rivalry. In November 1407, John the Fearless of Burgundy had Orléans assassinated, setting off a civil war between the Burgundians and the Armagnacs (named for the comte d'Armagnac, leader of the movement to avenge Orléans).

Upon his accession to the throne in 1413, Henry undertook a series of fruitless negotiations with the French. Not content with Aquitaine and the other lands ceded by the Treaty of Calais, Henry also demanded Normandy, Touraine, and Maine (the old Angevin empire consolidated by Henry II in 1152 and later returned to France by the 1259 Treaty of Paris, which retained Guyenne for the English).

The Men-at-Arms

The men-at-arms went into battle in medieval style. They wore sixty to seventy pounds of armor: steel plate down to the knee, steel leggings and helmets, face masks with visors. Each carried a heavy set of weapons, too: sword, dagger, mace, battleax, and lance. With all that armor, why weren't the French men-at-arms impervious to arrows? They probably were, at first. But arrows shot high in the air that then plunged downward would easily have penetrated the padding that was all the horses had to protect their backs. (They had armor on their heads and chests, protecting only against frontal attack.) Many horses bolted, the cavalry turned back in to the advancing lines of men-at-arms on foot, and the panic began. According to Desmond Seward, before long many of the armored French were lying on top of one another in piles as high as a man. Those still alive were led off as prisoners or stabbed to death through their visors.

The Archers

The French nobles regarded them, Alfred Burne tells us, as "the despised common breed of archers." However, with their English longbows they could and did do terrible damage. After the armies had faced each other for hours without moving, Henry decided to provoke the French into attacking. He gave the order to the archers' commander, Sir Thomas Erpingham, who signaled them to advance to about 250 yards from the French front line, the maximum arrow range. Quickly replanting the eleven-foot stakes they carried at an angle calculated to impale a horse, the archers resharpened the exposed ends and then, in unison, let fly their first volley.

There were five thousand English archers, each carrying one or two sheaves of twenty-four arrows. They could fire every ten seconds. So at the peak of the attack the French had five thousand arrows coming at them every ten seconds. When the arrow supply was exhausted, the archers moved in to kill the fallen French with cudgels and knives. They were barefoot in the mud.

mander, but they have other explanations for Agincourt: weapons, tactics, topography, weather, and the nature of the opposing forces.

As to the last, the French had raised troops hastily from all over a large country, and they had different commanders; the English were a trained army under unified command. Most of them were archers, and that made a crucial difference. The vast numbers of French men-at-arms resented the archers, ordinary men whom they considered ill-bred, preferring to fight the armored English gentry and nobility. Yet the archers were devastatingly effective. Placed at the ends of the thin English line and in the woods beyond on either side, they provoked the French to begin attacking with a volley of arrows. John Keegan, in *The Face of Battle*, states that the arrows were shot high in the air so that they made a sharp turn down on the front ranks of the French.

The French cavalry, armored men on armored horses, charged at the archers. They were a fearsome sight. But as they reached their goal, and only then, they found that the archers had planted among themselves long stakes with sharpened ends. Some of the horses were impaled on the stakes; the remaining cavalry turned and galloped back, riding through their own infantry. That was a first element in the disaster.

It had rained all night, and the field of Agincourt—newly planted—was mud. Some historians believe that this put the heavily armored French at a disadvantage: They were literally stuck in the mud. However, an English military historian, Lt. Col. Alfred H. Burne, writes: "The rain raineth on the just and the unjust alike, and though the English had had plenty of rain in the night they advanced farther through the mud than did their opponents. No, it was arrows not mud, that turned back the French horsemen and started the rot."

Another factor, an extraordinary one, was that there were simply too many French men-at-arms. They were crowded together; and as they advanced, the field narrowed, forcing them even closer together. As a result, many literally could not lift their arms to wield their swords. When an armored soldier fell, he often brought down those next to him, and once down no one could get up. Some suffocated from the weight of men falling on top of them, among them the highest English casualty, the duke of York.

The films do not show the fatal crowding of the French lines. But both Olivier and Branagh evidently had read some history to fill out Shakespeare's sparse account of the battle. Their films show the sharpened stakes and the massed flights of arrows. Olivier is particularly effective on the arrows, while Branagh emphasizes the mud. Both show what historians say was an important element in the battle: The archers, when they saw the confusion in the French ranks, ran in to climb among the encumbered French and kill them with short swords, axes, and mallets. The films omit a grisly chapter of Agincourt: A third line of French horsemen menaced the English as they were busy collecting prisoners. Henry feared that if his soldiers turned to fight the horsemen, they would be attacked from the rear by their prisoners (many still in armor), so he ordered the prisoners killed. The English soldiers were reluctant to carry out the order, because it meant losing ransom money, but the king sent a detail of two hundred archers to make sure it was done. The slaughter stopped only when the third French cavalry line withdrew from the field. (The English still had two thousand prisoners, who were taken to London. The duc d'Orléans, unransomed, remained a prisoner for twenty-five years.)

The two films reflect different views of history. Olivier's, made toward the end of World War II, is a patriotic pageant; it is about England as an idea, a spirit. In beginning at the Globe Theatre, Olivier makes us think of the Elizabethan Age. In that theater, without scenery, it makes sense to have the Chorus (superbly played by Leslie Banks) set the scene in words: glorious words. It makes little sense, in the Branagh version, to have the Chorus wandering about on a real battlefield or a modern sound stage. Branagh's film, made after Vietnam, shows us the brutality of war and the ruthlessness of ambitious kings. And in its way that is also faithful to Shakespeare. Olivier omits the scene in which Henry approves the hanging of Bardolph, his companion in the old Eastcheap days, for stealing from a church; Branagh includes the scene and has the camera linger on Bardolph's hanging body. (Historians say that Henry explicitly forbade stealing from French churches and punished transgressors.)

Poetry and acting have their claims as well as history. No one can show that Henry wooed Princess Catherine in bad French or that she countered in bad English. But after watching Renée Asherson and Olivier or Emma Thompson and Branagh, one has to believe that they—and England and France—lived happily ever after. Alas, history was and is bloodier.

The Dauphin

The French Court

There remains the question of the French court. Shakespeare shows us a king, a dauphin, and nobles who are effete and weak. Olivier makes Charles VI near mad, and that turns out to be historically accurate. Charles VI was intermittently insane from 1392 to his death in 1422. As for the dauphin, Shakespeare has the king forbid him pettishly to leave court for the battle; yet he turns up there, to be mocked behind his back by the constable of France. In fact, the dauphin was not at Agincourt. But who would deny us the pleasure of watching, in the Olivier version, Max Adrian as a foppish dauphin?

Background Reading

Alfred H. Burne, *The Agincourt War* (Essential Books, 1956)

John Keegan, *The Face of Battle: A Study of Agincourt, Waterloo, and the Somme* (Viking, 1976)

Margaret Wade Labarge, *Henry V: The Cautious Conqueror* (Secker & Warburg, 1975)

Desmond Seward, *Henry V: The Scourge of God* (Viking, 1988)

Henry V
1944/GB/Color
DIRECTOR: Laurence Olivier, Reginald Beck; PRODUCER: Laurence Olivier, Filippo Del Giudice; SCREENPLAY: Alan Dent, Laurence Olivier; STUDIO: Rank; VIDEO: Paramount; RUNNING TIME: 127 min.

Henry V
1989/GB/Color
DIRECTOR: Kenneth Branagh; PRODUCER: Bruce Sharman; SCREENPLAY: Kenneth Branagh; STUDIO: Curzon/Renaissance; VIDEO: Fox; RUNNING TIME: 138 min.

Later...

Henry V died of a sudden illness just seven years after Agincourt, in August 1422. He was succeeded by his son, Henry VI, a weak king whose reign saw England lose all its French conquests. With the death of Charles VI in October 1422, Henry VI also became the titular king of France by the Treaty of Troyes (May 21, 1420), which set aside the dauphin's claim to the throne in favor of Henry V, who married Catherine two weeks later. Of course, the dauphin refused to accept the Treaty of Troyes, but it was not until the emergence of Joan of Arc in 1429 that he found the means to recover his inheritance.

After Henry V's death, Catherine married Owen Tudor. In 1485, their grandson, Henry Tudor, defeated Richard III at the battle of Bosworth Field. Taking the throne of England for himself, Henry Tudor became Henry VII, founder of the Tudor line. The dynastic connection between the Lancastrians and the Tudors surely influenced Shakespeare—who, after all, lived in Tudor times and was bound to exalt the Tudor house.

JOAN OF ARC

Three Films

Gerda Lerner

Joan of Arc is singular among historic female figures in being celebrated as a heroic woman from the time of her death to the present. Even before her death, Joan was celebrated for her heroism by Christine de Pizan (1365–c.1430), the first self-consciously feminist writer in Europe. Joan was included in every compilation of celebrated women to be printed thereafter. In 1867, the aging feminist Sarah Grimké translated Alphonse de Lamartine's biography of Joan of Arc into English. By 1871, more than twenty-five hundred publications about her had appeared in print, including her appearance as a leading character in Shakespeare's *Henry VI,* a drama by Schiller, an epic by Voltaire, and a history by Mark Twain. During the twentieth century, she has been the subject of biographies and plays, operas and oratorios. There have been more than twelve films made about her, including a monumental Cecil B. DeMille extravaganza in 1916.

The facts about Joan of Arc's life rest almost entirely on the records of her investigation and trial, first published by Jules Quicherat in 1841, and on the eyewitness testimonies collected in connection with it and, later, with her vindication and sanctification. These are the reported facts: During the Hundred Years' War, the crown of France was in dispute between the son of Valois king Charles VI, known as the Dauphin, and the Lancastrian English king Henry VI. English armies, in alliance with those of Burgundy, were occupying much of France. The Dauphin's cause seemed hopelessly lost when Joan appeared on the scene in 1428.

Joan of Arc's Campaigns, 1429

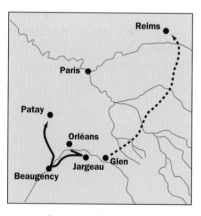

Route to Patay ———
Route to Reims ··········

An illiterate peasant girl, Joan had first heard "voices" three years earlier at the age of thirteen; she initially denied the voices but eventually accepted them. Following the urging of her voices—which she identified as those of St. Margaret, St. Catherine, and St. Michael—she overcame innumerable obstacles to reach the court of the Dauphin. There she was interrogated by various ecclesiastics, secured their support, and encouraged a wavering Dauphin to allow her to defend the city of Orléans, which had been under English siege for months. Overcoming the knights' resistance to being led by a girl, she won the support of the common soldiers and led attacks on the English at several points. Thus inspired, the French succeeded in lifting the siege of Orléans and went on to rout the English army at Patay. Yet the commanders refused to pursue this victory and failed to crush the invaders.

After much vacillation, the future Charles VII, at Joan's urging, continued to fight the English. The royal army soon reached Reims, which surrendered, and Joan was present when the object of her prophecies took

HISTORY

Monument to Joan of Arc erected at Orléans

From the transcript of Joan's trial: "Master Denis Gastinel, licentiate in civil and canon law, gave his opinion in the following form: . . . this woman is scandalous, seditious, and wanton, towards God, the Church, and the faithful. She takes herself for an authority, a doctor and a judge, when her very faith is suspect, and she herself persistent in schismatical and heretical error . . . she is seditious and a disturber of the peace."

HOLLYWOOD

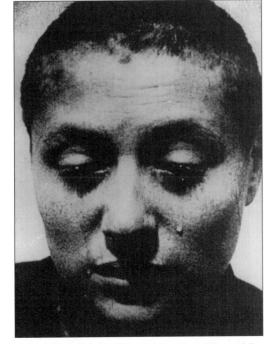

Renée Maria Falconetti in *The Passion of Joan of Arc*

Following the popularity in France of his film *Thou Shalt Honor Thy Wife* (1925), Carl Theodor Dreyer accepted an offer by the Société Générale des Films to direct a motion picture devoted to a great French historical figure. The Danish director chose Joan of Arc, who had recently been canonized, because, as he later wrote, "I wanted to interpret a hymn to the triumph of the soul over life." Almost instantly hailed as a classic, *The Passion of Joan of Arc* (1928) is a work of rare power.

Some Background on the Conflict

The so-called Hundred Years' War between England and France began in 1337. After 1407, a feud between the followers of the duke of Orléans (the Dauphin's party) and the Burgundians (allied with the English) led to civil war. In 1415 at Agincourt, English forces led by Henry V wiped out the French army. By the Treaty of Troyes (1420), the Valois Dauphin Charles (later Charles VII) was disinherited in favor of the English Lancastrian line. In 1420 Henry V married Catherine, the daughter of Charles VI; meanwhile, her sister married Philip the Good, duke of Burgundy. This established the Double Monarchy—France and England united under the English crown.

When Henry V died in 1422, leaving a nine-month-old heir (Henry VI), the Valois Dauphin challenged the infant's claim to the French crown. By 1428, however, the Dauphin had still not been crowned at Reims; Joan of Arc would shortly change that.

place—Charles was crowned at Reims. Joan wanted to continue to fight the English and take Paris, but Charles again held back and arranged a truce with the Burgundians. Several months later, however, Joan, without authorization, engaged the Burgundians and the British at Compiègne, where she was wounded and captured. After an attempt to escape failed, the University of Paris, which had taken the Burgundian side in the civil war, claimed the right to try her; the ecclesiastics there were determined to discredit Charles by showing that he owed his coronation to a heretic.

The bishop of Beauvais, in whose diocese Joan had been captured, bought her from the Burgundians for ten thousand francs and brought her before a Church court to be tried as a heretic. The outcome of the trial was never in doubt. Manacled, chained, and guarded by soldiers, Joan was interrogated for three months before the trial proper began. Her judges were the bishop of Beauvais and theologians of the University of Paris, who constructed a twelve-count indictment based on her claim that her voices were divine and superseded the authority of the Church. Joan defended herself steadfastly, but finally, when faced with torture and execution, she abjured her voices. The court nevertheless condemned her to life imprisonment. Three days later, she recanted her statement and reaffirmed the message of her voices. The court then turned her over to the civil authorities as a "relapsed heretic," and she was burned at the stake.

The primary sources contain a mix of verifiable facts as well as anecdotes of miraculous occurrences that seemed perfectly natural and factual to the medieval mind. Eyewitnesses repeatedly testified to miracles that Joan had performed, which explain her enormous authority over her contemporaries and her ability to turn military defeats into victories. Regardless of how twentieth-century historians view the likelihood of miracles, her historic role cannot be appreciated without an understanding that her contemporaries believed in their actuality.

Both Victor Fleming's *Joan of Arc* and Otto Preminger's *Saint Joan* adhere quite closely to the main historical facts of her story. They also succeed in creating a sense of historical veracity by getting superficial details right, such as the weapons and the costumes of the time. As George Bernard Shaw writes so scathingly and prophetically in his preface to *Saint Joan* (the play on which Preminger's film is based):

> The producers would build elaborate scenery, having real water in the river Loire and a real bridge across it, and stage an obviously sham fight for possession of it, with the victorious French led by Joan on a real horse. The coronation would eclipse all previous theatrical displays, showing, first the procession through the streets of Rheims, and then the service in the cathedral, with special music written for both. Joan would be burnt on the stage.

Indeed, this is precisely the approach to historical veracity in both films, but they differ greatly in how they portray the miracles and the inspirational aspects of Joan's leadership.

The Fleming picture enacts several of the miracles. It shows Joan trying to gain access to the commander of the garrison nearest her village in order to persuade him to lead her to the Dauphin. Refused, she sits outside the garrison, waiting. A strange event occurs—all the hens in the castle stop laying eggs while she is kept waiting, but once she is admitted the hens resume laying. Granted an escort of horsemen and wearing men's clothing, Joan makes her way to the Dauphin's palace at Chinon. Again denied access and threatened by a soldier, she predicts his imminent death and he drops dead. The guards, now convinced of her miraculous powers, admit her to the court. Put to a test, she recognizes the Dauphin, although he has changed garments and places with another courtier. She later persuades the knights, again by aid of a miracle, to let her lead them in battle. Fleming stages these events in a straightforward manner, so that they can be interpreted either as miracles or as fortuitous accidents.

The coronation and battle scenes are realistically portrayed and carry the main freight of establishing historical veracity. A narrator's voice occasionally offers historical background. The one dramatic event not verifiable in the historical record—the refusal of one of the judges to take part in the trial because of its procedural and legal flaws and his subsequent arrest by the bishop of Beauvais—is used to explain the grounds on which the trial would be declared illegal twenty-five years later. This invention works quite well dramatically and does no violence to history.

The scene at the stake looks like a medieval painting but flashes on quite briefly. Ingrid Bergman's luminous performance carries the drama forward and makes her pain and terror during the burning believable. Unfortunately, the "miraculous" ending—the cross held before her, now set against a golden sky in glory and supported by typical Hollywood music designed to signify exaltation—shatters that illusion.

Preminger, on the other hand, follows quite closely the tone and text of the G.B. Shaw play. Joan is presented as the sensible voice of the common people, her miracles are demystified as frauds, and those in power—clergy, military, and courtiers alike—are portrayed as self-seeking, corrupt villains. In his brilliant preface to the play, Shaw shows that he understood as well that the trial was fair for its day and its judgment rational. He treats Joan as a heresiarch and a forerunner of Luther. Yet in the play twentieth-century rationality prevails over medieval superstition. The dialogue, despite Shaw's stated intentions, is debunking and totally ahistorical. Shaw speaks but not Joan. Most of the lines—which include long, prescient monologues by Joan about her impending death—are not based on the trial transcript but are pure Shaw, much to the play's detriment.

Joan of Arc (1948)

A highly popular actress known for her fresh, radiant beauty, Ingrid Bergman was a natural for virtuous roles but equally adept at playing notorious women. After achieving international stardom during her seven-year association with producer David O. Selznick, Bergman went freelance, first playing a prostitute in Lewis Milestone's *Arch of Triumph* (1948) and then reprising her Tony Award–winning role in Victor Fleming's screen version of Maxwell Anderson's play *Joan of Lorraine*. For years thereafter, whenever Bergman traveled to France, customs officials would greet her with the same line: "Ah, Jeanne d'Arc! Welcome home." In 1949, Bergman left her husband, Dr. Peter Lindstrom, for Italian director Roberto Rossellini, by whom she had a child. She then married Rossellini, but the ensuing international scandal (she was even denounced in Congress) tarnished her wholesome image and led to the actress being blacklisted from American films for seven years. Bergman made a triumphant return to Hollywood with *Anastasia* (1956), garnering her second Academy Award, a sign that her "sins" had been officially forgiven.

A former race-car driver and chauffeur, *Joan of Arc* director Victor Fleming began his film career as a camera assistant in 1910 and later served as Walter Wanger's cameraman at the 1919 Versailles Peace Conference. Fleming's talent for spectacular action and ability to elicit strong performances from leading stars made him one of the most popular directors of the 1930s. Today, he is most widely known for two 1939 classics: *The Wizard of Oz* and *Gone with the Wind*.

Saint Joan (1957)

A former assistant to German stage producer Max Reinhardt, Otto Preminger began his directing career with the 1935 Broadway melodrama *Libel*. He subsequently found himself in demand as a Hollywood character actor, typically portraying villainous Nazis. His breakthrough as a director came with the critical and commercial hit *Laura* (1944). Preminger began independently producing his own films in the early 1950s and soon earned a reputation for controversial projects, such as *The Man with the Golden Arm* (1955), which broached previously taboo subjects such as drug abuse.

After a talent hunt that involved some eighteen thousand applicants and took the director to more than twenty cities, Preminger chose Jean Seberg for the title role in his screen version of George Bernard Shaw's classic *Saint Joan*. Seberg, a beautiful Iowa University freshman, had little acting experience. When *Saint Joan* proved a commercial and critical failure, her career briefly stalled, but her starring role in Jean-Luc Godard's landmark New Wave feature, *Breathless* (1959), brought her renewed international attention. In 1979, she was found dead of a barbiturate overdose in a Paris suburb. Estranged from second husband Romain Gary, Seberg had anguished over a 1970 miscarriage that had led to substance abuse and annual suicide attempts. Years later, the FBI admitted spreading a false rumor that Seberg had been impregnated by a prominent member of the Black Panther party, the purpose of the smear campaign being to "neutralize" the actress because she supported the Black Panthers financially.

Shaw included an epilogue informing the audience of the events after Joan's death. The film uses this device clumsily as a frame for beginning and ending the story. The effect is to distance the audience from the main events and to lessen the emotional and visual impact. It is as though we were seeing a film about the historiography of Joan of Arc, rather than about her life and death.

Preminger's public scenes and costuming are more modest than Fleming's, probably due to budget restraints. Jean Seberg's performance is occasionally stirring but mostly unconvincing. She plays the maid as a teenage waif and fails to convey her strength, drive, and force.

Danish director Carl Theodor Dreyer, in *The Passion of Joan of Arc*, takes an entirely different approach. This silent film encompasses only the time of Joan's interrogation, trial, and execution. The events preceding it are alluded to only as they appear in the interrogation. The story is told almost entirely in facial close-ups that are intercut dramatically to evoke an atmosphere of intense emotion. By alternating painfully slow images of Joan's agonized face with fast-paced intercutting of the faces of her tormentors, Dreyer conveys a sense of the innocent girl, alone and entrapped by evil men who surround and overwhelm her. An almost excruciating scene of three soldier-guards mocking the chained girl by crowning her and giving her a staff, in imitation of the scene of Christ mocked by the soldiers, illuminates Dreyer's main theme of Joan's martyrdom. The two other films do not come near the atmosphere of horror and ravaged innocence that Dreyer creates. The sparse intertitles consist almost entirely of lines from the actual record of Joan's interrogation, which gives the work a spare and appropriately medieval tone. Where the Hollywood pictures show Joan's triumph, her military victories, and her subsequent fall, Dreyer masterfully renders her saintliness.

Using only two sets, one exterior and one interior, Dreyer tells his story almost entirely from Joan's point of view and angle of vision. Only in the final scene, during and after her burning, is there a widening of focus to the common people, convinced of her innocence, rioting and being beaten by soldiers.

Fleming presents a spectacular coronation scene with thousands of extras, befitting his large budget, while Preminger endows the court scenes with interesting byplay, amusing bit parts, and extraneous dramatization. Yet it is Dreyer—in his low-budget film almost entirely devoid of scenery, costumes, and extras—who comes closest to conveying the historical truth: A peasant girl, a virgin, put on man's clothing; led an army to victory; crowned the weak, legitimate heir king of France; was betrayed by him and by some of her countrymen; and died a martyr's death. She was impelled to this by voices she heard; she believed the voices had come from God, and she made people in her time believe that they had. After she died with great courage, most of those present believed she was a saint. It took the Church longer.

The two Hollywood films imitate the life and times of Joan of Arc with varying degrees of success and some moments of verisimilitude. Dreyer, using film poetically and metaphorically, makes us suffer the agony of the peasant girl Joan and makes us feel the radiance of the presence of a saint. He has not only achieved a masterpiece of filmmaking, justly recognized as one of the great classics in film history, but also shown us how film can speak truth to history without a cast of thousands or a budget of millions.

Joan and Men's Clothing

Early in her crusade to save France, Joan decided to wear men's clothing. She did so as a practical matter because she lived continuously among soldiers, and she also claimed that it protected her. But her masculine appearance left her vulnerable because many considered it an offense against decency and a violation of the teachings of the Church. Her insistence on wearing men's clothing was cited in the indictment following her arrest, and it was a crucial element leading to her conviction.

On the afternoon of May 24, 1431, after she had renounced her "voices," Joan was returned to prison at the castle of Rouen. Several of the judges came to her cell. According to the official transcript: "She was told she must put off her male costume and take woman's dress, as the Church had commanded. Jeanne agreed and put on woman's dress." On May 28, they again came to her cell. She was once again wearing men's clothing. "Asked why she had resumed it . . . she answered that she had taken it of her own will, under no compulsion, as she preferred man's to woman's dress. . . . She said she had resumed it because the promises made to her had not been kept, which were to permit her to go to Mass and receive the Saviour, and to take off her chains." She then retracted her abjuration, saying that "what she had declared and recanted on Thursday was done only for fear of the fire. She said she would rather . . . die than endure any longer the suffering of her prison." Her sentence was carried out two days later.

Background Reading

Bernard Shaw, *Saint Joan: A Chronicle Play in Six Scenes and an Epilogue* (Brentano's, 1924)
Marina Warner, *Joan of Arc: The Image of Female Heroism* (Knopf, 1981)

The Passion of Joan of Arc
1928/France/B&W
DIRECTOR: Carl Theodor Dreyer; SCREENPLAY: Carl Theodor Dreyer; STUDIO: Société Générale des Films; VIDEO: New York Film Annex; RUNNING TIME: 127 min.

Joan of Arc
1948/USA/Color
DIRECTOR: Victor Fleming; PRODUCER: Walter Wanger; SCREENPLAY: Maxwell Anderson, Andrew Solt; STUDIO: RKO; VIDEO: Sterling; RUNNING TIME: 145 min.

Saint Joan
1957/USA/B&W
DIRECTOR: Otto Preminger; PRODUCER: Otto Preminger; SCREENPLAY: Graham Greene; STUDIO: Wheel; VIDEO: Warner; RUNNING TIME: 110 min.

Later...

Charles VII made no effort to save Joan, and on May 30, 1431, at the age of nineteen, she was turned over to the civil authorities and burned to death at the stake. Some twenty-five years later, however, the monarch did assist Joan's family in appealing the case to the pope, and in 1456 a papal court annulled the 1431 judgment. The case for Joan's canonization was placed before the Vatican in 1869, and on May 16, 1920, Joan of Arc was made a saint by the Roman Catholic Church.

CHRISTOPHER COLUMBUS

Two Films

Carla Rahn Phillips
William D. Phillips, Jr.

DESPITE THE SUPERHEATED EMOTIONALISM that marked much of the Columbian Quincentenary in 1992, scholars ended the year with a better understanding of Christopher Columbus and his times. The same cannot be said of the general public, especially in the United States, where the treatment of Columbus in schools has long been distorted to suit one political agenda or another. The two major motion pictures launched to coincide with the quincentenary had an opportunity to benefit from the work of generations of serious scholars and to present to the general public Columbus's life in all the complexity it merits. That they missed their opportunity should come as no surprise, though it is nonetheless disappointing.

The known facts surrounding Columbus's life, though minimal, do provide enough drama to sustain many films. Born in Genoa in 1451, he went to sea at an early age as a merchant mariner. Sometime about his twenty-fifth year, he settled in Lisbon and established himself within the Italian community there. During the nine years he spent in Portugal, he married into a family of minor Italo-Portuguese nobility, developed his plan to seek a westward route to Asia, and tried unsuccessfully to peddle that plan to the Portuguese court. Rebuffed, widowed, and perhaps caught up in political turmoil, he moved to southwestern Castile in 1485, taking his six-year-old son, Diego, with him. He was befriended by several learned monks, and, relying on powerful connections in Portugal and Castile, quickly gained an audience with the king and queen to present his scheme. A westward route to Asia would not only establish trade with the fabled East but also provide funds for the reconquest of Jerusalem from the Muslims and an opportunity to seek Christian converts across the seas, a notion dear to the queen's heart.

Isabel of Castile was deeply impressed by millennial prophecy, which accorded Spain a key role in preparing for the Last Judgment. Though she had many Jewish advisers, she would soon conclude that Spain's Jews must convert to Christianity or leave. Columbus may have shared her views in the mid-1480s; he certainly did later. The queen was occupied with war against Muslim Granada in 1485, but she appointed a panel of experts to study Columbus's ideas. She also provided periodic financial support during the seven years he awaited a royal decision. In that time, when he was not following the court, he maintained a household in Seville and fathered an illegitimate son, Hernando. Finally, after Castile won the Granadan War in 1492, Queen Isabel agreed to support a

From Portugal to Spain

In 1479, Portugal and Castile signed a treaty ending the war between the two countries. Portugal ratified Isabel's possession of the Castilian throne, and Castile agreed not to voyage in the Atlantic Ocean south and east of the Canary Islands. Thus was Castile excluded from the lucrative African coastal trade and what turned out to be the sea route to India. For Castile to develop any shipping trade with Asia, it would have to find a westward sea route.

Columbus arrived in Portugal about 1475 and during the next ten years made a number of local voyages to the Atlantic islands and the African coast. His marriage to Felipa Moniz, a well-connected Portuguese noblewoman, gave him access to the most current geographical information available at the royal court, but he remained unable to secure Portuguese backing for his expedition. In 1485, after political upheavals reduced the influence of his late wife's relatives, Columbus moved to Spain; here it is quite likely that he received his introduction to the Castilian court, and later assistance, from high-ranking Portuguese exiles holding important offices under Isabel and Ferdinand.

HISTORY

The Berruguete portrait

In the late 1980s a painting came to light that has been attributed to Pedro Berruguete, a Spanish artist who died two years before Columbus. The portrait agrees extraordinarily well with written descriptions of Columbus—showing a man with a long face, high cheekbones, gray hair, olive-green eyes, and a pronounced aquiline nose. If the new portrait is one day authenticated as a Berruguete beyond any shadow of doubt and the subject is agreed to be Columbus, the painting would be the only known portrait of the explorer created in his lifetime. Even if it is never authenticated, it will still be worthy of note because it follows the written descriptions of Columbus so closely.

HOLLYWOOD

Gérard Depardieu as Columbus

Although Gérard Depardieu handles his own language beautifully in many of France's most successful film exports, his awkward pronunciations of English words make his delivery in *1492* at times laughable: "Dee lund eez closh," he says at one point, expressing his faith that the journey will soon be over.

Columbus's Geography

Like many popular accounts through the centuries, both *Christopher Columbus: The Discovery* and *1492: The Conquest of Paradise* ask viewers to side with Columbus against the experts in Portugal and Spain who refused to accept his geographical ideas and support his voyage of discovery. Nonetheless, Columbus was wrong and his detractors were more nearly correct. The geographical dispute centered on the size of the world and the distance westward from Europe to Asia. All parties accepted the spherical nature of the earth.

Columbus shaped his geographical knowledge from evidence gathered during his travels, plus rumors about undiscovered islands in the Atlantic and a wide reading of the Bible and the works of ancient and medieval geographers. He found special inspiration in the writings of a contemporary, Florentine humanist/geographer Paolo del Pozzo Toscanelli, who described the feasibility of a westward route to Asia. On the basis of his own calculations, Columbus thought that Asia stretched much farther eastward than it does and that the earth was much smaller in circumference than it is. Thus he calculated a distance of only twenty-four hundred nautical miles from the Canary Islands to Japan, whereas the real distance is more than ten thousand nautical miles.

After assembling a learned committee to examine Columbus's ideas, King João II of Portugal refused to back him. In Spain, Ferdinand and Isabel twice appointed geographical commissions headed by Hernando de Talavera, a trusted royal official, and twice the commissioners concluded that Columbus's scheme was impractical. Nonetheless, Ferdinand and Isabel seem to have concluded that the slight possibility of success outweighed the risk of losing their small investment, and they gave Columbus permission for a first voyage. As luck would have it, he reached the Bahamas at about the point where he expected to find Asia. But for the unexpected presence of land in the Western Hemisphere, Columbus would probably have perished on his voyage long before reaching Asia, just as the Iberian experts had warned.

modest expedition, despite the well-reasoned skepticism voiced by many of her royal councillors. Columbus managed to find a sufficient crew for his expedition only after persuading several well-known mariners in southwestern Spain to join him, notably the Pinzón brothers of Palos.

After a largely uneventful, though occasionally tense, voyage of just over two months, Columbus reached an island in the Bahamas, believing it to be Asia. After exploring further and establishing friendly relations with some of the scattered local populations, he left behind thirty-nine men and returned to a hero's welcome in Spain. Though he quickly organized a large colonizing expedition, his primary aim was to continue exploring until he found the Asian mainland. Returning to the western islands, he discovered that all thirty-nine of his men had been killed, and the new colony he organized soon descended into chaos under his mismanagement. Leaving his brother Bartolomé in charge, Columbus returned to Spain in 1496 and organized a third voyage, while the colony suffered desertion and rebellion among the colonists and warfare with the local inhabitants. The crown took charge in 1500, with its agent sending the Columbus brothers home in chains to face royal justice. Although Columbus was allowed to make one more voyage in 1502, he was stripped of all his official responsibilities and died disillusioned and embittered, though wealthy, in 1506, blaming everyone but himself for his spectacular fall from grace.

The biography later written by Columbus's illegitimate son, Hernando, presented a sanitized, mythologized, and self-serving version of his father's life, and it is this mythic version that shapes both of the films under review. In both treatments, Columbus emerges as a surprisingly bland but generally good-natured individual, motivated by nothing especially compelling but desirous of doing well for his family and his royal patrons through his novel conception of world geography. Both films treat the historical record as mere raw material, to be adapted to the needs of the screenplay. Chronology is expanded, compressed, reversed, or falsified to suit the dramatic trajectory. Historical personages are revised, deified or demonized, conflated or created from whole cloth to serve the director's will.

Both films pay some attention to the visual evocation of time and place, sometimes producing stunning and unforgettable images; regrettably, those images are often hilariously overblown or just plain wrong. Almost no one in either cast can pronounce Spanish, and more than a few cannot speak understandable English. Occasionally, accurate scenes or bits of dialogue appear in the generally fanciful creations, but it takes considerable knowledge to separate the wheat from the chaff. The casual viewer would do well to disbelieve every word and virtually every scene in both films. They should not be viewed as historically based documentaries but as moral fables in a loosely structured historical context. The hero of both fables is, of course, Columbus, though the rest of the cast of characters, and the roles assigned them, vary according to each director's vision, as does the scope of the narrative.

In producer Ilya Salkind's *Christopher Columbus: The Discovery*, based on a Mario Puzo story, we follow Columbus from about 1480 until his triumph after the first voyage. Columbus (George Corraface) appears throughout as a brash and daring dark-haired young buck, energetic and engaging, sometimes down but never out. Neither he nor anyone else in the film seems to age. As the story opens, he is on the island of Chios on a trading voyage from Lisbon, accompanied by his loyal friend Diego de Arana. (He did not really meet Arana until several years later.) When Columbus goes to Spain with his young son, Diego, the monks who befriend him also persuade him to take his voyaging scheme to the Castilian court. Although Rachel Ward is too pretty to represent Queen Isabel at thirty-seven, who had at least ten pregnancies and a hard life in the saddle behind her, the dialogue is nonetheless believable. Isabel sees great advantages for Christianity in Columbus's proposal, despite the skepticism of her husband, Ferdinand of Aragon (Tom Selleck), and Tomás de Torquemada (Marlon Brando), head of the Spanish Inquisition. That these three pivotal figures are portrayed fairly accurately represents a rare victory for the film's historical advisers. Columbus's enemies at court are the haughty nobles, as well as the clerical commission of experts who reasonably oppose his scheme as ill-conceived. The seven frustrating years before 1492 are disposed of in a few scenes: Unable to launch his voyage, Columbus dallies with his mistress and works in Seville for a (fictitious) Jewish mapmaker, which allows the director to portray him (implausibly) as opposing the rising tide of sentiment against the Jews.

Once the crown backs his voyage, Columbus gains support by dazzling the locals with his wit (inaccurate, but nicely staged). The Pinzón brothers are surprisingly well characterized throughout the film. Considerable footage is devoted to the voyage itself, focusing on and embellishing two near-mutinies (real) and staging a near-execution of Columbus (fictitious) to build tension just before land is sighted. No one died on the real voyage, but in the film one (fictitious) traitor is murdered, and another eaten by sharks. On San Salvador (where the director has made mountains out of mud flats), initial encounters between Europeans and natives develop peaceably at first, with suggestions of disputes brewing. After Columbus leaves the thirty-nine men behind on Hispaniola, the film shows the deterioration of relations leading to their deaths (plausible but fictitious). The film ends with Columbus's triumphant reception at the royal court—though dark hints are dropped about disasters to come. Columbus has treated some of the natives cruelly and used threats and force to bully them into accepting Christianity. Near death, Martín Alonso Pinzón warns Columbus, "Don't let greed put you in chains"—a nice touch but somewhat obscure for those without a knowledge of Columbus's later life. The explorer emerges from Salkind's treatment a flawed hero but not a believable human being, much less the real human being who pursued a dream for most of his adult life.

Columbus, in chains, returning from his third voyage

Hispaniola

As a colonial founder and administrator, Columbus failed miserably. The wreck of the *Santa María* on the first voyage forced him to establish a settlement called La Navidad on the northern shore of Hispaniola (the island now shared by Haiti and the Dominican Republic). After hastily building a fortress, he left thirty-nine men behind in January 1493. When he returned less than a year later, all of them were dead.

In early January 1494, Columbus broke ground for La Isabela, named in honor of the queen and also located on the northern coast of the island. Even though Columbus chose a poor site for the settlement—a flat plain fully a mile away from the nearest fresh water—he laid out a grand classical grid of streets to define future construction. His Genoese companion, Michele de Cuneo, reported the more modest reality: "Here we made two hundred houses, which are as small as hunting cabins back home and are roofed with grass." In an attempt to make something of Columbus's ill-conceived and unpromising community, the colonists built irrigation canals, brickworks, and a flour mill at the same time they planted their crops. Despite these efforts, however, La Isabela did not last long due to disease as well as Columbus's inadequate provisioning and poor management.

Between his second and third voyages, Columbus left his brother Bartolomé in charge on Hispaniola. Bartolomé concentrated on exploiting the new gold fields in the south and establishing a new port, Santo Domingo, on the southern coast. The site chosen for the port was located beside a natural harbor at the mouth of a river and surrounded by fine arable land. Moreover, it was close to the gold fields. All these advantages made Santo Domingo vastly more suitable for settlement than La Isabela, which Bartolomé virtually abandoned. Santo Domingo remains the oldest continuously inhabited European settlement in the Americas.

The portrait by Piombo

Columbus Portraiture

Most of the portraiture of Columbus bears little relation to descriptions written by those who knew him. Bartolomé de Las Casas, who first saw Columbus and his Indian companions in Seville in 1493 and later wrote a history of the Indies, offered one of many similar descriptions: "In his external person and corporeal disposition [he was] tall rather than of middling height, his face long and commendable; the nose aquiline; the eyes gray-green; the complexion pale, tending to bright red; the beard and hair, when he was a youth, fair, but which soon became gray with his troubles." (Columbus reportedly went gray by the time he was thirty.)

Until the recent appearance of the Berruguete portrait, experts had long believed that no portrait was made of Columbus during his lifetime and that a painting by Sebastiano del Piombo was the earliest posthumous one. An inscription on Piombo's painting bears the date 1519 and the sentence, "This is the admirable likeness of the Ligurian Columbus, the first who entered the world of the antipodes in ships."

This portrait has greatly influenced popular imagery of the explorer. In the early 1980s, however, scholars challenged both the date and the identity of the portrait. Its gallery label in the Metropolitan Museum of Art in New York City now reads: "Portrait of a Man, Traditionally Called Christopher Columbus. . . . On the grounds of style this portrait of an anonymous cleric can be dated to the late 1520s. About seventy years later it was claimed to be a likeness of Columbus."

Ridley Scott's *1492: The Conquest of Paradise* is more inclusive, following Columbus from just before 1492 until just before he embarks on his fourth, and last, voyage across the Atlantic. In this version at least, Columbus and his supporting cast age. As Queen Isabel, Sigourney Weaver shows a wrinkle or two, though she wears coquettish off-the-shoulder gowns throughout the film, even in Segovia in the dead of winter. Thus shaped by the fertile imaginations of the screenwriter and costume designer, Weaver's character is hard to accept as the pious warrior-queen whom Columbus knew. The forceful Ferdinand of Aragon, a model for Machiavelli's *The Prince*, does not even have a speaking role. The commission of experts that sometimes met at the University of Salamanca is again portrayed as the collective villain, exemplifying the superstitious medieval mentality that supposedly gripped Spain during the late fifteenth century. In fact, the Spanish commission, like the Portuguese, had at its disposal the best geographical knowledge of the day, which cast justifiable doubt on Columbus's theories.

Physically, Gérard Depardieu is fairly well cast as Columbus, except for his nonaquiline nose and his irrepressible French accent. (Columbus spoke Castilian with an Italo-Portuguese accent, yet he must have been more understandable than Depardieu in English.) The least accurately portrayed of the major historical characters is Martín Alonso Pinzón (Tcheky Karyo), the case-hardened mariner whose support made Columbus's first voyage possible. In Ridley Scott's version, Pinzón seeks out Columbus in Seville, pliantly offering his assistance—in other words, playing the role of the hero's supportive sidekick. The drama that marked the recruitment of a crew is ignored, along with most of the epochal voyage itself. The focus is on the steamy islands and their inhabitants, and the edgy, exotic musical score further suggests that we are entering Joseph Conrad's *Heart of Darkness*.

Back in Spain after the first voyage, Columbus begins to win the grudging support of Gabriel Sánchez, the queen's household accountant, a minor figure in the historical record. Ably played by Armand Assante, Sánchez is used in the film to represent the court, at first highly skeptical of Columbus and his scheme but eventually won over by his accomplishments and impressive force of will. The large expedition formed for the second voyage includes Adrián Moxica, embodying the elite opposition to Columbus. The film sides with Columbus's version of events, in which his good intentions are deliberately subverted by greedy and evil Spaniards. By portraying Moxica as a strange-looking and even-stranger-behaving figure, the film focuses most of the opposition to Columbus's incompetent administration on one unsympathetic caricature. Though not all of it. Disgruntled colonists and disinterested friars take the message of Columbus's incompetence back to Castile, and the queen believes them, which agrees with the historical record. First chastened by an anachronistic hurricane, Columbus is then arrested by the royal emissary sent to replace him. In a final irony, the emissary informs him that another Italian sailing for Spain (Amerigo Vespucci) has discovered and claimed the mainland for Castile. The film ends with an aging and care-worn Columbus looking out to sea, planning his last voyage and recounting his earlier exploits for his biographer son. Though the lands Columbus discovered would be named for Amerigo Vespucci (by a German mapmaker in 1507), the film wrongly claims that Columbus's achievements were forgotten until his son Hernando's biography recounted them. In fact, Columbus was named and praised by virtually all of the sixteenth-century chroniclers.

Each of the 1992 films about Columbus has certain appealing qualities, yet neither captures Columbus's character or his probable physical appearance as well as the eponymous 1949 film biography starring Fredric March. Though less technically sophisticated than the 1992 efforts, it provides the most believable film characterization to date of the historical Columbus—brilliant, pious, cranky, self-assured, single-minded, irascible, rigid, and thoroughly irritating—the characteristics that shaped both his successes and his failures.

The Sons of Columbus

Columbus had two sons, both of whom served as pages in the Castilian court during their father's lifetime and had important later careers. The first was Diego, the product of Columbus's marriage to Felipa Moniz in Portugal. Diego married into the Castilian nobility, became the second Admiral of the Ocean Sea, and served as governor-general in the lands his father discovered.

Hernando was the illegitimate offspring of Columbus's liaison with Beatriz de Arana, a resident of Córdoba. Hernando accompanied Columbus on his fourth voyage and later wrote the best-known biography of his famous father. Hernando never married and used the wealth he inherited from Columbus to accumulate what was arguably the largest library in Europe owned by a private individual. Many of his books remain today in Seville's Biblioteca Colombina.

The death of Columbus

Later...

Queen Isabel died in 1504, two years before Columbus. King Ferdinand lived until 1516, ruling in Aragon, conquering Navarre for Castile, and acting as regent in Castile for his daughter Juana. The grandson of Ferdinand and Isabel, known as Charles I of Spain (and Charles V of the Holy Roman Empire), inherited Aragon and its Mediterranean empire as well as Castile and its American empire. Charles also inherited the Netherlands and many Habsburg lands in central Europe from his paternal grandparents. The union of these possessions created the first European superpower.

Columbus's voyages and colonizing efforts began Spain's American empire, but even during his lifetime dozens of other Spanish explorers followed him across the Atlantic Ocean. Eventually they created for Spain an empire stretching from northern California and the Mississippi Valley to Patagonia at the tip of South America. The colonial administrative structure established by Columbus's royal patrons lasted in one form or another until 1898.

Background Reading

Marvin Lunenfeld, ed., *1492: Discovery, Invasion, Encounter* (Heath, 1991)

William D. Phillips, Jr., and Carla Rahn Phillips, *The Worlds of Christopher Columbus* (Cambridge University Press, 1992)

Christopher Columbus: The Discovery
1992/USA-Spain/Color
DIRECTOR: John Glen; PRODUCER: Ilya Salkind; SCREENPLAY: John Briley, Cary Bates, Mario Puzo; STUDIO: Warner; VIDEO: Warner; RUNNING TIME: 120 min.

1492: The Conquest of Paradise
1992/USA-Spain-France-GB/Color
DIRECTOR: Ridley Scott; PRODUCER: Ridley Scott, Alain Goldman; SCREENPLAY: Roselyne Bosch; STUDIO: Paramount; VIDEO: Paramount; RUNNING TIME: 140 min.

ANNE OF THE THOUSAND DAYS

Antonia Fraser

TRUTH IS NOT ALWAYS STRANGER THAN fiction, but in the case of Henry VIII, with his infamous serial marriages, the old proverb has something to be said for it. The strangeness of the truth, however, has not stopped the creation of many, many fictional versions of this extraordinary melodrama—the story of a sixteenth-century monarch who, in order to marry six times, beheaded two wives and divorced two more (one died of natural causes and the last survived him)—and, in the course of all this, transformed the religion of his country. Probably the best known of these fictions is still the classic *The Private Life of Henry VIII*, starring Charles Laughton. For many, Laughton's obese, jocund, yet menacing image, glimpsed on late-night television in black and white, is the definitive Henry.

Derived from the play by Maxwell Anderson, *Anne of the Thousand Days* concentrates on one relationship only—that of Henry and Anne Boleyn. The director is Charles Jarrott, but the dominant force, one feels, is producer Hal B. Wallis, a man with a taste for historical epics. (Wallis went on to make *Mary, Queen of Scots* with Vanessa Redgrave and Glenda Jackson.) Although the film starts with King Henry hearing the guilty verdict on Queen Anne's "lovers," it moves quickly into flashback. In essence, the story begins with the moment at which Henry meets and falls in love with Anne.

The Six Wives of Henry VIII

(1) Catherine of Aragon (divorced 1533)
— MARY I

(2) Anne Boleyn (executed 1536)
— ELIZABETH I

(3) Jane Seymour (died 1537)
— EDWARD VI

(4) Anne of Cleves (divorced 1540)

(5) Catherine Howard (executed 1542)

(6) Catherine Parr (survived)

In historical terms, the date of this fateful encounter has never been definitely established, though the most likely moment is the Shrovetide of 1526, when the king was nearly thirty-five and Anne Boleyn about ten years younger. (Boleyn's birth date, like so much about her life, has been the subject of much dispute, but recent research points to about 1501.) In 1526, King Henry had been married to the Spanish princess Catherine of Aragon for over sixteen years. In that time, she had born him one healthy daughter, now aged ten. She had also born him several sons—one of whom, in the early days of their marriage, had lived for eight weeks; the rest were either late miscarriages or stillbirths. At forty, six years older than her husband, Catherine was widely regarded, no doubt with good reason, as beyond childbearing.

King Henry did have a living son at this point—an illegitimate boy of eight by his mistress Bessie Blount. Yet his dynastic ambitions were, of necessity, concentrated on the grandest possible marriage for his only legitimate child, Princess Mary Tudor. He had recently tried very hard to marry her to her first cousin, Holy Roman Emperor Charles V—Henry's goal being to establish a sort of pan-European kingdom under their joint

HISTORY

As the film suggests, the historical Anne was a graceful dancer. She had "passing excellent" skill at this and was often on the king's arm, noted a contemporary who called her a "fresh young damsel." Anne had long black hair, sparkling black eyes, and silky, well-marked eyebrows that were praised by another eyewitness as "the gift of Venus."

HOLLYWOOD

Much trouble was taken by the filmmakers regarding Anne's appearance and demeanor. Geneviève Bujold bears quite a resemblance to the famous portrait of Anne Boleyn with the letter B hanging from her neck. The French accent used by Bujold (who is French-Canadian) is correct because Anne was educated in France, a distinction that gave her an additional allure in the eyes of the English court.

The English Reformation

What began in the sixteenth century as a religious movement to reform the Roman Catholic Church resulted in the Protestant Reformation, with manifold political repercussions. The Reformation ended the ecclesiastical supremacy of the pope and resulted in the establishment of the Lutheran, Calvinist, Anabaptist, and Anglican churches. On the Continent, the religious break with the papacy precipitated political disaffection; in England, however, the political break came first.

On his father's death in 1509, Henry (1491–1547) succeeded to the throne of England as Henry VIII and promptly married his brother's widow, Catherine of Aragon, having been betrothed to her through a special papal dispensation secured in 1503. In 1527 Henry announced his desire to divorce Catherine on the grounds that the papal dispensation contravened ecclesiastical law. Holy Roman Emperor Charles V, Catherine's nephew, opposed the divorce, and Pope Clement VII, whom Charles had imprisoned, could not invalidate the marriage without displeasing his captor. When the prospect of securing a papal annulment seemed hopeless, Henry proceeded to dissolve England's ties to the papacy. With the aid of parliamentary legislation, he secured control of the clergy, compelling that group to acknowledge him as head of the English church in 1532. He then secretly married Anne Boleyn in January 1533, several months before his obedient archbishop of Canterbury, Thomas Cranmer, pronounced Henry's divorce from Catherine. Although Henry was immediately excommunicated, the king retaliated in 1534 when he had Parliament pass an act appointing the king and his successors supreme head of the Church of England, thus establishing an independent national Anglican church. Further legislation cut off the pope's English revenues and ended his political and religious authority in England.

Henry had no interest in going beyond these changes, which were motivated principally by political rather than doctrinal considerations. Although he had altered the church, he had no wish to introduce Protestant doctrine; rather, he desired to maintain the principles of the Catholic faith. The changes in Anglican religious doctrine came afterward, during the reigns of his children Edward VI and Elizabeth I.

rule. Alternatively, Mary might still have married another first cousin on her father's side, James V of Scotland, thus leading to a British union.

Again in historical terms, it is clear that the king's violent infatuation with Anne Boleyn, a passion that she refused to gratify in physical terms—at least completely—for some time, changed this scenario. By degrees, the king was led to believe that his marriage to Catherine was against God's will (hence the death of his sons), while his marriage to Anne would be very much to God's liking and would, for this reason, be sanctified by the birth of sons.

When we come to *Anne of the Thousand Days*, we find that the screenplay by Bridget Boland and John Hale does lay heavy emphasis throughout on the king's need of a son "to give the land peace after I am gone," as he observes more than once. It is also dated roughly correctly in 1527. However, Henry is assumed *already* to be searching for a son when he falls in love with Anne Boleyn, for which there is no evidence. *Already* he sees his marriage to Catherine of Aragon (played by a highly melancholy Irene Papas, her Greek accent standing in for Spanish) as "accursed." Once again, there is no historical evidence for this.

In the film, Henry's dynastic needs are contrasted with the needs of his sexual nature. Before the film opens, Henry seduces Anne's sister, Mary, who is now pregnant, then rejects her (and her unborn child) once his lust is satisfied. In truth, Mary Boleyn was Henry's mistress during a previous period, but she never conceived a child by him. A weeping pregnant Mary is, however, necessary to the film's plot: a totally unhistorical love affair between Henry and Anne in which somehow *The Taming of the Shrew* meets *Gone with the Wind*.

The insistence that Anne Boleyn initially rejected Henry—rejected him strongly, even violently—provides some good corny lines of dialogue ("Mistress, you will dance to my tune") and some tempestuous, even torrid, scenes. Here is masterful Henry, going for sexual conquest, with the ever-present warning sight of Mary Boleyn to remind us what will happen to Anne if she does give in.

Unfortunately, all this is very far away from history—and the mentality of the sixteenth century. It is a fact that chroniclers of women's lives during this time have to face: Monster that Henry might have been, all six of his wives married him willingly—they were, in fact, happy to dance to his tune—although at least two of them, Catherine Howard and Catherine Parr, were in love with other men at the time. The reason lay in the king's position as the very center of the world in which these women lived. In a material way, it was understood that the king would shower prosperity on every relative of his wife, something even daffy little Catherine Howard appreciated. Yet even more important was the psychological pressure of duty to the monarch; the effect of the king's courtship was to impress upon any woman the absolute impossibility of refusing him.

The real Anne Boleyn was delighted to receive the king's attentions; the originality of her (historical) character lay in the way she played her hand to achieve a royal marriage, having started with very few assets on her side. The film Anne Boleyn gives in to Henry only when she falls in love with him, for a reason that is never made quite clear—but it is definitely love, not ambition, that brings about her surrender. At which point Henry, in spite of such endearments as "you great big royal fool" (or, conceivably, because of them?), begins the long process of rejecting her. In short, Henry loses sexual interest, just as Anne's sister had warned her he would. Anne sums up the situation when she reflects sadly that, of her thousand days as queen, there was only one on which they loved each other equally.

This beating heart at the center of the film ("men want only one thing") is a pity because much of the detail is accurate as well as picturesque, including the appearances of the principals and the settings (such as Hampton Court and Hever Castle) that give a colorful, majestic, and historical feel to the enterprise. The film's account of Anne's fall is also one with which most historians would now agree. Her execution for adultery with assorted lovers is shown to have been engineered by Thomas Cromwell, acting on a hint from the king, who now wishes to marry the submissive Jane Seymour. That is, more or less, certainly what did happen: The king did reject Anne when she miscarried a son (having already born one healthy daughter, the future Elizabeth I). "She has miscarried of her saviour," says Anne's uncle in the film, a remark that may well be historically accurate. Be that as it may, it is certainly true.

Unfortunately, the prominence given to Maxwell Anderson's central love story means that any real political element is entirely missing from the film. A few murmurs about the dissolution of the monasteries have to stand for the whole process of the Reformation. Above all, Anne Boleyn's own commitment to reformist Protestant doctrines, which made her once again a female of noted independence and originality in her own time, is entirely omitted.

Thomas Cromwell

A disciple of Cardinal Wolsey before Wolsey's fall from power in 1529, Thomas Cromwell (1485?–1540) entered the king's service in 1530 and rose rapidly: He became privy councillor in 1531, master of the jewels in 1532, chancellor of the exchequer in 1533, king's secretary in 1534, and vicar general in 1535. During this time, he wrote most of the Reformation acts passed by Parliament and, from 1536 to 1539, put into effect the Act of Supremacy (1534) and carried out the dissolution of the monasteries.

After Jane Seymour's death, Cromwell urged the king to marry Anne of Cleves and thus gain an alliance with her German Protestant brother, but Henry hated his fourth wife from the start and the Protestant alliance was distasteful to him. Although Cromwell was created earl of Essex and lord great chamberlain in April 1540, his enemies persuaded Henry in June that Cromwell was a traitor to both his religion and his king. He was arrested on June 10, condemned without a hearing, and beheaded on July 28.

Later...

Edward VI (1537–53), the son of Henry VIII by Jane Seymour, became king upon Henry's death in 1547. Because Edward was only nine years old, his uncle Edward Seymour, duke of Somerset, ruled as regent, introducing the Protestant doctrines and practices so abhorred by Henry. Great things were expected of the young monarch, but he died of tuberculosis at the age of sixteen. Following her half-brother to the throne was Mary I (1516–58), also called Mary Tudor, though better known as Bloody Mary. The daughter of Henry and Catherine of Aragon, Mary at once made Catholicism the state religion. During her reign, many Protestants, including exhumed corpses, were burned at the stake. When Mary Tudor died, she was succeeded by Elizabeth I (1533–1603), Henry's Protestant daughter by Anne Boleyn. In 1559, Elizabeth reached a religious settlement with the Catholics that enforced Protestant religion by law and made celebration of the mass illegal but nonetheless permitted Catholics to pay a moderate fine in lieu of attending Anglican church services and permitted them to celebrate mass privately without interference.

Background Reading

Antonia Fraser, *The Wives of Henry VIII* (Knopf, 1992)
E.W. Ives, *Anne Boleyn* (Blackwell, 1986)

1969/GB/Color
DIRECTOR: Charles Jarrott; PRODUCER: Hal B. Wallis; SCREENPLAY: Bridget Boland, John Hale; STUDIO: Universal; VIDEO: MCA; RUNNING TIME: 145 min.

A MAN FOR ALL SEASONS

Richard Marius

IN 1534, SIR THOMAS MORE, FORMERLY THE lord chancellor of England, was imprisoned in the Tower of London for treason against Henry VIII. The charge derived from More's refusal to swear an oath supporting the king in his so-called Great Matter—the divorce from his first wife, Catherine of Aragon, and his subsequent marriage to Anne Boleyn. The Catholic Church wouldn't condone the divorce, so Henry separated England from papal rule and named himself "supreme head" of the Christian faith in England. More's silence on the subject, coming as it did from a man who had once been the king's closest adviser, implied his condemnation of Henry's actions. During his imprisonment, More was repeatedly interrogated by the king's aides, principally Thomas Cromwell, then tried and beheaded in 1535.

Henry VIII's Cunning

Henry VIII of England was certainly a man of primordial egotism, but he was hardly the raging maniac portrayed in *A Man for All Seasons*. In his later years, when he suffered from an ulcer on his leg that would not heal, Henry sometimes lost his temper in private and shouted at people. He once struck his secretary, Thomas Cromwell, on the head, and he raged to his ministers in 1541 when they revealed the adulteries of his fifth wife, Catherine Howard. When frustrated, he sometimes burst into tears.

However, in public, especially in his younger days, he could be viperlike in his cunning. Henry remained personally friendly, almost to the last, with many of the people he destroyed—including Cromwell and Thomas Cardinal Wolsey. And with Eustace Chapuys, the ambassador of Holy Roman Emperor Charles V (who was also the nephew of Catherine of Aragon), Henry played a resolute game of smiles, cajolery, and threats.

The historical Thomas More was witty, devout, principled, courageous, and faithful unto death—the perfect hero, except that he stood on the wrong side of the sixteenth-century religious revolution that carried England into an exuberant Protestant nationalism. The papal church became what Tarquin the Proud had been to the Romans or Nero's Rome to the early Christians, an overthrown tyranny remembered with proud hatred and triumphant contempt. To produce in sixteenth-century England a play about Thomas More would have been roughly equivalent to staging in contemporary Israel a drama about a principled Nazi martyr after the fall of the Third Reich.

Robert Bolt's play *A Man for All Seasons* exploded onto the London stage in 1960 and repeated its success in New York a year later for several reasons. At the time, a combination of tolerance, religious indifference, and the warm personality of Pope John XXIII had made Catholicism mainstream. (Americans had also elected their first Catholic president, John F. Kennedy, in 1960.) The horrors of the Hitler regime were still vivid, and Alexander Solzhenitsyn had recently revealed to the world in *One Day in the Life of Ivan Denisovich* the stifling of the soul in the Soviet Union.

Audiences were ready for the story of a heroic martyr to conscience struggling against the power of a tyrant, and Bolt gave it to them. Paul Scofield as Thomas More radiated a burning integrity and a stunning presence—not to mention a commanding voice. In 1966, director Fred Zinnemann's superbly filmed and acted version of the play swept the country, won a cluster of Academy Awards, and made More (again played by Paul Scofield) a household name. A couple of struggling schools even changed their names to Thomas More College.

HISTORY

Thomas More was most likely born in the early morning of February 7, 1478. He revered his father, a judge in the court of the King's Bench, and followed him into the law. More had also considered a clerical career, but he burned to marry and so resolved, as his friend Erasmus said, to become a good husband rather than a bad priest. He was married twice, first in 1504 to a country girl named Jane Colt, who bore him four children. Within a month of Jane's death in 1511, he married a widow, Alice Middleton. More served the City of London until 1517, when he became a member of the King's Council under Wolsey's direction. When Wolsey fell in 1529, the king appointed More to replace him. The symbol of More's authority was the Great Seal, which remained in the lord chancellor's possession during his tenure.

HOLLYWOOD

Paul Scofield as More on Broadway

The producers of *A Man for All Seasons* took a gamble when they bought the rights to Robert Bolt's play. Even though it was a stage hit in London and on Broadway, Hollywood insiders worried that the story of a sixteenth-century European martyr would not play in Peoria. Casting Paul Scofield as More was another risk. Although Scofield had won much praise for his handling of the role on stage, Richard Burton or Peter O'Toole (both of whom were briefly considered) would have been a more bankable choice. However, Scofield's casting turned out to be a wiser and more courageous one. Primarily a stage actor, Scofield was used to playing to the balcony; but under Fred Zinnemann's Oscar-winning direction, Scofield played such a strong, restrained More that he, too, picked up an Academy Award.

The Church of England

Thomas More became a martyr because he could not accept Henry VIII as Supreme Head of the Church of England, the title granted the king by Parliament in 1534. More adhered to an old and hard-won principle governing relations between the Church and the monarchs of the Catholic West. Kings were to protect the Church, but secular governments, ordained by God to suppress sin and keep order, had no authority to define theology.

The idea of a monarch—especially a king such as Henry—making theological decisions by whim horrified More. He thought that God's revelation inspired the Church as a whole and that whenever an issue arose that made consensus problematic, a general council of the bishops should define doctrine. Their definition represented a recognition of the consensus presumed to exist within the Church. Never did More suggest that one man had authority to make all the decisions that bound a community—whether that man be a mayor, a king, or a pope.

Cardinal Wolsey

Henry's government—led by his pliable archbishop of Canterbury, Thomas Cranmer—moved slowly to change old usages. The Eucharist remained the center of the worship service, and Henry held onto the doctrine of a "real presence" in the elements of the sacrament; that is, Henry believed that Christ was physically present in the bread and the wine. In 1538, splendidly arrayed in white robes, the king himself sat in judgment on John Lambert. Lambert taught that the bread and the wine were only symbols of the body and the blood of Christ. Henry condemned Lambert to death at the stake.

English did replace Latin as the language of worship, and the English monasteries were suppressed, their property confiscated by the government. However, oral confession in the sacrament of penance continued, priests were forbidden to marry, vows of chastity were required to be kept, and prayers for the dead—implying the existence of purgatory—continued. In the liturgy of worship, ordinary English Christians without taste for theology would have noted only slight differences between Henry's Church and the medieval Catholic Church it displaced.

The film provided viewers with the comfortable feeling that they knew all about More. He became a Catholic Abraham Lincoln, an icon of purity and principle who provoked reverence and affection. But to make his drama both a tract for the times and an appealing diversion to audiences, Bolt gave us a More who would have been scarcely recognizable in his own time and perhaps a scandal to More himself.

Some of the film's errors and distortions are harmless concessions to theatricality, and some are even plausible inferences from the *Life of More* written by More's son-in-law William Roper some two decades after the lord chancellor was executed. (Roper's tome seems to have been the chief source for Bolt's script.) More's eventual betrayer, Richard Riche (John Hurt), makes a superbly slimy movie villain. Roper naturally vilified Riche, and Bolt made the most of Roper's story. Yet Roper was not an eyewitness to the events he describes so powerfully. No doubt Riche was a man on the make, and no doubt he gained royal favor by his testimony, but examination of the fragmentary contemporary records shows that Riche's actual role was much more ambiguous; his testimony at More's trial (which was not before a jury of nonentities, as the film has it, but before eighteen respected noblemen) was far less malicious.

The film similarly reviles Cromwell, although his role in the whole affair is more unclear: Even the More family biographies were not hostile to him. Roper was on friendly terms with him before More's trial and remained friendly with him afterward. Nicholas Barker of the British Library tells me that a year or so after More's death, Cromwell stood as godfather to a child born to Roper and More's daughter Margaret (More had three other children the film chooses not to depict). Other factual errors abound, though they represent acceptable dramatic license. It is less easy to excuse Bolt's idolatry of More's character. The film adheres to Roper's contention that More sometimes opposed the then lord chancellor, Thomas Cardinal Wolsey (Orson Welles), even in Parliament. The film shows More railing against the cardinal, even though not a shred of contemporary evidence shows that More was anything but a docile servant to Wolsey in matters both public and private. He counted on Wolsey for advancement and never did anything to offend the cardinal until *after* Wolsey failed to gain papal acceptance of the king's divorce and thus fell from grace. The film is also silent on More's cruel and vindictive tirade against the cardinal in Parliament in his maiden speech as lord chancellor.

Later, More wrote with ironic wit of the flattery men heaped upon Wolsey in the days of the cardinal's power. However, it is clear even from these stories that More flattered along with the rest, and many flattering letters from More to Wolsey still exist. Flattery was the lubricant that oiled the wheels of court, and More used it as well as anyone. He was, as Geoffrey Elton has called him, Henry's "tame humanist."

Far more contemptible, however, is the saccharine picture that both play and film present of More's religion and his furious and cascading hatred of the Protestants. Bolt's More refuses to let his daughter Margaret marry Roper until after Roper has cast off a flirtation with

Lutheranism. (Roper's Lutheran episode almost certainly came after his marriage.) But in the film, More's attitude seems parallel to the polite but firm disdain we might expect of the head of a large corporation whose beloved daughter is about to marry a used-car salesman. Nowhere do we see the historical More who produced hundreds of pages of ugly polemics shrieking for the blood of Protestants. He wanted to destroy heresy by fire. Here is More in one of a thousand citations that could be drawn from his ranting works against the heretics: "The author showeth his opinion concerning the burning of heretics, and that it is lawful, necessary, and well done." When heretics were burned, More gloated.

Nowhere in the film is the More who raged against Luther's marriage to a nun. Nowhere is the More who after his resignation as chancellor went on pouring out works against heresy—even when the king was trying to negotiate an alliance with Protestants. These works, with their ominous demands on the king to do his duty against the heretics, could leave no doubt in anyone's mind about where More stood on the king's Great Matter. Finally, Henry's council had to order him to desist.

Nowhere in the film is the More who intended that his hatred for heretics be inscribed on his tomb. And, by the by, More was not a papalist as the film makes him. He believed that popes had erred, that the general council of bishops was superior to the pope in authority, that a council could depose a pope for any reason it wished, and that perhaps the Church could do without the pope altogether.

A Man for All Seasons gives us a More who died heroically for the sake of his conscience. It robs him of the dubious content of that conscience and thus robs us of the tragedy represented by the real Thomas More—and the catharsis as well. It leaves us not cleansed and thoughtful but with glowing confidence that right-thinking people like ourselves would have voted for the hero. In fact, most of us would have done what all More's family did—take the oath that he refused. We also would probably have voted—sheepishly perhaps—for his death so that England might continue to prosper without the threat of foreign invasion or civil war. Throughout the film the common people are depicted as ignorant trash, gullible, unable to bear ambiguity, incapable of thought, self-righteous, and transfixed by appearances. *A Man for All Seasons* was designed for just such an audience. It succeeds brilliantly because it judges us so well.

Background Reading

Richard Marius, *Thomas More* (Knopf, 1984)
J.J. Scarisbrick, *Henry VIII* (University of California Press, 1968)
Lacey Baldwin Smith, *Henry VIII: The Mask of Royalty* (Jonathan Cape, 1971)
Richard S. Sylvester and Davis P. Harding, *Two Early Tudor Lives* (Yale University Press, 1962)

1966/GB/Color

DIRECTOR: Fred Zinnemann; **PRODUCER:** Fred Zinnemann; **SCREENPLAY:** Robert Bolt; **STUDIO:** Columbia; **VIDEO:** Columbia Tristar; **RUNNING TIME:** 120 min.

More the Author

Woodcut from the first edition of *Utopia*

As a writer, Thomas More is best known for his *Utopia* (1516), a fictional account of an imaginary island republic off the coast of the New World. In *Utopia*, the individual is subordinated to the good of the community. All property is held in common, private life hardly exists, and the penalty for discussing political affairs in private is death. The Utopians are devout adherents of a mild and mystical philosophical paganism, but they are tolerant in their religious views—as they must be to receive the superior Christian faith brought by their European visitors.

The evenhanded idealism of *Utopia* gave credence to the notion that More was a gentle, noble thinker. Yet most of his books were screeds against Protestantism, which seemed to him a threat to both salvation in heaven and civilization on earth. More fiercely attacked Martin Luther, William Tyndale, and other Protestants, urging that they be burned alive. After he resigned as lord chancellor in 1532, he continued to pour out books against Protestants while Henry sought alliances with Lutherans in the affair of the divorce.

Later...

Anne Boleyn failed to produce a male heir to the throne, but she did give birth to England's greatest monarch, Elizabeth I. Unfortunately, Henry could not see the future and tired of Anne, accusing her of adultery and incest. He had her tried and condemned in a court presided over by her uncle, Thomas Howard, the duke of Norfolk. She was beheaded in 1536.

Cromwell's 1540 beheading at Henry's order remains mysterious. Hating Cromwell, Norfolk had accused him of both heresy and treason, and indeed Cromwell seems to have had Protestant leanings. But Norfolk soon encountered his own difficulties. Condemned to death in 1547, he was saved miraculously when Henry himself died the night before Norfolk was to go to the block.

Henry's government treated More's survivors lightly. His widow, Lady Alice, lived seventeen years after More's death. More's daughter Margaret died in 1544. In the meantime, her husband, "Son Roper," fell out with Dame Alice after More's death. A quarrelsome, litigious man, he sued her repeatedly for land that had belonged to More. Richard Riche bent happily to every wind and died wealthy as Baron Riche in 1567.

THE·RICHE·MINES·OF·POTOSS I·

AGUIRRE, THE WRATH OF GOD

Stephen Minta

C A S T

Lope de Aguirre	*(Klaus Kinski)*
Pedro de Ursúa	*(Ruy Guerra)*
Gaspar de Carvajal	*(Del Negro)*

Aguirre's Route down the Amazon

In total length, the Amazon is very slightly shorter than either the Nile or the Mississippi-Missouri, but the volume of water it carries far exceeds that of any other river in the world. From the time of its "discovery" by Europeans in the sixteenth century, it has seemed impossible that such a vast area of the world should not contain untold riches. From the early seekers after El Dorado to those who joined the gold rush in the late 1980s, the Amazon has been the site of enormous hopes and inevitable disappointments. In fact, as we now recognize, the land of Amazonia is generally poor, its fertility quickly stripped away by cultivation. Only once in its history has the promise of El Dorado been fulfilled: in the period after 1850, when Amazonia briefly had a monopoly on the world's rubber trade and a few grew fabulously rich on its profits.

ON SEPTEMBER 26, 1560, ONE OF THE largest expeditions ever to explore the Amazon River left its base camp in the Peruvian jungle and headed east. The party was made up of three hundred Spaniards, six hundred Indian servants, and twenty black slaves. It was under the command of Pedro de Ursúa, who at age thirty-five had been chosen to represent the authority of the king of Spain on a journey into an almost totally unknown world. The objective of the quest was the mythical kingdom of El Dorado, a golden land that would redeem all sorrows—and in which so many during the early sixteenth century believed, or pretended to believe. Ursúa brought to this expedition a lifetime's fighting experience, the self-assurance of high social status, and a reputation as one of Peru's greatest womanizers. But a few months later, in an insignificant Amazonian village somewhere between the modern jungle cities of Iquitos in Peru and Manaus in Brazil, he was assassinated. The unlikely ringleader of the assassins: a man named Lope de Aguirre.

A soldier of fortune, Aguirre came originally from the Basque country. He had spent almost a quarter of a century in the New World, fighting to win a share in the riches of the Conquest. Nearly fifty years of age, embittered by a lifetime's poverty, he finally took his chance. Having won power through the killing of Ursúa, he launched a reign of terror, murdering at least forty members of the expedition and creating a legend that survived in South America well into the nineteenth century. That Aguirre was mad, or became so on the Amazon, there can be no doubt. Yet he was something more than a pathological killer or a common criminal; he was also an astute politician and leader of men, and he found on the Amazon a theater he believed equal to the scale of his vast ambitions, a place where he could be, in his own words, both the "Prince of Freedom" and the "Wrath of God."

From the opening frames, it is clear that Werner Herzog's 1972 film *Aguirre, the Wrath of God* is searching for an authority that is imaginative rather than historical. "Late in 1560," we read, "a large expedition of adventurers, under Gonzalo Pizarro, set off from the Peruvian Sierras. The only document to survive from this lost expedition is the diary of the monk Gaspar de Carvajal." All this, historically speaking, is nonsense. Pizarro died twelve years before Ursúa set out, executed as a famous traitor to the king of Spain. Nor is there any historical place in the film for the Dominican friar Gaspar de Carvajal, who in 1560 was living safely in a monastery in Lima.

It soon becomes obvious that Herzog's film has brought together two quite distinct stories. First, there is the story of Gonzalo Pizarro's El

HISTORY

Although we know a great deal about the last ten months of Aguirre's life, we know almost nothing about the fifty or so years before that. All historians have been able to discover is that he was born in Spain, probably between 1511 and 1516; that he came to the New World when he was young, as so many did; and that for a quarter of a century he lived and fought as a mercenary soldier in South America. He was, says one of the chroniclers, "of medium height . . . lame, a great talker . . . with a *mestiza* daughter who was not at all bad-looking." Until his sudden emergence on the Amazon as the murderer of Pedro de Ursúa, almost everything else about him is pure conjecture.

Ironically, the only memorial to Aguirre anywhere in the world is this statue on the Venezuelan island of Margarita, which was devastated by Aguirre and his men in 1561.

HOLLYWOOD

Klaus Kinski as Aguirre

Along with countrymen Rainer Werner Fassbinder, Volker Schlöndorff, and Wim Wenders, maverick director Werner Herzog revitalized his country's film industry during the 1970s. Herzog, characterized as the "romantic visionary" of the German New Wave, put his heart and soul into the making of *Aguirre, the Wrath of God*, one of the most expensive independent productions of its time. Herzog reportedly pulled a gun on actor Klaus Kinski during the shooting of *Aguirre*, threatening to kill Kinski if he quit the film.

Kinski, whose piercing eyes and aquiline features were ideally suited to crazed or possessed roles, continued his acclaimed collaboration with Herzog in *Nosferatu* (1978) and *Fitzcarraldo* (1982). The latter's production difficulties were hauntingly revealed in Les Blank's documentary *Burden of Dreams* (1982). Kinski died in 1991.

Dorado expedition, which came down from Ecuador in February 1541. Pizarro faced the hardships, hunger, and disease that were to characterize all the later ventures into the eastern jungle, and he was forced to turn back with the main body of his expedition—more or less as he is shown to do in Herzog's film. But a small detachment of men, including the priest Carvajal, pressed on, followed the Amazon all the way down to the Atlantic, and arrived off the coast of Venezuela in September 1542. Carvajal's chronicle of the journey is the account of a born survivor—he lost one of his eyes during an Indian attack—and it provides a number of incidental details for the film. Much more important, though, the introduction of the anachronistic figure of Carvajal offers Herzog a standpoint of narrative sanity: Here is a man of intelligence who can watch and comment dispassionately while all around him dissolves into chaos.

The second story is the "true" story of Aguirre himself. There were at least five eyewitness accounts of what happened on the Amazon, told by men who knew Aguirre well and who inevitably found themselves implicated in his actions. However, Herzog makes little use of these accounts, and what happens in the film is often a world away from what the chroniclers have to say. For example, we are left at the end of the film with Aguirre marooned and mad in the middle of the Amazon; in reality, Aguirre brought his men down to the Atlantic following the same route that Carvajal had taken twenty years before. He reached the mouth of the Amazon on July 4, 1561, and from there sailed on to Venezuela.

The film also suggests a highly distorted, unhistorical view of the Spanish Church. "You know," says Carvajal in the midst of the apparently endless bloodletting, "the Church has always been on the side of the strong," a point that is dramatic enough in the context of the film but manifestly untrue in the context of the early sixteenth century.

Finally—and perhaps understandably—Herzog ignores the complex political aspects of Aguirre's adventure. Some historians have argued that Aguirre's rebellion against the king of Spain and, in particular, a speech he made calling on his men to relinquish their Spanish nationality should be seen as one of the earliest stages in the American colonists' long struggle for freedom. But Herzog stresses the mere theatricality of the events, denying them all significance.

What interests Herzog above all is the broad sweep of impressions, the drama of face and gesture, and the power of landscape. In three mesmeric scenes, we are given his sense of where the deeper meaning of the Aguirre story may lie. The first is the film's opening sequence, in which Herzog shows us the high Andes in cloud and then gradually lowers our gaze to a procession winding down the mountainside. This procession resolves itself into figures who will become familiar during the course of the film: Ursúa's lover, Doña Inés, in a sedan-chair; the hooded monk Carvajal; Aguirre, leading his daughter by the hand. All are struggling, all dominated by the towering mountains above and the mud of Peru's rainy season below.

The second moment occurs when Ursúa is taken away downriver to be executed. His face, as he lies in the boat, is serene, as though his death had long ago become inevitable. His acceptance of defeat seems to have as much to do with the awesome mystery of the rain forest that surrounds him as with the violence of his enemies. We see Ursúa as a man overcome by a world he cannot hope to understand, and this proves to be the fate of Aguirre as well. The third scene comes at the end of the film, when Aguirre treads his sinking raft, besieged by monkeys on an almost motionless river. As the camera turns in slow circles around him, the landscape shadows a descent into final madness.

It is at moments such as these, largely devoid of speech or commentary, that *Aguirre, the Wrath of God* is at its strongest. As we come to see the land of Peru through Aguirre's eyes, we do, through all the unhistorical details, glimpse a version of his adventure that is plausible in its own way. We shall never know what really happened to Aguirre on the Amazon. But at the very end of his life he wrote to the king of Spain a demented letter suggesting his immense disappointment that so many killings and so much effort should have given him so little reward.

"Never allow another fleet to be sent to this unhappy river," he wrote. "Even if one hundred thousand men went there, none would escape, for there is nothing on the river except despair." Aguirre had seen a world that, by its scale, denied a man's ability to believe in the value of his own actions, a world in which to be everything and nothing turned out to be distressingly the same. That apparent paradox is at the heart of Herzog's film and, in the final sequence, the distorted features of Klaus Kinski as he gazes out over the Amazon perhaps bring us as close to an understanding of Aguirre's psychology as we are likely to get.

El Dorado

The conquistadors were told a story, probably originating among the Chibcha Indians of the Andes, about a prince or priest who covered his body with resin before bathing in a sacred lake. Gold offerings were thrown into the lake, from which the prince emerged as the "gilded man," or *el dorado*. The idea became magnified in repeated tellings, and El Dorado took on the meaning "kingdom of gold," a place always just out of reach but tantalizingly real for several generations of immigrants to Peru. The myth of El Dorado was also encouraged by the Spanish authorities, who considered expeditions in search of El Dorado an ideal way of getting troublemakers out of Peru and into the jungle—from which, with luck, they would never return.

Later...

Herzog's film leaves us with Aguirre still on the Amazon, his journey apparently over. In fact, Aguirre went on to complete his navigation of the river and in July 1561 arrived with his expedition relatively intact on the Venezuelan island of Margarita. Here he instituted another reign of terror that matched in ferocity his behavior on the Amazon. He and his men finally moved on from Margarita at the end of August, leaving the place utterly traumatized and its economy in ruins. They sailed to the Venezuelan mainland, where Aguirre met his death at the hands of royalist forces in the inland town of Barquisimeto on October 27, 1561. His body was quartered and thrown into the street; then a solemn proclamation was issued requiring that any house belonging to Aguirre be leveled and strewn with salt so "that no trace or memory . . . should remain."

Background Reading

Bertram T. Lee, *The Discovery of the Amazon, According to the Account of Friar Gaspar de Carvajal and Other Documents* (American Geographical Society, 1934)

Stephen Minta, *Aguirre: The Re-creation of a Sixteenth-Century Journey Across South America* (Henry Holt, 1994)

1972/West Germany/Color
DIRECTOR: Werner Herzog; **PRODUCER:** Werner Hezog; **SCREENPLAY:** Werner Herzog; **STUDIO:** New Yorker; **VIDEO:** New Yorker; **RUNNING TIME:** 90 min.

BLACK ROBE

James Axtell

C A S T

Father Laforgue	*(Lothaire Bluteau)*
Daniel	*(Aden Young)*
Annuka	*(Sandrine Holt)*

The Iroquois and the Hurons

The Iroquois and the Hurons who clashed so tragically were more alike than different. Each was a confederacy of five tribes, or "nations," probably formed during the sixteenth century, numbering twenty to twenty-five thousand people. Each spoke languages of the Iroquoian family. Each farmed vegetables for the mainstays of their diet. Each reckoned kinship matrilineally (through the mother), and women owned the fields and longhouses. Clan mothers had a direct role in the appointment and removal of male chiefs and in the adoption of prisoners.

Despite these similarities, they were inveterate enemies by geography and history. When French traders settled Quebec in 1608, they had to ally themselves with the tribes north of the St. Lawrence River: the Algonquins and the Montagnais, who had access to the best furs. These tribes were, in turn, allies of the Hurons, who lived in southern Ontario near the Georgian Bay. All three groups were longtime foes of the Iroquois nations that stretched across central New York. Moreover, the Iroquois traded on the Hudson with the Dutch, from whom they obtained guns. When epidemic diseases scythed through Iroquois villages in the 1630s and 1640s, their war parties increased in size, range, and ferocity as they sought to capture culturally similar Hurons as replacements for their fallen kin.

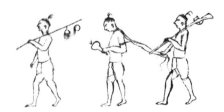

Iroquois warriors returning from a 1666 raid

IT'S ONE THING TO MAKE A MOVIE ABOUT A historical event; it's much harder to depict a cultural process. Brian Moore wrote the screenplay for *Black Robe* after writing a novel of the same name about Jesuit attempts to convert the Hurons of early Canada to Catholicism. Inspired by Graham Greene's essay on Francis Parkman, himself a keen critical student of *The Jesuits in North America,* Moore immersed himself in the Jesuit *Relations*—their field reports to their superiors in France and Rome—and located a storyline based not on the trials of an actual missionary but on the drama of one religious culture's attempts to understand, compromise, and transform another.

To personalize this clash of cultures, Moore hangs his tale on the physical and mental journey of young Father Laforgue, recently arrived in New France, to a distressed Huron Jesuit mission. He is accompanied by Algonquin trading partners, led by Chomina, and an Algonquin-speaking French youth, Daniel, who has his eye—and soon hands—on Annuka, the chief's daughter. After being deserted by most of the party as liabilities, the Frenchmen and their loyal Algonquin friends are viciously attacked and taken prisoner by an Iroquois war party. After they're tortured and Chomina's young son's throat is cut, the captives escape from the Iroquois village and make their way upriver to Huronia. When Laforgue finally reaches the mission, he finds it stricken with disease and despair and realizes that the Christian gains have come at tremendous expense to the Indians. The point is underscored by a postscript noting that the Christianized Hurons were subsequently wiped out by the Iroquois.

Director Bruce Beresford has taken great pains to recapture the spirit of the time, the place, and the cultural clash. The autumn beauty of the Lac St-Jean–Saguenay region—standing in for the Ottawa River Valley—is spectacular. The reconstructed Huron village at Midland, Ontario, lends authenticity, as do seventeenth-century buildings in Rouen, France, used for Laforgue flashbacks. Best of all is the film's evenhanded depiction of the baffling otherness of both native and French cultures. Neither culture is morally privileged; each is presented to the viewer in its undiluted strangeness, as it was to the other in 1634. Indian speech (Cree rather than Algonquin and Montagnais, as well as correct Mohawk) is translated in subtitles, though for non-Quebec audiences the Frenchmen speak English.

Because it is not strictly relevant to the plot, we are not told that the Jesuit missions to the five large Huron nations near Georgian Bay began

HISTORY

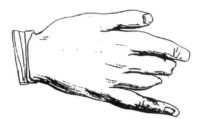

The stigmata of Indian torture are visible on the mangled hands of the artist, Father Francesco Bressani, who was captured by the Iroquois in 1644. "Of ten fingers," he wrote from captivity, "I no longer have five good ones." Rescued by the Dutch, Bressani served nearly four years among the Hurons before returning to Italy. More than one mutilated Jesuit appeared in European pulpits to edify the faithful with their wounds and to inspire other priests to answer the Canadian call.

HOLLYWOOD

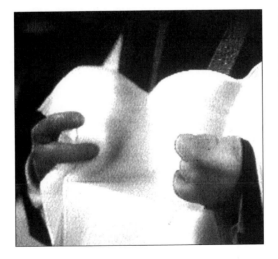

In Rouen Cathedral, novice Laforgue (Lothaire Bluteau) is impressed by a veteran priest who wants to return to Canada to convert the Indians who cut off several of his fingers and burned off his ear.

The Jesuits

Paul Le Jeune

The Black Robes in Canada were members of the Society of Jesus, an order of missionary priests founded in 1534 by Ignatius Loyola, a former Spanish soldier-courtier studying theology at the University of Paris. Six years later, the pope gave the order his blessing after its members took vows of perpetual poverty, chastity, and obedience. By 1626 the Jesuits numbered over fifteen thousand and had established Catholic missions not only in Reformation Europe but also in Asia, Africa, and the Americas.

The Jesuits were known for their educational foundations (some 444 colleges, 56 seminaries, and 44 houses of training by 1626), their service as royal confessors (especially to the French kings), and their international missions. Trained at length in their own schools, the Jesuits were among the most learned men in Europe. They were accomplished linguists who learned myriad native languages, practiced students of alien cultures, and keen debaters. Their task was to attack "paganism" by supplanting native religious leaders with their own evangelical authority and to lead entire tribes to embrace "the Faith."

The Jesuits served in French Canada from 1611 to 1613, 1625 to 1629, and 1633 to 1800. In the seventeenth century alone, 115 priests maintained thirty missions and baptized more than ten thousand healthy adult Indians after considerable catechizing and moral testing. The keystone of the Canadian mission was the Huron confederacy with its large sedentary villages of trading partners and allies. From their headquarters at Sainte-Marie, the Black Robes fanned out to villages in all five nations, where they built churches, cared for the sick, and baptized the dying.

Paul Le Jeune (1591–1664) was the Jesuit superior in Canada during much of the 1630s and the editor of the first eleven *Relations*. Published in Europe annually between 1632 and 1672, the *Relations* sought to publicize the Canadian activities of the Jesuits, raise funds for the order, and attract settlers and nuns to Canada to help civilize *les sauvages*. However, their efforts were halted by the ferocious Iroquois raids of the 1640s.

in 1623 with the Recollects, an understaffed mendicant order of Franciscans who invited the Jesuits to Canada to join them two years later. After the English captured New France in 1629 and expelled the French for the next three years, only the Jesuits returned to resume their assault on the "paganism" of their Huron trading partners. But we are shown in memorable detail just how durable and consistent native values and practices were. We are also made to see French culture through native eyes, just as we know Laforgue interprets theirs. Only Daniel, the new hybrid Canadian, navigates the cultural rapids as a surehanded relativist.

In the film, the Jesuits—and particularly Laforgue—have to overcome two major obstacles if they are to conquer the native religion: a dream and a shaman. Shortly after leaving Quebec, Chomina dreams of a black crow pecking out the eyes of an unidentified Indian on a deserted winter island. Because dreams were regarded as "wishes of the soul" that needed to be fulfilled to prevent misfortune, the Algonquins seek out a famous Montagnais shaman (anomalously) to interpret the dream. Laforgue and this dwarf sorcerer engage in a contest of will and power over the next few days. When Laforgue baptizes a dead Algonquin infant, the Indians decide that he has "cast a spell on it" and stolen its spirit. They then abandon the Jesuit.

> ## "I have in mind a *Heart of Darkness* tale, a story of a journey upriver."
>
> *Brian Moore*

Native life posed other challenges to French proselytizers. Endemic warfare hindered missions dedicated to the cause of peace, particularly when the "pagan" Iroquois conducted revenge raids against their age-old Huron rivals. Many native men also had more than one wife, which contravened the Catholic sacrament of marriage. Native warriors had difficulty appreciating French priests, who wore feminine robes, carried no weapons, and showed no interest in women, beaver skins, or hunting. Unlike Counter-Reformation Catholicism, native religion was inclusive and tolerant, adding new deities and rituals to old as hedges against the growing uncertainties of life.

But as *Black Robe* makes clear, the Jesuits had several weapons in their arsenal. They quickly learned the natives' languages. (At the Jesuit house in Quebec, Laforgue has studied Algonquin and Huron.) The desire for French trade goods—particularly cloth, metal tools, and guns (which the French initially sold or gave only to converts)—also gave the Jesuits leverage among the tribes and, historically, kept the Huron missionaries alive. In the film, one Jesuit is tomahawked by a grieving father who does not wish his dead child to be baptized. Imported epidemic diseases, which did not seem to afflict the French, frightened and weakened native villagers and disposed them to listen to explanations and spiritual remedies offered by the Black Robes, as the missionaries were known. So did the French possession and control of "miraculous" technology. In the film, Indian visitors at a Quebec church are astonished by the chiming of its clock—"Captain Clock is alive!"—and at the ability of the literate French to "read" minds at a distance, as only their own shamans supposedly could. The film rings true on such points as these.

Yet despite a valiant effort to be faithful to historical truth, *Black Robe* contains a number of anomalies. The plot turns around the fifteen-hundred-mile journey of an untried, rather wimpy Jesuit, accompanied by only a lovesick French lad lacking any religious convictions. But the *Constitutions* of the Jesuits mandated that priests be sent in pairs, partly to avoid the kind of sexual temptation to which Laforgue succumbs when he happens on a nocturnal bout of (missionary-position) lovemaking between Daniel and Annuka. Only in the late 1630s did the Jesuits resort to *donnés*—lay domestics who signed a civil contract and took a vow to serve the order in equal chastity, poverty, and obedience—to accompany them on missions. And no sensible Canadian would have embarked on such a long journey so close to the winter freeze-up. Scenes of the escapees dragging and paddling fragile bark canoes over and through the ice are simply ludicrous.

Less noticeable to most viewers are the unhistorical location of the Iroquois village on the Ottawa River west of Montreal (Algonquin territory) and the puzzling behavior of the Iroquois captors. The film shows scaffold burials outside longhouses, which (correctly) suggest that the Iroquois, too, were suffering from epidemics. However, they would never have gratuitously killed a young prisoner who could have been adopted into a family to replace a fallen kinsman. Nor would a guard have attempted to have sex with a female prisoner. A strict taboo applied to war prisoners in general throughout the native East, but the Iroquois in particular eschewed sex with future adopted kinswomen. The filmmakers also have no documentary grounds for depicting two incidents of Indian-Indian sex in the animal position. Finally, no Iroquois guard was ever posted in a scaffold tower in the cold dead of a winter night. Sensibly, native war parties stayed home in winter.

Background Reading

James Axtell, *The Invasion Within: The Contest of Cultures in Colonial North America* (Oxford University Press, 1985)

Bruce G. Trigger, *The Children of Aataentsic: A History of the Huron People to 1660* (McGill-Queen's University Press, 1976)

1991/Canada-Australia/Color
DIRECTOR: Bruce Beresford; PRODUCER: Robert Lantos, Stephane Reichel, Sue Milliken; SCREENPLAY: Brian Moore; STUDIO: Samuel Goldwyn; VIDEO: Vidmark; RUNNING TIME: 100 min.

Jesuit Baptisms

In the drawing above (from a map cartouche), a Jesuit missionary, wearing a distinctive Catholic biretta, baptizes a Canadian Indian. Unless the candidate was near death, the Jesuits in Canada did not baptize natives except after rigorous instruction and moral testing, sometimes for years. Those Indians who were converted worshiped their new Christian deity instead of (or perhaps in addition to) their ancient deity, the sun.

Later...

Large Iroquois armies, drawing warriors from all five nations, mercilessly attacked the disease-weakened Hurons. The Jesuits torched their headquarters at Sainte-Marie and fled west with their native converts, first to Christian Island in Lake Huron and then, the following year, to Quebec. Several priests were captured and martyred, often with tortures mocking Christian ceremonies. Resisting Huron villagers were either killed or marched to Iroquoia, where they were adopted en masse. Those who fled south and west became known as Wyandots and figured in eighteenth-century Anglo-French rivalries.

After the Iroquois destroyed Huronia, the Jesuits moved on to other tribes in the Great Lakes region, Illinois, and later Louisiana. When New France fell to the British in 1763, the Indians were allowed to keep their Jesuit priests but not replace them. The last French Black Robe died in service in 1800, twenty-seven years after the pope had officially suppressed the order worldwide.

CAST

Nathaniel Poe   *(Daniel Day-Lewis)*
Cora Munro   *(Madeleine Stowe)*
Chingachgook   *(Russell Means)*
Uncas   *(Eric Schweig)*

The Book

Although on its original publication James Fenimore Cooper's *The Last of the Mohicans* met a mixed critical reception, it enjoyed immediate popular success. "Mr. Cooper," W.H. Gardiner noted in the July 1826 *North American Review*, "has the almost singular merit of writing American novels which everybody reads." What everybody read about in *The Last of the Mohicans* was a romance of the forest, of Indians and Natty Bumppo (the white man who learned from them), of a society barely gone. Cooper's Bumppo was inspired by scouts: men who prepared the way for civilization and in doing so destroyed the very world they valued. Gardiner did not see the scouts as tragic, but we read Natty's story as a tragedy: Natty Bumppo, the white Indian, put Indian knowledge to work to eliminate Indians who opposed the British; in eliminating them, he eliminated the world he loved.

THE LAST OF THE MOHICANS

Richard White

MICHAEL MANN'S *THE LAST OF THE MOHICANS* is a third-generation fiction: a film adapted from a film that was adapted from a novel. Uncas, Natty Bumppo (now Nathaniel Poe), Chingachgook, Magua, and Colonel Munro's daughters, Alice and Cora, are all creations of James Fenimore Cooper. For this effort, they have been redesigned in Hollywood and located on the New York State frontier at the besieged Fort William Henry during the French and Indian War. They move through the film's historical setting as tourists move through Colonial Williamsburg—like modern people in an artfully re-created simulation of the past.

With its mixture of period setting and fictional characters, *The Last of the Mohicans* is a costume drama. People just like us, except more beautiful, dress up in exotic outfits and pretend, well, that they are just like us except more beautiful. And because they walk like us, talk like us, and share our values and prejudices, the setting, the scenery, and the costumes become essential for creating the illusion that this is history.

The performers have to *look* exotic because they sure don't *act* exotic. For example, the basic character traits of English colonial officials appear to have been lifted from a close study of Monty Python skits: The officers are, without exception, supercilious twits. The Indians are also quite a piece of work: They are a modern version of what Mark Twain called "Cooper Indians." These aborigines, who possess an unfailing if occasionally loony woodcraft, come in two types—noble savages and ignoble savages. Mann has added a dose of twentieth-century spirituality to bring the noble savages up-to-date. The ignoble savages are Huron and Catholic; the most noble savages are Uncas and Chingachgook.

The relation of these Indians to historic Indian peoples of the region is, to put it generously, postmodern. For *The Last of the Mohicans*, history is a junkyard full of motifs and incidents that can be retrieved, combined, and paired with new inventions as Mann sees fit. It is not that all the details are all wrong; it is that they never were combined in this fashion. It is like having George Washington, properly costumed, throwing out the first ball for a 1843 Washington Senators baseball season opener. Sure, there was a George Washington; sure, there once were Washington Senators; sure, the president throws out the first ball; sure, there was an 1843. So what's the problem?

Magua, the film's Huron villain, exemplifies the problem. There were fifty-two Hurons from Detroit and Lorette with the marquis de Montcalm. They were, indeed, Catholics. But they lived in mission towns adjacent to

HISTORY

A Cooper woodsman

"Cooper's gift in the way of invention was not a rich endowment. In his little box of stage-properties he kept six or eight cunning devices, tricks, artifices for his savages and woodsmen to deceive and circumvent each other with, and he was never so happy as when he was working these innocent things and seeing them go. . . . He prized his broken twig above all the rest of his effects, and worked it the hardest. It is a restful chapter in any book of his when somebody doesn't step on a dry twig and alarm all the reds and whites for two hundred yards around."

Mark Twain

HOLLYWOOD

Daniel Day-Lewis as Nathaniel Poe

Director Michael Mann's memory of *The Last of the Mohicans* begins with the 1936 version starring Randolph Scott. "*The Last of the Mohicans* is probably the first film I saw as a child," Mann says. It was this memory that led Mann back to Cooper's novel. "I found parts of it very provocative and powerful," he says, "but the novel was written in an age which romanticized the events of seventy-five years earlier. It also diminished complex and powerful native cultures into simplistic and two-dimensional villains." Mann began his own research, supplementing Cooper's prose with accounts by historian Francis Parkman, the diaries of the comte de Bougainville, and the work of Simon Schama and Howard Zinn. "I wanted history to become as vivid and real and immediate as if it were being lived right now," says Mann. "I wanted people to be as intelligent, capricious, humane, venal, and libidinous as anybody else in any other time frame."

The French and Indian War

The French and Indian War, more properly called the Seven Years' War, was the culminating struggle between France and England in North America. Like earlier imperial wars, it was part of a much wider conflict fought in Europe, on the seas, and wherever the competing empires reached.

The French and Indian War was, however, unique in several significant ways. Earlier wars had begun in Europe and then reached North America; the French and Indian War began when the French, fearing the loss of their Indian allies in the Ohio Valley, moved to stop the penetration of English traders into western Pennsylvania and the Ohio country. They built Fort Duquesne on the site of modern Pittsburgh, prompting the ill-fated English expedition led by Gen. Edward Braddock. All of this fighting preceded a formal declaration of war.

Unlike the earlier wars and contrary to the popular legend of colonial soldiers firing from behind trees at massed ranks of regulars, the French and Indian war was dominated by European soldiers, tactics, and resources. Ironically, a war begun with colonial initiatives and marked by the initial triumph of colonial and Indian fighters over European troops became, as one scholar has noted, a "gladiatorial" war fought largely according to European norms. British prime minister William Pitt asserted centralized control from London and poured troops and money into the colonies while the English fleet blockaded Canada. The French, beset by constant food shortages and dwindling aid, lost most of their Indian allies. Angry at Montcalm over their treatment at Fort William Henry and deprived of presents and supplies, most Indians retreated into neutrality. The war ended with a complete English victory and the near total disappearance of French influence from North America.

the French and not in the Hollywood Indian village of the movie, and they had no great chief who could decide all. As for the rest, from Magua's personal history (he was a slave of the Mohawks), to the treatment of prisoners, to the rather astonishing suggestion that the fur trade was alien to Huron ways, it is as though we are watching Washington throw out that first ball. These Indians are a wild hodgepodge of borrowed detail, pure invention, and startling juxtapositions of time and place.

However, the film is a romance, and romances *can* be rearranged. Not surprisingly, Mann changes Cooper's plot. As *Soap Opera Digest* might have it: Duncan no longer loves Alice; he proposes to Cora. Cora falls in love with Nathaniel. Uncas *seems* to be interested in Alice. Colonel Munro quite literally loses his heart to Magua. Magua hates everyone.

Rearranging these relationships in turn rearranges the meaning of the story. The new plot now explains, for instance, why we needed a revolution: to protect our democratic, freedom-loving, interracial society from supercilious twits. Nathaniel, the white raised by Indians, is the emblem of this egalitarian society. Cora symbolizes the rejection of her dead (quite literally, by the end) European past. In its place, she embraces Nathaniel and America.

The movie conveys this happy, multicultural America in one particularly bizarre scene during which British recruiters seem to intrude on the first Thanksgiving, which then breaks up into an interracial lacrosse game involving the Mohawks (noble Indians) and white settlers. Thanksgiving and athletics are, of course, currently our only two symbols of interracial harmony. Mann simply transports them back to the eighteenth century.

Things were a little different back at the real Fort William Henry. One of the problems the English faced in 1756 and 1757 was that the Mohawks refused to scout for them. Their only effective scouts were New Hampshire frontiersmen and Stockbridge Indians, among whom were some Mohicans. Nor were New York frontiersmen very prominent during the siege; the garrison was largely British regulars and New England militiamen. The fort couldn't hold them all, so many were camped outside. Showing the actual layout of the siege in the movie would ruin the spectacular attack on the isolated fort, so everyone is packed inside.

The actual siege of the fort was both nerve-wracking and dull. Lt. Col. George Munro watched helplessly as the French, under the marquis de Montcalm, pounded his fort while extending their trenches closer and closer. Gen. Daniel Webb had promised to reinforce Munro, but the Indians so effectively disrupted communications that Webb's mobilization was delayed.

The key historical scene in the movie is the massacre following the surrender. Indeed, it was Cooper's novel that gave the massacre a permanent place in the American imagination. Yet the movie's depiction of events is wrong in virtually every detail. The basic cause of the attack on the English was a conflict between European military etiquette and the customs of the Indian allies of the French. The Indians expected to be allowed to plunder the fort, and they had expected prisoners who could be adopted or ransomed. They were enraged that the English, who had suffered few casualties, might be allowed to depart with their arms and equipment intact.

In the movie Magua, with Montcalm's encouragement, lays an ambush and slaughters the British some distance from the fort, but the actual fighting was more like a one-sided brawl. It began as the British left their entrenchments. The French-allied Indians, many of whom had been drinking, fell upon the provincial wounded, killing seventeen of them, and then seized Indian allies of the English as well as black slaves and female camp followers. They also robbed the paroled soldiers, killing some of them. They concentrated on the militia at the rear of the column who were not protected by the small French guard. The Indians were largely after prisoners and booty.

The actual assault lasted only a short time, but the provincials understandably panicked and ran. The flight of so many soldiers created an exaggerated impression of the extent of the "massacre." Jonathan Carver wrote a famous eyewitness account that put the number of dead and prisoners at 1,500. More careful scholarly accounts estimate that at most 300 of the garrison were killed or missing, plus an unknown number of camp followers. Because the French retrieved many of these prisoners, a possible maximum of 185 people died or spent their lives in captivity; the minimum number was far less, perhaps 69 or 70.

Despite the dramatic "massacre," interracial harmony and common values remain the messages of this well-intentioned if silly movie. Mann realizes that in the movies, if you don't like the first take of the past you can reshoot it. And Daniel Day-Lewis can be the lead, and Russell Means, the American Indian Movement activist, can star in the movie instead of demonstrating against it. And the nasty stuff in the story? Why that's all the fault of supercilious twits from England.

Background Reading

Ian K. Steele, *Betrayals: Fort William Henry and the "Massacre"* (Oxford University Press, 1990)

1992/USA/Color
DIRECTOR: Michael Mann; **PRODUCER:** Michael Mann, Hunt Lowry; **SCREENPLAY:** Michael Mann, Christoper Crowe, Philip Dunne; **STUDIO:** Twentieth Century-Fox; **VIDEO:** Fox; **RUNNING TIME:** 122 min.

Jonathan Carver's Eyewitness Account

By this time the war-hoop was given, and the Indians began to murder those that were nearest to them without distinction. It is not in the power of words to give any tolerable idea of the horrid scene that now ensued; men, women, and children were dispatched in the most wanton and cruel manner, and immediately scalped. Many of these savages drank the blood of their victims, as it flowed warm from the fatal wound.

An engraving from *The Last of the Mohicans*

Later...

Colonel Munro, far from being killed, was at the head of the column and probably never witnessed the brief attack on the rear or saw the panicked flight.

After the victory at Fort William Henry, the French retreated. It was the high-water mark of the marquis de Montcalm's advance. General Webb's decision to allow Fort William Henry to fall and concentrate his forces on defending the approaches to Albany proved a wise one. The next year British advantages in men and material came into play. Montcalm would die in the decisive battle at Quebec in 1759.

As for the Indians, most of the westerners, angry at their treatment by Montcalm, largely withdrew from the war. The last I heard of the Mohicans, they were operating a casino in Connecticut.

THE SCARLET EMPRESS

Carolly Erickson

SINCE BIBLICAL TIMES, WOMEN WHO LOVED too much—and too many—have been linked with the color of blood. Hence Nathaniel Hawthorne's *The Scarlet Letter*, Scarlett O'Hara, and Josef von Sternberg's 1934 film, *The Scarlet Empress*. The empress in question is Catherine II, known after her death as Catherine the Great, who became notorious for doing what most male rulers of her time did: She had many lovers.

Of this fact there can be no dispute. However, the historical Catherine was nothing like the kittenish, pouting, vamping heroine played by Marlene Dietrich, and the real Catherine's early life was not a romp through a fantastic Russian pleasure garden but a trail of tears.

Born Sophia Fredericka, daughter of an insignificant German nobleman of slender means, the girl who became Empress Catherine was large and boisterous and slightly walleyed. She was a tomboy, but along with her earthy physicality went an avid curiosity and a love of deep thoughts. In the film, the child Sophia—who is blonde and ringletted, very much on the model of Shirley Temple—is asked what she would like to be when she grows up. "I want to be a toe-dancer," she says. The Sophia of history announced at fourteen, "I am a philosopher," and wrote a long treatise to prove it.

The budding philosopher was summoned to Russia to marry the heir to the imperial throne, the strange tormented half-mad boy Peter. For a number of years Sophia—rechristened Catherine on her baptism into the Orthodox Church—struggled to please the capricious Empress Elizabeth, Peter's aunt, and to endure her husband's adulteries and cruel whims. In her misery she found consolation in books, educating herself and developing her political skills to counteract the vicious palace intrigues that threatened to ensnare her.

I n the film, Catherine must ward off a would-be Russian seducer even before she sets foot on Russian soil. In actuality, she was a faithful wife caught in a terrible impasse: Her sole purpose in life was to give birth to an heir to the throne, yet her husband would not share her bed—and appeared to be impotent in any case. Ought she risk death by taking a lover, and bearing his child, or continue to suffer the empress's anger at her barrenness?

Covertly encouraged by the empress, the historical Catherine eventually had three lovers, while continuing to be Peter's wife, each of whom gave her a child. In giving birth the first time she nearly died of neglect and mistreatment, and the experience toughened her. Kept away from her children, alternately humiliated and exploited by her increasingly

The Young Catherine

Catherine the Great was born into obscurity. Her father was co-ruler of the tiny and poor principality of Anhalt-Zerbst, a postage-stamp realm subject to the all-powerful Frederick of Prussia. As a child, Sophia was aggressive, precocious, and unattractive, but King Frederick was impressed with her mind and arranged her marriage to the heir to the Russian throne. Her father, an upright man with a mediocre military career, tried to guide Sophia's morals while her mother, an egotistical and frivolous woman starved for attention and power, was eager to use her daughter to advance her own position. Sophia was one of many German princesses with title but little wealth or status who became brides to foreign monarchs during the eighteenth century. That she gained influence, wealth, and fame was partly a matter of luck, partly the result of her own extraordinary intelligence and power of will.

HISTORY

The historical Catherine II was a tireless reader who devoured the works of the French Enlightenment; her favorite writers were Montesquieu, Voltaire, and Diderot. With Voltaire she carried on a clever and mutually congratulatory correspondence. Diderot she persuaded to come to Russia and stay for several months, but while he admired her intellect he ultimately found her conversation tiresome; she thought him rude and bombastic and was relieved when he left.

Catherine wrote many plays, poems, and essays, and found literary work a pleasing diversion from the labor of governing. One of her favorite pastimes was to gather together a group of cultivated friends and collectively translate a novel from French into Russian.

HOLLYWOOD

After acting under the tutelage of the renowned Max Reinhardt, Marlene Dietrich began her German film career in 1923 with *The Little Napoleon* and made more than a dozen pictures before being discovered by director Josef von Sternberg (he added "von," as did Erich von Stroheim, to lend glamour to his name). In Germany to cast the female lead in *The Blue Angel* (1930), von Sternberg realized that Dietrich's talents were ideally suited to the role of Lola, an amoral dance-hall girl who drives Emil Jannings to the most extreme humiliations in the name of love. Hearing Dietrich's sultry version of "Falling in Love Again" for the first time, the entire world fell in love with her.

The Empress Elizabeth

Empress Elizabeth of Russia was Catherine II's nemesis yet also her mentor. Born the illegitimate daughter of Peter the Great, her mother a beautiful peasant woman, Elizabeth seized the throne in a military coup in 1741. As vain as she was ambitious, Elizabeth was suspicious of everyone, especially other attractive women. She never married but had male concubines and may have been secretly married to one of them.

Unlike Catherine, Empress Elizabeth ruled through terror and caprice. Her beauty belied her very unlovely qualities: malice, spite, vengefulness, and a deep and pervasive fearfulness. Having no children of her own, she appropriated Catherine's, allowing them only rare visits with their mother. When Catherine became empress, she used to her advantage what she had learned from watching Elizabeth, avoiding the older woman's cruelty and personal excesses.

Peter's Murder

Shortly after Catherine became empress in a military coup, her imprisoned husband, Peter III, died in a brawl with his guards—a political murder unconvincingly disguised as an accident. It was widely believed at the time that Catherine had ordered the killing, and historical opinion concurs that she was, at least, complicit. Thus murder was added to the list of her scarlet sins. Her son and heir, Paul I, sought to avenge the barbarous assassination of his putative father (Paul was in actuality the son of Catherine's lover Sergei Saltykov) and nursed a lifelong grievance toward his mother.

hostile husband and menaced by dangerous enemies at court who sensed her astuteness and growing power, Catherine managed to keep a cool head and bide her time. She was fearful, though, for Peter threatened to send her to a convent once Empress Elizabeth died and he was on the throne.

The film virtually eliminates Catherine's children, reduces her lovers to shadowy nonentities, and portrays Catherine as more blatantly seductive than Mae West—whose films, like those of Shirley Temple, were a major box-office draw in the year *The Scarlet Empress* was released. Catherine is shown sleeping her way to the top, relying on her beauty to make men fall at her feet and the throne fall into her lap. The historical truth is more complex. One of Catherine's lovers, Gregory Orlov, a nobleman with whom she had a long-term monogamous affair that was in most respects a marriage, helped her gain the political loyalty of key regiments and these soldiers staged the coup that made her empress.

In some of its details, the film draws on Catherine's memoirs, and these provide a sprinkling of authenticity. Peter's obsession with toy soldiers, Elizabeth's harem of handsome young officers, Catherine's wearing a guardsman's uniform on the day she took the throne: such images help to resurrect the eighteenth-century court as it actually was.

Overall, however, *The Scarlet Empress* is a gross distortion of the times in which Catherine lived. Instead of the restrained, elegant classical palaces in which Catherine's actual story played

> ## "I am an aristocrat; it is my profession."
>
> *Catherine II*

itself out, the film's extravagant sets are neo-Gothic monstrosities in which looming life-size gargoyles steal scene after scene from the actors. Instead of the dry, tinkling delicacies of harpsichord and string orchestra—the quintessential sound of Catherine's youth—we are bathed in a lush soundtrack of Mendelssohn, Tchaikovsky, Rimsky-Korsakov—and, inevitably, the *1812 Overture* and Wagner's "Ride of the Valkyries."

Absurdities abound. One of Catherine's admirers chides her for resisting him by saying, "Those ideas are old-fashioned. This is the eighteenth century!" Peter's mistress, a dark-eyed starlet in a clinging costume apparently borrowed from a Busby Berkeley movie, fails to recognize Catherine and unwittingly tells her, "Peter's going to marry me when the old bat dies." Empress Elizabeth herself talks with a tough, streetwise New York accent. Hordes of Cossacks ride madly across the screen time and again—always the same hordes.

Historical gaffes apart, *The Scarlet Empress*, while memorable and intermittently entertaining—and made luminous by the entrancing Marlene Dietrich and the grinning, lunatic Sam Jaffe as Peter—betrays the real woman who became Catherine the Great. Gritty, clever, courageous, and ultimately magnificent, the historical Catherine had brains and character—and breathtaking daring. By the time she gained the throne at age thirty-three she had lost her looks, her youth, even her health. She won the admiration of her troops not by sexual allure but by earning their respect, and ultimately their devotion.

Hollywood mythmaking reduces Catherine's life—and an important era in Russian history—to a dark fairy tale in which a charming innocent, forced to marry a troll and pitted against a wicked court, uses her beauty and her wiles to overturn the forces of evil. But the factual story of Catherine's life was more compelling than any myth, its flawed heroine all the more admirable for enduring and ultimately transcending the sordid cruelties of the Russian court.

Catherine's Reputation

When the French Revolution broke out in 1789, Catherine II was still empress of Russia. The French iconoclasts, bent on destroying not only the French monarchy but all monarchy everywhere, made the famed Russian empress a target of their campaign. Journalists repeated all the unsavory stories that had accumulated about her over the years and invented outrageous new ones. The legend of the voraciously libidinous, sexually deviant empress is a product of their fictions.

Later...

After her coup in 1762, Catherine II ruled Russia for thirty-four years, surviving rebellions and assassination attempts and continuing the work begun by her idol Peter the Great in bringing Russia into the community of the rationalist West. Her law code, administrative reforms, and appeals for humane social principles were to endure until the 1917 revolutions.

Catherine continued throughout her life to seek her ideal mate. Twice she thought she had found him. Gregory Potemkin, a wayward genius with a huge appetite for life, matched her best—they may have been secretly married—but his dark moodiness made life with him impossible. In the end, they parted amicably, while remaining political partners. Alexander Lanskoy, a handsome poet, was the darling of her later years; had he not died young, she might have remained faithful to him as her final consort.

Background Reading

John T. Alexander, *Catherine the Great: Life and Legend* (Oxford University Press, 1989)
Carolly Erickson, *Great Catherine* (Crown, 1994)

1934/USA/B&W
DIRECTOR: Josef von Sternberg; PRODUCER: Adolph Zukor; SCREENPLAY: Manuel Komroff; STUDIO: Paramount; VIDEO: MCA; RUNNING TIME: 110 min.

1776

Thomas Fleming

The Second Continental Congress

The Second Continental Congress assembled in Philadelphia on May 10, 1775, in the aftermath of the bloodshed at Lexington and Concord. Radicals in favor of independence had a far stronger voice than they had manifested in the Continental Congress of 1774. But they were opposed by conservatives and moderates led by John Dickinson of Pennsylvania, who argued that a solution to the quarrel short of war could still be found. The shattering failure of the American attempt to annex Canada made others wary of radical predictions of

an easy victory. The Declaration of Independence by no means healed these political divisions. After the virtual collapse of the American army in 1776, the radicals' vision of a short violent war was replaced by George Washington's doctrine of a protracted conflict. By 1779 the radicals were in disarray. Samuel Adams was contemptuously called "Judas Iscariot" by conservative congressmen. Men such as financier Robert Morris, who believed in order and system and took a dim view of radical enthusiasm, displaced Adams and his circle and brought the war to a successful conclusion.

A MUSICAL ABOUT THE DECLARATION of Independence? The first time composer Sherman Edwards and librettist Peter Stone proposed this improbable notion, their friends must have recommended intensive psychotherapy. Still, they amazed everyone, creating a Tony Award–winning show. The inevitable film version of *1776* closely follows the stage production. The camera never leaves Philadelphia and seldom departs from Independence Hall and its gardens.

From a historical point of view, Stone, who adapted his Broadway success for the screen, gets a number of things right. He conveys not a little of the confusion, hesitation, and conflict that raged among the Founding Fathers in the spring of 1776 as they wrestled with the question of whether to declare the independence of thirteen barely united American colonies or try one more time to achieve a reconciliation with Great Britain. Two of the leading protagonists for independence—the hotheaded, loquacious John Adams and the diffident, reticent Thomas Jefferson—as well as their chief opponent, starchy, pompous John Dickinson of Pennsylvania—are deftly and, on the whole, accurately depicted. The quarrel between northerners and southerners over slavery, one of the major differences that almost wrecked the enterprise, is starkly dramatized. The swarming flies and beastly temperatures of Old Philadelphia in July are also vividly rendered.

There is little doubt that the creators of *1776* hoped to give their audience a history lesson as well as a good time. This makes all the more regrettable the historical lapses that mar the story. The most egregious error is the utter hash the film makes of the Continental Army's role during these tense weeks. By the spring of 1776, the Americans, having imbibed the heady antimonarchical vitriol of Tom Paine's *Common Sense*, were already fighting a full-scale war. Their invasion of Canada was faltering, but they had driven the British army out of Boston and were busily fortifying New York City against an almost certain British attack. Gen. George Washington was more than a little hopeful that his twenty-three-thousand-man army could make a good showing against the oncoming enemy army and fleet. Despondence did not set in until the Americans were routed in the Battle at Long Island, seven weeks *after* July 4.

None of this military optimism, however, penetrates *1776*. Instead, Washington sends a series of lugubrious letters detailing the parlous state of his troops. The communiqués are read aloud by Charles Thomson, the secretary of the Continental Congress, to a chorus of hoots and groans from the sweaty solons. Someone grouses that Washington

HISTORY

Backed by ex-presidents Thomas Jefferson and John Adams, John Trumbull was commissioned by Congress to create this painting for the Capitol Rotunda. In it the members of the drafting committee—John Adams, Thomas Jefferson, Benjamin Franklin, Roger Sherman, and Robert Livingston—present the Declaration of Independence to John Hancock, president of the Congress. Along with the work, Trumbull provided a key that identified all the delegates but one—the man wearing a hat in the rear. He remains a mystery.

HOLLYWOOD

1776 on Broadway

Aging Hollywood lion Jack L. Warner, never bothered by such trifling matters as historical accuracy, spent well over one million dollars on the screen rights to Peter Stone and Sherman Edwards's play, hoping to duplicate its considerable success on Broadway, where it ran for some twelve hundred performances following its opening on March 16, 1969. (Warner's previous musical triumphs had included *Yankee Doodle Dandy* [1942], *My Fair Lady* [1964], and *Camelot* [1967].) Despite its cast of distinguished stage performers, the resulting five-million-dollar film version, released through Columbia Pictures (Warner had already retired from the famous company that bore his name), was a resounding critical and commercial failure, a most unworthy swan song for Warner, who died in 1978.

John Dickinson

John Dickinson was born in Maryland and raised in Delaware but moved to Philadelphia to practice law after studying for three years in London. Conservative by nature, he opposed Benjamin Franklin's attempts during the 1760s to oust the proprietary government of the descendants of William Penn. Despite his unpopularity among local democrats, Dickinson remained an influential force in Pennsylvania's politics, which inevitably made him a power in the Continental Congress. He was a gifted writer, and Congress turned to him repeatedly to draft public documents. Defeated in the independence struggle, he volunteered for military duty to prove his patriotism. After the war he was elected president of Pennsylvania and was a delegate from Delaware to the 1787 Constitutional Convention.

Lewis Morris

Lewis Morris was the third lord of the manor of Morrisania, which composed a good chunk of the present-day Bronx and Westchester County. Strongly anti-British in his sentiments, he overcame considerable local resistance among his tenants and neighbors to get himself elected to the New York Provincial Congress, which sent him to the Continental Congress. There he served competently on several committees though was absent when the vote on independence was taken, having been appointed a brigadier general of the militia. Later in the summer he returned to Congress and signed the Declaration, one of many who did not get around to contributing their signatures until months after July 4.

Richard Henry Lee

Richard Henry Lee was the eldest of the four political sons of Thomas Lee. A tall, austere man, sometimes described as a southern Puritan, he was an early supporter of independence and subsequently played a key role in persuading Virginia to give up its grandiose claims to western lands, enabling Congress to ratify the Articles of Confederation. With his trou-  blemaking brothers, Arthur and William, he became deeply embroiled in the controversy over funds spent in France by American representatives, a quarrel that generated much heat and little light in the Second Continental Congress. After the war he joined Patrick Henry in opposing the Constitution—but served briefly as Virginia's first U.S. senator.

needs to learn to write more upbeat letters to the delegates and stop "depressing" them.

Before independence can be voted, therefore, the filmmakers must solve the problem they've created of Washington's supposedly collapsing army. To do so, they send Samuel Chase of Maryland, a wavering moderate, along with Adams and Benjamin Franklin on a visit to a "training camp" in New Brunswick, New Jersey, which Washington has reported in one of his lamenting letters to be full of disorder and prostitutes. Chase returns to tell everyone his worries have been resolved. The camp was disorderly, but when a flock of ducks flew over, the hungry Americans shot them out of the sky. Thus does the film enshrine the myth of American marksmanship as the key not only to victory in the war but also to the vote for independence—piling myth upon myth.

On many other occasions, Sherman and Stone seem to view the Continental Congress as an early version of *Animal House*. When Thomas Jefferson says he is going home to see his wife, Stephen Hopkins of Rhode Island, who is portrayed as an unkempt drunk (the real Hopkins did like his rum), yells: "Give her a flourish for me." Even more imaginary is the depiction of Richard Henry Lee, that austere Virginia Puritan, who was heart and soul with the pro-independence New Englanders from the moment he entered Congress. Humorless, high-minded, intense, Lee was, after Adams, the most powerful orator in Congress. In the film he is portrayed as a giggling buffoon who makes endless puns on the name Lee. When Franklin and Adams suggest he procure a resolution for independence from Virginia, he acts as though the idea would never have occurred to him in a million years and rides wildly off to do their bidding.

Perhaps aiming at a warts-and-all realism, the authors similarly downgrade other characters. The brilliant Lewis Morris is depicted as an idiot who repeatedly says: "New York abstains—courteously." James Wilson, the shrewd and contentious lawyer from Pennsylvania, perhaps the greatest intellect in America after James Madison, is portrayed as a timid fool. The magisterial Robert Livingston of New York, the man who would negotiate the Louisiana Purchase in 1803, comes across as an utter twit. Benjamin Franklin, portrayed by the veteran actor Howard Da Silva, is full of sly winks and leers about assignations with women—which is not a complete caricature; Ben did have his racy side—but the authors miss the bitter seriousness with which Franklin backed independence. He was an angry man, out to even the score with a British government that had hauled him before the Privy Council in 1774 and called him a liar and a thief.

The worst departure from reality, however, is the film's handling of Jefferson's relationship with his wife, Martha. Jefferson was deeply worried about her health during the weeks he struggled with the Declaration of Independence. She was at Monticello, too ill and depressed even to write him a letter. In the film we see him discarding draft after draft of the manifesto, which begins to look stillborn. Then comes a knock on the door: There stands a radiant Blythe Danner as Martha. John Adams has "sent for her," as though she were a package of sweetmeats. The Jeffersons embrace passionately while Adams and Franklin giggle and snigger. Presto! Within a day or two, Tom's sexual frustrations have been relieved, and we have the great document, followed by an inane song from Danner, "He Plays the Violin."

1776 is at its best in the final scenes, which cover the first four days in July, when the vote on independence was debated. At the end of the first day, defeat seems inevitable. However Edward Rutledge procures an overnight delay to rally the wavering South. Meanwhile, Franklin manipulates Pennsylvania into a yea, and Caesar Rodney arrives with the vote that swings Delaware into line. The film combines the decision for independence on July 2 with the approval of Jefferson's document on July 4, which were actually two distinct procedures, but this dramatic license is hardly objectionable.

During the movie debate over Jefferson's paragraph on the evils of slavery, which was in fact excised, John Adams defends it with all-or-nothing rhetoric and Rutledge stalks around a darkened chamber declaiming with operatic intensity that northern ship owners and southern slave owners are equally responsible for the incubus. While Jefferson did praise Adams's stout defense of his original antislavery draft, these histrionics are a good deal stronger than Jefferson's own recollection that the paragraph was cut because South Carolina and Georgia objected to it and some northern states "felt a little tender" on the subject. This is a quibble, to be sure, but it concerns the origins of this nation's most divisive issue.

In spite of these departures from the historical record, *1776* manages to convey the peculiar mixture of bravado, wily politicking, and hardheaded courage that produced an epochal moment—and a historic document—that continues to reverberate around the world. It would take an enervating seven-year war to guarantee the United States of America's survival. But, as the self-same screenwriter would be quick to tell you, that's another story.

Background Reading

Thomas Fleming, *1776: Year of Illusions* (Norton, 1975)
H. James Henderson, *Party Politics in the Continental Congress* (McGraw-Hill, 1974)

1972/USA/Color
DIRECTOR: Peter H. Hunt; PRODUCER: Jack L. Warner; SCREENPLAY: Peter Stone; STUDIO: Columbia; VIDEO: Columbia Tristar; RUNNING TIME: 141 min.

Edward Rutledge

Edward Rutledge had a poor opinion of New England men, their "low cunning" and their "levelling principles." John Adams had an equally poor opinion of Rutledge, calling him "jejune, inane and puerile." Educated for the law at the Temple in London, Rutledge ably represented in Congress the planter oligarchy of his native South Carolina. He was no enthusiast for independence, finally voting for it because he saw disunion as a worse evil. He continued to harbor grave doubts about what might happen to South Carolina in a government dominated by Yankees. He spent most of the war years in the army as an artillery captain. Captured when Charleston surrendered to the British in May 1780, he survived to serve as a postwar state senator and governor.

Caesar Rodney

Caesar Rodney was described by John Adams as "the oddest looking man in the world; he is tall, thin and slender as a reed, pale; his face is not bigger than a large apple, but there is sense, fire, wit and humor in his countenance." Rodney's midnight ride to cast a tie-breaking vote and bring Delaware into the independence camp made him persona non grata in his state. During the following year, he was defeated in contests for a number of political offices, and he did not return to Congress until late 1777. He died in 1784 of cancer of the face, a disease that had tormented him for a decade.

Later...

The Declaration of Independence acquired a history of its own, becoming over the course of the next two centuries one of the primary documents of Western civilization. In 1776 the signers saw it largely as an attempt to explain the decision to sever their loyalty to the king. What has made the Declaration endure are its opening paragraphs, in which Thomas Jefferson states the fundamental premises of American nationhood: that all men are created equal; that they are endowed by their creator with inalienable rights; and that to secure these rights, governments are instituted among men, deriving their just powers from the consent of the governed. These ideas became the driving force of the American experiment—and reverberated throughout the nations of the world. They were at the heart of Lincoln's address at Gettysburg. In ten classic sentences Lincoln made it clear that the Civil War was being fought for "a new birth of freedom" in which the principles of the Declaration would be paramount.

C A S T

Gilbert Martin	**(Henry Fonda)**
Magdelana Martin	**(Claudette Colbert)**

DRUMS ALONG THE MOHAWK

Anthony F. C. Wallace

Sir William Johnson

In 1756, Sir William Johnson (1715–74), a prosperous Irish fur trader in the Mohawk Valley, was appointed superintendent of Indian affairs north of the Ohio River. His military exploits during the French and Indian War earned him a baronetcy. After the death of his first wife in 1759, he entered into a common-law marriage with a young Mohawk woman, known among whites as Molly Brant (1735?–96). Molly's younger brother, Joseph Brant (1742–1807), was sent to England in 1776 in the company of Guy Johnson, the late Sir William's nephew and soon-to-be Indian superintendent himself, to establish an understanding about the Six Nations' role in the troubles between Great Britain and her rebellious colonists. Joseph was presented at court to George III, to whom he pledged the continued loyalty of the Mohawks.

IN 1939 TWENTIETH CENTURY-FOX RELEASED a modest contribution to the historical film genre: *Drums Along the Mohawk*, starring Henry Fonda and Claudette Colbert, based on the 1936 novel by Walter D. Edmonds. Set during the American Revolution, Edmonds's book made a serious effort to show the sufferings and fortitude of ordinary people, the sturdy yeoman settlers in the valley of the Mohawk River west of Albany in upstate New York. Beset by raiding parties of Indians led by British officers, the frontiersmen fought back and, in the end, prevailed.

Edmonds based his work on a personal familiarity with the landscape and on careful research among documentary sources. The movie, up to a point, follows Edmonds pretty closely, even using some of his dialogue, and it tries hard to catch the spirit of the book—and of the times the book depicts. It maintains a narrow focus on the lives of ordinary people, particularly Gilbert Martin and his bride, Magdelana, as they build and then lose their little farm far out on the edge of settlement. Yet it is the narrowness of this focus that ultimately trivializes the events the film portrays.

The Mohawk Indians were the aboriginal inhabitants of the Mohawk Valley. By 1775, they had sold much of their land to the Crown, but many still remained in ancient settlements; these Mohawks were devoted to the British and to the famous superintendent of Indian affairs, Sir William Johnson. Johnson maintained close ties with "the faithful Mohawks" and was married (in Indian fashion) to a Mohawk woman, Molly Brant. Her brother, Joseph Brant, who was educated at Eleazar Wheelock's school in Connecticut (later renamed Dartmouth College), became a principal leader among his people.

When the split between the Americans and the British degenerated into war in 1775, the Mohawks were in a quandary. Sir William had died in 1774 and his successor had not yet been appointed. Both sides publicly urged the Indians to stay neutral, but the Americans were so suspicious of Indian intentions that the uneasy Mohawks gradually drifted away to take refuge near British posts to the north and west. Farther west, other Iroquois—the Oneidas, Onondagas, Cayugas, Tuscaroras, and Senecas—maintained neutrality for a time. However, by 1776 the situation had become unstable. In his bill of particulars against George III (the preamble to the Declaration of Independence), Thomas Jefferson accused the king of inciting "merciless savages" to attack the Americans. By 1777, many of the warriors of the western Iroquois had gone over to the British, along with Joseph Brant's Mohawks. The Oneidas wavered and then joined the Americans.

HISTORY

The military force that the Americans put into the field was composed of two elements: the militias and the Continental Army. The militias were local men who traditionally supplied their own arms and chose their own officers; all able-bodied male citizens were liable to be mobilized for militia duty. Militiamen tended to fight best defending their own neighborhoods; they were undisciplined, untrained, and apt to take leave without notice to care for farm and family. By 1777 the Continental Congress realized, reluctantly, that the nation needed a large, regular, paid standing army, with competent officers committed to definite terms of service and professional military training. Some of the soldiers in this "continental" army were volunteers; others were recruited by "persuasion" or even drafted from the ranks of the militias according to quotas.

HOLLYWOOD

The classic western *Stagecoach* marked John Ford's 1939 return to American history as a major source for his work. Henry Fonda—who starred in Ford's two other historical films that year, *Young Mr. Lincoln* and *Drums Along the Mohawk*—would become, like *Stagecoach* star John Wayne, a Ford regular until their famous feud during the filming of *Mister Roberts* (1955).

Ford filmed *Drums Along the Mohawk* in northern Utah's high country, where roads had to be cut for the equipment trucks. According to one report, more than two hundred thousand board feet of lumber were used to build the reproductions of Fort Stanwix and several frontier homes. Because the entire production was filmed on government land, Ford was obligated to dismantle the sets following the completion of principal photography. He simplified matters by inserting into the script a scene in which the fort is destroyed with gunpowder. After the explosion, Ford's crew merely picked up the pieces and went home.

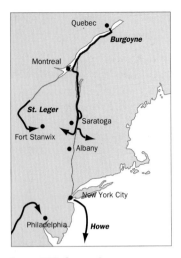

The 1777 Campaign

The failure of three British armies to unite at Albany, and so divide the southern colonies from New England, was in large measure the result of British underestimation of the strength of the rebels, their readiness to fight, and their competence in guerrilla warfare. Lord George Germain, the colonial minister in charge of war plans, expected British regulars to defeat with ease the disorganized American rabble. Neither he nor his generals were prepared psychologically or logistically for the realities of the American war.

A principal case in point was the conduct of the Mohawk Valley campaign. A supercilious officer, St. Leger thought poorly of the martial abilities of the provincials—even those fighting on his side. He did indeed crush the relief force under General Herkimer at Oriskany, but he was not able to bring the siege of Fort Stanwix to a successful conclusion. That failure was a direct result of his contempt for the rebels. So confident was he of an easy victory that he did not bother to bring heavy artillery with him, and the light artillery that he did bring was completely ineffective against the sturdily rebuilt fort. The British bombardment of Stanwix, their Indian allies said, was like "Apples that Children were throwing over a Garden Fence."

"Gentleman Johnny" Burgoyne descended along the Lake Champlain–Lake George–Hudson River trade route and seized Fort Ticonderoga at the head of Lake George. He unwisely chose to travel the remaining miles to Albany through the wilderness. His nine-thousand-man army far outnumbered the three thousand or so Continentals opposing him, but his supply trains and foraging parties were decimated by the hit-and-run attacks of lightly armed but elusive militia units. Burgoyne was forced to surrender at Saratoga, a disaster that convinced France to enter the war formally on the American side. Meanwhile, Gen. William Howe, who was supposed to have moved up the Hudson River from New York City, chose instead to move south, defeating Washington's army in pitched battle at the Brandywine and then occupying Philadelphia (while Washington made camp at Valley Forge north of the city). Howe seems to have thought that St. Leger and Burgoyne could triumph over the fumbling Americans without him.

Attacks on exposed Mohawk Valley settlements began in earnest in the summer of 1777 and continued off and on until 1781. Farms were burned; livestock slaughtered; men, women, and children killed. Settlers took refuge in small forts, and their militiamen fought back with, at first, minimal aid from Congress and the Continental Army. A combined force of Indians and British rangers laid siege to Fort Stanwix and inflicted a bloody defeat on a relief army of militia under Gen. Nicholas Herkimer at Oriskany in August 1777. Thereafter, Indian raids devastated the valley. In 1779, however, major continental armies, including continental regulars under Gen. John Sullivan, as well as local militias, burned most of the Iroquois towns. When the war ended, the surviving settlers returned to their farms and the drive west began again.

The problem faced in the production of a movie about these events lies not so much in the historical accuracy of detail. Re-creating colonial forts, farmsteads, and mansions; displaying colonial garments and equipment; portraying hard work on the frontier, felling trees, grubbing stumps, gathering hay, spinning yarn; and following the personal lives of the two typical protagonists, present no difficulty. Nitpicking about such things as having General Herkimer die the night after the Oriskany battle or mislocating Fort Stanwix (around which all of the action occurs) as an unnamed stockade in German Flats would perhaps be unfair. As usual, the Native Americans are depicted as either figures of fun or savage killers. And the final dramatic scene in which Henry Fonda as Gil outruns the fastest Indian warrior to summon help from Fort Dayton (thirty miles away) seems to make the war for the Mohawk Valley depend on a local footrace. The Revolution in the film ends immediately after the relief column reaches Fort Stanwix (an event that occurred in the fall of 1777), when an officer announces that Cornwallis has surrendered at Yorktown (which actually took place four years later).

The scholar's major complaint against the movie, however, must be its utter failure to convey the strategic importance of the Mohawk Valley during the Revolution. As the campaign of 1777 began, the British hoped to end the rebellion by a three-pronged attack: Gen. William Howe was to advance up the Hudson River from New York City, while Gen. John Burgoyne moved south from Montreal via Lake Champlain, and Col. Barry St. Leger, with his brigade of Iroquois warriors, marched east from Lake Ontario. After taking Fort Stanwix, St. Leger was to proceed down the Mohawk River to Albany, where he would rendezvous with Howe and Burgoyne. The plan was designed to cut the northern colonies in two, isolating the southern colonies from New England. By clearing the Americans out of the prosperous Mohawk Valley, St. Leger would also deprive the Continental Army of one of its major sources of food and supplies.

The plan failed because Burgoyne was forced to surrender at Saratoga, because Howe attacked Philadelphia instead, and because St. Leger's force, while it devastated the militia army at Oriskany, could not maintain the siege of Fort Stanwix. When rumors began to circulate of a huge army approaching under Benedict Arnold (false ones planted by the small relief column at Fort Dayton), St. Leger's Indian allies slipped away to their villages and the colonel decided to withdraw. Only after St. Leger's retreat did the British strategy turn to full-scale raids on settlements in the Mohawk Valley and elsewhere. The raids were so devastating that the major American military goal for the summer of 1779 was the coordinated scorched-earth invasion of the Iroquois country by three armies, their intention (copied from the British) being to destroy the enemy's sources of food, shelter, and supply.

Edmonds's novel conveyed these larger strategic issues to the reader by the use of appropriate dialogue and by stretching the time span to cover the full sweep of events. In the book, the impact of the larger war on local communities becomes plain. In the movie, with its narrow focus on the summer of 1777 and on the homey details of frontier life, that sense of history is lost. It is a classic example of not being able to see the wood for the trees.

Background Reading

Anthony F.C. Wallace, *The Death and Rebirth of the Seneca* (Knopf, 1970)

1939/USA/Color
DIRECTOR: John Ford; **PRODUCER:** Raymond Griffith; **SCREENPLAY:** Lamar Trotti, Sonya Levien; **STUDIO:** Twentieth Century-Fox; **VIDEO:** Key; **RUNNING TIME:** 103 min.

Fort Stanwix

Fort Stanwix, constructed in 1758, was not intended as a place of refuge for farm families but rather as a major fortress. It stood thirty miles beyond the nearest settlement astride the strategically important mile-long portage between the Mohawk River and a series of streams that emptied into Lake Ontario at Oswego. Thus Fort Stanwix controlled the main route for the canoe-borne fur trade between Indians to the north and west and Dutch and English traders at Albany.

Stanwix, which also guarded against invasions from the north and west, was a substantial fort, approximately one hundred yards square with projecting corner bastions. The parapets were constructed of planed logs two feet thick and about fourteen feet high. Inside was a parade ground, a bombproof magazine, and cannon, as well as barracks and officers' quarters for up to four hundred men. Surrounding the walls was a dry moat, bristling with wooden stakes, and beyond the moat was an earthen rampart or glacis. Fort Stanwix was garrisoned by the British from 1758 until about 1769, when it was abandoned; it was restored by the Americans in 1777, temporarily renamed Fort Schuyler.

Later...

After the fighting ended in 1781, the Mohawk Valley was quickly repopulated. In 1825 the valley became the route of the Erie Canal. (Walter Edmonds wrote about the canal and the lives it affected in another novel, *Rome Haul*, which was made into a movie called *The Farmer Takes a Wife* [1935].) With the canal came the Industrial Revolution, and a string of manufacturing towns sprang up west of Albany, including Schenectady, Utica, Rome, Syracuse, Rochester, and Buffalo.

The fate of the Indians was mixed. The Mohawks and many of the Cayugas, Onondagas, and Senecas took refuge with the British in Canada, and many of their descendants still live on the Grand River reservation in Ontario. Most of the remaining Iroquois lands in New York State were purchased between 1784 and 1797, but Onondagas, Tuscaroras, and Senecas still reside on reservations in the western part of the state.

Mohawks from reservations along the St. Lawrence River have benefited from the industrialization of America, becoming well known as workers in skyscraper construction. Senecas easily gained industrial employment as the railroads expanded across New York. Recently, a small Mohawk community has sprung up at Canajoharie, site of the old Mohawk "castle." And the council fire of the ancient League of the Iroquois, temporarily extinguished during the Revolution, still burns at Onondaga.

MUTINY ON THE BOUNTY

Greg Dening

CAST

William Bligh *(Charles Laughton)*
Fletcher Christian *(Clark Gable)*
Roger Byam *(Franchot Tone)*

The Morning After

It is eight o'clock in the morning on April 28, 1789. The mutiny is over. Capt. William Bligh stands in the open launch of the HMS *Bounty* as the mutineers set him adrift with eighteen companions. Bligh and his loyalists are about to begin their epic four-thousand-mile voyage to Timor, but few of the mutineers can expect them to survive.

The first thing Bligh does is record his thoughts on what he believes to be the real reason for the mutiny: the luscious attractions of Tahiti. Then he composes a description of each mutineer. Of Christian, Bligh writes: "He is subject to violent perspiration and particularly in his hands so that he soils anything he handles."

This July 1790 aquatint by Robert Dodd, *Lieutenant Bligh Leaving the Bounty*, was the first graphic representation of the *Bounty* mutiny. The Royalty Theatre, London, had already staged the first *Bounty* play with Ralph Wewitzer as the first Captain Bligh and William Bourke as Fletcher Christian. Later there were ballets, aquaballets, poems, novels, histories—and five films.

FILMS ABOUT A MUTINY HAVE A PROBLEM: On what side lies political correctness—the order being sustained by the institution or the injustices being suffered by the individuals? When Irving Thalberg, the creative genius of Metro-Goldwyn-Mayer, suggested to Louis B. Mayer that MGM make a film about the *Bounty* mutiny, Mayer was very reluctant. He did not want his studio to produce a film in which mutineers would be heroes.

Louis B. Mayer was born in Russia—one of several Eastern European Jews who, as Neal Gabler writes, "invented Hollywood." Entrepreneurs all, they worshiped the opportunities the Land of the Free and the Home of the Brave had given them—Louis B. Mayer more than any.

Thalberg knew that Mayer would never bless a film about revolution, mutiny, or even social change, so he looked for heroes other than the mutineers. What he found was the British Royal Navy, which he made the true hero of *Mutiny on the Bounty*. In its scrolling preface, the film contends that the mutiny "helped bring about a new discipline, based on mutual respect between officers and men, by which Britain's sea power is maintained as security for all who pass upon the sea."

Thalberg himself was a centrist. While traveling in Nazi Germany, where he was refused surgery because he was a prominent Jew, he saw storm troopers in the streets. Back in Hollywood, he experienced firsthand the leftist movement among screenwriters being led by Upton Sinclair. For Thalberg personally, the middle ground between fascism and Communism was to be found in stable institutions that could sustain good order and bend to legitimate demands. That's why Thalberg made Charles Laughton's Bligh so horrendous: His horrible behavior makes mutiny against him understandable, if not excusable. It also allows the British Admiralty to support Bligh's authority while distancing itself from his practices.

In this analysis, master's mate Fletcher Christian (played by Clark Gable) becomes yet another tragic hero, unrewarded except by his sense of honor. In Christian's place as the real hero of shining goodness is an entirely invented character, Roger Byam (Franchot Tone), who never raises a hand against Bligh yet suffers anyway because of his commitment to the ideals of the navy. The Byam character was created by Charles Nordhoff and Norman Hall, who used him as the fictional narrator of their three *Bounty* novels. (The script for Thalberg's film was based on this popular trilogy.)

When several of the real *Bounty* mutineers were captured on Tahiti and brought back to England, midshipman Peter Heywood, sixteen at

HISTORY

John Smart painted this watercolor of Bligh around 1803 to commemorate the captain's brave actions at the battle of Camperdown (1797), where Adm. Horatio Nelson singled him out for praise. Fourteen years after the *Bounty* mutiny, Bligh looks a young forty-nine years old. He has—for those of us raised on Charles Laughton's mythologized Bligh—a look of unexpected serenity, slightly teasing.

When he posed for this painting, he was on the eve of his appointment as governor of the penal colony in New South Wales. Bligh served three years in that post before Lt. Col. George Johnston mutinied against him in 1808 and sent Bligh back to England under arrest. Johnston and the other mutineers were subsequently found guilty of conspiracy. Meanwhile, Bligh was promoted to rear admiral.

HOLLYWOOD

This face of Bligh—Charles Laughton's—is the one most deeply etched into our mythic consciousness. Comedians of the day made much of Laughton's aura of menace and hatefulness. Laughton himself was crippled with self-doubt during the filming and said he hated the character he was playing. The Hollywood crew, however, was awed by Laughton's English composure and cultural knowledge. He even knew what the *Book of Common Prayer* was!

An Account of the Mutiny

In 1786, British plantation owners in the West Indies needed cheap subsistence food for their slaves. Cut off from their American suppliers by the Revolutionary War, they thought the wondrous breadfruit of Tahiti would do as a replacement. A reluctant Admiralty, lobbied by Sir Joseph Banks, gave the command of a small ship, the *Bounty*, to William Bligh, a naval lieutenant on half pay. Bligh was working the West Indies trade at the time.

Embittered by a lack of recognition for his achievements as master aboard James Cook's *Resolution*, the thirty-two-year-old Bligh was determined to make this apparently insignificant voyage a perfect one. But the odds were against him. He had an incompetent crew, and though not violent himself, he violated most of the rules of command.

A five-month stay in Tahiti waiting for breadfruit cuttings to strike gave the crew a taste of hedonism, yet they were in fact eager to return home, not least because curios they had collected would make them a small profit. On the voyage back, Bligh was in a constant

rage at their incompetence, and Fletcher Christian seemed to feel more needled than most. On April 28, 1789, he led a mutiny that was totally unexpected and bloodless. Bligh, with eighteen others and five days' worth of supplies, was set adrift in an open twenty-one-foot launch off Tofua, near Tonga. When one of the launch people was killed at Tofua by the islanders, Bligh determined to sail four thousand miles west to Timor. This terrible journey was made worse by much accusatory hatred among the group.

By March 1790, Bligh was back in England. Almost immediately, the Admiralty returned him to the Pacific in the *Providence* to get the breadfruit. The Admiralty also sent Capt. Edward Edwards in the *Pandora* to capture the mutineers. Edwards found fourteen on Tahiti and imprisoned them in appalling conditions in "*Pandora*'s box." Returning to England, the *Pandora* was wrecked off the Australian coast, and four of the "pirates" were drowned. The survivors, in chains, then made their own voyage to Timor on the bottom of open boats. Ten "Bounties" were eventually tried, and six condemned to hang. Of these, three were hanged from the yard of the *Brunswick* on October 29, 1792; two were given king's mercy; and a third escaped on a legality.

the time of the mutiny, became the dramatic focus of their court-martial. Events that had actually happened to Heywood were transferred to Byam by Nordhoff and Hall. The real Heywood had protested his innocence, been condemned to die, and then been given king's mercy. Byam is also pardoned, but not before he delivers an entirely fictional court-martial speech in which Thalberg makes all his didactic points.

The film ends with "Rule Britannia" playing and the Union Jack flying, leaving the audience with a warm feeling of reassurance and the knowledge that the navy can see true virtue and respond to it. Fade out. It doesn't matter that British sailors were still flogged fifty years after the *Bounty* mutiny or that the entire fleet mutinied just ten years later. The theater of the film—its cathartic point—is that submission to legitimate authority, even at the cost of personal sacrifice, is the first step of reform.

However, the cathartic point of a film is not necessarily our cultural memory of it. The cultural memory of the 1935 Laughton/Gable *Mutiny on the Bounty*, for instance, is a mythical cliché. Doing a "Captain Bligh" quickly became twentieth-century shorthand for the pathologically cruel use of inept authority. The later *Bounty* films offered different contexts, but film critics couldn't shake the cultural memory of the 1935 film. Some even berated the remakes for being unhistorical because they omitted some of the inventions of the Laughton/Gable film!

Although the 1935 filmmakers believed historical realism was one of their film's most salable features, they were not at all bashful about admitting they made some of it up to "produce an effect." For marketing purposes, they created a *Teaching Manual for U.S. High Schools*, which suggested appropriate readings and provided some reflective questions about the relationships among the Nordhoff and Hall novels, the script, and the historical record. The manual's authors justify loading Bligh down with the sadistic acts of other English captains by claiming "it allowed a close-knit, strong, and more comprehensive study of Bligh's character." To have told the actual story "might have confused the issue." They were not embarrassed to stress that the film's priority was to "produce effects" rather than record facts.

Telling the actual story, even if it confused the issue, might have been a more appropriate historical ambition. If one can create a historical fact simply by counting, then Bligh was one of the least violent of captains in the Pacific. He flogged only 10.9 percent of the *Bounty* crew. In comparison, James Cook flogged 25.6 percent of the *Resolution* crew, and George Vancouver, 52.8 percent of the *Discovery*'s. If Bligh was indeed known to contemporary seamen as the Bounty Bastard, it was not because he was inordinately violent in a violent navy. It was because of something else.

That something else, they said, was Bligh's bad language, and—when he was court-martialed (but acquitted) for unbecoming conduct in 1805—his gestures. At first glance, bad language might not seem a very convincing reason for three successful mutinies against Bligh's authority (not to mention several unsuccessful ones). After all, sailors seemed to have endured much worse in the eighteenth-century navy. However, Bligh's "bad language" has to be understood as his failure to speak his roles properly in the theater of his command. The one grace of physical punishment was its finality, but Bligh also wanted his men to feel guilty for what they had done and grateful to him for what he had not done.

Where the abuses of other captains flowed over the sailors, Bligh's stuck and picked at the scabs of wounds he had already inflicted. His very gestures, idiosyncratic though they were, breached a personal space, as did his intrusive rules and regulations. "Sailors [are] like children," he once wrote to Sir Joseph Banks. And, in fact, there were many crews proud to call their captains Father, but not the *Bounty*'s. "Captains [create] their own mutinies," Admiral Collingwood said at the time, and this was almost certainly true of Bligh as well. The actual story of the *Bounty* mutiny is likely to have been that Bligh created his own mutiny, not with pathological violence but with the banality of his command.

W riting the history of a cultural memory created by a film can be difficult because films as cultural artifacts have a disembodied feel. Their function is to be seen, not read. A film in a can is not like a book on a shelf or a manuscript in an archive. It requires a cinema in which to be seen and cinematic conventions in which to be understood. The seeing of a film is mostly a one-time experience. Using the fast-forward and rewind buttons to study a film on video is not the same experience as seeing a film in a cinema, where we see films with other people and then discuss what we have seen.

Fortunately for historians, even these shared experiences leave behind some texts. The 1935 *Bounty*, for example, produced an abundance of texts: the film scripts; MGM's Campaign Books, which outline the studio's marketing strategy for the film (including "news" items fed to the media that betray messages the film was meant to convey); and its Press Books, which record the cultural response to the film.

Films probably make myth by becoming such total cultural events that they create a lasting cultural memory. In this process, the making and marketing of a film, as well as the social context of its launch, play their part alongside the actual narrative. The Campaign Books for *Mutiny on the Bounty* show how such a "total event" was created: They are full of "amazing facts" that were distributed by the studio to newspapers around the world, such as the fact that twenty-five million people had already read the Nordhoff and Hall novels. These books also suggested "catchlines" for newspapers: "44 Men on a 90-Foot Hellship." "Round the Clock with Gable," one bit of gossip proclaims: "6:00 rise; 7:00 cold shower; 8:00 into speedboat; 9:00 sharkshooting, 10:00 sets. . . ."

Above all, the Campaign Books championed the filmmakers' dedication to historical research: The noted naval historian C.N. Robinson spent an entire year performing the scrupulous work of historical verifi-

Clark Gable as Christian

The Real Fletcher Christian

The only image we have of the historical Fletcher Christian is this enlargement from Robert Dodd's watercolor *Lieutenant Bligh Leaving the Bounty*. Note that Dodd shows Christian wearing a hat, the symbol of radical politics. At the time, the Royal Navy was seen as Britain's only defense against the revolution across the Channel in France. There was no way that this unpolitical mutiny on an unimportant ship at the ends of the earth could go unpunished. Thus, the navy lost fifty more lives and one more ship dragging back all the *Bounty* mutineers it could catch.

The real master's mate was an English gentleman who belonged directly to the Isle of Man's line of the Deemsters. Although his immediate family had fallen on hard times, his relatives included three bishops, a lord chief justice, a high sheriff, and two members of Parliament. His brother Edward was a professor of law at Cambridge University, and his brother Charles, a psychologically disturbed ship's surgeon. At the mouth of the Thames, the *Bounty* crossed paths with Charles's ship returning from India, and Fletcher learned that his brother had been charged with mutiny on the voyage back. One wonders whether Fletcher told Bligh this.

Clark Gable was a reluctant Christian. He did not want to lose his mustache ("damned lucky for me"), and he worried how his bandy legs would look in costume. He also didn't know how to play Good against Bligh's Evil without appearing feminine, so he acted the part with a rascally swagger. The result is the most cheerful press-gang officer ever seen on the *Bounty*—in part because the ship had no impressed sailors.

Trevor Howard and Marlon Brando in the 1962 *Bounty*

The 1962 and 1984 Versions

Marlon Brando, star of the 1962 *Mutiny on the Bounty*, was, like Gable, a reluctant Christian. He preferred the part of John Adams, the last surviving mutineer on Pitcairn, who—after years of murder and mayhem—finally found God. There was "more philosophy" in this role, Brando said. Furthermore, he had no interest in cloning Gable, and he disliked Eric Ambler's screenplay, which he felt turned the *Bounty* tragedy into an action movie. Five hundred thousand dollars persuaded him otherwise.

Once the filming got under way, Brando drove Carol Reed, the original director, off the set, and chased away Reed's replacement, Lewis Milestone. He then self-directed what may be the most bizarre death scene ever committed to film. There was never a past more imperfect than Brando's *Mutiny*. Everything was bent to the mad logic of his idea that Christian, being a gentleman, was wealthy and foppish.

Not to be outdone by his predecessors, Mel Gibson, star of the 1984 *Bounty*, was also a hesitant Christian. Perhaps he saw too great a gap between his Mad Max persona and the petulant, posturing Christian—or he may have been concerned with the homoerotic relationship between Bligh and Christian posited by the script. But the producers wanted him for his olive complexion and his height. (Bligh had described the five-foot-nine-inch Christian as "swarthy" and "dark.") As the story goes, Gibson decided to take the role after he found that his footprint fitted the tracing supposedly made by the historical Christian in the leaden guttering of Christian's Moreland Close home.

The Bounty notwithstanding, there has never been much doubt about Christian's heterosexual propensities. According to one of his contemporaries, "He was one of the most foolish young men I ever saw in regard to the sex." That statement gave license to much ribald invention and prompted a considerable literature describing, in a soft pornographic way, Tahitian native life. On the other side, the evidence for a homoerotic relationship between Christian and Bligh is slight. Considering that, at the time, about three sailors a year were hanged for sodomy and hundreds more flogged for the less lethal offense of "uncleanness," it would not have been a matter passed over lightly.

cation. The studio commissioned not one, but two reconstructions of the *Bounty*: One was a full-sized replica; the other, an eighteen-foot model sailed by two men crouched under her deck and lost at sea for a few days off Catalina Island. One news item, headlined "Original Bounty Logs Discovered," told the story of director Frank Lloyd meeting a mysterious "white-haired lady" in the Blue Lagoon Cafe, Papeete, on Tahiti. (She was Ida Leeson, librarian of the Mitchell Library in Sydney.) Another tells of Charles Laughton's discovery of Bligh's actual measurements at Gieve's Military Tailors in London, which convinced him to lose fifty-five pounds for the role. MGM even took special pains to use bona-fide eighteenth-century wooden legs as props for the *Bounty*'s surgeon (who had both his legs in real life!). The historical triumphs in the Campaign Books are endless, but most betray the fact that for the filmmakers historicity was a prop man's concern rather than a scriptwriter's.

"Producing effects," such as the imprinting of the Captain Bligh image on the cultural consciousness, is a complicated business. The mythologizing of Laughton's Bligh owes much to the confidence created by the public knowledge that the *Bounty* mutiny was an actual historical event. The process was also speeded along by Laughton's overwhelming performance, which quickly became the subject of much nightclub, stage, and radio comment. Bligh's violence was made the more believable by the counterfoil of comedy as much as by Laughton's histrionics. Herbert Mundin as Bligh's innocent, incompetent servant makes the captain even more outrageous, and Dudley Digges, who plays the one-legged surgeon Bacchus (Thomas Huggan in real life), uses his character's own human weakness to make Bligh seem the more inhumane. Even Gable's Americanism lent perspective to Bligh's strict Britishness. The filmmakers thus produced the "effect" of Bligh's extravagance, and perhaps the cultural memory of it, by contrasting his behavior with the ordinary humanity of others. There is a lot of myth-value in believing that evil is somehow Other and not like Us.

Beyond these effects internal to the film, there were others produced by making the film a cultural event. The novelty of many of its marketing strategies has worn off now, but at the time the studio's efforts to bend the gaze of the widest possible public were considered both inventive and remarkably successful. For example, *Mutiny on the Bounty* was the first film released simultaneously in every Loews movie theater across the country. Half a million people saw it in a month. For a Depression-era film, its two-million-dollar cost was extravagant, but over four and a half million in quick profits made the picture an entrepreneurial triumph trumpeted in newspapers abroad. Stores located near cinemas even reported thirty to forty percent increases in sales, generated by moviegoers, and this, too, helped etch the film into cultural memory. There is "strong stuff at the Capitol," one critic said, and "the public are eating it up," all "this flogging and torture stuff."

Thalberg wasn't at all surprised. "People are fascinated by cruelty," he said, and professional that he was, he kept the studio's publicity department busy. Newspapers were fed with even more stories about the eighty-eight days the crew spent filming on location—both on Catalina and in Tahiti, where two thousand natives were fitted out with every spear that Thalberg could find in the Hollywood warehouses. One would be hard put to disentangle all the webs of memory in which the cliché of Captain Bligh has become caught. On reflection, though, it seems that the twentieth century has found it easier to mythologize the extravagant violence of evil than its banality. If the past created by Hollywood is indeed imperfect, then a past-perfect Bligh might be more banal than pathological. Perhaps there should be a sixth *Mutiny on the Bounty* film to mythologize that one.

Franchot Tone as Byam beside Charles Laughton

The Byam Character

In this court-martial scene, Franchot Tone as the fictional Roger Byam delivers one of those famous "Cut it! Can it!" Hollywood performances. His speech allowed Thalberg the "out" he needed to win Louis B. Mayer's approval. Critics said the scene was all part of the 1935 film's crush on empire, and perhaps *Mutiny on the Pinafore* could be expected next. They also pointed out the amount of screen time given to Gable's "gams" and Tone's "manly stems," and they thought they knew why (wink, wink).

Later...

William Bligh endured other mutinies: one at Great Nore in 1797 and then the Rum Rebellion against his governorship of New South Wales in 1808. In 1814, he was made a vice-admiral, but he did not live long enough to enjoy his promotion. He died in 1817 and was buried in St. Mary's Church, Lambeth.

Fletcher Christian first took the *Bounty* to Tubuai after the mutiny, though his settlement there failed because the *Bounty* crew could not persuade the island women to liaise with them. Sixteen voted to go back to Tahiti. Christian demanded the *Bounty* and promised anybody who went with him that he would find some isolated island. Stopping at Tahiti, he kidnapped twelve Tahitian women and six men and took them with eight mutineer companions to Pitcairn Island. Pitcairn was hell on earth until John Adams made it heaven. In the meantime, Christian was murdered by the Tahitians he enslaved. His grave has not been definitively identified.

Background Reading

Greg Dening, *Mr. Bligh's Bad Language: Passion, Power and Theatre on the Bounty* (Cambridge University Press, 1994)

1935/USA/B&W
DIRECTOR: Frank Lloyd; PRODUCER: Irving Thalberg; SCREENPLAY: Talbot Jennings, Jules Furthman, Carey Wilson; STUDIO: MGM; VIDEO: MGM/UA; RUNNING TIME: 132 min.

DANTON

Robert Darnton

Declaration of the Rights of Man and of the Citizen

In *Danton*, a child hesitatingly recites for Robespierre's approval the first four articles of the Declaration of the Rights of Man and of the Citizen. The Declaration's articles (seventeen in all) enunciated the principles that inspired the French Revolution. They were adopted by the National Assembly between August 20 and August 26, 1789, and later served as the preamble to the Constitution of 1791.

1. Men are born and remain free and equal in rights. Social distinctions can be based only on public utility.

2. The aim of every political association is the preservation of the natural and imprescriptible rights of man. These rights are liberty, property, security, and resistance to oppression.

3. The source of all sovereignty resides essentially in the nation. No body, no individual can exercise authority that does not explicitly proceed from it.

4. Liberty consists in being able to do anything that does not injure another; thus the only limits upon each man's exercise of his natural rights are those that guarantee enjoyment of these same rights to the other members of society. These limits can be determined only by law.

AT THE BEGINNING OF THE POLITICAL YEAR in September 1983, when Frenchmen returned from their vacations to face a declining franc, an escalating arms race, and trouble everywhere on the home front, François Mitterrand summoned his ministers and lectured them on the sorry state of history—not the current turn of events, but the history that French children were failing to learn in school. No doubt the president had other worries. But the crisis that he placed at the top of his agenda was the inability of the electorate to sort out the themes of its past. What would become of a citizenry that could no longer distinguish between Louis XIII and Louis XIV, between the Second and Third Republics, or (and this seems to have been what really hurt) between Robespierre and Danton?

Mitterrand may not have mentioned the controversy aroused by Andrzej Wajda's film, but he probably had *Danton* on his mind. He had disapproved of it when he saw it at a private screening before its release in January 1983. It had outraged his supporters on the Socialist-Communist left when it was shown at the Assemblée Nationale. While the opposition gloated, the left-wing intellectuals thundered with indignation and scored points in the popular press by demonstrating their ability to set the historical record straight.

Such vehemence may seem puzzling to American viewers of *Danton*. We know that the French take their history seriously and that it doesn't do to tamper with their Revolution. But why should the Socialists disavow a version of the feud between Danton and Robespierre that puts Danton in a favorable light? Could not Danton's attempts to stop the Terror be seen as a heroic foreshadowing of the resistance to Stalinism? Is not Wajda a hero of Solidarity? And shouldn't Wajda's Danton be expected to appeal to the moderate left in France, the champions of socialism with a human face? It seems appropriate to pursue these questions, for they take us into the strange symbolic world of the European left, a world in which intellectuals become entangled in the myths they've created.

The film *Danton* opens with some grim scenes in the streets of Paris at the end of 1793. Danton arrives from his country estate to turn back the Terror that he himself helped to create after the overthrow of the monarchy in August 1792. Soon he is engaged in a desperate struggle over the course of the Revolution, which pits the moderates (or Indulgents) against the hard-liners around Robespierre in the Committee of Public Safety. The film dramatizes Danton's inability to stop the guillotining and ends with his own execution on April 5, 1794.

HISTORY

After the outbreak of the Revolution in July 1789, twenty-nine-year-old attorney Georges Danton joined the *garde bourgeoise* (civic guard) of the Cordeliers district. Less than a year later, with some other militants of the district, he founded the Club of the Cordeliers. During the crisis that followed Louis XVI's flight to Varennes in June 1791, Danton became an increasingly important orator of the popular revolutionary movement. On April 7, 1793, he joined the first Committee of Public Safety, charged with managing the revolutionary government's foreign and military affairs. His attempts to negotiate a peace with the invading armies of the First Coalition went nowhere, however, and when his term expired in July, his committee membership was not renewed. By October 1793, Danton's disapproval of the Reign of Terror had become so great that he withdrew from public life, citing reasons of health and family. Yet he returned to Paris six weeks later and quickly became a leader of the moderate opposition.

HOLLYWOOD

Gérard Depardieu as Danton

Andrzej Wajda, the best-known Polish director of his generation, has become, in both his life and his work, a symbol of the political progress his beleaguered country has made in recent years. Following the Communists' December 1981 military crackdown in Poland, Wajda moved to France, where he made *Danton*, a cinematic version of the 1931 play by Stanislawa Przybyszewska. Although Wajda's interest in Danton predated the suppression of Solidarity and the imposition of martial law in Poland (he had already staged Przybyszewska's play three times), many read into *Danton* a condemnation of Communist party practice—including the Polish government, which postponed the film's theatrical release there. In 1989, however, in the wake of the astounding liberalizations that had swept through Poland, Wajda was elected as a Solidarity member to the Sejm (the Polish parliament), and he subsequently announced his retirement from filmmaking.

ROBERT DARNTON

The execution of Louis XVI, 1793

Before the Reign of Terror

On January 21, 1793, Louis XVI was executed by order of the National Convention, the representative body then ruling France. The death of the king marked a turning point for the revolutionary government. It signaled the decline of the moderate Girondins and the rise of the radical Montagnards, who had opposed the Girondins in the Convention and voted overwhelmingly for the king's execution (the death sentence passed, after an endless roll call, by a vote of 387 to 334).

The Girondins were mostly rich professionals who had participated in Louis's final government and controlled the Legislative Assembly, then France's governing body, from its creation in October 1791 until the overthrow of the monarchy on August 10, 1792. At that time, the Constitution of 1791 (which had chartered the Legislative Assembly) was suspended, universal suffrage was instituted, and elections were held for the new National Convention.

The Girondins had risen to prominence because of their agitation for war with Austria, which they had thought would unite the country behind the Revolution. Their inability to prosecute that war successfully, however, undermined their popularity, as did their policies, which stopped short of social and economic equality. The Montagnards, closely associated with the Jacobin Club of Paris and led by Robespierre and Saint-Just, drew their support from the artisan class and the sansculottes.

In March 1793, republican France lost a series of battles to the First Coalition, which represented the foreign (conservative) reaction to the radicalism in France. That same month, counterrevolutionary uprisings against military conscription broke out in the western Vendée region. These crises produced a popular insurrection in Paris, encouraged by the Montagnards, which in turn led to the expulsion of the leading Girondins from the Convention.

Many Girondins fled Paris for the provinces, where they fomented rebellion against the Convention. Meanwhile, the Montagnard and Jacobin bourgeoisie set about consolidating their power, which remained dependent on the revolutionary fervor of the sansculottes. After joining the Committee of Public Safety in July 1793, Robespierre worked with others to create an emergency government whose instrument of power would be "coercive force"—that is, the Terror.

Wajda refuses to let history fall into a simple formula—the apparatchik versus the man of the people—and produces plenty of incriminating evidence against Danton. Gérard Depardieu's powerful acting makes Danton the dominant and more sympathetic figure, but Depardieu's insistence on Danton's self-indulgence can also be taken as evidence of the character's bourgeois decadence. When Danton meets Robespierre for dinner to discuss their differences he gets sloppily drunk. His inability to take decisive action against the Reign of Terror in the crisis of March and April 1794 might even suggest the failure of the West to rescue Solidarity in 1981. But the film is too ambiguous to provide a precise moral for the present. One cannot even gauge how much Wajda cast his weight on the side of Dantonism, because the texts of the original Polish drama by Stanislawa Przybyszewska and Jean-Claude Carrière's screen adaptation are not available for comparison. Nonetheless, one can spot the points at which the film deviates from the historical record. Three of them would probably stand out clearly to a Polish audience for their allegorical content.

Near the beginning of the film, a small boy, the picture of innocence, stands naked in a tub, trying to recite the Declaration of the Rights of Man while his older sister bathes him. Whenever the words fail to come, he holds out a hand and she slaps him over the knuckles. She is not so much washing him as brainwashing him in order to ingratiate herself with her father's distinguished boarder, Citizen Robespierre.

Soon afterward, Robespierre orders some thugs from the secret police to destroy the shop in which Camille Desmoulins has been printing *Le Vieux Cordelier*, the journal that popularized the Dantonists' attempt to turn back the Terror. Having dwelled on the pain etched on the face of the boy, the camera picks up every detail of the smashing of the presses. Neither episode took place, but the Polish viewer would not have to know that Wajda invented them in order to see them as a comment on thought control at home.

The third episode provides an even clearer indictment of Stalinist indoctrination. Robespierre, wrapped in the robes of Caesar, is posing for neoclassicist painter Jacques-Louis David. He stops to berate the prosecutor of the Revolutionary Tribunal, who is having difficulty rigging Danton's trial. Then he notices a gigantic canvas on which David has begun to paint his famous version of the Tennis Court Oath. In the crowd of patriots, Robespierre spies the freshly painted head of Fabre d'Eglantine, who is then being tried along with Danton. "Wipe it out," he orders. "But he was there," David objects. Nonetheless, Robespierre insists, and so Fabre disappears like all the victims of Stalinist historiography. Yet this scene never happened. Fabre did not participate in the Tennis Court Oath because he was not a deputy to the Estates General in 1789. Wajda seems to have been so intent on exposing the falsification of history by the Stalinists that he was willing to falsify it himself.

Although the film allows Robespierre a few moments of triumph from the rostrum, its camera work undoes the effect of his words. While he

HISTORY

Maximilien de Robespierre

From July 1793 to July 1794, Maximilien de Robespierre (1758–1794) used his dominance of the Committee of Public Safety to direct the revolutionary government—and the committee's Reign of Terror to control France. The son of a lawyer, Robespierre had been raised in Arras but he studied in Paris, where he earned degrees in law and philosophy. In 1783, he was admitted to the Arras Academy for the advancement of the arts and sciences; he became its chancellor and, later, its president. When the king summoned the Estates General in 1788 (for the first time since 1614), the citizens of Arras chose Robespierre to represent them as a member of the Third Estate, thus beginning his political career. In 1792, as a leader of the Jacobin Club, Robespierre opposed the war with Austria that Girondin leader Jacques-Pierre Brissot was advocating as a means of spreading the Revolution. When the French army subsequently lost a series of battles and invasion threatened, the masses abandoned Brissot and looked to Robespierre for leadership.

Louis de Saint-Just

The father of Louis de Saint-Just (1767–1794) was a captain in the cavalry; his mother, the daughter of a wealthy local notary. (A woman of strong political opinions, she believed that the nobility should be reduced to the level of the bourgeoisie.) At nineteen, Saint-Just ran away to Paris, was found by his mother, and spent most of the next year in a reformatory. When released, he studied the law and received his degree in April 1788. France was then suffering from a poor harvest and a difficult winter. When the Bastille was stormed the following year, Saint-Just was too young to serve as a deputy in the National Assembly (the legally required age was twenty-five). "I am a slave of my adolescence!" he cried. However, he did make a reputation as the municipal corporation council of Blérancourt, and in September 1792, shortly after his twenty-fifth birthday, he was elected to the National Assembly, where he rose by degrees, joining the Committee of Public Safety in May 1793.

Camille Desmoulins

Camille Desmoulins (1760–1794) was one of the Revolution's leading journalists and pamphleteers. Although admitted to the bar in 1785, he struggled as a lawyer because of a stammer. Nevertheless, on July 12, 1789, he successfully urged a crowd of Parisians to take up arms against the king; two days later, the Bastille was stormed. In the months that followed, Desmoulins published *La France libre*, which summarized the failures of the ancien régime, and *Discours de la lanterne aux Parisiens*, which championed the bourgeois reforms of the National Assembly. After Louis XVI's flight to Varennes in June 1791, Desmoulins stepped up his campaign for the creation of a republic. With the overthrow of the monarchy in August 1792, he formed an alliance with Danton, under whom he served in the Ministry of Justice. In late 1793, after the June 2 expulsion of the Girondin leaders from the National Assembly, he and Danton became leaders of a moderate faction, known as the Indulgents, within the Jacobin Club.

French Historians of the Revolution

Even though the debate about *Danton* seemed to turn on questions of fact that could be settled from the primers of the Third Republic, it really concerned symbolic power. In appealing to the facts, however, the Socialist politicians exposed themselves to some difficulties raised by their fellow travelers among the intelligentsia: The primers were out of date. Worse, factuality itself had been consigned by the avant-garde to the scrap heap of outmoded notions like liberalism and positivism. Michel Foucault and a host of literary critics had dissolved facts into "discourse," and the most fashionable historians, those identified with the *Annales* school and based in the Ecole des Hautes Etudes en Sciences Sociales, had turned their backs on politics and events in order to study social structures and *mentalités*.

Long before the opening of *Danton*, the split between the new and the old history had been dramatized by a feud between two of the leading historians of the Revolution: Albert Soboul and François Furet. Soboul, a Communist and professor at the Sorbonne, stood in the direct line of descent from Albert Mathiez, who had tried to knock Danton off his perch by proving that he had sold himself to the counterrevolution. In his place, Mathiez had erected Robespierre, the ideological strategist who formed an alliance with the common people in order, Mathiez maintained, to force France down the road to social revolution. Furet, a former Communist and eminent Annalist from the Ecole des Hautes Etudes, attacked the entire tradition from Mathiez to Georges Lefebvre as a myth perpetuated in the cause of Stalinism.

The polemics shook the Left Bank for several years in the 1970s, but they had subsided by the time the Socialists and Communists cooperated to elect Mitterrand. In the autumn of 1982 Soboul died. His funeral was a sad affair, a high Communist mass with red roses and black suits at the Mur des Fédérés, the most sacred territory of the Left in the Cimetière du Père-Lachaise. It seemed to mark the end of a vision of the Revolution that had inspired Frenchmen for more than a century.

cows the deputies of the Convention with the official line on Terror and Virtue, the screen fills with a close-up of his dainty shoes. He rises to the climactic movements of his speech on tiptoe, more like a dancing master than a champion of the people, in contrast to Danton, who roars at the crowd in the courtroom like a caged lion.

If Robespierre scores any points in the debates, they are wiped away in the end by the guillotining. The blade comes down on Danton's neck with sickening inexorability. Blood gushes into the hay below the scaffold. The executioner holds the severed head before the crowd, and the camera dwells upon it in a sequence of overexposed shots that leave the viewer feeling dizzy and nauseated. Then the scene shifts to Robespierre, sweating like a madman in his bed, while the young boy, who at last has learned his catechism, recites the Declaration of the Rights of Man and of the Citizen. As the boy parrots the words, his voice is drowned out by dissonant background music, and on that harsh note the film ends.

In France, everything seemed disposed to make *Danton* a hit: Wajda was lionized; Solidarity had captured the heart of the public; and the newly elected Socialist government was eager to present the film as its overture to the bicentennial of the French Revolution in 1989.

Yet *Danton* created a scandal, especially on the left, where the uneasy alliance between the Socialists and Communists left some uncertainty about who represented the Revolutionary tradition. The Communists tried to mount the strongest condemnation: "It is counterrevolutionary," wrote a critic in *L'Humanité*. The Socialists replied in kind: "It disfigures everything most beautiful [in the Revolution]," Philippe Boucher declared in *Le Monde*. Pierre Joxe added, "[Wajda's] history is not ours."

The Revolution established the basic categories of French politics, beginning with the distinction of left and right, which derives from the seating pattern of the Constituent Assembly. The politicians sitting in the Assemblée Nationale two hundred years later understood that they could head off political challenges by manipulating these categories. Like Robespierre, they tried to speak in the name of the sovereign people and so outflank their enemies on the left.

The left flank of the Socialists looked vulnerable when *Danton* opened in January 1983. The government had changed course and adopted economic policies closer to those of Margaret Thatcher than to the radical program on which Mitterrand had been elected. Its temporizing smacked of Dantonism, and the Communists began to snipe at it from the left, just as Robespierre had done when he attacked the moderates in the Convention, aligning himself with the sansculottes. The Socialists needed to prove their ideological purity, so they rushed to defend the orthodox view of the French Revolution. They fell over themselves in the scramble to denounce the heresies in *Danton*. Every point scored against Wajda could be counted toward a victory over the opposition and a demonstration of one's superior faithfulness to the true revolutionary tradition.

Wajda, it was charged, had made the Terror seem gratuitous by eliminating all reference to its context: the civil war in the Vendée, the federalist revolts in the provinces, the counterrevolutionary intrigues in Paris, and the invasion about to burst across the border. Wajda had ignored Robespierre's campaign against the left-wing extremists led by Jacques René Hébert, thereby making nonsense of the leftist opposition to Robespierre in the Committee of Public Safety and obscuring the political rationale for Robespierre's stroke against the Dantonists: a need to preserve the allegiance of the sansculottes and to prevent the Revolution from veering to the right after the purge of the Hébertist left. Wajda had even cut out the sansculottes themselves. The common people hardly appear in the film, yet the French Revolution was an uprising of the masses, not a parliamentary duel between a few bourgeois orators.

Finally, the critics raked over the film in search of anachronisms. Unlike the grim "Angel of Death" of orthodox history, Wajda's Saint-Just wears an earring and cavorts about like a modern hippie. Furthermore, Billaud-Varenne is too unshaven, Desmoulins too weak, and Danton too drunk. These details offended the critics not because of their inaccuracy but because they made the leaders of the Revolution look more familiar and less heroic than the figures in the history books.

Wojciech Pszoniak's portrayal of an icy, neurotic, inhuman Robespierre seemed especially offensive, because Robespierre was the touchstone of orthodoxy in interpretations of the Revolution. Equally important, he was the model of the modern French intellectual. He personified engagement. A theorist turned man of action, he laid out party lines and devised strategy in the interest of the masses. The Socialist leaders thought of themselves as intellectuals of this kind.

In debating *Danton*, the politicians were caught in a double bind. They appealed to an old-fashioned kind of history that no longer seemed tenable to their intellectual avant-garde and no longer existed for their children or grandchildren. They had brought that trouble on themselves, however, for the French Ministry of Culture had given Wajda— a hero of the left, an intellectual of the purest anti-Stalinism—three million francs to celebrate their Revolution, and he had denigrated it. What was the world coming to? The Socialists could only shake their heads and lecture one another on Wajda's heresies, unaware that their indignation demonstrated how much they remained prisoners of their own mythology.

Background Reading

Robert Darnton, *The Kiss of Lamourette: Reflections in Cultural History* (Norton, 1990)

William Doyle, *The Oxford History of the French Revolution* (Oxford University Press, 1989)

1983/France-Poland/Color
DIRECTOR: Andrzej Wajda; **PRODUCER:** Margaret Menegoz; **SCREENPLAY:** Jean-Claude Carrière, Andrzej Wajda, Agnieszka Holland, Boleslaw Michalek, Jacek Gasiorowski; **STUDIO:** Gaumont; **VIDEO:** Columbia Tristar; **RUNNING TIME:** 136 min.

The execution of Robespierre

Later...

Danton was warned several times of his imminent arrest, but he paid little heed: "They will not dare!" he said. In fact, the Jacobins arrested Danton, Desmoulins, and the other Indulgents during the night of March 29–30, 1794. Danton defended himself vigorously before the Revolutionary tribunal, provoking the Convention to exclude him from the debate. "I will no longer defend myself," Danton responded. "Let me be led to death. I shall go to sleep in glory." Danton and his fellow Indulgents were guillotined on April 5. "Show my head to the people," Danton instructed his executioner. "It is worth the trouble."

Now even more firmly in control of the government, Robespierre and Saint-Just enjoyed a number of immediate triumphs. On June 4, the National Convention elected Robespierre its president with 216 votes out of a possible 220. On June 26, the French army defeated the Austrians at Fleurus in the Austrian Netherlands (modern Belgium). Yet the success of the Jacobins ironically figured in their downfall. As France's military victory became more certain, the Convention increasingly protested the dictatorial Jacobin rule.

By June 1794, Robespierre's unremitting work schedule had undermined his health, and he ceased making appearances, first before the Convention and then before the Committee of Public Safety. During July, public opinion began to turn against him. On July 26, he appeared before the Convention and made what would be his final speech. The following day he was arrested— although the warden at Luxembourg prison, uncertain whether the arrest order would be confirmed, refused to jail him. Robespierre then went to the Hôtel de Ville (city hall). Armed supporters gathered there, awaiting his instructions, but Robespierre refused to lead an uprising. Instead, after hearing that the Convention had declared him an outlaw, he wounded himself severely with a pistol shot. On July 28 (10 Thermidor by the revolutionary calendar), soldiers of the National Convention attacked the Hôtel de Ville and seized Robespierre. He was guillotined that evening along with Saint-Just, their deaths marking the onset of the bourgeois Thermidorian reaction.

THE BUCCANEER

Two Films

Sean Wilentz

THE STORY OF MAJ. GEN. ANDREW JACKSON, privateer Jean Laffite, and the battle of New Orleans has the makings of an epic film: larger-than-life characters, piracy and political intrigue, and a fierce military engagement of world-historic importance. Not satisfied with all that, Hollywood has twice offered up *The Buccaneer*, a semifictional rendering that invents some star-crossed love affairs and makes them central to the plot. Uninformed viewers may come away from either film thinking that New Orleans (and, in all likelihood, the entire Mississippi Valley) escaped British conquest during the War of 1812 largely because of Laffite's longings for an American belle. Still, the films are worth a look. Their treatments of key historical events preceding the battle and of the battle itself contain some reliable history, and their starkly different love stories mark some deeper changes between the late 1930s and the late 1950s in how American films approached sex and sexual symbolism.

In emphasizing the importance of the New Orleans battle, the films are actually more trustworthy than many standard history textbooks. After burning Washington, D.C., and setting the federal government to flight in August 1814, the British military was in a strong position to seize command of the Mississippi basin and thus negate Thomas Jefferson's Louisiana Purchase of 1803—a purchase that the British government (with justice) had always regarded as illegitimate. Because control of New Orleans would effectively guarantee control of the entire Mississippi River Valley, military attention focused on the city and its surrounding bayous. Simultaneously, American and British peace commissioners were meeting at Ghent to negotiate an end to the hostilities—but their discussions had no bearing on the New Orleans crisis. Had the British forces captured the city, the British government was prepared, treaty or no treaty, to seize the advantage, declare the Louisiana Purchase a dead letter, and redraw the political map of North America. Numerous scholars have assumed, wrongly, that because the battle ended after the Treaty of Ghent was signed, Jackson's victory had minimal military or political significance. In fact, the fate of the United States—indeed, of the Western world as we know it—may well have hung on the battle's outcome.

Fresh from his triumphs over the Creek Indians at Horseshoe Bend and over the British at Pensacola, Jackson took personal command of the defense of New Orleans on December 1, 1814. He found a desperate situation: a city lacking adequate troops and munitions, with a French and Spanish Creole population of dubious loyalty—and, to the south, a treach-

"You are uneasy; you never sailed with me before, I see."

Andrew Jackson

HISTORY

Born probably in France of uncertain parentage, Jean Laffite emigrated to New Orleans sometime around 1806 and quickly became the leader of a band of desperadoes that preyed on Spanish shipping. From his base on Grand Terre Island about fifty miles south of New Orleans, Laffite controlled shipping into and out of the city. He converted his plunder into cash through unscrupulous New Orleans merchants, the most notorious being his brother Pierre. After the battle of New Orleans, Laffite went to sea for three years in search of a new base of operations. In 1817, he finally settled on the island that is now Galveston, Texas. Four years later, Lt. Lawrence Kearney of the U.S. Navy ordered Laffite off the island, and the pirate relocated once again, this time to Mujeres Island off the Yucatán coast. By this time, however, his forces were much diminished. He died in about 1826 at Teljas on the Yucatán mainland.

HOLLYWOOD

A distinguished stage actor and one of the most versatile stars of Hollywood's Golden Age, Fredric March played in a wide range of genres—from light comedy to horror to melodrama. His classically trained voice and patrician good looks graced a number of period pieces, including *Anna Karenina* (1935), but March seemed most comfortable playing contemporary characters, such as the fading matinee idol in *A Star Is Born* (1937) and a World War II veteran in *The Best Years of Our Lives* (1946).

Born Taidje Khan in 1915 off the coast of Siberia, Yul Brynner took up acting after an accident curtailed his career as a circus acrobat. He emigrated to the United States in 1940 but failed a 1947 screen test at Universal because he looked "too Oriental." In 1951, he began a 4,625-performance run on Broadway as the king of Siam in Rodgers and Hammerstein's *The King and I*. Trading on his exotic appearance and imperious manner, Brynner starred in a number of films as a succession of royals, secret agents, and gunslingers, notably in *The Magnificent Seven* (1960) and *Westworld* (1973).

The War of 1812

In the decade preceding the War of 1812, a gigantic conflict raged between Great Britain and Napoleonic France. On October 21, 1805, the English took control of the seas with a victory over the combined French and Spanish fleets at Trafalgar. A few weeks later, Napoleon gained the upper hand on land when he defeated the Austrians and Russians at Austerlitz. Henceforth, Britain avoided engaging France on land and France did not challenge Britain at sea. However, believing that the source of Britain's strength lay in its commerce, Napoleon closed European ports under his control to British goods. In retaliation, the British forbade neutral vessels to trade at ports closed to Britain unless they had first touched at a British harbor and paid duties to the British government. Both national policies were flagrant violations of international law. But where France's favored American shipping, Britain's harmed it and gave rise to anti-British sentiment in the United States.

At this time, Andrew Jackson was a successful businessman, slave owner, and land speculator. He was also major general of the Tennessee militia, and he longed to play a greater part in his nation's affairs. When the War of 1812 broke out, Jackson immediately volunteered his services and those of his militiamen to the federal government. In 1813, Jackson commanded a long and spectacularly successful campaign against the Creek Indians, who were allies of the British. In August 1814, he moved his army to Mobile, Alabama, where he made preparations for an unauthorized invasion of Spanish Florida (Spain was also allied to Britain). On November 7, Jackson's troops occupied Pensacola. Then they immediately turned around and marched to New Orleans, where they arrived in early December.

erous patchwork of swamps and waterways known as Barataria, under the control of the outlaw smuggler Laffite and his brothers Pierre and Alexandre (better known by his *nom de guerre*, Dominique You). Relations between the American officials and the Baratarians were particularly testy. Earlier, the British had offered Laffite thirty thousand dollars, land grants, and a naval commission if he and his men would aid the invasion. The haughtiness of the British may have offended the privateers; without question, the offer amounted to a trifle. (Laffite's men, one thousand strong, were already fabulously rich from the plunder of Spanish ships in the Caribbean and the Gulf of Mexico, and they had little use for land.) Laffite was also concerned about the fate of his brother Pierre, whom the Americans had arrested and jailed in New Orleans. While the British awaited his reply, Laffite reported the British offer to the American governor, William Claiborne, and pledged his services to the American side, in exchange for Pierre's release.

Suspecting some sort of ruse, Claiborne's military advisers responded to Laffite's overture by unleashing U.S. warships under the command of Daniel Patterson, who had orders from Washington to destroy the privateers' base of operations on Grand Terre Island. Eighty Baratarians, including Dominique You, fell prisoner; the rest retreated into the bayous. Jackson, who arrived soon thereafter, had no sympathy for pirates who had dickered with the British, and in his first proclamation to rally the New Orleans citizenry he denounced Laffite and the Baratarians as "hellish banditti" courted by an invading army that hoped to "prostrate the holy temple of our liberty."

Jackson soon changed his mind. Laffite, an indifferent sea captain but a shrewd businessman, wanted what the Americans had—his men; and he had what the Americans wanted—a large supply of munitions and hundreds of battle-hardened fighters. Disregarding the assault on Grand Terre, Laffite again offered his full cooperation, this time in exchange for a full pardon for all the Baratarians. Jackson had little choice but to agree.

Eventually thousands of volunteers and militiamen arrived in New Orleans from Kentucky and Tennessee—Jackson's famous buckskinned squirrel shooters. Yet the Baratarians' contributions were vital to the American success, not least their expert cannoneering under the command of You, who had learned the arts of artillery in service to Napoleon Bonaparte. Advancing up the Mississippi via Lake Borgne, the British met with murderous barrages from the polyglot American forces, who stood well protected behind canal ditches, freshly dug earthworks, and bales of commandeered cotton. After their final retreat from the field on January 8, the British counted more than twenty-four hundred casualties in the New Orleans campaign; American losses amounted to about one-tenth that number. As promised, Laffite and his men received their pardons from President James Madison—plus warm public thanks from an admiring Jackson.

The first version of *The Buccaneer*, directed by Cecil B. DeMille, appeared in 1938. Fredric March acquits himself well in the film as Jean Laffite, speaking with a plausible Creole accent and affecting the raffish, gentlemanly air of the original privateer. In the role of Jackson, Hugh Sothern (a collateral descendant of the general) effectively conveys the admixture of gallantry and explosiveness that was Jackson's hallmark. The script silently alters some important historical facts: Pierre Laffite, for example, drops out of the story completely; events that occurred over several days are telescoped together; a few scenes (notably Laffite's initial meeting with Jackson) get doctored into stagy melodrama. However, the account of the major incidents that actually *did* occur is for the most part reliable, including bits of dialogue lifted directly from surviving eyewitness reports.

Somewhere along the line, DeMille and company decided that they needed to add some romantic interest in order to explain Jean Laffite's American allegiance—and, no doubt, to help the picture at the box office. They wound up concocting several romances. As the film begins, Laffite is in love with a reputable New Orleans mademoiselle, Annette de Rémy, who refuses to marry him until he turns respectable. In an early scene, Annette bids farewell to her sister, who sails off for Havana with her fiancé aboard the fictional *Corinthian*. Before the *Corinthian* gets very far out to sea, a renegade Baratarian ship, commanded by one Captain Brown (another invention), robs and sinks her, in defiance of Laffite's standing order banning attacks on American vessels. Brown's men kill everyone aboard the *Corinthian* save one passenger, a pert young Dutch woman named Gretchen—whom Brown promptly forces to walk the plank.

With the *Corinthian* still ablaze, Laffite's own ship shows up. He and his men pluck Gretchen from the ocean, and Laffite summarily hangs the fractious Captain Brown, thereby establishing himself once and for all as the sole boss of Barataria. Gretchen joins the smugglers and falls in love with Laffite. Yet his heart remains with Annette de Rémy, whom he succeeds in winning over by siding with the Americans and fighting valiantly in the great battle.

At the victory ball, Laffite and Annette are at last about to become engaged when, suddenly, Dominique You appears on the dance floor, arm-in-arm with Gretchen (in whom *he* has taken a fancy). A gentleman recognizes Gretchen as a passenger who sailed aboard the *Corinthian*, and he grows suspicious. One question leads to another; at last, Laffite (a pirate with honor) confesses that the *Corinthian* was sunk, that only Gretchen survived, and that he, as boss of Barataria, accepts full responsibility. Protecting Laffite from the outraged crowd, Jackson gives him an hour's head start to clear out of New Orleans. The film cuts to You, Gretchen, and Laffite, standing on the deck of a Baratarian ship, headed out to sea. Gretchen snuggles up to Laffite, clasping his hand, and the credits roll.

Pirates and Privateers

International law defines piracy as the crime of robbery, or any other act of violence for private ends, on the high seas, committed by the captain or crew of a ship outside the normal jurisdiction of any nation, and without authority from any government. The people who engage in such acts are called pirates. A pirate has no valid commission either from a sovereign state or from an insurgent or belligerent group engaged in hostilities with a sovereign state. The buccaneers of the sixteenth and seventeenth centuries were pirates who preyed mostly on the commerce between Spain and its American colonies. Piracy waned with the development of the steam engine and the growth of the British and American navies in the later eighteenth and early nineteenth centuries.

The term *privateer*, by contrast, applies to a privately owned army vessel whose captain and crew have been commissioned by a belligerent state to carry on naval warfare. Privateering is thus distinguished from piracy by its governmental sanction. During the Middle Ages, European states with few or no warships hired merchant vessels for hostile purposes; these ships were issued letters of marque authorizing them to prey on enemy commerce. (Laffite himself received a letter of marque from Cartagena, an independent province of Colombia.) As compensation, the privateers were allowed to share in the booty they captured. Privateering flourished during both the American Revolution and the War of 1812. Even Jean Laffite, one of history's most legendary pirates, insisted that his captains operate legally as privateers. The Declaration of Paris abolished the practice in 1856, but the United States was not a party to that agreement. As a result, in 1863 Congress authorized President Lincoln to commission privateers. Lincoln never exercised the power, but the Confederacy did engage in some privateering during the Civil War.

Jackson's New Orleans headquarters

New Orleans

Although southeastern Louisiana was originally explored by the Spanish in the sixteenth century, Sieur de la Salle claimed it for France in 1682. The decision to found New Orleans was made in Paris in 1717; its purpose was to serve as a "port of deposit" for furs traveling down the Mississippi. Jean-Baptiste le Moyne chose a spot on the eastern bank of the Mississippi, 110 miles north of the Gulf of Mexico, where the river bends sharply (hence its Crescent City nickname). The clearing of underbrush probably began in March 1718. The work went slowly. Among the problems were an uncooperative labor force made up mostly of convicts, a shortage of supplies, difficult living conditions (the environs were mosquito-infested swamps), and two severe hurricanes.

By November 1721, New Orleans had a population of 470: 277 whites, 172 blacks, and 21 Indian slaves. After 1731, more "respectable" settlers began to arrive, but the city nevertheless acquired an international reputation for corruption, graft, and lavish displays of wealth. Balls, parties, and banquets were everyday pastimes for the early colonists, many of whom were criminals and political exiles. At the end of the Seven Years' War in 1763, France ceded to the English all of its lands east of the Mississippi; Louis XV, however, had already agreed to transfer New Orleans to Spain by a secret treaty with Charles III. When the Creoles (the French population of Louisiana) learned of their new Spanish governor, they revolted, but the resistance didn't last long. An Irishman in service to Spain, Don Alexander O'Reilly, crushed the rebellion and later became the Spanish governor of Louisiana.

In 1958, twenty years after the first *Buccaneer*, DeMille supervised the production of a Technicolor remake, with Anthony Quinn directing. (Quinn had played a small part in the original and was now DeMille's son-in-law.) The two leading roles went to the stars of DeMille's enormous hit of two years earlier (yet another remake), *The Ten Commandments*. Yul Brynner's Laffite is more soulful and brooding than Fredric March's, but Brynner also has some charming lighter scenes—all despite the preposterous wig forced upon him by the filmmakers. As Jackson, Charlton Heston, who has been made up to look as though he has just stepped off a twenty-dollar bill, barks orders and lurches about. The main supporting actor, Charles Boyer, plays Charles Boyer playing Dominique You, and he is a sweet, roguish presence. Inger Stevens and Claire Bloom play the female leads.

The historical portions of the second *Buccaneer* largely repeat those of the first, including the lapses. Once again, Pierre Laffite never appears. Gov. William Claiborne is made to seem much more constructive and sympathetic to the Baratarians than he was either in the original film or in actual fact. In a new apocryphal touch (with hints at support for the 1950s civil rights movement), Governor Claiborne's house slave, Cato, serves as a volunteer in the American army. (Slaves were actually kept well away from the action in New Orleans, lest they turn their guns against their masters; however, in compliance with Jackson's orders, two battalions of "free men of color" *did* fight on the American side.) Early in the film, Brynner's Laffite is stirred when one of his company reads him the opening passages of the American Declaration of Independence, adding a bit of democratic idealism to the mix of Laffite's motivations for joining Jackson. Otherwise, most of the accurate historical essentials remain in place.

The major changes have to do with the fictional love stories and their sexual overtones. By 1958, commercial American filmmaking had begun to reflect some of the troubled, rebellious sexual spirit that had been simmering beneath the bland stereotypes of the Eisenhower years and that would boil over in the decades to come. As the biker Johnny in *The Wild One*, Marlon Brando epitomized the charismatic sexual outlaw; *Rebel Without a Cause*, *The Blackboard Jungle*, and lesser "youth-oriented" ventures included tough girls as well as tough boys in the delinquent milieu, alienated from the world of "neat neck-tied producers and commuters of America and Steel civilization" (as the Beat writer Jack Kerouac put it). Intentionally or not, the romances in the second *Buccaneer*—especially the contrast between Claire Bloom and Inger Stevens—dramatized the gathering tensions between rough and respectable.

Stevens—as the governor's daughter and Laffite's love interest, Annette Claiborne (*not* de Rémy)—is an archetypal American object of desire, a fair-haired 1950s "proper" young lady, decked out in Regency dresses—beautiful, graceful, and repressed. Even more than the original version's Annette, she is an improbable catch for Laffite, well above his social station; however, he wins her on the condition that he find a more elevated line of work. The innocent Gretchen character, meanwhile, is eliminated in the remake in favor of Bonnie Brown, daughter of the mutinous pirate Captain Brown. As played by Bloom, she is a brunette spitfire—tomboyish, defiant, and violent. (Her white skin is also slightly darkened, suggesting ever so gently that she may be a mulatto—and thus all the more taboo.) During the first half of the film, while Brynner mopes over his blonde goddess, Bloom hurls abuse at him (and, in one scene, a dagger) for what he has done to her father. The stage is set for a 1950s pop Freudian twist, as Bloom discovers that beneath her rage lies an irresistible passion for her father's executioner. At the film's conclusion, Brynner and Bloom, joined by fate, stand on deck and glare out at the horizon, outlaws forever, sailing (it seems in retrospect) into the 1960s.

With all of these heavy-handed fabrications, it is hard to keep a straight face through an entire screening of the second *Buccaneer*. And even if the original version is less blatantly allegorical, the tampering with the past evident in both films can only offend historical purists. Yet it would be unfair to dismiss the films completely, for both manage to narrate some important episodes in our history with reasonable accuracy and dramatic brio, true to the spirit of the events if not to all the facts. If one concedes that most historical films range along a spectrum from factual, interpretive documentaries *(Eyes on the Prize, The Civil War)* to outright propaganda *(The Birth of a Nation, JFK)*, then the *Buccaneer* films would fall somewhere in the middle. Neither version ranks as a premier piece of filmmaking, but both certainly have their moments, moments arresting enough to encourage some viewers, especially uncynical younger viewers, to learn more about what actually happened. Or so it seems to someone who, at age seven, saw the second *Buccaneer* at a Brooklyn matinee, got hooked on history and the story of Andrew Jackson, and has never looked back at that afternoon—or that movie—until now.

Background Reading

Jane Lucas de Grummond, *The Baratarians and the Battle of New Orleans* (Louisiana State University Press, 1961)

Robert V. Remini, *Andrew Jackson and the Course of American Empire, 1767–1821* (Harper & Row, 1977)

1938/USA/B&W
DIRECTOR: Cecil B. DeMille; **PRODUCER:** Cecil B. DeMille; **SCREENPLAY:** Edwin Justus Mayer, Harold Lamb, C. Gardner Sullivan; **STUDIO:** Paramount; **VIDEO:** none; **RUNNING TIME:** 124 min.

1958/USA/Color
DIRECTOR: Anthony Quinn; **PRODUCER:** Henry Wilcoxon; **SCREENPLAY:** Jesse L. Lasky, Jr.; Bernice Mosk; **STUDIO:** Paramount; **VIDEO:** Paramount; **RUNNING TIME:** 121 min

Later...

When Spain ceded Florida to the United States in 1821, President James Monroe appointed Andrew Jackson territorial governor. In 1823, to promote himself for a possible presidential nomination, Jackson accepted a seat in the U.S. Senate. The following year, he indeed ran for president. With the demise of the Federalist party, the sixth president of the United States would certainly be a Democratic-Republican. However, there were four Democratic-Republicans running in what quickly became a regional race. Secretary of State John Quincy Adams had the solid backing of New England, Speaker of the House Henry Clay took his support from the West, and Secretary of the Treasury William Crawford drew on the South. Only Andrew Jackson, the war hero, could count on votes from all over the country. (The election of 1824 was the first in which the popular vote was considered important enough to be counted.)

Jackson won more electoral votes than any other candidate, but he had only a plurality—not a majority—so the election was thrown into the House of Representatives. There Clay's support brought Adams a narrow victory; Adams reciprocated by naming Clay secretary of state. Jackson, furious, took every opportunity to criticize the president. As 1828 approached, the verbal barrages between the two men intensified. Because the candidates took similar positions on the issues, the campaign consisted of little more than personal attacks. Jackson repeatedly hammered Adams for the "corrupt" bargain he had made with Clay in 1824, while the Adams campaign accused the general of executing soldiers for minor offenses during the War of 1812. They also portrayed Jackson as crude, uneducated, and always ready for a brawl—a characterization that may have disturbed New England businessmen and clergy, but perhaps contributed to Jackson's popularity on the frontier. In what was the first truly grass-roots campaign, Jackson's managers played on their candidate's populist image, hosting local picnics, sponsoring parades, and even handing out souvenirs. Jackson won in a landslide.

SEAN WILENTZ

THE ALAMO

Marshall De Bruhl

C A S T

Col. David Crockett   *(John Wayne)*

Col. James Bowie   *(Richard Widmark)*

Col. William Travis   *(Laurence Harvey)*

Stephen F. Austin

The Texas Revolution

The Texas Revolution was brief but bloody. It lasted from October 1835 until April 1836. Most of the engagements were massacres rather than battles, and the Alamo was the first.

The chief architects of the revolution were Americans who had migrated south to take advantage of the Mexican government's generous land offers. Mexico, anxious to colonize the remote northeastern province of Tejas, granted enormous tracts of land to *empresarios*—most notably to Stephen F. Austin, whose first settlers arrived in 1822.

Many thousands followed, and though they suffered the requirements of Mexican citizenship and conversion to Catholicism, their loyalties remained north of the border. Many at once agitated for secession from Mexico and annexation by the United States. They led small uprisings and encouraged other forms of disobedience to the central government in Mexico City.

THE STORY OF *THE ALAMO* WAS THE paradigmatic American heroic legend for its director, producer, and star—John Wayne—who lobbied for more than ten years to get the picture made. The actor succeeded well as producer, somewhat less well as star, and not well at all as director.

Duke Wayne was a card-carrying American supremacist and a virulent anti-Communist who stood out even in an era noted for red-baiting and witch hunts. Because his public and private personas were one, he often used his movies to propagate his simplistic though widely shared views. *The Alamo* is not just a film but a call to the barricades.

Given Wayne's worldview, it was perhaps inevitable that he would be drawn to this great story, the most famous—but by no means most important—event of the Texas Revolution. Yet like most Americans he fell under the spell of the Alamo of legend and not the Alamo of history.

The issues that divided the American settlers from an increasingly repressive and remote Mexican government—education, taxation, religion, civil law, and slavery (the Texans favored it)—were, for the most part, irreconcilable. Especially so after the rise to power of the despotic Generalissimo Antonio López de Santa Anna, who promised to treat the rebel Texans as common criminals.

In early 1836 Santa Anna marched his army north. The largest town in Texas, San Antonio de Bexar, lay directly in his path. Although the revolution was centered in Anglo settlements farther east, the Mexican dictator had sworn to kill every Texan who resisted, and there were 184 of them at San Antonio de Bexar, barricaded inside the Alamo. It is their deaths—or their martyrdom, if you will—that have engaged the popular imagination for a century and a half.

Wayne's film dispenses with the preliminaries of Texas history and begins with Sam Houston, commander-in-chief of the Army of Texas, arriving grandly in San Antonio de Bexar with a large entourage. (Although Houston was indeed given to outsized gestures, he habitually traveled with just an aide.)

The general has come to the headquarters of Maj. William Barret Travis, the commander in Bexar, to enjoin him to hold back Santa Anna's army "right here on the Rio Grande." Travis's delaying action, says Houston, will give him time to raise, equip, and train a proper army to defend Texas. (San Antonio, of course, lies not on the Rio Grande but some 130 miles north; this is the first of many geographic lapses that infect the film.)

HISTORY

The real Davy Crockett was born in Hawkins County, Tennessee—not in Kentucky, as *The Alamo* suggests. Though barely literate, he served three terms in the U.S. Congress and was the putative author of three best-selling books. Indeed, he was one of the best-known people in America—perhaps the first of a breed that would become all too familiar, a person who is famous for being famous.

Early in the film, John Wayne's Crockett informs Laurence Harvey's Travis rather slyly that he does indeed understand the issues (which was true). Most of the volunteers who came to Texas knew very well why they had come. Stephen F. Austin had returned to the United States in December to drum up support, and his passionate appeals, invoking the spirit of the American Revolution, had received a great response. There had also been the promise of land, as much as 640 acres per enlistee.

HOLLYWOOD

In *The Alamo*, John Wayne failed to translate into a coherent narrative film his belief that the defense of the Alamo was a heroic act worthy of emulation—rather than the military folly it was. Even worse, Wayne repeatedly undercut the gritty bravery of the doomed men with hackneyed sentimentalism and inappropriate Hollywood-style hijinks. Nevertheless, *The Alamo* received seven Academy Award nominations, including one for Best Picture, which may have had more to do with Wayne's jingoistic politics and Hollywood loyalties than with art. An advertisement for the film in the trade papers suggested that for Academy members not to vote for the film was un-American. Evidently, the ads failed: The picture received just one Oscar—for sound.

Sam Houston

Sam Houston's greatest task was to raise and train an army capable of turning back Santa Anna's seasoned six-thousand-man force. Houston's troops were generally ragtag frontiersmen who wanted to fight but did not want to learn how. The spirit and independence of the volunteers, including Jim Bowie and Davy Crockett, have been much romanticized, but these qualities were no match for trained soldiers, and Houston's regular army troops were not much better. No doubt they deserved Gov. Henry Smith's dismissive remark that they were "a mob nicknamed an army." Indeed, Houston had just as little control over the commissioned officers as he did over the volunteers. Travis and fellow commander James Walker Fannin ignored their orders as a matter of course.

Sam Houston was never in San Antonio de Bexar during the Texas Revolution, though he did travel south in January 1836 to rally the troops. While in Goliad on January 17, Houston dispatched Bowie and James Butler Bonham to Bexar with orders to remove the captured Mexican armaments from the Alamo and blow up the place. Travis and Bonham arrived at the Alamo the following day and found James Clinton Neill in command. After Neill left Bexar on February 11, Travis and Bowie settled their argument over the succession of command when it was agreed that Bowie would command the volunteers and Travis the regular troops. Travis soon had the command to himself, however, when typhoid fever confined Bowie to bed for the duration of the siege.

Houston's January 1836 inspection trip ended abruptly at Refugio when he learned that the revolutionary government had effectively relieved him of his command by placing Fannin in charge of a proposed invasion of Mexico. Houston promptly returned to the seat of the provisional government at Washington-on-the-Brazos, where he busied himself until late February 1836 negotiating a neutrality treaty with the thousands of Texas Indians who could do more mischief than any invading army.

Another Texas legend, James Bowie, is introduced, though not seen because he is too drunk to attend the conference. Houston nevertheless recommends Bowie to Travis as a man to whom he would entrust the fate of Texas: "He took this town from General Cos," says Houston (thus removing from the historical record another revolutionary hero, Ben Milam, who captured San Antonio for the Texans in December 1835).

Travis, who insists that he is senior to Bowie, orders the frontiersman to meet him at the "ruined mission" of San Antonio de Valero (the Alamo). The rough-hewn Bowie, jealous of his autonomy, grudgingly agrees. However, when Bowie arrives he immediately challenges Travis's plan to turn the long-abandoned mission into a defensible fortress. Their animosity is a recurring theme in the film, and an accurate one, but their disagreement was over command, not strategy. Both men felt that the Alamo should be defended.

Soon Davy Crockett (played by Wayne) and his Tennessee volunteers arrive, apparently to hunt and raise hell. Instead of checking in with the army, they repair to the local cantina. Crockett sobers up long enough to deliver a few rather windy odes to freedom and republican government.

Next comes a vast Mexican army, and an officer appears before the walls of the Alamo to demand its surrender. Travis listens impassively, then replies by setting off a cannon with his lit cigar. (This was indeed Travis's reply.) The shot roars over the head of the Mexican envoy, and the siege is on.

When the hopelessly outnumbered defenders grow restive, Travis reveals his rationale for holding the Alamo: "Santa Anna cannot go round and leave a fort on his lines of communication." If the Texans can hold out, the Mexican army will be immobilized before the Alamo. (The real Santa Anna would, of course, have been wiser to leave a small troop behind to besiege the Alamo while his main force pursued Houston's army; instead, his stubbornness cost him two weeks and a thousand men.)

Bowie again threatens to quit the Alamo, but Crockett averts the crisis by breaking out the whiskey jugs. There is some evidence that this behavior is pretty much on the mark. If the Mexican army had arrived in San Antonio just a few hours earlier, they could have easily overcome the Texans, most of whom were whooping it up at a fandango in the town.

The Mexican dictator's emissary again appears below the wall and reads Santa Anna's offer of safe passage out of the Alamo for all noncombatants. A line of carriages miraculously appears to take out wives, children, servants, etc. (Noncombatants were never an issue at the Alamo, with two exceptions: Suzannah and Angelina Dickinson, the wife and daughter of Travis aide Lt. Almaron Dickinson.) Then the women and children leave the fort (actually, the Dickinsons stayed), the Mexicans commence a fearsome bombardment, and they charge forward, only to be repulsed. Night falls, and the defenders ponder their predicament (actually, the infantry assaults, three in number, all came on the final morning).

With no prospect of reinforcements, Bowie once again resolves to leave, and this time Crockett decides to go with him. Crockett even says something about "the better part of valor." Travis then appears in the courtyard of the mission. Every schoolboy knows what is supposed to happen next—but it doesn't. Unaccountably, Travis does not draw the famous "line in the sand." It is a myth, perhaps, but it is as true to Texans as Pickett's charge at Gettysburg or the raising of the flag on Iwo Jima.

Screenwriter James Edward Grant was reportedly adamant in his belief that only Texans knew of this famous story, so he refused to include it. Apparently he felt that his own words could do the job just as well, and he did provide Laurence Harvey with the best speech in the film. Travis extols the bravery of the departing troops and wishes them well. As for himself, he says, he will remain with his command. He orders the gates opened. But Bowie dismounts and goes to stand by him. One by one, the men follow Bowie's lead.

The final Mexican attack begins with a spectacular artillery barrage. Early in the battle, Bowie is wounded and put to bed in the chapel, but he defends himself heroically and dies fighting. Travis is equally brave: He dies at the gate, defending himself with only his sword. Crockett, carrying a flaming torch, retreats to the powder magazine. At the door, he is impaled by a Mexican lancer, but he frees himself, staggers into the powder room, and blows up the place.

This is nearly all wrong. If Santa Anna had as much artillery as this film suggests, the Alamo would have been reduced to rubble in a matter of minutes. Bowie was not confined to his bed by a wound; rather, he had spent the entire siege there, suffering from typhoid. Travis died early in the assault, falling backward from the wall with a bullet through his head. And Crockett, according to Mexican accounts, surrendered. Gen. Manuel Castrillon interceded with Santa Anna to save Crockett's life, but Santa Anna, who had vowed to spare no prisoners, summarily executed Crockett and the other survivors.

Background Reading

Marshall De Bruhl, *Sword of San Jacinto: A Life of Sam Houston* (Random House, 1993)

1960/USA/Color
DIRECTOR: John Wayne; **PRODUCER:** John Wayne; **SCREENPLAY:** James Edward Grant; **STUDIO:** Batjac; **VIDEO:** MGM/UA; **RUNNING TIME:** 192 min.

Santa Anna

Later...

In an effort to buck up his besieged men, the film Travis tells them that James Walker Fannin is preparing to march south from Goliad with a thousand men to help defend the Alamo. Actually, there were only four hundred men at Goliad (and they would have had to march northwest to reach the Alamo). The film Bonham eventually rides in with the news that Fannin and his men have been ambushed and murdered. In fact, the Goliad massacre took place three weeks after the fall of the Alamo. Fannin and his army were captured at Coleto Creek and marched back to Goliad, where—on March 27, 1836—they were butchered on Santa Anna's orders.

The insubordinations of Travis at Bexar and Fannin at Goliad resulted in more than five hundred deaths, which reduced the Army of Texas during the spring of 1836 to just 375 men. It is little wonder that Houston railed against those who would fight before Texas was ready—and, in particular, those foolhardy enough to allow themselves to be "forted up" and destroyed by a besieging army.

Houston himself pursued a delaying course until he was ready to fight. The evacuation of Gonzales began a five-week strategic retreat across Texas that ended on April 21, 1836, when Houston turned and annihilated the Mexican army at San Jacinto (outside present-day Houston). The Mexican prisoners taken that day included Santa Anna himself.

The Republic of Texas was now free and independent, and Houston was twice elected its president. But the new nation was hardly viable: It limped along until its annexation by the United States in 1845, an act that led directly to the Mexican War. Houston continued his service to Texas, first as a U.S. senator and then as governor, but his pro-Union views cost him both positions.

THE CHARGE OF THE LIGHT BRIGADE

Richard Slotkin

CAST

Geoffrey Vickers *(Errol Flynn)*
Elsa Campbell *(Olivia de Havilland)*

Alfred, Lord Tennyson

The Charge of the Light Brigade

I
Half a league, half a league,
Half a league onward,
All in the valley of Death
Rode the six hundred.
"Forward the Light Brigade!
Charge for the guns!" he said.
Into the valley of Death
Rode the six hundred.

II
"Forward the Light Brigade!"
Was there a man dismay'd?
Not though the soldier knew
Someone had blunder'd.
Theirs not to make reply,
Theirs not to reason why,
Theirs but to do and die.
Into the valley of Death
Rode the six hundred.

Alfred, Lord Tennyson, 1854

WARNER BROTHERS' LAVISH 1936 *Charge of the Light Brigade,* directed by veteran helmer Michael Curtiz, provides an excellent illustration of how and why historical films were made under Hollywood's studio system. The "real story" counts for something: It provides a premise, guarantees the "importance" of its subject, and gives the production people a set of authentic period details, which the studios lovingly (and often very carefully) re-created on screen. However, historical fiction usually approaches the past with a presentist agenda: a search in the past for pathways to the present. This is especially true in a commercial medium such as the movies, which has to attract audiences presumably uninterested in history for its own sake. As a result, the themes of Hollywood's history films usually have some obviously timely aspect, and the period text usually has a contemporary subtext. Finally, the way in which the story is told is inevitably shaped by Hollywood storytelling conventions—most significantly, by the operation of the star system and by the narrative formulas of film genres.

Warner Brothers chose to make *The Charge of the Light Brigade* because it wanted to exploit (and exceed) the success of Paramount's *Lives of a Bengal Lancer* (1935), an action-adventure set on the frontiers of British India. Warners required a story that would justify opulent production values, epic length, and the use of a new pair of romantic stars, Errol Flynn and Olivia de Havilland. *Bengal Lancer* concerned the dirty routine of imperial warfare, with the "great game" of British-Russian rivalry in the background. *Light Brigade* would make the worldwide implications of the border war explicit by developing a fictional connection between this frontier war and the larger Great Power confrontation. The Crimean War of 1853–56 was chosen because it provided a spectacular conclusion toward which the film could build: the celebrated cavalry charge at Balaklava, immortalized in Tennyson's poem as "The Charge of the Light Brigade."

The studio research department outdid itself in providing proper period costumes and weaponry. Replicas of Victorian postage stamps were used on interoffice correspondence to build a sense of authenticity in the company, even though these stamps would never appear on screen. But the film's account of the battle of Balaklava has little or nothing to do with historical reality.

The historical plot of *The Charge of the Light Brigade* has one purpose only: to provide the "reason why" the Light Brigade makes its suicidal charge. Yet the answer offered by history (and Tennyson)—that "some-

HISTORY

Battle of Balaklava, 1854

power as well as the imperial interests of France and Great Britain in the Near East, these two traditional enemies formed an unlikely alliance to aid Muslim Turkey against Christian Russia.

The Crimean War was marked by scandalous mismanagement and military incompetence on both sides. The British army was commanded by superannuated veterans of Waterloo (1815) and officered by a system that favored social rank, influence, and privilege over professionalism. (Promotions as high as colonel could be gained through purchase.) Only the greater incompetence of the Russian army—and the professionalism, courage, and morale of the enlisted men and junior officers—allowed the Allies to triumph after much needless suffering and the waste of many soldiers' lives.

In 1853 Russian tsar Nicholas I attacked the Ottoman Empire, hoping to liberate Eastern Orthodox Slavs in the Balkans from Turkish rule and gain access to world sea-lanes by controlling the Dardanelles. Because Russian expansion threatened the European balance of

HOLLYWOOD

Cecil Woodham-Smith's *The Reason Why* is a superb analysis of the charge, of the British army at the time of the battle of Balaklava, and of the Victorian culture that produced both. The 1968 British remake of *The Charge of the Light Brigade* follows Woodham-Smith's account

fairly closely, though it does add some fictional romance. The original Warner Brothers film has almost nothing to do with any of this. It gets the place and date of the battle about right, also the costumes—but absolutely nothing else. The Chukoti massacre that is the film's centerpiece has a probable historical source in the Cawnpore Massacre that occurred during the 1857 Sepoy Mutiny, which involved rebellious native troops led by Nana Sahib rather than wild hill tribesmen from "Suristan." The details of this massacre, as given in G.O. Trevelyan's *Cawnpore*, a likely source for the studio research department, closely resemble the scenario and imagery of the fictional Chukoti massacre.

Balaklava Heights

The Battle of Balaklava

In September 1854, a small Allied army under British command invaded Russia's Crimean Peninsula. Its aim was to capture the great Black Sea naval base of Sebastopol, without which Russia could not prosecute its war against Turkey. The Allies succeeded in besieging Sebastopol but could not adequately protect their base of supplies at the small coastal village of Balaklava. On October 24, 1854, a large Russian force of infantry and cavalry advanced against Balaklava and seized four small artillery redoubts on the Causeway Heights. The Russians were checked by a single regiment of Highland infantry (the famous "thin red line"), but they had taken crucial positions blocking the main road between the British army and its base.

The British response was hesitant and muddled; none of the senior officers had thought to scout either the terrain or the enemy. At the urging of his staff, the British commander, Lord Raglan, eventually agreed to order the Light Brigade to charge and retake the captured redoubts. From his position on a hill above the battlefield, it seemed obvious to Raglan that the Light Brigade would charge the redoubts along the Causeway Heights, where the Russians were in some disarray and possessed only a single line of guns. And here the famous "blunder"—or series of blunders—occurred. The order was vaguely worded, the staff officer who carried it was angry and impatient, and the commanders of the cavalry (Lords Lucan and Cardigan) were so incompetent as to be unable to interpret it properly.

From Lucan and Cardigan's position, the Russians on the Causeway Heights were invisible; they believed the order required them to charge down the North Valley between the two lines of guns and make a frontal assault on the Russian batteries at the far end—a mode of attack they must have known would result in the annihilation of their regiments. It may or may not be admirable that the troopers rode, as ordered, to their deaths without asking "the reason why." In their commanders, under the circumstances, such a response was brainless at best—the dereliction rather than the apotheosis of military duty. Although the Russian attack on Balaklava was repulsed, the mismanaged battle left the Russians in command of the Allied supply route. The resulting dearth of supplies nearly destroyed the Allied army and literally worried Lord Raglan to death.

one had blundered"—is insufficiently heroic to sustain the plot of an epic movie. Nor does it comport with the kind of heroism associated with the "star" persona of an Errol Flynn. Traditional Hollywood heroes cannot be blunderers; their actions must be not only intelligible but also in accord with a higher reason. In searching for a proper "reason why," Warner Brothers looked not to British history and the Crimean War but to American historical mythology—specifically to the myth of the frontier and the formulas of the western movie, which see history as a racial struggle between savage Indians and civilized whites for control of an undeveloped New World. It is worth noting that when a British production company made its own *Charge of the Light Brigade* in 1968 (directed by Tony Richardson), its major concern was not with "Indian frontiers" and race but with the cruelties and absurdities of Victorian class structure.

The Warners movie at first transports us to India's northwest frontier, where we find the Twenty-seventh Lancers escorting a diplomatic mission to the Muslim hill-chieftain Surat Khan, emir of "Suristan" (Afghanistan). The emir has the manners of a gentleman, coupled (as he himself smugly admits) with the cruelty "natural" to his "ancient race." The opening scenes reveal a sharp split between the politicians—a set of elderly and effete armchair warriors—and the virile soldiers, particularly Capt. (later Maj.) Geoffrey Vickers (Flynn), who is not only brave but also a realist who "knows Indians." His advice is to deal from strength, to strike rather than temporize—but he is ignored.

Surat Khan then makes a secret alliance with the Russian tsar; with the aid of Count Volonoff, a Russian military adviser, he leads an uprising of the hill tribes against the Chukoti garrison while most of the regiment is on maneuvers. After the British surrender on the promise of safe conduct, the Khan orders a massacre of the garrison's men, women, and children. Nevertheless, Vickers manages to rescue Elsa Campbell (Olivia de Havilland)—his colonel's daughter and also his fiancée. Subsequently, the British defeat the Suristanis and hound the Khan out of India, but the massacre remains unavenged; Vickers is ready to protest the regiment's transfer to the Crimea until he discovers that Surat Khan has accompanied Count Volonoff to Sebastopol.

And *here* is the reason why: Vickers learns that Surat Khan and Volonoff are actually on Balaklava Heights. He forges his commander's signature, changing a retreat order into an attack; then sends a belated warning to the commander so that he can use the charge as a diversion for a successful attack on the Russian lines. Vickers leads the charge and kills Surat Khan amid the Russian batteries with a cast of his lance, falling mortally wounded by the Khan's pistol shot. In the final scene, we learn why the "real story" of the charge was not previously known: Sir Charles Macefield, the army chief of staff, burns Vickers's confession because it would taint the public memory of his heroism.

Racial and sexual imagery is crucial to the development of the film's political theme, which is that a Great Power must take a strong military stance against colonial "savages" and their European sponsors. The soldiers who speak for or embody this principle are seen as virile, insightful, and heroic. Oriental despots and temporizing politicians bent on appeasement are identified with women; and femininity, even as idealized in the female lead Elsa, is seen as shallow and fickle by nature: Elsa betrays her engagement to Vickers by falling in love with his effete "political" younger brother, Perry.

Details of imagery and echoes of contemporary slogans (for example "peace at any price") are also used to suggest that the film's "history" should be understood as an allegory of contemporary politics. In particular, the role of the Russian adviser Volonoff—who looks remarkably like Stalin—suggests that the audience watch for connections to the politics of Europe in the mid-1930s. The years 1935 and 1936 saw German remilitarization; aggressive posturing by the Soviets (coupled with Stalin's internal purges); fascist Italy's invasion of Ethiopia; fascist and Russian surrogacy in the Spanish Civil War; and Japanese advances in China— "peripheral" conflicts that threatened to provoke a world war, pitting the West against any or all of the world's totalitarian powers. Thus the explanatory historical fiction offered by *The Charge of the Light Brigade* can be read not only as a rendering of the historical past but also as the use of a mythologized past to interpret a present crisis: the choice between appeasement and rearmament. At the same time, the displacement of this crisis into "history" clouds the allegory and evades the danger of offending particular European audiences.

Background Reading

Nick Roddick, *A New Deal in Entertainment: Warner Bros. in the 1930s* (British Film Institute, 1983)

Richard Slotkin, *Gunfighter Nation: The Myth of the Frontier in Twentieth–Century America* (Atheneum, 1992)

Cecil Woodham-Smith, *The Reason Why* (Dutton, 1960)

1936/USA/B&W
DIRECTOR: Michael Curtiz; PRODUCER: Samuel Bischoff; SCREENPLAY: Michael Jacoby, Roland Leigh; STUDIO: Warner; VIDEO: MGM/UA; RUNNING TIME: 115 min.

Cary Grant in *Gunga Din*

Later...

The success of *The Charge of the Light Brigade* was widely imitated between 1936 and 1941, and a new genre formed that might be called the "British empire film" or, more generally, the "imperial epic." These movies usually involved a historical crisis in which civilization—symbolized by the Victorian Empire or its equivalent—found itself threatened by an alliance between unruly "savages" (often led by a "khan" of some sort) and the agents of an "evil empire"—Russia, Germany, Imperial China. The Victorian—or civilized—order is embodied by a military outpost, whose values are those of a liberal and progressive imperium, in which a justified soldiers' warrior-patriarchy rules over consenting white women and childlike brown races. However, these soldiers are in danger of massacre because the politicians in Whitehall (or Washington) are too corrupt, inept, or tangled in red tape to take action against the khan and the evil empire.

The only one who can save them is the hero, a soldier who knows the natives well enough almost (or actually) to pass for one and who fights the enemy with his own weapons and methods. We *are* saved, although often at the cost of the hero's sacrificial death, together with those of his picked band of men, in some heroic last stand or suicidal charge.

In addition to *The Charge of the Light Brigade*, representative titles of this genre include *The Lives of a Bengal Lancer* (1935); *Wee Willie Winkie* and *Another Dawn* (1937); *Drums* (1938); *The Four Feathers, Beau Geste, The Sun Never Sets,* and *Gunga Din* (1939). The genre persisted through the 1950s and 1960s in *Kim* (1950); *King of the Khyber Rifles* (1954); *55 Days at Peking* (1963); *Guns at Batasi* and *Zulu* (1964); *Khartoum* (1966), and the like. Crucial features of the genre also show up in other kinds of films, particularly such westerns as *They Died with Their Boots On* (1942) and *The Alamo* (1960)—and more recently in sci-fi films like *Star Trek II: The Wrath of Khan* (1982).

THE YOUNG LINCOLN

Two Films

Mark E. Neely, Jr.

LITERATURE AND THEATER LED POPULAR taste during the 1930s, while the movie industry followed along, capitalizing on themes already tested for success. It's difficult to imagine a historical subject more tempting to Hollywood at that time than the life of Abraham Lincoln. Gone was the debunking spirit of the 1920s; instead, American historians were becoming more patriotic. Among them, none could quite match the patchwork of folklore, poetic language, and history woven by Carl Sandburg into his monumental six-volume life of Lincoln. Sandburg published *Abraham Lincoln: The Prairie Years* in 1926 and the four-volume *Abraham Lincoln: The War Years* in 1939. The period in between constituted, as historian Merrill D. Peterson maintains, the zenith of Lincoln's reputation. Sandburg himself did more to promote Lincoln's reputation than any other person since John Wilkes Booth.

Sandburg's volumes on Lincoln's presidency appeared too late to influence the two films considered here—*Young Mr. Lincoln* was released in 1939 and *Abe Lincoln in Illinois* a year later—but his view of the prairie years largely dictated the content of these movies. Neither deals with Lincoln's presidency; rather, both offer a folk hero who bears only a passing similarity to the real Lincoln.

Director John Ford's *Young Mr. Lincoln* depicts the young Abraham as a true son of the frontier, twanging a Jew's harp as he rides in a wagon or working with his feet on his desk. Although Ford's movie constantly surrounds Lincoln (Henry Fonda) with rustics in coonskin caps, these characters are far from idealized. In fact, the heart of the film is a courtroom drama, and the townspeople are clearly eager for a hanging, legal or otherwise. The murder trial depicted in the film was based very loosely on the Duff Armstrong case tried in Beardstown, Illinois, in May 1858. Lincoln represented Armstrong for no fee because his mother was an old friend. During the trial, the forty-nine-year-old Lincoln discredited the testimony of an eyewitness by producing an almanac and proving that on the night of the murder the moon had been so low on the horizon that it couldn't have produced enough light for the prosecution's chief witness to have seen the murder.

The film's screenwriter, Lamar Trotti, who wrote two or three film scripts a year during the 1930s, didn't have time for elaborate research, so he opted to make the trial fictional, naming the victim Scrub White (his real name was James Preston Metzker) and greatly altering the nature of the murder and the trial. In *Young Mr. Lincoln*, the film Abe first saves his client from a lynch mob attempting to break into the jail,

The Armstrong Case

On August 29, 1857, while a camp meeting revival roared nearby, William "Duff" Armstrong, James Norris, and James Preston Metzker fell into a drunken brawl. After Norris hit Metzker with a piece of wood, Armstrong followed with a frontier blackjack. The dazed Metzker managed to mount his horse and ride away, but he fell off several times and later died. Norris, who had previously killed a man, was convicted of manslaughter. Armstrong—tried separately in Beardstown, Illinois, on May 7, 1858—engaged Lincoln as his counsel (his mother knew Lincoln from his New Salem days, some twenty years before).

The prosecution's most important witness, Charles Allen, testified that he saw the fatal blow struck, even though the event occurred at night, because a bright moon had shone overhead. Lincoln then produced an almanac proving that the moon had been near the horizon at the time and could not have produced enough light. In truth, the prosecution's case was not strong. More than one man had struck Metzker, and a doctor testified that the victim might have died from falling off his horse. The defense also produced a witness who testified that he had the alleged murder weapon—the blackjack, or "slung shot," as it was called—in his possession at the time of the murder. The jury subsequently found Armstrong not guilty.

HISTORY

This daguerrotype, taken in 1846, is the earliest-known camera portrait of Lincoln, who was a thirty-seven-year-old prairie lawyer at the time.

HOLLYWOOD

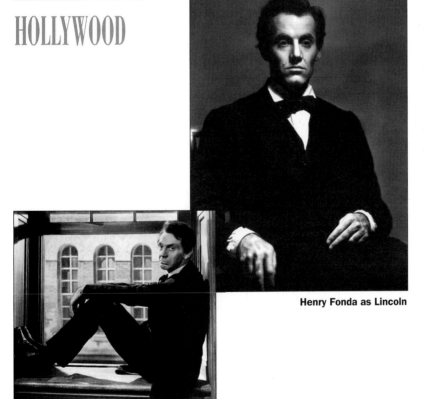

When Henry Fonda was first offered the title role in *Young Mr. Lincoln*, he turned it down, being too much in awe of Lincoln to believe he could play the part convincingly. Unwilling to accept Fonda's decision, director John Ford called the rising young star into his office. "What's all this bullshit about you not wanting to play Abraham Lincoln?" Ford erupted. "You're not playing the Great Emancipator. You're playing a jacklegged lawyer from Springfield, Illinois, a gawky kid still wet behind the ears who rides a mule because he can't afford a horse!" (This is the bowdlerized version of Ford's tirade fed to the gossip columnists; the director was typically not so polite.) Ford himself had doubts about the project before he began. The recent success of two Broadway plays about the young Lincoln, including Robert E. Sherwood's *Abe Lincoln in Illinois*, had convinced Ford that the subject had been "worked to death"—until Lamar Trotti's screenplay convinced him otherwise.

Henry Fonda as Lincoln

Raymond Massey as Lincoln

Lincoln debating with Douglas

The Reality of Illinois Politics

U.S. senators were not popularly elected in Lincoln's day; they were chosen by the state legislatures. So the famed 1858 campaign waged in Illinois between Lincoln and Stephen A. Douglas, with its immortal debates, in fact hinged on the outcome of dozens of races run by unknowns for seats in the Illinois legislature.

In the closest of these races, politicians, including Lincoln, were tempted to play their dirtiest tricks. When Lincoln heard that gangs of itinerant Irish-American railroad workers—famous for their steadfast adherence to the Democratic party—were arriving in certain highly contested electoral districts in late October 1858, he suggested a scheme to Republican henchman Norman B. Judd:

> What I most dread is that they will introduce into the doubtful districts numbers of men who are legal voters in all respects except residence and who will swear to *residence* and thus put it beyond our power to exclude them. They can & I fear will swear falsely on that point, because they know it is next to impossible to convict them of Perjury upon it.
>
> Now the great remaining part of the campaign is finding a way to head this thing off. Can it be done at all?
>
> I have a bare suggestion. When there is a known body of these voters, could not a true man, of the *"detective"* class, be introduced among them in disguise, who could, at the nick of time, control their votes? Think this over. It would be a great thing, when this trick is attempted upon us, to have the saddle come up on the other horse.

None of the other discussions of this idea was committed to paper, and the outcome is unknown. In the end, Lincoln lost the election, despite beating Douglas in the statewide popular vote, because of Democratic holdovers in the state senate. Neither the Democrats nor the Republicans cried foul or called for an investigation of voter fraud.

then saves him again in the courtroom, proving not only that the state's eyewitness could not have seen the event by moonlight but also that he had committed the murder himself!

Lawyers were probably as despised during the 1930s as they have been at any other time in American history, so it may have seemed odd even for a heroic rendering of Lincoln's life to focus on his law practice. Historians have generally avoided discussing Lincoln's law career and concentrated instead on his politics, which has also helped preserve Lincoln's heroic image. The filmmakers, of necessity confined to Lincoln's pre-presidential career by the Sandburg scenario and knowing well the power of courtroom drama, avoided this difficulty by making Lincoln a lawyer less interested in law than in justice. "I may not know so much of law, Mr. Felder," he says to the prosecutor, "but I know what's right and wrong."

The character of Ann Rutledge, depicted wearing improbable lipstick and eye shadow, plays a significant role in Lincoln's life in both films. She was purported to be Lincoln's first love and is portrayed in these films as the guiding spirit of his career. She died at the age of nineteen and left behind not a single document from which historians might learn about her from direct testimony, but this dearth made her the perfect character for Hollywood's imagination to embellish. In fact, John Ford's film was mostly fiction, and corny fiction at that, and it is redeemed only by the director's eye for landscape, the folk tunes in the musical score, and Henry Fonda's considerable acting ability. Incidentally, the actor who played Lincoln's Democratic political rival, Stephen A. Douglas, does bear a very strong resemblance to the real Douglas as he appeared in early photographs.

Abe Lincoln in Illinois is a superior film with regard to history, Raymond Massey's wooden performance in the title role notwithstanding. Based on Robert Sherwood's adaptation of his own successful play and directed by John Cromwell, *Abe Lincoln in Illinois* portays Lincoln as unfailingly solemn, a sort of statue hiding in homespun. Massey's Lincoln mouths liberal pieties and blandly inclusive religious views and tries to avoid politics. The antiparty sentiment of the film is one of its most strikingly inaccurate qualities. In one scene, Uncle Ben, a town character dressed in a colonial uniform, says to Lincoln, "Don't let 'em get you in politics." The visual effect is as though one of the country's founders has appeared to warn Lincoln against political parties. Of course, nothing could miss the spirit of the true Lincoln more than to put him at a remove from the electioneering techniques of the antebellum United States. He is distinguished in our history because he combined policy substance with vast electioneering skills. But Mr. Sherwood preferred a statue, and early in the film a rustic Lincoln says, "I don't want to be no politician."

To get him to his political destiny without ambition or a taste for electioneering required two women: Ann Rutledge, who foresees Lincoln's destiny, and his future wife, Mary Todd, who, somewhat unpleasantly, forces him to realize it. Lincoln, of course, had plenty of ambitions of his own—to leave the log cabin of his birth and never look back, to marry a woman who could speak French and had attended finishing school, to send his son to Exeter prep school and to Harvard. In fact, Lincoln's ambition, as his law partner, William Herndon, said after his death, was "a little engine that knew no rest." But such a person is not discernible in *Abe Lincoln in Illinois*; instead, Lincoln is pushed by his wife and pulled by political bosses who finally get him to "play the game" with them.

Films didn't bother with historical advisers fifty years ago, and none is listed for either of these ventures. Ford's version of the young Lincoln made little attempt to get the facts of his life straight, and *Abe Lincoln in Illinois* confused the chronology of Lincoln's early life so much that it is a muddle. For example, Lincoln met the only intimate friend of his life, Joshua Speed, when he moved to Springfield from New Salem, though in the film Speed appears in New Salem. Films have always been largely indifferent to the accuracy of narrative, but always interested in proper atmosphere and increasingly obsessed with what might be called "accuracy in antiques"—having no anachronistic objects appear in the frames of pictures about the past. Of course, we see no clouds of mosquitoes or flies and no horse dung in the towns' dirt streets in either of these films. The scenery is as sanitized as the historical narrative.

Background Reading

John J. Duff, *A. Lincoln: Prairie Lawyer* (Rinehart, 1960)
Benjamin P. Thomas, *Abraham Lincoln: A Biography* (Alfred A. Knopf, 1952)

Young Mr. Lincoln
1939/USA/B&W
DIRECTOR: John Ford; **PRODUCER:** Kenneth Macgowan; **SCREENPLAY:** Lamar Trotti; **STUDIO:** Twentieth Century-Fox; **VIDEO:** Fox; **RUNNING TIME:** 100 min.

Abe Lincoln in Illinois
1940/USA/B&W
DIRECTOR: John Cromwell; **PRODUCER:** Max Gordon; **SCREENPLAY:** Robert E. Sherwood, Grover Jones; **STUDIO:** RKO; **VIDEO:** Turner; **RUNNING TIME:** 110 min.

Later...

The peculiar timing of American elections during the nineteenth century afforded President Abraham Lincoln many opportunities to "play the game" of politics. Put simply, elections did not come in neat two-year intervals, timed to coincide with the presidential and midterm congressional elections. The states determined when their elections would be held with the result that, of the forty-eight months that the Civil War lasted, twenty-four of them saw a major election somewhere in the United States. In the presidential election year of 1864, some states—Indiana, for one—held their gubernatorial elections in October, before the November presidential polling day.

Indiana, therefore, received an inordinate share of attention from politicians throughout the country who wanted to see this important swing state go their party's way shortly before the national election. Among those politicians was the one occupying the White House and running for reelection in 1864. President Lincoln was also commander-in-chief of the Union Army, yet putting that role aside he wrote Gen. William T. Sherman on September 19, 1864:

> The State election of Indiana occurs on the 11th of October, and the loss of it to the friends of the Government would go far towards losing the whole Union cause. The bad effect upon the November election, and especially the giving of the state government to those who will oppose the war in every possible way, are too much to risk, if it can possibly be avoided. The draft proceeds, notwithstanding its strong tendency to lose us the State. Indiana is the only important State, voting in October, whose soldiers cannot vote in the field. Any thing you can safely do to let her soldiers, or any part of them, go home and vote at the State election, will be greatly in point. They need not remain for the presidential election, but may return to you at once. This is, in no sense, an order, but is merely intended to impress you with the importance, to the army itself, of your doing all you safely can, yourself being the judge of what you can safely do.

Sherman, who liked Lincoln but distrusted politicians in general, was occupying Atlanta and planning his famous March to the Sea. In the end, only sick and wounded Indiana soldiers were furloughed from his army to return home before the election—which the Republicans won.

GLORY

James M. McPherson

C A S T

C A S T

Robert Gould Shaw	*(Matthew Broderick)*
Trip	*(Denzel Washington)*
Cabot Forbes	*(Cary Elwes)*
Rawlins	*(Morgan Freeman)*

CAN MOVIES TEACH HISTORY? FOR *GLORY*, the answer is yes. Not only is it the first feature film to treat the role of black soldiers in the American Civil War, but it is also one of the most powerful and historically accurate movies ever made about that war. After more than fifty years on the screen, Scarlett O'Hara and Rhett Butler are still teaching false and stereotyped lessons about slavery. Perhaps *Glory* can restore the image of courageous black soldiers that prevailed in the North during the latter war years, before the process of romanticizing the Old South obscured it.

Glory tells the story of the Fifty-fourth Massachusetts Volunteer Infantry from its organization during the winter of 1862–1863 to its climactic assault the following summer against Fort Wagner, a massive earthworks guarding the approach to Charleston harbor. The Union's naval effort to capture Charleston failed earlier in 1863—and so did the assault on Fort Wagner led by the Fifty-fourth, which suffered nearly fifty percent casualties. Among those killed was Col. Robert Gould Shaw, *Glory*'s protagonist, who died leading his men over the parapet.

However, if in this sense the attack was a failure, in a more profound sense it was a success of historic proportions. The unflinching behavior of the regiment in the face of an overwhelming hail of lead and iron answered the skeptic's question, Will the Negro fight? It demonstrated the courage of the race to millions of white people in both the North and the South who had doubted whether black men would stand in combat against soldiers of the self-styled master race.

Will the Black Soldier Fight?

One of the most effective scenes in the movie depicts the Fifty-fourth Massachusetts marching proudly through Boston, having completed its training in May 1863. About the same time, the *New York Tribune*, the leading northern newspaper and a supporter of arming blacks to fight, observed that most Yankees, while endorsing the policy, still wondered whether blacks would make good soldiers. A war correspondent for the *Tribune* soon answered those doubts when he vividly described the assault on Fort Wagner. "Who asks now in doubt and derision, 'Will the Negro fight?'" commented one abolitionist. "The answer is spoken from the cannons's mouth . . . it comes to us from . . . those graves beneath Fort Wagner's walls, which the American people will surely never forget."

The recruitment of black combat troops was still regarded as a risky experiment when the Fifty-fourth's six hundred men moved out at dusk on July 18 to attack Fort Wagner. During the next few hours they more than justified that experiment. Forced by the ocean on one side and swamps on the other to approach the fort along several hundred yards of narrow, exposed beach, the regiment moved steadily forward through bursting shells and murderous musketry. Losing men every step of the way, they nevertheless continued right up the ramparts and breached the parapet before the immense strength of the works stopped them. The portrayal of this attack in *Glory* is the most realistic combat footage in any Civil War movie.

The white officers of the Fifty-fourth represented the elite of New England society. Some, including Shaw, were Harvard alumni and sons of prominent families. Several, also including Shaw, had already fought with white regiments during the first two years of the war. Antislavery in con-

The attack on Fort Wagner

The Case of Black Soldiers

The events that led to the action on Fort Wagner, an epochal moment in African-American history, represented a radical evolution of the scope and purpose of the Civil War. The original war aims of Abraham Lincoln's administration had been to suppress an insurrection in eleven southern states and restore them to their place in the Union. The North conceived of this war as a limited one that would not fundamentally alter the American polity or society—including slavery. The four slave states that remained loyal to the Union would not have supported a war in 1861 to abolish slavery. Neither would have the Democrats, who constituted nearly half the northern electorate. Furthermore, the Constitution that the North was fighting to defend guaranteed the protection of slavery in states that wanted it. Therefore, despite Lincoln's personal abhorrence of slavery, he could not willfully turn this war for the Union into a war against slavery. Nor could his War Department in 1861 accept black volunteers in the Union army, for to do so would have sent the signal that this was to be an abolitionist's war.

By 1862, though, the conflict was becoming just such a war. It was a total war now, not merely a militia action to suppress an insurrection. And when northern troops invaded portions of the South, thousands of slaves flocked to Union army posts. Abolitionists and Radical Republicans insisted that these slaves must be granted freedom. At the same time, the success of Confederate military offenses in 1862 convinced Republicans, including Lincoln, that the

North could not win the war without mobilizing all of its resources. They also concluded that they would have to strike against every southern resource used to sustain the Confederate war effort.

The most important of the South's resources was slavery, since slaves constituted the majority of the southern labor force. In the summer of 1862, Congress enacted legislation confiscating the property of Confederates, including slaves. Lincoln followed this with the Emancipation Proclamation to free the slaves, invoking his power as commander-in-chief to seize enemy property used to wage war against the United States. The Emancipation Proclamation also stated that blacks would be "received into the armed services of the United States."

These events underlay the decision of Gov. John Andrew of Massachusetts to organize a black regiment, which became the Fifty-fourth Massachusetts. A bold experiment, black soldiers could be made acceptable in the context of the time only if they were commanded by white officers. Andrew was determined to appoint officers "of firm antislavery principles . . . superior to a vulgar contempt for color." In Robert Gould Shaw, son of a prominent abolitionist family, he found his man. As black volunteers came into the training camp near Boston during the spring of 1863, Shaw shaped them into a high-morale outfit eager to prove their mettle.

The First Black Regiments

The Fifty-fourth was neither the first black regiment organized nor the first to see combat. To test the waters, the War Department had quietly allowed Union commanders of forces occupying portions of the lower Mississippi Valley, the Kansas-Missouri border, and the South Carolina sea islands to begin organizing black regiments in the fall of 1862. Four of these regiments fought in actions connected with the Vicksburg campaign during May and June 1863, winning plaudits for their performance. However, these episodes received little publicity in the northern press.

The Draft Riots

The Fort Wagner attack came just days after terrible draft riots shook New York City. The July 13–16 riots were fueled in part by the racism of Irish Americans who wanted no part of a war to free slaves. Black New Yorkers were the chief victims of the rioters, who feared freed slaves would come North to compete for jobs and social space. On July 15, a mob beat to death the nephew of Robert Simmons, a sergeant in the Fifty-fourth; three days later, Simmons was mortally wounded in the assault on Fort Wagner.

The draft riots occurred within the context of northern Democratic opposition to the Lincoln administration's war policies, including emancipation, the enlistment of black soldiers, and the draft. Democrats had done much to stir up the racial hatreds manifested by the rioters, who chanted the antiwar and antiblack slogans of the Copperhead wing of the party. In the aftermath, few Republican commentators missed the opportunity to juxtapose the draft riots with the heroic conduct of the Fifty-fourth at Fort Wagner, and to point out the moral: Black men who fought for the Union deserved more respect than white men who rioted against it.

viction, they had willingly risked stigma and ridicule to cast their lot with a black regiment.

The Confederate defenders of Fort Wagner stripped Shaw's corpse and dumped it into an unmarked mass grave with the bodies of his black soldiers. When the Union commander sent a flag of truce across the lines a day later to request the return of Shaw's body (a customary practice for high-ranking officers killed in the Civil War), a Confederate officer replied contemptuously, "We have buried him with his niggers."

The performance of the Fifty-fourth Massachusetts at Fort Wagner not only advanced the liberation of slaves but also helped to liberate President Lincoln from certain constitutional and political constraints. These restraints had earlier inhibited the president from making this war for the Union a war against slavery, an institution that Lincoln had often branded a "monstrous injustice."

If it is not literally true, as the movie's final caption claims, that the bravery of the Fifty-fourth at Fort Wagner caused Congress to authorize more black regiments—this had happened months earlier—the example set by the Fifty-fourth did help transform potential into policy. However, *Glory* does not go into detail about the impact of the battle on northern opinion, nor does it provide much political context for the black soldier issue. In

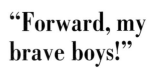

"Forward, my brave boys!"

Col. Robert Gould Shaw

fact, the movie ends with the attack on Fort Wagner, although the Fifty-fourth continued to serve throughout the war, fighting in several more battles and skirmishes.

Except for Shaw, the principal characters in the film are fictional: There was no real Maj. Cabot Forbes; no Emerson-quoting black boyhood friend of Shaw's named Thomas Searles; no tough Irish Sgt. Maj. Mulcahy; no black Sgt. (and father figure) John Rawlins; no brash, hardened Private Trip. Indeed, there is a larger fiction involved here. The movie gives the impression that most of the Fifty-fourth's soldiers were former slaves. In fact, this atypical regiment was recruited mainly in the North, so most of the men had always been free. Some came from prominent northern black families; two of Frederick Douglass's sons were among the first to sign up. The older son was sergeant major of the regiment from the start. (The regiment's young adjutant, wounded in the Fort Wagner assault, was Garth Wilkinson James, brother of William and Henry James.)

Real historical figures such as these could have provided the framework for a dramatic and important story about the relationship of northern blacks to slavery and the war—and about the wartime ideals of New England culture. But the story that producer Freddie Fields, director Edward Zwick, and screenwriter Kevin Jarre chose to tell is not simply about the Fifty-fourth Massachusetts but about blacks in the Civil War.

Most of the 178,000 black soldiers (and 10,000 sailors) *were* slaves until a few months, even days, before they joined up. They fought for their freedom and for the freedom of their families and their people. This was the most revolutionary feature of a war that wrought a revolution in America by freeing four million slaves and uprooting the social structure of half the country. Arms in the hands of slaves had been the nightmare of southern whites for generations. At Fort Wagner, the nightmare came true. Fighting for the Union bestowed upon former slaves a new dignity, self-respect, and militancy, which helped them achieve equal citizenship and political rights—for a time—after the war.

Many of the events described in *Glory* are also fictional: the incident of the racist quartermaster who initially refuses to distribute shoes to Shaw's men; the whipping Trip receives as punishment for going AWOL; the regiment's dramatic refusal on principle to accept less pay than white soldiers, which shames Congress into equalizing the pay of black soldiers (this actually happened, but at Shaw's initiative, not Trip's); the religious meeting the night before the assault on Fort Wagner.

However, there is a larger truth. *Glory*'s point is made symbolically in one of its most surreal and, at first glance, irrelevant scenes. During a training exercise, Shaw gallops his horse along a path flanked by stakes, each holding aloft a watermelon (in February in Massachusetts?). Shaw slashes right and left with his sword, slicing and smashing every watermelon. The point becomes clear when we recall the identification of watermelons with the "darky" stereotype. If the image of smashed watermelons in *Glory* can replace that of moonlight and magnolias in *Gone with the Wind* as America's cinematic version of the Civil War, it will be a great gain for truth.

Background Reading

James M. McPherson, *Battle Cry of Freedom: The Civil War Era* (Oxford University Press, 1988)

1989/USA/Color
DIRECTOR: Edward Zwick; **PRODUCER:** Freddie Fields; **SCREENPLAY:** Kevin Jarre; **STUDIO:** Tri-Star; **VIDEO:** Columbia Tristar; **RUNNING TIME:** 122 min.

Equal Pay

The federal government promised the black soldiers of the Fifty-fourth the same pay as their white counterparts: thirteen dollars a month. However, they received only ten; three dollars was docked from each of their salaries, supposedly to pay for their uniforms. The soldiers refused to accept these terms and campaigned for eighteen months until the government finally granted them equal pay.

Saint-Gaudens's monument in Boston honoring Col. Robert Gould Shaw

The death of Robert Gould Shaw made a deeper impression on Yankee culture than that of any other New Englander killed in the Civil War. Clergyman Henry Ward Beecher wrote that Shaw's martyrdom had regenerated Boston's past glory as America's cradle of freedom: "Our young men seemed ignoble; the faith of old heroic times had died . . . but the trumpet of this war sounded the call and Oh! how joyful has been the sight of such unexpected nobleness in our young men." Both Ralph Waldo Emerson and James Russell Lowell extolled Shaw in verse. Lowell wrote:

Right in the van,
On the red rampart's slippery swell, he fell
With heart that beat a charge, he fell
Forward, as fits a man;
But the high soul burns on to light men's feet
Where death for noble ends makes dying sweet.

GONE WITH THE WIND

Catherine Clinton

C A S T

Rhett Butler   *(Clark Gable)*
Scarlett O'Hara   *(Vivien Leigh)*
Mammy   *(Hattie McDaniel)*

Margaret Mitchell, 1938

The Novel

Atlanta newspaper reporter Margaret Mitchell spent ten years working on *Gone with the Wind*, which she based on stories she had heard as a child. In April 1935, Mitchell impulsively entrusted her tattered manuscript to Harold Latham, vice president of Macmillan Books, who suggested changing the title from *Tomorrow Is Another Day* and the main character's name from Pansy to Scarlett. When the novel was published in July 1936, it broke every sales record (its millionth copy appeared that December). More than twelve thousand of Mitchell's fans gathered in December 1939 for the film's premiere in Atlanta, where Mitchell took a bow and expressed her gratitude "for the grand things these actors have done." Mitchell was killed by a drunk driver in August 1949 before she could complete her next work. Alexandra Ripley's *Scarlett*, a sequel belatedly authorized by Mitchell's estate, appeared in 1991, and the original *Gone with the Wind* (with fifty million copies already in print) once again topped best-seller lists.

GONE WITH THE WIND REIGNS UNCONTESTED as the most popular American historical film ever made. The single most influential interpretation of the Civil War in twentieth-century popular culture, the film has defined that war for a mass audience. Boldly laying claim to historical veracity, *Gone with the Wind* inserts dates and other historical material before key scenes, using such "history" to legitimize its Hollywood version of the plantation past.

The filmmakers may have proclaimed their commitment to authenticity, but their penchant for accurate detail extended only so far. In the film's opening scenes, blacks pick cotton despite the fact that plantations never harvested cotton in spring. (We know it's spring because the drama opens with news of the April 1861 attack on Fort Sumter.) In this case, as in many others, producer David O. Selznick sacrificed accuracy to suit his larger goals.

Gone with the Wind was designed to succeed simultaneously as a war film (perennially a male favorite) and as a "woman's picture." In telling the story of Rhett Butler's heroic role in the Civil War and Scarlett O'Hara's emotional saga, Selznick combined two winning formulas of Hollywood's Golden Age. All else is merely backdrop for the characters' tempestuous struggles.

The film's hyperbolic prologue ("There was a land of Cavaliers and Cotton fields called the Old South. . . . Look for it only in books, for it is no more than a dream remembered, a Civilization gone with the wind") heralds the quixotic tone of Confederate nostalgia that saturates the drama. Historian Henry Steele Commager, an early and enthusiastic reviewer of the novel, commented: "It is one of the virtues of Miss Mitchell's book that she presents the myth without being taken in by it or asking us to accept it, and that she makes clear the reasons for both its vitality and its ultimate demise." This cannot be said of the motion picture, however, which indulges in Lost Cause romanticism, especially in relation to the roles of blacks and whites.

The film's most controversial aspect remains its portrayal of race relations. *Gone with the Wind* may have been the first plantation film to feature African-American characters who *don't* spontaneously burst into song, but the picture still reflects historian U.B. Phillips's "plantation school" view of the African-American experience, which portrayed happy-go-lucky "darkies" loyal to benevolent masters. This view dominated the study of U.S. history during the first half of this century. Although Selznick consulted with the NAACP, he nevertheless concentrated on his

HISTORY

A Civil War belle, 1863

Daily life on a plantation was not all balls and barbecues. Young girls might be freed from the drudgery of running the estate, but when they married (usually around the age of twenty) southern brides became saddled overnight with the responsibilities of plantation management. The plantation mistress was expected to safeguard the care and feeding of her family, as well as tend to the domestic requirements (food, clothing, shelter, and medical care) of her husband's slaves. The planter's wife kept the keys to the pantry, the smokehouse, the candlebox, and the medicine chest about her person at all times. Although laundry, cooking, and house cleaning were generally undertaken by slaves, the mistress supervised the gardens, the dairy barn, and the slaughterhouse, and she performed many unglamorous agricultural tasks. For women on antebellum slave-owning estates, a season of belledom was followed by a lifetime of hard work.

HOLLYWOOD

Vivien Leigh (center)

Before the release of *Gone with the Wind*, legendary Hollywood mogul Louis B. Mayer proclaimed, "You can never make a nickel on a Civil War picture." Of course, producer David O. Selznick chose to defy this Hollywood logic, and *Gone with the Wind* remains the most popular American historical film ever made. Recent polls conducted by the American Film Institute showed that *Gone with the Wind* is, in fact, the favorite movie of most Americans. It ranks in the top twenty moneymaking films of all time (and would probably rank first if inflation were taken into account). The film opened during the second week of December 1939 and sold a million dollars' worth of tickets before New Year's Day. It won an unprecedented thirteen Academy Award nominations and eight Oscars. *Gone with the Wind* opened in London in 1940 and played for a record 232 consecutive weeks. Its 1976 American television premiere was the highest-rated single network program ever broadcast.

David O. Selznick with Vivien Leigh at the 1939 Academy Awards

The Search for Scarlett

Even before David O. Selznick snapped up the screen rights to Margaret Mitchell's book for fifty thousand dollars, Americans had begun to cast their favorite actors and actresses in the film's leading roles. A canny publicist, Selznick milked the public speculation and anticipation: The Search for Scarlett dominated the trade press as fourteen hundred candidates were tested. In June 1938, Clark Gable signed on to play Rhett Butler, but the female lead remained uncast. On December 10, 1938, Selznick shot the famous "burning of Atlanta" scene using stunt doubles for Scarlett and Rhett. In the light of the flickering flames, his agent brother, Myron, introduced Selznick to his new client, a British actress named Vivien Leigh; to her Selznick gave the coveted part of Scarlett.

The scale of Selznick's production was unprecedented. The cast included at least fifty-nine leading and supporting players, as well as twenty-four hundred extras. Of the two hundred sets Selznick had designed, ninety were actually built, using nearly a million board feet of lumber. Production costs topped three and a half million dollars, with yet another half million spent on prints, publicity, and advertising. When the film was completed, the rough cut of six hours was reduced to its final running time of 220 minutes.

white audience, not the black protesters, and the film reflects his cavalier (in every sense of the word) attitude. Pork's comic relief, Big Sam's allegiance, Prissy's imbecility, and Mammy's fidelity ring true to Hollywood's typical betrayal of African Americans.

The film weighs in with stock images—slave children fanning sleeping belles, a loyal slave being rewarded with his late master's watch, a grinning black carpetbagger riding in a fine carriage beside an unscrupulous white man, and freedmen open-mouthed at the promise of forty acres and a mule if they "vote like [their] friends do." The movie never attempts to highlight the racial struggles of the day. Nor does it make any effort to address the very articulate and eloquent challenges made by African Americans seeking their own autonomy.

Gone with the Wind's "all the blacks were childlike and devoted" subtext by no means refutes the cinematic sensationalizing exemplified by such earlier films as D.W. Griffith's *The Birth of a Nation* and their caricatures of bestiality in blackface. Nor does it address contemporary concerns about the treatment of African Americans. Hattie McDaniel's portrait of Mammy may have won her a coveted Oscar for 1939 (the first black performer to win such an honor), but because of Georgia's segregation laws she didn't attend the film's Atlanta premiere. Decades later, Malcolm X recalled cringing in a Detroit theater when he first saw the film, and *Gone with the Wind* continues to incite anger and discomfort as it subjects new generations to its racist stereotypes.

Not surprisingly, the film fares better when depicting the white South. Its glimpses of the O'Hara household reflect the historical reality of an up-country plantation in prewar Georgia. Gerald O'Hara's humble foreign origins mirror the experiences of a large percentage of antebellum planters, Ireland and Scotland being the main sources of southern immigrants. Furthermore, in one of the film's early scenes, ne'er-do-well overseer Jonas Wilkerson reports to Ellen O'Hara on his daily planting, demonstrating the plantation mistress's authority on the estate—a fact rarely reflected in historiography, although frequently underscored in historical fiction.

Ellen O'Hara's brief appearances demonstrate the mistress's competent and crucial role in managing her husband's property—as well as in caring for the infirm, delegating responsibility, ministering to neighbors, and enforcing moral standards both by example and by dictum. Mrs. O'Hara is the very soul and engine for not only her family but also her husband's slaves and employees. Her character conveys the tone and spirit of idealized plantation life. In fact, the job of mistress of the house was so rigorous and demanding that many women checked out of the process altogether, opting instead for a life that involved lots of smelling salts and reclining on fainting couches. As hundreds of diaries and letters from the era testify, Scarlett's dilemma at her mother's death, her father's breakdown, the O'Hara family's decline, and the general hardships faced during wartime are all true to life.

Scheming southern women have long been a popular focus of fiction (Lillian Hellman's *The Little Foxes*, for example). Thus Scarlett O'Hara's famed conniving and fierce independence are often seen as just another instance of literary fantasy. However, Scarlett's transformation in the face of calamity from southern belle to towering matriarch was not unusual during Reconstruction. Like most women of her time, Scarlett found herself forced by economic necessity into a male domain, and she used whatever feminine wiles she could, playing a scheming vamp one moment and a vulnerable damsel in distress the next.

Scarlett's desire to protect her home, Tara, and her family (indeed, even to commit murder); her mercenary marriage and scalawag business deals; her exploitation of convict labor; and her flaunting of gender conventions create a heroine both unforgettable and quite faithful to the historical record. After the war, poverty forced many women into unfamiliar or unsuitable jobs and marriages. At the outset of the war, Sen. James Henry Hammond of South Carolina (famous for telling his fellow senators, "Cotton is king") declared that the South would triumph. Because Hammond died during the war, he never had to endure any of the postwar hardships; his family was not so lucky. Hammond's granddaughter, Katherine, was forced to train as a nurse in order to support herself during the deprivation that accompanied Reconstruction.

Rhett Butler's character is even more accurately grounded. At the outset, he recognizes, as did many southern moderates, that "the Yankees are better equipped than we. They've got factories, shipyards, coal mines, and a fleet to bottle up our harbors and starve us to death." However, once Butler witnesses the heartbreak of impending defeat ("Take a good look, my dear. It's a historic moment. You can tell your grandchildren how you watched the Old South disappear"), the former cynic heroically treks off to enlist in a noble nod to southern honor. Butler's conversion experience—to sacrifice for a higher cause—symbolized that of thousands of volunteers whose tramping off to war redefined mid-century America. Butler's soul is the soul of every soldier. Scarlett's more complex trials and tribulations touched a similar chord with the public. Thus, despite flawed historical interpretation, the movie still flourishes and entertains. Its Technicolor historical pageantry is every bit as seductive now as when the film premiered in 1939.

Background Reading

Richard Harwell, ed., *Gone with the Wind as Book and Film* (University of South Carolina Press, 1983)

Darden A. Pyron, ed., *Recasting: Gone with the Wind in American Culture* (University Presses of Florida, 1983)

1939/USA/Color
DIRECTOR: Victor Fleming; PRODUCER: David O. Selznick; SCREENPLAY: Sidney Howard; STUDIO: MGM; VIDEO: MGM/UA; RUNNING TIME: 220 min.

Epic Authenticity

The movie's set and costume design had to be exacting for a number of reasons. It was likely that most viewers had read Margaret Mitchell's richly detailed novel, and Mitchell herself demanded authenticity from the filmmakers. If that weren't enough, Selznick was determined to achieve perfection.

In addition to the usual Hollywood talents, Selznick hired a retinue of advisers to keep his production historically "accurate"—including southern dialogue coach Will Price, etiquette expert Susan Myrick (who became known as the Emily Post of the South), and Wilbur G. Kurtz, a historical artist/architect specializing in the Civil War. Costume designer Walter Plunkett undertook extensive research in Atlanta museums, collecting swatches that he sent to a textile mill for reproduction. The women's costumes for *Gone with the Wind* cost nearly one hundred thousand dollars to make, and an additional ten thousand was spent on laundering them during the six months of filming.

Later...

Although not as successful as the western, the "southern" was a popular product during the first half of this century. From the start, nickelodeon operators banked on the South's commercial potential, a holdover from the minstrel tradition on stage. Edwin S. Porter's popular *Uncle Tom's Cabin* (1903) and D.W. Griffith's three-hour *The Birth of a Nation* (1915) electrified audiences. Later, *Gone with the Wind* became the crowning jewel in a string of popular plantation epics that included *So Red the Rose* and *Jezebel*. After World War II, protests over Hollywood's racist stereotyping tainted this popular genre. Disney's *Song of the South* (1946), the animated version of Joel Chandler Harris's popular Uncle Remus tales, was perhaps the last gasp of Hollywood's love affair with plantation settings.

THE BIRTH OF A NATION

Leon F. Litwack

CAST

Elsie Stoneman	(Lillian Gish)
Flora Cameron	(May Marsh)
Ben Cameron	(Henry B. Walthall)
Austin Stoneman	(Ralph Lewis)
Silas Lynch	(George Siegmann)
Gus	(Walter Long)

Thomas Dixon, Jr.

The Book

After his ordination in 1886, Thomas Dixon, Jr., achieved popularity in the North as an evangelist preaching the Social Gospel. Sensitive to criticism of his native South, Dixon vowed after attending a stage revival of *Uncle Tom's Cabin* in 1901 that he would respond with a novel telling the true story of slavery and Reconstruction. *The Leopard's Spots*, published in 1902, dramatized the need to segregate, repress, and expel blacks. *The Clansman*, which appeared three years later, related the version of Reconstruction that would become the basis for *The Birth of a Nation*. As a novel, and subsequently as a 1906 stage play, *The Clansman* was particularly vicious in its depiction of black people, reflecting Dixon's growing alarm over the black menace. When *The Birth of a Nation* premiered in Los Angeles in 1915, it was initially entitled *The Clansman*, but Dixon persuaded D.W. Griffith to adopt a more powerful and grandiose title, perhaps to underscore the importance of its message for the entire nation.

WITH THE RELEASE OF *THE BIRTH OF a Nation* in 1915, the motion picture as art, propaganda, and entertainment came of age. Reviewers were ecstatic in their praise, audiences unrestrained in their enthusiasm. This was the movie everyone had to see, a unique and awesome experience for Americans, the first film spectacular, technically and artistically superior to anything they had ever viewed on the screen. Employing a multiplicity of cinematic techniques, director D. W. Griffith profoundly influenced filmmaking throughout the world. His epic film proved to be an extraordinary success, the first—and one of the greatest— box-office attractions in the history of motion pictures. From 1915 to 1946, some two hundred million people viewed the film in the United States and overseas, where it scored particularly impressive triumphs in Germany and South Africa. President Woodrow Wilson had a private showing of *The Birth of a Nation* in the White House. It was the first feature film shown there and an appropriate one for a president who embraced the ideology of racial segregation and maintained a discreet silence on the triumph of white terrorism in his native South. "It is like writing history in lightning," he reportedly said of the film. "My only regret is that it is all so terribly true." (Some years later, after the film had inflamed racial tensions, Wilson called it an "unfortunate production.")

From the very outset, the film mesmerized and misled Americans, revealing the extraordinary power of the cinema to "teach" history and to reflect and shape popular attitudes and stereotypes. Earlier public entertainment—such as minstrel shows, "coon" songs, and vaudeville—depicted blacks as clowns and buffoons, as essentially passive objects. *The Birth of a Nation*, however, introduced still another dimension: The grinning and obsequious demeanor of black men often masks a vicious bestiality, at no time more vividly manifested than after emancipation. The film is based on *The Clansman*, a novel by Thomas Dixon, Jr., a native of North Carolina and popular Baptist preacher who wanted to awaken the American people to the nature of the Black Peril. To Dixon, this was a national problem. The presence of the Negro, North and South, endangered American civilization and the sanctity of white womanhood, and it posed as great a threat in 1900 as it did in 1868. "There is enough negro blood here," a Dixon character warns, "to make mulatto the whole Republic." That obsession consumed Dixon, and the film—true to his intentions—plays on the presumed primitive sexuality of the subhuman black man and its implications for the survival of the

136

HISTORY

On the night of April 14, 1865, President Abraham Lincoln attended a performance of the comedy *Our American Cousin* at Ford's Theater in downtown Washington. During the third act, actor John Wilkes Booth entered the presidential box (he had earlier tampered with the door) and shot the unguarded president through the back of the head. Grappling briefly with an audience member, Booth swung himself over the balustrade and leaped onto the stage shouting, "Sic semper tyrannis! The South is avenged!"

HOLLYWOOD

The adoring son of a former lieutenant colonel in the Confederate cavalry, David Wark Griffith (1875–1948) was born on a farm in Oldham County, Kentucky. His films reflected a special fondness for rural life, and he clearly identified with southern attitudes toward the proper places of whites and blacks. But if Griffith was a racist, he was also a populist, suspicious of big business and meddlesome government, as *A Corner in Wheat* (1910), adapted from Frank Norris's *The Pit*, brilliantly confirmed. After six frantic years as a staff director, mostly for Biograph, averaging two films a week, Griffith shot *The Birth of a Nation* over the final six months of 1914, at a cost of more than one hundred thousand dollars, which the director had to hustle to raise.

Harper's Weekly cover, 1867

Radical Reconstruction

None of the Reconstruction governments was completely dominated by blacks. Even where blacks comprised a majority of the voters, the number of black officeholders was never commensurate with their electoral strength. Only in South Carolina did black legislators outnumber whites (eighty-eight to sixty-seven), but in no state did blacks control the executive mansion. *The Birth of a Nation* makes much of the black-dominated South Carolina legislature that abolished the ban on interracial marriages. However, black legislators emphasized that they were only purging the statute books of all racial distinctions. This was a sensitive subject, and whites perceived it as an open invitation to interracial liaisons. But blacks sometimes used the issue to underscore white hypocrisy: When a white Republican in Alabama proposed an ordinance banning racial intermarriage, a black legislator moved an amendment that stipulated life imprisonment for any white man found living with a black woman. The convention chose to drop the issue altogether.

Censorship

The opening frame of *The Birth of a Nation* anticipated much of the controversy over censorship that the film would precipitate:

A PLEA FOR THE ART OF THE MOTION PICTURE

We do not fear censorship for we have no work to offend with improprieties or obscenities, but we do demand, as a right, the liberty to show the dark side of wrong, that we may illustrate the right side of virtue, and the same liberty that is conceded to the art of the written word— that art to which we owe the Bible and the works of Shakespeare.

Anglo-Saxon race. The message is driven home in imagery no audience could easily forget. Before riding off to redeem the white South, klansmen dip their emblem into the blood of a blonde white virgin who has been terrorized to death by a black brute.

The credits do not list Dixon or President Wilson as consultants, but their influence hovers over the film. Dixon supplied the plot; Wilson, the scholarly footnotes. Intent on assuring the public of the film's historical credibility, Griffith went to extraordinary lengths. On Reconstruction, Wilson's *A History of the American People* was cited to underscore and authenticate the vivid scenes depicted on the screen. The end result was not simply a flawed but a profoundly perverted history. It was a history, however, that Americans found easy to absorb. "My object," Dixon said of the earlier stage version of his novel, "is to teach the North . . . what it has never known—the awful suffering of the white man during the dreadful Reconstruction period . . . to demonstrate to the world that the white man must and shall be supreme."

The Birth of a Nation appeared during the most repressive and violent period in the history of race relations in the South. Between 1890 and 1915, in the face of racial tensions heightened by growing evidence of black independence and assertiveness (the New Negro), whites acted on the prevailing racial orthodoxy to ensure their absolute supremacy and the permanent political, economic, and social subordination of the black population. To achieve this objective, the white South systematically disenfranchised black men, imposed rigid patterns of racial segregation, corrupted the judicial system, and sustained extraordinary and unprecedented levels of violence and brutality, culminating in the public burnings and lynchings of black men and women. At the same time, the findings of "science" and the learned professions and the dissemination of dehumanizing caricatures reinforced and comforted whites in their racial beliefs and practices.

This was the America *The Birth of a Nation* explained, vindicated, and celebrated. What more effective way to awaken the American people to the nature of the Black Peril and justify their racial atrocities than to remind them of what had happened during Reconstruction? Through the lives and relationships of two families—the Camerons of South Carolina (the plantation ideal) and the Stonemans of Pennsylvania (the abolitionist Radical Republican impulse), *The Birth of a Nation* depicts a tragic era in the history of "the Aryan race," when a misguided North, under the spell of radical zealots like Austin Stoneman (a thinly disguised Thaddeus Stevens) and mulatto demagogues like Silas Lynch (Stoneman's protégé), along with their carpetbag and scalawag colleagues, used the votes of duped and ignorant newly freed slaves to fasten a black despotism onto the South.

Through its vivid and unforgettable images, the film impressed on Americans a certain version of reality. Reconstruction, proclaimed one of the intertitles, was "the agony which the South endured that a nation might be born." The camera graphically captures the lurid details of that "agony": Impudent, ungrateful, venal black men, their ambitions bloated by emancipation and civil rights, terrorize helpless whites, shoving them off the sidewalks, blocking their access to the ballot boxes, and leering at their women. Blacks brandish signs reading, "Equal Rights, Equal Politics, Equal Marriage." They ridicule and chain their old masters. They abuse those "faithful souls" (the Cameron servants) who still take pride in their white folks. They make a mockery of democratic government, sitting shoeless in legislative chambers, drinking whiskey from bottles, and eating chicken off the bone while enacting a statute legitimizing interracial marriage. Finally and inevitably, maddened by power and lust, blacks strike out at the most valued possessions of white men—their women. Gus, a depraved "renegade Negro" and former Cameron slave, forces a white girl (the Cameron's youngest daughter) to leap to her death in order to preserve her purity. And Silas Lynch, whose election as lieutenant governor only heightens his lust, seeks to force marriage on a virginal, limp, gagged, and helpless young white woman (none other than Austin Stoneman's daughter). "I will build a Black Empire," he tells her, "and you as my queen shall rule by my side."

Barely suppressing a nostalgia for slavery, *The Birth of a Nation* paints its black characters literally and figuratively. While exploiting every traditional racial stereotype, most of them passive and unthreatening, the film introduces the relatively new image of the Negro as aggressor ("the bad nigger"), assuming in this picture the guises of revolutionist (Lynch) and sexual brute (Gus). No matter whether black people are depicted as evil or sympathetic, they are all dehumanized, from the blindly faithful, submissive, and pampered house servants to the wretched, dim-witted, insolent, and brutish mass of newly freed slaves. Yet the ultimate and most dangerous villain is unmistakably the mulatto (Silas Lynch), who combines the sexuality and lust of the savage Negro with the intellectual and organizing prowess that could be explained only by his white blood.

Like an "Anglo-Saxon Niagara" (as Vachel Lindsay called it), the Ku Klux Klan (the freedom fighters of the 1870s) mobilize and pour down the road to rescue the South from the "anarchy of black rule" and to reestablish white supremacy. Clearly, this film suggests, only the end of Reconstruction deserves to be commemorated—a triumphant redemption of honor, virtue, and race, when, in the words of Woodrow Wilson, "Negro rule under unscrupulous adventurers was finally [ended], and the natural, inevitable ascendancy of the whites, the responsible class, established."

Evoking the film's spirit and principal theme, the beleaguered Cameron family finds refuge in a log cabin occupied by two Union veterans, and they join forces to resist pursuing black soldiers. The intertitle says it all: "The former enemies of North and South are united again in

NAACP Protest

Despite its enormous popularity, *The Birth of a Nation* aroused controversy from the very outset. An outraged NAACP, for example, was galvanized into action. Protesting the film's blatant racism, it established picket lines outside theaters and petitioned legislators and city officials to ban the film as an incitement to violence. (The film was said to have inspired the revival of the Ku Klux Klan in the 1920s.) The protests did result in the deletion of some particularly objectionable footage, including a rape scene, but efforts to ban the film itself generally failed. D.W. Griffith defended himself against the NAACP's charges of racism and accused the organization of threatening his freedom of speech. After all, he noted, if such protests succeeded, Indians would claim that films also defamed them, "for in most Western pictures they are depicted killing white men."

The Progressive Era

That *The Birth of a Nation* coincided with the Progressive Era should be in no way surprising. Even as the South sought to resolve the "Negro problem," the North confronted waves of strange-looking immigrants from southern and eastern Europe, and the West tried to deal with the growing presence of unwanted Asians. Many who called themselves Progressives expressed deep concern over inferior racial groups whose very presence posed grave dangers to the social and political order. Blacks and "new" immigrants were said to be particularly susceptible to political corruption. Both groups challenged the idea of the United States as a predominantly Anglo-Saxon nation, and by the early twentieth century the growing presence of such marginal and allegedly inferior groups suggested to many whites intellectual, spiritual, and racial decline and degradation. To press their case, in fact, immigration restrictionists constructed a racial ideology based on various stereotypes of immigrant groups that resembled the stereotypes southern whites had drawn of blacks. Appreciating that similarity, a Mississippi Democrat could declare with absolute confidence on the floor of the Senate, "I stand with the State of California in opposition to mixed schools. I stand with Californians in favor of the proposition that we want a homogeneous and easily assimilated population of white people in the Republic."

The Use of Blackface

The principal "black" performers in *The Birth of a Nation* were blackfaced whites; actual African Americans appear mostly in the crowd scenes. After "careful weighing of every detail concerned," Griffith later remarked, "the decision was to have no black blood among the principals." Some were to argue, in defense of Griffith, that he was the first director to employ Negro extras. (He housed them in segregated barracks near the Griffith lot.) The use of these extras did pose some problems, however. In one of the fight sequences involving both blacks and blackfaced white players, the combat became so realistic that several actors had to be hospitalized.

Gone with the Wind Reconstructed

The portrayal of history in *Gone with the Wind* was no more enlightened than that in *The Birth of a Nation*, but Hollywood made it more acceptable to modern audiences and the characterizations of blacks were thought to be less racially offensive. In her novel, Margaret Mitchell reiterated a perverted version of Reconstruction that compared the freed slaves to "monkeys or small children turned loose among treasured objects whose value is beyond their comprehension. . . . Here was the astonishing spectacle of half a nation attempting, at the point of a bayonet, to force upon the other half the rule of negroes, many of them scarcely one generation out of the African jungles." Such passages did not appear in the film, but they accorded fully with the popular version of Reconstruction.

common defense of their Aryan birthright." By the conclusion of the film, even those naive and misled northerners (the Stonemans) who had initially embraced Reconstruction come to see their folly. The redemption of the South—and the nation—is given a biblical sanction as well, with Jesus Christ in the "halls of brotherly love" overseeing (or so it seems) the glorious triumph of the Ku Klux Klan and white supremacy. In this redemption, according to Dixon and Griffith, the American nation is truly born: that is, only after whites regained absolute supremacy on the basis of a nationalized racial consciousness, and only after the North acquiesced in the South's "final solution" to the "race problem."

Stripped of complexity, the history reenacted in *The Birth of a Nation* is easy and simpleminded. It took another generation to expose the myths, falsehoods, and fantasies on which the film is based. Few historians still accept the perverse view of Radical Reconstruction as an unrelieved orgy of black misrule. The motives and conduct of the much-reviled carpetbaggers and scalawags were as varied as their social make-up. The much-publicized corruption of the era was biracial and bipartisan, polluting politics in both the North and the South, and the principal beneficiaries everywhere were businessmen and speculators, among them members of some of the South's most distinguished families. While in power, the Radical state governments, even those tainted with corruption, enacted much needed democratic reforms, including universal manhood suffrage, equal access to the courts, and the first public school systems. The black legislators and officeholders, although initiated into the political process during a period of corruption, learned the uses of political power and ruled as competently—and, in some instances, as incompetently—as their white counterparts. The Radical governments were overthrown not because they were corrupt but because the reforms they instituted threatened the supremacy of whites and the subordination of black labor.

Few if any films in the history of the cinema had such tragic and far-reaching consequences. "Chicago went wild," one observer wrote. "It started people to thinking. . . . The people of Chicago saw more in *The Birth of a Nation* than a tremendous dramatic spectacle. They saw in it the reason the South wants to 'keep the Negro in his place.' They saw in it a new conception of southern problems." More than any historian or textbook, the vivid images conveyed by *The Birth of a Nation* shaped American attitudes toward Reconstruction and the "Negro problem." With that version of history firmly fixed in their minds, most Americans could readily understand why black southerners were unfit to exercise political rights and why the white South had to go to such extraordinary lengths to control and contain its black population. And for much of the twentieth century, *The Birth of a Nation* molded and reinforced racial stereotypes, distorting the physical appearance of black men and women, making a mockery of their lives and aspirations, and fixing in the public mind the image of a race of inferiors—sometimes amusing and comical, sometimes brutal and subhuman, but in either case less than white men and women.

"Art is always revolutionary," D.W. Griffith remarked in 1915, "always explosive and sensational." He left his generation with a classic example. Yet for African Americans, the film remains one of the principal artifacts of a racial ideology that denied them their very humanity. With *The Birth of a Nation*, Ralph Ellison wrote, "the propagation of subhuman images of Negroes became financially and dramatically profitable. The Negro as a scapegoat could be sold as entertainment, could even be exported. If the film became the main manipulator of the American dream, for Negroes that dream contained a strong dose of such stuff as nightmares are made of."

Stepin Fetchit

Background Reading

Eric Foner, *Reconstruction: America's Unfinished Revolution, 1863–1877* (Harper & Row, 1988)

Seymour Stern, "The Birth of a Nation," in *Film Culture*, 36 (Spring–Summer 1965)

1915/USA/B&W
DIRECTOR: D.W. Griffith; PRODUCER: D.W. Griffith; SCREENPLAY: D.W. Griffith, Frank E. Woods; STUDIO: Epic; VIDEO: Republic; RUNNING TIME: 154 min.

Later...

The consequences of *The Birth of a Nation* endured for nearly half a century. The controversy over the film, kept alive by NAACP protests, no doubt influenced the Motion Picture Association of America in the early 1920s and again in 1933 when it adopted a production code prohibiting negative depictions of black people. But even as the film industry abandoned the image of African Americans as sexual and political monsters, it proceeded to entertain generations of Americans with degrading portraits of black men and women as clowns, buffoons, and nitwits, often listing them in the screen credits only by some demeaning first name, such as Napoleon or Flossie. During the 1920s and 1930s, for example, Stepin Fetchit (Lincoln Theodore Monroe Andrew Perry) became the first black actor to be accorded featured billing, appearing as the slow-witted, lazy caricature of a black man, shuffling and stammering and rolling his eyes through a host of films. He would later defend these roles: "I went and kicked open the door in Hollywood. I went in the back door so now Sidney Poitier can come in the front door."

After World War II, virtually any showing of *The Birth of a Nation* encountered organized resistance. The Museum of Modern Art withdrew the film in 1946, at least temporarily, because of "the potency of its anti-Negro bias." In 1992, the Library of Congress placed *The Birth of a Nation* on the National Film Registry, certifying it as a classic. The NAACP protested the action, but Librarian of Congress James H. Billington defended the decision while acknowledging the explosive nature of the film. "Bigoted and racist as its treatment is of African Americans, *The Birth of a Nation* is an inescapable part of our history." The inclusion of the film in the National Film Registry, he added, should not be interpreted as "some kind of national honor" but rather as a necessary action to preserve the film.

THE MOLLY MAGUIRES

J. Anthony Lukas

CAST

James McParlan   *(Richard Harris)*
Jack Kehoe   *(Sean Connery)*
Mary Raines   *(Samantha Eggar)*

The Real Molly Maguires

Who was Molly Maguire? And who were the men who took her name? These questions still elicit fierce historical debate. According to one version, Molly was a poor Irish widow whose brutal eviction from her land inspired rage among her neighbors. By the time of the Great Potato Famine in the 1840s, the name was invoked by agrarian insurgents in the counties of Cavan, Longford, Donegal, and Tyrone. In 1847, a Tyrone landlord received a threatening letter ending: "Molly Maguire and her children have been watching you." On the roster of Irish secret societies—Whiteboys, Tibbonmen, and Hearts of Steel—the Mollies gained a reputation as particularly bloodthirsty. They first cropped up in the United States in 1857 when a society of that name was said to be working for Pennsylvania Democrats.

It wasn't until after the Civil War that the first reports of Mollies in western Pennsylvania's anthracite mines were documented. The Mollies were believed to operate within a benign group called the Ancient Order of Hibernians, which provided fraternal aid to Irish immigrants. The Mollies soon became an instrument of vengeance against oppressive mine owners and managers, but historians still disagree about how lethal they really were.

THE LEGEND OF THE MOLLY MAGUIRES was nineteenth-century America's favorite detective story: the saga of a vengeful band of western Pennsylvania coal miners whose murders of mine bosses and policemen was quelled by the derring-do of a Pinkerton detective. In barbershops, hotel lobbies, and Pullman cars throughout the land, Americans voraciously consumed this tale, repeated incessantly in penny dreadfuls and dime novels. Ironically, for a yarn so embedded in the American vernacular, this film's most effective sequence is a twelve-minute prologue in which not a single word is uttered.

In the pale dawn sky, a yellow sun burns through the coal dust as a lute renders a haunting Irish ballad. Ever so slowly, the camera pans down a chute into a mine shaft as we hear the clank of wheel and winch, the drip of mine water, the hacking of a miner's cough, the crunch of pickaxes, the clunk of a wooden stanchion, the clank of lunch pails, the crunch of boots on gravel, the shriek of the mine whistle, the flare of a match, the fizz of a fuse, and finally, the roar of an explosion that rips through subterranean chambers as the titles, superimposed on flame, read: "Pennsylvania 1876."

Director Martin Ritt's wordless opening may have struck some viewers as a piece of cinematic affectation, but it impressed me as the most telling—and authentic—episode in *The Molly Maguires*. No audience of today can comprehend the Mollies without feeling the damp, drear, dangerous world of the nineteenth-century coal miner. Ritt's twelve minutes of chop, drip, and hack evoke that world with precision and empathy. From then on, however, the film is less effective in capturing the famous story's shadings and complexities. For a start, it utterly omits the context of the Molly investigation, which was prompted by the convergence of two corporate imperatives.

The 1873 depression confronted Pinkerton's National Detective Agency with a critical cash shortage. The summer before, its president, Allan Pinkerton, had confided to an aide: "We are in great want of money." The agency borrowed heavily, but by May 1873 Pinkerton feared bankruptcy. "Go to Franklin Gowen," he told a deputy. "I have no doubt he will give us work." Gowen, the president of the Philadelphia and Reading Railroad, was already one of the agency's best clients: In 1870, he had hired Pinkerton operatives to sniff out fare-pocketing by railroad employees; two years later, several more Pinkertons were dispatched to investigate the beating of mine supervisors and derailing of rail cars at Glen Carbon, Pennsylvania. Those operatives' reports led a Pinkerton

HISTORY

During the nineteenth century, most anthracite mines in Pennsylvania were poorly ventilated. Methane gas, which the miners called "firedamp," is lighter than air, and it tended to build up in pockets high in the manways. Occasionally, a miner's lamp would accidentally ignite one of these pockets. The explosion usually killed everyone nearby. Because of firedamp and other hazardous gases, miners sometimes lowered dogs into suspected areas to test the air. Others carried caged canaries with them into the mines. It was believed that, because of the their smaller lung capacity, the birds would be overcome by poisonous gases before humans were. The mines remained dangerous places, however, where a roof might fall on you or a mine car run you over in the dark. On average, more than ten miners were killed each week in Pennsylvania's anthracite fields, and many more were maimed.

HOLLYWOOD

The Molly Maguires was shot almost entirely on location in Pennsylvania, and the film's eleven-million-dollar budget (in 1970 dollars) reflected the cost of shooting so much of it away from Hollywood. Unfortunately for the producers, the wonderful scenery didn't help much: *The Molly Maguires* performed dismally at the box office, returning less than two million dollars. Among the film's problems were its lighting and dialogue. Director Martin Ritt allowed both his male leads, Sean Connery (playing Kehoe) and Richard Harris (as McParlan) to lapse into dialect at will. These speech patterns may have been authentic, but they also made certain conversations nearly unintelligible. Ritt also determined, along with cinematographer James Wong Howe, to film the mine scenes "authentically" using only contemporary available light. During the 1870s, that meant torches and helmet lights (small candles worn on the miners' helmets), neither of which could adequately light a feature film—as Ritt and Howe discovered.

We never sleep.

The Pinkerton Agency

The private detective has deep roots in Anglo-Saxon history. As early as the seventeenth century, the English evinced acute distaste for the notion of an efficient, professional, state-controlled police force—both because it would require new taxes and because it smacked of authoritarian rule. Deep into the eighteenth century, much of English and, later, American law enforcement was the work of private informers, bounty hunters, and "thief-takers." If these private detectives were often no more morally upstanding than their prey, they were effective, precisely because law enforcement often benefits from maintaining intimate relations with the criminal classes.

In America, private detective agencies sprouted like mushrooms in the 1870s. Fourteen flourished in Chicago alone, among them the nation's largest, Pinkerton's National Detective Agency, founded in 1850 under a different name by Allan Pinkerton, a thirty-one-year-old Scottish immigrant. Pinkerton won national renown as the Union army's intelligence chief during the Civil War. He exploited that fame to build his hugely successful agency. On the facade of his three-story Chicago headquarters was the company slogan, "We Never Sleep," stripped above a huge, unblinking black-and-white eye. This is the origin of the phrase *private eye*.

Among the Pinkertons' best-known cases were the foiling of an assassination plot against President-elect Abraham Lincoln in Baltimore (February 1861); the pursuit of Frank and Jesse James (1867–75); and the search for Oliver Curtis Perry, the so-called "gentleman desperado," who had performed several spectacular robberies on the New York Central Railroad (1891–92). In July 1892, the Pinkerton agency, which often supplied "watchmen" to break strikes at embattled corporations, sent three hundred men by river barge to the Carnegie steel works in Homestead, Pennsylvania, after striking workers took over the town and laid siege to the works. As the Pinkertons attempted to land their barges on July 6, the workers fired cannons, lobbed dynamite, and launched a flaming raft toward them. The Pinkertons returned fire. The day-long battle ended with nine workers dead and several more injured, while seven Pinkertons were killed and many more were severely beaten by townspeople as they surrendered and made their way off the field of battle.

superintendent to write in October 1873 of "the rumored existence at Glen Carbon of an organization known as the 'Molly Maguires,' a band of roughs joined together for the purpose of instituting revenge against any one of whom they may take a dislike."

For the Philadelphia and Reading Railroad, the violence attributed to the Mollies—acts of sabotage like removing railroad spikes and blowing up bridge trestles, which escalated to attacks on railroad and colliery staff—was only the latest sign of restiveness among the workers at its extensive holdings in Pennsylvania's anthracite region. Gowen was already embroiled in a struggle with the Workingman's Benevolent Association, a union that had led the miners in a costly 1871 strike. To Gowen, the Mollies' depredations presented an intriguing opportunity: By linking the union to these "criminals," he could tarnish the group, if not break it altogether.

The Pinkerton agency found the railroad more than receptive to a formal investigation of the Mollies. In mid-October 1873, Allan Pinkerton himself journeyed to Philadelphia for a conference with Gowen. There they decided to send an undercover operative into the anthracite region with instructions to infiltrate the Mollies and obtain evidence on which to convict them of murder. To fill this demanding position, Pinkerton turned to a twenty-nine-year-old recruit in Chicago, still pulling a tenderfoot's duty spotting crooked conductors on the city's trolleys: one James McParlan (played by Richard Harris). On October 27, the new operative, under the alias James McKenna, boarded a Reading coach bound for the coal country.

The film skips all these preliminaries, beginning the story as McParlan alights in Port Clinton, Pennsylvania, and finds his way to a tavern where he makes contact with the Mollies. Not surprisingly, the script juggles the historical events and characters as we know them from McParlan's actual reports. The detective's initial contact with the Mollies occurred not at Port Clinton's Emerald House but at the Sheridan House in nearby Pottsville. Moreover, his critical penetration of the secret society occurred in one of its "hotbeds," Shenandoah, where the so-called bodymaster (master of the membership) was "Muff" Lawler, who took his nickname from the fighting gamecocks he trained. It was Lawler—not, as in the film, Jack Kehoe (Sean Connery)—who eventually brought McParlan into the secret society.

The film's focus on Kehoe is understandable, since press and prosecution alike depicted him as the master conspirator, "the arch-fiend of the century." Allan Pinkerton, in his semifictional account of these events, pictured Kehoe as a nearly diabolical figure. There is good reason to suspect this caricature; to the film's credit, its portrait of the man is more complex.

But *The Molly Maguires* washes away many other complexities. It barely mentions the private squabbles, workplace quarrels, ethnic resentments, and class grievances that gave rise to much of the violence in the coal patches. Instead, it reduces the tale to the collision of two Irishmen—Kehoe and McParlan—representing the two poles of the Irish immigrant experience: fierce loyalty to blood and clan versus relentless assimilation to the values of the larger society.

If Kehoe represents the atavistic Celt, then McParlan is the successful professional rising rapidly in the New World, even though it means betraying his countrymen. By any standard, his penetration of the Mollies for two and a half years must rank with the niftiest bits of detective work in the nation's history. Certainly it was one of the most dangerous. Had his coreligionists smoked out his identity, they almost surely would have killed him.

Instead, McParlan lived to tell his tale in court. It would be going too far to say, as some have suggested, that McParlan singlehandedly eradicated the secret Irish society, but of the twenty men who died on the gallows, McParlan's testimony accounted for the fate of twelve. Indirectly, he paved the way for the execution of the other eight and the jailing of twenty-six more.

One wonders how the sight of these men walking to the gallows in the pale light of dawn, often holding a single rose sent by their wives or girlfriends, affected the detective who sent them there. After all, these were the men with whom McParlan had lived for years, with whom he had worked in the mines, sung ballads, swapped yarns, and gotten drunk. It's here that the film is least satisfactory. The best stab the movie makes at an answer to this question is the motive McParlan offers to the character Captain Davies (ostensibly Robert J. Linden of the Pinkertons): "I'm tired of looking up, I want to look down."

However, neither money nor position quite explains the risks McParlan was prepared to run as an informer, the most loathed of all Irish vocations. If the film never quite grapples with these issues, it resists the temptation to label one man a hero, the other a villain. It thus manages to preserve a moral ambiguity. When, in the film's last words, McParlan says to Kehoe, "See you in hell," one can well believe he will.

Background Reading

Wayne G. Broehl, *The Molly Maguires* (Harvard University Press, 1964)
Franklin P. Dewees, *The Molly Maguires* (J.B. Lippincott, 1877)

1970/USA/Color
DIRECTOR: Martin Ritt; PRODUCER: Martin Ritt, Walter Bernstein; SCREENPLAY: Walter Bernstein; STUDIO: Paramount; VIDEO: Paramount; RUNNING TIME: 124 min.

The Love Interest

The only female role in *The Molly Maguires* of any substance is that of Mary Raines (Samantha Eggar), the Irish-American beauty with whom McParlan has a poignant flirtation. This relationship is presumably based on McParlan's courtship of Mary Ann Higgins, sister-in-law of one of the leading Mollies, Jimmy Kerrigan. The historical romance was one that furthered the investigation, probably nothing more, but Hollywood may be excused for building it into a tragic love story.

Mollies being led to the gallows in Pottsville, Pennsylvania

Later...

Franklin B. Gowen lost his job with the Reading Railroad in 1883. Returning to his private law practice, Gowen appeared to thrive. But on December 13, 1889, he locked himself in a hotel room and shot himself in the head. Jack Kehoe was convicted of the 1862 killing of a mine foreman and on December 18, 1878, was hanged. Due to a hangman's error, however, Kehoe's body swung to and fro for three minutes before he was strangled to death.

James McParlan—who subsequently changed the spelling of his name to McParland—rose relentlessly in the Pinkerton ranks, ultimately becoming the manager of the agency's Western Division, based in Denver. In 1906–7, he once again gained national renown for his investigation of the murder of Frank Stuenenberg, the ex-governor of Idaho. On the basis of evidence gathered by McParlan, "Big" Bill Haywood was tried for commissioning the murder but was acquitted.

MASSACRED

GEN. CUSTER AND 261 MEN
THE VICTIMS.

NO OFFICER OR MAN OF 5
COMPANIES LEFT TO
TELL THE TALE.

CAST

George A. Custer *(Errol Flynn)*
Libbie Custer *(Olivia de Havilland)*

THEY DIED WITH THEIR BOOTS ON

Alvin M. Josephy, Jr.

A WARNER BROTHERS "EPIC," RELEASED IN the post–Pearl Harbor days of 1942 when America needed the inspiration of military heroes, *They Died with Their Boots On* is a sympathetic screen biography of George Armstrong Custer and his wife, Libbie. A rousing adventure film, it is famous among the many students of the battle of the Little Bighorn for its climactic scene depicting Custer, played by Errol Flynn, emptying his revolvers at an encircling horde of Indians and then sinking in death as Sioux chief Crazy Horse sends him to his glory.

No one knows how Custer died. But never mind. That scene, based on history (after all, Custer and his men *were* overrun and killed), typifies the entire film. The screenwriters and director Raoul Walsh based much of the production on known historical facts, though they embellished, refashioned, twisted, and distorted most of these facts into their own hodgepodge of truth and melodramatic fairy tale.

Custer has always been a hard fellow for historians and biographers to deal with. He was raised in a family of male practical jokers (including, most of all, his farmer/blacksmith father) who drew attention to themselves by the pranks they played on one another. Nevertheless, Custer managed to end up, and stay, at West Point, despite being a dreadful clown, cutup, and student (last in his class). The movie covers this unpromising side of Custer with a few contrived-in-Hollywood episodes that are faithful to the spirit of the facts but not to the facts themselves.

Item: Historically, Custer, who came from "the other side of the tracks," went to West Point primarily because it afforded him a free education and an opportunity to improve his social and economic status. Later in life he was regarded widely as a chaser of glory, which led him inevitably to the tragedy at the Little Bighorn. In the film, Custer's glory-chasing—as well as his daring, fun-loving nature—are points established at once with a colorful yet fictitious version of his 1857 arrival as a plebe at West Point, on horseback and dressed in plumes and gold braid. Accompanied by a pack of hounds and a servant carrying his luggage, Custer shocks everyone with his flamboyant, comic-opera conduct. When one of the cadets asks why he has chosen the army as a career, Custer responds, "Glory. I want to leave a name behind me that the nation will be proud of."

Such contrived distortions and dramatic liberties tumble one upon another in *They Died with Their Boots On*. When the Civil War comes, Custer gets his first assignment with the help of General-in-Chief

The Black Hills Expedition of 1874

Historically, Custer laid the groundwork for his own death when he invaded the Sioux's sacred, treaty-protected Black Hills in 1874 and announced that he had found gold there. Unable to halt the ensuing gold rush, the government tried unsuccessfully to buy the Black Hills from the angry Indians, then ordered the Sioux off their hunting grounds and onto reservations. When many of the Indians—under such chiefs as Crazy Horse and Sitting Bull—did not comply, the government deployed troops, including Custer's Seventh Cavalry, to enforce the reservation order. Sent out ahead to find the Indian's whereabouts, Custer discovered the huge camp on the Little Bighorn, where he attacked and was swallowed up by the stiff resistance and overwhelming numbers of Sioux and Cheyenne.

HISTORY

The movie attributes Custer's abrupt rise in rank to a mistake caused by a clerk's accidental mix-up of dispatches. The truth: Gen. Alfred Pleasonton, invigorating the cavalry arm of the Army of the Potomac, deliberately elevated Custer and several other fiery young officers to the rank of brevet brigadier general so that they could command his expanding number of cavalry brigades.

Although Custer incurred huge casualties in reckless charges, his bravery and several spectacular victories gained him fame and the respect and loyalty of his men and superiors. He fought in scores of battles and skirmishes, from the first Bull Run to Appomattox. The movie flirts excitingly with his war record, often inflating to absurdity Custer's role and exploits, but it remains generally faithful to the historical course of events.

HOLLYWOOD

Studio boss Jack Warner originally hired Michael Curtiz to direct *They Died with Their Boots On*, but Errol Flynn, already cast as Custer, told Warner that he would break his contract rather than work with the "mad Hungarian" again. Unwilling to lose Flynn, Warner replaced Curtiz with Raoul Walsh.

Walsh filmed the exteriors for *They Died with Their Boots On* about forty miles north of Los Angeles in a wide valley that passed for the Dakota plains. For the Sioux warriors, he hoped to cast actual Sioux, though only sixteen answered his call to the reservation at Fort Yates. These sixteen Indians were used again and again in the close-ups, while hundreds of Filipino extras filled out the landscape.

Libbie Custer

Although Custer's later commander and protector, Gen. Phil Sheridan, was still an obscure lieutenant at a fort in Oregon when Custer was at West Point, the movie makes him the pre–Civil War commandant at the Point and the admiring mentor from the picture's start—not only of Custer ("You know, there's something about that fellow I like," he says after one of Custer's bold brushes with authority) but also of Libbie Bacon (played by Olivia de Havilland), who happens to show up at West Point with her father.

Historically, Custer met Libbie at a Thanksgiving party in her hometown of Monroe, Michigan, while he was on furlough from the Union Army in 1862, long after he had left the Point. But for added entertainment value, the movie depicts Libbie meeting cadet Custer at West Point during one of his awkward episodes of punishment. It is love at first sight on the part of both of them. Libbie then explains to George that she and her father are visiting an old friend of the family, none other than "Uncle Phil" Sheridan.

Crazy Horse

Crazy Horse often spoke with contempt of Indians who made deals with *wasichus*, or white men: "One does not sell the earth upon which the people walk." In 1877, a year after the events on the Little Bighorn, a frontier character named Frank Grouard, who had lived with the Oglala Sioux, delivered a message from Crazy Horse to Gen. George Crook. Crook had wanted to know whether the Oglalas would ride with him against their common enemy, the Nez Perce. Although Crazy Horse had said he would fight until *not a Nez Perce lived*, Grouard told Crook that Crazy Horse had said he would fight until *not a white man lived*. It is a matter of dispute whether Grouard made a mistake or lied; in any case, an irate Crook decided to have Crazy Horse arrested. On September 6, the Sioux leader, escorted by fellow chiefs Spotted Tail and Touch-the-Clouds, rode to Fort Robinson to explain himself. When he realized that the soldiers meant to imprison him, Crazy Horse pulled out a knife, but Little Big Man grabbed his arm and Pvt. William Gentles speared him with a bayonet. Crazy Horse was carried to the post adjutant's office, where he died.

Winfield Scott (true, but misrepresented in the movie by a silly sequence in which the brash, newly minted Lieutenant Custer wins the friendship of "Old Fuss and Feathers" Scott by catering to his taste for creamed onions). Scott (played by Sidney Greenstreet) remains as general-in-chief of the army until well after the end of the Civil War, although historically he resigned in November 1861 and was succeeded in the course of the war by such men as Henry W. Halleck and Ulysses S. Grant.

Despite his miserable record at West Point, the real-life Custer quickly became a Civil War hero and, at twenty-three, the youngest general in the U.S. Army. After the Civil War, however, there emerged a different Custer, one entirely ignored by the movie. Although still in the army, he was now a postwar lieutenant colonel who was cruel to his men and hated by many of them. Sent first to Texas to cope with former secessionists and then to Kansas to fight Indians, he became a controversial figure who seemingly thirsted for the fame and glory that had vanished with the end of the Civil War.

It is at this point that the movie runs completely amok historically, turning into a cock-and-bull melodrama. The shift is signaled in the film when Custer takes to drink to soothe his let-down feeling after Appomattox. (The truth: After an 1862 binge when he made a humiliating spectacle of himself on the streets of Monroe, Michigan, Custer swore that he would never take another drink in his life, and he never did.) Skipping the reality—Custer's duty in Texas, his frustrating campaigns against Indians in Kansas, his court-martial and reinstatement, his massacre of Cheyenne families at the Washita, and his confrontations with the Sioux while guarding Northern Pacific Railroad surveyors in the Yellowstone Valley—the picture has Libbie, with the help of Sheridan, snapping Custer out of his alcoholic gloom by getting him back on active duty and sent to Fort Abraham Lincoln in present-day North Dakota to take command of the Seventh Cavalry and pacify the Sioux.

The film tells not only a totally different, made-up story, but one that reflects how Hollywood, until only recently, played fast and loose with American Indian history, culture, and sensibilities. If the producers gave any thought to what Indians in the audiences might have known or felt about how they or their history were portrayed, there is no evidence of it in *They Died with Their Boots On*.

On his way to Fort Lincoln, the film Custer and his entourage are attacked by Sioux, led by a goofy-looking, goofy-talking Chief Crazy Horse (in real life, even today, perhaps the most revered patriot of the western Sioux). After being captured and then escaping, the ersatz Crazy Horse (Anthony Quinn in an atrocious wig) sues for peace, and in a fictitious meeting with Custer (Crazy Horse never parleyed with whites), the chief announces that the Indians will give up all their lands to the whites (!) except the sacred Black Hills, which the united tribes will defend to the death. Seeing the folly of risking a disastrous war, the film

Custer now suddenly becomes a noble friend of the Indians, promising to protect the Black Hills for the Sioux.

Of course, he fails. Evil developers who want to open up the Black Hills spread rumors that start a gold rush (in truth, the gold rush was started by Custer himself), and the Indians prepare to fight. The film Custer, meanwhile, strikes one of the villains and is ordered to Washington, where a congressional hearing, and even President Grant, are against him. Custer finally persuades Grant to send him back to the Seventh Cavalry; he returns to Fort Lincoln just in time to say an ominous farewell to Libbie, who, like her husband, knows that they will never see each other again. To the strains of Custer's favorite song, "Garry Owen," the regiment rides off at dawn to its legendary appointment at the Little Bighorn.

In an egregious final scene, Libbie visits General Sheridan and reads him a letter left by the fallen Custer, demanding that the government "make good its promise to Chief Crazy Horse. The Indians must be protected in their right to an existence in their own country." Sheridan, the man who in real life was purported to have said, "The only good Indian is a dead one," replies solemnly to Libbie that he has the promise of the Grant administration—"from the president himself"—that Custer's demand will be carried out. "Come, my dear," he says in the film's most incongruous and shamelessly fraudulent line, "your soldier won his last fight after all."

Later...

Background Reading

Elizabeth Bacon Custer, *"Boots and Saddles," or Life in Dakota with General Custer* (Harper & Brothers, 1885)

Alvin M. Josephy, Jr., *The Patriot Chiefs* (Penguin, 1993)

Jay Monaghan, *Custer: The Life of General George Armstrong Custer* (Little, Brown, 1959)

Robert M. Utley, *Cavalier in Buckskin* (University of Oklahoma Press, 1988)

1942/USA/B&W
DIRECTOR: Raoul Walsh; **PRODUCER:** Hal B. Wallis; **SCREENPLAY:** Wally Kline, Aeneas MacKenzie; **STUDIO:** Warner; **VIDEO:** MGM/UA; **RUNNING TIME:** 140 min.

The defeat of Custer shocked the American people, who had happily been celebrating the nation's centennial year. Far from protecting the Indians' right to their lands, the Grant and Hayes administrations, responding to the public's demand for revenge, waged a harsh and punitive campaign against the Sioux, scattering them across the wintry plains and forcing their small, starving bands, one by one, to come to the reservations.

Breaking a previous agreement, government commissioners coerced some of the now-powerless chiefs to sign a new treaty, giving up the Black Hills. Eventually, with government connivance, both Crazy Horse and Sitting Bull, the principal Indian leaders at the Little Bighorn, were murdered. Today, more than a century after the battle, the Sioux are still struggling to recover from the federal government even a small part of their sacred Black Hills.

Within the army, an attempt to fix the blame for what became known erroneously as the "Custer Massacre" divided the colonel's friends and enemies. In this long and unseemly quarrel, Custer's widow, Libbie, played a leading role, defending her husband fiercely for more than half a century until she died in 1933, two days before her ninety-second birthday. Even today, Custer remains an enigma to many, with both detractors and defenders. Arguments over what kind of man he was, and what he did or did not do at the Little Bighorn, still go on. However, one thing is sure: Custer now symbolizes for many the white men's sins against the Indians, an ironic reversal of the American hero glorified in *They Died with Their Boots On* fifty years ago.

CAST

Lt. Col. Owen Thursday (Henry Fonda)

Capt. Kirby York (John Wayne)

Philadelphia Thursday (Shirley Temple)

Sgt. Maj. O'Rourke (Ward Bond)

Lt. Michael O'Rourke (John Agar)

FORT APACHE

Dee Brown

WITH THE PASSAGE OF SEVERAL generations, director John Ford's films of the Old West have become as legendary as the legends he loved to portray. During the half-century spanned by his career, which began in 1917 with *Straight Shooting* and ended in 1966 with *Seven Women*, Ford probably did more than any other filmmaker to fix images of a romantic West in the minds of American moviegoers. Other directors borrowed from Ford, just as writers of western scripts and novels did, but Ford was the original. Like Frederic Remington, whose paintings he often used as models for scenes, Ford used reality as he needed it to create pictures of heroic myth.

The opening of *Fort Apache* is pure John Ford: Lt. Col. Owen Thursday—accompanied by his daughter, Philadelphia—is traveling by stage to take command of Fort Apache in remote eastern Arizona. Spectacular rock formations relieve the otherwise barren countryside, but the colonel has no interest in the scenery; rather, he expresses his low opinion of the terrain and goes on to criticize the War Department for assigning an officer of his stature to so scruffy a post. When the prim, rigid Thursday arrives at the stage station, he is further offended to find that the only transport to the fort is meant for Lt. Mickey O'Rourke, fresh from West Point. (Because the telegraph wires are down, news of Thursday's posting has not yet reached Fort Apache.) At the station, Philadelphia meets Lieutenant O'Rourke, thus beginning the tangled love interest in the story. When Colonel Thursday finally arrives at Fort Apache that evening, he finds in progress a Washington's Birthday ball at which he meets Capt. Kirby York, acting commander of the post and a capable, experienced Indian fighter.

Arizona Apache Country

Owen Thursday is a fiction writer's composite of a frontier military officer, with broad hints of Custer. We learn that Thursday, like Custer, rose during the Civil War to the rank of brevet general and is now determined to win the permanent rank. Also like Custer, he is willing to risk his own life and the lives of his men to gain fame and promotion. Both Thursday and Custer are undoubtedly brave men, both die in suicidal battles, and both become national heroes. However, there are important differences: Thursday hates frontier dress, while Custer reveled in it. And Thursday has a dour manner with very little sense of humor, while Custer was a practical joker and a cutup.

Thursday's command is also grounded in reality. Shot in black and white, *Fort Apache* bears a remarkable resemblance to surviving glass-plate photographs of the period and place. The best examples appear

HISTORY

Unfortunately, not many photographers made the difficult journey to Fort Apache during the 1870s, when its namesakes still threatened the local stage routes. This photograph, taken perhaps a decade later, shows wooden officers' quarters that were built about 1873 or 1874.

HOLLYWOOD

The first three-quarters of *Fort Apache*, depicting life on a cavalry post, are well done with skillful re-creations of period atmosphere. The two dances staged by Ford deserve an A$^+$, especially the Grand March performed at the non-commissioned officers' ball on the night before Thursday rides out to face the Apaches. The last quarter of the film, however, although exciting to watch, should be viewed as bad mythology. A true portrayal of the Apache wars it is not.

DEE BROWN

The Real Fort Apache

The film's Lt. Col. Owen Thursday, played by Henry Fonda, bears little resemblance to the real commanders at Fort Apache during this period. Their names and deeds can be found throughout the military annals of the West—cavalrymen Eugene A. Carr and George W. Schofield and infantryman George M. Randall. (Two or three infantry companies were usually stationed at the fort, although none is shown in the film.)

The real Fort Apache was not so named until five years after the death of Cochise. In 1870, when the post was known as Camp Ord, the famous Chiricahua made a peaceful visit there. During the following year, as a gesture of friendship, the post's name was

Infantry soldiers at Fort Apache ca. 1895

changed to Camp Apache. It was not designated a fort until 1879. Because John Ford set *Fort Apache* about the time of Custer's 1876 death, Geronimo and Cochise's son Naiche would have been better choices historically for the role given Cochise in the film.

One documented military clash involving Fort Apache occurred in 1881 when Colonel Carr led a force to nearby Cibecue to arrest a prophet of an early ghost dance movement. The arrest was ordered because of an Indian agent's fallacious belief that the prophet was planning to attack the fort. The result was a fight between the Apaches and Carr's soldiers in which a troop commander and six enlisted men were killed. A general outbreak of fighting followed, ending with a real but unsuccessful attack on the fort, which never would have been threatened if not for the ill-considered arrest. In the hands of a good scriptwriter, this episode could have been as exciting as Thursday's fictitious charge and a more accurate representation of Apache history.

early in the film when the script accurately describes nineteenth-century life on a southwestern cavalry post. The most careful attention is paid to details as the characters are being developed. Drills and assemblies, the training of new recruits, and social customs among the military (particularly between enlisted men and officers) are depicted in an entertaining and sometimes humorous fashion. One of the more effective points about class difference is made when Thursday barges into the family quarters of Sergeant Major O'Rourke (father of Mickey) in search of his daughter. Although Mickey O'Rourke is a junior officer, the fact that his father is an enlisted man makes Mickey's prospective relationship with Philadelphia a difficult one for Colonel Thursday to accept.

It is not until we are well into the film that we see any evidence of Apache hostilities. When Lieutenant O'Rourke escorts Philadelphia on a horseback ride outside the fort, the pair comes upon the tortured bodies of two cavalrymen who had been sent out to repair the telegraph wires. Mickey and Philadelphia gallop back to the fort, where the lieutenant makes his report. Judging by the arrows used to kill the men, Captain York determines that the Indians must have been Mescaleros. An armed pursuit follows.

Sinister Indian reservation agents are favorite villains in western movies, and one such agent plays the heavy in *Fort Apache*. He has been selling rifles and whiskey to his Mescalero charges, while at the same time cheating them of government food rations. It is made clear that this treatment of the Mescaleros provoked them to abandon their reservation and kill the soldiers. We also learn that, earlier, Cochise and his Chiricahua Apaches left the reservation for many of the same reasons.

It is true that during the 1870s and 1880s many Indian tribes did leave their reservations because of poor treatment by the goverment. Historically, Indian agents were political appointees, and often they were corrupt. In addition, many knew nothing of the tribes they were sent to oversee. An inept agent at the Pine Ridge reservation, for example, bears much of the responsibility for the events that led to the 1890 Wounded Knee massacre. The agent in *Fort Apache* fits this authentic profile. He also becomes the dramatic machine leading to catastrophe.

It is important to keep in mind that Thursday desperately wants War Department recognition and promotion, just as Custer did. Because Cochise is well known across the country as a leader of renegade Indians, Thursday believes that bringing in Cochise will win him national prestige and a transfer back to Washington. The fact that Cochise and his Chiricahuas have fled the reservation because of ill treatment by the agent seems not to concern Thursday. When he learns that Captain York knows Cochise and can act as an intermediary, it is in character for Thursday to order York to coax Cochise back to the reservation.

Cochise is portrayed sympathetically, but with his appearance reality gradually falls away from the story. In western movies, vast distances are often foreshortened, and this occurs more than once in *Fort Apache*. For example, Captain York would have required a week for his journey to Cochise's stronghold in Mexico, and Cochise would have needed much longer than that to bring the tribe north. Nor would Cochise have moved his people until he had received personal assurances from Thursday that the reservation agent would be removed.

Exaggeration of numbers also occurs. As Thursday prepares for an ill-advised final attack (following the breakdown of negotiations with Cochise), York warns that the regiment is outnumbered four to one. In other words, York estimates that Cochise's band numbers about twenty-five hundred warriors, almost as many as Custer faced at the Little Bighorn. However, Apaches rarely fought in massed groups; instead, they usually attacked in raiding parties of fewer than one hundred warriors, using guerrilla tactics.

Thursday's final mounted charge is the story's culminating event. Despite repeated warnings from his subordinates, especially York, the colonel leads a grand charge down a canyon against enemies who cannot be seen and whose strength is unknown. Echoing Custer at the Little Bighorn, Thursday disregards all the rules of military engagement. Perhaps the screenwriter meant to intimate that Thursday had gone mad; or perhaps Thursday, so filled with hubristic confidence in the superiority of white soldiers, believes that only glory awaits him. In any case, what follows after Thursday draws his saber is a dramatic series of Frederic Remington images: swiftly galloping horsemen, Apaches firing from high ground, falling cavalrymen, Apaches charging on fast mounts. The sequence concludes with a hopeless encirclement that reminds one of the many paintings of Custer's last stand.

The film closes with a coda, set a few years after Thursday's charge. A group of newspapermen have come to Fort Apache to report on a new campaign against Geronimo, and they question post commander Kirby York about his illustrious predecessor, whose courage and sacrifice journalists and artists have made famous across the country. Ignoring the irony of the situation, York praises Thursday sincerely, thus preserving the nation's admiration for the man who has become "every schoolboy's hero." As one of John Ford's own characters says in *The Man Who Shot Liberty Valance*, "When the legend becomes fact, print the legend."

Background Reading

Dee Brown, *Bury My Heart at Wounded Knee* (Holt Rinehart, 1971)

1948/USA/B&W
DIRECTOR: John Ford; PRODUCER: John Ford, Merian C. Cooper; SCREENPLAY: Frank S. Nugent; STUDIO: RKO; VIDEO: Turner; RUNNING TIME: 127 min.

Later...

After Cochise's death (from natural causes) in 1874, his eldest son, Taza, became chief of the Chiricahua Apaches. But Taza was not the chief his father was. Bands of Chiricahuas soon rejected his leadership and resumed their practice of raiding ranches and stage routes. (Cochise had strictly forbidden these raids in order to obtain peace with whites.) In 1876, the year of Custer's defeat at the Little Bighorn, the Commissioner of Indian Affairs ordered the Chiricahuas removed from their reservation at Apache Pass to dry, dusty San Carlos in the White Mountains, already the administration point for seven different Apache bands.

Geronimo

Rather than move to San Carlos, however, the forty-six-year-old Geronimo led a band of recalcitrant Chiricahua across the border to Mexico.

In September 1882, Gen. George Crook assumed command of the Department of Arizona. Crook had won fame during the early 1870s hunting down Cochise, though he changed his harsh ways during a tour of duty among the Sioux and Cheyenne, who convinced him that Indians were human beings. Under Crook's leadership, the Apaches at White Mountain were treated with respect, while corrupt reservation agents were fired. Crook's treatment of these Apaches convinced Geronimo to surrender in February 1884.

The peace held until May 1885, when Geronimo left the reservation for Mexico, fearing that scurrilous newspaper stories about invented Indian atrocities might incite white men to arrest and hang him. During the summer of 1886, Crook's replacement, Gen. Nelson "Bear Coat" Miles, put five thousand soldiers in the field to catch Geronimo and his "army" of twenty-four warriors. With thousands of Mexican troops also chasing him, Geronimo surrendered to Miles for the last time in September 1886. President Grover Cleveland believed all the tales printed about Geronimo and wanted him hanged. Instead, Geronimo and his surviving warriors were sent to Fort Marion, Florida. So many Apaches died in this unfamiliar, hot, and humid climate that in 1894 their traditional Kiowa and Comanche enemies took pity on them and offered the Chiricahuas a part of their Oklahoma reservation. (Arizonans had refused to allow the Chiricahuas to return to their homeland.) Geronimo led the survivors to Fort Sill, where he died in 1909.

THE TALE OF WYATT EARP

Seven Films

John Mack Faragher

Wʏᴀᴛᴛ Eᴀʀᴘ, ᴛʜᴇ ᴍᴏsᴛ ꜰᴀᴍᴏᴜs ᴏꜰ ᴀʟʟ frontier lawmen, has been the subject of at least two dozen Hollywood westerns. The mere mention of his name immediately evokes the image of a sharpshooting marshal bringing law and order to the wild towns of the West. "This may not be Dodge City," said a spokesman for the U.S. Marines occupying war-torn Mogadishu, Somalia, in 1993, "but Wyatt Earp's in town."

Yet Earp, unlike other frontier legends in their own time, was a minor figure until a popular writer named Stuart Lake concocted a legend for him. In 1931, Lake published *Wyatt Earp: Frontier Marshal*, which featured a hero who single-handedly cleaned up the worst frontier hellholes. This book subsequently became the authority for nearly all the film portraits of Earp. Acknowledging Lake's biography on screen lent a kind of historical authenticity to these films, but the trouble was that the book was an imaginative hoax, a fabrication mixed with just enough fact to lend it credibility. Although he claimed to have interviewed his subject—and used Earp's authoritative first-person voice throughout his narrative—Lake later confessed that "as a matter of cold fact, Wyatt never 'dictated' a word" to him.

L ake created his legend from whole cloth. The real Earp was a man of the frontier demimonde—sometime lawman but full-time gambler, confidence man, and associate of prostitutes and pimps. Born on an Illinois farm in 1848, Wyatt Earp was introduced to the Far West in 1864 when his wanderlust father moved the family across the continent to southern California. The post–Civil War years were western history's most tumultuous period. They included the wars against the Plains Indians, the construction of the transcontinental railroad, the slaughter of the buffalo, the rise and sudden collapse of the open-range cattle industry, and the mining rushes from the Black Hills to the southwestern deserts. Earp and his brothers threw themselves into the thick of the plunder, working as stage drivers and teamsters, night watchmen, and bartenders.

For a few brief months in 1870, Wyatt experimented with steady living, marrying a Missouri girl and settling down in a small town. With her unexpected death, however, he returned to the transient life of the frontier. Arrested in Indian Territory for horse stealing, he jumped bail and fled to Kansas, where he became a buffalo hunter. In 1874, he turned up in the booming cow town of Wichita, where his brother James was tending bar and James's wife ran a brothel. Wyatt found work as a town policeman, but he kept company with the saloon crowd and quickly

Frederic Remington's *Fight in the Street*

The Western Duel

Few quarrels in the West were settled by the classic face-offs of Hollywood legend. Gunplay was common in the cow towns, but historians have found no evidence to support the numerous deaths by firearms portrayed in westerns. During his years as a Dodge City lawman, for example, Wyatt Earp is thought to have killed only one man. More frequently he used his guns to pistol-whip "hurrahing" cowboys. The famous gunfight at the O.K. Corral lasted only a few seconds and was so confusing that even eyewitnesses could not agree on what they had seen.

The convention of the gunfight between two men facing off in the middle of a dusty street probably derives from the confrontation between the villain and the hero in Owen Wister's influential western novel *The Virginian* (1902). Wister adapted his story for the Broadway stage, and it was made into several silent movies before the first sound version, with Gary Cooper, was released in 1929.

HISTORY

Doc Holliday

Wyatt Earp

These photographs show Wyatt Earp and John "Doc" Holliday as they appeared in the early 1880s. Earp was both a lawman and a gambler; he found his associates among the saloon crowd in the cattle and mining towns of the frontier. Holliday, a former dentist, came to the West to relieve his tubercular condition, took up gambling, and built a reputation as a cold-blooded killer. They became friends in Dodge City, Kansas, and stood together at the O.K. Corral gunfight in Tombstone, Arizona.

HOLLYWOOD

Victor Mature as Holliday

Henry Fonda as Earp

Although most critics rank *My Darling Clementine* among the very best of John Ford's fifty-six westerns, the great director never wanted to make the film. He owed Twentieth Century-Fox one more picture before his contract expired, however, and *My Darling Clementine* was it. Ford was reportedly none too pleased when Fox studio chief Darryl F. Zanuck cut thirty minutes from the director's original edit because Zanuck thought it "overlong." The principal photography certainly didn't take very long: The entire picture was shot in Monument Valley (Ford's favorite location) in just forty-five days.

FRONTIER MARSHAL

Wyatt Earp	(Randolph Scott)
John "Doc" Holliday	(Cesar Romero)

1939/USA/B&W
DIRECTOR: Allan Dwan; PRODUCER: Sol M.
Wurtzel; SCREENPLAY: Sam Hellman; STUDIO:
Twentieth Century-Fox; VIDEO: none; RUNNING
TIME: 71 min.

Tombstone, Arizona, as it appeared in 1881

Tombstone

The town was named by prospector Ed Schieffelin,
who discovered silver there in 1877.
(Acquaintances had told Schieffelin that all he
would find there would be his own tombstone.)
During the early 1880s, about seven thousand
people lived in or near the boom town, but most
moved away within a few years when lower silver
prices, labor unrest, and floodwaters in the mines
drove down profits. The town was declared a
National Historic Landmark in 1962.

developed a reputation as a hard case. Earp often pulled his long-barreled Colt on drunken cattle hands, usually not to fire but to "buffalo," or pistol-whip, those who stepped out of line.

In 1876, Wyatt moved on to Dodge City, where both he and his brother Morgan found jobs as deputy marshals. The Earps considered themselves "sporting men," cavorting with the likes of John "Doc" Holliday—a tubercular gambler with a reputation for violence—and prostitutes such as Doc's woman, Kate Elder (also known as Kate Fisher), and Mattie Blaylock, who became Wyatt's common-law wife. Hostile ranchers called the Earp brothers the "fighting pimps."

Meanwhile, older brother Virgil had won an appointment as deputy U.S. marshal in southern Arizona Territory, where a silver strike had spawned the boomtown of Tombstone. In 1880, the three Earp brothers joined him there, followed by friends who included Doc Holliday. The Earps continued to run with the saloon crowd, but in Tombstone they also made a serious bid for respectability, aligning themselves with the town's Republican establishment. Working as bank guards and deputies, they invested in real estate and local mining properties.

Southeastern Arizona at the time was torn by conflict between the Republican business community and the mostly Democratic ranchers of the arid countryside. The "cowboys," as the Republican *Tombstone Epitaph* labeled the ranchers, were led by Newman "Old Man" Clanton and his hot-headed sons and were backed by such violent gunmen as "Curly" Bill Brocius and Johnny Ringo. The trouble in Tombstone was just

> ## "I am not ashamed of anything I ever did. Notoriety has been the bane of my life."
>
> *Wyatt Earp*

one episode in a series of local wars that pitted men with traditional rural values and southern sympathies against mostly Yankee capitalist modernizers. As the hired guns of the businessmen in town, the Earps became the enemies of the Clantons.

In 1881, Wyatt ran for county sheriff against the incumbent, John Behan, an ally of the rural Democrats. Earp charged that Behan was protecting the Clantons and other cowboys responsible for a series of stage robberies, while the Democrats countered that Holliday and possibly the Earps themselves were behind the crimes. The political competition between the candidates became personal when Earp took up with Behan's lover, the beautiful Josephine Marcus. Wyatt lost the election but won the woman, and the confrontation became a bitter feud, reaching its climax in October 1881, when Virgil and Wyatt buffaloed a drunken Ike Clanton and his friend, rancher Tom McLaury, in Tombstone.

Licking their wounds in a vacant lot next to the O.K. Corral with a small group that included their brothers, Clanton and McLaury suddenly found themselves confronted by three heavily armed Earp brothers accompanied by Doc Holliday. "You sonofabitches have been looking for a fight, and now you can have it!" Wyatt reportedly shouted. Shots rang out, and in a few seconds it was all over. Tom and Frank McLaury and Billy Clanton were dead, Virgil and Morgan Earp wounded.

Reaction to the shootout among Tombstone's citizens varied according to political loyalty. Democrats, who claimed the Earps had fired on unresisting and innocent ranchers, brought charges of murder, but when a Republican justice of the peace refused to indict them, the Earps and Holliday walked. The feud continued. Within weeks Virgil was gunned down and badly wounded, and Morgan was killed by unknown assailants. Wyatt secured an appointment as a deputy U.S. marshal and led Holliday and others on a rampage during which they killed at least three of their cowboy enemies, then fled the territory.

The historical facts are very messy, unlike the squeaky clean Earp of Stuart Lake's book. "In the confused political, economic, and social climate of the frontier," historian Paula Mitchell Marks wrote in her fascinating study of Tombstone, "men could not agree on right and wrong." But western myth demanded simple tales of good and evil. As Josephine Marcus Earp herself reminded Lake when he was about to complete his book, "It must be a nice clean story."

And so it was. The first film to feature Wyatt Earp by name, *Frontier Marshal* (1939), was based on Lake's biography. Veteran director Allan Dwan had met Earp when the old man visited the sets of Dwan's silent westerns to talk of old times and drink with the cowboy extras. Wyatt was "as crooked as a three-dollar bill," Dwan remembered. "He and his brothers were racketeers, all of them." Yet that didn't prevent Dwan from turning his screen Earp into a paragon of virtue. Randolph Scott played Earp the town-tamer, the man who reluctantly but effectively brings law and order to Tombstone. The script simplified the story by erasing Earp's brothers, and it sanitized Wyatt by linking him to frontier lowlifes only through his loyalty to Doc Holliday (Cesar Romero), whom he seeks to reform. *Frontier Marshal* is a thoroughly forgettable film.

Not so the remake, John Ford's poetic *My Darling Clementine* (1946). In Ford's hands, Earp's story takes on deep significance. His Tombstone becomes, in the famous phrase of historian Frederick Jackson Turner, "the meeting point between savagery and civilization." Metaphorically framing this central conflict is the rugged Monument Valley location. In one of the most famous sequences in American film, Henry Fonda's Wyatt dances with his "lady fair" on the floor of Tombstone's unfinished church, its bare frame silhouetted against the magnificent buttes. These visual elements reinforce the contrasting relationships among the central characters. The good Earp brothers, frequently shown in the town hotel's dining room and the barbershop, fight the brutish Clantons, who

GUNFIGHT AT THE O.K. CORRAL

Wyatt Earp	**(Burt Lancaster)**
John "Doc" Holliday	**(Kirk Douglas)**

1957/USA/Color
DIRECTOR: John Sturges; PRODUCER: Hal B. Wallis; SCREENPLAY: Leon Uris; STUDIO: Paramount; VIDEO: Paramount; RUNNING TIME: 122 min.

I Married Wyatt Earp

Josephine Marcus Earp (1861—1944) was the daughter of a Jewish pioneer merchant from San Francisco. In 1879, she ran off with a troupe of actors and ended up in Tombstone, where she became the mistress of the sheriff of Cochise County, John Behan. A striking beauty, she took up with Wyatt Earp when her romance with Behan soured. Although Josephine and Wyatt never formally married, they lived as man and wife for the rest of their lives.

After Wyatt's death, his widow complained about the errors in each of the books and films about him, and in the late 1930s she wrote her own version of the Earp legend: *I Married Wyatt Earp*, an engaging account that not surprisingly covers up many of the details the old woman found embarrassing. A television movie, *I Married Wyatt Earp* (1983), starring Marie Osmond, marked the first time that Josephine Marcus was featured in an Earp film.

HOUR OF THE GUN

Wyatt Earp   (James Garner)
John "Doc" Holliday   (Jason Robards, Jr.)

1967/USA/Color
DIRECTOR: John Sturges; PRODUCER: John
Sturges; SCREENPLAY: Edward Anhalt; STUDIO:
UA; VIDEO: none; RUNNING TIME: 101 min.

The Western Wars of Incorporation

In the years following the Civil War, both the South
and the West went through a turbulent and often
violent process of incorporation into the economic
life of the nation. In the far West, small ranchers
and farmers, many of them Democrats from the
South, were pitted against northerners,
Republicans, big ranchers, and industrialists.
Historian Richard Maxwell Brown places the
Tombstone conflict in the middle of what he calls
the Cochise County War. Other local wars included
the Johnson County War in Wyoming (loosely the
subject of the classic 1953 western *Shane*) and
the Lincoln County War in southern New Mexico
(from which sprang the legend of Billy the Kid).

These class and political conflicts were also
cultural ones. The agrarian, or cowboy, faction represented premodern cultural values focusing on
small community relationships, friendships, and
kin. Their opponents represented modernizing
influences, industrial development, and capitalism.

are at home in the arid countryside. Doc Holliday (Victor Mature) inspires Wyatt with his urban cultivation even as he backslides toward self-destruction. The Clementine of the title (Cathy Downs) is the eastern lady who comes West to save her beloved Doc, only to discover and then challenge his Mexican whore (Linda Darnell).

"It's always simplicity that you should go after," Ford once told an interviewer, and in *My Darling Clementine* he strips the Earp story to its bare essentials. The Clantons murder the youngest of the Earps in the first reel, leading the three surviving brothers to pin on badges and gather evidence against the ranchers. But Ford's Wyatt is not simply after revenge; he wants something larger. "We're gonna be around here for a while," he promises at his brother's grave. "Maybe when we leave this country, young kids like you will be able to grow up and live safe." Contemporary audiences surely linked this monologue to speeches that Fonda delivered in earlier Ford films—at the graveside of his dead sweetheart in *Young Mr. Lincoln* (1939), for example, or at the stirring conclusion of *The Grapes of Wrath* (1940). When Wyatt finally finds the proof he needs, he tries to arrest the Clantons, provoking the fatal gunfight that provides the film's climax.

None of this, of course, has anything to do with the messy historical facts, but that did not keep Ford from proclaiming the authenticity of his film. During his early days as a director, Ford claimed, Earp would stop by his sets and tell him about the old days in the West. But if that were so, film historian John Tuska once asked Ford, why didn't he shoot the film the way it actually happened? Never one to be questioned, the great director grew testy. "Did you like the film?" he sputtered, and when Tuska admitted it was one of his favorites, Ford shot back, "What more do you want?" As Tuska concluded, Ford didn't give a damn for the messy historical facts. What mattered in *My Darling Clementine* was the historical interpretation, the meaning that Ford gave to his story about the coming of civilization to the West. He expressed a similar sentiment in *The Man Who Shot Liberty Valance* (1962), one of his last films: "This is the West, sir," says a newspaperman. "When the legend becomes fact, print the legend."

The next significant addition to the Tombstone canon came ten years and half a dozen minor Earp movies later. *Gunfight at the O.K. Corral* (1957), written by Leon Uris and directed by John Sturges, follows Earp from the Texas town where he meets Doc to Dodge City and then to Tombstone for the finale. Dozens of small authenticating details, many taken directly from Stuart Lake's biography, seek to establish the picture's verisimilitude. The climactic shootout, filmed as a paramilitary confrontation, takes up a full six minutes of screen time, as the picture moves from the tedious to the overblown. But the movie's concentration on the psychology of the relationship between Wyatt (Burt Lancaster) and Doc (Kirk Douglas) makes *Gunfight at the O.K. Corral* enduringly fascinating.

The film provides an explanation for their friendship when Holliday rescues Earp from a murderous crowd, but there are hints of a deeper attraction. "I like you, Wyatt Earp," Doc says, primping before a barber's mirror, "I like your cut." Breaking into a toothy smile, just about the only one in his dour portrayal of Earp, Lancaster replies coyly, "Let's say I like your cut, too." Doc's woman, Kate (Jo Van Fleet), clearly considers Wyatt her competitor, and she conspires to have him killed. Discovering her plan, Doc stalks Kate with the fury only Kirk Douglas can bring to a role. "I thought if Wyatt were out of the way," Kate shrieks, "you'd come back home."

These psychologizing elements signaled the revisionism that would transform westerns over the next generation. A decade after *Gunfight at the O.K. Corral*, Sturges filmed a sequel, *Hour of the Gun* (1967), which *begins* with the famous gunfight and goes on to detail its violent aftermath. James Garner plays Wyatt as an avenger whose moral decline is highlighted by the growing humanity of Jason Robards's Doc. Advertising banners for the film proclaimed: "Wyatt Earp—Hero with a Badge or Cold-Blooded Killer?"

This preoccupation with debunking continued in the most downbeat of all Earp films, Frank Perry's *Doc* (1971). Newspaper ads for the picture played to the cynical mood of the time: "On a good day he might pistol-whip a drunk, shoot an unarmed man, bribe a politician, and get paid off by an outlaw. He was a U.S. Marshal." The plot deliberately jumbles the elements of the traditional Earp story—primarily by making Doc, not Wyatt, the hero. Played as a romantic loser by Stacy Keach, Doc drifts into Tombstone with Kate (Faye Dunaway), in this film a vibrant and life-affirming whore. Harris Yulin's Wyatt, an opportunistic schemer, is running for town marshal. When Doc expresses surprise at his friend's new respectability, Wyatt assures him that it is all part of a plot to corrupt the town and make them both rich. "We sound like bad people, Wyatt," Doc replies in a world-weary tone. "We are, John," says Earp with a malicious wink.

Tombstone's cowboys may be crude in *Doc*, but this time around it's the Earps and their associates who are the criminals. At the O.K. Corral, the Earps produce shotguns and mow down their opponents. Screenwriter Pete Hamill explicitly linked his story to the cultural and political turmoil surrounding the Vietnam War. "We were continuing to fight [in Vietnam] because of some peculiar notions of national macho pride," Hamill wrote. "Indochina was Dodge City, and the Americans were some collective version of Wyatt Earp."

In both *Doc* and *Hour of the Gun*, history becomes exposé and truth myth-busting. "This picture is based on fact," an opening caption in *Hour of the Gun* declares. "This is the way it happened." Viewed with the postmodern detachment made possible by videocassettes and remote fast-forward, *Hour of the Gun* and *Doc* are fascinating, especially when seen with the other Earp offerings very much in mind. Yet both were box-office flops. Although all westerns are concerned with history, no one

DOC

Wyatt Earp	**(Harris Yulin)**
John "Doc" Holliday	**(Stacy Keach)**

1971/USA/Color
DIRECTOR: Frank Perry; PRODUCER: Frank Perry; SCREENPLAY: Pete Hamill; STUDIO: UA; VIDEO: none; RUNNING TIME: 89 min.

TOMBSTONE

Wyatt Earp	**(Kurt Russell)**
John "Doc" Holliday	**(Val Kilmer)**

1993/USA/Color
DIRECTOR: George P. Cosmatos; PRODUCER: James Jacks, Sean Daniel, Bob Misiorowski; SCREENPLAY: Kevin Jarre; STUDIO: Hollywood; VIDEO: Hollywood; RUNNING TIME: 128 min.

WYATT EARP

Wyatt Earp	**(Kevin Costner)**
John "Doc" Holliday	**(Dennis Quaid)**

1994/USA/Color
DIRECTOR: Lawrence Kasdan; PRODUCER: Jim Wilson, Kevin Costner, Lawrence Kasdan; SCREENPLAY: Lawrence Kasdan, Dan Gordon; STUDIO: Warner; VIDEO: Warner; RUNNING TIME: 189 min.

An Earp By Any Other Name . . .

In addition to those movies featuring Wyatt Earp by name, the Earp character appears under a pseudonym in a number of other Hollywood efforts. In fact, Earp was rechristened for Edward L. Cahn's *Law and Order* (1932), the first film to feature elements of Wyatt's story. Based on W.R. Burnett's novel and starring Walter Huston, this dark and moody drama was adapted for the screen by Huston's son John (who would later script and direct Burnett's *The Asphalt Jungle*). The picture was remade twice: in 1940, with the lead played by cowboy star Johnny Mack Brown, and in 1953, with Ronald Reagan.

Ronald Reagan in *Law and Order*

Earp was also renamed in the first film version of Stuart Lake's *Frontier Marshal* (1933). Fox was forced to take that step when Josephine Marcus Earp, Wyatt's widow, threatened to sue over the film's "unauthorized" portrayal. Five years later, during the craze for biopics inspired by the success of the picture *Jesse James* (1939), Darryl Zanuck determined to remake *Frontier Marshal* using Earp's name. Mrs. Earp threatened once again to sue, but this time she was appeased with a five-thousand-dollar check.

The Man Who Invented Wyatt Earp

In 1927 Stuart Lake was writing for films and magazines when he learned that Wyatt Earp was still alive and living in Los Angeles. After visiting the old man, he set to work on what would become *Wyatt Earp: Frontier Marshal* (1931), one of the most successful western biographies of all time.

Lake later became a successful screenwriter of Hollywood westerns—credited with *Wells Fargo* (1937), *The Westerner* (1940), and *Winchester '73* (1950), among others. During the 1950s, he served as an adviser on the sets of a number of Earp pictures, including *Gunfight at the O.K. Corral*, and he created the enormously popular television series *The Life and Times of Wyatt Earp* (1955–61), for which he wrote more than two dozen scripts. Lake died in 1964 at the age of seventy-four, but his influence continues, for even the most recent Earp films draw heavily on the details in his Earp biography.

goes to the movies for a cynical history lesson. Audiences don't want history's messy facts; they want its meaning. The most enduring westerns—*My Darling Clementine* is one of them—feature this metahistorical element. In contrast, the revisionist Earp films, which clearly reject the progressive interpretations of Stuart Lake and John Ford, have little to offer in their place. Mired in the disillusionment of their own times, they find nothing significant to say about the American past.

During the 1970s and 1980s, film critics pointed to the failure of these debunking pictures as important evidence of the much-noted "death of the western." Perhaps it was inevitable that during the equally heralded rebirth of the genre in the 1990s Hollywood turned once again to Wyatt Earp. Neither of the most recent Earp films succeeds, however, in resolving the debunker's dilemma. The stars of both *Tombstone* (1993) and *Wyatt Earp* (1994) claimed that their pictures were the most historically accurate in sixty years. "We hope we've found the Wyatt Earp who actually existed," opined Kurt Russell (the Wyatt of *Tombstone*), and Kevin Costner declared that his Earp (in *Wyatt Earp*) was constructed "within the boundaries of historical fact."

> # "I'll be damned."
>
> *Doc Holliday's last words*

Certainly there was a good deal of promotional bombast in such remarks, but just as earlier films had depended on Stuart Lake for their authenticity, these movies relied on new historical research. Both thoughtfully re-create a considerably more complex social and cultural frontier milieu, utilizing new and more inclusive multicultural western history. They are the first big-screen features to showcase Wyatt's relationship with Josephine Marcus and to depict both the shootout *and* the vengeful aftermath.

The historicity of *Tombstone*, however, is merely skin deep. Its heart belongs to the pop culture of today. George P. Cosmatos, who grew up in Italy, directs in over-the-edge emulation of Sergio Leone's spaghetti westerns. *Tombstone*'s cowboys wear gang colors, Josephine (Dana Delany) wonders aloud whether Wyatt is "really happy," and Doc (Val Kilmer) spouts some of the campiest dialogue west of TriBeCa. "You're a good woman," he mumbles to Kate. "Then again, you may be the Antichrist."

Lawrence Kasdan's *Wyatt Earp* is as self-important as *Tombstone* is unpretentious. Crawling along for more than three hours, it tells viewers far more than they ever wanted to know about Earp. The filmmakers clearly did their research well, taking their commitment to history seriously. Too seriously. *Wyatt Earp* is truer to the messy historical facts than any previous Earp film, but it's lifeless. Loading us down with facts, it presents very little of what Earp's life might have *meant* and finally has nothing important to say.

So fifty years after its release, the artistic benchmark of the Wyatt Earp films remains *My Darling Clementine*. John Ford's picture lies about the past but locates in the Earp story a *logos* for American history. A yawning divide separates us from the metahistorical confidence of *Clementine*. The trick for future westerns will be to tell truer tales that also inspire audiences with their breadth of vision about the meaning of the American past. To paraphrase John Ford, when the facts outgrow the legend, revise the legend.

Wyatt Earp in Hollywood

By the time Wyatt Earp reached his mid-sixties, he and Josephine had settled down in the Los Angeles area. He spent a good deal of his last decade hanging around with the frontier types who worked as actors and extras on the sets of Hollywood westerns. "His wife was a very religious woman," John Ford recalled. "She'd go away on these religious conventions, and Wyatt would sneak into town and get drunk with my cowboys." Wyatt tried to interest someone in making a picture of his life, but before the publication of Stuart Lake's biography few people had heard of him. Earp became friends with cowboy stars William S. Hart and Tom Mix, who were both pallbearers at his 1929 funeral. Blake Edwards' *Sunset* (1988), an enjoyable fantasy set in 1920s Hollywood, spins a yarn in which Wyatt Earp (James Garner, reprising his role in *Hour of the Gun*) and Tom Mix (Bruce Willis) solve a murder mystery together.

Wyatt Earp in his later years.

Later...

Although Wyatt Earp failed to gain respectability in Tombstone, he did accumulate considerable capital. Josephine Marcus's well-to-do San Francisco family also may have helped support the couple, and they provided strategic business introductions for Wyatt. He and Josephine continued to pursue the sporting life in mining towns from Nevada to Alaska until they finally settled down in southern California in 1906.

Virgil Earp left Tombstone to become the sheriff of Colton, California, where he also ran a successful saloon before his death in 1906. Mattie Blaylock went back to prostitution after Earp abandoned her in Tombstone, and in 1885 she killed herself with a drug overdose. Two years later, Doc Holliday died of tuberculosis in a Colorado sanitarium. Kate Elder went on to run a prosperous boarding house in Prescott, Arizona.

Background Reading

Richard Maxwell Brown, *No Duty to Retreat: Violence and Values in American History and Society* (Oxford University Press, 1991)

Paula Mitchell Marks, *And Die in the West: The Story of the O.K. Corral Gunfight* (Morrow, 1989)

My Darling Clementine
1946/USA/B&W
DIRECTOR: John Ford; PRODUCER: Samuel G. Engel; SCREENPLAY: Samuel G. Engel, Winston Miller; STUDIO: Twentieth-Century-Fox; VIDEO: Fox; RUNNING TIME: 97 min.

KHARTOUM

David Levering Lewis

As *KHARTOUM* ENDS, CHARLES GEORGE Gordon stands alone at the top of his palace stairs. Resplendent in a dark-blue uniform, saber unsheathed, the governor general of the Sudan (played by Charlton Heston) watches impassively as invaders faithful to the Sudanese Mahdi scale the garrison walls, overwhelm its Egyptian defenders, and surge toward him. When they hesitate for a moment, this high-suspense confrontation between the eminent Victorian and the Sudanese dervishes becomes an occidental cinematic cliché in splendid culmination: the lone white man who attempts to quell the menacing tumult of dark-skinned peoples by sheer *presence*, by the adamantine superiority of all that his person embodies. Then the dervishes spear the white commander in the chest, lop off his head, and stick it on a six-foot pole. A sepulchral voice-over warns, "A world without Gordons would return to the sands," as the fading sun extinguishes a bronze equestrian statue of the general and the credits roll across a darkening screen.

Victorian England saw in Gordon's martyrdom one more grand gesture legitimating the burden of empire. Director Basil Dearden's *Khartoum* finds in Gordon's sacrifice a reassuring message for the European world of the late 1960s (a time of Third World impertinence and Marxist contagion): that civilization as we know it depends, *au fond*, on values peculiar to Europe and its offshoots. Yet the historical verity underlying this film ultimately subverts its Eurocentric premise because *Khartoum* the cinematic saga, like the historical saga on which it is based, depends at one level of agency on the dogmatic beliefs and charismatic force of two remarkable men.

Gordon's desert analog was a thirty-seven-year-old Dunqulawi Arab named Muhammed Ahmad (Laurence Olivier). Ahmad had called for a holy war to drive the British and their Egyptian allies from the Sudan. In November 1881, the Egyptians sent a company of infantrymen to arrest Ahmad at his island sanctuary in the Nile, but Ahmad's forces slaughtered the attackers, badly shaking the Egyptians and puzzling the custodians of the British Empire. An ascetic who became increasingly exalted by virtue of his *baraka* (supernatural power), Ahmad audaciously proclaimed himself the Mahdi, the Expected Guide, claiming he was sent by the Prophet to return the *ansar* (the faithful) to the true tenets of Allah—and, above all, to deliver the Sudan from rapacious Egyptian (and ultimately British) exploitation. During the next two years, the Mahdi and his hordes swept through the Sudan, winning one stunning victory after another against the infidels and forcing the Egyptians to cede territory to the Sudanese.

HISTORY

Charles George Gordon

Khartoum gives audiences relatively unschooled in the eccentricities of Victorian biography and the vagaries of imperial real estate a credible initiation into Gordon's character. He was a second lieutenant during the Crimean War (1853–56) and distinguished himself by his reckless courage, becoming a national hero in Britain and earning the nickname Chinese Gordon for his role in suppressing the 1864 Taiping Rebellion. The real-life Gordon, if we take Lytton Strachey's famous portrait as accurate, was a repressed pedophile subject to fits of black, immobilizing depression followed by bursts of weird inspiration and brilliantly focused achievement, during which brandy-and-sodas and the Bible were consumed in about equal quantities.

HOLLYWOOD

Charlton Heston as Gordon

Khartoum's producer, Julian Blaustein, was a stickler for authenticity, and much about the film, from the armaments to the costumes, is accurate. He even sent a copy of the film script to the Mahdi's grandson, who returned it with a note that although, as far he was aware, his grandfather and Gordon never met, "It's an extremely fine script." When Blaustein expressed his regret that the screenplay erred on this point, the grandson replied, "Ah, but Mr. Blaustein, they should have!"

The death of General Gordon

A City Under Siege

Upon his arrival in Khartoum, Charles Gordon did evacuate about two thousand people from a population that may have been as high as forty thousand. He also ordered channels dug that would allow the Nile to flood moats around the city. In the early days of the siege, there was great confidence in Gordon's leadership and the city's propects for deliverance.

The Slave Trade

Heavy taxation certainly played a part in stirring the Sudanese uprising. As a London *Times* correspondent wrote at the time, "If the crop is good, [peasants] pay double taxes (one for the private purse of the Pasha and one for the government at Cairo). If they don't grow the corn, they can't pay taxes at all, and are kourbashed (whipped with good hippopotamus hide) and put into prison." Yet although the peasantry suffered terribly under Egyptian rule, it was the cumulative rage of Sudanese *jallaba* (merchants in the towns) and *ta'isha* (cattle herders)—cut off from the lucrative Saudi Arabian and Cairene slave markets by the very Egyptian officials who were supposed to enforce the Khedive's 1877 ban on the slave trade—that ultimately created the preconditions for *Mahdiya*, the polity set up by the Mahdi. Brown Arabs of the north had been forced from their slave-trade monopoly over black animists of the south by the superior firepower of Egyptian armies. Although Ahmad made no explicit appeal to those whose profitable slave raiding had been suppressed, it was obvious that his triumphs would mean the return of such revenues.

The economic and political history behind the Mahdi's spectacular *jihad*—a convoluted story originating with Egyptian penetration into the Sudan during the 1820s and largely devoid of redeeming characters, whatever their color or mission—has almost no place in the film. Detailing the connections among finance capital, technology diffusion, and national self-determination was much too tall an order for the filmmakers. Yet these factors can't be ignored entirely. Through body language, voice tones, and sound bites, the film tries to suggest in a few frames the paramount importance of the Suez Canal, the impaired sovereignty of the Egyptian Khedive, and the de facto supremacy of Her Majesty's resident in Cairo.

The history left out of the story is riveting. In order for Egypt to leap several stages of modernization, its government borrowed prodigiously from European banks; and in the scramble to finance this massive debt, the Khedive's Circassian bureaucrats taxed and plundered the life out of the common people of Egypt and the Sudan. Meanwhile, bankers in London, Paris, and Berlin, increasingly anxious about interest payments, brought ever-greater pressure to expropriate Egypt's customs revenues. But "efficient" European collection of revenues for bankers only spurred corrupt Egyptian pashas to greater extremes of despoilment, causing unrest from Alexandria to Wadi Halfa and deposition of the Khedive Ismail, who dared to abrogate Egypt's pact with the bankers.

All this led ultimately to the cry, "Egypt for the Egyptians," then to Col. Ahmed Bey Urabi's nationalist coup d'état in September 1881. Political instability in Egypt unleashed Islamic revolution in the Sudan, and Sir Evelyn Baring ("Lord Overbearing") arrived with red-coated regiments to protect the Suez Canal and run the dominion for Britain as proconsul.

Khartoum's action begins with Col. William Hicks and his fellow British officers on horseback bellowing commands to parched *fellahin* infantry and yawning camel corpsmen. The time is November 1883; the place, near Obeid, the capital of Kordofan province, almost two thousand Nile miles south of Cairo. In a battle scene of surpassing realism, the Mahdi's *ansar* (numbering around eighty thousand) massacre almost to a man Hicks's army of eight thousand, capturing five artillery batteries and nearly ten thousand Remington repeater rifles. "Explain to me," booms the film's mutton-chopped Prime Minister Gladstone (Ralph Richardson), "how a rabble of tribesmen armed only with spears, swords, and rocks can destroy a modern army? A British officer commanding!" In the end, Downing Street satisfies itself with a mad-mullah explanation. (The real Gladstone's revealing aside about the Sudanese being "a people struggling to be free, and rightly struggling to be free," goes unmentioned by scriptwriter Robert Ardrey, who no doubt regarded it as a complicating excess of high-mindedness.)

In 1884, when Khartoum, the administrative capital of Egyptian-ruled Sudan, is threatened by the Mahdi's forces, Her Majesty's Government dispatches Gordon to evacuate the European and Egyptian populations there. According to Anthony Nutting's 1966 book, *Gordon of Khartoum: Martyr and Misfit*, the general never intended to obey these orders.

Instead, Gordon wagered his life and the lives of thousands of Khartoum's citizens on a high-stakes gamble to preserve British influence in the Sudan. He decided to hold the city rather than evacuate it.

In the movie's two apocryphal meetings between Gordon and the Mahdi, the didactic script hammers home the point that, despite their profound cultural and religious differences, the Englishman and the Sudanese understand that they are fellow fanatics, one predestined to self-destruction because of the other's conquering vision. Lisping through the gap between his incisors and rolling his eyes out of trances, with a face badly daubed from the same pot of makeup he used for *Othello*, Olivier measures his *baraka* against Heston's destiny. On the eve of the Mahdi's order to attack the city and end the 317-day siege, Gordon warns Ahmad that the Mahdi, too, will perish as a result of the Englishman's death. Whatever dramatic benefits derive from such confrontations, they beggar the inherent significance of the Mahdi's rise and Gordon's fall. In their different ways, both the Islamic zealot and the old-style Victorian imperialist tried to resist the onslaught of modernization, which was running at full tilt in the 1880s as a result of the industrial revolution.

Progress, however, could not be halted. Seven years after Gordon's death, the British commander at Suakin forwarded an intriguing report to Sir Evelyn Baring in Cairo: "It is too soon to speculate yet, but with the gradual disappearance of religious fanaticism as the source power, with the establishment of practically a military despotism, with the revival of trade, and with the counsels of merchants receiving daily more attention, to the neglect of more restless and ambitious fighters, . . . the day may come when the earthly ruler at Omdurman may listen to a proposal to come to terms, if the Egyptian Government entertain such an idea."

Such speculations may take us far beyond the scope of *Khartoum*, yet they are highly germane to the premise of worlds returning to sand, as expressed by the narrator at the film's conclusion. In place of the corrupt, somnolent regime imposed by Egypt's Turkish-Circassian rulers, there was now in East Africa an emerging nation-state, a modernizing theocracy rising out of the sands. Yet because the film has little aptitude and even less concern for the dynamic forces propelling its characters, *Khartoum*'s attempt at larger-than-life portrayals of Gordon and the Mahdi has the unintended consequence of depriving them of their epochal resonance.

Background Reading

P.M. Holt, *The Mahdist State in the Sudan* (Clarendon Press, 1970)

David Levering Lewis, *Race to Fashoda: Colonialism and African Resistance* (Holt, 1995)

Anthony Nutting, *Gordon of Khartoum: Martyr and Misfit* (Clarkson N. Potter, 1966)

1966/GB/Color
DIRECTOR: Basil Dearden; PRODUCER: Julian Blaustein; SCREENPLAY: Robert Ardrey; STUDIO: UA; VIDEO: MGM/UA; RUNNING TIME: 134 min.

The tomb of the Mahdi

Later...

Although *Khartoum* suggests some mystical nexus between the deaths of Gordon and the Mahdi, in reality the Mahdi's demise several months after Gordon's was probably attributable to typhus. (After its victory, the Mahdi's army was decimated by a plague spread by rats who fed off the slaughtered corpses that lay in the ravaged city's streets.) The fall of Khartoum on January 26, 1885, led to an unprecedented reverse of British imperialism—the city's collapse coming just two days before the arrival of two gunboats sent ahead from Gen. Garnet Wolseley's vast approaching army. Thirteen years would elapse before Lord Kitchener's Maxim guns obliterated the legions of the Khalifa Abdullahi, Muhammad Ahmad's successor, on Omdurman plain.

Meanwhile, the grand design of Cecil Rhodes and other British Empire architects to build an uninterrupted rail-and-telegraph network from the Cape of South Africa through Cairo to Alexandria was put indefinitely on hold. The French, sorely aggrieved at being ousted from Egypt, conceived a daring plan to weave a network of alliances from Ethiopia into the Sudan in order to compel their British rivals to the conference table. Out of such a scheme came the improbable Congo-Nile expedition led by Marine Capt. Jean-Baptiste Marchand. At the same time, Leopold of Belgium hatched equally ambitious schemes to foreclose British reentry into the Nile Basin by extending his vast real estate possessions beyond the Congo into lands claimed by the Mahdiya.

MURDER BY DECREE

David Cannadine

CAST

Sherlock Holmes *(Christopher Plummer)*
Dr. Watson *(James Mason)*
Charles Warren *(Anthony Quayle)*

THE YEAR 1888 WAS ONE OF THE MOST varied, remarkable, and traumatic in London's nineteenth-century history. Charles Booth, aided by the young Beatrice Potter (later Webb), was working on his survey of metropolitan life and labor. Gilbert and Sullivan produced *The Yeomen of the Guard*, the closest they ever came to a sad and serious opera. There was a long and bitter strike of women workers at Bryant & May's match factory at Bow. Sherlock Holmes appeared for the first time in hardback, in a novel coyly entitled *A Study in Scarlet*. And a notorious, unidentified serial killer called Jack the Ripper terrorized a part of the East End called Whitechapel.

For more than a century, the British have been repelled, haunted, and fascinated by the Ripper murders, rather in the same way that the American public has been fixated by the assassination of President Kennedy. To this day, self-styled and self-appointed Ripperologists continue to debate his identity, his motives, and the number of murders he actually committed. There is general agreement that between August 31 and November 10, 1888, there were at least five victims, all poor, all prostitutes, and all grotesquely mutilated: Mary Ann Nicholls, Annie Chapman, Elizabeth Stride, Catharine Eddowes, and Mary Kelly.

The perpetrator of these terrible atrocities—and it is generally assumed there was only one murderer at work—was never caught, hence the hundred-year open season on morbid and macabre speculation. Some have argued that the Ripper was a well-connected aristocrat, possibly motivated by a perverse desire to save those even more illustrious than himself from scandal. Some have suggested that he was a demented doctor, a real-life version of Robert Louis Stevenson's *The Strange Case of Dr. Jekyll and Mr. Hyde*, published just two years prior to the murders. Others have asserted that such fiendishly un-English crimes could have been committed only by a foreigner—perhaps a Russian, perhaps a Portuguese, probably a Jew.

It has even been proposed that the villain was none other than His Royal Highness Prince Albert Victor, duke of Clarence and Avondale, elder son of the prince of Wales (the future King Edward VII), grandson of the Queen-Empress Victoria, and thus himself in direct line of succession to the throne of Great Britain. Prince Albert Victor was a sad, vacant, lethargic boy who grew up to be the despair of his parents and his grandmother, not the least because of his wayward and irresponsible sexual proclivities (he was once apprehended by police after a raid on a homosexual club at 19 Cleveland Street). Much to the royal family's guilty

Contemporary woodcut from *The Police Gazette*

Naming the Killer

The Whitechapel murders struck Londoners with equal measures of horror and terror. There was deliberate and very distinctive method in the murderer's work, but no apparent reason. After the first two murders, local Whitechapel streetwalkers nicknamed the killer Leather Apron because there were rumors that the police were searching for a man who had been seen wearing a butcher's apron. The killer's more famous nickname derived from a series of anonymous, taunting letters sent to the police, the media, and local vigilance committees. One of them read, "I am down on whores and shan't quit ripping them till I get buckled." All were signed, "Jack the Ripper." The first was received by the Central News Agency on September 28, 1888, just two days before the murders of Elizabeth Stride and Catharine Eddowes.

HISTORY

Commissioner Sir Charles Warren was head of the Metropolitan Police and the most senior officer in charge of the Ripper investigation. It was he who bore the brunt of the fear and panic. By the time of the third murder, the policemen assigned to patrol the streets of Whitechapel (including more than one hundred on plainclothes duty) almost outnumbered the public, yet the Ripper was still able to commit his lengthy butcheries undetected. What few records remain from the case suggest the hunt for the Ripper was neither efficient nor effective, and many of the detectives located the incompetence at the highest level—particularly Warren. The commissioner's main contribution to the search was to make a fool of himself when he let two bloodhounds chase him through Regent's Park (the dogs were being tested to see whether they could sniff out the Ripper). In their desperation to find the killer, Scotland Yard even turned to a spiritualist, clairvoyant Robert Lees (portrayed by Donald Sutherland in the film).

HOLLYWOOD

**Christopher Plummer as Holmes
and James Mason as Watson**

The first serious attempt to portray Arthur Conan Doyle's fictional detective on screen, *Sherlock Holmes* (1932), featured Clive Brook in the title role. In 1939, Basil Rathbone and Nigel Bruce starred in *The Hound of the Baskervilles*, which was quite faithful to Conan Doyle's original stories. During World War II, Universal updated the characters, producing a dozen amiable, morale-boosting movies in which Rathbone and the bumbling Bruce uncovered a Nazi spy ring (*Sherlock Holmes in Washington*), unmasked Lord Haw Haw (*Sherlock Holmes and the Voice of Terror*), and saved a stolen bombsight from falling into enemy hands (*Sherlock Holmes and the Secret Weapon*). In *The Seven-Per-Cent Solution* (1976), an attempt to deconstruct the Holmes myth, Watson (Robert Duvall) lures Holmes (Nicol Williamson) to the Vienna office of Sigmund Freud (Alan Arkin) in order to cure his persecution complex and cocaine addiction. In the comedy *Without a Clue* (1988), it is Watson (Ben Kingsley), not Holmes (Michael Caine), who is the sharp one.

The Theories

Because of the grisly nature of the murders, some theories about the identity of Jack the Ripper have presumed he was a member of the medical profession. Dr. Alexander Pedachenko was one of the first Ripper suspects, supposedly sent by the tsarist police either to embarrass their English counterparts or to discredit London's burgeoning anarchist movement. Then there was Dr. Stanley, a Harley Street surgeon and close friend of London coroner Cedric Saunders. According to this now-discredited theory, Dr. Stanley began his killing spree as an act of revenge against the prostitutes who gave his son syphilis (from which he later died). There was also speculation that the Ripper might be a woman, perhaps a midwife.

In fact, the brutal murders showed little evidence of medical knowledge—the mutilations merely demonstrated that the killer knew roughly where the vital organs were located. Other theories suggested that the murders were the work of a "sexual maniac," but at no time during any of the five inquests was sexual assault reported or even suggested.

When someone, presumed to be the Ripper, scrawled the phrase "The Juwes are the men that will not be blamed for nothing" in chalk on a wall near the spot where Catharine Eddowes was murdered, attention turned to Jewish suspects (perhaps the word *Jews* was misspelled because the murderer was a recent immigrant) and to the Freemasons (because the word *Juwes* is part of their initiation ritual). Speculation regarding the Freemasons increased when it was learned that Commissioner Warren, a known Freemason, had ordered the graffito erased. One hypothesis pinned the crimes on Charles Ludwig, a German hairdresser who had terrorized prostitutes in the past. Queen Victoria was much convinced by the idea that the Ripper was a foreign sailor. She even asked her home secretary whether foreign ships were being searched (they were).

The first suspect brought in for questioning after the first two murders was John Pizer, a Polish Jew who worked in the leather trade. He had alibis—including a policeman—for both nights and was soon released. The case notes of Sir Melville Macnaghten, a former head of the Criminal Investigation Department, suggest that there were three other prime suspects: a lawyer named Montague John Druitt, who was supposedly driven half insane by the failure of his practice (he committed suicide in December 1888); another Polish Jew named Kosminski, who ended up in a public asylum; and a homicidal Russian doctor referred to as Michael Ostrog (who is often identified as Pedachenko).

relief, he died in 1892, allegedly of influenza. His betrothed, Princess Mary, then married his younger brother, the duke of York, who later became King George V.

The duke of Clarence may have been delinquent, even demented, but the evidence against his being Jack the Ripper is overwhelming, not least because he was miles away from London when some of the murders were committed. Nevertheless, in 1976 Stephen Knight wrote a book infelicitously titled *Jack the Ripper: The Final Solution*, which offered an alternative and more plausible version of the Clarence story. Knight postulated that the killings were a series of ritual executions carried out to protect the prince of Wales's eldest son, and thereby the monarchy itself, from exposure to a public scandal. The plot was supposedly conceived and discharged under the direction of the secret society of Freemasons, some of whose members held high positions in both the police force and the British government.

According to Knight's book, Jack the Ripper was really three people: royal physician Sir William Gull, painter Walter Richard Sickert, and a coachman, John Netley. Among them, they sought to deal with a serious problem. In addition to his other misdoings and misdemeanors, Prince Eddy (as the duke of Clarence was known) had clandestinely married a Catholic commoner named Annie Crook and by her had fathered a daughter. Soon after, Annie Crook was incarcerated in an asylum, from which she was never to emerge. Meanwhile, her child was left in the care of Mary Kelly (a friend and a witness to the wedding), who placed it in a convent.

The book contends that when news of these events reached the government and the royal household, certain figures (most of them Freemasons) decided that peremptory action should be taken. In order to avoid the risk of blackmail, Mary Kelly had to be silenced, and so must other street women to whom she had confided her secret. Hence the Masonic conspiracy to make the grotesque Ripper murders look like the work of a madman. Meanwhile, Annie Crook's daughter survived, protected by Walter Sickert, who in his turn fathered a child by her. It was this Joseph Sickert, claiming to be the grandson of the duke of Clarence, who provided Stephen Knight with most of his information.

But what, meanwhile, of Sherlock Holmes? Inevitably, as the renown of Sir Arthur Conan Doyle's fictional sleuth grew, there were those who sought to connect the world's most famous serialized detective with the world's most famous serial killer. Some have argued that Holmes solved the crime but the perpetrator was so famous that the matter was hushed up. Some have argued that Holmes caught the criminal and executed the killer himself. Some have even dared to suggest that Holmes himself was the Ripper. After all, he had a considerable knowledge of anatomy, he was a master of disguise, he was clever enough to avoid capture, he was vain enough to taunt the police, and he was a self-confessed misogynist.

Murder by Decree, released a mere three years after Knight's book, takes his version of the Ripper murders virtually unaltered but gives Sherlock Holmes (Christopher Plummer) the responsibility and the credit for solving them. More than in any of the original Conan Doyle stories, Holmes is on the side of the underdog and in a crusading mood against the British ruling establishment. Director Bob Clark's depiction of 1880s London is no comfortable, escapist piece of gaslit Victorian nostalgia. The poverty of the East End and the barbarity of the murders are accurately and horrifyingly conveyed. The men in high places are depicted as paranoid, irresponsible monsters. At the heart of the world's greatest empire is corruption and covering-up.

However, for all the power and integrity of the film, *Murder by Decree* takes too many liberties with late nineteenth-century London. Burlington House becomes the Royal Opera in Covent Garden, the Royal Hospital at Greenwich is transported to the very center of the city, and Tower Bridge is in existence several years before it was actually completed. And the underlying concern of the governing class for the safety and security of the throne seems overdone. To be sure, the monarchy had been unpopular during the 1870s, but only a year before the Ripper murders Queen Victoria celebrated her Golden Jubilee and was rapturously received in the streets of London.

Indeed, when Knight's book first appeared, this was one of the original criticisms leveled at it. The fact that Annie Crook was not done away with also seemed rather curious (an omission that the film takes pains to rectify). But there was worse to come. In 1978, Joseph Sickert admitted, "It was a hoax. I made it all up." By then, *Murder by Decree* was already in production. The Holmes-and-Watson element in the film is, of course, pure fiction. The Sickert-based story is at best impure fantasy. The Ripper alone was real. But who was the Ripper? And was he alone? We do not know. And, notwithstanding *Murder by Decree*, it seems highly unlikely we ever will.

1880s London

Crime was rampant in the East End during the 1880s. Whitechapel, in particular, was a rat's nest. Gangs from outside London—from Nichol and Hoxton—raided the dimly lit district, terrorizing streetwalkers, mugging passersby, and demanding protection money from shopkeepers. Most of Whitechapel's prostitutes, including the Ripper's victims, were far from the glamorous street urchins depicted by Hollywood. Rather, they were squalid paupers, gap-toothed fifty-year-olds who sought solace in cheap gin. (The twenty-four-year-old Mary Kelly was an exception.) Venereal disease was almost as widespread as the poverty in Whitechapel's overcrowded slums. In London alone, it was estimated that 1,500,000 fresh cases of syphilis were reported every twelve months.

Later...

The failure to apprehend Jack the Ripper nearly brought the Metropolitan Police to its knees. Sir Charles Warren was forced to resign as commissioner, and the botched operation led to a complete review of criminal-investigation techniques. Thanks to the skillful and diligent work of Warren's successor, James Monro, the Met's reputation survived the decade. Scotland Yard never issued an official statement about the Ripper investigation, and so many documents have been lost over the years that it is difficult to shed any new light on the murders. The Ripper investigation continued long after the November 9 murder of the final victim, Mary Kelly. Extra police were still assigned to patrol Whitechapel as late as July 1889.

Background Reading

W. J. Fishman, *East End 1888: A Year in a London Borough Among the Labouring Poor* (Duckworth, 1988)

Stephen Knight, *Jack the Ripper: The Final Solution* (Harrap, 1976)

Philip Weller, *The Life and Times of Sherlock Holmes* (Bracken, 1992)

1979/GB/Color
DIRECTOR: Bob Clark; **PRODUCER:** Rene Dupont, Bob Clark; **SCREENPLAY:** John Hopkins; **STUDIO:** Avco Embassy; **VIDEO:** Embassy; **RUNNING TIME:** 121 min.

DAVID CANNADINE

FREUD

Peter Gay

CAST

Sigmund Freud   *(Montgomery Clift)*
Cecily   *(Susannah York)*
Josef Breuer   *(Larry Parks)*

THE IDEA OF MAKING A FILM ABOUT Sigmund Freud (1856–1939), the legendary founder of psychoanalysis, is not immediately attractive. After all, until the Nazis' absorption of Austria in March 1938 forced the elderly Freud from his home into exile in England—he was almost eighty-two then and very sick—nothing much happened to him. He was a Jewish doctor who overcame the distinct disadvantages that being a Jew in Vienna entailed. However, there were other doctors who could say the same. And yet Freud changed the world, changed it in very internal ways: by brooding about his dreams and his slips and his father's death; by putting his neurotic patients on the couch and listening to them in concentrated silence; by lecturing and writing about his cases; by fighting—no other word will do—against the medical, and notably the psychiatric, establishment.

It is great drama, but a closet drama, in which most of the action takes place within the mind. The question is how to translate this action into a viable script that would produce a film from which audiences would not flee. One can appreciate the difficulty of this assignment by reading the two scripts that Jean-Paul Sartre wrote at John Huston's request in the late 1950s: Sartre took considerable liberties. To give but one example, he takes Freud's most controversial case, commonly known as "Dora," sets it in 1892, and has Freud massaging the back of his almost completely naked analysand. The historian, however, will note that the real Dora spent some eleven weeks as Freud's patient late in 1900, when he had not been doing any sort of massage for years. Furthermore, in Freud's published account of 1905 it is perfectly clear that he never laid a hand on Dora. Indeed, even in 1892 Freud never had his patients undress and never massaged anything but their foreheads. A pretty analysand who wears nothing but her stockings may capture a certain attention in the movie house; her scanty attire may even hint at an erotic undercurrent in Freud's treatment of Dora, for which there is some warrant. Yet the scene represents the triumph of dramatic license over historical truth.

Huston liked Sartre's screenplay but could not agree with the esteemed author on cuts and changes; Sartre's second attempt, designed to be shorter, was actually longer, and in the end Huston turned to reliable word merchants Charles Kaufman and Wolfgang Reinhardt to repair Sartre's work. The result appeared in 1962, first plainly called *Freud* and soon thereafter (in an attempt to cash in on Freud's reputation as the sex doctor) *Freud: The Secret Passion*.

A clinical lecture by Jean-Martin Charcot

Hysteria

The ailments known together as hysteria had been diagnosed, under one name or another, many centuries before Freud. In the nineteenth century, however, they secured particular attention among medical researchers. Some physicians broadened the meaning of *hysteria* beyond all recognition, but in general parlance the term meant excessive response to stimuli and paralysis inexplicable by physiological causes.

Contrary to a widespread belief, physicians from the seventeenth century on were confident that men could be as hysterical as women. When Freud went to Paris in the fall of 1885 to work for several months with the celebrated neurologist Jean-Martin Charcot, he saw this idea amply confirmed.

HISTORY

Sigmund Freud was born Sigismund Schlomo Freud on May 6, 1856, to an impecunious Jewish cloth merchant, Jacob Freud, and his third wife, Amalia Nathanson Freud, at Freiberg in Moravia. When he was four, Freud moved with his family to Vienna and soon proved himself an immensely gifted pupil with as great a future as a Jew in Vienna might hope for. He entered the University of Vienna in 1873, at first studying humanistic subjects but soon turning to medicine. It was a fortunate choice: His professors, nearly all of them imports from Germany, were at the top of their profession and worked within a tough-minded scientific universe that Freud found most congenial. He did some notable empirical research in biology, which confirmed his positivist inclinations—the diligent search for evidence and the distrust of grandiose philosophical theories.

HOLLYWOOD

Along with Marlon Brando and James Dean, Montgomery Clift epitomized the new breed of brooding young stars whose naturalistic acting style and nonconformist behavior greatly influenced an entire generation of filmgoers. When Hollywood first approached Clift in 1941, the stage-trained and classically handsome actor flatly refused to sign a seven-year contract with MGM. Several years later, though, he accepted Howard Hawks's offer to star opposite John Wayne in *Red River* (1948). With his faint air of sexual ambiguity, Clift demonstrated a combination of sensitivity and sensuality rarely, if ever, seen before. He also excelled at playing sensitive loners and idealists, imbuing these characters with a jittery, contemporary psychological edge. According to director John Huston, who had severe difficulties with his tormented star, "the combination of drugs, drink, and being homosexual was a soup that was too much for him." Clift died of a heart attack in 1966 at the age of forty-five.

Freud's couch

The Origins of Psychoanalysis

Psychoanalysis was not a thunderbolt but an evolution. Freud did not coin that name until 1896, although he had been inching toward it for years. After going into private practice in 1882, he began to specialize in the treatment of what were plainly mental problems. When he started, there was, in that vast area, only vagueness in nomenclature and confusion about treatment. *Neurasthenia*, the favorite term of the day, could mean almost anything. But Freud brought a measure of clarity into the picture and developed sweeping theories about the causes of what he was calling "neuroses."

From the early 1890s, he began to write down his dreams and learn from his patients. In 1895, he published—with his older, well-to-do, and munificent friend, Dr. Josef Breuer—the first collection of case histories, all of them women, all of them hysterics. Earlier, Breuer had told Freud about the strange case of Anna O. This, as Freud would later say, was the first case of psychoanalysis. Breuer—baffled by his patient's waxing and waning paralyses, her inability to speak her native language, and other peculiar symptoms—introduced (with the active collaboration of his highly intelligent patient) what he called the "talking cure." Breuer got Anna O., mainly through hypnosis, to recall events she had done her utmost to banish from her mind. In this way, according to Breuer's account, he managed to free her of her symptoms, one by one. Although the case report Breuer published in 1895 (in *Studies in Hysteria* with Freud) was far too sanguine—Anna O. still needed much further treatment—it nevertheless set the stage for the development of psychoanalytic techniques.

Sartre's successors discovered three ways to make the tragicomedy of Freud's heroic years filmworthy: First, they depict Freud thinking to himself as he stalks around Vienna at night, in top hat and overcoat, almost desperately trying to resolve the contradictions in the theories he is evolving. They show him thinking out loud at home, pacing the room as he speaks before, rather than to, his wife, who (though jealous of Freud's rich and good-looking patients and put off by his preoccupation with obscene topics) leaves no doubt that she believes in him. Freud's nightmares, as he stumbles on the terrible truths of human nature, belong to this display of the intrepid searcher into the abyss of love and aggression. This technique of dramatizing historic thought processes led Huston to have Montgomery Clift, who portrays Freud, do a great deal of staring. He stares as he watches the great Jean-Martin Charcot in Paris dissolve and create hysterical symptoms in a few minutes, and he stares as he watches the most prominent analysand in the film, a lovely young woman partly invented by the screenwriters and partly pulled together from some of Freud's cases, tentatively move her legs for the first time in years.

Second, the screenwriters make use of the open conflict between Freud and the Vienna medical establishment by drawing on, and shamelessly exaggerating, its response to two of Freud's lectures, showing the physicians shouting, jumping to their feet, and ostentatiously leaving the auditorium. Not even Freud, at once daring in the face of opposition and just a bit inclined to feel sorry for himself, ever reported anything like this brutal, downright physical rejection of his provocative assertions that all neuroses are sexual in origin and that sexual feelings begin not in puberty but in early childhood.

Obviously, though, the third (and least fallible) way to show Freud working out the great mysteries of human neuroses—and, for that matter, the even greater mysteries of normal human behavior—is to show him treating his patients, and these encounters take up a good deal of *Freud*. Evocative as these vignettes are, as cleverly as they allow Freud to make one discovery after another about analytic technique and the mind at work, they also become the source of much confusion. They leave the uninformed viewer with all sorts of incorrect notions about the evolution of psychoanalysis from the late 1880s to the late 1890s, and the better-informed one racing for a reliable biography of Freud to make sure he remembers the history correctly.

It is not pedantry to object to the inaccuracies that Huston and his crew have introduced into their history of psychoanalysis; rather, it is an attempt to warn audiences that what they are seeing is well-meaning pseudo-history. A few instances may give the sense of the wreck that the makers of *Freud* have left behind. Anna O., the founding patient of psychoanalysis, was (as the film correctly notes) the patient of Josef Breuer, Freud's generous friend and patron. She may claim priority among psychoanalytic patients because it was with her, between 1880 and 1882, that

Breuer used hypnosis to reach the sources of her symptoms and discovered that when she talked out the precipitating moments, these symptoms would disappear. She is important also because Breuer reported this case to Freud in detail and, at Freud's request, often. However, contrary to the representation in *Freud*, Freud never treated her, let alone met her.

Nor did Freud ever pursue—in the interest of psychoanalysis or otherwise—a female analysand, as the film depicts him doing with the character Cecily, brazenly following her into town at night. According to the film, Freud hypnotizes Cecily to get to the root of her traumatic experiences, during a period that must be the end of the nineteenth century; he does so after his father's death, which occurred in 1896. However, once Freud discovered the value of sitting behind his patients he proceeded to give up hypnosis, and in real life he had done both years earlier.

Yet again, when the film has Freud discover what he calls the Oedipus complex (a term, incidentally, he didn't employ until years later) it makes him feel horrendously guilty and ready to abandon his enterprise because it reveals his latent hatred of his own father. In reality, there is no evidence that Freud's oedipal theory in any way depressed him. On the contrary, he was pleased to note that every man has been a little Oedipus at some time in his life.

What *Freud* does relatively well is depict a brilliant man's search— even though his discoveries, like Charcot's treatments of hysterics, come a bit too easily and too casually. However, for anyone eager to establish a useful timetable of early psychoanalysis, a good biography remains indispensable.

Background Reading

Peter Gay, *Freud: A Life for Our Times* (Norton, 1988)
Ernest Jones, *The Life and Work of Sigmund Freud* (Basic Books, 1953–57)

1962/USA/B&W
DIRECTOR: John Huston; PRODUCER: Wolfgang Reinhardt; SCREENPLAY: Charles Kaufman, Wolfgang Reinhardt; STUDIO: Universal; VIDEO: none; RUNNING TIME: 140 min.

Dora

Among the controversial case histories that Freud was to publish, "Fragment of an Analysis of a Case of Hysteria," known popularly as "Dora," remains the most disputed. Dora, an attractive young hysteric, was in treatment with Freud toward the end of 1900; she broke off the analysis, still far from complete, eleven weeks later. Freud's daring interpretation of his patient's communications, his bullying, and his lack of sensitivity to Dora's pressing psychological needs have long aroused criticism—and not from feminists alone. Freud had an inkling of his failure and did not publish the case until 1905. Then, bravely, he published the case anyway, taking it as an instance of having failed to deal with what he called the patient's "transference"—the bestowal of feelings onto the analyst, both amorous and hostile, that are really intended for others. Thus Freud turned defeat into a technical advance.

Freud, ca. 1930

Later...

Psychoanalysis had been the victim of its own success. In the 1950s, it seemed not only a fashionable mind cure but also the solution to political and social problems. This overestimation necessarily had to give way and illusion turned into disillusionment. In addition, advances in the neurological study of the brain and the emergence of mood-altering medications raised serious questions about the future place of analysis in mental healing. But the obituaries of psychoanalysis have all proved premature; among young physicians, interest in analysis seems to be growing once more, and while the prospects remain clouded, it seems probable that the psychotherapy of the next decades will be a combination of medication and the "talking cure." And even if the psychoanalytic session disappears, the contribution that Freud's science can make to an understanding of the mind will likely remain indispensable.

YOUNG WINSTON

William Manchester

CAST

Winston Churchill *(Simon Ward)*
Lady Jennie Churchill *(Anne Bancroft)*
Lord Randolph Churchill *(Robert Shaw)*

**Randolph Henry
Spencer Churchill**

Tory Democracy

Churchill liked to quote his father's championship of "Tory democracy." Actually, Randolph scorned democracy; his explanation of this odd phrase was that England's upper and lower classes should unite in "frank immorality" against the "greasy hypocrites" of the middle class. In a true democracy, he would never have been elected to Parliament. In today's England successful candidates must please constituencies of about fifty thousand people; back then, there were only 1,071 qualified voters in the Churchill family borough, of whom just 565 voted for him. The upper class controlled both houses of Parliament; three out of every four members of the Commons were related in some way to Lords sitting in the upper house.

YOUNG WINSTON RAISES THE QUESTION OF whether any film, however spectacular its story or distinguished its makers, should try to meet the standards of the cinematographic art and the exacting historian. If we're to judge by this example, the answer is that those who try to do both may end in producing neither.

Undeniably, Winston Churchill's early life was dramatic. Although the grandson of a duke, he nevertheless endured an unhappy childhood. When he reached young manhood his goals, then as later, were political, and he believed the quickest way to attain them was to achieve military fame. He did it and won a seat in the House of Commons.

The film opens on V-E Day, the Prime Minister's finest hour, then takes us back to the early 1880s. We see Winston being birched by a cruel master and baffled in examinations while at the same time admiring his mother's excursions into London society and his father's masterful performances in Parliament. Randolph takes a kindly interest in his son's future but then, tormented by illness, turns on the boy.

The father dies. The son, commissioned at Sandhurst, answers the call of imperial trumpets in India, the Sudan, and South Africa. Director Richard Attenborough uses all the colorful paraphernalia of the Victorian army in scenes supported by the strains of "The British Grenadiers" and "Soldiers of the Queen." Our hero doubles as a war correspondent, and his dispatches offend Lord Kitchener; nevertheless, when Kitchener and his army avenge Chinese Gordon at Omdurman, Churchill is there, galloping forward and swinging his saber in history's last great calvary charge.

He runs for Parliament and loses. Next, we see him embroiled in the Boer War. Captured, he manages a sensational escape across three hundred miles of enemy territory. The press acclaims him, he wins a second election to the House of Commons, and delivers his maiden speech.

All this is more or less true, although some liberties have been taken. The maiden speech is completely bogus, and he could not have glimpsed his future wife in the Stranger's Gallery, as the film depicts, because he did not meet her until three years later. There's also a scene in which a journalist asks Lady Churchill about Randolph's syphilis, yet it's inconceivable that a reporter in the 1890s would have quizzed the wife of a cabinet minister about her husband's VD. Nevertheless, errors of commission are few.

Errors of omission, on the other hand, are legion. Screenwriter Carl Foreman relied almost entirely on a single source—Winston's charming

HISTORY

Winston Churchill after his graduation
from Sandhurst

Churchill once wrote an article for *Pall Mall Magazine* about one of his typical days at Sandhurst, the British equivalent of West Point. Reveille sounded at 6:00 A.M., and forty-five minutes later the study halls were filled with cadets in immaculate blue uniforms, "deep in the wiles of tactics or the eccentricities of fortifications." Breakfast was served at 8:00 A.M. Morning parade came an hour later, followed by gymnastics, the formation of skirmishers beyond the cricket pavilion, bayonet practice, lectures on outposts and attacking enemy positions, and lunch. Riding school was held in the early afternoon and was mandatory, even for the infantry cadets; those who lacked mounts, like Winston, hired "screws" at the local livery stables. Sports began at 4:00 P.M. Tea and study preceded mess, the school's only formal meal. Evenings were devoted to reading, talking, playing whist and billiards, and, sometimes, watching boxing matches between cadets.

HOLLYWOOD

Simon Ward on the set of *Young Winston*

After Winston Churchill saw *The Guns of Navarone* (1961) for the first time, he knew that he had found the right man to adapt and produce a film about his own early life. Churchill personally offered *Guns of Navarone* producer Carl Foreman the rights to his 1930 memoir, *My Early Life*, but Foreman was busy at the time and could not take on the project right away; Churchill died in 1965 before the film could be shot. *Young Winston* was finally completed in 1972. It featured a script by Foreman and direction by Richard Attenborough, often considered the foremost practitioner of the historical epic.

WILLIAM MANCHESTER

British soldiers during the Boer War

The Great Escape

It is widely known that Winston Churchill rocketed to fame and was first elected to Parliament after his spectacular breakout from a Boer prisoner-of-war camp. The film makes much of this heroic feat. Less understood are the ludicrous circumstances of his capture.

In November 1899, the Ladysmith province of South Africa was invaded by Boers. Among the British trapped inside the province was a young Winston Churchill, formerly a cavalry officer but now a civilian, a war correspondent for the *Morning Post.* He was impatient to see action, and when invited to ride aboard an armored train patroling the front, he immediately accepted.

That was unwise. The train was a monstrosity, a tribute to the dense military mind of one Col. C.J. Long. It consisted of a locomotive and three cars, all shielded by great slabs of blue-gray iron. Slits permitted the soldiers to fire out. No mounted troops accompanied them because, Long claimed, the train was invulnerable.

In fact, it was a pushover. Moments after the Transvaaler guerrillas saw the train steam past, they threw a few rocks on the tracks, just around the bend. When the lumbering engine's whistle tooted on the return trip, the Boers opened fire, provoking the engineer to pour on steam. When the train rounded the curve, it hit the rocks and was derailed, ending, among other things, the inventive colonel's career.

Instinctively, Winston took charge, calling for volunteers to right the cars. He was in the midst of this highly partisan activity when he found himself staring into the muzzles of two Boer Mauser rifles.

Belatedly, and disingenuously, he argued that as a newspaper correspondent he was exempt from arrest. His captors would have none of this; they had been watching him. Later, however, when their commandant-general learned that their prisoner was the son of an English lord, he decided to let him go. Then came an ironic twist: Before the order for Winston's release could reach his POW camp, he was over the wire and on his way to freedom. Had the edict arrived twenty-four hours earlier, instant fame would have eluded him. He would have had to look for another way to reach the House of Commons. Of course, being Churchill, he would have found one.

1930 memoir, *My Early Life*, published in the United States under the title *A Roving Commission.* The great man's recollections are invaluable, of course, but they present the past as he remembered it, which is not always as it actually was.

We have a fairly clear idea of what it was, in part because Churchill himself left behind an extraordinary trail of documents—his family seems to have saved everything of his except the tissue paper in the loo. Most of these records may be found in the eight-volume *Official Biography* and its fourteen *Companion Volumes*, comprising 20,827 pages. We can also pore over contemporaneous sources: newspapers, diaries, letters, autobiographies, and some 217 collections of private papers now preserved in archives as various as the National Library of Scotland and the University of Texas Library.

The past they reveal is both deeper and darker than Foreman's valentine would have us believe. To understand young Winston's early life one must grasp the real character of his parents. In his eyes, Lord Randolph Churchill was and would always be a great man. In fact, Randolph was a shallow demagogue whose star briefly crossed England's political firmament in the mid-1880s and then, owing to his extraordinarily bad judgment, plunged out of sight.

Winston reached the age of awareness at the peak of his father's parliamentary fame and became his most ardent champion, writing adoring letters and fighting boys who criticized him. Randolph ignored his son. He couldn't remember whether he had sent Winston to Eton or Harrow; he didn't even remember his son's age. Once he kept an appointment just across the street from one of Winston's schools and didn't bother to look in on him. After his fall from power, an embittered Randolph actually came to hate his son.

Winston's American-born mother was cut from similar cloth. Lady Randolph Churchill—Jennie—was a beautiful, shallow, selfish, diamond-studded panther of a woman. Later, when Winston grew to manhood, she found him "interesting," as she put it, but she didn't like children. Instead, she enjoyed parties, social intrigue, and romantic adventures. The novelist George Moore estimated that Jennie had slept with some two hundred men. Doubtless that was an exaggeration, but unquestionably she was generous with her favors. The names of nineteen of her lovers, including the Prince of Wales, later Edward VII, have survived. Winston knew some of them and at least one was kinder to him, and had more time for him, than his own father.

Beginning when he was seven, the boy wrote his mother often, sometimes daily. Most of his pitiful letters, begging for attention, went unanswered. Other boys' parents visited them on special days; his own were absent. He wasn't permitted to come home for Christmas because the house was full of guests. When vacation time arrived, Jennie sent him to France, promising him a week at home when he returned and then breaking the promise.

YOUNG WINSTON

Ignored, Winston blamed himself. Needing outlets for his own welling adoration, he enshrined his parents, creating images of them as he wished they were, and the less he saw of them, the easier the transformation became. His resentment had to be directed elsewhere. Thus he became a difficult child and a wretched student. In 1895, his father's death emancipated him, but all his life he would be plagued by spells of depression. "Black Dog," he called them. Love, he had come to believe, was something that had to be earned, and he sought it in achievement, becoming a creature of ambition and raw energy.

In Foreman's tale, parental neglect is mentioned only briefly. Jennie appears as a long-suffering woman with a tremulous, vacuous smile; at times, she looks embalmed. Toward the end of the film she has the chutzpa to deplore Lloyd George's "annoying way of looking at women." One would never suspect that she herself had been a crotch-watcher since puberty.

Entire dimensions of Winston are omitted as well. In fact, one is tempted to conclude that presenting such finite characters is almost an imperative of the screen. How, if Winston was such a miserable scholar, did he become so learned? The answer—that he became an autodidact, studying through the long, sweltering siestas in India—is not here. And what of his emerging literary genius? He became, after all, a Nobel Laureate. At one point we are told, without any preparation, that he has had a book published. The subject is then dropped.

Sterile, devoid of genuine conflict, tacitly endorsing nineteenth-century imperialism, the movie rolls along like a well-made Pinero play, occasionally hitting us over the head with thudding reminders of the towering figure our hero will someday become, all unaccompanied by any explanation of why. To be sure, *Young Winston* avoids being reverential or servile. It's entertaining, relaxing, and inoffensive—and perhaps we should settle for that. But given the tale and the talent, one had hoped for far more.

Background Reading

William Manchester, *The Last Lion—Winston Spencer Churchill 1874–1932: Visions of Glory* (Little, Brown, 1983)

1972/GB/Color
DIRECTOR: Richard Attenborough; **PRODUCER:** Carl Foreman; **SCREENPLAY:** Carl Foreman; **STUDIO:** Columbia; **VIDEO:** Columbia Tristar; **RUNNING TIME:** 145 min.

Salisbury's Stakes

William Gladstone

William Gladstone's Liberals were in power when Randolph Churchill rose to prominence as an energetic parliamentary tactician and a colorful Tory gadfly, baiting the Grand Old Man mercilessly while exploiting the issue of Home Rule for Ireland. Churchill played a conspicuous role in the June 1886 Tory landslide—newspapers called him Gladstone's "great adversary"—and this gave him inflated ideas. He believed he could oust the new Prime Minister, Lord Salisbury, and succeed him.

Salisbury, well aware of this, named his thirty-seven-year-old challenger Chancellor of the Exchequer. The Prime Minister was just giving him rope, with which Randolph hanged himself in six months. He resigned from the cabinet, hoping to set off a Tory revolt. Salisbury accepted the resignation, there was no revolt, and Randolph's political career was over.

Jennie Churchill

Later...

Randolph Churchill died of syphilis in 1895. Jennie lived until 1921, remarried twice, and even acted in a movie. In 1910, Winston and fellow liberal firebrand Lloyd George laid the foundation for England's welfare state; Lloyd George then went on to become Britain's World War I Prime Minister. Before his own World War II premiership, Churchill held every cabinet post except foreign secretary. In the end, he saw Hitler defeated, but the Empire he loved was forever lost. He died in 1965 and was buried next to his parents in Bladon Churchyard, less than a mile from his Blenheim Palace birthplace. The entire nation, led by the Queen, mourned.

HESTER STREET

Joyce Antler

CAST

Gitl   *(Carol Kane)*
Jake   *(Steven Keats)*
Bernstein   *(Mel Howard)*
Mamie   *(Dorrie Kavanaugh)*

PRODUCED INDEPENDENTLY ON A shoestring budget, Joan Micklin Silver's 1975 film, *Hester Street*, is scrupulously adapted from an 1896 story by the influential editor and novelist Abraham Cahan. While the film lacks the biting irony of Cahan's tale, Silver, who both wrote and directed the movie, has shown unusual sensitivity to the nuances of immigrant life portrayed in the story.

Distributed by Silver's husband, Raphael, after Hollywood turned it down, *Hester Street* was filmed mostly on Morton Street in Greenwich Village (the real Lower East Side appeared too modern). Shot in black and white and using much subtitled Yiddish, the film derives its authenticity as much from the bemused tone it takes toward its characters' antics as from its setting and period look. As opposed to most Hollywood depictions of the immigrant experience, *Hester Street* avoids sentimentalizing either the *shtetls* of the Old World or the urban ghettos of the New.

Focusing on love and marriage as inevitable casualties of the immigrant struggle to adapt to modernity, *Hester Street* provides an unusual glimpse into the traumas of Jewish acculturation in turn-of-the-century New York. Jake, formerly Yekl, the film's protagonist, has not only renamed himself since his arrival in the United States three years earlier but also cast aside all traces of his former religious beliefs. His jaunty mustache, sporty cap, and dapper clothes belie the fact that he is only a sweatshop tailor; likewise, his flirtation with Mamie, a stylish dance-hall girl with whom he is smitten, belies the fact that he already has a wife, Gitl, in the Old Country. Though he accepts Gitl when she arrives unexpectedly with their young son, Yossele, Jake fears that their presence will impede his own Americanization.

The contrast between Mamie and Gitl, who thinks Mamie must be "nobility" because she wears an elaborate feathered hat and an expensive dress, is starkly drawn. "Stop being a greenhorn," Jake tells Gitl. "In America, anyone can dress like that." Focusing his anger on Gitl's dowdy appearance, Jake insists that she remove her wig (or *sheitel*—which Orthodox married women wore for reasons of modesty) and dress like an "edicated" American woman. Initially resistant, Gitl soon dispenses with the wig, then the kerchief that replaces it. Jake resists her attempt to please him, spitting out that she looks like a "wet cat" in her own hair. In his eyes, Gitl will always be a greenhorn.

With Mamie's years of hard-earned savings offered as a settlement, Gitl reluctantly agrees to a divorce. In the film's final scene, Mamie, in bridal veil and dress, strolls with Jake to City Hall. Now penurious, she

Immigration

From 1880 to 1920, more than two million eastern European Jews—about one-third of the entire Jewish population there—immigrated to the United States. This mass migration, following smaller migrations of German and central European Jews during the mid-nineteenth century, was sparked by a series of violent pogroms and the passage of laws restricting Jewish employment, education, and settlement after the 1881 assassination of Russian tsar Alexander II. In 1880, the Jewish population of the United States, about 250,000, constituted three percent of world Jewry. By 1924, when Congress passed legislation drastically restricting immigration from eastern Europe, the number of Jews in the United States had swelled to four million, or almost twenty-five percent of the world's Jewish population.

HISTORY

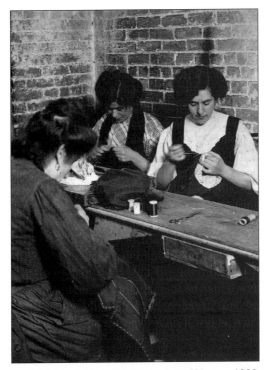

Jewish women on the Lower East Side, ca. 1900

Hester Street's use of clothing as an expression of the immigrant struggle to acculturate is well founded. In *The Promised Land*, a classic tale of assimilation, Mary Antin recalls her father's insistence that her Orthodox mother discard her *sheitel*, which she does reluctantly. A measure of devoutness in the Old World, the *sheitel* represented backwardness and foreignness in America. Getting rid of it indicated that an immigrant woman was on her way to becoming an American; shaving one's beard and *payess* (earlocks) meant the same for a man. In a telling moment in *Hester Street*, Jake meets Gitl on Ellis Island. The first thing he notices about her is her voluminous wig, which repulses him; the first thing she sees, with alarm, is that he has shaved his beard. Like language, religious custom, and the practice of love and leisure, costume reflects a fundamental aspect of identity.

HOLLYWOOD

Carol Kane as Gitl

Writer/director Joan Micklin Silver chose the topic of immigration because she wanted to make a movie "that would count" for her family. Hollywood studios, which did not welcome her efforts, advised Silver that the best she could hope for in the way of distribution was the synagogue circuit. However, after *Hester Street* found an enthusiastic audience at Cannes, the Silvers were able to place the film in several European markets. The profits from these foreign sales financed the first New York City screenings of the film, and finally *Hester Street* came home.

The Dance Halls

Jake's infatuation with Mamie and the glittering modern world of the dance hall rings true. At the turn of the century, the Lower East Side was filled with dance halls. As commercialized expressions of the new American notions of leisure, dance halls were frequented most often by native-born citizens and assimilated immigrants. They offered unmarried working-class men and women the opportunity to socialize outside family-sanctioned gatherings, and they reflected yet another aspect of many young immigrants' desire to cast aside their pasts and become "real" Americans. As a single, independent working girl, the glamorous Mamie represents to Jake the enticing promise of New World liberation.

Jewish Marriage and Divorce

Unlike Jake and Mamie, who are to be married at City Hall in a civil ceremony, Jake and his first wife, Gitl, were undoubtedly married in the Old Country according to Orthodox Jewish custom. The traditional wedding ceremony takes place under a *chuppah* (canopy) and involves the reading of the *ketubah* (marriage contract), the recitation of several blessings, and the breaking of a glass placed under the bridegroom's foot—a symbolic reminder of the destruction of the Temple and, some say, of the fragility of all relationships. Should the marriage come apart, Jewish law dictates that the couple obtain a *get* (divorce) from a *Bet Din* (religious court). According to Jewish law, marriages and divorces are contracts entered into by mutual consent, yet only the husband may initiate a divorce, to which the wife must consent. A woman whose husband leaves her but refuses to divorce her is called an *agunah* ("anchored" woman) and is forbidden to remarry.

refuses to spend a nickel for carfare; her dream of establishing a dancing academy must be deferred. Gitl walks off with Bernstein, a pious scholar who had come to board with Jake and Gitl. She promises that Bernstein can continue his studies after they marry and start a grocery shop—with Mamie's money. In a tailored shirtwaist, her hair upswept in a stylish pompadour, Gitl is well on her way to becoming as much of an "uptown lady" as Mamie. She has "ausgreened" herself, as Mamie predicted.

Hester Street, its director has acknowledged, is a "little film." Its small scope—focusing on the lives of a few ordinary immigrants—parallels its small budget. Yet in portraying the relentless progress of assimilation and its destructive effects on family life, *Hester Street* provides an accurate historical template of the stresses of Americanization.

In spite of the much-heralded strength of the Jewish family, divorce and desertion were common among Jewish immigrants at the turn of the century. The Lower East Side, home of the Jewish ghetto ("Where are all the Gentiles?" a puzzled Gitl asks her husband. "Do they live in another place?"), registered one of the highest divorce rates in the city; desertion was so serious a problem that the *Jewish Daily Forward*, the paper Cahan edited, ran a regular feature entitled the "Gallery of Missing Men," which printed photographs of deserters and pleas that they contact their wives. By 1902, the number of desertions in New York City had become so alarming that the United Hebrew Charities established a department to deal with the problem; the department received thousands of applications for relief each year.

One of the chief causes of desertion and divorce was the fact that husbands and wives acculturated at different rates. Husbands often migrated first; many assimilated so rapidly that they felt estranged from spouses who came later. Since husbands, as breadwinners, usually experienced the family's first regular contacts with Americans, the acculturation gap was felt even by couples who migrated together. Like Gitl, wives often seemed perpetual "greenhorns" to their husbands, reminders of the traditional past that immigrant men sought to jettison. Even though the majority of husbands neither deserted nor divorced their wives, stresses engendered by the exigencies of acculturation profoundly affected immigrant marriage.

While most attention has been devoted to the generational conflicts that arose as a consequence of migration, the sphere of love and marriage—as *Hester Street* reveals—was thus also profoundly and disproportionately affected. "In America," Jake tells one of his dance-hall buddies at the start of the film, "they marry for love." Captivated by the ideology of romantic love and the more open expression of sexual desire in the New World, he imagines himself a "regular American fella," a "Yenkee," free to embrace the new American mores even at the cost of giving up his son, whom he loves, and Gitl.

Cahan's story, "Yekl," ends with Jake emerging from the house of the rabbi who has granted Gitl a religious divorce—or *get*—with the feeling that he is a "victim" who has suffered an "ignominious defeat" rather than a "conqueror." There is no parallel awakening in *Hester Street*; even though he has fallen down the economic ladder as Gitl has risen up it, Jake is apparently content to walk off with Mamie. Although the film shies away from presenting a typical "happy" Hollywood ending, Cahan's version, leaving Jake to confront a future that is "dark and impenetrable," is less upbeat.

Like Cahan's story, *Hester Street* succeeds in portraying the inexorable process of assimilation, while suggesting that it affects males and females differently. Refusing to blame women for progressing too rapidly (like Mamie) or too slowly (like Gitl), the film implies that these women will have a powerful hand in determining their families' American futures; in both the story and the film, it is Jake who is ultimately more bewildered than either Gitl or Mamie. In indicating the hardships experienced by women and their resiliency, as well as the deep strains assimilation posed to masculinity, *Hester Street* touches on a fundamental cultural challenge confronting immigrants.

Background Reading

Jules Chametzky, *From the Ghetto: The Fiction of Abraham Cahan* (University of Massachusetts Press, 1977)

Gerald Sorin, *A Time for Building: The Third Migration, 1880–1920* (Johns Hopkins University Press, 1992)

Sydney Stahl Weinberg, *The World of Our Mothers: The Lives of Jewish Immigrant Women* (University of North Carolina Press, 1988)

1975/USA/B&W
DIRECTOR: Joan Micklin Silver; PRODUCER: Raphael D. Silver; SCREENPLAY: Joan Micklin Silver; STUDIO: Midwest; VIDEO: Live; RUNNING TIME: 90 min.

Abraham Cahan

Born in 1860 in Vilna, Lithuania, Abraham Cahan was already a socialist when he arrived in the United States in 1882. Active in party politics, he helped organize the first garment workers unions, taught English in night schools, and wrote for several American newspapers. In 1897, he helped  found a Yiddish-language newspaper, the *Jewish Daily Forward* (*Forvarts*), which he edited from 1903 until his death in 1951. Dedicated both to propagating socialism and to helping Jews Americanize, the *Forvarts* became the most widely read Yiddish newspaper in the world—its lively news items, stories, and innovative *bintl brief* (bundle of letters) column being especially popular among immigrants. In addition to his many short stories, Cahan authored one of the first and most highly acclaimed immigrant novels written in English, *The Rise of David Levinsky* (1917). Chronicling an immigrant's rise to affluence, the novel—like "Yekl"—explores the emotional and cultural costs of assimilation.

Later...

During the peak years of mass immigration at the turn of the century, a quarter of a million Jews— almost seventy-five percent of New York City's Jewish population—lived on the Lower East Side, making it the most densely crowded area in Manhattan. In 1924, fewer than one-quarter of the city's Jews still lived there. In the meantime, immigrants and their families had flocked to new, largely Jewish neighborhoods in upper Manhattan, the Bronx, and especially Brooklyn. To many, the tree-lined avenues of Eastern Parkway and the Grand Concourse were the "Jewish suburbs."

This transplantation, which continued through the 1920s and 1930s, reflected the rise of American Jews, primarily of the second generation, to middle-class status. For those who could afford it, leaving the Lower East Side symbolized not just their relative prosperity but, even more important, their Americanization.

GALLIPOLI

Kenneth T. Jackson

CAST

Frank Dunne   *(Mel Gibson)*

Archie   *(Mark Lee)*

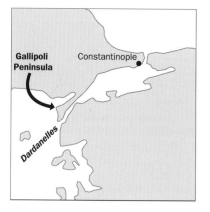

The Dardanelles

When the Great War began in August 1914, Turkey was ruled by a group of progressives known as the Young Turks, who had deposed the ruling sultan six years earlier and sought to modernize the nation. Initially, they kept Turkey neutral, but in late October 1914, the Young Turks ordered their fleet to attack Russian ports and shipping in the Black Sea. Russia, Britain, and France immediately declared war. First Lord of the Admiralty Winston Churchill persuaded the British government to attempt a naval bombardment of Constantinople and thus knock Turkey out of the war. On March 18, 1915, more than a dozen English and French warships attempted to force their way past Turkish defenses along the narrow Dardanelles. After three big ships were sunk, the attack was called off.

THE WINDING ROADS OF KING'S PARK, near the center of Perth in western Australia, are bordered by closely spaced gum trees. At the base of each is a small plaque with the name and unit of a World War I soldier, the date and place of his death, and the name of the person, usually a mother or wife, who planted the tree in his memory. The markers and trees are in good condition; those that have withered or weathered in the intervening seventy-five years have been replaced. The trees stretch as far as the eye can see, and this impressive commemoration is one among many in Australia because that thinly settled outpost of the British Empire suffered inordinately between 1914 and 1918. It sent three hundred thousand men overseas to fight for king and country. Almost sixty thousand of them never came home again and were buried with their comrades in far-off lands.

Although Australia suffered terrible losses on the Western Front, the nation's remembrance of the Great War has focused on Gallipoli—a barren, hilly, and generally godforsaken peninsula in Turkey. Even today, young Australians traveling around the world typically set aside one day for a bus ride and pilgrimage to the place known as ANZAC Cove (ANZAC being the acronym for Australian and New Zealand Army Corps), where row upon row of well-tended graves remind them of the sacrifice of their ancestors. April 25, the anniversary of the ANZAC landing in 1915, remains the country's most important national holiday. In short, Gallipoli is to Australia at least what Gettysburg is to the United States.

Directed by Peter Weir, the film *Gallipoli* concentrates on the ill-fated campaign of the same name. The plan for the attack was conceived by Winston Churchill, then the first lord of the Admiralty, as an easy way both to knock Turkey out of the war and to open the way to the Black Sea and Russia. His hope was that Royal Navy battleships could steam through the Dardanelles, point their massive guns at a vulnerable Istanbul, and quickly convince the Turks to abandon their German allies. Unfortunately for Whitehall, Turkish shore batteries on the Gallipoli peninsula and minefields in the Dardanelles prevented the passage of the British warships. So Churchill and his advisers decided to take Gallipoli by invasion and thus open the sea route to the Ottoman capital.

The invasion was a disaster from the start. The British landings at Cape Helles stalled a few miles from the tip of the peninsula, while the Australians and New Zealanders were even less fortunate. They landed at the wrong place and spent the next eight months clinging to a narrow

Australian soldiers at ANZAC Cove, 1915

Daily life in the Gallipoli trenches was every bit as oppressive as trench life on the Western Front—perhaps more so. A billowing gray dust swirled along the coast, choking the soldiers and coating their food, clothes, and skin. Water was scarce. Cape Helles was supplied by tankers carrying water from the Nile, seven hundred miles away. Summer temperatures soared well into the nineties and brought tarantulas, scorpions, and flies that fed on the unburied corpses in No Man's Land. The forces dug in on Gallipoli were further plagued by an outbreak of dysentery. Sir Ian Hamilton, the British commander of the invasion, was himself stricken with the disease: "It fills me with a desperate longing to lie down and do nothing but rest. This, I think, must be the reason the Greeks were ten long years in taking Troy."

HOLLYWOOD

Mel Gibson (left) and Mark Lee

The release of *Gallipoli* in 1981 marked the peak of the Australian film invasion, the so-called "uprising from down under." Previous Australian exports had included Weir's *Picnic at Hanging Rock* (1975) and *The Last Wave* (1978), as well as Bruce Beresford's *Breaker Morant* (1979). In *Gallipoli*, Weir used the tragic story of the failed campaign to explain Australia's isolationism and, perhaps, to support his country's burgeoning republican movement with its antimonarchist (and thus anti-British) manifesto. Weir's interest in moviemaking developed while on board a Greek ship bound for Britain. He discovered an unused closed-circuit TV camera and, together with several friends, created shows for the other passengers. On his return to Australia, he joined the Commonwealth Film Unit as an assistant cameraman before directing short movies and, finally, features.

Churchill with Kaiser Wilhelm II shortly before World War I

Churchill and Gallipoli

In September 1914, Winston Churchill, then first lord of the Admiralty, thought that Turkey, the perennial Sick Man of Europe, could be easily toppled. "A good army of fifty thousand and sea power; that's the end of the Turkish menace," he proclaimed. He hatched the plan for the naval attack on Constantinople, and when that failed he endorsed the amphibious invasion of Gallipoli. When the British and ANZAC armies were forced to settle into a deadly stalemate with the Turks, Churchill was removed from his post. Even years after the war, critics challenged him during speeches with shouts of "What about the Dardanelles?"

The Cost of War

Gallipoli gives the impression that the English shirked the fighting. One scene shows the Australians being swept by murderous machine-gun fire when a field telephone rings in an Australian dugout. The radioman calls out the news to his commander:

"Sir, the British are ashore at Suvla."
"Are they meeting heavy opposition?"
"None, sir. Apparently they're just sitting on the beach drinking cups of tea."

In fact, the British did their share of fighting at Gallipoli. Casualty figures are very inexact, but the British suffered twice as many deaths as the Australians and New Zealanders combined. The Lancashire town of Bury, with a 1914 population of fifty thousand, sent some seven thousand volunteers overseas during the first nine months of the war, most of them dispatched to Gallipoli. Of the thousand men of the town's First Battalion, which landed in April 1915, only forty-three remained on active service on Armistice Day 1918. The Gallipoli campaign resulted in three hundred thousand Turkish casualties and nearly as many on the Allied side.

beachhead under the guns of tenacious Turkish defenders. Moreover, they had to contend with a determined enemy commander, Mustafa Kemal, who later changed his name to Kemal Atatürk and became the father of modern Turkey.

Despite heroic thrusts and tragic losses on both sides, the stalemate continued through the spring and early summer of 1915. Finally, the British decided to make new landings closer to Istanbul at Suvla Bay in early August. To confuse the Turks and prevent them from moving in reinforcements, the British commander-in-chief ordered his Australian and New Zealander forces to launch a series of frontal assaults at ANZAC Cove.

None of these attacks was more suicidal than that of the Australian Tenth Light Horse Regiment. They were superb soldiers, but even under the best of circumstances their assignment was probably impossible. They had to charge uphill on foot (their horses were left behind in Egypt because of the steep Gallipoli terrain) across a narrow neck of land in the face of murderous Turkish machine-gun and rifle fire. Their only hope was that a ferocious artillery bombardment, lasting until exactly 4:30 P.M., would pin down the Turkish defenders in their trenches and foxholes until just before the Australians overwhelmed them.

Inexplicably, the barrage lifted at 4:23 P.M. In those seven minutes of quiet, the Turks scrambled back to their positions and set the sights of their weapons. On schedule, the first Australian wave came over the top at 4:30. The Turkish defenders calmly mowed them down. Three additional waves followed at two-minute intervals, with the same result. On each occasion, the Australians were slaughtered almost as soon as they left their trenches. More than ninety percent of them became casualties in the space of ten minutes. Theirs are the names below the trees in King's Park, and theirs are among the graves at Gallipoli.

By examining in detail this one incident (which played a relatively minor role in the vast global conflict), the film uses the devastating experiences of the Tenth Light Horse Regiment to highlight the awful human cost of war. An early scene shows the two stars, Mel Gibson and Mark Lee, in the Australian desert as they are making their way to a recruiting station. They encounter a prospector who inquires about their purpose. He doesn't know about the assassination of Archduke Ferdinand, the Kaiser, or the Rape of Belgium. When told of the war he remarks, "I knew a German once." What, he wonders, does war in Europe have to do with Australia? And why are these young men anxious to enlist? "Because if we don't stop the Germans there," the pair argue, "they will come over here." The prospector slowly looks around at the arid vastness and comments, "They are welcome to it."

Gallipoli shows how the promise of adventure and travel, combined with a burgeoning national pride, encouraged bored youth to enlist for what they expected would be a short and glorious war. Leaving by ship to the cheers of their countrymen, they crossed the Indian Ocean to the pyramids of Egypt, where they underwent final combat training (plus the obligatory visits to Egyptian brothels and lectures about the dangers of unprotected sex). The movie correctly portrays the boisterous behavior of the tanned, proud, and tough Australians, as well as their lack of military courtesy for arrogant British officers.

All too soon, the Tenth Light Horse Regiment is sent to Gallipoli and given its hopeless task. In the film's climactic scene, Gibson, who is temporarily serving as a messenger at the command post, is given the order to call off the attack. He races back with the news that would save his mates who wait in the trenches, fully aware that the first three assaults have been disasters. Conscious of their imminent death, they push letters, rings, and watches into the earth, leaving them behind for their mothers, wives, and girlfriends. Gibson arrives too late to stop the men from being ordered over the top, and most of the regiment is cut down instantly. Only Gibson's best friend, fueled by terror and heroism, is left to sprint through the murderous fire, proof that youth, courage, and beauty will ultimately prevail in the glory of war. Instead, he, too, is shredded, and the film ends.

> ## "I don't order you to attack; I order you to die."
>
> *Mustafa Kemal*

In the main, *Gallipoli* stays faithful to the historic record, but there are some glaring omissions: For example, the movie gives the impression that a British general stubbornly refused to call off the hopeless August attack. In fact, an Australian officer made the fateful decision. More seriously, the film fails to explain the purpose of the attack, how the campaign fit into the larger context of the war, or even the location of the battle. Nor does the viewer learn that the entire invasion force was withdrawn in December 1915, its mission a total failure. The film, however, does accurately depict the competition to enlist, the camaraderie in the ranks, and the soldiers' quiet courage in the face of death. It is superb in conveying the tragic futility of the Great War and thus ranks with *All Quiet on the Western Front* and *Paths of Glory* as one of the greatest anti-war movies of all time.

Background Reading

Alan Moorehead, *Gallipoli* (Harper, 1956)
Geoffrey Moorhouse, *Hell's Foundations: A Social History of the Town of Bury in the Aftermath of the Gallipoli Campaign* (Holt, 1992)

1981/Australia/Color
DIRECTOR: Peter Weir; **PRODUCER:** Robert Stigwood, Patricia Lovell; **SCREENPLAY:** David Williamson; **STUDIO:** Paramount; **VIDEO:** Paramount; **RUNNING TIME:** 110 min.

The Gallipoli Peninsula

On April 25, 1915, British soldiers landed at five beaches near Cape Helles, the southern tip of the Gallipoli peninsula; meanwhile, Australian and New Zealand troops landed farther north, at Ari Burnu. Neither invasion force was able to break out of its enclave. On August 6, another British force landed farther north at Suvla Bay to trap the Turkish armies to the south. In order to prevent the Turks from repulsing the Suvla invasion, the British at Cape Helles and the ANZACs at ANZAC Cove were ordered to attack—the reason for the suicidal effort depicted in *Gallipoli*. The Suvla Bay initiative caught the Turks by surprise, and the British landed with little opposition. However, the Turkish commander, Mustafa Kemal (later Kemal Atatürk), threw his men quickly into battle and another bloody stalemate ensued.

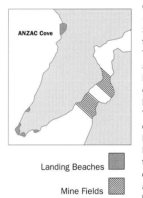

ANZAC Cove

Landing Beaches

Mine Fields

Later...

Despite the sacrifices of the Australian and New Zealander troops, as well as the equally serious losses of the British army at Cape Helles and Suvla Bay, the Gallipoli campaign was a total failure. After the Allies withdrew their forces from the peninsula in December 1915, no further combat took place there during World War I.

The successful leader of the Gallipoli defense, Mustafa Kemal, went on to lead the revolution that abolished the Ottoman sultanate in 1922. A year later, he became the first president of the new Turkish republic. Revered as the father of modern Turkey, he sent an extraordinarily gracious message to the Australian people before his death. On behalf of his nation, he promised to honor the memory of the Australians who had fought in Gallipoli, and he personally approved changing the name of the battlefield to ANZAC Cove. In gratitude, Australia built a monument to him adjacent to its National War Museum in Canberra. Can any American imagine the United States building a monument to George III, Santa Anna, or Tojo?

WORLD WAR I

Five Films

Tom Wicker

My father, a railroad conductor by trade, served in France during the First World War in an American railway unit based in Dijon. Later, he was an enthusiastic member of the American Legion. In the 1930s, therefore, his son became an unenthusiastic member of the Sons of the Legion. Back and forth we marched over the barren grounds of the Hamlet, N.C., high school, as patriots like my father prepared their offspring for another go at the Huns.

Most of us were certain it could never happen; surely the world had learned its lesson. In not too many years, however, many of my marching companions left for World War II; some never came back. More than half a century later, I am still amazed at how little those who barked our marching orders told us about what's usually called in Europe, and with good reason, the Great War. None ever explained to us—though surely some must have known—not only that war is hell but that long before Buchenwald or Auschwitz the Western Front was a foul monument to both the killer soul and the blind stupidities of mankind. Before that monument, the age-old notion of "glorious war" fell like a boy riddled by machine-gun bullets.

Maybe our drill instructors had willed themselves not to talk or even think about men existing like moles in the earth, in the mud and stench of trenches scarring Europe from the English Channel to the Swiss border, about bodies by the tens of thousands mangled in the shellholes or draped like bloody laundry on the barbed wire of a moonscape called No Man's Land—the grim debris of a single day or a single hour of fighting, in which no ground had been gained or lost, no advantage won, no purpose served.

Western Front 1914–16 ———

It was not for nothing that Churchill opposed as long as he could the World War II invasion of France, for which the Americans and Russians were so eager. It was for the memory of slaughter at Passchendaele and Ypres and the fear that a "second front" would be stalemated, then bog down in trench warfare like the Western Front, with another British generation destroyed in another No Man's Land.

Perhaps, too, in making their World War I films, the moguls of Hollywood—some of whom must have served in the Great War, on one side or the other—calculated that Great Depression– or World War II–era Americans would not be much entertained by movies about the grisly horrors of the Western Front. Better to make films about heroes and heroism, sacrifice and glory, boys becoming men and women waiting faithfully—or perhaps not—for their return to a world made safe for democracy.

HISTORY

German soldiers on the Western Front

Casualties in the Great War were unlike anything previously known to human history. During the first five months of the war, the French lost three hundred thousand dead and six hundred thousand wounded, captured, or missing. The French death toll in that brief period exceeded the total number of British dead in the entire Second World War.

On July 1, 1916, the first day of the battle of the Somme, after a five-day barrage from more than fifteen hundred guns, British troops attacked across a twenty-five-mile front. In the bloodiest single day of battle in the Great War, more than a thousand officers and twenty thousand enlisted men were killed; twenty-five thousand more were seriously wounded. A breakthrough was not achieved. When the battle of the Somme ended four months later, the Allies had advanced six miles—a gain for which 95,675 Britons and 60,729 Frenchmen paid with their lives. The German death toll in defense was 164,055.

HOLLYWOOD

Lew Ayres in *All Quiet on the Western Front*

Moviegoers of a certain vintage may get a few goosebumps of reminiscence if they watch *The Dawn Patrol* (1938) and *The Fighting 69th* (1940). Both are Warner Brothers productions featuring that studio's familiar "stock company" of players. In addition to lead performances by James Cagney and Pat O'Brien, *The Fighting 69th* boasts such well-remembered names as Dennis Morgan, George Brent, Alan Hale, Jeffrey Lynn, Dick Foran, and Frank McHugh. Few Warner films of the era appeared without one or more of these actors in the cast. For *The Dawn Patrol*, about a British air squadron in France, Warner Brothers trotted out an equally familiar array of English and Irish accents to back up leading players Errol Flynn, David Niven, and Basil Rathbone: Donald Crisp, smoking his inevitable pipe; Melville Cooper, at his Cockney best; and Barry Fitzgerald, mugging shamelessly as usual. Watching both of these films is like a memory course in the Hollywood of half a century ago.

The Western Front

The German Schlieffen Plan worked well in August 1914 to carry the Kaiser's armies through Belgium and deep into France. The result of twelve years of work by Gen. Alfred von Schlieffen, chief of the general staff from 1891 to 1905, the plan called for a massive wheel by the German right wing, bypassing the fortified German-French frontier. The sleeve of the last man on the right, von Schlieffen decreed, should brush the English Channel.

Despite unexpected resistance from the Belgian army and the appearance of the British Expeditionary Force in France, the gigantic turning movement succeeded until German advance patrols moved within eight miles of Paris. On September 5, the French and British struck at the German flank, which had been exposed north of Paris by the continuation of the great wheel. In the ensuing battle of the Marne—four days of fierce fighting involving 1,275,000 Germans, 1,000,000 French, and 125,000 British—the invasion was turned back.

A "race to the sea" followed, with the Germans hoping to take the Channel ports and thus cut the BEF off from resupply and reinforcement. But the race was won by the British, and on October 21 both armies began to dig trenches in the later-famous Ypres area. By early 1915, historian John Buchan has written, "the fronts had been stricken by their vastness into stagnation. . . . A man could walk by a chain of outposts from Switzerland to the Vosges, and in a ditch from the Vosges to the North Sea." The war of maneuver was over; thereafter, the fight on the Western Front was between armies dug into trenches stretching for hundreds of miles but sometimes only yards apart.

At any rate, several Hollywood films about the Great War that I recently viewed—*The Big Parade*, *All Quiet on the Western Front*, the 1938 remake of *The Dawn Patrol*, *The Fighting 69th*, and *Paths of Glory*—conveyed too little sense of that war as a low point of human history. Not that they are bad movies (save *The Fighting 69th*) or even bad history. Inaccuracies, if any, are not glaring; battle scenes are usually graphic; the antiwar message is loud and clear (again, save in *The Fighting 69th*, filmed in the early days of World War II); and all emphasize one of the Great War's most memorable elements—the constant mud in which men slogged to their deaths or lived in misery.

The Fighting 69th is the most stereotypically "Hollywood" movie of the five. It features big stars, James Cagney and Pat O'Brien—Cagney playing as usual a tough-talking wise guy, O'Brien as usual a fatherly priest. Predictably, the wise guy turns coward in battle; predictably, the wise priest tries to save his soul; predictably, the coward finds God and courage in the end. And when all else fails, as it usually does, the film throws in Frank McHugh for wisecracks and funny faces. Cagney plays a coward as intensely as he has played killers in other films but deserves better than this hackneyed yarn.

The problem with the other, better films is that they are *war* movies more nearly than *Great War* movies. The best of them, Stanley Kubrick's *Paths of Glory* (featuring a typically jut-jawed performance by Kirk Douglas), is about the arrogance and inhumanity of commanding officers anxious for promotion and reputation, even at the expense of their troops' lives. In what war has this not been a factor? *Paths of Glory*, though an impressive film, could have been set in any of them.

Kubrick's film does have some powerful opening battle scenes of a French attack that goes nowhere and accomplishes nothing except the deaths of many of the attackers. That was typical of the Great War, but the result is attributed neither to the nature of trench warfare nor to the bitter stalemate into which the Western Front settled after 1914. Rather, it's shown as the result of a French officer's desire for rank and promotion. Some of the attacking troops are arrested and tried for cowardice in order to cover up the officer's criminal order to attack; the trial—with Douglas for the defense—and its results form the meat of the story.

Based on an actual Great War incident, *Paths of Glory* is strikingly like *Breaker Morant* (an equally powerful Australian film set during the Boer War), another true story of individual lives ruthlessly sacrificed to a commander's or a nation's vanity and indifference to justice and humanity. This story is no less grim for being a recurring truth of all wars; however, except for scenes of men in the uniforms of 1914–18 and in an unmistakable Great War landscape, *Paths of Glory* conveys less a sense of the Western Front than of French army bureaucracy.

The Dawn Patrol, which is about early aerial warfare, not only has splendid scenes of rickety old flying crates and "dogfights" in the clouds but also seems downright prophetic. The makers of the 1938 *Dawn*

Patrol, based on the 1930 film starring Douglas Fairbanks, apparently were convinced that World War II was just around the corner; so the movie's characters—the most prominent played by Errol Flynn, David Niven, and Basil Rathbone—constantly warn that the tragedies and stupidities they witness are certain to be repeated by the unnamed "maniacs" who will surely start another war (in the context, this could refer to Churchill as easily as to Hitler).

A movie about the first aerial war could only be about the Great War, and in this respect *The Dawn Patrol* is more faithful to its ostensible subject than some of the other films. It focuses on the uncertainties, the anxieties, and the raw courage of men who fought a new kind of war—not only human enemies in the air and the faceless bureaucracy of faraway "staff" but also the fallibility of their flimsy machines.

Men facing such trials probably did turn to drunkenness and horseplay to conceal or counter their fears, but this aspect of *The Dawn Patrol* is marred by Hollywood excess. Flynn and Niven too often appear to be jolly good fellows enjoying a jolly good adventure rather than desperately harried and fearful men at war. The film constantly leavens the tension and/or tragedy with wisecracks and schoolboy heroics (such as a ridiculous episode in which Flynn is shot down but survives, Niven lands under fire to pick him up, and both have a simply grand old time at derring-do).

I had never seen the legendary *Big Parade* or its star, silent-screen idol John Gilbert, whose career and high-pitched voice went out with the advent of the talkies. The movie begins rather badly, in Hollywood's idea of military hijinks—war as frolic, fun, and games. It proceeds, however, to some magnificent episodes. One is a suspenseful advance of an American battle line through a seemingly empty wood, which ultimately erupts in sniper and machine-gun fire. Another is a wonderfully filmed night battle scene that compares favorably, for sheer spectacle, with the burning of Atlanta in *Gone with the Wind*.

The advance through the woods, though I don't doubt such actions occurred in France, seemed to me more typical of, say, conflict in the American Civil War than in the Great War. The night battle scene, however, is one of the few in any of these films that caught, for me, the nightmarish quality of war on the Western Front. And from scenes in which Gilbert finds himself cowering in a shellhole with the corpse of a German he's just killed, the fear and filth and agony of No Man's Land seem to rise like a stench.

All Quiet on the Western Front is, of course, unique among these films in that it's about German soldiers and told from a German point of view. Nevertheless, it seems to have been something of a model for many later American movies about World War II—the story begins with a group of innocent and eagerly patriotic youths, follows them through military training, then on into the real thing, death and desolation.

The difference is that such World War II movies usually hailed or promised heroism and victory; yet *All Quiet on the Western Front* far

No Man's Land

Most of the Great War on the Western Front was fought in trenches or between trench lines. Dug deep enough to shelter men from enemy fire, with a parapet of earth in front of them, the trenches were continuously muddy, sometimes flooded, clogged with the bodies of wounded or dead men and animals, foul with the stench of brief life and violent death. Tormented by rats, lice, shell fire, "trench foot," and enemy snipers, men of both armies slept, ate, and died in the gouged earth.

To attack, troops carrying rifles and heavy packs had to go "over the top"—climb from the trenches, over the protective parapet, and advance into No Man's Land toward opposing entrenchments only yards away, usually through barbed-wire entanglements and always into a blaze of machine-gun and rifle fire, with shells, grenades, poison gas, and flamethrowers making the defense unbelievably murderous.

No Man's Land was a sea of mud pocked with shellholes, lit at night by the infernal glare of aerial flares, swept by crisscrossing lines of fire, littered with corpses from both armies, unburied after earlier attacks. The dead frequently hung like rotting fruit from accordion-tangles of barbed wire.

Attacks across this hellish ground were usually preceded by thunderous bombardments from artillery—guided, for the first time in war, by observation planes. On March 10, 1915, at Neuve Chapelle, 342 British guns fired, in one thirty-five-minute barrage, more shells than were fired in the entire Boer War fifteen years earlier. Through miscalculation, these terrifying bombardments often fell on advancing troops of the gunners' own side.

The Big Parade

1925/USA/B&W
DIRECTOR: King Vidor; SCREENPLAY: Harry Behn; STUDIO: MGM; VIDEO: MGM/UA; RUNNING TIME: 142 min.

All Quiet on the Western Front

1930/USA/B&W
DIRECTOR: Lewis Milestone; PRODUCER: Carl Laemmle, Jr.; SCREENPLAY: Del Andrews, Maxwell Anderson, George Abbott; STUDIO: Universal; VIDEO: MCA; RUNNING TIME: 140 min.

The Dawn Patrol

1938/USA/B&W
DIRECTOR: Edmund Goulding; PRODUCER: Hal B. Wallis, Robert Lord; SCREENPLAY: Seton I. Miller, Dan Totheroh; STUDIO: Warner; VIDEO: MGM/UA; RUNNING TIME: 103 min.

The Fighting 69th

1940/USA/B&W
DIRECTOR: William Keighley; PRODUCER: Hal B. Wallis; SCREENPLAY: Norman Reilly Raine; Fred Niblo, Jr.; Dean Franklin; STUDIO: Warner; VIDEO: MCM/UA; RUNNING TIME: 90 min.

Paths of Glory

1957/USA/B&W
DIRECTOR: Stanley Kubrick; PRODUCER: James B. Harris; SCREENPLAY: Stanley Kubrick, Calder Willingham, Jim Thompson; STUDIO: UA; VIDEO: MGM/UA; RUNNING TIME: 86 min.

more boldly carries its protagonists into disillusionment—not with the Kaiser's Germany, for which they continue to fight, but with war itself. The justly famous final scene, in which Lew Ayres reaches out of a trench to capture a butterfly, only to be shot and killed, wordlessly passes judgment on war as wanton waste of life and beauty—and reminds us of the camera's unmatched power to convey such images.

Like *The Big Parade*, this film—based on Erich Maria Remarque's novel—occasionally looks with compassion and disgust on the peculiarly subhuman life of the Western Front: the trenches, the mud, the half-buried remains, the landscape like a rotting corpse, the terror and the ever-present danger and misery, the meaninglessness amounting at a distance to absurdity. Alone among these films—perhaps, to be fair, because it's about Germans—*All Quiet on the Western Front* also has the courage to attack patriotism, that powerful, sometimes mindless surge of pride in race or creed or country or region or flag—in *something*—that so often drives humanity to war and inhumanity.

In *The Great War and Modern Memory*, Paul Fussell argues that man's consciousness of life and civilization was changed by a cataclysm that had, to that time, no parallel in human experience. In *The Shooting Party*, novelist Isabel Colegate portrays the essential innocence of the world of 1914, as it was about to be introduced by the Great War to machine guns and poison gas and tanks and airplanes throwing "like King Billy bombballs in." Ford Madox Ford in his Tietjens novels manages somehow to achieve a vivid sense of the degradation of human life reduced to a filthy struggle for survival in the primordial mud of the trenches.

Barbara Tuchman details in *The Proud Tower* how in 1914 Europe actually welcomed what neither side could imagine would be the worst extension of human experience in history. The Great War generations seem to have marched into the soulless technology of the lethal twentieth century as innocently as in my youth we bumble-footed Sons of the Legion stumbled about the high school grounds playing at war. For them, the unspeakable Western Front, the destruction of innocence, lay just ahead; for us, it was as if the pit of horror over which the world hangs suspended had to be glimpsed again before it could be believed, or even sensed.

These worthy films, with rare and notable exceptions, do not afford viewers that glimpse. Their makers had other purposes, as men usually do. What is missing, therefore, is not accuracy but the difference between accuracy and truth.

Background Reading

Paul Fussell, *The Great War and Modern Memory* (Oxford University Press, 1975)
Martin Gilbert, *The First World War* (Henry Holt, 1994)
Barbara Tuchman, *The Guns of August* (Macmillan, 1962)

Technological Innovations

The machine gun (both the Lewis, invented in the United States, and the Maxim, a European product) was perhaps the most effective but not the only new development of the Great War. In late 1914, bombs from German airships—zeppelins—killed the first three British civilians to die in warfare in the home islands since 1690. Zeppelin raids forced the British and French to devise anti-aircraft defenses. Biplanes, first used for reconnaissance, became effective fighting machines once machine guns were synchronized to fire through their whirling propellers.

Women were first employed in making munitions in Britain in June 1915. That same month, steel helmets were first issued to British and French troops. In July 1915, the Germans used the first flamethrower, in a battle in the Ypres Salient. Also that year, a clever British cabinet minister suggested to Prime Minister Herbert Asquith that "steam tractors" be fitted with armored shelters, machine guns, and caterpillar tracks—the first step in the development of the tank, which was used effectively on the Western Front beginning in 1916 and later became the major weapon of World War II. The clever cabinet minister was Winston Churchill, who was himself to serve in the trenches.

Later...

By the Treaty of Versailles, signed on June 28, 1919, Germany's home territory was diminished, its armed forces disbanded, and its responsibility for the war defined by the heavy reparations it was forced to pay to the victorious allies. Germany was forbidden to unite with Austria, deprived of all colonial possessions, and barred from importing war materials or building submarines. This punitive treaty is generally regarded as having fueled the German resentment that led to World War II.

The allies set up the League of Nations, but neither Germany nor Russia was allowed to join. The United States later rejected both the Treaty of Versailles and the League, though President Woodrow Wilson, who participated in the peace conference, had been instrumental in devising both.

REDS

Christine Stansell

Louise Bryant

Louise Bryant was born in San Francisco in 1885 to a family of the liminal social stratum between working class and solidly middle class that produced so many radical intellectuals prior to World War I. A graduate of the University of Oregon, she married Paul Trullinger, a prominent Portland dentist, in 1909. Her labor sympathies and bohemian notions inspired her to stake herself as an artist with a little studio on Portland's waterfront. She also peddled subscriptions to the radical New York monthly *The Masses* and wrote for the San Francisco anarchist newspaper *The Blast*. In 1915, she met John Reed when he returned to Portland to visit his family.

REDS IS SOMETHING OF A MARVEL, POSSIBLY the only big-budget Hollywood film to take socialists, feminists, and Communists—"Reds"—and package them gorgeously and sympathetically for a mass audience. The film concerns John Reed and Louise Bryant, radical writers who figured prominently in the "lyrical Left" of Greenwich Village during the mid-1910s and, as journalists, became leading American supporters of the 1917 Bolshevik Revolution. True, David Lean's *Doctor Zhivago* had already proved that the October Revolution could sell tickets—but only framed within an anti-Communist idiom. In *Reds*, the Reds themselves triumph, if not quite as desirable political leaders, at least as pioneers of modern marriage.

Over three hours long, *Reds* divides with an intermission into what are essentially two stories. The first concerns the vicissitudes of a heterosexual romance based on the ideals of free love, equality between men and women, and companionship in work. Resonating with feminist concerns of the 1970s and early 1980s, this might be called the tale of a two-career commuting couple. Reed meets the would-be bohemian artist Bryant on a trip home to Portland, Oregon, in 1915. Married at the time to a dentist, she follows Reed back to Greenwich Village, where he has already established himself as a successful writer and serious politico. While Reed orates for the Industrial Workers of the World, hobnobs with the *Masses* crowd, and conspires with Emma Goldman, Bryant tags along, jealous of his fame yet insufficiently grounded in her own writing to make a go of it. For both, political principle merges with an inability to "commit," in modern parlance. Bryant uses free-love ethics to rationalize her affair with playwright Eugene O'Neill; Reed cites political duty to justify his constant trips out of town. They marry to shore things up, but Reed's suspicions about O'Neill and Bryant's continuing resentment of his absences precipitate a breakup.

Bryant flees to Europe to work as a war correspondent. Prospects for the couple look bleak, but revolution is brewing: Reed follows her to Europe and lures her to Russia promising the biggest scoop of her career and an egalitarian, professional relationship. She will be her own woman, she demands, and he pledges: "Miss Bryant" and not "Mrs. Reed," with her own byline, expenses kept separately, and sleeping together out of the question. In St. Petersburg, elated by the revolutionary events and their reportorial coup, they reconcile. Dispatches fly out of their typewriters; they scribble clipped, efficient emendations on each other's writing; they gambol in the snow and make love to the strains of "The Internationale."

HISTORY

John Reed was born in 1887 to a substantial family in Portland, Oregon. Sent to an eastern prep school and then to Harvard, he found himself an outsider in the world of the East Coast patriciate. Cheerful and enthusiastic, with an unquenchable hankering to belong, he tried to ingratiate himself with the campus elite at Harvard. His encounters with socialism, feminism, and literary realism, however, alerted him to an alternative order of status and achievement centered in Greenwich Village, where Reed moved upon graduating. His reports on the Mexican Revolution (he traveled with Pancho Villa's troops) soon made him the most celebrated young journalist in the country. Vivid, powerful human-interest stories followed: the bitter mineworkers' strike in Ludlow, Colorado, then the action on the Serbian battlefront in Europe.

HOLLYWOOD

Long one of the most politically active members of the Hollywood community, Warren Beatty starred in two of the more politically astute films of the 1970s: *The Parallax View* (1974), about an organization of political conspirators, and *Shampoo* (1975), a satire on the amorality of the Nixon era. Beatty's filmmaking efforts coalesced in *Reds*, a labor of love that consumed four years. After cowriting the screenplay with British playwright Trevor Griffiths, Beatty hired Elaine May and Robert Towne, both uncredited, to polish it. Paramount put up thirty-four million dollars for the production but came close to canceling it on several occasions as costs soared to an estimated forty-five million. One unusual production cost would have made Reed himself proud: After Beatty explained to extras for the Baku conference scene how Reed championed the workers' struggle for better salaries and working conditions, the extras took Reed's principles to heart, went on strike for higher wages, and got them.

CHRISTINE STANSELL

The Testimony of the Witnesses

Reds' most innovative device is the inclusion of a chorus of "witnesses," now-elderly people who (supposedly) participated in the events narrated in the film. This technique, lifted from documentaries, underscores the historical reliability of the scripted story with the testimony of living memory, introduced as disembodied voice-overs or in studio shots of talking heads. Because by the time *Reds* was made most of the principals were dead, the producers seem to have issued a general casting call for radicals of a certain age and ended up with an odd assortment, most of whom had little or nothing to do with Reed, Bryant, Greenwich Village, or the lyrical Left.

The Greenwich Village of the 1910s has, for almost a century now, spawned a profuse tradition of memoirs to which countless hangers-on and pretenders have attached themselves; the *Reds* witnesses fall squarely within this camp. Of the thirty-some people, only two or three really figured in the lives of Bryant and Reed—and only a handful more were part of the early Village scene. Several were, in actuality, children at the time; the gabbiest of the group, Rebecca West, lived in England; Henry Miller, who authoritatively psychoanalyzes Reed as if they were intimates, could hardly have known him. The person closest to the main characters is painter Andrew Dasburg, Reed's friend and Bryant's lover before she followed Reed to Moscow in 1920. Curiously, Dasburg does not speak of his intimacy with either, as if a mention of this biographical twist would have disturbed the symmetry of the film's Bryant/Reed/O'Neill triangle.

Yet the very shakiness of the witnesses' testimony, though never acknowledged in the film, works subliminally to buttress the authority of the fictionalized narrative. As the opening credits roll, cracked old voices speak in voice-over of their confusion about the historical task they're supposed to be performing: "I've forgotten all about them," someone querulously insists. "Were they socialists?" "It never impinged on my own personal life," seconds someone else. With memory rendered as faint, cracked, and reticent, the fictionalized story, cast in such beautiful detail, becomes all the more credible.

The pairing of an ambitious female and a sympathetic yet unwittingly condescending male is a classic Hollywood conceit, dating back to the Tracy-Hepburn comedies. *Reds* taps into this tradition and handles its elements nicely. Warren Beatty's Reed is a well-meaning, cheerful, slightly oblivious New Man with a sexual gaze that could melt a stone. Diane Keaton plays Bryant, the New Woman, with an interesting mixture of bravado, vulnerability, sexual opportunism, and ditziness. Today, the story still seems fresh and compelling in its treatment of the stresses of sexual modernism, especially in contrast to the hackneyed Hollywood treatment of ambitious, evil, and deluded career women and their unwitting male victims so prominent during the 1980s and 1990s.

Yet *Reds* runs into trouble after the intermission, in part because its historical ambitions are so large. After 1917, Reed's story veered away from Bryant as he submerged his deepest energies into socialist and, later, Communist politics. Rather than ignore this central aspect of the man's life, *Reds* takes on the task of representing the internecine fights of the Left into which Reed plunged himself in 1919. This is no easy matter when what requires depiction is the battle for Comintern recognition between one American sect and another, a struggle played out in convention halls, smoky backrooms, and the offices of Soviet bureaucrats.

The pace of the film inevitably slackens, and *Reds* compensates by shifting to the proven dramatic motif of star-crossed lovers separated by the epic of war. Bryant's New Woman persona fades as she becomes an onlooker marginalized by Reed's fervor, the resentful wife of a workaholic. The two once again separate when Reed travels—illegally, since all borders have been sealed—to Russia to arrange Comintern recognition for his Communist Labor Party.

The film picks up the pace by shifting, *Zhivago*-like, to panoramic cinematography and the theme of missed connections. Wide-angle shots of the snowy wastes of Finland and Russia feature tiny heroic trekkers: first Reed as he tries to get to Moscow, then Bryant as she tries to get to Reed. Invariably, she arrives in places shortly after his departure; he cables home frantically and believes she has left him. Finally, they fall into each other's arms at the Moscow train station. Cut to a hospital ward in 1920, where Reed is dying of typhus and Bryant gazes remorsefully at a child, the baby she never had.

Except for the melodrama at the end, most of this is more or less correct: The most important distortion is of Bryant's motives for returning to Russia, which had as much to do with recovering her position in the select circle of writers inside the country as with her desire to reunite with Reed. Bryant was a devoted nurse at Reed's sickbed, but she scarcely skipped a beat in her career, keeping an appointment for an interview with Lenin shortly after Reed's death.

For the most part, however, *Reds* is scrupulous about historical fact, displaying an unusual depth of exact detail. Secondary characters, for instance, are actual historical personages, even those who speak only a line or two; the dialogue also often invokes contemporaneous events. These techniques can sometimes seem extraneous or merely discursive (Emma Goldman rattling off her philosophy of birth control agitation as she bids Reed goodnight), but the precision can also be satisfying and even provocative of historical reflection. In a scene in Portland, for example, Bryant tries to make Reed attend to her as a serious writer. He is about to leave when she mentions she has been published in *The Blast*. He wheels around, his interest hooked: "Berkman's *Blast*?" Her association with Alexander Berkman's anarchist journal might indeed have transformed Bryant in Reed's eye from a provincial *litterateur* to a serious radical.

Yet too often in *Reds* the enthralling politics of the 1910s, both domestic and foreign, become a mere foil for the trials and triumphs of the lovers rather than the opposite way around. Two complex lives are reduced to a manageable plot line, shrinking history to biography and biography ultimately to cliché. Bryant suffers the most; still, in its determination to retain some complexity—who could imagine the conflict between the Communist Labor Party and the Communist Party figuring in a Hollywood script?—*Reds* holds considerable interest. And in its excitement over how *different* people could be in the past—its wide-eyed discovery that, in 1916, interesting people actually embraced ideals of free love, women's equality, and human brotherhood—the film breathes the charms of the otherness of history.

The Film's Palette

The costuming and interior set design are brilliant. If the Great Depression happened in black-and-white, then after seeing this film you'll know the 1910s occurred in rich browns, mauves, and creams. Indoors, life is cast in the glow of a Stickley lampshade. The Greenwich Village and Provincetown sets are exquisitely dressed in a manner that uncannily anticipates the 1990s upscale vogue for peeling paint, stressed wood, and battered, tattered, fading antiques. Costumes, subtly colored, play off this visual scheme. Do historical characters seem more "real" when they color coordinate with their surroundings? The Provincetown sequence, especially, places actors dressed in delicately varied creams and whites in and around an old shingled beach house replete with layers of pearly grays, pale blues, and beiges.

Later...

Bryant resumed her journalistic career after Reed's death in 1920, embarking within a short time on a long, adventurous, and hazardous stint in Asiatic Russia. (She became one of the few Western correspondents to travel through that region.) Later she married William Bullitt, a wealthy but disgruntled former aide to Woodrow Wilson (and, in the future, FDR's ambassador to the Soviet Union). Living in Europe and Manhattan within a conventional marriage, the wife of a rich man, Bryant allowed her career and political involvements to lapse. She became increasingly devoted to Reed's memory, however, abetted by Bullitt—who, in his own way, was drawn to Reed as a leftist alter ego. Bryant divorced Bullitt and spent her last years alcoholic and poverty-stricken; she died in Paris in 1936. As for Reed, his star rose as the American Communist Party lionized him as a hero of the revolution, founding John Reed Clubs during the 1930s so that artists and writers could follow his example.

Background Reading

Virginia Gardner, *"Friend and Lover": The Life of Louise Bryant* (Horizon, 1982)
Robert A. Rosenstone, *Romantic Revolutionary: A Biography of John Reed* (Knopf, 1975)

1981/USA/Color
DIRECTOR: Warren Beatty; **PRODUCER:** Warren Beatty; **SCREENPLAY:** Warren Beatty, Trevor Griffiths; **STUDIO:** Paramount; **VIDEO:** Paramount; **RUNNING TIME:** 200 min.

CHRISTINE STANSELL

CAST

Rosa Luxemburg *(Barbara Sukowa)*
Leo Jogiches *(Daniel Olbrychski)*
Karl Liebknecht *(Otto Sander)*

ROSA LUXEMBURG

John Patrick Diggins

Freedom for the supporters of the government, only for the members of one party—however numerous they may be—is no freedom at all. Freedom is always and exclusively freedom for the one who thinks differently.

Rosa Luxemburg

ALTHOUGH WE LIKE TO CLAIM IT AS OURS (the "American Century," Henry Luce once called it), the twentieth century has actually been the century of Communism. For three-quarters of the century (1917–89), Communism seemed in ascendance, first in the vast spaces of Russia, then in the land mass of China, and later possibly spreading through the Third World. Today, it is gone for good in eastern Europe, ready to topple in Cuba, and on the way to some inevitable transformation in China. If everywhere the brave new future has failed so miserably, how could any intelligent person ever have believed in it?

Among the many virtues of *Rosa Luxemburg* is the aesthetic and political sense it makes of the beliefs and behavior of people who once lived to make a better world. No figure personified so passionately as Luxemburg the ideals of the radical movements that swept Europe at the turn of the century. The film, directed by Margarethe von Trotta and featuring Barbara Sukowa as Luxemburg, avoids what might have been mere propaganda, not only to deal with history in all its messy complexities but also to portray its heroine as a tragic figure who inadvertently unleashed the forces that destroyed her.

Rosa Luxemburg (1871–1919) was one of the most talented women of her era. Having been born in Russian Poland to a family of wealthy merchants, she became interested in socialism and, at eighteen, was forced to flee to Switzerland because of her revolutionary activities; three years later, she helped found the Polish Socialist Party. A symbol of courage and rectitude, she fought against every prejudice and handicap. Born with a deformed foot, Luxemburg walked with a limp (in the film she refers to herself as "a lame duck") and was regarded as too young to be a serious political thinker, even though she had made outstanding contributions to the study of political economy in her early twenties. In 1898, she married Gustav Lübeck, a German national, relocated with her husband, and became active in the German Social Democratic Party (SDP). The ultimate foreigner, Luxemburg was a Pole in Berlin, a Jew in Germany, and a woman in a political world dominated by men.

Particularly illuminating are the film's scenes dramatizing the meetings and debates of the SDP, the strongest socialist party in Europe during the early twentieth century. Von Trotta skillfully interposes cultural settings amid the political dialogue; in one instance, Luxemburg turns down an invitation to dance with Eduard Bernstein, her rival for leadership of the Social Democrats. Bernstein prevailed over international social democracy as a revisionist, convinced that Marx's predictions of

HISTORY

Rosa Luxemburg

Can a film treat adequately the complexities of political ideas and their movements? In *Reds*, when director Warren Beatty attempts to deal with the differences between factions of the emerging American Communist Party, he completely loses the audience. If *Rosa Luxemburg* succeeds it may be due to the fact that the formation of American Communism was a Byzantine affair that waited on orders from Moscow, whereas German socialism was debated boldly, out in the open, with a roaring lioness like Luxemburg.

HOLLYWOOD

Barbara Sukowa as Luxemburg

Perhaps the best-known female director to emerge from the New German cinema, Margarethe von Trotta frequently examines the uses and effects of violence. Von Trotta's solo directorial debut, *The Second Awakening of Christina Klages* (1978), describes the odyssey of a feminist militant whose fierce determination to save her "alternative" day-care center leads her to bank robbery. With *The German Sisters* (1981), von Trotta dramatizes the plight of Gudrun Ensslin, one of the three Baader-Meinhof terrorists who died in Stammheim prison, and her sister Christiane, who campaigned tirelessly to discredit the official claim that Ensslin and her comrades committed suicide. Based on extensive research into the theoretical writings and personal letters of its protagonist, *Rosa Luxemburg* continued von Trotta's presentation of political and social issues on a human, personal scale.

The Socialist Left During World War I

In February 1917, the tsarist autocracy in Russia fell, leading to the establishment of a moderate provisional government under Alexander Kerensky that was itself overthrown in October by the Bolsheviks, a minority party that claimed to speak not only for the whole of Russia but also for the meaning and revolutionary direction of history. The October Revolution brought to a head a split that had divided democratic socialists from revolutionary militants ("minimalists" from "maximalists"). Many of the intellectuals on the Left, in America as well as in Europe, were swept away by V.I. Lenin's daring seizure of power in a country where revolution had not been supposed to happen. If in Russia, why not here?

Before 1917, Luxemburg had expressed differences with Lenin over his theory of a small revolutionary "vanguard." After the October Revolution, however, she extended to him tentative support. Although she regarded herself as a revolutionary, she remained more consistent with orthodox Marxism, believing that socialist consciousness would arise within the working class. On these grounds, she opposed Lenin's dictatorship and continued to believe in the power of mass strikes and strategic demonstrations. Tragically, she sought to take politics to the streets, and it was in those streets that she was killed.

the pauperization of workers and the polarization of classes were problematic and that socialism could be reached through piecemeal, parliamentary reforms. By way of contrast, Sukowa portrays Luxemburg as a captivating orator and fresh, provocative thinker who justly made party theoreticians nervous. In one particularly vivid scene, Luxemburg stands before a transfixed audience as she hammers out her own position, which called for continuous revolutionary struggle on the part of the workers themselves.

Despite *Rosa Luxemburg*'s focus on complex theoretical matters, von Trotta makes numerous skillful transitions from the political to the personal. Looking at a portrait of her lover, Leo Jogiches, she remembers her activist days in Poland with him. Jogiches was a workaholic dedicated to the revolutionary movement and, according to Clara Zetkin, a "rare" masculine personality who could tolerate "a great female personality" without feeling his ego threatened. Their affair was stormy; despite protestations of free love, each became jealous and possessive when the other took a lover. In the film, Jogiches demands of Luxemburg, "Do you want to be a mother or a revolutionary?" "Both," she answers. "Your vocation is to bring ideas into the world—these are your children," Jogiches shouts back, at which point Luxemburg returns to the present and lashes out at his photograph.

In 1914, Luxemburg and her fellow internationalists despaired at the outbreak of World War I. When socialist leaders in Germany and other European states failed to oppose the conflict in their respective parliaments and workers rose to the call of nationalism, Luxemburg denounced their actions. For this, she was tried for treason and repeatedly imprisoned by German authorities.

The film opens with Luxemburg in a Berlin prison during the snowy winter of 1916, writing to friends as a voice-over conveys her thoughts about history and politics. Suddenly, her female cellmates rush to their windows to watch in horror the execution in the yard of several political prisoners. Then, in a scene that could have been lifted from Dostoyevsky, Luxemburg is marched blindfolded into a room and forced to stand against a wall as the order "Fire!" is given. She flinches and her thoughts flash back to her childhood, but the feigned execution fails to terrify her into informing on her comrades.

During her prison years, Luxemburg cultivates plants and gardens with a reverence for flowers, animals, and all things natural. The conservative officials show their respect for the quality of her mind as she makes pleas in court, yet when she becomes caught up with the 1917 revolutions in Russia and calls for mass strikes in Germany, they call her "Red Rosa" and nervously plot to contain the danger she represents.

After the armistice is signed in 1918, Luxemburg is released from jail and immediately joins Karl Liebknecht in founding the German Communist Party. Very quickly, a fanatical faction of the party, the Spartacus League, moves to overthrow the new German republican government, which at the outset was headed by socialists with the support of the workers. Luxemburg argues passionately with Liebknecht against premature revolutionary adventurism, but it's all in vain. After the failure of the Spartacist Revolt in Berlin, the prevailing forces of order hunt down Liebknecht and Luxemburg. In the film's last scene, Luxemburg is arrested, clubbed, shot in the skull, and dumped into a canal.

Although *Rosa Luxemburg* deals successfully and accurately with the political circumstances of the time and with the real Luxemburg's complex personality, it neglects her unique contribution to radical political thought. Specifically, her devastating critique of Lenin's theory of party dictatorship goes unmentioned. It is for this critique that she remains the conscience of any revolution made in the name of freedom.

German police during the Spartacist Revolt

The Spartacist Revolt

Officially founded in 1916 by Karl Liebknecht, Rosa Luxemburg, Clara Zetkin, and Franz Mehring, the Spartacus League developed as an offshoot of the more moderate Social Democratic Party. Its members accepted the October 1917 Bolshevik Revolution and saw in the unstable post–World War I political climate an opportunity to realize the international proletarian revolution. Luxemburg drafted the program accepted by the Communist Party of Germany, into which the Spartacus League was transformed at the party congress held from December 30, 1918, to January 1, 1919. Meanwhile, the Spartacists encouraged demonstrations that culminated in an abortive attempt to overthrow the Socialist Democratic Provisional Government. On January 15, 1919, Luxemburg and Liebknecht were arrested and executed by members of the conservative Freikorps, who had seized control of Berlin's police presidium.

Later...

In a way, [Rosa Luxemburg] was lucky to have died at the hands of the reactionaries. Had she lived another twenty years and sought refuge in Stalin's Russia from Hitler's gas chambers, she would have been shot as an "agent of British and American imperialism." For though she had acclaimed the Bolshevik Revolution, she by no means approved of the totalitarian methods inaugurated by Lenin and Trotsky, and her posthumous pamphlet about the Russian Revolution, which contained some of the most pungent criticisms of Communist party dictatorship, was violently attacked by all Russian Communists.

Max Nomad, 1960

Background Reading

J.P. Nettl, *Rosa Luxemburg* (Oxford University Press, 1966)

1986/West Germany/Color
DIRECTOR: Margarethe von Trotta; **PRODUCER:** Eberhard Junkersdorf, Martin Wiebel; **SCREENPLAY:** Margarethe von Trotta; **STUDIO:** Bioskop; **VIDEO:** New Yorker; **RUNNING TIME:** 122 min.

THE FRONT PAGE

Arthur Schlesinger, Jr.

The Sacco-Vanzetti Case

On May 5, 1920, Italian immigrants Nicola Sacco and Bartolomeo Vanzetti were arrested and charged with killing a factory paymaster and his guard during a robbery in South Braintree, Massachusetts, two weeks earlier. In July 1921, a jury found both men guilty. The case became controversial, however, when left-wing political groups began charging that Sacco and Vanzetti, both anarchists, had been convicted because of their political views.

In 1925, a condemned inmate, Celestino Madeiros, testified that the murders had actually been committed by the Morelli gang, but trial judge Webster Thayer refused to reopen the case and the Massachusetts Supreme Court declined to order another trial. On April 9, 1927, Sacco and Vanzetti were both sentenced to death. The sentences, which provoked worldwide protest, were duly carried out the following August, but the question of whether justice was done continued to be debated. In July 1977, the state of Massachusetts finally reversed itself when the governor declared that Sacco and Vanzetti had been improperly tried.

THE FRONT PAGE WAS NOT FOUNDED ON any particular historical incident. Its aim was not to reconstruct an event but to re-create a city and an era—Chicago in the 1920s, a roaring, brawling town run by demagogic politicians, crooked municipal officials, and cynical newspapermen, while a wondrous collection of writers, artists, and rogues observed from the sidelines. It was the time of the Chicago Renaissance—of Carl Sandburg and Frank Lloyd Wright, of Ring Lardner and Harriet Monroe, of Clarence Darrow and Al Capone, of Mr. Dooley and Ernest Hemingway, of Benny Goodman and Bix Beiderbecke, of John Gunther and J.P. McEvoy, of Burton Rascoe and Harry Hansen, of Lowell Thomas and Meyer Levin—celebrated names once, though mostly forgotten today. Chicago in the Twenties was a fascinating city, brilliant and corrupt, and in the second decade of the century it weaned two avid young newspapermen, Ben Hecht and Charles MacArthur.

Hecht and MacArthur had dreams beyond journalism. Although they soon escaped the bondage of the city room, they never sought to escape the gaudy memories of their Chicago apprenticeship: "We were both obsessed with our youthful years. . . . We remained newspaper reporters and continued to keep our hats on before the boss, drop ashes on the floor and disdain all practical people. . . . We were both full of nostalgia for the bouncing days of our servitude."

In 1928, having safely fled to New York, Hecht and MacArthur distilled their memories of newspapering in Chicago into a play they called *The Front Page*, their tribute to the romantic but intolerable past. Jed Harris produced *The Front Page* on Broadway, and George S. Kaufman directed. In it Osgood Perkins as Walter Burns, the demonic editor, and Lee Tracy as Hildy Johnson, his star reporter, made their reputations. *The Front Page* remains one of the most celebrated American plays of the century, often revived in the United States and abroad, most recently in London in 1994.

Most of the characters depicted on the stage were based on real reporters in Chicago; in some cases, the names were hardly changed. It was one of the marvels of *The Front Page*, Jed Harris said later, that "although all the characters were actual people, nobody ever thought of suing us for invasion of privacy."

Walter Burns was inspired by Walter Howey, the editor of William Randolph Hearst's *Chicago Examiner*, for whom MacArthur had worked after he returned from World War I. Ben Hecht, who was on a rival Chicago paper, the *Journal*, described Howey this way: "He cooed like a

HISTORY

Walter Howey

In 1902, after an unsuccessful year at the Chicago Art Institute, Walter Howey got a job as a reporter on his hometown newspaper, the *Fort Dodge* (Iowa) *Messenger*. Two years later, Howey stormed back into Chicago "like thunder out of China," according to Charles MacArthur. In 1906, he became the youngest city editor in the country, and in 1917, after quitting as city editor of the *Tribune*, Howey accepted William Randolph Hearst's offer to become managing editor of the *Examiner*.

It has been said that Walter Howey, who served as the model for the Walter Burns character, competed for stories as though he were waging a war. Focusing on scandals, crimes, and human-interest pieces, Howey loved stories that his reporters could follow up for weeks, and he typically put police switchboard operators on the *Examiner* payroll so they would tip off his reporters first. Howey's support for Big Bill Thompson in the 1919 mayoral election paid off handsomely when a grateful mayor ordered the police to keep rival reporters away from disaster and crime scenes.

HOLLYWOOD

Adolphe Menjou as Walter Burns

Louis Wolheim, a character actor who had recently enjoyed a great success in Milestone's *All Quiet on the Western Front*, was signed for the part of Walter Burns, but he died of a stroke three weeks into production, triggering a frantic search for a replacement. Milestone's recruitment of Adolphe Menjou surprised many Hollywood tongue-waggers, who thought him too debonair for the part. The indefatigable Menjou adapted well, however: His first day on the set, he found Pat O'Brien shooting craps with a few members of the cast. Kneeling down on the knifeblade creases of his pants, Menjou greeted them briskly. "Hi, suckers," he said. "Save the introductions for later. I await my turn at the dice!"

The Remakes

Nine years after Milestone's *Front Page*, another top director, Howard Hawks, proposed a remake in which Hildy Johnson would be a woman and, not only that, the divorced wife of Walter Burns, no longer a misogynist. Hawks's *His Girl Friday* thus fused the scorching Hecht-MacArthur newspaper drama with the screwball comedies of the 1930s. Despite the valiant efforts of Rosalind Russell, Hildy Johnson does not quite work as a woman, and for all his easy charm Cary Grant lacks the icy gravitas of Adolphe Menjou. The Chicago atmosphere mostly disappears. Still Howard Hawks masterfully sustains the nonstop pace required by the script, and the film has its rewards as entertainment, even if politics is subordinated to farce and the wonderful last line is sacrificed to the need to unite Walter Burns and Hildy Johnson in holy rematrimony.

In 1974, nearly half a century after *The Front Page* first opened on Broadway, director Billy Wilder offered another remake, this time in Technicolor. Wilder and his frequent collaborator, I.A.L. Diamond, wrote the screenplay. Their version is more faithful to the Chicago of the Twenties than *His Girl Friday*, but *The Front Page* is one of those stories that cry for black and white; color drains the sordid goings-on of credibility. Walter Matthau, though he has personal authority, plays Walter Burns as a rumpled slob rather than as a natty boulevardier, and Jack Lemmon plays Hildy Johnson as a jaunty vaudevillian rather than as a rough-and-tumble reporter. In deference to a changing world, the homosexual theme cursorily suggested in the character of Roy Bensinger of the *Tribune* receives disproportionate emphasis. Seeing the Wilder version again after twenty years, I found it better than I had remembered; but, overall, it is a disappointment for Wilder admirers.

dove, smiled like a wide-eyed sightseer in from the sticks. He wore a polka-dot bow tie, neat linen and a pressed suit. . . . Yes, Mr. Howey, God rest his wild bones, had a soft benevolent look and air, voice and manner. But the Assyrians menacing Sinai were casual folk beside him. He could plot like Cesare Borgia and strike like Genghis Khan."

In the play, Hildy Johnson—in love with Peggy Grant, a demure young woman—prepares to leave the newspaper racket, marry Peggy, take a job with a New York advertising agency, and embrace suburban domesticity. But there are problems in Chicago: A philosophical anarchist has inadvertently killed a black policeman and is awaiting execution in the city jail. He is a hapless fellow named Earl Williams, modeled on Bartolomeo Vanzetti, who had been electrocuted in Massachusetts the year before. An election impends, the black vote is vital, and Williams's hanging is deemed essential to the reelection of the mayor and the sheriff.

The mayor is modeled on Big Bill Thompson, famed for winning the job on his promise to biff King George of England on the snoot should he ever set foot in Chicago. In the play, the mayor has been persuaded by the sheriff to forgo King George and seek reelection on a promise to drive radicals out of Chicago under the slogan "Reform the Reds with a Rope." The Friends of American Liberty and other "Bolshevik organizations" are demanding clemency for Williams.

The action takes place in the press room of the criminal courts building, a bare, grimy, disordered room peopled by newspapermen in need of shaves, pants pressing, and small change. There the cynics play poker, drink, sleep off jags, and jeer impartially at the mayor, the sheriff, Earl Williams, and the streetwalker Mollie Malloy, who has befriended Williams and whom the reporters play up (falsely) as Williams's lover. Their derisive badinage is interrupted periodically by the ghastly thud of crashing weights as the executioner tests the gallows outside their window.

Hildy Johnson, Peggy, and Peggy's mother have tickets on the night train to New York, where Hildy and Peggy are to be married the next day. Walter Burns, a misogynist of the first water, is determined to stop the marriage and keep Johnson on the Williams story. There follow frantic complications—an alienist asks Williams to reenact the crime and hands him the sheriff's gun; Williams shoots and escapes; a citywide manhunt ensues; Williams enters the press room to be discovered by Hildy Johnson and hidden in a rolltop desk; Walter Burns arrives, persuades Johnson to stay on the story, does his best to deflect Peggy Grant and her mother; Burns and Johnson are arrested for obstructing justice; and finally they triumph over the mayor and the sheriff.

Hildy Johnson can still make the New York train, and in an apparent rush of sentimentality Burns ceremoniously blesses the young couple and presents his prize watch to Johnson. Johnson happily departs for the railroad station. In the famous last line, Burns orders a wire to be sent to the train's first stop calling for the arrest of Hildy Johnson: "The son of a bitch stole my watch."

The coruscating Hecht-MacArthur dialogue, the breakneck pace, the sardonic political commentary, and the swift and wholly persuasive shifts in mood between farce and melodrama transfixed audiences. The rapid-fire dialogue would have been too much for silent pictures, but the arrival of talkies made *The Front Page* a screen possibility. In 1930 Howard Hughes (yes, the same one) bought the rights from Jed Harris for $125,000—around $2,500,000 in the debased currency of the 1990s. The director was Lewis Milestone, fresh from making *All Quiet on the Western Front*, with *Rain*, *Of Mice and Men*, *A Walk in the Sun*, and other fine films in his future. Bart Cormack, a contemporary of Hecht and MacArthur in Chicago journalism, wrote the screenplay.

It is a brilliant movie. Adolphe Menjou as Walter Burns stalks balefully through the film with dapper dress, gimlet eye, caustic speech, and total lack of scruple—a marvelously exact and strong performance. Pat O'Brien is a brash, fast-talking Hildy Johnson in the Lee Tracy vein. The boys in the press room are splendidly rendered by Walter Catlett, Edward Everett Horton, Frank McHugh, and other old pros. George E. Stone is an appropriately forlorn Earl Williams.

But what makes the film memorable is Milestone's direction. The fluidity of the camera movement, the audacity of the cutting, the starkness of the black-and-white photography—all give the rip-roaring Hecht-MacArthur lines their ideal context. Even the last line is rescued from the censorship of the Hays Office by the business of Menjou's fist crashing down on a typewriter as he utters the forbidden word "bitch."

Several directors have remade *The Front Page*, but Milestone's remains the classic version. It has the occasional crudities characteristic of early talkies, but it is the closest to the historical period and catches best the legend of Chicago in the Roaring Twenties—Chicago, that stupefying city, as Julian Street said, "an Olympian freak, a fable, an allegory, an incomprehensible phenomenon . . . monstrous, multifarious, unnatural, indomitable, puissant, preposterous, transcendent," a myth not too far from reality, forever enshrined in the vivid and romantic memories of Ben Hecht and Charles MacArthur.

Background Reading

Ben Hecht, *Charlie* (Harper, 1957)
Ben Hecht and Charles MacArthur, *The Front Page* (Covici & Friede, 1928)
William MacAdams, *Ben Hecht: The Man Behind the Legend* (Scribners, 1990)

1931/USA/B&W
DIRECTOR: Lewis Milestone; **PRODUCER:** Howard Hughes; **SCREENPLAY:** Bartlett Cormack; **STUDIO:** UA; **VIDEO:** Pearl; **RUNNING TIME:** 101 min.

Big Bill Thompson

William Hale Thompson, called Big Bill because of his size and athleticism, won his first election as mayor of Chicago in 1915. He ran as a reformer, promising to clean up the police department and appoint a woman to the school board. He did neither. Instead, he funded an elaborate public works campaign, bestowing the most lucrative contracts on his political supporters. Reelected in 1919 by a much slimmer margin, Thompson came under increasing attack for his corrupt spending. The *Chicago Tribune* even sued the mayor, charging him with conspiracy to defraud the city of two million dollars.

When a jury convicted Thompson's political mentor, Republican party boss Fred Lundin, of robbing the school treasury, the mayor was forced to withdraw from the 1923 race. But Thompson was back again in 1927, this time supported by mob money (particularly Al Capone's). Attacking Prohibition, the League of Nations, and the king of England, Thompson won yet another term, during which he became the laughingstock of the nation when he fired the Chicago superintendent of schools for introducing pro-British history textbooks.

Later...

Like all renaissances, that of Chicago ran its course. Its luminaries migrated to New York or to Hollywood and eventually to heaven or, very possibly, to the Other Place. The onset of the Great Depression altered the city's—and the nation's—mood. As early as 1931, Lewis Milestone's *Front Page* began with the words: "This story is laid in a Mythical Kingdom." Chicago became thereafter a city of solid and sober intellectuality, the pyrotechnics that lit up the sky during the 1920s having long since vanished. Eight dailies were represented in the Hecht-MacArthur press room; today Chicago has only two, and even Col. Robert R. McCormick's unbridled *Tribune* is now moderate and responsible.

After joining the *Examiner* in 1917, Walter Howey spent most of his working life editing Hearst publications. He started the tabloid *New York Mirror* for Hearst in 1924, reportedly in just ten days. After losing decisively in the 1931 mayoral election, Big Bill Thompson for the most part faded from public view. He did resurface briefly in 1937, however, when a judge required him to pay the American Red Cross seventy-three thousand dollars, about half the amount he had raised for the organization ten years earlier and never remitted.

CAST

Joe Kenehan   *(Chris Cooper)*
Danny Radnor   *(Will Oldham)*
Sid Hatfield   *(David Strathairn)*

MATEWAN

Eric Foner

MATEWAN TELLS THE STORY OF A BITTER 1920 strike in the coal mines of southern West Virginia. The struggle culminates in the Matewan Massacre, a violent (and historically accurate) confrontation in which the town's mayor, seven armed guards hired by the coal operators, and two miners lose their lives. However, this film does more than chronicle a particularly dramatic episode in American labor history. In the hands of director John Sayles, *Matewan* offers a meditation on broad philosophical questions rarely confronted directly in American films: the possibility of interracial cooperation, the merits of violence and nonviolence in combating injustice, and the threat posed by concentrated economic power to American notions of political democracy and social justice.

Although *Matewan* is peopled with actual historical figures—notably Sid Hatfield, the town's pro-union chief of police and the central protagonist in the massacre—Sayles uses two fictional characters to propel the plot. One is Danny Radnor—a boy preacher, miner, and union supporter—in whose voice as narrator, looking back from fifty years later, the story of Matewan is told. The second is the film's main character, Joe Kenehan, a World War I veteran, former member of the Industrial Workers of the World, organizer for the United Mine Workers of America, and committed pacifist. Joe urges nonviolence upon miners skilled in the use of dynamite and subjected on a daily basis to intimidation by the armed guards who patrol the town's streets and assault and murder strikers. He also preaches racial tolerance. When the company brings in black and Italian strikebreakers to keep the mines operating, Joe persuades the strikers to invite them into the union. The first quarter of the film centers on this confrontation, culminating in the "scabs" joining the strike. When the miners are evicted from company-owned housing and erect a tent city outside the town, Joe goes with them, continuing to counsel nonviolence even as company guards assault the strikers from nearby woods. There follows the film's only false step, an implausible subplot in which a company agent has Joe falsely accused of raping a miner's wife. Once Joe has been cleared, the film hastens to its violent conclusion, in which Joe is accidentally killed. The film ends with Danny recalling that, in the massacre's aftermath, he dedicated himself to preaching the gospel of "one big union."

In the world of contemporary filmmaking, John Sayles is unique. Proud of his independence, he runs his own production company and does not accept studio financing. Sayles is attracted to working-class subjects (as in *The Return of the Secaucus Seven*, his 1980 feature debut) and

Company Towns

Those attempting to organize a mine workers union in West Virginia faced daunting obstacles, not least the tight control of local communities and state government by coal operators and railroad companies. In West Virginia, far more miners (over ninety percent) lived in towns where housing was owned by the companies than in any other state. On any given day, their homes were subject to unannounced searches by company agents, and they were often paid in scrip redeemable only at company stores.

HISTORY

Blacks formed a major part of the work force in southern West Virginia. In some mines, they were a majority of the laborers. Although some blacks were brought into the area as strike breakers, many became active supporters of the union. Despite segregation of schools and housing in company-dominated towns, black and white miners shared an experience of powerlessness and exploitation. This engendered a sense of interracial solidarity reflected in the determined effort of the United Mine Workers of America to bring black miners into its ranks. When the union came to southern West Virginia, it actively enlisted the support of black miners, and blacks held offices throughout the union's local organizational structure. At a time when the craft unions of the American Federation of Labor erected insuperable barriers to black participation, the UMWA, as an industrial union, made it a point of pride to include all mine workers—black and white, immigrant and native.

HOLLYWOOD

James Earl Jones as "Few Clothes Johnson"

John Sayles was already a critically acclaimed novelist and short-story writer when he joined Roger Corman's stable of B-movie screenwriters in the late 1970s, penning *Piranha* (1978), *The Lady in Red* (1979), and *Battle Beyond the Stars* (1980). Sayles marked his feature directorial debut with *Return of the Secaucus Seven* (1980), a witty and poignant look at a reunion of 1960s activists on the verge of adulthood. Almost a "talking heads" film, it was shot for a reported forty thousand dollars and used few sets, sparse camera movement, and little action. Nonetheless, Sayles received the Best Screenplay award from the Los Angeles Film Critics Association and quickly established himself as one of America's most widely admired independent filmmakers.

West Virginia Politics

From the 1890s to the 1930s, West Virginia's U.S. senators were generally officials of coal companies, as were most of its governors. The state legislature, dominated by representatives of agricultural counties, was less reliably favorable to the coal interests. It was not uncommon, however, for lawmakers to accept bribes from coal companies (five were arrested in 1913 for accepting payments from a coal operator running for the U.S. Senate). Perhaps even more important, the coal companies dominated county government, choosing sympathetic sheriffs and other officials. The companies were the main source of county funds, which gave them a powerful voice in local affairs. Not infrequently, deputy sheriffs were paid directly by the coal companies. Even legislation intended to assist miners could be turned to the companies' advantage.

The Workmen's Compensation Law of 1913, for example, relieved the coal operators of responsibility for job injuries, for which local juries had previously awarded compensation to miners. Laws restricting child labor were weak and systematically ignored. They failed to provide educational requirements for working children and did not specify dangerous occupations from which they should be barred. Mine safety laws were notoriously unenforced; West Virginia had the highest death rate of any mining state, and the

proportion of miners who died in accidents far exceeded that of any European country. "One cannot imagine the power of the mining companies," a U.S. senator from Wisconsin wrote in 1913 after visiting West Virginia. The companies, he added, "own both the Republican and Democratic parties in the state."

American history, especially moments that expose a gap between the country's myths and its reality (*Eight Men Out* is his account of the 1919 Black Sox World Series scandal). Sayles has never had a bona-fide hit, although *Matewan* is widely admired. Asked to name their favorite movie about the United States, a group of American historians recently ranked *Matewan* fifth, after *Gone with the Wind*, *Citizen Kane*, *The Grapes of Wrath*, and *Glory*.

Also unusually among filmmakers, Sayles, an O. Henry Award–winning prose writer, has published a book, *Thinking in Pictures*, about the making of *Matewan*. Apart from the script itself, which takes up half the volume, the book mostly explains how Sayles financed *Matewan* (its four-million-dollar budget might have been a pittance by Hollywood standards, but it far exceeded the cost of any of his previous films) and offers insights about such technical matters as casting, shooting, and lighting. It also tells how Sayles became fascinated with West Virginia's coal-mining district, its people, and their traditions after hitchhiking through the region in the late 1960s. This experience may help to explain the film's greatest strength—its evocation of the texture of the miners' world. Through music, regional accents, and numerous local characters, Sayles successfully creates a sense of the Matewan community. Visually, too, the film is remarkably effective, thanks to Haskell Wexler's careful and deliberate cinematography. Dramatic as it is, *Matewan* is not "entertaining" in a conventional sense. With its accented dialogue often difficult to follow and its slow-moving pace, it demands concentration on the part of the viewer. But partly because of this, it succeeds admirably in creating a sense of time and place.

Yet the relentless concentration on the local community, *Matewan*'s greatest strength, also contributes to its most glaring weakness—the absence of context, both historical and political. *Matewan* is uncompromising in exposing the mechanisms used by the coal operators to control and intimidate the workers, from payment in scrip usable only in company stores to control of housing, the use of strike breakers, and the ubiquitous private police forces. Indeed, by the end of the film, the viewer has come to appreciate that the massacre was less an irrational episode than an explosion of the violence that had long simmered just beneath the surface of the town's life. But the coal operators themselves are absent from the story, and so, too, is their domination of West Virginia's state government. Sympathy for the union among local officials, including the mayor and the police chief, was not unusual in mining communities; what the film does not show is that their authority was often overridden by the courts and state and federal authorities.

Nor was the Matewan strike an isolated local incident, as portrayed in the film. Rather, it formed part of a prolonged struggle for unionization that lasted for decades. Unionism in 1920 was hardly new to the miners of southern West Virginia, and it did not require someone from outside the community to bring its message to Matewan. The regionwide 1912 strike had inaugurated a period of intensely violent struggle between the union and mine owners. In the years that followed, moreover, the mine workers union, perhaps the most racially integrated labor organization in the nation, succeeded in uniting black and white miners, as well as natives and immigrants. The problem is not that Sayles does not trace these earlier events but that he gives the miners no sense of their own history, forcing them to rely on an outsider for lessons in union organizing and racial tolerance.

Simply to make *Matewan* in the seventh year of Ronald Reagan's presidency—the most antilabor administration since the 1920s—was itself a remarkable accomplishment. Yet implicitly, the film's power rests on nostalgia for a bygone era of militant organizing and muscular labor. At a time when more Americans work in McDonald's restaurants or as secretaries than in steel mills or coal mines, *Matewan* evokes a period in history when the brawny industrial worker stood at the heart of the working class, when men did the "real" work and women occupied subordinate places in cohesive, family-oriented communities. The film presents several female characters, some of them heroic, but all, essentially, are loyal helpmates to the men who do the work, organize meetings, and confront the bosses. Women did not, in fact, work underground in the mines. However, one would never know from *Matewan* that one of West Virginia's most celebrated union organizers was the eloquent and outspoken Mother Mary Jones. For Sayles, as for many in Hollywood (one need only think of other films with labor subjects, such as *F.I.S.T*, *Blue Collar*, and *Hoffa*), the working class is by definition male.

Nonetheless, if the house of labor has been transformed since the events depicted in *Matewan*, the film's pleas for nonviolence, interracial harmony, and economic justice are hardly irrelevant today. It is sobering to reflect that these ideals seem as utopian to contemporary viewers as when they were propounded by the I.W.W. and United Mine Workers of America nearly a century ago.

Background Reading

David A. Corbin, *Life, Work, and Rebellion in the Coal Fields: The Southern West Virginia Miners 1880–1922* (University of Illinois Press, 1981)

John Sayles, *Thinking in Pictures: The Making of the Movie Matewan* (Houghton Mifflin, 1987)

1987/USA/Color
DIRECTOR: John Sayles; PRODUCER: Peggy Rajski, Maggie Renzi; SCREENPLAY: John Sayles; STUDIO: Cinecom; VIDEO: Lorimar; RUNNING TIME: 132 min.

Mother Jones

Born in Ireland, Mary Jones (1830–1930) was brought to Canada as a young girl and moved to the United States shortly before the Civil War. Her husband and four children died in a yellow fever epidemic in 1867. She then worked in Chicago as a seamstress and later emerged as one of the most prominent union organizers in the nation's coal fields and a speaker on behalf of social causes ranging from the abolition of child labor to the Mexican Revolution.

As a paid organizer for the United Mine Workers of America, Mother Jones worked among miners from Pennsylvania to Colorado. She was active in West Virginia in a 1901 organizing drive, during the 1912 strike, and again after the Matewan Massacre. Jones's actions challenged conventional definitions of a woman's place, but she had little interest in women's suffrage and effectively played upon traditional gender roles (including wearing Victorian dresses) in constructing her own image as a "mother" to male miners, whom she referred to as her "boys."

Later...

The events that followed the Matewan Massacre were even more dramatic than those recounted in the film. Indicted for his part in the bloodshed, Matewan chief of police Sid Hatfield was murdered by company operatives on the courthouse steps—a demonstration, in the miners' eyes, of the owners' utter contempt for legal processes. There followed the Great Coalfield War, in which the operators flooded the region with strike breakers and armed guards, while strikers blew up mines and other property and fought pitched battles with company forces and state troopers. In 1921, the violence culminated in the armed march on Logan—"the greatest domestic armed conflict in American labor history," according to historian David A. Corbin—in which some ten thousand armed miners clashed with company forces. With the miners apparently gaining the upper hand, President Warren G. Harding placed the entire state under martial law, brought in federal troops, and broke the strike. Not until the 1930s would unionization come to the coal fields of southern West Virginia.

ERIC FONER

SHANGHAI EXPRESS

Jonathan D. Spence

CAST

Shanghai Lily *(Marlene Dietrich)*
Capt. Donald Harvey *(Clive Brook)*
Hui Fei *(Anna May Wong)*
Henry Chang *(Warner Oland)*

THE BASIC EVENT FROM WHICH THE IDEA for *Shanghai Express* springs is an especially dramatic one: the May 1923 seizure by Chinese bandits of the so-called Blue Express on its northward run from P'u-k'ou on the Yangtze River to Tientsin. The story made world headlines for a few days when twenty-six of the Western passengers on the train were held for ransom, along with some one hundred Chinese passengers.

However, in adapting this story for the screen, director Josef von Sternberg and screenwriter Jules Furthman faced a significant problem of name recognition. Most Westerners have never heard of P'u-k'ou, a small town on the northern shore of the Yangtze, across from Nanking. In those days, in the absence of any railway bridges across the Yangtze, which is about half a mile wide at that point, P'u-k'ou was the terminus for trains moving south. Passengers had to alight there and cross the river by ferry to Nanking station, whence a branch line took them to Shanghai. Yet *P'u-k'ou Express* was hardly a memorable title, and *Tientsin Express* was little better. *Peking Express* might have served, but after 1928, when Chiang Kai-shek formally established the Nationalist capital in Nanking, Peking's name was changed to Peiping. Since von Sternberg clearly intended the film to be topical, hence setting the story in 1931 (the film was released in 1932), this meant he would have had to name his film *Peiping Express*, which has a decidedly weak ring. So despite the fact that the train had been traveling from south to north at the time it was seized, if it was to be the *Shanghai Express* for filmic purposes it had to be going from north to south.

The plot of *Shanghai Express* was also given a distinctly political twist: As the train roars south out of Peiping toward Shanghai, it is stopped by Nationalist troops for a check of passengers' identification papers. One young man, Li Fung, is found to be carrying secret documents and is arrested. Observing the arrest, a Chinese passenger, Henry Chang, sends a cipher telegram message to his followers, ordering them to board the train farther down the line and hold the passengers hostage. After the train is successfully boarded at a watering stop, Chang sets up a temporary headquarters inside the rural station, revealing himself to be the "commander-in-chief of the Revolutionists."

He interrogates the Western passengers one by one and finds to his great delight that one of them, a British army doctor, is on his way to Shanghai to perform crucial surgery on the governor-general. Here is the perfect refinement to the hostage situation. While the delicate negotiations on the doctor's fate drag on through the night, Chang first tries to

Sun Mei-yao (seated) after the release of the hostages

The Warlords of North China

The militarization of China was one of the utterly unexpected consequences of the Qing dynasty's fall in early 1912—although even before 1912 local military leaders had begun pushing for power in their regions. Many had been trained in the military academies that began to proliferate in the late nineteenth century, while others studied at Japanese academies that had gained a new and bittersweet prestige after Japan smashed the Chinese army and navy in the short war of 1894. By 1915, when the fledgling Republic of China lay in shambles, large areas of the country were already under the de facto control of military bosses, who found their recruits and their antagonists among the hundreds of thousands of men left jobless or landless after the crises of the Republican revolution.

HISTORY

Women in Shanghai, 1920

During the late 1920s, the Western presence in China was obvious in many different guises. The world of business changed rapidly, as foreign companies expanded their operations and Chinese chambers of commerce established their own shares of the new markets. Railway building, coupled with the expanded use of steamships on Chinese rivers, dramatically changed the patterns of both business and tourism. Missionary schools, reinforced by church-related groups including the YMCA, brought reformist thinking to China's youth. Shanghai became a new kind of city for China, its three million people divided among foreign concession areas and Chinese administrators—a system made to order for the expansion of racketeers, who swiftly took over the lucrative trade in narcotics, gambling, and prostitution.

HOLLYWOOD

Anna May Wong (left) with Marlene Dietrich

Born Wong Liu Tsong in the Chinatown district of Los Angeles, Anna May Wong first broke into films as a twelve-year-old extra in *Red Lantern* (1919). After playing a number of featured parts, she finally attracted widespread attention as the Mongol slave girl in Raoul Walsh's lavish 1924 *Thief of Baghdad*, starring Douglas Fairbanks as the swashbuckling hero. A subsequent vogue for Oriental mysteries boosted her to international stardom by the end of the decade. Crossing the Atlantic, Wong starred in a number of inconsequential European films. Upon her return to the United States, she gave what is perhaps her best-known performance in *Shanghai Express*. Unfortunately, her subsequent Hollywood films (she retired in 1942) were mostly cheap crime melodramas in which, more often than not, she was relegated to the role of the mysterious villainess.

The Account of Lucy Truman Aldrich

I had given a small S.O. dinner party the night before and we were awfully tired, so I decided to go to bed early. I went to sleep almost immediately and was aroused by the train stopping with a jerk. I got up, half asleep, put on a thin silk wrapper and bed-slippers, and without speaking to Mathilde, who was over my head, went into the corridor. Everything was quiet except for a (to me) queer crackling noise outside; but no one was in sight. I was just going to open the door and go back, when Miss MacFadden grabbed me, dragged me into her stateroom, slammed the door, and said in a queer breathless whisper, "They are attacking the train and are just outside." I peeked out through the curtain and saw a crowd of people. It was still dark and I could only see dimly, but they seemed to be swarming into the train. . . . In a minute the room was filled with a wild crowd, slashing, threatening, and snatching. One man had cut his hand quite badly. He looked at it stupidly for a minute and then went on pawing things over with the blood streaming. They cut and ripped the bags open with long knives, growling like tigers. When they emptied Miss MacFadden's handbag, I saw one take the red case with my letters of credit and Japanese money, and I tore it out of his hand. Another took her precious string of jade and I managed to get it away from him, only to have it snatched in a minute by another. He bent my fingers back, and in wrenching it out of my hand, broke the string, and the beads went all over the floor. I was furious and sternly told him to pick them up. Before he realized what he was doing, he did pick up a few of them, then straightened and held a revolver to my head, while I groped for as many as I could find, myself.

November 1923

seduce Shanghai Lily, played with an exquisite blend of humor and sensuality by Marlene Dietrich. When she confesses her love for the doctor, however, Chang assuages his lust by raping a Chinese woman who shares Shanghai Lily's compartment. Li Fung is released, but before Chang can celebrate fully he is murdered by his rape victim "to settle their account." As the train once more hurtles south, Shanghai Lily and the doctor rekindle their passionate love.

This is a wonderful film, with great performances by both Dietrich—"it took more than one man to change my name to Shanghai Lily"—and Anna May Wong. Von Sternberg's opening shots—of the bustling and chaotic preparations for the train's departure and its slow shunting progress through densely crowded alleys, where townspeople and farmers drift across the tracks almost under the train's wheels as soldiers on guard duty absent-mindedly spear bits of food from peddlers' stalls with their bayonets—are surely as good as anything in his oeuvre. But the historian cannot help asking, despite the screenplay's dramatic strengths, whether the reality of the 1923 train hijacking does not offer a story even more adventurous and strange.

The leader of the bandits who seized the Blue Express near the Shantung town of Lincheng at 2:50 A.M. on May 6, 1923, was named Sun Mei-yao. He was about twenty-five years old and had no political agenda or connections at all; rather, he presided over a loosely federated force of close to one thousand rootless followers, refugees from famine and civil war, who were themselves but one of scores of bands that roamed northern China during the warlord period. The capture and ransoming of travelers on China's roads and rivers by such bandits had become commonplace, along with the mutilation or murder of those whose families would not or could not pay. There had also been a few attacks on trains. Yet the impact of Sun Mei-yao's raid came from the daring scale of the operation and the large number of foreigners involved.

The train was first derailed by the removal of steel brace plates that held the tracks rigid, after which the bandits fanned down the corridors of the first-class sleeping compartments, rousing the passengers and ransacking their possessions. One Englishman was killed in the preliminary skirmish, after which twenty-six of the foreign passengers—nearly all in their nightclothes or underwear, some with coats or capes thrown hurriedly round their shoulders—were dragged or hustled at gunpoint across the bleak countryside. Famished and exhausted, they were secured in various bandit hideouts while the ransom negotiations proceeded through American and Chinese intermediaries. (The women were kept for a few days, and the men up to five weeks.) The Chinese authorities finally provided about ninety thousand dollars in ransom money and granted the bandits their main wish, which was a full pardon and their induction en masse into the "regular army" of the region, controlled by northern Chinese warlords. Sun Mei-yao was named to the rank of brigadier general, but he enjoyed his new honor for only a few months before he was murdered on his commander's orders.

The surviving reminiscences of the Western hostages make absorbing reading and constitute a major source for the history of Chinese banditry and village life during the early 1920s. Almost certainly, neither Furthman nor von Sternberg knew of these writings or they surely could not have resisted incorporating some of them into their story. Most astonishing in its irony, given the context of the ransom negotiations, is the fact that among the women captives—though her name meant nothing to the bandits—was Lucy Truman Aldrich, sister of Mrs. John D. Rockefeller, Jr. Her account shows that the women—although they suffered miseries of exhaustion, hunger, thirst, extreme discomfort from the burning sun, embarrassment at their scanty attire, and rude treatment—were not sexually abused in any way. Indeed, like several of the men, they built up an odd sort of bond with their captors, whom they saw as poor, uneducated, desperate, and almost as hungry and miserable as themselves. Accounts by several male hostages and the photographs that some of them managed to take corroborate the outlines of Lucy Aldrich's story and add vivid descriptions of how the bandits draped themselves in their stolen finery, marching across the country in beribboned hats and flowing shawls, with silken brassieres slung around their bodies like bandoliers, bulging with ammunition or food looted from the first-class dining cars.

One upshot of the international furor and diplomatic pressures following the train seizure was the imposition of rigorous new rules for the presence of armed troops aboard the Tientsin–P'u-k'ou railway trains and greatly stiffened safety procedures at stations along the route. Thus von Sternberg's magnificent opening shots of the troops who crowd the engine and cars of his 1931 *Shanghai Express* are an anachronistic but accidentally accurate depiction of the only "constructive" change that came from Sun Mei-yao's daring raid.

Background Reading

Phil Billingsley, *Bandits in Republican China* (Stanford University Press, 1988)

1932/USA/B&W
DIRECTOR: Josef von Sternberg; **PRODUCER:** Josef von Sternberg; **SCREENPLAY:** Jules Furthman; **STUDIO:** Paramount; **VIDEO:** MCA; **RUNNING TIME:** 80 min.

Later...

One outcome of the simultaneous growth of the Communist and Nationalist parties in China was the emergence of an alliance between the two groups, formalized in 1923. Each side hoped to use the other to cement its own power. However, the two parties were also, to some extent, sincere in their desire to pool strengths: They both wanted to curb foreign imperialism on the one hand and Chinese militarists on the other.

Aided by Comintern advisers from the Soviet Union, the United Front organized a small but formidable army, led by military cadets from the Whampoa Academy and directed by Sun Yat-sen's protégé, Chiang Kai-shek. In 1926, Chiang led his forces in a march through South China to the Yangtze River. In the spring of 1927, however, convinced that the Communists now posed the greatest threat to China's future, Chiang turned on his allies, who were killed by the

Chiang Kai-shek

thousands in Shanghai and other major cities by a combination of Nationalist troops, warlord armies, and gangs coordinated by organized-crime leaders.

By 1928, building on his dramatic reversal of policy against the Communists, Chiang managed to bring an appearance of unity to the country. But his success was, in fact, a fragile one. In many areas of central China, he had chosen to make alliances with warlord armies, and in North China, strongly entrenched Japanese forces had impeded his advance, forcing him to make humiliating concessions. Meanwhile, the Japanese moved rapidly to establish a virtual colony in Manchuria.

Even the Communists showed surprising resilience. Giving up most of their bases in the cities, they found new sanctuary in the poorest areas of the Chinese countryside. There, finding recruits among the desperate peasants, landless laborers, and rootless vagrants—many of whom had earlier served with the warlords' forces—they created a new system of linked rural soviets that proved able to resist all of Chiang's attempts to destroy them. From this series of rural guerrilla bases, Mao Zedong created the disciplined fighting force that successfully resisted the Japanese and ultimately destroyed Chiang Kai-shek's Nationalist government.

CAST

Harry Houdini (*Tony Curtis*)

Bess Houdini (*Janet Leigh*)

HOUDINI

John F. Kasson

IF HOLLYWOOD IS HARDLY SCRUPULOUS IN its treatment of history, what then should we expect of its handling of biography? The makers of Paramount's *Houdini* might have thought themselves positively scholarly compared to many film biographers: Not only had they read a book, Harold Kellock's *Houdini: His Life-Story* (1928), prepared with the assistance of Houdini's widow; but they had also hired a magician, Joseph Dunninger, inheritor of many of Houdini's illusions, to serve as technical consultant. A box-office success, *Houdini* immediately became, and to a large extent remains, the dominant popular version of its subject's life. Yet the film is inaccurate in virtually every respect, and it offers an interpretation of Houdini's life that Houdini—himself not always meticulous with the facts—would have loathed.

"Don't insult me by calling me a magician," Harry Houdini once told reporters. "I am an escape artist." He was indisputably the greatest escape artist in the history of illusion and one of the most spectacular performers of the twentieth century. He began as a struggling conjurer, performing with his wife, Beatrice (known as Bess), in dime museums, beer halls, and traveling circuses through much of the 1890s. His vaudeville stardom and international celebrity lasted from 1900 until his untimely death in 1926.

Suspended Animation

A short man, Harry Houdini forged his body into a powerful instrument of escape. His arms were thick and muscular, and his immensely strong fingers could work their way through canvas. With constant training, his toes acquired the dexterity of fingers. He could open knots and buckles with his teeth. Houdini practiced holding his breath underwater for long periods, and he learned to conserve his energy by never giving way to fear.

A struggling entertainer through most of the 1890s, happy to make $50 per week and often receiving much less, Houdini ultimately claimed fees as high as $3,750 per week. He captured the imagination of millions on both sides of the Atlantic with his daring challenges and aura of invincibility, retaining his popularity by repeatedly introducing highly publicized stunts, such as his stupendous aerial straitjacket escapes. He performed these in numerous cities beginning in 1914, shrewdly suspending himself from newspaper buildings and attracting as many as fifty thousand spectators. Trussed in a thick canvas-and-leather straitjacket, he violently twisted and tugged his way free, extended both arms outward as a victory salute, then dropped the jacket to the cheering crowd.

Houdini suspended, 1922

During the course of his extraordinary career, Houdini freed himself from restraints of every conceivable sort: the most cunningly designed handcuffs and leg irons; massive packing crates and zinc-lined piano cases; office safes and bank vaults; a rolltop desk; a huge government mail bag; a riveted iron boiler; a gigantic football; the jail cells of notorious criminals; and straitjackets, first on stage and then suspended upside-down high above city streets. Wrapped with chains and ropes or locked inside a weighted box, he plunged into rivers and swam free. Lashed against the open barrel of a cannon with a time fuse, he vowed to release himself or "be blown to Kingdom Come." Once he even consented to be buried under six feet of earth and clawed his way back to life.

This was scarcely ordinary work, but Houdini was no ordinary man. Born Ehrich Weiss in 1874 in Budapest and raised in Wisconsin and New York City, the son of a failed rabbi and an intensely doting mother, Houdini was wracked with psychological conflicts. His escape art teemed with elements of perverse anxieties, including exhibitionism, mutilation, entrapment, criminality, insanity, and death.

The film *Houdini* does its best to reduce such perversity to the conventional terms of post–World War II domesticity, using the turn-of-the-

HISTORY

Houdini, clothed for a change, before one of his jail-cell escapes

Houdini dramatized his naked body as audaciously as any performer of his time. At a San Francisco police station in 1899, he took off all his clothes, demanded a thorough body search to prove he had no concealed pick or key, and then challenged officials to lock him in their toughest handcuffs and leg irons to see whether they could hold him. His only condition was that he be allowed to work unobserved. In 1906 at Boston's Tombs prison, Houdini stripped and left his clothes in a locked cell. He was searched, then handcuffed, shackled, and locked naked into a cell on the second tier. The superintendent of police retired to his office, confident that Houdini would be defeated. Only sixteen minutes later, Houdini, now fully clothed, scaled the prison yard's outer wall and climbed into a waiting car. From his dressing room at Keith's Theater, five miles away, he telephoned the startled superintendent, who thought Houdini was still snugly locked in jail.

HOLLYWOOD

Tony Curtis as Houdini

In the film *Houdini*, Harry accepts a challenge to escape from a jail administered by London's famed Scotland Yard. Although Tony Curtis has an athletic build, his body is not displayed in this scene. The warden, not the escape artist, sets the terms of the search. He empties Harry's pockets; confiscates his hat, jacket, belt, collar pin, tie, and shoes; looks into his mouth, and frisks him—a quite superficial search compared to what Houdini actually demanded. Curtis's Harry quickly sheds the single pair of handcuffs but struggles agonizingly to pick the lock outside the cell with a piece of wire from his trousers. Unlike the real Houdini, he permits himself to be observed: A prisoner in the cell facing his comically mimics Harry's every move in his own effort to escape. Although Harry eventually frees himself, the task takes not minutes but hours.

Houdini's Chinese Water Torture Cell

Introduced in 1912 and thereafter a mainstay of his act, the Chinese Water Torture Cell was perhaps the most compelling stage trick Houdini ever devised. The cell itself was an imposing metal-lined mahogany cabinet, less than six feet high and roughly three feet square at its base. In its front panel was an inch-thick plate-glass window. Houdini himself solemnly described the challenges of the escape: He would be locked upside-down inside the box, his ankles shackled and, as if these tortures were not fiendish enough, his body completely immersed in water. He offered a thousand dollars to anyone who could prove he received air while inside the tank. "We all know accidents will happen—and when least expected," he explained, before introducing an assistant who would stand ready with an ax to smash the cell's glass front if that became necessary. Although the tank had a full-length steel grille—to protect Houdini from broken glass should the assistant's services become necessary—this cage ostensibly restricted his movements and made escape that much more difficult.

While Houdini changed into a bathing suit off-stage, volunteers from the audience examined the tank, and his assistants filled it to the brim with water. Houdini then had his ankles secured in heavy wooden stocks, which in turn were fitted into a solid steel frame. He was hoisted aloft and lowered head-first into the cell, his entire body visible underwater through the glass. Assistants quickly locked the frame in place, fastened the tank with padlocked steel bands, and curtained it off from view. With grim humor, the orchestra played "Asleep in the Deep." A minute passed . . . two minutes . . . as many as three. Spectators invited to hold their breath had long since given up. The assistant with the ax raised it anxiously—until Houdini suddenly thrust aside the curtain and strode forward, dripping wet but smiling triumphantly. The empty cell behind him stood as strongly locked as before. He was inevitably greeted by tumultuous applause.

century setting principally as an excuse for lavish costumes by Edith Head. The drama of Houdini and Bess, as played by the newly married young stars Tony Curtis and Janet Leigh, becomes the problem of reconciling love and career, marriage and show business, security and success. Rather than exploring the dimensions of Houdini's intense, driven personality, the film concocts a fictitious account of the couple's marriage. The threat comes not in the form of another woman, but in the siren call of the supernatural, urging Harry to flirt with death as the price of fame. Houdini's childhood is totally ignored: His poverty, his immigrant Jewishness, and even the name Ehrich Weiss are airbrushed away (like Tony Curtis's own impoverished Jewish childhood as Bernard Schwartz).

While Hollywood's Harry is willing to do anything to please the crowd, the more levelheaded Bess nags him to take a normal day job—at a safe and lock factory, no less. Meanwhile, at a magicians' society dinner, he spontaneously performs a straitjacket escape, aided by a strange and unbidden hypnotic power. Impressed by this amazing feat, an old magician tells Harry of a Berlin conjurer named von Schweger who once escaped from a gigantic sealed bottle, reportedly by dematerializing himself. Alarmed by his own powers, von Schweger quit performing. "Drop it, drop it," the old magician similarly warns Harry. "It will make you famous, but it will kill you." Prophecy in this film is not subtle.

As Harry rockets to fame, the film presents, though alters the terms of, many tricks that the real Houdini performed, often reducing their force and drama in the process. "Metamorphosis," for example, was an integral part of the act that Houdini performed with Bess from the beginning of their marriage. The trick began with Houdini submitting to multiple layers of restraint. With his wrists tied behind his back, he was fastened in a sack and locked inside a trunk secured with rope. Bess and assistants concealed the trunk behind curtains. On the count of three, Houdini threw back the curtains to reveal himself free of all bonds. Then he untied the trunk, opened it, and disclosed Bess inside the sack with her hands bound precisely as his had been.

Performed with lightning speed and cunning showmanship, the trick mesmerized audiences. The illusion of "Metamorphosis" could be read in two alternative ways: as the magical release of a man from redoubled confinement and a woman's corresponding capture or as a still more magical sex change between Houdini and his wife. The latter possibility, hinted at in the title of the act, led spectators all the more comfortably to see a man freed and a woman confined as a restitution of order. But the film unaccountably reverses these roles: Bess is freed and Harry takes her place. Instead of an escape artist, he becomes an enterologist, and the drama fizzles.

At the same time the film insists on Harry's deepening pact with the supernatural and with death. The retired magician von Schweger dies in Berlin only days before Harry can speak with him, leaving behind a model of a water torture cell and a faithful assistant, Otto, who immediately transfers his allegiance to Harry. Back in America, Harry continues to woo the crowds by promising to perform an escape in the icy Detroit River. On November 27, 1906, fettered by manacles and two sets of handcuffs, Houdini did actually jump off Detroit's Belle Isle Bridge. Later accounts by Houdini and others elaborated the stunt, turning the water into thick ice, locking Houdini in a trunk, and having him conduct an excruciating underwater search for a hole in the ice. The film *Houdini* incorporates all these fictional elements and moves the event to his allegedly "unlucky" day of Halloween. It even adds its own fillip to the legend: Harry is directed toward the opening in the ice by his mother's voice—only to learn later that she died in New York at that precise moment.

When Houdini's mother did die—in 1913, seven years after the Detroit jump—it was unquestionably the greatest loss in his life. He was so desperate to communicate with her that he employed spirit mediums, even though he and Bess had worked briefly as sham mediums during the 1890s and knew firsthand the tricks of the trade. When these séances proved fraudulent, Houdini mounted a passionate crusade against such poseurs.

Although few things in Houdini's life were uncontroversial, the cause of his death was among the least mysterious. While on tour in Montreal, he exhibited his strength by allowing a medical student to strike him in the abdomen. But the blows came before Houdini had time to prepare himself, and they ruptured his appendix. Houdini fiercely disregarded his own physical ailments, continuing the tour until he collapsed and subsequently died of peritonitis in a Detroit hospital on Halloween, 1926.

Houdini's death is the event toward which the entire film has been steering. While obliquely acknowledging that Harry did have appendicitis, *Houdini* makes the real culprit von Schweger's water torture cell and the dark forces it represents. Despite Bess's forebodings and frantic protestations, Harry attempts the trick for the first time near the end of the film. (In fact, Houdini developed his water torture cell escape fourteen years before his death and performed it hundreds of times.) The film Harry attempts the water torture cell escape to satisfy the lust of the crowd and dies as a result. His last words to Bess are, "If there's any way, I'll come back, I'll come back." If the historical Houdini does indeed come back from the dead, he might make his first visit a vengeful one to Paramount Studios.

Background Reading

Milbourne Christopher, *Houdini: The Untold Story* (Thomas Y. Crowell, 1969)
Kenneth Silverman, *Houdini (Ehrich Weiss)* (HarperCollins, forthcoming)

1953/USA/Color
DIRECTOR: George Marshall; PRODUCER: George Pal; SCREENPLAY: Philip Yordan; STUDIO: Paramount; VIDEO: Paramount; RUNNING TIME: 105 min.

Debunking Spirit Frauds

Modern spiritualism began in 1848 in Hydesville, New York, as a girlish hoax. Catherine Fox and her sister Margaret claimed they had established contact with a mysterious spirit in their house that communicated through strange rappings. Soon they were charging admission and became celebrities. Countless other mediums quickly discovered similar gifts, and spiritualist societies spread across the country. Especially after his mother's death in 1913, Houdini deeply craved the "scientific" confirmation of immortality that spiritualism promised, but he was pitiless in exposing its deceptions. For the rest of his life, while he sought an authentic spiritualist contact with his mother, he devoted considerable energy to unmasking spiritualist charlatans with all the drama and publicity at his command. Wearing disguises, he attended séances and caught mediums red-handed. When *Scientific American* offered prizes for "an authentic spirit photograph" and for "the first physical manifestation of a psychic nature produced under scientific conditions," Houdini joined its investigating committee and prevented it from being duped. On the lecture circuit and in stage performances, he duplicated their effects for all to see.

Houdini preparing for an underwater escape

Later...

Houdini's widow, Bess, tried dutifully to contact her late husband after 1926, but her willingess succeeded only in attracting frauds. A hoax staged by one such medium was exposed in 1929. Five years later, Bess moved to Hollywood where, on the tenth anniversary of Houdini's death, she participated in a widely publicized séance broadcast from the roof of the Knickerbocker Hotel. Nothing happened. She died, still waiting, in 1943.

C A S T

John L. Sullivan (Joel McCrea)
The Girl (Veronica Lake)

The Commercial Apotheosis

When the plot requires that Sullivan (McCrea) end up in a southern chain gang, he knows what hell is like—unrelenting for the convicts, except for an occasional excursion to see a film in a black church. While watching his fellow prisoners taken, briefly, out of their misery, McCrea suffers what one may call the Commercial Apotheosis—except that, in the film's dark context, he realizes that what makes the men laugh is far better than the Man's Fate sort of film he had wanted to make. (In this scene, Sturges also provides a daring note for those days: The blacks have more compassion for the convicts than the whites.)

I suspect that the sly Sturges was able to persuade Paramount to make so downbeat a film by convincing them, in this scene, that, "Well, after all, I show that it's pop lowbrow entertainment that the folks out there want, and I'm all for it, too."

SULLIVAN'S TRAVELS

Gore Vidal

PLACE: EXETER, NEW HAMPSHIRE. Circumstances: I am in my lower-middle-year at the Phillips Exeter Academy. I am fifteen years old. The Japanese have already attacked Pearl Harbor. I know that by the time I am seventeen I shall be in the army. Meanwhile, I sit in the cold gymnasium and watch *Sullivan's Travels.* I don't much like it. The director/writer, Preston Sturges, keeps sliding from farce into grim realism—well, stern pathos—and I am having a hard time keeping up with him.

The story begins in the best Sturges comic style: A popular film director, Joel McCrea, wants to become Serious and adapt for the screen what sounds like a gorgeously awful novel called *Oh Brother, Where Art Thou?* The studio wants him to make one of his usual mindless comedies. McCrea, separated from avaricious wife, consults his "family" retainers, Eric Blore and Robert Greig. Blore is a comic genius whose rabid ferret eyes glare with paranoia while Greig is a solemn bullfrog of a butler, filled with Johnsonian commentaries on the human condition and the nature of vanity. When McCrea announces that he will take to the road as a tramp and make his way penniless in a world of poverty, his advisers try to dissuade him. He persists. When they see his tramp's costume, they sigh and moan. The poor, Greig observes sententiously, do not like to be mocked. Identification is placed in McCrea's shoe, a key plot point.

McCrea then takes to the road followed by a large trailer containing most of the studio's publicity department. He gives the trailer the slip; ends up chopping wood for a randy widow; escapes; meets Veronica Lake, playing an actress who can't get her foot onto a studio lot. (Lake was known for her long straight blonde hair that covered one eye. During the first year of the Second War, women on the assembly line wore their hair like Veronica Lake's, and many were scalped by the relentless machinery. Finally, the Roosevelt administration got Lake to cut her hair. Rosie the Riveter followed suit, and thus the war was won.) In the film, Lake buys McCrea breakfast, and he takes her home—back to Hollywood where all roads lead. So far, so good—that is, funny. But McCrea persists in his quest. Implausibly disguised as a boy, Veronica Lake goes with him. They hop a freight train.

In those days movies were filled with hoboes, comic and otherwise, traveling the rails as they had been doing since the 1870s, when Civil War veterans went looking for work. In that icy gymnasium, I was distinctly uncomfortable with the low-life scenes, while I found them every bit as menacing as I had the actual Bonus Army that converged on

HISTORY

A hobo convention in St. Louis, 1937

The word *hobo* is of obscure origin. It is first sighted around 1890, when it meant an out-of-work man on the move in search of any sort of odd job. The first wave of hoboes appeared after the Civil War, when jobless veterans were dumped on a country and an economy at whose center was the railroad. The second wave was after World War I, again mostly veterans, faced with Depression and Dust Bowl. By and large, hoboes traveled with the complaisance of the authorities. After World War II the U.S. government showed that it had, ever so slowly, learned a lesson: The G.I. Bill of Rights offered free education to the veterans while Harry Truman et al. thoughtfully provided us with a permanent war-time economy, still in place.

HOLLYWOOD

The famous Veronica Lake hair is shorn so that she will look, not too convincingly, like a boy hobo as she joins Sullivan in his pursuit of hell. Writer/director Preston Sturges wanted Lake for the part of the waiflike actress after seeing her in Paramount's *I Wanted Wings* (1941), about three air force recruits. What Lake didn't tell Sturges at first was that she would be six months pregnant when shooting began. Lake's condition forced Sturges to rewrite some scenes, and he ordered costume designer Edith Head to create for Lake gowns and a floppy hobo costume that wouldn't show her condition.

The Bonus March

"The Boners are coming!" That cry is my first political memory. I was six years old. The people of my hometown—Washington, D.C.—were terrified. An army of World War I veterans was marching on the city to demand a bonus for services rendered in the recent war. They were called Boners for short. At six, I thought they were Halloween skeletons: I was terrified, too. The grownups were fearful that, at last, in those bad days, revolution had begun. Only fifteen years earlier the Russian Revolution had taken place. The same thing could happen here, everyone agreed. There were thirteen million unemployed, a number that might bring a quiet smile of satisfaction to Mr. Greenspan's lips but a frown to President Hoover's brow.

On June 17, 1932, I drove with my grandfather, Senator Gore, to the Capitol, where the Senate would vote whether or not to grant the bonus. Gore was known to be antibonus. As we approached the Capitol, I was pleasantly surprised to find that the Boners were not skeletons but plain, if shabby, everyday people. One recognized Gore, and a rock came in through the car window. Grimly, Gore entered the heavily guarded Capitol and voted against the bonus. A benevolent government offered to pay the fare home for each Boner, and all but two thousand left the city. When those who remained refused to abandon their Anacostia village, the army chief of staff, Gen. Douglas MacArthur, with his aide, Maj. Dwight Eisenhower, dispersed them forcefully. There were accidental deaths. This was the background to the age of Franklin Roosevelt that began, four months later, with his election.

MacArthur (left) with Eisenhower (right) at the Bonus March

Washington, D.C., in the summer of 1932. Sturges's tramps lived in makeshift shanties just like the Boners, our name for those veterans of World War I who had come to town in search of bonuses to help them survive the deepening depression.

One morning my father and I flew low over the Anacostia Flats to see how some seventeen thousand Americans were living. Now Sturges had put this poverty—in eloquent black and white—on the screen. I longed for Eric Blore to show up and be funny, but Sturges kept tightening the screw: McCrea's shoes are stolen. The tramp who stole them is killed. From the identification tag in the shoe, McCrea is thought dead. But he is actually in a southern prison camp, at hard labor. For some infraction, he is placed in an upright metal coffinlike structure and sweated nearly to death. Brutal realism takes over the screen. I wonder when—not if—the inmates will take over this camp and kill the guards. A question I still ask myself in other, similar, regards.

On rare occasions, the convicts are allowed to see a movie in a black church. The movie is always a simpleminded comedy, but the prisoners are delighted to be taken, briefly, out of grim reality. In a Damascene flash, McCrea realizes that the world does not need his lugubrious Serious film but more comedy. A series of quick comic turns and McCrea is back to Hollywood, turning out commercial comedies.

At fifteen, I didn't entirely buy this. But I have never forgotten the Boners in life or the hoboes and convicts on the screen. For more than half a century their images keep coming back to me—and always, curiously enough, in black and white—even those scenes recalled from life. Finally, last spring, as a television documentary maker, I returned to the Anacostia Flats for the first time since 1932, and there they still were, the poor, only now they are all black and far more numerous than then—and one knows pretty much what is to be.

Background Reading

Jacqueline Jones, *The Dispossessed: America's Underclass from the Civil War to the Present* (Basic Books, 1992)
Gore Vidal, *Screening History* (Harvard University Press, 1992)

1941/USA/B&W
DIRECTOR: Preston Sturges; PRODUCER: Paul Jones; SCREENPLAY: Preston Sturges; STUDIO: Paramount; VIDEO: MCA; RUNNING TIME: 91 min.

Army troops evict the Boners.

Later...

May 1932
Bonus Army evicted from Anacostia Flats.

Douglas MacArthur: "The misguided men have refused to listen to persuasion. Now they must submit to compulsion."

President Herbert Hoover: "The government cannot be coerced by mob rule."

September 1932
General James Mitchell: "The Bonus Army brought to the city of Washington the largest aggregation of criminals that had ever assembled in the city at any one time."

November 1932
H.L. Mencken: "Hoover had to defame the poor idiots he had gassed."

Herbert Hoover defeated by Franklin D. Roosevelt.

1933
President Roosevelt: "No person, because he wore a uniform, must thereafter be placed in a special class of beneficiaries over and above all other citizens."

Roosevelt signs Economy Act of 1933, which cuts allowances for service-related disabilities by 25 percent. A second, smaller group of Boners marches on Washington; Roosevelt shunts the veterans fifteen miles away to a camp at Fort Hunt; the protest fizzles.

1944
Congress passes the G.I. Bill.

1945
Robert J. Watt, American Federation of Labor: "If we give special status to veterans today, we are faced with the problem of special consideration for minority groups tomorrow."

CAST

Clyde Barrow	*(Warren Beatty)*
Bonnie Parker	*(Faye Dunaway)*
C.W. Moss	*(Michael J. Pollard)*
Buck Barrow	*(Gene Hackman)*

BONNIE AND CLYDE

Nancy F. Cott

Bonnie horsing around with Clyde

Bonnie and Clyde and Frank Hamer

At one point in the film, Bonnie and Clyde capture Texas Ranger Frank Hamer, who has been pursuing them. More than any other scene in *Bonnie and Clyde*, this one proposes Bonnie as a liberated woman, free to taunt even the male authority represented by Hamer. Her affectation of a cigar, as well as her insolence in kissing Hamer on the mouth, express this liberation symbolically. (The real Hamer did return to the Rangers in 1934, leaving other work at the state's request to hunt down Bonnie and Clyde, but he was never personally humiliated by them.)

That Bonnie Parker smoked cigars was often noted in the press, though the only basis for this was a photo, found after a stakeout of the Barrow gang's lodgings, showing Bonnie, fooling around, with her foot on a car bumper, a revolver in her hand, and Buck Barrow's cigar in her mouth. Thereafter, she was frequently identified as a cigar-smoking moll, which made her and her family irate.

PERHAPS NEVER WAS A "HISTORICAL" FILM less intended and less inclined to make a point about its ostensible subject than director Arthur Penn's *Bonnie and Clyde*. In an interview published in *Cinema* in 1968, the year after the film was released, Penn readily conceded that he "wanted to make a modern film whose action takes place in the past." The narrative of *Bonnie and Clyde* indeed follows the exploits of Clyde Barrow and Bonnie Parker, who evaded police capture between spring 1932 and May 1934 while robbing banks, filling stations, dry-cleaners, and grocery stores in ten states and killing at least a dozen people as they went. However, the film takes great artistic liberties with the history of Bonnie and Clyde, imprinting it with 1960s themes of youth revolt and women's liberation.

These themes are suggested in the film's opening scene, when a restless, virtually naked Bonnie stalks about her bedroom, incoherently discontented; the camera focuses on her as she lies back on the bed and gazes through the bed rails, as though imprisoned by her routine life. (This shot also displays her 1960s eye makeup, making no concession to period style.) Looking out the window, she spies Clyde Barrow attempting to steal her mother's car, and the relationship between them begins. Bonnie is intrigued, not intimidated, by Clyde's admission that he has recently spent time in state prison for armed robbery; she finds the figure of the outlaw magnetic. In possibly the film's sexiest moment, Clyde shows Bonnie his gun, which she strokes with awe. This early scene sets up an important dynamic between the two, for it is upon Bonnie's mild taunt—"You wouldn't have the gumption to *use* it"—that Clyde resumes his life of crime by robbing the store across the street. Their getaway, which ends with Bonnie throwing herself amorously on Clyde, confirms the point that she finds an erotic charge in his gun-handling. His rejection of her kisses, however, and his admission that he's "not much of a lover boy" confound audience expectations of a conventional romantic screen pairing.

Clyde abdicates both the appeal of sexual pleasure and the power of sexual violence over Bonnie. Instead, he challenges her psychologically, divining her mental rather than bodily needs and offering her the possibility of leaving routine behind and becoming someone special and notorious if she sticks with him. As Bonnie responds to this approach—obeying Clyde's command to get rid of the spit-curl on her cheek, the mark of her desultory life as a waitress—he appears to have reestablished his male authority. But as the movie proceeds, it becomes unclear just who is on top: Clyde's lack of interest in heterosexual sex means that Bonnie

Bonnie Parker, who grew up in working-class Cement City outside Dallas, was a twenty-year-old unemployed waitress when she met Clyde Barrow in 1930 and fell in love with him. At the time she was still married to her high school sweetheart, whom she had wed at sixteen, but that marriage was over in all but name. (Her husband was in jail for robbery.)

The product of a more impoverished background than Bonnie's, Clyde was twenty-one years old when they met. He had already had a series of love affairs and was thought to be very charming (despite his large ears). His strongest commitments to women, however, seemed reserved for his mother and his older sister, Nell, who were both fanatically devoted to him. Bonnie's closeness with her own mother is often referred to in the film, but Clyde's sustaining relationships with his mother and sister are left out.

HOLLYWOOD

Faye Dunaway as Bonnie

Using myth, violence, and moral ambiguity, director Arthur Penn has often dealt with contemporary issues through the lives of social outcasts. In the two films he made after *Bonnie and Clyde*, Penn sustained his theme of the outcast's relationship to conventional society. In its story about a commune of hippies, *Alice's Restaurant* (1969) portrayed the metaphorical death of 1960s idealism. And the sometimes lyrical, often brutal *Little Big Man* (1970)—narrated by the only white survivor of Custer's famous last stand—was one of the first Hollywood productions to undermine the romantic myths of the American West.

When *Bonnie and Clyde* was criticized for its graphic brutality, Penn defended the violence as an element of human nature. Eliminating violence from the film, Penn said, would be "like eliminating one of the primary colors from the palette of the painter."

The Women's Movement

As *Bonnie and Clyde* was being made and released, a resurgent feminism was causing seismic shifts in the social roles of women and their relationship to men. Beginning in the early 1960s, federal policy paid new attention to women's rights: President John F. Kennedy's Commission on the Status of Women documented women's continuing legal and economic inequality, and the Equal Pay Act of 1963 mandated that women be paid the same as men doing the same work. More important, the Civil Rights Act of 1964, which was supposed to root out discrimination on the basis of race or color, included "sex" in its purview as the result of unexpected collusion between southern congressmen hoping to load down the bill (and thereby defeat it) and congresswomen directly pursuing women's rights. In 1963, Betty Friedan's best-selling *Feminine Mystique* analyzed the constraints that kept educated middle-class women at home as wives and mothers, their potential as individuals unrealized. A few years later, she and others founded the National Organization for Women to pursue women's "full participation in the mainstream of American society."

While NOW mobilized women's rights advocates in public policy occupations, labor unions, and the professions, a younger generation of women (mostly students at universities) were being radicalized by their immersion in the southern civil rights movement, the student New Left, and the growing opposition to the Vietnam War. Meanwhile, the youthful counterculture, aided by access to the new birth-control pill, rejected parental sexual mores. By the mid-1960s, young women radicals were claiming their own right to free sexual and political expression. Frustrated by their relegation to second-class status in male-dominated movements for social change and feeling sexually objectified rather than free, they analogized their own oppression to that of racial minorities or colonized peoples and demanded "women's liberation." Using the networks established by student radicals and the tactic of small-group "consciousness-raising," pockets of activists spread the women's liberation movement nationwide by the end of 1967.

cannot bend him to her will by exerting typical feminine "wiles"; what she can and does do, however, is challenge his masculinity (especially his apparent lack thereof), inciting outlawry of the kind that first attracted her to him. In this way, guns substitute for sex, and the next-to-last scene confirms early hints that Bonnie's challenges have set Clyde on his increasingly deadly crimes. As the couple drives along in a carefree mood—their car taking them, unknowingly, to their deaths by police ambush—Bonnie picks a piece of fruit out of a paper bag, bites into it, and hands it to Clyde for him to take a bite. Clearly this Eve has led Adam astray.

In fact, Clyde Barrow was a confirmed criminal when he first charmed Bonnie Parker, two years before they embarked on their travels together. His stint in the Texas state penitentiary came between their meeting and the parole that freed him to begin adventuring with her. Their relationship seems to have been a good deal more conventional, in terms of gender roles, than the movie version suggests—that is, Clyde called the shots and Bonnie went along. She was a tiny person, only four feet ten, and weighed less than ninety pounds—not nearly as statuesque or glamorous as Faye Dunaway, but pretty, with curly blonde hair and blue eyes. The presence of this golden-haloed accomplice among the Barrow gang (over time, Clyde worked with several different men, including his brother, Buck) became central to their infamy. Yet the film's implication that Bonnie inflated Clyde's criminal ambitions is false—perhaps borrowed from the history of Kathryn Thorne, who married small-time bootlegger George Kelly Barnes and egged him on to become the well-known gangster Machine Gun Kelly.

The film also imports, from another outlaw's personality, a Robin Hood theme that seems to exonerate Bonnie and Clyde from any imputation of evil—that is, their sympathy for the dispossessed. However, the real Bonnie Parker and Clyde Barrow never displayed motives or sympathies of this sort; rather, it was their contemporary, John Dillinger, who did—as his biographer, John Toland, forcefully insisted in response to the public's embrace of this movie. (*Bonnie and Clyde*'s screenwriters had indeed used Toland's biography as a source for their screenplay.) Unlike Dillinger, who conducted mainly high-class heists and tried to avoid killing, Clyde Barrow was a careless and remorseless killer in pursuit of small stakes; this, together with his tremendous skill driving speeding Ford V-8s (he once wrote a letter of appreciation to Henry Ford!) and the way Bonnie shouldered her own gun next to him, made them legendary.

Bonnie and Clyde was severely criticized at first for glamorizing the lives of two hardscrabble criminals and portraying their multiple felonies as picaresque adventures set to banjo music. Yet the enormous box-office success of the movie forced even these critics to come to grips with its appeal. Through the film's veneer of 1930s decor and costume, a 1960s sensibility shimmers. If Depression folk had gotten some vicarious plea-

BONNIE AND CLYDE

sure (and horror) from the Barrow gang's exploits, 1967 audiences identified with Bonnie and Clyde, even if they recoiled from the violence they engendered, fatal to others and finally to themselves. *Bonnie and Clyde* was seen as a rumination on this violence as well as on the nature of power: Did it come from the barrel of a gun? Or from "the law" and its settled structures of authority? Only a few years before, President Kennedy had been shot (indeed, Clyde's screen death borrows a gory detail from the assassination); now black ghettos were going up in flames and the war in Vietnam was escalating. Violence, both popular and systematic, was very much on people's minds.

Just as important, 1967 was a watershed year for student protest against the Vietnam War, the youth counterculture, and the civil rights movement. The perception that constituted authorities were unreasonable had reached a new level of intensity, but the fractures within these movements were still hidden, and the cataclysmic assassinations of Martin Luther King, Jr., and Robert Kennedy as yet unforeseen. Bonnie and Clyde's defiance, insouciance, and feeling for the oppressed captured the contemporary sensibility of revolt—and, not least, the revolt of women. Bonnie's multivalent character—simultaneously punk and moll—suggested both the threat and the promise of changing the gender order. Frolicsome in spirit while deadly in implication, *Bonnie and Clyde* offered no resolution for these refractory issues. Instead, the historical record provided its spectacular doomsday ending.

The Farmhouse Scene

In another invented scene that takes place after their very first getaway, Bonnie and Clyde are hiding out in an abandoned farmhouse when its former owner stops by to find them at shooting practice. The couple soon discovers that the farmhouse is empty because a bank has foreclosed on the farmer's mortgage. It's a "pitiful shame," Bonnie declares, and Clyde announces, "We rob banks," as though they had chosen their targets in retaliation for cases such as the farmer's. Clyde then invites the farmer and his black sharecropper to shoot at the bank's sign, which apparently gives them all satisfaction. Later scenes pick up this theme of Clyde's supposed sympathy for the impoverished.

Peter Simon bought Bonnie and Clyde's bullet-riddled car at auction in 1973 for $175,000.

Later...

Bonnie and Clyde met violent deaths on May 23, 1934, when they were ambushed outside the small town of Arcadia, Louisiana, by four men: Dallas sheriff's deputies Ted Hinton and Bob Alcorn; former Texas Ranger Frank Hamer; and Hamer's assistant, Manny Gault. After the ambush, some lionized these Texas lawmen as heroes; others condemned them as cowardly murderers. The *Dallas News* marveled at "the glamour that small minds saw in the sneaking and bloody exploits" of the Barrow gang. That same year, "Public Enemy Number One" John Dillinger was gunned down by agents of the Federal Bureau of Investigation. Dillinger's death at the hands of the FBI augured the end of an era when criminals could evade the law simply by crossing state lines.

Background Reading

Alice Echols, *Daring to Be Bad: Radical Feminism in America, 1967–1975* (University of Minneapolis Press, 1989)
John Treherne, *The Strange History of Bonnie and Clyde* (Jonathan Cape, 1984)

1967/USA/Color
DIRECTOR: Arthur Penn; **PRODUCER:** Warren Beatty; **SCREENPLAY:** David Newman, Robert Benton; **STUDIO:** Warner; **VIDEO:** Warner; **RUNNING TIME:** 111 min.

NANCY F. COTT

THE GRAPES OF WRATH

Alan Brinkley

CAST

Tom Joad   *(Henry Fonda)*
Ma Joad   *(Jane Darwell)*
Casey   *(John Carradine)*

NEITHER JOHN STEINBECK, IN WRITING THE novel *The Grapes of Wrath*, nor John Ford, in translating it to the screen, believed he was producing a work of history. The book and the film were attempts to reveal an aspect of life in the 1930s, one that both Steinbeck and Ford considered morally and dramatically compelling. To modern readers and viewers, however, *The Grapes of Wrath*, in all its versions, has become an unusually vivid historical document: a portrait of a portion of American society in the Great Depression and of a political sensibility that continues to resonate (if only faintly at times) in the contemporary world.

More than a million people, most of them dispossessed farmers, uprooted themselves from the barren lands of the Dust Bowl during the 1930s and moved to California. They were known as Okies, even though as many came from Texas, Arkansas, and western Missouri as from Oklahoma. Steinbeck became aware of them as they poured into the agricultural areas surrounding his home in northern California. Their story possessed him, and he distilled it into an account of the fictional Joad family's troubled journey from drought-stricken Oklahoma to the false promise of the West. The novel had a sensational impact, greatly strengthened by the strikingly faithful 1940 film adaptation, directed by John Ford, a four-time Academy Award–winner who is better known today as the auteur of several classic westerns. Both the book and the film were among a relatively small number of popular works of the Great Depression centrally concerned with issues of social and economic justice.

For Steinbeck, publication of *The Grapes of Wrath* was the culmination of a long and, at times, tortured search for an answer to the question of what Americans really valued. The Great Depression, he believed, had exposed the hollowness of the "American dream" of individualism and material success. Steinbeck wanted there to be something more, but it took him most of the 1930s to find it. *The Grapes of Wrath* was his third attempt at using the Okies to assess the meaning of the Great Depression. In it, he found at last a philosophical stance that expressed both his outrage at social injustice and his belief in the possibility of transcending it.

There were signs of hopelessness, to be sure: The main characters, the Joads, come to the end of their long ordeal in worse shape than when they began it—the family dispersing, their possessions washed away in a flood, their prospects bleak. There were signs, too, of anger—in the unvarying harshness of Steinbeck's portraits of bankers, landowners, local sheriffs, and other capitalist flunkies; in the bitter commentary on the human costs of industrial "progress" (explicit in the novel, implicit in the film); and in the radicalization of Tom Joad, who, having killed a policeman (justifiably,

Farmhouse near Dalhart, Texas, 1938

The Dust Bowl

The calamitous drought that prostrated the Great Plains during the 1930s—and produced the Dust Bowl migration of which the Joads became a symbol—was beyond human control. The devastation it caused was not. Most of the agricultural lands that constituted the Dust Bowl (roughly 150,000 square miles in western Oklahoma, the Texas Panhandle, and parts of Colorado, New Mexico, and Kansas) had been relatively recently settled—in the late nineteenth century or later. The newly arrived farmers had torn up the deeply rooted natural sod that had protected the soil from drought for many centuries (hence the term *sodbusters),* cultivated the land, and left it unprotected against aridity and wind. The results were the great dust storms of the 1930s—storms so terrible that they blotted out the sun and suffocated any animals and people unable to take protection from them.

HISTORY

Migrant Mother **by Dorothea Lange**

John Steinbeck was not the first chronicler of the plight of migrant workers. A group of extraordinary documentary photographers—among them Walker Evans, Margaret Bourke-White, Roy Stryker, Arthur Rothstein, and Ben Shahn—recorded some of the most memorable images of the Okies beginning in the mid-1930s. Many of them found employment with such New Deal agencies as the Farm Security Administration.

One of the most talented was Dorothea Lange, whose famous photograph *Migrant Mother* has become an icon of the era. Lange was a portrait photographer in San Francisco in the early 1930s until she became so distressed by the suffering around her that she resolved to "capture somehow the effect of the calamity which overwhelmed America." For the next several years, she worked at documenting the lives of migrant farmworkers, mostly through portraiture, creating a body of work that was both polemically effective in its own time and timeless in its emotional power.

HOLLYWOOD

The Joad family in *The Grapes of Wrath*

There is about *The Grapes of Wrath* an affecting optimism, a joy in life and community, that is central to John Ford's work in the 1940s. Nonetheless, it took considerable courage for him to undertake a film that bordered on indicting the capitalist system and served almost as a cry for socialism. Twentieth Century-Fox chieftain Darryl F. Zanuck adopted the film as his personal project and involved himself with every aspect of its production. He took great pains to preserve Steinbeck's novel, for which he paid a then-staggering one hundred thousand dollars, including in the contract the promise that the film would "fairly and reasonably retain the main action and social intent of said literary property." Zanuck personally emended Nunnally Johnson's screenplay and, with Steinbeck's approval, inserted Jane Darwell's famous "We're the people" speech. Ford lauded Zanuck's efforts, stating: "The way Zanuck changed it, it came out on an upbeat."

Doctors immunize children at an FSA camp.

The Farm Security Administration

One of the few happy moments in *The Grapes of Wrath* is the Joad family's arrival at a federally run camp for migrants, which appears almost utopian compared to the grim campsites depicted elsewhere in the film. It was clearly meant to represent the string of camps established in California by the New Deal's Farm Security Administration, the most important government agency concerned with the plight of the Okies. The FSA camps were intended both as a solution to the migrants' problems and as a symbol of enlightened social planning. Just as in the film, the real camps had common washrooms and community facilities designed to promote a sense of cooperation and mutual obligation.

Radicalism During the Great Depression

Contemporaries sometimes called the 1930s the Red Decade because radical politics in those years achieved an intensity and a popularity perhaps unprecedented in American history. Although radical sentiment took many forms, the growth of the American Communist party was perhaps the most visible sign of its strength. The party's formal membership peaked at approximately one hundred thousand in the mid-1940s, but its reach was far greater than that. It was a critical force in the union battles of the Depression era, including the attempts to organize farmworkers. It also had great appeal among intellectuals, many of whom saw the Depression as evidence of the failure of capitalism and the need for a radically different economic and social order. The party experienced its greatest influence during its Popular Front period, when it temporarily muted its calls for revolution, worked to produce an alliance of "Anti-Fascist" groups, and even supported Franklin Roosevelt. After the 1939 Nazi-Soviet pact, party leaders (complying with directives from Moscow) abandoned the Popular Front and resumed their traditional revolutionary stance.

Steinbeck suggests), leaves the family late in both the novel and the film to join an unspecified movement committed to social struggle. He promises his mother: "Wherever they's a fight so hungry people can eat, I'll be there. Wherever they's a cop beatin' up a guy, I'll be there."

At first, Ford's film adaptation seems to mute the despair and the anger of the novel. Gone are the terrible flood that devastates the Joad family at the end and some of the harshest scenes of legal and political brutality. At times, the film suggests that the suffering it portrays is simply a result of forces beyond anyone's control. But the occasional note of fatalism in the film is, in the end, less powerful than the frequent scenes of cruelty, prejudice, and evil, which are almost as harsh as those in the novel itself: a gas-station operator casually observing that "them Okies got no sense and no feelings. They ain't human"; brutish police shooting and killing a mother in a transient camp in a bungled effort to stop a fleeing "agitator," then commenting, "Boy what a mess those .45s make"; landowners and the tame local officials in California using any pretext to exploit and degrade the migrant workers. "They're working away on our spirits . . . our decency," Tom Joad tells his mother later in the film. Ford, like Steinbeck, makes clear that it is not just impersonal social forces but human selfishness and cruelty that are responsible for the human misery.

To both Steinbeck and Ford, however, neither despair nor rage could adequately convey the real meaning of the Great Depression. Instead, the novel and film suggest, the true lesson of the times was the importance of community: not community defined in traditional, geographical terms; not the community of a neighborhood, or a town, or a region—but a community of the human spirit, for which the only real model was the family. The apostate preacher Jim Casy (an allegorical figure whose principal function is to convey Steinbeck's spiritual yearnings) expresses something of this idea in his diffident way: "Maybe it's all men an' all women we love," he says in the novel. "Maybe all men got one big soul ever'body's a part of." In the film, he wears the perpetual gentle smile of a secular saint and says at one point, "All that lives is holy," as if to suggest that true religion is a love less of God than of humanity and a respect for the decency of all people.

Yet while the men in *The Grapes of Wrath* may talk at times about a transcendent vision of community, they seem unable to do much to help achieve it. The male characters die, run away from responsibility, get into trouble and disappear, or descend into helplessness and paralysis. It is the women who have the strength to endure and to lay the foundation of a new human community based on universal love. Ma Joad, the center of both the family and the story, gradually redefines her own notion of "fambly" to include "anybody": "It used to be the fambly was first," she says. "It ain't so now. Worse off we get, the more we got to do." In the novel's closing scene, her daughter, Rose of Sharon, helps a starving stranger by allowing him to nurse at her breasts. (Ford, a conservative Catholic, omitted this scene entirely from his film.) When Pa Joad despairs late in the film, admitting, "I ain't no good no more," Ma replies, "A woman can change better than a man. Man, he lives in fits and jerks. Woman, it's all one flow, like a stream."

To their many critics, both the novel and the film are hopelessly romantic. The treacly optimism and boundless generosity of its beleaguered characters often strain credulity. The political message seems muddled and at times naive. But the occasional bathos is part of what makes *The Grapes of Wrath* such an important document of the Great Depression. Analysts of the 1930s have long struggled to understand why, in the face of such misery and distress, the United States experienced so little genuine upheaval—such relatively limited radicalism, such modest violence. The most frequent answer has been the power of individualism—the tendency of desperate people to blame themselves for their problems, Americans' cultural inability to think in collective terms. *The Grapes of Wrath* suggests another answer to that question.

Steinbeck embraced, and John Ford faithfully re-created, a social vision no less deeply rooted in American culture than the individualistic ethos with which it competed. It rested on an almost romantic notion of the natural goodness of "the people." It imagined a culture in which a simple, folkish patience and warmheartedness—a spontaneous generosity— would compensate for and eventually overcome the cruelty and oppressiveness of the economic system. The story of *The Grapes of Wrath* is a harsh one, to be sure; but in many ways the message was as comforting to Americans of the 1930s as that of Frank Capra's warm, hopeful, populist comedies—and not, in the end, very different from it. In 1936, poet Carl Sandburg—as sentimental a cultural figure as one can imagine— published his own paean to Depression-era radicalism, an optimistic, self-consciously uplifting book entitled *The People, Yes!* John Steinbeck and John Ford were saying essentially the same thing: "We keep a comin'," Ma Joad affirms in the film's closing lines. "We're the people that live."

The enduring appeal of *The Grapes of Wrath* suggests the fascination with which Americans still regard the Great Depression. But the novel and the film are more than intriguing period pieces. Despite their occasional clumsiness and sentimentality, they speak to modern audiences, as they did to audiences in the 1930s, by evoking one of the most consistently cherished American faiths. They suggest that running like a river beneath the surface of the nation's cold, hard, individualistic culture lies the spirit of Ma Joad, a spirit of "fambly" and community that, once tapped, might redeem us all.

Background Reading

James N. Gregory, *American Exodus: The Dust Bowl Migration and Okie Culture in California* (Oxford University Press, 1989)

1940/USA/B&W
DIRECTOR: John Ford; PRODUCER: Darryl F. Zanuck; SCREENPLAY: Nunnally Johnson; STUDIO: Twentieth Century-Fox; VIDEO: Key; RUNNING TIME: 129 min.

Steinbeck and the Migrants

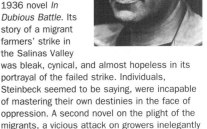

Steinbeck's first attempt to tell the story of the migrant workers in California, and to discern some meaning in it, was his 1936 novel *In Dubious Battle*. Its story of a migrant farmers' strike in the Salinas Valley was bleak, cynical, and almost hopeless in its portrayal of the failed strike. Individuals, Steinbeck seemed to be saying, were incapable of mastering their own destinies in the face of oppression. A second novel on the plight of the migrants, a vicious attack on growers inelegantly titled *L'Affaire Lettuceberg*, was bitter, angry, and so unsatisfying to the author that he burned the manuscript. Steinbeck later described it as a "mean, nasty book." In *The Grapes of Wrath* (1939), he found what he considered a proper balance between outrage and faith.

Later...

The story of the Dust Bowl migration, *The Grapes of Wrath* suggests, was one of great personal hardship and loss. But it was also part of a broad demographic shift that affected the entire United States during the 1930s and 1940s: the movement of people off increasingly unprofitable farms and into factories and other occupations. Throughout the Midwest and Southwest (not just within the Dust Bowl region), hundreds of thousands of sharecroppers, tenant farmers, and small landowners, black and white, lost their land and moved to towns and cities.

Those like the Joad family who moved to California suffered more than most, but in the long run, at least, the Dust Bowl migration may not have been a true disaster for many of the Okies and their descendants. Beginning in 1940 and accelerating thereafter, California became the fastest growing industrial state in the country— with massive new defense plants and other facilities employing many thousands of formerly jobless people. In this booming new world, which continued for several decades after the war, most of the Dust Bowl migrants eventually built lives of at least modest comfort and dignity for themselves. Whether their economic gains were adequate recompense for the pain of being uprooted from their land and their culture is not, perhaps, for historians to judge.

ALAN BRINKLEY

TORA! TORA! TORA!

Akira Iriye

CAST

Husband E. Kimmel	*(Martin Balsam)*
Yamamoto Isoroku	*(Soh Yamamura)*
Walter C. Short	*(Jason Robards, Jr.)*

The New Asian Order

U.S.-Japanese relations deteriorated during the 1930s as Japanese forces first conquered Manchuria and then, in 1937, invaded China, threatening American lives, interests, and prestige. In the United States, public opinion turned decisively against Japan as news spread of the atrocities committed against Chinese civilians (particularly the December 1937 "rape of Nanking"). The situation grew worse after 1940, when Japan allied itself with Germany and occupied the northern part of French Indochina. The Japanese justified this action in the name of a new Asian order that would free Asians from Western colonialism and exploitation. The Chinese did not share this vision and turned to the United States, the Soviet Union, and Great Britain for help. Because the European nations were enveloped in their own war, only the United States stood in Japan's way. Even before Pearl Harbor, President Roosevelt kept the bulk of the U.S. fleet in the Pacific as a deterrent and banned the shipment of most goods to Japan. The Japanese thus came to view the United States as the main obstacle in the way of their ambitions.

"TORA, TORA, TORA" WAS THE CODE THE Japanese pilots who bombed Pearl Harbor on December 7, 1941, used to signal their mission's success. Focusing on the attack on the U.S. Navy's Pacific headquarters, this film devotes almost an hour to scene after scene of Japanese planes flying over the harbor and targeting the battleships cooped up there, unable to escape or offer much resistance.

The background to the attack is presented from both the Japanese and the American perspectives. Adm. Yamamoto Isoroku, commander-in-chief of Japan's combined fleet and architect of the plan to attack Pearl Harbor, is presented as a brilliant strategist who nevertheless opposes war with the United States. In the film, Yamamoto (played by Soh Yamamura) even says that it is a great mistake to underestimate the fighting potential of the Americans, who—though seemingly easygoing, materialistic, and unwilling to make sacrifices for their country—will make a fierce opponent if aroused. The real Yamamoto, though keenly aware of the grave consequences of war (he had gone to school in the United States), dutifully worked out the Pearl Harbor attack plan throughout 1941. By the time the orders were confirmed in late November, he was ready to execute the plan.

In the film, Yamamoto insists that the Japanese deliver an ultimatum to the U.S. State Department one hour before the attack, scheduled to commence at 1:30 P.M. eastern standard time (8:00 A.M. in Hawaii). He later becomes furious when he learns that Japanese ambassadors Kichisaburo Nomura and Saburo Kurusu submitted the message to Secretary of State Cordell Hull at 2:20 P.M.—some fifty-five minutes *after* the attack (the assault began five minutes ahead of schedule). "To awaken a sleeping giant and fill him with a terrible resolve," Yamamoto tells other naval commanders as they celebrate the success of the Pearl Harbor mission, "is sowing the seed for certain disaster." And with this remark, the movie ends. Everything after December 7, 1941, happened as the admiral predicted.

The Japanese ultimatum was delivered late because the embassy was instructed not to entrust its decoding and typing to clerical staff. To illustrate this, the film shows a young diplomat typing the lengthy fourteen-part message with one finger as the minutes tick past. By focusing the coming of the war on so trivial a matter as incompetent typing skills, *Tora! Tora! Tora!* gives the impression that if the Japanese typist had been a little faster, the Americans might have fought less passionately and the course of history would have been quite different. Such a scenario loses sight of the larger picture. Yamamoto keeps saying, "If Japan

HISTORY

Adm. Yamamoto Isoroku (right)

After Pearl Harbor, Admiral Yamamoto basked in the glory of his success, but the advantage he had gained did not last long. As early as April 1942, U.S. forces launched a dramatic counterattack when planes from the aircraft carrier *Hornet* bombed Tokyo. In June of that year, Yamamoto, along with several Japanese army commanders, attempted to capture Midway Island, which they hoped to use as a base for their planned invasion of Hawaii. Yamamoto's strategy failed, however, when U.S. forces, making judicious use of intercepted military cables, sank four Japanese carriers, a major loss that compelled Japan to give up any hope of expanding its Pacific conquests. In April 1943, the United States, again making timely use of decoded intercepts, ambushed a plane carrying Yamamoto over the Solomon Islands and shot it down, killing the admiral.

HOLLYWOOD

Soh Yamamura as Yamamoto

It took several years of negotiation between Japanese and U.S. investors to get *Tora! Tora! Tora!* off the drawing board. Twentieth Century-Fox decided to produce two separate movies: A Japanese film depicting one side of the story and an American film showing the other. Producer Elmo Williams picked Richard Fleischer to direct the U.S. tale, while the Japanese story would be told by Akira Kurosawa, whose *Rashomon* (1951) and *The Seven Samurai* (1954) had made him the first Japanese director to win international acclaim. Kurosawa's film progressed painfully slowly, however, and its cost mounted. The producers finally dismissed the director and replaced him with Toshio Masuda and Kinji Fukasaku. The U.S. and Japanese films were finally spliced together into two slightly different versions, one for each country.

The Magic Intercepts

The Japanese used many codes in their diplomatic and military messages. One in particular, called Purple, was supposed to be the most advanced of its day. It was used by the foreign ministry in Tokyo to communicate with its embassies abroad. The fateful fourteen-paragraph ultimatum of December 7 breaking off further negotiations with the United States was encoded in Purple. It was so sensitive that Tokyo ordered its representatives in Washington not to use American secretaries to type it but to do so themselves. This led, in part, to the delay depicted in *Tora! Tora! Tora!* (An internal foreign ministry investigation conducted just after the war blamed the delay on the inefficiency and ineptness of two young diplomats.)

The Americans, however, had already intercepted and deciphered the message's fourteen parts, thanks to a decoding device known as Magic. The Magic intercepts were the result of arduous work by the U.S. Army's signal intelligence service, which by mid-1940 was circulating decoded messages among a few top officials. (The Hawaiian commanders, Adm. Husband Kimmel and Gen. Walter Short, were not among them.) In a controversial decision, the top military officials in Washington had decided not to forward Magic intercepts to Hawaii as a safeguard against the Japanese learning that the secrecy of Purple had been breached. Messages decoded in Washington were summarized and, when deemed important, forwarded to Honolulu by military cable. It so happened that on the morning of December 7, a Sunday, no means was available to send the gist of the decoded ultimatum to Hawaii—except by Western Union. (Military radio was out due to bad weather conditions.) By the time the telegram arrived, Pearl Harbor was a war zone.

is forced to enter into war against the United States . . . ," but the passive voice is misleading; it was the United States, not Japan, that was forced to go to war in the Pacific. While the film shows Secretary of State Hull and Ambassador Nomura engaging in endless and futile negotiations to avert war, the fundamental obstacles to peace are never clarified. Nothing is said about Japanese aggression in China or the much-publicized atrocities committed by the Japanese during their occupation. It was American outrage at these events that precipitated war in the Pacific.

There is casual mention of Japan's invasion of Indochina and the retaliatory U.S. oil embargo, although this is technically incorrect: There was no formal embargo, only a de facto prohibition of oil shipments through the denial of export licenses. The film also refers to the Japanese alliance with Germany, depicting the Japanese army as aggressively seeking a treaty with the Nazis despite the navy's opposition. These digressions, however, are never placed in a coherent picture, and the viewer has no way to make the connections among them.

In reality, Japan sought an alliance with Germany for a number of reasons: Among them was the belief that a pact with Germany would keep the United States out of a war it would be forced to fight on two fronts. The Japanese navy, which had different and conflicting aims, initially opposed the alliance. Some senior officers thought it would actually increase the chances of war with the United States (for which the navy was not yet prepared), while others thought the continuation of the war in China *without* the threat of a Pacific war would mean more money for the army and severe cutbacks for their own service.

Instead of depicting these disputes, the film remains preoccupied with the Pearl Harbor attack itself and the question of why it was not prevented, or at least predicted in sufficient time to minimize damage. At times, the story comes close to embracing a conspiracy theory—namely, that Washington did not forward to its Hawaiian commanders pertinent information obtained from decoded secret Japanese messages (the so-called Magic intercepts, made possible by a major American cryptographic breakthrough) for fear that such information might alert the Japanese to change their codes. Yet the overall impression the film conveys is less one of conspiracy than of ineptitude, bureaucratic and otherwise. Except for a few middle-ranking and low-level officers, the American military is portrayed as either complacent or ignorant. Although the commanding officers in Washington know the bilateral relationship has reached a critical point, they do little or nothing to alert Hawaii.

Those responsible for the defense of Hawaii, too, are depicted as unimaginative, bureaucratic types. For instance, the movie accurately locates a Japanese submarine in the vicinity of Pearl Harbor on the morning of December 7. The submarine, engaged in a scouting mission, was sighted and immediately sunk by a U.S. patrol boat. However, the report of this incident is not taken seriously by the senior officers in the film. In fact, *Tora! Tora! Tora!* repeatedly contrasts determined Japanese initiatives with the complacent American responses (or lack thereof).

Within this narrow framework, the film stays fairly close to the known facts. All the characters are based on real people and on the whole they conform to the historical record. It is certainly true that, before the attack, the U.S. military was both shortsighted and nonchalant. Its commanders utterly underestimated the Japanese war machine's strength and ability, and even after the attack several prominent U.S. military advisers thought Germany must have been behind it; ironically, they doubted that Japan had the technology or the engineering skill to create such an effective assault force.

Tora! Tora! Tora! is a binational movie, giving the Japanese side of the story as much authenticity as the U.S. side. The translation of Japanese conversations is fairly accurate but greatly abbreviated, omitting several key passages. (For instance, the poem the emperor actually recited at the meeting where the decision for war was taken was not his, as is indicated in the subtitles, but his grandfather's.) Also, the Japanese keep referring to the date of the Pearl Harbor attack as December 8 (which it was in Japan, across the international date line), but the translation always comes out as December 7. These, however, are minor problems, and on the whole we can applaud the filmmakers' sincere effort to be evenhanded in presenting the Pearl Harbor tragedy.

The movie was released in 1970, when U.S.–Japanese relations were cordial and uncontroversial. American scholars and the public were eager to solidify the Pacific alliance through a better understanding of the causes of the war. The Cold War was still the basic framework for U.S. foreign policy, and there were as yet no overtures to the People's Republic of China. Despite—or one might say, because of—the Vietnam War, both countries sought a stable relationship.

Today, in the changed atmosphere of the post–Cold War era, a Pearl Harbor movie might well take a different form. It is doubtful that Yamamoto would be portrayed as a hero, as this film does, and it certainly would contain some information on Japanese aggression in Asia, as this film does not. In many ways, therefore, the movie is an interesting source not only for the Pearl Harbor attack but also for the atmosphere in the two countries around 1970.

Background Reading

Gordon W. Prange, *At Dawn We Slept: The Untold Story of Pearl Harbor* (McGraw-Hill, 1981)

Roberta Wohlstetter, *Pearl Harbor: Warning and Decision* (Stanford University Press, 1962)

1970/USA-Japan/Color
DIRECTOR: Richard Fleischer, Toshio Masuda, Kinji Fukasaku; **PRODUCER:** Elmo Williams; **SCREENPLAY:** Larry Forester, Hideo Oguni, Ryuzo Kikushima; **STUDIO:** Twentieth Century-Fox; **VIDEO:** Fox; **RUNNING TIME:** 143 min.

The Result

The U.S. Navy had eight battleships and seventy-odd smaller vessels docked at Pearl Harbor just before the early-morning attack (its aircraft carriers were all at sea). The 350 Japanese dive bombers, fighters, and torpedo planes that took off from six Japanese aircraft carriers sank three of those battleships and damaged two more. Another nineteen U.S. ships were sunk or disabled.

Later...

Ten days after the Pearl Harbor attack, Admiral Kimmel was relieved of his command and replaced by Adm. Chester Nimitz, who led the navy's counterattack against Japan. Kimmel was recalled to Washington for a series of congressional hearings to determine why he and General Short had not taken steps to prevent the Pearl Harbor disaster. Throughout, Kimmel defended himself valiantly, arguing that, given the scanty information with which he had been provided, there was little else he could have done. He implied that authorities in Washington should have alerted him to the danger of an impending Japanese attack. Both Kimmel and Short were found guilty of dereliction of duty by a military board of inquiry, although Congress changed this verdict in 1946 to "errors of judgment."

After the war, Kimmel repeated his charges, fueling conspiracy theories. According to one of these theories, the White House and the nation's top military officials kept the Hawaiian commanders ignorant of the expected Japanese attack so they could portray it as a "sneak" attack, thus inflaming American opinion and making it easier for the nation to enter the war. Today, most historians give this theory little credence.

PT 109

Richard Reeves

CAST

Lt. John F. Kennedy   *(Cliff Robertson)*
Ens. Leonard J. Thom   *(Ty Hardin)*
Ens. "Barney" Ross   *(Robert Culp)*

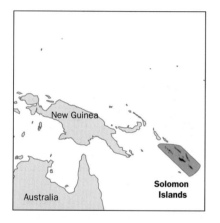

The Solomon Islands

After their defeat at Guadalcanal in February 1943, the Japanese withdrew farther west among the Solomon Islands. By the summer of 1943, their major garrisons at Vila on Kolombangara and Munda Point on New Georgia were preparing for an imminent U.S. invasion. On August 1, the U.S. military intercepted an enemy radio message ordering Japanese ships to move down Blackett Strait and deliver reinforcements and supplies to Vila that evening. A squadron of PT boats, stationed some thirty miles to the south, was directed to intercept and sink the Japanese supply ships. At 6:30 P.M., fifteen PT boats, including PT 109, sailed north through the Ferguson Passage and began to patrol Blackett Strait. The boats soon became separated, however, due to poor visibility and that night's thick cloud cover.

PT 109 IS A WORLD WAR II MORALE MOVIE made twenty years too late. It is the kind of film some people would call propaganda—full of clean-cut young American officers, their cranky superiors, witty gobs, and a few sneaky "Japs." There are also some good sunsets and more than a little flag-waving.

The film was made out-of-time in 1963 because the twenty-six-year-old commander of Patrol Boat 109, Lt. John F. Kennedy, grew up to become president of the United States. His political quest was certainly helped by his well-covered (if not quite as well-documented) heroism in the South Pacific. The *New York Times*, *The New Yorker*, *Reader's Digest*, and a book by Robert J. Donovan of the *New York Herald Tribune* all presented long and glowing accounts of Lieutenant Kennedy's exploits in the Solomon Islands during the first days of August 1943, exploits that were certainly courageous if not strictly speaking heroic.

"They had to give me a medal or throw me out," said the young navy lieutenant after he had somehow let his eighty-foot boat get run over and sliced in two by a Japanese destroyer, without a shot or torpedo being fired. The courage of the movie's JFK (played by Cliff Robertson) is shown in his determination to get himself and his men back to their base before they drown, or starve to death on some barren little island, or are found and captured or killed by the Japanese soldiers all around them. Perhaps the movie's quintessential scene is one in which Kennedy gives yet another pep talk to his desperate men. Half-dead after relieving Jack Kennedy—who had been swimming out into the night sea with a flashlight and a revolver, treading water for hours in the hope of signaling a rescue boat or plane—Ens. George "Barney" Ross (most of the names are real) gasps out: "Boy, you kill me! We're beat, burned, and given up for dead, living on green coconuts and no water, surrounded by fifteen thousand Japs, and you think the odds are with us!" "It's a flaw in my character," Kennedy replies.

People talk like that all the time in this film, which was directed by Leslie H. Martinson and apparently liked by the real Kennedy—who was then, of course, the commander-in-chief of all the military services. Martinson and screenwriter Richard L. Breen, who adapted Robert J. Donovan's book, obviously rearranged words, facts, and timing, in the grand Hollywood tradition. The film's dialogue sounds pretty corny today, but it gets to the truth of John F. Kennedy: The man had an iron will. No matter how you rearrange the facts of his life—including the fact that his health was such that he never should have been in the navy, particularly in the PT service—JFK was not an easy man to discourage.

Kennedy had no business being in the military, much less on a PT boat. Prior to joining the navy, he was plagued by fevers, abdominal pain, venereal disease, back problems, and Addison's disease. He couldn't even obtain life insurance. He failed at least one navy physical and passed another only through the influence of his father. He lied about his medical record to get on a PT boat.

As president, Kennedy continued to deceive the public about his health, and photographs of him playing touch football were part of the act. Just after his election in 1960, Kennedy responded to a reporter's question: "I never had Addison's disease. . . . My health is excellent." Yet as an adult Kennedy had received the last rites of the Catholic Church at least four times. And as president, he often spent half of each day in bed, frequently receiving daily injections of novocaine and ingesting a special concoction of amphetamines. Once he was so debilitated by back pain that a cherry picker had to lift him into Air Force One.

Cliff Robertson with Rose Kennedy at the *PT 109* premiere

The casting director for *PT 109* was John F. Kennedy. Daily rushes of auditions were flown overnight to the White House. Kennedy chose Cliff Robertson (over Warren Beatty), saying, in his navy way, "He wears his equipment on the same side of his pants as I do." The president also liked the dialogue coach, a man named Lou Gallo, who threw lines to Robertson during the audition. Kennedy told producers to use Gallo, too—which they did. *PT 109* was released in June 1963, less than a year before the first primaries of the 1964 presidential campaign. The movie was a box-office success, but critics complained about its obvious political purposes. *Time* magazine considered *PT 109* acceptable fluff but thought that it had been blown up "out of proportion in deference to the man who is now the Great Big Skipper." The movie was "a wide-screen campaign poster," filmed with "a reverence usually reserved for a New Testament spectacle."

Lieutenant Kennedy receiving a navy medal for gallantry

The Ramming of PT 109

Shortly after midnight on August 2, 1943, the captain of a radar-equipped PT boat tracked four blips moving along the coast of Kolombangara. He thought they were barges and moved in for the attack. When they began shooting at him, he realized they were Japanese destroyers, fired his torpedoes, and scampered back to base. The crew of PT 109 spotted the fire flashes in the east but didn't know what they signified. The Japanese destroyers proceeded to Vila, unloaded one thousand troops and supplies, and raced back through Blackett Strait to return to their base before daybreak, when the skies would fill with American bombers. Suddenly, a sailor aboard PT 109 saw a large black shape looming straight ahead and screamed out a warning. Kennedy pushed the throttle forward, but the engine hesitated and the Japanese destroyer sliced through the starboard bow.

The boat burst into flames, killing two men. Several of the eleven surviving crew members were badly burned, yet they managed to cling to what was left of PT 109. By noon the next day, the survivors began to worry that the currents would carry them to Japanese-occupied Gizo Island, so they abandoned the flotsam and swam toward the tiny island of Plum Pudding. With the straps of a life jacket clenched in his teeth, Kennedy dragged one of his wounded crewmen as he swam. After four hours, they all made it to Plum Pudding. That evening Kennedy threaded his way past the coral reef and swam into Ferguson Passage hoping to hail a PT boat, but none came. Later, he swam to Olasana and Naru islands, where he met natives working for Allied coastwatchers. They arranged a rescue mission that arrived one week after the initial attack.

The PT boats were thrown together with plywood and typically twelve-man crews to hide the fact, from both the Japanese and the American people, that the U.S. Pacific Fleet had been almost totally destroyed at Pearl Harbor. The film's opening narration is quite accurate: "Their job was to harass the enemy and buy time for a navy that was still on the drawing boards." In real life, the testimony of another celebrated PT captain, Leonard Nikoloric—who became a Washington lawyer and was interviewed by Joan and Clay Blair, Jr., for their 1976 book, *The Search for JFK*—tells a slightly different story: "Let me be honest. Motor torpedo boats were no good," he said. "You couldn't get close to anything without being spotted. I suppose we [Squadron Three] attacked capital ships maybe forty times. I think we hit a bunch of them, but whether we sank anything is questionable. The PT brass were the greatest con artists of all times. They got everything they wanted—the cream of everything, especially personnel. But the only thing PTs were really effective at was raising War Bonds."

Well, the military is like that. And war is hell. It is always hard to find out what actually happened in combat—often because the men involved don't know themselves. What Kennedy did know was that the best slots in postwar America, particularly in public businesses like politics, would be reserved for those who had served in the military. He had to share in his generation's great shared experience. With the help of his father, the former U.S. ambassador to Great Britain, and family friends, JFK used his rich and powerful connections to get into the navy and into combat without ever taking a medical examination—which he would certainly have failed because of chronic back trouble and other maladies unknown or concealed.

Frail health was Kennedy's great secret. He lied about it his whole life and cheated to get into the service. This movie is part of that deception. As PT 109 is struck by the destroyer, Robertson grabs at his back in pain, affirming the official line that Kennedy had old football injuries that were aggravated during the war. In fact, JFK had back troubles and an array of other medical problems from birth. He was a brave man, in pain most every day, but determined to live every minute he had. "He feigned being well," wrote his executive officer, Leonard Thom, to his wife back in Ohio.

Kennedy's movie war begins with a scene on the way to the Solomons. A seaman asks him to "tell the old man to drop the word in somebody's ear" and get them both desk jobs somewhere safe. At that moment Japanese Zeroes hit the ship and Kennedy runs off, quite literally, to pass the ammunition. The movie extols Kennedy's leadership. He reassures a frightened sailor who is convinced that his days are numbered. "You better talk to him, he's afraid they're going to mail him home," says another seaman. Kennedy says he's afraid, too, and the boy asks, "What can a man do, Mr. Kennedy, except pray?" "You can do your job," the skipper says in his best Mr. Roberts manner, "like all the rest of us."

All of that may have really happened, and if it didn't, something like it might have. The film, however, does take a few liberties with the recorded facts, such as the scene depicting PT 109 bravely rescuing a cut-off platoon of Marines trapped on a Japanese-occupied island called Choiseul. In real life, the Marine rescue came months *after*, not before, the ramming of PT 109 (the times are switched so that the film can end with the survival of the lieutenant and his crew after the sinking of the 109). That's okay, I think, but what PT 109 and its skipper actually did is grossly exaggerated. The movie shows Kennedy's boat out there alone, when in fact a small flotilla came to get the Marines out of harm's way.

The movie also does not let its audience know that the survival of Kennedy and his crew was special enough that correspondents from the Associated Press and United Press International hopped on the rescue PTs when they realized the marooned skipper was Ambassador Kennedy's son. That, however, does not change the real-life fact that his father was not with him when he jumped into a burning sea (exploded gasoline) to save his own men and then swam miles with one of them strapped to his back.

The film ends with Lieutenant Kennedy deciding to stay on rather than take leave after the sinking of PT 109. In life, that was when he took over PT 59. Never mentioned is a piece of history I found fascinating in researching the incidents: His crew and a lot of PT men amused themselves by talking about the bright and likable young lieutenant, and many of them were convinced that one day he would be president of the United States. Bets were taken and a small pool was started over when he would run.

Later...

On August 5, while Kennedy was still swimming around Ferguson Passage, an American attack force overwhelmed the Japanese garrison at Munda Point. Toward the end of August, the Japanese evacuated Kolombangara, and by April 1944, they were gone from the Solomon Islands entirely. After his rescue, Kennedy was taken to a hospital suffering from (according to a doctor's report) "many deep abrasions and lacerations of the entire body, especially the feet." The lieutenant was awarded the U.S. Navy and Marine Corps medals for heroism and returned to PT duty.

Kennedy's well-publicized exploits in the Pacific contributed to his postwar electoral success. He never lost an election. In 1946 he campaigned for the House of Representatives with a slogan designed to appeal to voters and their families: "The New Generation Offers a Leader." After several terms in the House, he was elected to the Senate in 1952 and reelected by a huge margin six years later. In 1960, ex-lieutenant Kennedy ran for president against another former navy lieutenant, Richard Nixon, who had been a supply officer in the Pacific. Nixon's "I Served" campaign showed him standing at attention in dress blues. Kennedy's campaign poster showed him barechested and grinning in the cockpit of PT 109, wearing sunglasses and a fatigue cap—the movie before the movie.

For their part, U.S. Navy commanders learned a lot from the failed August 1 PT boat mission: They learned that the PT boats were hopelessly impotent and vulnerable. Of the thirty torpedoes the PT boats in the attack force fired, not one hit a target.

Background Reading

Walter Lord, *Lonely Vigil: Coastwatchers of the Solomons* (Viking, 1977)
Richard Reeves, *President Kennedy: Profile of Power* (Simon & Schuster, 1993)

1963/USA/Color
DIRECTOR: Leslie H. Martinson; PRODUCER: Bryan Foy; SCREENPLAY: Richard L. Breen, Howard Sheehan, Vincent X. Flaherty; STUDIO: Warner; VIDEO: Warner; RUNNING TIME: 140 min.

RICHARD REEVES

CAST

Col. Benjamin Vandervoort *(John Wayne)*

Brig. Gen. Norman Cota *(Robert Mitchum)*

Brig. Gen. T. Roosevelt, Jr. *(Henry Fonda)*

Brig. Gen. James Gavin *(Robert Ryan)*

THE LONGEST DAY

Stephen E. Ambrose

THE LONGEST DAY HELPS US VISUALIZE the Allied invasion of Normandy, which marked the beginning of the end of Nazi control in the West. A three-hour blockbuster, the film re-creates on a grand scale the largest amphibious invasion in history. The deployment of thousands of troops and vast amounts of equipment, in addition to the technical wizardry of exploding shells, produced Academy Awards for cinematography and special effects. I can still recall the sense of pride I felt in the autumn of 1962 when I saw *The Longest Day* for the first time. It is one of the great epics of the Second World War.

The film's producer and driving force, Darryl F. Zanuck, based his story on Cornelius Ryan's enormously successful book of the same name, which had sold eight hundred thousand copies during its first year in print. Ryan had covered the Normandy invasion in 1944 for the London *Daily Telegraph* and later, over the course of a decade, he interviewed nearly one thousand survivors. In his book, published in 1959, Ryan ingeniously combined these personal reminiscences with a compelling account of the invasion. How to make use of those individual stories within a coherent, integrated story line was one of the major challenges faced by the filmmakers. It was a challenge they never quite met.

The other major challenge, of course, was re-creating the spectacle of the June 6 invasion. In this, the filmmakers were tremendously successful, and *The Longest Day* remains one of Hollywood's most remarkable logistical achievements. The D-Day invasion force—composed primarily of American, British, and Canadian troops—numbered nearly 175,000 men. They were ferried across the channel and supported by more than three thousand ships and landing craft. Thousands more Allied aircraft flew some fourteen thousand sorties. On the first day, the initial beachhead was secured. Then the Germans' primary line of defense, the fortifications of the so-called Atlantic Wall, were breached. Within a month, more than one million Allied troops surged into France.

The film's theme is a patriotic one: the triumph of democracy over dictatorship. The Allied soldiers in *The Longest Day* are bold, confident in their leaders and their cause, and eager to seize the initiative, while the German soldiers are confused, fearful of opportunity, and deeply suspicious of the principles they serve. This theme is often underscored visually by the immense fleets that rise up behind the invading soldiers. They are a miracle of industrial production, expressing perfectly Dwight Eisenhower's 1942 warning: "Beware the fury of an aroused democracy."

The Invasion

At a June 1943 interservice conference, codenamed Rattle, the planners of the cross-Channel invasion chose the Normandy coast between Cotentin and Dieppe as the site for Operation Overlord. Focusing their resources on the task of choosing appropriate beaches, intelligence officers began studying prewar tide tables, Michelin Guides, picture postcards, and snapshots taken by tourists, as well as airplane and midget submarine reconnaissance photos. French Resistance artists and photographers with box cameras provided images of German defenses from behind the lines. Eventually, it was decided that the U.S. First Army would land at beaches code-named Utah and Omaha, while the British Second Army and allied Canadian units would attack coastal sectors Sword, Juno, and Gold.

HISTORY

On June 6, 1944, 5,000 invasion craft landed British, Canadian, and U.S. troops on five Normandy beaches. They were supported by 1,200 warships and 10,000 aircraft. It was by far the largest naval invasion in history. Before D-Day, some officers had feared the invasion would produce another Gallipoli, but casualties turned out to be less than expected. The exception was Omaha Beach, where rough seas and strong German resistance resulted in about two thousand American casualties, compared to only two hundred at Utah Beach.

HOLLYWOOD

Dubbed "The Longest Film" by some critics, *The Longest Day* was more expansive and expensive than any film made to date. Its cost climbed to nearly ten million dollars by the time it premiered on October 1, making it the most expensive black-and-white film ever made. Its producer, Darryl F. Zanuck, one of Hollywood's toughest moguls and a longtime executive at Twentieth Century-Fox, had previously spawned such war films as the Revolution-era *Drums Along the Mohawk* (1939) and *Twelve O'Clock High* (1949), about the Allied bombing of Germany. For this outing, Zanuck hired three directors—Ken Annakin, Andrew Marton, and Bernhard Wicki—and then directed several major scenes himself. Elmo Williams coordinated the battle scenes.

The Puzzle Scare

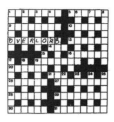

On May 2, 1944, Scotland Yard's counterespionage department, M.I.5, began a discreet investigation of Leonard Sidney Dawe, a schoolteacher who doubled as senior crossword compiler for the London *Daily Telegraph*. For more than twenty years, Dawe had chosen the clues for each morning's puzzle. Military intelligence was interested in Dawe because, during the last month, his puzzles had included a number of unusual word choices. The May 2 *Telegraph* puzzle included this clue (as seventeen across): "One of the U.S." The answer was "Utah." On May 22, the clue "Red Indian on the Missouri" produced "Omaha." On May 30, "Mulberry," the code-name for the artificial Normandy harbors, appeared in the puzzle, and on June 1 so did "Neptune," the code-name for the invasion's naval operations. Even worse, the prize competition puzzle in the May 27 *Telegraph* included this clue (at eleven across): "But some big-wig like this has stolen some of it at times." The answer, published on June 2, was "overlord," the code-name for the entire Allied invasion.

On June 4, a Sunday morning, two agents from M.I.5 visited Dawe at his home and asked him for an explanation. Dawe had none. "How can I tell what is being used as a code word and what isn't?" he asked them. The agents went over the words one by one, but Dawe soon pointed out that the puzzles in question could have been composed six months before. In the end, he could suggest only one rationale, which the agents finally accepted: The use of the code words was a complete coincidence.

Zanuck tells his viewers that most of what they see really happened, and the credits underscore the point with a long list of the film's military consultants, including some of the most famous men of D-Day. They made an impressive roster, including Gen. James Gavin, Lord Lovat, Maj. John Howard, Cmdr. Philippe Kieffer of the French commandos, Gen. Pierre Koenig of the Free French forces, Adm. Friedrich Ruge of the German navy—and Frau Lucie Rommel, widow of the Desert Fox.

Early on, Zanuck decided to shoot the film in black and white, which saved a good deal of money. (As one of my students told me recently, "World War II? Isn't that the one fought in black and white?")

> ## "There is nothing duller on the screen than being accurate but not dramatic."
>
> *Darryl F. Zanuck*

Zanuck also saved money when it came to his military advisers: He didn't pay them. He did, however, throw wonderful parties. John Howard recalled being treated like royalty while he was in France serving as technical adviser for the opening combat scene at Pegasus Bridge. Zanuck put the advisers in the best hotels and gave fabulous dinner parties. Quite intentionally, the mingling together of these erstwhile enemies symbolized the postwar reconciliation between Germany and the Allies. So did the movie itself.

Major Howard told me, however, that the military advisers were not always heeded. On D-Day night, Howard's first task had been to seize Pegasus Bridge before it could be blown up. (Allied intelligence believed that the bridge was rigged for demolition in the event of a Resistance raid.) After securing the bridge, he had to search for and remove the explosives thought to be under the girders. Following orders, Howard secured the bridge, but his engineers found no explosives underneath it. Instead, the charges were found in a nearby shed, ready to be moved.

The engineers reported that there were no charges under the bridge. This was welcome news to Howard in 1944, but not to Zanuck in 1962. The producer insisted that there had to be explosives in place so that his engineer stuntmen could climb hand-over-hand from the bank of the canal to the girders, remove the charges, and throw them into the canal. The scene was shot as Zanuck wanted it, Howard looking on in disbelief.

However, the scene at Pegasus Bridge is not the worst distortion in the film. That takes place on Omaha Beach. The original plan in 1944 had been for bulldozers to open "exits" from the beaches so that tanks could drive up the draw and reach the top of the bluff, with the infantry following behind. That plan was an immediate bust because neither the bulldozers nor the tanks made it ashore, and the "exits" were heavily fortified to the point of being impregnable to attack from the front or the sides. They were vulnerable from the rear, however, which meant that infantrymen had to work their way up the bluff before descending on the fortifications from behind. That is what happened. Junior officers and NCOs took charge and led their infantry companies up and around and down behind the German fortifications. Unfortunately, this was not the dramatic episode that Zanuck wanted.

Perhaps Zanuck had too many generals and too few enlisted men among his advisers. (After the assault, the generals pretended that the original plan had worked.) More likely, it was Zanuck's judgment that a few groups of men crawling up a bluff and down behind the enemy line would not provide sufficient visual impact. His sense of showmanship probably required a final big bang. Whatever the reason, the climax to the movie comes when a cement barrier is blown up, the rubble cleared, and the men of the First and Twenty-ninth Divisions come rushing from behind the sea wall and, in a grand charge, dash up the bluff. It is precisely what the viewer expects and makes a wonderful scene. That nothing remotely like it ever happened never bothered Zanuck, whose stock reply to such criticism was, "Anything changed was an asset to the film. There is nothing duller on the screen than being accurate but not dramatic."

Surprisingly, in one instance Zanuck did underplay a scene that is nevertheless one of the most memorable in the movie. Shortly after midnight, as Pvt. John Steele (Red Buttons) hangs helplessly in his parachute, which is caught on the steeple of the church in Ste-Mère Eglise, he watches, horrified, as a firefight in the square wipes out his buddies.

That is the scene in the film, although there was more to it than Zanuck knew. In 1944, a second paratrooper caught his chute on that church: His name was Ken Russell, and he told his story in a 1988 interview. As he neared the ground, he saw his buddies being sucked into a fire in the barn near the square. Jerking on his risers, Russell came down instead on the roof of the church. "I hit and a couple of my suspension lines went around the church steeple, and I slid off the roof. I was hanging off the edge. And Steele, he came down, and his chute covered the steeple."

Sgt. John Ray landed in the church square, just past Russell and Steele. A German soldier came around the corner. "I'll never forget him," Russell related. "He was red-haired, and as he came around, he shot Sergeant Ray in the stomach. Then he turned to me and Steele and brought his machine pistol up to shoot us. And Sergeant Ray, while he was dying in agony, he got his .45 out, and he shot the German soldier in the back of the head and killed him."

If Zanuck failed to include the complete drama of Ste-Mère Eglise, he made up for it with other out-and-out inventions. The one that most distresses veterans of the invasion force involves men coming off the Higgins boats—the smallest landing craft, each of which carried thirty-

Ste-Mère Eglise

Café Vérité

The Gondrée Café at the Pegasus Bridge caught Zanuck's attention because it was the first building the Allies liberated in France. The Gondrées were also part of the French Resistance, which made them and their small children an irresistible subject. Moreover, their café was charmingly French, unchanged since 1944 (and still unchanged in 1994).

However, café owner Mme. Gondrée made certain that the auteurs of The Longest Day remained faithful to reality. During the Nazi occupation, the Gondrées had served members of the local German garrison in their café. Because M. Gondrée spoke German (unbeknownst to the Nazis), they were able to pass information along to the British. The Gondrées were somehow able to prevent German soldiers from being billeted in their home by giving each of their small daughters a room of her own, thus having none to spare.

The attack on the Pegasus Bridge and the liberation of the café make up the opening sequence of the movie. It was a memorable piece of high drama in 1944 and would have been again in The Longest Day. Yet Zanuck wanted more. He wanted half-dressed German soldiers jumping out of the café's windows when it came under fire. However, when Zanuck started to shoot the scene, Mme. Gondrée insisted that there had never been any Germans sleeping in her house. Zanuck had no choice but to surrender, or lose her permission to film in the café.

Making the Movie

When *The Longest Day* was first released in 1962, it was suggested that the film was meant to commemorate the approaching twentieth anniversary of the invasion. But the real explanation for Zanuck's interest in D-Day had more to do with Twentieth Century-Fox's financial difficulties. For Zanuck, who was sixty years old in 1962, it was up or out. First he paid $175,000 for the screen rights to Cornelius Ryan's book. Then, before he was done, he had five scriptwriters (including Ryan, James Jones, and Romain Gary), a battle-scenes coordinator, thirty-seven military advisers, and forty-two international stars with speaking parts. So many stars, so much spectacle, such dynamic special effects, and such faithful reproduction in moving images of familiar still photographs of D-Day helped make *The Longest Day* a major success at the box office. The film grossed seventeen and a half million dollars, nearly double its original cost.

The International Cast

Producer Darryl Zanuck's decision to use famous stars, not only for the principal historical figures but also for cameos as average soldiers, had great audience appeal. Moviegoers in 1962 were overwhelmed by a cast that included John Wayne, Robert Mitchum, Henry Fonda, Robert Ryan, Rod Steiger, Robert Wagner, Mel Ferrer, Jeffrey Hunter, Sal Mineo, Roddy McDowall, Eddie Albert, Edmund O'Brien, Red Buttons, Richard Burton, Kenneth More, Peter Lawford, Sean Connery, Curt Jurgens, Paul Anka, and Fabian. Zanuck justified his use of so many stars in terms of showmanship: "I wanted the audience to have a kick. Every time a door opened, in would come a famous star."

two men. In the movie, these soldiers leap into the water, rush through the waves, dash across the beach, throw themselves down behind the sea wall, and start firing at the enemy. In reality, they plunged in over their heads, inflated their life jackets, struggled to shore, hid behind the beach obstacles, crawled forward to the sea wall, and threw themselves down, exhausted.

Another deception involved the depiction of death. Lots of men are killed in the movie, but always with a clean shot that brings instant death. There are no wounds to speak of, no blood, and no scenes depicting the damage that bullets and high explosives can do to the human body. In this sense, the movie is so far removed from reality that it seems little more than Hollywood fantasy.

Of course, many people like Hollywood fantasy. In his 1962 review, film critic Bosley Crowther of the *New York Times* could not restrain himself. Twentieth Century-Fox publicists might have blushed to have written such a review themselves. *Highly suspenseful, exciting, smashing, a perfect blend of history and drama*, and *breathtaking* were but a few of his words of praise. Crowther concluded, "The total effect of the picture is that of a huge documentary report, adorned and colored by personal details that are

> ## "Good luck! And let us all beseech the blessing of Almighty God upon this great and noble undertaking."
>
> *Gen. Dwight D. Eisenhower*

thrilling, amusing, ironic, sad." *The New Yorker*, however, was highly critical. "It struck me as I watched the Zanuck juggernaut," its reviewer noted, "that the fumbling of the German High Command upon discovering the Allied armada off the Norman beaches was being played, at least in part, for laughs." Actually, Zanuck's portrayal of the indecisive German High Command was one of the most accurate parts of the film.

By way of contrast, the American officers in *The Longest Day* are all determined and in control. When Brig. Gen. Theodore Roosevelt, Jr., (Henry Fonda) lands a mile south of his planned point of attack on Utah Beach, he immediately jettisons his plans. "We'll start the war from right here," he says. Never mind that in reality Col. James van Fleet made the actual decision. The truth was that Allied commanders at various levels were not afraid to act on their own.

The Longest Day was made long enough after the end of World War II to allow Zanuck to depict German soldiers with relative impartiality. By 1962, the war had been over for nearly two decades. During that time, West Germany had been rearmed and brought into the NATO alliance to block a possible invasion by the Soviet Union. Thus, the larger political purpose of the film, with its forty-two international stars, was to show that Germans, British, French, and Americans could now "act" together against the Communist threat from the East.

As a result, a number of German soldiers were portrayed sympathetically, including Gen. Erwin Rommel. Zanuck hired Rommel's widow less to ensure accuracy than to underscore Rommel's connection to the July 20, 1944, plot to kill Hitler that led to the general's death and his subsequent martyrdom to the cause of the German resistance. Germany had to be defeated if Nazism were to be destroyed, but *The Longest Day*, by making the enemy soldiers so approachable, offers a kind of exculpation for this worthy, chastened, and now useful former foe. As Gen. Gunther Blumentritt (Curt Jurgens) explains in the film, "We are disillusioned witnesses of a fact that will seem hard to believe to future historians, but it is still the truth: No one must wake up the Führer."

One can note in passing that the refusal in June 1994 to allow the Germans to participate in the fiftieth-anniversary celebrations of D-Day suggests that Zanuck offered a greater forgiveness in 1962 than has proved possible thirty years *after* the film was made.

Background Reading

Stephen E. Ambrose, *D-Day: June 6, 1944* (Simon & Schuster, 1994)
Cornelius Ryan, *The Longest Day* (Simon & Schuster, 1959)

1962/USA/B&W
DIRECTOR: Andrew Marton, Ken Annakin, Bernhard Wicki; **PRODUCER:** Darryl F. Zanuck; **SCREENPLAY:** Cornelius Ryan; **STUDIO:** Twentieth Century-Fox; **VIDEO:** Fox; **RUNNING TIME:** 180 min.

The Horsa Gliders

When it came to equipment, Zanuck sought total authenticity. In 1944, Maj. John Howard and his men had used Horsa gliders to cross the English Channel and land in occupied France. But in 1962, there was none left intact, so Zanuck obtained the blueprints and had one built in Britain. When he applied for a permit to tow it by air across the Channel, the British air ministry claimed that the design was inherently bad and the glider was not airworthy, something the thousands of men who made the crossing that day would have been surprised to learn. Zanuck then dismantled the Horsa, brought it over by ship, and put it together again in France.

Later...

The resupply of the Normandy beachhead was a crucial part of Allied invasion planning. Although divisions landed with full gas tanks and a week's rations, once the Germans were engaged, the troops would use up their ammunition at a prodigious rate. Just sitting on the beaches, the soldiers would require a considerable stockpile of rations and supplies. It was estimated that the invasion force would need three thousand additional tons of supplies daily by D-Day-plus-four and seven thousand tons by D-Day-plus-eight.

The resupply problem was solved by two artificial harbors, called Mulberries, each the size of the port of Dover. Assembly of the Mulberries began on D-Day plus one. The first convoy of blockships arrived in the assault area at 1230 hours on June 7. These ships were sunk to create a breakwater. Between the breakwater and the beach were placed huge concrete boxes, three stories tall, which had been towed across the Channel by tugs; these Phoenixes were used to form an outer sea wall. Within the sea wall, tugs positioned floating roadways, called Whales, which could move up and down with the twenty-three-foot Normandy tide.

PATTON

CAST

George S. Patton, Jr.	(George C. Scott)
Omar N. Bradley	(Karl Malden)
Bernard L. Montgomery	(Michael Bates)

Paul Fussell

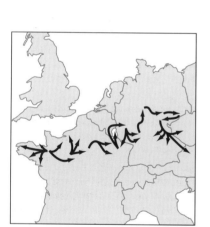

Patton's Advance into Germany

Military historians consider Patton's relentless 1944 drive through Europe to be one of the most spectacular assaults of all time. It took Patton's Third Army just ten months to storm through parts of six countries—France, Belgium, Luxembourg, Germany, Austria, and Czechoslovakia. The general's daring tank strategies—based on the rapid, saberlike cavalry charges he studied at West Point—continually caught the Nazis off guard.

PATTON IS SO LONG (ALMOST THREE HOURS) and so rich in incident and texture that one tends to recall it as a film biography spanning the entire career of Gen. George Patton. Actually, it deals with only a brief slice of his extraordinary military life, from February 1943 to October 1945, but depicts his public behavior during those months with remarkable fidelity.

As the film shows, Patton had already earned a reputation as a disciplinarian when he was ordered to Tunisia to arrest the rot undermining the Second Corps. In mid-February 1943, its four divisions had been routed at Kasserine Pass and forced into a humiliating retreat. The British were beginning to think, and to say out loud, that the Americans could only run away. As corps commander, Patton imposed the discipline that his predecessor, Gen. Lloyd Fredendall, had allowed to grow slack. He immediately made himself unpopular by insisting on punctuality, proper uniforms, and saluting, and his remarkable success in bringing this corps up to a standard of soldierly pride was demonstrated when his men defeated the Tenth Panzer Division at the battle of El Guettar.

Such successes earned Patton rapid promotion, and soon he was planning the invasion of Sicily—and opposing British Gen. Bernard Montgomery's wish to assign Patton's new command, the Seventh Army, a subordinate role. When the invasion took place in July 1943, Patton set himself and his troops the task of beating Montgomery to Messina, the goal of the whole campaign. Remarkably, Patton reached Messina first, but an incident along the way almost terminated his career. Always romantic about bravery and self-sacrifice, he struck two hospitalized soldiers he assumed were malingering. The slaps soon became public, and Allied commander Dwight Eisenhower allowed Patton to remain as an army commander only after he apologized in person to each of his divisions and their medical personnel.

After this humiliation, it was not clear what job could be found for him, and he waited in Sicily for five months before being ordered to England to command the Third Army, consisting of four corps comprising twelve divisions. The plan was for Patton's troops not to land on D-Day but to be introduced afterward to conduct the pursuit and, it was hoped, envelopment of the German forces. While waiting to enter the Continent, Patton slipped up again, announcing that the British and the Americans were going to rule the world after the war. His proclamation angered the Russian allies and brought another rebuke from Eisenhower and a renewed warning about governing his tongue.

The Third Army joined the battle on August 1, and its rapid, inventive, and risky advance surprised only those unacquainted with its comman-

HISTORY

"In any war," George Patton once said, "a commander no matter what his rank, has to send to certain death, nearly every day, by his own orders, a certain number of men. Some are his personal friends. All are his personal responsibility. . . . Any man with a heart would like to sit down and bawl like a baby, but he can't. So he sticks out his jaw, and swaggers and swears."

HOLLYWOOD

When George C. Scott was nominated for his first Oscar in 1959 (Best Supporting Actor for *Anatomy of a Murder*), he called the Academy Awards a "meat race." Having lost to Hugh Griffith, who benefited from the *Ben-Hur* sweep, Scott vowed "never again to have anything to do with the Oscar." Two years later, when he was nominated for *The Hustler*, he asked to have his name withdrawn—a request that was refused by Academy president Wendell Corey. Although Corey told him he could refuse the award, the point became immaterial when Scott lost again, this time to George Chakiris for *West Side Story*. In 1970, when he received his first Best Actor nomination for *Patton*, Scott cabled the Academy from Spain, requesting again that his name be withdrawn and saying he would not attend the ceremony. When Scott did finally win the Oscar for *Patton*, approving peers saw his victory as an end to studio manipulation of the awards. After all, why else give a statue to someone who doesn't play the game?

Patton's Early Years

George Smith Patton, Jr., was born in 1885 to a rich Southern California family. Much of his later insecurity, for which his flagrant profanity and obscenity overcompensated, was caused by his boyhood dyslexia. He learned to read late, and his spelling was always atrocious. But he soon became obsessed with military and heroic narratives, and he determined to perform deeds such as those ascribed to Scipio and Hannibal, Caesar and Napoleon, Lee and Stonewall Jackson.

The destiny of such a boy was clearly West Point, though because of scholarly deficiencies he had to spend a prepatory year at the Virginia Military Institute. (It also took him five years, instead of the normal four, to graduate.) At the academy, Patton developed traits that would mark his adulthood: absolute precision in the wearing of his uniform, a demand for rigid discipline in himself and others, and an obsessive attentiveness to duty. In a personal notebook, he commanded himself, "Always do more than is required of you." As a cadet officer, Patton was described by his subordinates as "too damned military," and he was widely disliked. He solaced himself by marrying Beatrice Ayer, the daughter of a family as rich as his own. This match made Patton the richest officer in the army.

His first experience of something like battle came while serving as an aide to Gen. John J. Pershing during Pershing's punitive 1916 expedition into Mexico. Patton distinguished himself as a cavalry officer, and when tanks began to displace horses, he threw himself enthusiastically into mastering this new weapon. During the First World War, he rose to the rank of lieutenant colonel and command of the U.S. Tank Corps. Leading an attack on foot, he was shot through the thigh and soon celebrated by the press as a "Hero of the Tanks." Between the wars, he commanded various cavalry units, and as the Second World War neared, the army assigned him to run a special training center for its armored divisions. Here (with ample publicity) Patton developed tank tactics and prepared himself for combat duty in North Africa, where he found himself able to act on his advice to others: "When in doubt, ATTACK!"

der. Patton was convinced that, if unleashed, he could reach Berlin within a few weeks, even though his supply lines were stretched to the limit and his armored vehicles finally ran out of gas.

After his rush to the German border was stopped by the enemy's winter counterattack in the Ardennes, Patton achieved the rare military feat of quickly turning his divisions' axis of advance by ninety degrees and heading north instead of east. He now was able to batter the left flank of the German salient and (attended by immense publicity) to relieve the besieged town of Bastogne.

The film adds no events to these, but it omits much, dispensing with incidents irrelevant to its implicit theme of disgrace followed by redemption. (The explicit theme, the displacement of the traditional warrior-general by the diplomat-general, is too obvious and too clumsily propelled to count for much.)

For instance, when Patton felt sexually lonely in England and France, his niece Jean Gordon was available nearby as a Red Cross doughnut girl. She and the general had long been intimate, to the outrage and fury of his wife. The film makes no allusion to this interesting matter. Nor does it include reference to the mad, private, gravely ill-advised tank raid Patton undertook in March 1945 to rescue his son-in-law from a German prisoner-of-war camp deep in enemy territory. The raid was a disaster, killing and wounding many Americans. The son-in-law was seriously wounded, though not freed.

As the invasion of Germany proceeded in the spring, his army came upon German concentration camps. Patton was so overcome at Buchenwald that he vomited, but the film passes over his retching, as it does his later anti-Jewish ravings and his outspoken opposition to de-Nazification, born of his hatred of the Russians and respect for German efficiency.

The result of these omissions is a simplification that supports the always popular folk theme of the redemption of the bad boy. Historiography and responsible biography would exhibit a different Patton, specifying more spots and stains but also evoking more of adult interest. They would note, for example, that for Patton, much of Eisenhower's conduct revealed him as simply "yellow" and that Patton believed George VI was just one notch above a moron. And there are other real moments that the film wouldn't think of including, such as the

> **"At the close of this war, I will remove my insignia and wristwatch. I will continue to wear my short coat so that everyone can kiss my ass."**
>
> *George S. Patton, Jr.*

sotto voce remark of one disgruntled junior officer to another after being forced to listen to a vainglorious Patton harangue: "What an asshole!" That would constitute an interesting cinematic moment. I know it took place because I was the one who said it.

World War II veterans and historians will note the numerous anachronisms in *Patton* that do the film no damage whatever. For example, in Patton's opening address to his green troops in front of that immense flag, he wears the uniform of a four-star general and sports all the orders and decorations lavished upon him after the war by European countries. Actually, that speech was delivered on June 4, 1944, when Patton was still only a lieutenant general and hadn't won any continental victories. Similarly, the tanks in the film, rented from the Spanish army, are German, not American. George C. Scott's body is heavier and wider than Patton's, and his head is noticeably larger. Patton, as Scott has said, "had a high, squeaky voice. . . . The more excited he got, the higher it got. I didn't use that." But for most purposes, Scott's Patton has quite effaced the actual one, and the myth solidified by the film is likely to become the whole key, or at least an indispensable element, in the interpretation of Patton.

Among critics raised on Aristotle's *Poetics,* it is a commonplace that art is more real than life. Such critics would also be likely to hold that history is available only as myth, with *myth* meaning something like "moral plot." Patton's grandson, Robert H. Patton, finally consented to see the film, which for years his family had tried to block and undo. For him, ironically, *Patton* had the effect not of misrepresenting his grandfather but of making him real. Using *myth* in the common, erroneous sense of "lie," he said of the film, "Despite the obscuring, myth-making inflation that *Patton* brings to its subject, it led me to consider for the first time in my life that my grandfather was somebody real." And it has been said that Gen. Norman Schwarzkopf, preparing himself for command in the Gulf War, was more influenced by Scott's impersonation of Patton than by his own military experience. Literary wit might seem at some distance from the making of popular movies, but an observation of Logan Pearsall Smith's may illuminate the issue: "People say life is the thing, but I prefer reading."

Background Reading

Martin Blumenson, *Patton: The Man Behind the Legend* (Morrow, 1985)
Roger H. Nye, *The Patton Mind* (Avery, 1993)
Robert H. Patton, *The Pattons* (Crown, 1994)
Charles M. Province, *The Unknown Patton* (Hippocrene, 1983)

1970/USA/Color
DIRECTOR: Franklin J. Schaffner; PRODUCER: Frank McCarthy; SCREENPLAY: Francis Ford Coppola, Edmund H. North; STUDIO: Twentieth Century-Fox; VIDEO: Fox; RUNNING TIME: 170 min.

Patton and Montgomery

Given two characters of such determined eccentricity as Field Marshal Sir Bernard Law Montgomery and Lt. Gen. George S. Patton, rivalry would seem inevitable. Both shared, in intensified form, the views of their respective armies: The British, who had been fighting more than two years longer than the Americans, regarded the newcomers as incompetent amateurs. The Americans, for their part, considered the British stuffy, pompous, and snobbish, as well as too cautious in combat.

The opinion of the Americans held by Gen. Sir Harold Alexander in 1943 was close to Montgomery's: The Americans, he declared, "simply do not know their job as soldiers. . . . [They] are soft, green, and quite untrained. Unless we can do something about it, the American army in the European Theater of Operations will be quite useless. They have little hatred of the Germans and Italians and show no eagerness to get in and kill them."

Stung by such condescension, Patton determined to refute it by demonstrating his troops' superiority over the British at every opportunity. He said, "I can outfight that little fart Monty anytime."

Later...

The war won, General Patton's hatred of the Russians and his latent anti-Semitism burst out, and it became embarrassingly clear that his admiration for German efficiency made it hard for him to administer the official Allied anti-Nazi policies. As a result, he was relieved of command of his beloved Third Army and rusticated to a unit compiling a history of the European campaign. His death from a freak auto accident near Mannheim in southwest Germany on December 21, 1945, was a relief to many. He was buried in Luxembourg. Patton's memoirs, *War As I Knew It,* were published two years later.

FAT MAN AND LITTLE BOY

Mark C. Carnes

CAST

Gen. Leslie R. Groves   *(Paul Newman)*
J. Robert Oppenheimer   *(Dwight Schultz)*
Kitty Oppenheimer   *(Bonnie Bedelia)*
Michael Merriman   *(John Cusack)*

JUST BEFORE MIDNIGHT, LIGHTNING RIPS through the clouds and briefly illuminates a solitary derrick in the New Mexico desert. J. Robert Oppenheimer, scientific director at Los Alamos, peers through a curtain of rain and lights another cigarette. Scientists fidget with their equipment, worried that the storm has damaged the circuitry. They debate whether radioactive fallout from the world's first atomic blast, carried by wind and rain, will endanger Amarillo, Texas. Some suggest that the Trinity test be called off. Gen. Leslie Groves, military commander of the Manhattan Project, paces furiously, mindful that President Truman is holed up with Stalin in Potsdam and wants desperately to know whether the bomb works. Groves decides to postpone the test for several hours. Just before sunrise, the rain stops, and Groves resumes the countdown. Scientists smear their faces with suntan lotion, put on welding goggles, and take up positions behind sandbags. With sixty seconds to go, loudspeakers at the site accidentally pick up a distant radio signal that overlays the countdown with music. Technicians try to get rid of it but cannot, so mankind approaches the threshold of the nuclear age to the "Dance of the Reed Flutes" from the *Nutcracker Suite*. Then everything is seared by a blinding light and, moments later, a metallic scream.

In this, the final scene of *Fat Man and Little Boy*, director Roland Joffe makes a strong case for his claim that the film is "more truthful to what actually happened than any documentary will ever be." He has depicted many of the details and much of the drama of the July 16, 1945, Trinity test at Alamogordo, New Mexico. Government photographers took hundreds of pictures of the test, but this documentation provides little insight into the fascinating relationship between Oppenheimer and Groves, or into any of the other human demons and dilemmas that give depth and substance to drama, and to life. Joffe has re-created, often with painstaking authenticity, the moments leading up to the Trinity explosion.

With one exception: It was not Tchaikovsky's "Dance of the Reed Flutes" that accompanied the countdown, but a dreamy waltz from his "Serenade for Strings." This is to pick, surely, the tiniest of nits. Compared to the wholesale fabrications of some Hollywood history, Joffe's invention is modest; certainly it warrants no suspension of his dramatic license. He has altered no one's personality, words, or actions. Does it even matter which of Tchaikovsky's pieces was broadcast by radio station KCBA of Delano, California, half a century ago?

The Bombs

Fat Man contained a hollow ball of plutonium surrounded by explosives. When these explosives were detonated, the resulting force, focused inward, compressed the plutonium, thereby initiating a chain reaction. A bomb such as this was detonated during the Trinity test, then dropped on Nagasaki.

Little Boy had as its fissionable core a rare and unstable isotope of uranium called U-235. To achieve the critical mass necessary for a nuclear reaction, one chunk of U-235 was fired down a tube into another piece of U-235. On August 6, 1945, a U-235 bomb was dropped on Hiroshima, killing eighty thousand people.

HISTORY

When World War II broke out, Leslie Groves, whose career had languished in the corps of engineers, longed to lead combat troops. However, his most recent success—the building of the Pentagon—made him the most likely candidate to take on the monumental construction operations of the two-billion-dollar Manhattan Project. On being offered the job, he replied, "Oh, that thing," and later chafed at being taskmaster to "the largest collection of eggheads in the world." But soon he saw the project as his opportunity for glory and worked unceasingly to that end. He spent so much time on the phone that his elbows bled; secretaries had to sew padding into his sleeves.

HOLLYWOOD

"Oh, my God, what're my liberal friends going to say?" Paul Newman recalled of his decision to play Groves. His concern must have influenced his performance: Newman portrayed the snarling Groves unsympathetically, though not inaccurately, with sufficient gruffness if insufficient girth. (Bonnie Bedelia's flirtation with Newman seems plausible; that the real Kitty Oppenheimer made a pass at General Groves, as the movie suggests, does not.) For Dwight Schultz, *Fat Man and Little Boy* was an unusual experience, since it was his first feature film after four years playing Howling Mad Murdock on television's "The A-Team." Schultz, a conservative, remarked that he thought the film had been too rough on Groves and too easy on the scientists.

Klaus Fuchs

The movie openly sides with the scientists, who complain of Groves's paranoid preoccupation with security, yet never mentions that Groves's harsh measures were, in fact, inadequate. Despite the general's precautions, Los Alamos employees Klaus Fuchs and David Greenglass (Julius Rosenberg's brother-in-law) were still able to pass details of the bomb to the Soviets.

The Death of Louis Slotin

Louis Slotin, a thirty-four-year-old Canadian physicist, specialized in one of the most dangerous experiments: He called it "tickling the dragon's tail." While other scientists watched in tense silence, Slotin delicately manipulated a screwdriver barely separating two silvery-gray globes of fissionable plutonium. One time he slipped, the globes touched, and radiation flooded the laboratory. Slotin lunged forward and pushed the plutonium apart, saving the others. His own dosage of radiation, he knew, was lethal; with chalk, he marked the positions of others in the room and calculated on a nearby blackboard that they would live. Then he became nauseated. His arms, legs, and face swelled hideously. Within a week, he became incoherent and died. A nurse wept.

Joffe depicts all of this with terrible accuracy but gives the scientist the fictitious name of Michael Merriman and has him plead with Oppenheimer, while dying, not to let the bomb be dropped on Japan. Oppenheimer ignores him, and Merriman dies just minutes before the Trinity explosion, neatly underscoring Joffe's point: Los Alamos represented the triumph of death over life. There is no evidence, however, that Louis Slotin opposed use of the bomb; in any case, his death provided no cautionary warning to Oppenheimer, for it occurred on May 30, 1946, nearly a year after the destruction of Hiroshima and Nagasaki.

Surely not. The problem, however, is that this alteration of the historical record, like nearly all Joffe's "improvements" (there are many, it turns out), sustains a particular political viewpoint. Released in 1989, after the Reagan administration had increased the absurdly immense American nuclear arsenal to exceed twelve thousand bombs and missiles, *Fat Man and Little Boy* argued that the frenzied nuclear-weapon expansion had from the outset been driven by pigheaded militarists (such as Groves) who intimidated morally sensitive people (Oppenheimer) into doing what they knew to be wrong. The Trinity test marked the fateful triumph of nuclear death over human life. (When the blast goes off in the movie, Oppenheimer's head becomes a skull, his face blanched by the fireball's brilliant glare, his goggled eyes becoming dark sockets.) To accompany this horror with the dreamy violins of a Tchaikovsky waltz would have been all wrong. So Joffe substituted the traipsing lilt of the "Dance of the Reed Flutes" and thereby gave the scene an ironic twist: God snickering at mere mortals playing with fire. Joffe's film is drenched in moral pieties, many of them sensible in their own right, though the history from which they are squeezed is misleading and often wrong.

> **"Mr. President, I have blood on my hands."**
>
> *J. Robert Oppenheimer*

Fat Man and Little Boy pits the heavyset, pugnacious Groves against the gaunt, transcendental Oppenheimer. But it's no contest: "Fat Man" Groves runs roughshod over "Little Boy" Oppenheimer and all his little friends. He censors the scientists' mail, imprisons them behind barbed wire in a remote desert compound, and imagines conspiratorial cabals nearly everywhere. When Oppenheimer objects to these excesses, Groves resorts to blackmail, threatening to reveal that Oppenheimer's mistress, Jean Tatlock, was once a card-carrying Communist. Trapped, the film Oppenheimer builds the bomb against his better judgment. In one late-night scene at Oppenheimer's house, as scientists heatedly debate the morality of the bomb, Oppenheimer excuses himself to quiet his restless son, who says he doesn't want to go to sleep. "There are lots of things we don't like," Oppenheimer intones, "but we have to do them." Thus is mankind dragged into the moral abyss—or so Joffe contends.

The movie's unflattering portrait of Groves is not far off the mark. His chief aide, Maj. Gen. Kenneth Nichols, called him "the biggest sonovabitch I've ever met in my life. I hated his guts, and so did everybody else." Yet Groves was no strutting martinet. Even Nichols conceded that his commander was one of the "most capable individuals" he'd ever met. The general was an organizer without equal as well as a tireless leader who held together the far-flung elements of the Manhattan Project, which employed 125,000 workers at facilities throughout the nation.

Though Groves was indisputably relentless, he never had to browbeat Oppenheimer—or any other scientist at Los Alamos—into building the A-bomb. After failing earlier in his career to reach the highest echelon of physicists, Oppenheimer craved the top job at Los Alamos; to curry favor with Groves, he even let it be known that he would be interested in obtaining an army commission. After Groves hired him in late 1942, Oppenheimer continued to show appropriate martial zeal. In 1943 he came up with the idea of poisoning the German food supply with radioactive strontium and asked Groves to explore the possibility: "We should not attempt a plan unless we can poison food sufficient to kill half a million men," Oppenheimer wrote. It would be hard to imagine two more different personalities, yet the boorish Groves and the cerebral Oppenheimer worked well together because they both wanted the same thing.

It is true, as the film points out, that after Germany surrendered, a Chicago-based group of Manhattan Project scientists signed a petition asking Truman to provide Japan with adequate opportunity to surrender before the bomb was dropped. But the film neglects to mention a subsequent poll of this group indicating most favored using the bomb on Japan. At Los Alamos, physicist Robert Wilson found that nearly all his colleagues believed that "yes, we should keep doing this work." After the bombs were dropped and Japan surrendered, they all joined in the wild celebrations. Oppenheimer, off in a corner, confided to a reporter that he was "a little scared" of what he had made but insisted that the decision to build the bomb was correct.

Only *after* the horrors of Hiroshima and Nagasaki became known—and hundreds of thousands of people were dead—did Oppenheimer's initial anxiety crystallize into abject guilt. When he met with Truman in March 1946, he was overwrought: "Mr. President, I have blood on my hands." "It'll all come out in the wash," Truman replied sharply. Once Oppenheimer left, Truman told an aide, "Don't you bring that fellow around again."

By fastening the blame on Groves (and, by implication, his successors in the military), *Fat Man and Little Boy* mostly absolves the scientists of the moral responsibility for the nuclear build-up of the Cold War era. But they should not be let off so easily—nor should we.

Background Reading

Leslie R. Groves, *Now It Can Be Told* (Harper & Row, 1962)
Richard Rhodes, *The Making of the Atomic Bomb* (Simon & Schuster, 1986)

1989/USA/Color
DIRECTOR: Roland Joffe; PRODUCER: Tony Garnett; SCREENPLAY: Bruce Robinson, Roland Joffe; STUDIO: Paramount; VIDEO: Paramount; RUNNING TIME: 126 min.

Science According to Hollywood

Fat Man and Little Boy correctly points out that the chief scientific breakthrough at Los Alamos was implosion, the squeezing together of a hollow ball of plutonium to create critical mass. The technical details are mostly accurate and unusually demanding. (Of implosion, for example: "It's so simple. It just swings the shock wave from convex to concave.") But the movie illustrates this scientific creativity with melodramatic clichés: Physicist Seth Neddermeyer comes up with the idea of implosion while tossing an orange into the air. Catching it, he squeezes the fruit—and suddenly Newton's apple drops. He races to Oppenheimer's house and blurts out his brainstorm. "Oh, God," Oppenheimer responds in hushed awe, "this could be very sweet." He hastens to the lab, leaving his wife, Kitty, alone on the sofa. In fact, the idea of implosion, like most scientific breakthroughs, came only gradually to Neddermeyer, who could never recall any revelatory moment. Moreover, according to a Manhattan Project report, "No one took implosion very seriously at first."

Later...

Following the Japanese surrender, Groves became an instant celebrity, lionized by the media as the Atom General. Groves opposed arms control negotiations with the Soviets and insisted that the U.S. monopoly on atomic weapons would last at least fifteen years. He retired from the army in 1948. A year later, the Soviets detonated their first atomic bomb.

J. Robert Oppenheimer resigned as scientific director of Los Alamos in October 1945, but he continued to work as a high-level consultant on atomic issues, speaking out within the government for international control of atomic energy. In 1953, after his Communist associations during the 1930s became known, Oppenheimer became a

target of the anti-Communist hysteria, and his security clearance was revoked. At Oppenheimer's hearing, Groves said that he had no doubts about the physicist's loyalty, though under prevailing security standards he "would not clear Dr. Oppenheimer today."

THE HUMAN CONDITION

Carol Gluck

C A S T

Kaji   *(Tatsuya Nakadai)*
Michiko   *(Michiyo Aratama)*
Okishima   *(Soh Yamamura)*

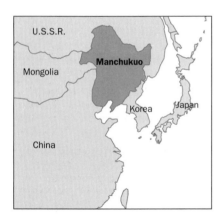

Northeast Asia

Consisting of three provinces in northeastern China between Siberia and Korea, Manchuria became the object of imperialist rivalry between Russia and Japan in the late nineteenth century. The Treaty of Portsmouth, which ended the Russo-Japanese War in 1905, brought Japan colonial territory in South Manchuria. Japan seized the whole of Manchuria in 1931 and established the puppet state of Manchukuo. The Soviets occupied Manchuria in 1945, and it was finally returned to Chinese sovereignty one year later.

THIS FAMOUS JAPANESE FILM RE-CREATES THE brutal end of World War II in Manchuria. Powerful in image and message, the movie is also long. Its three parts, lasting more than nine hours, present an often riveting, nearly unrelenting depiction of the inhumanity of war.

Americans and Japanese have long tended to think of the Second World War in Asia in terms of the Pacific War—from the attack on Pearl Harbor in December 1941 to the atomic bombing of Hiroshima in August 1945. But Japanese aggression began in Manchuria in 1931 and escalated to total war against China in 1937. The China War, in fact, was the reason for Pearl Harbor, which was a preemptive attack to knock out the United States so that Japan could prevail in the war on the continent.

Japan's "Fifteen-Year War" in Asia, which began in Manchuria, came to a particularly bitter end there—an end that this film shows to have epitomized the cruelty of Japan's military adventurism. Japan had touted Manchuria, a Japanese puppet state since 1932 under the supposed rule of China's "last emperor," as the jewel in its colonial crown—its defensive "lifeline," industrial showcase, imperial granary, and racially harmonious "new paradise" for hundreds of thousands of Japanese peasant-settlers. But the paradise, which was grim from the start for Chinese caught in the iron grip of Japan's Kwantung Army, became, in the last years of the war, a living hell for everyone—Chinese, Japanese, and Koreans alike—as the Kwantung Army, the war, and the empire descended together to the lowest depths and then collapsed.

The film begins in 1943, well after Japan's early victories have turned into a string of bloody and irreversible defeats. Taxed by the demands of a losing war, the colonial machines of wartime Manchuria grind on as they had before, but more brutally. Into this world comes Kaji, the idealistic hero of the film, who stands for decency and humanity in a military system that has no room for such niceties.

In Part I (the part most frequently seen), Kaji is a civilian employee of a state-connected steel company in Manchuria, who is sent off to the mines with a derisory challenge: to put his high-minded ideas for improving labor conditions into actual practice. Like many Japanese university students who had espoused socialism before the war, Kaji disagreed with the militarists but did not, in his words, have the courage to go to prison to resist them. Now he commits himself to do all he can to help the exploited workers, by acting at least like "a good dog who can lead the sheep to greener pastures."

But there are no greener pastures in the desolate expanses of a mine run like a prison camp, where Kaji finds ten thousand local workers,

HISTORY

Japanese troops on the mainland, 1937

The 1,500,000 Japanese left in Manchuria at the end of the war included 600,000 military prisoners, of whom huge numbers were shipped to Soviet labor camps in Siberia. Of the civilian population of 270,000 Japanese settlers, 80,000 died—some at the hands of the Chinese and the Russians, others from starvation or suicide. About 140,000 civilians were eventually repatriated to Japan, only to find that their contributions toward building the "new paradise" in Manchukuo were little appreciated at home. The jewel in Japan's imperial crown had turned to paste at a terrible cost to both Chinese and Japanese.

HOLLYWOOD

Tatsuya Nakadai as Kaji (left)

The film (1959–61) was based on Junpei Gomikawa's six-volume novel of the same title (1956–58)—which, despite its formidable length, sold 250,000 copies. The movie, listed for a time in the *Guinness Book of Records* as the longest feature film ever made, was also a surprising success despite its length and subject. For years it was possible to revive a Tokyo theater's fortunes with a through-the-night showing of all three parts of *The Human Condition*. The film made actor Tatsuya Nakadai famous and gave director Masaki Kobayashi a basis for future cinematic expressions of social protest—including his masterpiece, *Harakiri* (*Ritual Suicide*, 1962).

Japanese soldiers leading prisoners, 1937

Empire of the Sun

In the 1850s, Japan felt the threat of Western imperialism as European powers began new encroachments into Asia. Japan was spared the experience of colonization—partly because the United States, which took the main initiative in approaching Japan, wanted trade more than territory and partly because Japan responded rapidly by adopting the ways of Western civilization, which included seeking an empire of its own. That empire was near-flung, encompassing Asian territory mostly close to home: Taiwan, Korea, southern Sakhalin (from Russia), South Manchuria, and after World War I the former German islands in the South Pacific. Manchukuo, established in Manchuria in 1932, was different. Mixing military empire, economic planning, and social utopianism, Japan undertook the prototype of what it later vainly promoted as the Greater East Asia Co-Prosperity Sphere.

World War II As We Don't Know It

As its name indicates, the Second World War was a global conflict. For the United States, the end of the war meant the defeat of the Axis powers and the start of the Cold War. But for Asia it meant that and much more, as even the single case of Manchuria shows. Its empire gone, Japan moved toward peace, democracy, and alliance with its former enemy, the United States. Meanwhile China, finally freed from its Japanese predators, was engulfed in a civil war, which the Communists won in 1949, their strong support among the peasantry having been greatly expanded by the experience of fighting the Anti-Japanese War (the Chinese name for World War II). The ensuing struggle among Soviet, Chinese, and Korean Communists to establish their respective versions of socialism continued for decades, and a divided Korea represented a postwar legacy still unresolved more than a half century later.

scores of so-called "comfort women" (Asians recruited to serve the Japanese army as prostitutes), and six hundred "special laborers," half-starved Chinese civilians transported from Japanese-occupied areas in North China. These prisoners become Kaji's charges, and in their defense he confronts the limits of his own humanism, which falters in his inability to stand up to the military authorities. In retaliation for a foiled escape, three Chinese are executed while Kaji is forced to watch. As punishment for his attempted intervention in the execution, Kaji himself is drafted. Leaving his wife, depicted as the sentimental embodiment of Japanese woman- and wifeliness, Kaji becomes part of the heartless military machine that he—and the director—so despise.

Part II is all heartlessness as army order unravels during 1944 and 1945. Short now of men, materiel, and discipline, the Japanese military command calls troops away from Manchuria to defend Okinawa and the home islands, replacing them with young boys and middle-aged men who are supplied with birch lances as weapons against Soviet tanks. Once again Kaji tries to reconcile his sense of duty with his idealism: He is both a model soldier and the defender of his squad of brutalized recruits. When Soviet tanks roll into Manchuria on August 9, 1945, they literally (in a stunning scene) roll over the trenches of Kaji and his men. He has told them to hold their fire and save themselves, but only three survive, and Kaji himself has learned to kill.

Part III is about surviving and killing of a different sort. With the war over and Manchuria in Soviet hands, the Kwantung Army and Japanese civilian settlers are fleeing, like Kaji, toward the south. Brutality, so recently the specialty of the Japanese military, has become a free-for-all. Not only retreating Japanese soldiers but also Chinese peasants, guerrillas, and advancing Russian troops join in rape, murder, and pillage in the Manchurian countryside. Having expected more humane behavior from his Soviet socialist comrades, Kaji experiences yet another disillusionment.

When Kaji's continuing good intentions land him in a POW camp doing the sort of forced labor he had once directed, a Japanese soldier turned collaborator calls him naive "for trying to lead a serious life in mad times." In the end even Kaji cannot keep it up and finally deserts, stumbling deliriously homeward toward his wife through the vast Manchurian winter. He dies alone, the snow soon mounding over his corpse.

This last scene is powerful and famous—but is it history? The answer, in general, is yes. Much of the book on which the film was based—though not the death scene in the snow—derived from the author's own experience in wartime Manchuria. He had, so to speak, been there. The director was there, too, if only for a short time as one of the green recruits he portrays sympathetically. Both author and director knew the personal pain of the young leftist intellectual who deplored and opposed, but did not resist, the regime of empire and the depredations of war.

THE HUMAN CONDITION

While the main outlines of the story are accurate, the brush of characterization is broad. The hero, of course, is superheroic, his marriage sentimentalized, and Manchuria itself the stuff of inverted colonial romance. Stereotypes of Korean thugs, Chinese harlots, cruel Soviet officers, and even brutal Japanese military police present a cardboard parade of figures (and prejudices) marching in nasty unison. Still, to say that not every Soviet foot soldier was a rapist is not to gainsay the general fact that everything in the film probably happened—and not just once but repeatedly. At issue is not the reality of one scene or another but the way in which we remember war.

The Human Condition is one of the most important antiwar films of postwar Japan. It reflects the sense during the 1950s that what Japanese call the "personal experience of war" could act as a lodestone for memory against the recurrence of such a catastrophe. The military (and, by extension, Japanese society as a whole, which exacted similar obedience to obligation) was cast as the villain. The ordinary recruit (or the ordinary Japanese) thus became the victim—and the ordinary Chinese, the victim once removed. Humanism, which meant treating human beings as valuable in themselves, appeared as an antidote to the mindless triumphs of the imperial system.

Now, many decades later, this view of the human condition seems too simple. Antiwar films that concentrate on the human dimension, like the Vietnam movies depicting war at the platoon level, can leave unasked and unanswered the larger question of how wars come about in the first place and what might have been done—by human beings—to prevent them. Kaji's tragedy was his heroic ability to go the distance without questioning the direction of the road others had laid for him to travel.

Background Reading

Saburo Ienaga, *The Pacific War* (Pantheon, 1978)
Louise Young, *Total Empire* (Harvard University Press, 1996)

1959-61/Japan/B&W
DIRECTOR: Masaki Kobayashi; PRODUCER: Shigeru Wakatsuki; SCREENPLAY: Zenzo Matsuyama, Masaki Kobayashi; STUDIO: Shochiku; VIDEO: Sony; RUNNING TIME: 208 min. (Part 1); 180 min. (Part 2); 190 min. (Part 3)

Later...

Public memory of the Second World War has a history of its own. In 1995, the fiftieth anniversary of the end of the war revealed how much had changed since the 1950s, when this film was made—and how much had not. For decades Japanese had kept the focus of memory fixed on the Pacific War, the Japanese-American part of the conflict. In this respect the film's stark remembering of Japanese actions in Manchuria was a worthy exception to the more general forgetting of the China War. Chinese, Koreans, and other Asians had not, of course, forgotten what Japan had done to them. But it was only with the end of the Cold War and the growing importance of Asia during the 1990s that Japanese memory began to shift. The military exploitation of Asian "comfort women" depicted in this film had long been officially ignored or denied. But it became an international issue during the early 1990s, when Korean women demanded compensation for the horrors visited upon them. Japanese prime ministers embarked on a series of "apology tours" to Asian countries, and people began to speak of the Asia-Pacific War, restoring at least the name of the war to its proper place.

Other parts of the story remained immobile in the amber of memory. The controversy in the United States over the planned 1995 exhibit of the *Enola Gay*, the airplane that dropped the atomic bomb on Hiroshima, demonstrated again how deep emotions run in any national memory of war. In Japan, one of the deepest was the sense of victimization that this film portrays so hauntingly. The Japanese people felt victimized by their leaders, by the military, by the system. This "victim consciousness," as it is called in Japanese, had a double consequence during the postwar years. First, people paid less heed to the foreign victims of Japanese militarism than they did to their own experience. (The Japanese suffering at the end of the war in Manchuria, for example, obscured what the Chinese had endured for many years.) Second, the Japanese themselves did not feel responsible for the war that their leaders had brought upon them. Like Kaji in the film, they felt helpless before the authorities. And while this feeling had not disappeared in the fifty years after the war, neither had the deep pacifism that was based on it. Indeed, the antiwar message had become integral to ordinary Japanese understanding of the postwar human condition.

GANDHI

Geoffrey C. Ward

CAST

Mahatma Gandhi *(Ben Kingsley)*
Pandit Nehru *(Roshan Seth)*

Amritsar, India, May 1919

Jallianwalla Bagh

One of the most affecting scenes in Attenborough's *Gandhi* is the harrowing re-creation of the massacre at Jallianwalla Bagh in April 1919. That spring Gandhi had called for all Indians to refuse to obey the Rowlatt Acts, which had extended the wartime suspension of civil liberties into peacetime. The British prepared for trouble. At Amritsar, the holy city of the Sikhs, posters went up forbidding public meetings of any kind, but some two thousand people, many of them pilgrims, gathered nonetheless in a walled garden (or *bagh*) near the Golden Temple.

Gen. Reginald Dyer, a veteran of fighting on the Northwest Frontier, blocked the only exit to the garden and without so much as a word of warning ordered his men to open fire. Some four hundred men, women, and children were killed, another twelve hundred wounded and allowed to writhe helplessly while the troops marched away without offering aid. Dyer was forced to retire from the army, though not before the House of Lords presented him with a jeweled sword inscribed, "Saviour of the Punjab." Moderates within the Indian National Congress who had once hoped for a gradual and amicable parting with Britain now began to demand immediate independence.

IN THE AUTUMN OF 1963, ACTOR/ producer Richard Attenborough called on Prime Minister Jawaharlal Nehru of India to talk with him about making a film on Mahatma Gandhi. Nehru gave his blessing to the project but also issued a warning: "Whatever you do, do not deify him—that is what we have done in India—and he was too great a *man* to be deified." Attenborough would later claim that Nehru's admonition remained his "touchstone" through the nearly twenty years it took him to finance and make the film. As with a good many mantras, repetition eventually leached it of its meaning.

Gandhi has many virtues: It is beautifully shot and handsomely mounted, and it features a luminous performance by Ben Kingsley that was justly rewarded with one of the eight Academy Awards the film garnered in 1982. Its epic scenes—the 1919 British butchery of unarmed civilians at Jallianwalla Bagh, the 1930 Salt March that was to the Indian independence movement what the Boston Tea Party was to ours, Gandhi's assassination in a lovely New Delhi garden, and his gigantic funeral—all carry undeniable emotional power. For millions of Western viewers, the film provided a painless, affecting introduction to a history woefully unfamiliar to most of them, and on those grounds alone it may seem churlish to be critical of it.

However, *Gandhi* is a work of worship, not art, a portrait of a saint so uniformly worthy—save for one testy outburst at his wife early on—so brave and self-deprecating, good-humored and wise, that when he is murdered the audience is left with only the fuzzy notion that Gandhi was just too good for this wicked, wicked world.

There was much more to Gandhi and his world than that, of course, and it is a pity that Attenborough settled for being what an on-screen disclaimer calls "faithful in spirit" rather than true to the facts of his subject's life. Time must always be telescoped in films; drama requires that issues and motives be simplified, and important events must be omitted if they don't further the central narrative. But there should be at least a little room for the ambiguity and inconsistency that make human even the most lofty historical figures.

In *Gandhi*, everything is reduced to black and white. The film begins in South Africa, where its hero first developed his technique of satyagraha, and one of its most memorable scenes shows him being repeatedly beaten to the ground by white policemen for publicly burning the special passes that local law required him and his fellow Indians to carry. In fact, although South African policemen did once eject him from a whites-only railroad compartment, they otherwise evidently never laid a hand

HISTORY

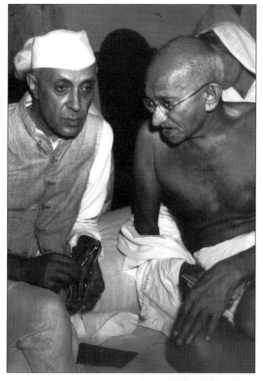

Nehru with Gandhi in 1946

Jawaharlal Nehru (1889–1964) first met Gandhi in 1916. The young Harrow- and Cambridge-educated lawyer was skeptical of Gandhi's idealization of the simple life, but he was impressed by the Mahatma's insistence on action. (Nehru himself was jailed nine times between 1921 and 1945 for his political activities.) Although he sought to make India a democratic socialist state, tolerant of all religions, Nehru refrained from taking any leadership role in Indian politics until 1929, when he presided over the historic Lahore session of the National Congress that proclaimed independence as India's political goal. Calculating that Nehru would draw India's leftist-minded youth into the mainstream of the Congress movement, Gandhi shrewdly favored him over other senior members. Although Gandhi did not officially designate Nehru as his political heir until 1942, observers quickly perceived in him the natural successor to Gandhi. On August 15, 1947, when India and Pakistan emerged as two independent countries, Nehru became India's first prime minister.

HOLLYWOOD

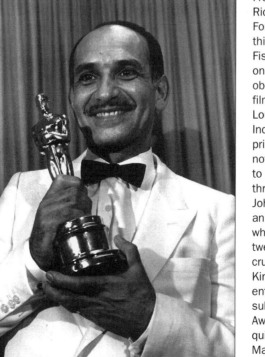

Ben Kingsley with his Academy Award for *Gandhi*

Frustrated by the staid British film industry, Richard Attenborough teamed with Bryan Forbes to form Beaver Films in 1959. By this time Attenborough, inspired by Louis Fischer's biography, had already embarked on the project that was to occupy him obsessively for the next two decades: a film biography of Gandhi. Through Lord Louis Mountbatten, the last viceroy of India, he was introduced to Nehru, but the prime minister's blessing and support was not enough to raise the huge sums needed to start production. Attenborough's breakthrough came years later when screenwriter John Briley introduced him to Jake Eberts, an enterprising British production executive who raised two-thirds of Attenborough's twenty-two-million-dollar budget. Another crucial advance was the discovery of Ben Kingsley, an accomplished stage actor but entirely unknown to film audiences, who subsequently received the 1982 Academy Award for Best Actor for his meticulous, quietly compelling performance as the Mahatma.

The Salt March

In the spring of 1930, Gandhi found a symbolic issue that galvanized India. The British had forbidden Indians to make salt on their own; all salt had to be purchased from government shops, where it was heavily taxed. The Mahatma determined to defy this law. First he politely warned the viceroy of his plans, then he led a steadily swelling throng on a two-hundred-mile march from his ashram at Sabarmati to Dandi, on the shore of the Arabian Sea. There, on April 5 he made salt from sea water, expecting to be arrested.

The British held off for a time, hoping Gandhi's bizarre crusade would fizzle. Instead, hundreds of thousands of people all over India followed his lead, defiantly making salt wherever they could. The British finally clapped Gandhi in jail in May, and by midsummer some one hundred thousand nationalists had joined him behind bars. Hundreds of thousands more were in the streets. Clearly, Gandhi could no longer be ignored; when the first Round Table Conference on India's future began in London without him, one observer compared it to trying to stage *Hamlet* without the Prince of Denmark.

Gandhi on Satyagraha

"Satyagraha is referred to in English as passive resistance. The term denotes the method of securing rights by personal suffering; it is the reverse of resistance by arms. When I refuse to do a thing that is repugnant to my conscience, I use soul-force. For instance, the Government of the day has passed a law which is applicable to me. I do not like it. If by using violence I force the Government to repeal it, I am employing what may be termed body-force. If I do not obey the law and accept the penalty for the breach, I use soul-force. It involves a sacrifice of self. . . . Moreover, if this kind of force is used in a cause that is unjust, only the person using it suffers."

on him during his nearly two decades in their country. He was beaten unconscious twice, once by white civilians—from whom the English wife of a police superintendent saved him by interposing her parasol—and once, by Indian Muslims, who thought he'd sold out their cause to the government.

Things are no more accurate after he returns to India in 1914. Virtually all the Britons he encounters there are dolts, buffoons, or bigots, and with the exception of Roshan Seth's intelligent portrayal of Nehru, even the actors who play the other leaders of India's independence movement—Vallabhbhai Patel, Maulana Kalam Azad, J.R. Kripalani, Abdul Gaffar Khan—are reduced to walk-ons whose sole function is by turns to be dazzled or bewildered by the Mahatma.

Indian audiences loved *Gandhi*, and little wonder, since in it all of India's faults are blamed on her British rulers. Hostility between Hindus and Muslims, for example—which still accounts for the loss of hundreds of lives a year nearly half a century after the British withdrawal—is blamed exclusively on the colonial policy of Divide and Rule. The genuine fears of the Muslim minority are never presented, and the brilliant lawyer who became the leader of the Muslim League, Mohammed Ali Jinnah, is portrayed as nothing more than a languid and malevolent fop—which makes the subsequent success of his campaign for Pakistan inexplicable. Nor is there any mention of the Congress Party's colossal wartime blunders—its precipitous withdrawal from the interim provincial governments that might have led to independence for a united India, and its demand that Britain "Quit India" just as the Japanese were closing in on her eastern frontier—both of which Gandhi enthusiastically supported, and which put him and all the other important Congress leaders in prison for the duration, leaving the field wide open for Jinnah and his followers to whip up Muslim support for carving up the country.

Gandhi's assassin is never named, let alone given a motive, even though Nathuram Godse was the enthusiastic instrument of a sizable conspiracy among members of a fundamentalist Hindu organization whose direct political descendants now threaten what is left of India's unity.

Gandhi fought two lifelong struggles: one for freedom from the British and the other, more intense, for his own liberation from worldly desires. The second, private struggle—the one that occupied most of Gandhi's time, meant most to him, and profoundly affected his politics—is simply left out of the film. So are other hard facts about him: He was difficult and demanding, a tyrannical and emotionally abusive father, obsessed with the workings of his own and other people's bowels, subject to long bouts of depression during which he refused to speak to even his closest associates, who were themselves notoriously quarrelsome and mutually envious.

Gandhi did aspire to be a saint, but no one knew better than he how short of that goal he fell. As the film memorably reminds us, when his dream of a nonviolent and united India began to die, he faced down bloody-minded mobs with astonishing courage, purchasing the lives of thousands of innocent Muslims and Hindus by risking his own, over and over again. Yet there is no hint of the real cause of the special anguish he felt. With the sort of self-referential thinking that denotes either sainthood or egomania, Gandhi had convinced himself that he was personally to blame for the chaos that accompanied independence, not because he had made political blunders but because he had failed somehow to be fully faithful to his vows of renunciation. And so, to demonstrate to God (and to himself) that at nearly eighty he had finally, irrevocably risen above the realm of the flesh, he took to sleeping naked alongside the young female disciples who were his constant companions.

Nehru was right: Gandhi was too much of a great *man* to be deified.

Jinnah

Mohammed Ali Jinnah is remembered as the *Quaid-i-Azam*, or Supreme Leader, of Pakistan, which was carved from the Muslim-majority regions of northern India in 1947. It seems unlikely that Pakistan would ever have come into existence without him. Yet nothing about Jinnah's background suggested that he would ever become the father of a purely Muslim nation: He was a worldly British-trained barrister who drank, was married to a non–Muslim, wore Savile Row suits, and spoke Urdu, the official language of the country he created, only with difficulty. He began as an eloquent spokesman for Hindu-Muslim amity within the Indian National Congress, withdrew from politics for a time when Gandhi—whom he considered a devious Hindu obscurantist—began to dominate its councils, and did not begin to call for a separate nation for his coreligionists until 1940. But his elegant exterior hid a steely core, and once he had set his course not even the Mahatma's offer of the prime ministership of a still-united India could sway him.

Gandhi's funeral procession, 1948

Later...

A good deal of lip service is still paid to Gandhi in India, where he is officially revered as The Father of the Nation. But since his death his message of nonviolence has been largely ignored in his native land even as it has served to inspire others overseas. Nelson Mandela drew strength from Gandhi's example while leading, from a prison cell, the struggle against apartheid in South Africa. Dr. Martin Luther King, Jr., based his campaigns of nonviolent resistance to segregation laws on Gandhi's peaceful assaults on British rule. "He was probably the first person in history," King said of Gandhi, "to lift the love ethic of Jesus above mere interaction between individuals to a powerful effective social force on a large scale."

Background Reading

Judith M. Brown, *Gandhi: Prisoner of Hope* (Yale University Press, 1989)
Mohandas Karamchand Gandhi, *An Autobiography: The Story of My Experiments with Truth* (Navajan, 1927–29)

1982/GB/Color
DIRECTOR: Richard Attenborough; PRODUCER: Richard Attenborough; SCREENPLAY: John Briley; STUDIO: Columbia; VIDEO: Columbia Tristar; RUNNING TIME: 188 min.

CAST

Laura Reynolds	**(Deborah Kerr)**
Tom Robinson Lee	**(John Kerr)**
Bill Reynolds	**(Leif Erickson)**
Herb Lee	**(Edward Andrews)**

Anthony Perkins (as Tom Lee) and Dick York in *Tea and Sympathy* on Broadway

The Stage Production

When the House Un-American Activities Committee began searching for Communist infiltrators in Hollywood, "boy genius" Elia Kazan was an obvious target. Like many of his former Group Theater colleagues, the stage and film director had been a member—from 1934 to 1936—of the Communist Party U.S.A. At first Kazan resisted the HUAC subpoena but then reversed himself and in April 1952 he "named names." Although the controversy temporarily jeopardized Kazan's career, he rebounded with *On the Waterfront* (1954) and later turned his attentions to directing the Broadway production of Robert Anderson's autobiographical *Tea and Sympathy*. Despite prodding from Anderson, his good friend, Kazan agreed only reluctantly to consider Deborah Kerr, already an established film star, for the pivotal role of Laura Reynolds. Decades later, in his autobiography *Elia Kazan: A Life*, Kazan credited Kerr and her "immaculate delicacy" with making the stage production a success.

TEA AND SYMPATHY

George Chauncey

ALTHOUGH NOT TIED TO A PARTICULAR historical incident, *Tea and Sympathy* offers a powerful indictment of male tribalism, conformity, and homophobia in Eisenhower's America. That its critique is so powerful is all the more surprising—and telling—because Hollywood's censors almost succeeded in keeping the film from being made.

Based on a highly acclaimed 1953 Broadway play by Robert Anderson, *Tea and Sympathy* (1956) tells the story of Tom Lee, a "sensitive" boy tormented by his boarding school classmates for refusing to behave like a "regular guy." A loner and an intellectual, he spends time by himself listening to classical music, reading poetry, and singing folk songs; he sews curtains for his dorm room and folds his sweaters neatly. For this he pays the terrible price of being ostracized and bullied by his classmates. The major adult authority figures in Tom's world, including his housemaster, join the boys in insisting that Tom conform. Even his father, horrified to hear his son mocked as a "sister-boy," demands that Tom cut his hair, drop out of the school play (in which he is supposed to wear a dress!), and act like a "regular guy."

Although Tom's classmates never quite call him a homosexual, that is clearly the implication of their taunts. The film makes it obvious that Tom's few supporters fear the other boys suspect this—and that even Tom has begun to doubt his sexual "normality." In one scene, Tom's sole friend among the boys, the captain of the baseball team, tries to help him deflect such suspicions by teaching him how to "walk like a man." However, it's clear that even his friend thinks Tom needs to prove something when he also advises Tom to have sex with the town prostitute, who is notorious for telling tales the morning after. When Tom flees from her in revulsion, the housemaster's wife—the one person wholly sympathetic to Tom—offers herself to him sexually to prove that he can love a woman.

The film's sympathies are clearly with Tom. It depicts his tormentors as jerks and, by most accounts, managed to make even the men in its audience feel protective of poor Tom and outraged at the boys' certainty that Tom's queer habits mean he *is* a queer.

The writer and filmmakers had reason to indict their society for its attacks on homosexuals and its stigmatization of nonconformists as homosexual. The 1950s were the most virulently homophobic decade of the twentieth century, in part in reaction to the growing visibility of the gay scene and the disruption of gender conventions during World War II. Joseph McCarthy accused the State Department of harboring homosexu-

HISTORY

Will H. Hays (right) beside Eric Johnston, his successor as head of the MPPDA

HOLLYWOOD

The Production Code Administration

Demands for the censorship of films arose almost from the moment of their appearance at the turn of the century in cheap theaters in immigrant neighborhoods. Those demands only grew as movies became one of the nation's preeminent forms of entertainment and as the Hollywood studios produced more and more films dealing with sexual matters, gangsters, and a host of other risqué topics. By the mid-1920s, eight states and more than two hundred municipalities had established censorship boards, each with its own set of standards.

By 1930, the studios realized they had to take steps to respond to the chaos produced by scores of local censorship policies and to avert the growing threat of federal censorship. Under the leadership of Will Hays, the head of the Motion Picture Producers and Distributors Association, they adopted their own production code, which they hoped would establish a single national standard for the creation of morally acceptable films. The code allowed the representation of adultery, murder, and many other immoral practices, so long as they were shown to be wrong, but it prohibited any reference whatsoever to homosexuality, or "sex perversion," along with a handful of other practices judged irredeemably immoral. When it became clear, though, that the studios were not abiding by the code, the Catholic Legion of Decency persuaded millions of people to pledge their support for a national boycott. This forced the studios in 1934 to establish an independent Production Code Administration, which had to approve studio films before they could be released.

While most people think of Hollywood censorship in terms of sex, the PCA intruded on political and social matters as well, softening depictions of poverty and race relations and downplaying labor and political strife. The PCA further encouraged studios to avoid overt criticism of government institutions, big business, and religion. The Production Code's stranglehold on movie morality began to loosen in the early 1950s when several Supreme Court decisions remade the law on censorship. In 1968, the Production Code was finally replaced by the Motion Picture Association of America ratings system.

Deborah Kerr and John Kerr

Joseph McCarthy and the Cold War

Joseph McCarthy, the junior senator from Wisconsin, burst onto the national stage in February 1950 when he told a startled group of Republican women in Wheeling, West Virginia, that he had a list in his hand of Communists in the State Department. Each time he repeated the charge in the following days he mentioned a different number of Communists on that list. Yet his charge still seemed plausible to many Americans because it came at the height of the postwar Red Scare, when labor unions, Hollywood studios, civil rights groups, and tenant organizations were regularly smeared as Communist fronts. Republicans had regained control of the Congress in the 1946 election (the year McCarthy won his seat) in part by charging the Truman administration with lax security.

McCarthy also claimed to know of homosexuals in the State Department. Local and state governments around the nation had already launched crackdowns on gay life, and other Republican senators seized on these charges and made them more forcefully. When the State Department admitted a few days after McCarthy's speech that it had fired ninety-one homosexuals as security risks, senators pushed for a full investigation. Later that year, a Senate subcommittee published a report on the "Employment of Homosexuals and other Sex Perverts in Government." Thousands of homosexuals were subsequently forced out of government jobs.

als as well as Communists, and every year thousands of lesbians and gay men were arrested by police in raids on gay bars, cruising areas, and private parties. The threat of facing ridicule or losing their jobs and homes led most gay people to keep their homosexuality hidden from nongay outsiders—and kept most people from doing anything that might mark them as "queer." Every boy knew that crossing his legs the wrong way might get him in trouble.

The film indicts this homophobic culture by indicting Tom's tormentors. But it hedges its bets: It does not defend Tom's right to be homosexual; it defends his right to be a nonconformist without being vilified—unfairly—as homosexual. Indeed, its main criticism of homophobia is that it threatens nonconformist heterosexuals. Tom may be cultivated and "soft," the film insists, but he prefers the company of women to men and is the only male in the film capable of having a mature relationship with a woman.

I t's the cult of male bonding in team sports, the prep school, and—by extension—the military that the film depicts as seething with homoerotic energy. While Tom falls hopelessly in love with the housemaster's wife, the housemaster himself clearly prefers the company of boys. In one remarkable scene, he kisses his wife on the cheek when she offers him her lips, then runs off to the beach to frolic with the boys and stroke their half-naked torsos. Tom's father is depicted as virtually an effeminate queen, waving his arms and crossing his legs the wrong way at the very moment he, too, insists that Tom visit the town prostitute. The playwright Anderson, a navy veteran, links his indictment of the boys' tribal masculinity to the military when he has a group of them march military-style to a bonfire where they engage in an annual school ritual—stripping and assaulting the freshmen.

Tea and Sympathy recapitulated a common critique of McCarthyites: that they were bullies whose attacks on dissenters as Communists manifested the same totalitarian instincts and techniques for which they vilified Communists. The film also gave public voice to the normally censored critique of McCarthy, J. Edgar Hoover, Roy Cohn, Cardinal Spellman, and other well-known antigay crusaders: that these men attacked in others the thing they most feared in themselves.

The very homophobia the film indicts, however, almost prevented it from being made. The Hollywood censorship code, in place since 1930 and strictly enforced by the Production Code Administration since 1934, prohibited films from condoning sexual immorality and from even mentioning homosexuality. The PCA initially refused to allow *Tea and Sympathy* to be made because the film focused on the subject of homosexuality and—secondarily—seemed to justify the woman's adultery by showing that "it solves the boy's problem"—that is, saves him from his incipient homosexuality.

It took three years for the filmmakers to come up with a script acceptable to the PCA. They did so by never letting Tom be called a homosexual and by cutting from the play a scene in which the housemaster's wife directly questions his heterosexuality. They also added a postscript in which Tom—now a decade older and happily married (thus vouchsafing his heterosexuality)—returns to the school and reads a letter from the woman denouncing her adultery and lamenting that it has ruined her life and that of her husband. In the incessant negotiations over the film, the PCA repeatedly insisted that "there should be no spot where it could be inferred that anybody is afraid [Tom] is a homosexual."

The only trouble was that most people who saw the film still inferred precisely that. As one trade journal put it, "nothing has been added or deleted that obscures the basic theme, that of a young man suspected by his schoolmates of being a homosexual and who is proved 'normal' by the wife of an instructor by the forthright if not moral expedient of seducing him." When the *New York Times* reported that the film's discussion of homosexuality marked a turning point in PCA policy, the PCA and the filmmakers both felt obliged to object that the film discussed no such thing.

Both sides were right. While the censorship board could prevent the characters in the film from *saying* they thought Tom's gender nonconformity meant he was gay, it could not prevent American audiences from inferring that. Given the tenor of American culture during the 1950s, audiences could hardly think otherwise. Even audience members who perceived that Tom was really a heterosexual hopelessly in love with his housemaster's wife nonetheless recognized that Tom's tormentors had—however mistakenly—leapt to the opposite conclusion. The very inability of the film censorship board to contain this implication makes the film a particularly rich document of Cold War homophobia, indicating how habitual it had become for people to stigmatize "sissies" as homosexuals—and to think this was the worst thing one could be.

Background Reading

George Chauncey, "The Postwar Sex Crime Panic," in William Graebner, ed., *True Stories from the American Past* (McGraw-Hill, 1993)

Leonard J. Leff and Jerold L. Simmons, *The Dame in the Kimono: Hollywood, Censorship, and the Production Code from the 1920s to the 1960s* (Grove Weidenfeld, 1990)

Vito Russo, *The Celluloid Closet: Homosexuality in the Movies* (Harper & Row, 1981)

1956/USA/Color
DIRECTOR: Vincente Minnelli; PRODUCER: Pandro S. Berman; SCREENPLAY: Robert Anderson; STUDIO: MGM; VIDEO: MGM/UA; RUNNING TIME: 122 min.

Later...

As the weakening of the studio system gave producers and actors more artistic autonomy and Hollywood as a whole sought ways to deal with the growing competition from television, filmmakers began to produce more critical films about serious social issues, including homosexuality. *Tea and Sympathy* was followed in the late 1950s and early 1960s by several films dealing more directly with homosexual matters: *Suddenly Last Summer* (1959) hinged on a mother's attempt to hide the secret of her late son's homosexuality; *The Children's Hour* (1961) depicted two schoolmistresses ruined by rumors of lesbianism; and Jo, the madam of the brothel in *Walk on the Wild Side* (1962), was represented as a butch lesbian.

Most of these films included isolated characters whose homosexuality was never made explicit, but in the late 1960s a new generation of films began to feature openly gay characters who were part of a gay subculture. This new explicitness became possible once the Production Code's ban on indecent films was replaced by the now-familiar graded scale, which allowed previously prohibited films to be released with an R or X rating. *The Killing of Sister George* (1968) was one of the first feature films to receive an X rating—not because of its two-minute lesbian sex scene but simply because it focused on lesbians and included scenes actually filmed in a lesbian bar.

Hollywood studios began to produce more films about gay life in the early 1980s. Most early efforts, such as *Making Love* (1982) and *Personal Best* (1982), simply showed men and women struggling with their homosexual desires, while more recent films, such as *Philadelphia* (1993), have gone on to show them dealing with AIDS and antigay discrimination. Almost all of these later Hollywood films have depicted a narrow range of respectable white middle-class gay characters. During the 1990s, however, the filmmakers of the "new queer cinema" began to depict more varied and unconventional gay characters, from the Harlem drag queens of Jennie Livingston's *Paris Is Burning* (1990) to the angry and irresponsible HIV-positive drifter of Gregg Araki's *The Living End* (1992).

THE LONG WALK HOME

Jacqueline Jones

AT LAST—A HOLLYWOOD FILM THAT GETS pretty nearly right a small but compelling piece of southern history: *The Long Walk Home* is an understated though powerful film about the Montgomery bus boycott. Two women—one white, the other black—take center stage, and the story of their developing relationship reveals much, and suggests much more, about the ironies and contradictions embedded in the larger struggle for civil rights and human dignity.

Initiated in December 1955, when Rosa Parks refused to give up her seat on a city bus to a white man, the boycott launched a decade of activism on the part of southern blacks determined to dismantle Jim Crow, bit by bit. In boycotting the municipal bus system and walking to work instead, blacks in Montgomery organized and sustained the first successful challenge to southern apartheid. During the thirteen long and bitter months that passed before the Supreme Court decided in the protesters' favor, the fledgling civil rights movement took flight and a young Baptist preacher named Martin Luther King, Jr., became its acknowledged leader.

Yet rather than cast the spotlight directly on Dr. King or Mrs. Parks, screenwriter John Cork and director Richard Pearce decided to investigate the boycott's impact on two (fictional) Montgomery households—the Cotters and the Thompsons. Whoopi Goldberg plays Odessa Cotter, a maid with nine years' service to the affluent suburban Thompsons. Her employer, Miriam Thompson (Sissy Spacek), is a June Cleaver–style southern housewife who has been trying to live up to the responsibilities of both her family and her privileged social position.

As the film chronicles the progress of the boycott—and the trials and tribulations of domestic servants forced to find alternate ways of getting to work each day—it also explores the rising tensions within the two households. Gradually, Miriam Thompson comes to see Odessa Cotter not merely as hired help but also as a wife and mother like herself. In the process, Miriam becomes estranged from her husband, a successful real estate developer who yields easily to the blandishments of the racist White Citizens Council.

Although idealized somewhat by the filmmakers, the Cotter family is still represented in a three-dimensional way. The household—consisting of two hardworking parents, two sons, and a daughter—is financially strapped but proud. At first, the oldest child, a teenager named Selma, expresses her hostility toward the boycott: She worries about getting out to see her friends and mocks the preachers who urge everyone else to walk but continue to drive their own cars. While Selma and her brothers

CAST

Miriam Thompson *(Sissy Spacek)*
Odessa Cotter *(Whoopi Goldberg)*

Montgomery in 1955

On a typical day in 1955, of the fifty-two thousand people who rode the segregated buses of the Montgomery City Lines, forty thousand were black.

E.D. Nixon with Rosa Parks in March 1956

Yet there were no black bus drivers, and whenever a white person needed a seat, a black person would have to stand. Occasionally, someone refused. Early in 1955, for example, fifteen-year-old Claudette Colvin refused to get up when the bus driver snarled the conventional command, "Nigras, move back!" She stayed in her seat until the police came. "I done paid my dime, I ain't got no reason to move," she said repeatedly.

E.D. Nixon, former president of both the state and the local NAACP chapters, prepared to take on Colvin's case and raise the half million dollars he thought necessary for a defense fund—until he found out she was pregnant. Worried that the case could be dismissed by the white press as that of a "bad girl" looking for trouble, Nixon continued his search for the perfect defendant. He turned down the cases of two more women before he learned that Rosa Parks had been arrested.

HISTORY

Montgomery bus, early 1950s

For Montgomery's blacks, riding on the city's buses was a daily ordeal. Being forced to sit at the back of the bus was often the least of the relentless indignities. Even during inclement weather, blacks were required to pay their fares, then exit and reenter the bus through its rear door. During rush hour, bus drivers would sometimes pull away quickly before the black passengers, having already paid their fares, could reach the rear door. Only a few months before Rosa Parks's arrest, one bus driver slammed the door on a blind black man and dragged him along the street. Other drivers beat blacks, and one even shot a black passenger during a quarrel.

HOLLYWOOD

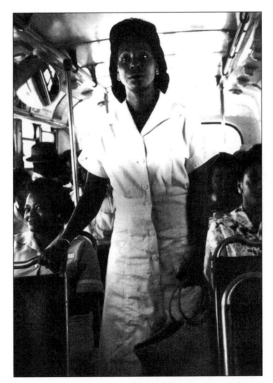

Whoopi Goldberg as Odessa

The Long Walk Home contains some moments that might be mistaken for melodrama, yet even these ring true historically. As a servant in 1950s Montgomery, Odessa must hold her tongue despite being repeatedly subjected to racial insults. During a Christmas dinner, for instance, Norman and Miriam's guests feel free to express their contempt for black people while Odessa and another maid serve them a lavish meal. The banter soon turns to the "laziness" of blacks, as the two working women stand stony-faced in the same room. Wherever Odessa goes, the treatment is the same.

Martin Luther King, Jr., 1956

The Montgomery Bus Boycott

On Thursday, December 1, 1955, Rosa Parks boarded a bus at Court Square in Montgomery's shopping district. She had just finished her work-day at a downtown department store, where she was employed as a tailor's assistant. She sat in a middle row of seats that were available to blacks as long as no whites were standing. At the next stop, some whites got on, filling all the white seats and leaving one man standing. Bus driver James Blake told the four blacks in Parks's row to stand up; only three of them complied. When Blake warned her that he was going to call the police, Parks told him to go ahead.

After her arrest, Parks, a longtime member and former secretary of the Montgomery NAACP, agreed to let her old friend E.D. Nixon turn her case into a cause. Beginning at five o'clock that Friday morning, Nixon called nineteen of the most influential black ministers in town and invited them to a meeting that night, where it was decided to call for a one-day boycott of the buses. The date of the boycott was set for the following Monday, December 5. Among those in attendance at the Friday-night meeting was the Reverend Martin Luther King, Jr., who had been called to the Dexter Avenue Baptist Church only the year before.

When the Monday boycott proved nearly one hundred percent successful, the ministers met again and agreed to form the Montgomery Improvement Association to coordinate future efforts. Martin King was the unanimous choice for MIA president. That evening, Dr. King chaired a public meeting at the Holt Street Baptist Church, where the capacity crowd inside and the thou-sands outside voted overwhelmingly to continue the boycott.

Although King never appears on screen, *The Long Walk Home* features original recordings of several of his speeches, including his address to the Holt Street mass meeting on December 5, 1955. Twenty-six years old when the boycott began, King was the middle-class son of a promi-nent Atlanta preacher. During one scene in the film, Miriam gets in her car and drives alone past the King home to see for herself the damage caused by a firebombing. On the night of January 30, 1956, a bomb was indeed thrown onto the porch of King's house; it caused substantial dam-age, but no one was injured.

generally ignore their mother's sacrifices, Odessa carries on unper-turbed. Each day she makes a heroic effort to get to work, and in the evening she returns home to begin a second workday cooking and clean-ing for the family.

Likewise, the Thompson family is given emotional range and depth. Norman Thompson is shown to be a warm and loving father, totally devoted to his wife and two daughters yet ultimately weak-willed and eas-ily swayed by the goadings of his racist brother. Seven-year-old Mary Catherine Thompson, now grown, provides the film's voice-over narrative as she watch-es the boycott polarize the three people she loves most—her mother, her father, and Odessa. Although Miriam Thompson begins driving Odessa to work, she has by no means reached an awakening. In fact, she keeps this breach in the wall of white solidarity secret from her husband. Only after he angrily confronts her does she begin to sort out her loyalties to him, to her children, to her race, and to her class.

> ## "My feets is tired, but my soul is rested."
>
> *Mother Pollard*

Interestingly, the husbands share a common skepticism about con-necting, on a personal level, with people of the other race. Norman Thompson tells his wife that picking Odessa up for work several times a week isn't "the right thing to do. . . . We don't know her, can't ever know her." Of Miriam, Odessa's husband, Herbert, notes, "She don't know us, and she don't want to know us." Against this backdrop, Miriam begins to assemble bits and pieces of the history of the South and the history of her own family. Sitting alone in her living room one day, she pulls out a photo album filled with pictures of family members and their black maids. Of her accommodation with segregation she says to Odessa, "We didn't know any better. . . . [As a white person] you don't question it." Recalling the time that Odessa had cared for Mary Catherine when she was sick with the chicken pox, Miriam wonders aloud, "Would I have done that for your daughter?"

M iriam's emerging consciousness soon takes the form of a solitary journey: Her husband moves out of the house, and she becomes alienated from her white friends when they continue to express their deep-seated prejudices in remarkably offhanded ways. In contrast, Odessa is embraced by a larger community that sustains her in her weariness. The proof of this fellowship is the support that the boycott eventually garners from every segment of the Montgomery black com-munity—the working class and the middle class, the young and the old, the men and the women. To dramatize this camaraderie, the film re-creates the regular evening meetings held in local churches that were attended so faithfully by the boycotters.

In this and many other respects, *The Long Walk Home* aims for historical accuracy. Some parts of the movie even have the look and feel of a documentary. For example, the very first scene, shot in black and white, shows a 1950s-era bus rumbling up the early-morning streets of Montgomery (the film was shot on location). Others that help sustain the film's authenticity include scenes of black working women paying their fares at the front of a bus, exiting, then boarding again at the rear; of a massive White Citizens Council rally; and of a grim parking lot where drivers congregate each day to take boycotters to work.

This parking lot figures prominently in the film's last scene when it becomes the site of a violent confrontation between angry white men and the beleaguered domestics. Intending to shut down the taxi service, the white men scream, "Walk, nigger, walk!" Frightened but determined, the black women clasp hands and step forward, singing a gospel song. Odessa reaches out, takes Miriam's hand, and draws her into the line. Mary Catherine joins her mother, and together they face down the hostile mob that includes Norman and his brother. As the startled white men behold this novel, and to them frightening, scene, the film achieves an oddly satisfying "Hollywood ending," affirming the power of song and solidarity in countering hatred and racial prejudice.

As far as I know, such a confrontation never occurred during the boycott; and, indeed, no white woman has yet emerged out of the shadows of history as a principled driver during the year-long ordeal (although at least some white women, like Miriam early on, did drive their maids to work so that they would not have to wash their own dishes and scrub their own floors). For my part, I choose to believe, perhaps foolishly, that some nameless white housewife did undergo a personal transformation and, in the process, impart lessons of fundamental human decency to her children. You never know. In this instance at least, hooray for Hollywood!

Background Reading

Taylor Branch, *Parting the Waters: America in the King Years 1954–63* (Simon & Schuster, 1988)

Juan Williams, *Eyes on the Prize* (Viking, 1987)

1990/USA/Color
DIRECTOR: Richard Pearce; **PRODUCER:** Howard W. Koch, Jr.; Dave Bell; **SCREENPLAY:** John Cork; **STUDIO:** Miramax; **VIDEO:** Live; **RUNNING TIME:** 97 min.

The Women's Political Council

Although central to the history of the Montgomery bus boycott, the black maids and white housewives were not the only groups of women to play leading roles. Jo Ann Gibson Robinson, a professor of English at Alabama State College in Montgomery, was serving at the time as the head of the Women's Political Council, a group of the city's leading black women professionals. Late on the night of December 1, 1955, Robinson received a telephone call from Fred Gray, a lawyer working with E.D. Nixon, who told her of Rosa Parks's arrest a few hours earlier. Independently, Robinson began to organize a bus boycott for the following Monday. She went to the Alabama State campus, cut some stencils, and used the school's mimeograph machine to run off thirty-five thousand copies, which her students distributed around town on Friday. By the time Montgomery's black ministers met that evening , the boycott was already a fait accompli.

Rosa Parks riding a Montgomery bus after desegregation

Later...

The 382-day-long Montgomery bus boycott ended on December 21, 1956, when Dr. King and several other black leaders ceremoniously boarded a Montgomery city bus and sat wherever they pleased. The desegregation of the Montgomery buses followed a November 13 Supreme Court decision declaring the Montgomery bus laws unconstitutional under the Fourteenth Amendment. But the boycott was successful on its own terms as well, enjoying close to ninety-nine percent effectiveness. The elaborate taxi network set up by the MIA's Transportation Committee sustained the boycott and nearly bankrupted the bus company in the process. Of course, running the network was expensive, but the twice-weekly mass meetings raised enough money to keep it going. "This movement was made up of just ordinary black people," one Montgomery reporter recalled, "some of whom made as little as five dollars a week, but they would give one dollar of that to help support the boycott."

DR. STRANGELOVE

Paul Boyer

CAST

Dr. Strangelove	*(Peter Sellers)*
Gen. "Buck" Turgidson	*(George C. Scott)*
Gen. Jack D. Ripper	*(Sterling Hayden)*
Col. "Bat" Guano	*(Keenan Wynn)*
Maj. T.J. "King" Kong	*(Slim Pickens)*

Two Hours to Doom

Peter George's *Two Hours to Doom*, published in Great Britain under the pseudonym Peter Bryant, appeared in the United States as *Red Alert*. Up to a point, *Dr. Strangelove* closely follows the plot of George's novel, in which a demented SAC commander orders the 843rd Bomber Wing to launch a nuclear attack on the Soviet Union, unaware that the Russians have deployed an automated retaliation system. But Kubrick made a crucial change in the ending: In *Two Hours to Doom*, the nuclear bomber crashes and humankind is spared. In the novel's final paragraph, the U.S. president, shaken by the close brush with disaster, pledges to devote the remainder of his term to the search for peace. Kubrick offered no such pat ending or heavy-handed didactic message: Faithful to his darkly comic vision, he grimly followed the ultimate logic of deterrence theory to its horrifying conclusion.

AMERICA'S TOP MILITARY AND CIVILIAN leaders gather for an urgent secret session in the nation's capital. An unexpected Cold War crisis threatens to lead to a world-destroying thermonuclear war. A long, rambling message arrives from Moscow, with the Soviet leader alternately blustering indignantly and stammering with fear of what may lie ahead. American strategists solemnly ponder the message: Has the Soviet premier cracked? Is he drunk? With humanity's fate hanging in the balance, the hours tick by and the world edges ever closer to nuclear Armageddon.

This may seem like a scene from Stanley Kubrick's *Dr. Strangelove*, but it really happened. During the October 1962 Cuban Missile Crisis, the White House received a long, almost incoherent message from Nikita Khrushchev, prompting President John F. Kennedy's top decision-makers to wonder whether the Soviet leader was drunk. To a greater extent than many might believe, *Dr. Strangelove* faithfully mirrors this historic epoch in which the world's fate often seemed hostage to accident, miscalculation, and human fallibility.

Of course, *Dr. Strangelove* is not a historical movie in the conventional sense; the precise events it portrays never actually occurred. But this black comedy does have historical resonances. It captures a specific moment and offers a satiric but recognizable portrait of the era's strategic thinking and cultural climate. Director Stanley Kubrick and his co-writers convey all too accurately the weird logic of deterrence theory, the paranoia of the Cold War, and the nuclear jitters of the early 1960s.

Atomic fear, having diminished somewhat from the immediate post-Hiroshima level, increased dramatically after 1954 as hydrogen-bomb tests in the Pacific spread deadly radioactive fallout across North America. While activists demanded a test ban, novelists, magazine editors, science-fiction writers, and moviemakers publicized the threat. Neville Shute's *On the Beach* (1957), made into a 1959 movie, was one product of this apprehensive climate. Another was Peter George's novel *Two Hours to Doom* (1958), the basis for *Dr. Strangelove*.

Fear intensified during the early 1960s as President Kennedy, having charged in his 1960 campaign that America faced a "missile gap," approved a nuclear build-up to close it. After sparring with Khrushchev over Berlin in July 1961, Kennedy warned Americans of the dangers of nuclear war and called for an urgent program of fallout-shelter construction. Schoolchildren hid under desks during nuclear drills and learned to "duck and cover" from Bert the Turtle in an animated civil-defense film.

HISTORY

Henry Kissinger

Long before he became President Richard Nixon's top foreign-policy adviser, Henry Kissinger made a reputation for himself as a diplomatic historian and then as a nuclear strategist. His first book, *A World Restored,* was a scholarly study of the conservative statesmen who reordered Europe after Napoleon, and it won him a professorship at Harvard. Turning from history to contemporary strategic issues in *Nuclear Weapons and Foreign Policy* (1957), Kissinger urged the United States to deploy a smorgasbord of tactical nuclear weapons to provide additional deterrence in the face of the Soviet threat. In *The Necessity for Choice* (1961), he warned darkly of a growing "missile gap" that invited Soviet expansionism and even nuclear blackmail of the United States.

Edward Teller

A native of Hungary who, like Kissinger, fled Europe after Hitler's rise to power, Edward Teller was a brilliant physicist who worked during the war on the Manhattan Project. While at Los Alamos, Teller was convinced of the feasibility of a far more powerful thermonuclear weapon. At the University of California's Lawrence Livermore Radiation Laboratory, he oversaw the development and 1952 testing of the first hydrogen bomb. An avid Cold Warrior, he used his considerable clout to push for continual expansion of America's nuclear arsenal, fiercely opposing the 1963 limited test-ban treaty. Teller—who had piercing, deep-set eyes and beetling eyebrows—epitomized the politicized scientists who helped drive the nuclear arms race forward. Antiwar critics recognized his influence and in 1970 sardonically presented him with the Dr. Strangelove Award.

Wernher von Braun

Blond, blue-eyed, and handsome, Wernher von Braun was a twenty-one-year-old scion of minor Prussian nobility when Adolf Hitler came to power in 1933. An early rocket enthusiast, the "boy wonder" von Braun became a key technician in the Nazi rocketry program at Peenemünde on the Baltic Sea. Joining the Nazi party in 1940, he helped persuade Hitler to give the program top priority. In September 1944, the Peenemünde team launched the first V-2 rocket against London. At the war's end, von Braun fled to Bavaria so he could surrender to the Americans rather than to the Russians. Late in 1945 he signed a contract with the U.S. Army. "The next time, I wanted to be on the winning side," he later recalled. By 1950, he was stationed at the army's Redstone Arsenal in Hunstville, Alabama, directing more than one hundred German scientists and engineers with whom he had worked in Hitler's day.

HOLLYWOOD

In *Dr. Strangelove*, Peter Sellers plays a triumvirate of characters: the phlegmatic President Muffley; General Ripper's lugubrious exec, Group Capt. Lionel Mandrake; and the titular Dr. Strangelove, a former Nazi who changed his name from Unwertigliebe after the war. President Muffley often calls upon Strangelove, as the Pentagon's top weapons guru, to explain the intricacies of nuclear strategy. For this horribly disabled but ever-smiling character, Kubrick combined elements of Henry Kissinger, physicist Edward Teller, and former Nazi rocket scientist Wernher von Braun.

Gen. Curtis LeMay

The Real General Ripper

As the near-legendary head of the Strategic Air Command during the 1950s, cigar-chomping Curtis LeMay provided an easily recognizable prototype for the film's fanatical general Jack D. Ripper. LeMay never met a bombing plan he didn't like. In 1957 he told two members of the Gaither Commission, which had been formed to assess U.S. military policy, that if a Soviet attack ever seemed likely he planned to "knock the shit out of them before they got off the ground." Reminded that a preemptive first strike was not U.S. policy, LeMay retorted, "No, it's not national policy, but it's my policy." In 1962, as a member of EXCOM, the top-level team that advised President Kennedy during the Cuban Missile Crisis, LeMay urged a preemptive air strike on the missile sites in Cuba, followed by an invasion of the island. Having retired from the Air Force, he ran for vice president in 1968 on a ticket headed by Alabama demagogue George C. Wallace. Asked what he would do about the war in Vietnam, LeMay said he would "bomb North Vietnam back into the Stone Age."

Sterling Hayden, the actor who played General Ripper, signed his first Paramount contract in 1940. The following year, he made two B-grade films, *Virginia* and *Bahama Passage*, before joining the Marine Corps after Pearl Harbor. He was soon transferred to the Office of Strategic Services, the forerunner of the CIA. Between 1943 and 1945, Hayden served in Greece and Yugoslavia with the partisans; out of sympathy for Tito's cause, he even joined the Communist Party for six months during 1946. Four years later, he was blacklisted, but he cleared his name in 1951 when he agreed to turn state's evidence before the House Un-American Activities Committee. Saying that he wanted to remove the "cloud over my name," Hayden called his party membership "the stupidest, most ignorant thing I have ever done in my life," adding that "I was the only person to buy a yacht and join the Communist Party in the same week."

The Cuban Missile Crisis was only the most scary in a long series of events that made the nuclear threat terrifyingly real. *Dr. Strangelove*, released in January 1964, grew out of this accumulation of nuclear alarms.

However, *Dr. Strangelove* does more than reflect the generalized nuclear anxiety of the time; it also offers insight into the strategic debates of the day. During the 1950s, U.S. policy makers developed deterrence theory as the surest means of avoiding a nuclear war. They believed that the fear of massive retaliation offered the most credible deterrent to nuclear attack. But how could such a retaliatory threat remain credible if an attacker could destroy the command-and-control centers responsible for launching the counterattack? This dilemma led to studies of automated response systems requiring no human intervention. In *On Thermonuclear War* (1960) and *Thinking About the Unthinkable* (1962), RAND Corporation strategist Herman Kahn coolly discussed (though ultimately rejected) such a strategy. This arcane debate fascinated Kubrick—in 1963, he wrote that he owned "70 or 80 books" on nuclear strategy—and in *Dr. Strangelove* he simply translated his fascination into black comedy.

Basing his plot on George's novel, Kubrick portrays a nuclear holocaust arising from the intersection of contemporary nuclear strategy and human fallibility. The action begins as the demented Gen. Jack D. Ripper, in charge of a Strategic Air Command unit at Burpelson Air Force Base, launches an unauthorized nuclear attack on Russia. Under the provisions of Wing Attack Plan R, designed as a retaliatory safeguard should Washington be destroyed, only General Ripper has the code necessary to recall the planes. When President Merkin Muffley contacts an inebriated Soviet premier Kissov to warn him of the danger, we learn that the Soviets have built a "doomsday machine." In the event of a U.S. attack, this huge bomb will automatically explode, creating a "doomsday shroud" of fallout that will encircle the earth and kill all life on the planet.

Is *Dr. Strangelove* historically accurate? In a larger sense, yes. The information on the U.S. nuclear arsenal and the capability of B-52 bombers is factual. The billboard at Burpelson AFB proclaiming "Peace Is Our Profession" actually adorned some SAC bases. Gen. Buck Turgidson's rantings about "doomsday gaps" and "mine-shaft gaps" directly echo Kennedy's 1960s "missile gap" rhetoric, and Turgidson's description of U.S. casualties in a nuclear war as "get[ting] our hair mussed" caught the lingo of such military men as former SAC commander Gen. Curtis LeMay.

Yet the Air Force angrily challenged the movie's basic premise—an attack order that could not be countermanded. No way, insisted U.S. strategists: Air Force crews in such a situation would attack *only* if they received explicit additional instructions confirming the original order. But even if *Dr. Strangelove* misrepresented nuclear command policy, it accurately captured deepening popular uneasiness about science and technology, as well as growing fears of an arms race escalating out of control. As nuclear stockpiles mounted and ICBMs cut attack time from hours to minutes, the potential for catastrophe soared.

Though an expatriate living in England, Kubrick brilliantly limned U.S. Cold War paranoia. General Ripper, brooding in his claustrophobic office, is a walking embodiment of free-floating cultural fears. Linking his anti-Communist obsessions to his anxieties about water-supply fluoridation, Ripper concludes that only a preemptive strike can save America and assure the continued purity of its citizens' "precious bodily fluids." The scenes in which the world's fate hangs on the availability of a dime for a pay phone and President Muffley's ability to reach Omsk Information epitomize both the horror and the absurdity of the nuclear arms race.

Kubrick was also among the first to explore the macho nature of nuclear strategy, a topic much discussed later by psychiatrists and feminists. The movie's title and most of the characters' names suggest a perverse eroticism, and beginning with the celebrated B-52 refueling sequence behind the opening credits, the movie is saturated with sex. General Ripper grips a large phallic cigar while pondering his sexual problems. As the holocaust looms, the ever-resourceful Dr. Strangelove describes how the War Room elite might survive in deep mine shafts, where it could replenish the human race by copulating nonstop with voluptuous women chosen for their sexual appeal. And in the movie's finale, the B-52 captain played by Slim Pickens mounts a hydrogen bomb and rides it down to its target, waving his cowboy hat in orgiastic pleasure.

Finally, *Dr. Strangelove* went a long way toward demolishing the traditional war-movie genre. The attack on Burpelson by army troops trying to capture General Ripper is filmed as a grainy newsreel and staged as a hackneyed combat set piece. Aboard one of the B-52s winging toward Russia, muted drum rolls and the strains of "When Johnny Comes Marching Home Again" echo in the background as Slim Pickens inspires his crew with a cornball homily on the importance of their mission. When the mushroom clouds erupt at last, Vera Lynn croons "We'll Meet Again"—a 1939 song indelibly associated with England's heroic stand during World War II. All of this, of course, is weirdly out of place in the context of global annihilation. Not only war but also war movies, suggests Kubrick, will never be the same.

Background Reading

Paul Boyer, *By the Bomb's Early Light: American Thought and Culture at the Dawn of the Atomic Age* (University of North Carolina Press, 1994)

George W. Linden, "Dr. Strangelove Or: How I Learned to Stop Worrying and Love the Bomb," in Jack G. Shaheen, ed., *Nuclear War Films* (Southern Illinois University Press, 1978)

1964/USA/B&W

DIRECTOR: Stanley Kubrick; PRODUCER: Stanley Kubrick; SCREENPLAY: Stanley Kubrick, Peter George, Terry Southern; STUDIO: Columbia; VIDEO: Columbia Tristar; RUNNING TIME: 93 min.

Another Version of Armageddon

Two 1964 movies explored the theme of accidental nuclear devastation. The other, *Fail-Safe*, was based on a best-selling 1962 novel by Harvey Wheeler and Eugene Burdick. While *Dr. Strangelove* presented nuclear holocaust as black comedy, *Fail-Safe* played the story straight. (Interestingly, *Fail-Safe* followed Peter George's *Two Hours to Doom* so closely that George sued for plagiarism; the suit was later settled out of court.) Although directed by Sidney Lumet and starring Henry Fonda as the president of the United States, *Fail-Safe* did not capture the public imagination. Instead, it was Kubrick's sardonic version of Armageddon, not Lumet's earnest treatment, that became a classic.

Later...

Dr. Strangelove appeared at a transitional moment in America's nuclear history. Nuclear terror, eased by the Limited Nuclear Test Ban Treaty of 1963, diminished still further during the détente of the Nixon years as more arms-control agreements were signed. But in the early 1980s, fears revived sharply amid the military build-up and belligerent rhetoric of Ronald Reagan's first term. Once again, reawakened nuclear anxieties produced a cultural fallout of novels, poetry, movies, and—something new—television specials about thermonuclear war.

In the early 1990s, the end of the Cold War heralded the dismantling of many nuclear arsenals, but as the nuclear threat eased, the dangers of earlier decades loomed even larger in retrospect. Stories of nuclear accidents and miscalculations surfaced for the first time, and revelations from within the Soviet Union suggested that at one time the Soviets may, in fact, have deployed (or at least developed) a fully automated retaliatory system that would have been triggered independently in the event of an attack—the dreaded "doomsday machine" that is the ultimate deus ex machina of *Dr. Strangelove*. Stanley Kubrick, it now appears, was closer to the truth than even he realized at the time.

PAUL BOYER

JFK

Stanley Karnow

SINCE ITS BIRTH, THE MOVIE INDUSTRY HAS spawned evangelists of nearly every stripe. D.W. Griffith asserted that he had been ordained by Christ to produce pictures exalting the "brotherhood of man." Chaplin's later films preached world peace, Louis B. Mayer celebrated middle-class virtue, and John Wayne personified patriotism. Oliver Stone's lofty purpose, he has asserted, is to "start to change things" by "looking at the '60s not as history but as a seminal decade for the postwar generation coming into power in the '90s." Without crediting either, he cites Shakespeare and George Santayana to punctuate his point: "What is past is prologue. To forget that past is to be condemned to relive it." Yet Stone's cinematic crusade often borders on the zany.

His defining moment was Vietnam, where he served as an infantryman. He won Academy Awards for directing two fine war pictures, *Platoon* and *Born on the Fourth of July*, but flopped with *Heaven and Earth*, a commendable attempt to recapture the ordeal of a Vietnamese woman trapped in the conflict. In between he made *JFK*, which deals with Vietnam as well. Stone based *JFK* on the book *On the Trail of the Assassins* by Jim Garrison, who also features as the movie's hero. A controversial former New Orleans district attorney, Garrison had a checkered career debunking the Warren Commission's version of the Kennedy assassination. The film, embracing his interpretation, indicts a cabal of high-level hawks for covertly engineering Kennedy's murder to prevent him from pulling out of Southeast Asia after his 1964 reelection. The culprits supposedly responsible for this "coup d'état" range from the military and the Dallas police to the intelligence community and multinational corporations, with Lyndon Johnson and J. Edgar Hoover "accomplices after the fact."

Released in 1991, the movie was widely excoriated by politicians, commentators, and scholars as a preposterous, even alarming, deformation of reality. The outcry boosted Stone's stature in Hollywood, which thrives on publicity. But Stone isn't gratified by mere attention. Far more than his show-business colleagues, many of whom believe fame makes them experts on everything from health care to arms control, Stone desperately yearns to be respected. He went ballistic over a piece in the *Washington Post* by George Lardner, who referred to *JFK* as "the edge of paranoia." Such attacks seem to confirm Stone's view of himself as a victim of the entrenched Establishment. In a furious response to Lardner, he evoked the campaign by the Hearst newspapers to suppress *Citizen Kane*. By implication, the same demons who plotted Kennedy's death are out to demolish him.

The "magic bullet"

Garrison and the Media

In *JFK*, Jim Garrison shows his indignation at an NBC News report attacking his investigation. (The actual report aired June 19, 1967, and accused Garrison of trying to bribe witnesses.) The film does not show, however, Garrison's own manipulation of the media. Between Clay Shaw's arrest on March 1, 1967, and the opening of his trial on January 21, 1969, the New Orleans district attorney conducted his own publicity campaign. On Johnny Carson's "Tonight Show" and in *Playboy* magazine, Garrison implicated Lyndon Johnson, the CIA, and the FBI, as well as unnamed neo-Nazis. He told Jim Phelan of the *Saturday Evening Post* that the Kennedy assassination was "a homosexual thrill-killing" concocted by David Ferrie, Shaw, Jack Ruby (whose gay name Garrison claimed was "Pinkie"), and Lee Harvey Oswald ("a switch-hitter who couldn't satisfy his wife," Garrison told Phelan).

HISTORY

Jim Garrison

Six-foot, seven-inch Earling Carothers "Jim" Garrison served in the National Guard during World War II before entering Tulane Law School in the fall of 1946. After graduation, he worked as an FBI agent for two years until, bored with routine loyalty checks, he returned to active service with the Guard. In October 1952, army doctors relieved him of duty after they diagnosed a "severe and disabling psychoneurosis." Garrison later claimed he had been sick with amoebic dysentery, which the doctors mistook for acute anxiety.

In 1954, Garrison joined the staff of New Orleans district attorney Richard Dowling. He served as an assistant DA until 1958, when he returned to private practice. In 1961, after failing to win a criminal court judgeship, Garrison beat Dowling in a four-way race for district attorney. Once in office, he quickly established a reputation for bringing sensational charges—and winning front-page headlines—although these cases rarely produced convictions.

HOLLYWOOD

Oliver Stone

Although *JFK* focuses on the investigation conducted by Jim Garrison (played by Kevin Costner), the film also includes numerous flashbacks. For his reenactment of the Kennedy assassination, director Oliver Stone placed a gunman behind the stockade fence on the famous "grassy knoll" in Dealey Plaza. Railway signalman Sam Holland had told the Warren Commission of "a puff of smoke" he had seen there just after the shots. Many conspiracy theorists believe Holland's story to be evidence of a second assassin. While filming the scene, however, Stone had difficulty finding a rifle that would produce enough smoke for a puff to be seen on film. To produce the necessary visual effect, Stone had a props man pump smoke from a bellows.

Members of the Warren Commission outside the Texas School Book Depository

The Warren Commission

On November 29, 1963, one week after the assassination, Lyndon Johnson signed Executive Order 11130, creating a presidential commission to investigate the events in Dallas. The seven-member panel, chaired by Supreme Court chief justice Earl Warren, included Representatives Hale Boggs and Gerald Ford; Senators John Sherman Cooper and Richard Russell; former CIA director Allen Dulles; and John J. McCloy, the former World Bank president who had coordinated disarmament activities for the Kennedy administration. The Warren Commission, which Oliver Stone repeatedly attacks in *JFK*, had a dual mandate: to discover the facts of the assassination and to dispel rumors that might, according to Allen Dulles, interfere with the functioning of the government, at home and abroad.

Beginning with Marina Oswald on February 3, 1964, commission lawyers spent six months deposing 552 witnesses. Gerald Ford had the best attendance record, hearing seventy-five percent of the testimony; Richard Russell, the worst, hearing just six percent. Meanwhile, the FBI conducted twenty-five thousand of its own interviews and submitted more than twenty-three hundred investigative reports.

Despite this deluge, the FBI still withheld important information, as did the CIA. The FBI, for instance, deleted the name, address, and phone number of Dallas special agent James Hosty from Oswald's address book before sending it to the commission. (Ten days before the assassination, Hosty had received from Oswald a note he later destroyed at the direction of Dallas FBI chief J. Gordon Shanklin. He never mentioned the note to the commission, and its existence was not revealed until 1975.) Meanwhile, the CIA and Commissioner Dulles never revealed the existence of CIA-Mafia plots to kill Fidel Castro.

On September 24, 1964, the commission delivered its 888-page report to President Johnson, whose initial comment was, "It's heavy."

I lack the credentials to judge Stone as a filmmaker—though many critics, including some who regard its thesis as repugnant, applaud *JFK* as a technical masterpiece. Nor am I competent to assess the picture's rendition of the Kennedy assassination, which has been scrutinized and debated again and again, yet still perplexes most Americans. However, I feel qualified to comment on the movie's Vietnam perspective, having covered the wars there for more than forty years—from France's futile struggle to retrieve its Asian empire to the helicopters frantically lifting off the roof of the U.S. embassy in Saigon. I reexamined the subject in depth while preparing my book *Vietnam: A History*, as well as for the PBS documentary series "Vietnam: A Television History."

Central to *JFK* is Stone's premise that Kennedy, had he lived, would have abandoned Vietnam. As evidence he cites a Kennedy plan to repatriate one thousand U.S. advisers by the end of 1963 as the prelude to a complete withdrawal. But Johnson, he alleges, was determined to intensify the war and, shortly after taking office, countermanded the order. I appreciate the difficulty of coping with complicated situations on the screen. Yet Stone, to buttress his proposition, twists the episode out of all recognition.

Early in 1963, South Vietnam's rigid President Ngo Dinh Diem was cracking down on internal dissidents, throwing the country into chaos. Fearing that the turmoil would benefit the Communist insurgents, Kennedy conceived of bringing home one thousand of the sixteen thousand American military advisers as a way of prodding Diem into behaving more leniently. Kennedy's decision was codified in National Security Action Memorandum, or NSAM, 263. Its aim was to "indicate our displeasure" with Diem and "create significant uncertainty" in him "as to future intentions of the United States." Kennedy hoped that the scheme, which also scheduled a reduction of the U.S. force over the next two years, would give the South Vietnamese the chance to strengthen themselves.

Nothing in Kennedy's public utterances, however, suggested that he even remotely envisioned scuttling Vietnam. During an interview with Walter Cronkite in early September 1963, he affirmed his faith in the domino theory, adding, "I don't agree with those who say we should withdraw." He echoed that line in a talk with Chet Huntley: "We are not there to see a war lost." Had he delivered the address he was slated to give in Dallas, he would have declared that the involvement in Southeast Asia might be "painful, risky, and costly . . . but we dare not weary of the task." Robert Kennedy repeated the same thesis in an oral history interview, saying that the president "felt that he had a strong, overwhelming reason for being in Vietnam, and that we should win the war. . . ." When asked if his brother ever contemplated "pulling out," Bobby replied, "No."

Three days after Kennedy's assassination, the Johnson administration issued its initial Vietnam directive, NSAM 273. With slight modifications, it perpetuated the Kennedy policy. A six-second bit in *JFK* shows the two documents—an effort by Stone to dramatize Johnson's switch to a new, more belligerent approach. But Professor Larry Berman of the University of California at Davis, an assiduous student of the war, has tapped virtually every available source on the period without discovering any evidence of a real change.

President Kennedy had made it plain that the repatriation of the U.S. advisers depended on the performance of the South Vietnamese troops; unless they were trained to take over, the Americans would stay. Johnson carried out the U.S. withdrawal, though it was essentially an accounting exercise. As one thousand men returned home, another thousand arrived; by December 1963, the force was the same as it had been.

In one of *JFK*'s most pivotal scenes, a secret agent tells Garrison about a late 1963 White House reception at which Johnson told the joint chiefs of staff, "Just let me get elected, and then you can have your war." Stone, by his own admission, borrowed the anecdote from my book, and I am convinced of its accuracy, having heard it from Gen. Harold K. Johnson, then the army chief of staff and a guest at the party. I used the story to illustrate Lyndon Johnson's practice of making different promises to different factions. In this instance, he estimated that by placating the brass he could rally their conservative allies on Capitol Hill behind his liberal social agenda. At the same time, as I wrote, he confided to members of Congress who had qualms about Vietnam that he had no intention of getting immersed in that "damn pissant little country." However, Stone, to depict Johnson as a warmonger, lifted the story out of context.

Quite apart from *JFK*, there remains the question of what Kennedy would have done had he lived: Would he have pulled out of Vietnam or, as Johnson did, escalated the war? Nobody will ever know. My guess is that he would have behaved just as Johnson did, given the Cold War climate of the time. But Stone may have the final word. Friends who teach high school and college courses on Vietnam tell me that, for most of their students, *JFK* is the truth.

Background Reading

Stanley Karnow, *Vietnam: A History* (Viking, 1983)
Gerald Posner, *Case Closed* (Random House, 1993)

1991/USA/Color
DIRECTOR: Oliver Stone; **PRODUCER:** A. Kitman Ho, Oliver Stone; **SCREENPLAY:** Oliver Stone, Zachary Sklar; **STUDIO:** Warner; **VIDEO:** Warner; **RUNNING TIME:** 189 min.

"You Can Have Your War"

Johnson subscribed to the adage that "wars are too serious to be entrusted to generals." He knew, as he once put it, that armed forces "need battles and bombs and bullets in order to be heroic" and that they would drag him into a military conflict if they could. But he also knew that Pentagon lobbyists, among the best in the business, could persuade conservatives in Congress to sabotage his social legislation unless he satisfied their demands. As he girded himself for the 1964 presidential campaign, he was especially sensitive to the jingoists who might brand him "soft on Communism" were he to back away from the challenge in Vietnam. So, politician that he was, he assuaged the brass and the braid with promises he may never have intended to keep. At a White House reception on Christmas Eve 1963, for example, he told the joint chiefs of staff: "Just let me get elected, and then you can have your war."

From Stanley Karnow's
Vietnam: A History

Later...

Once it came to trial, Jim Garrison's case against Clay Shaw quickly fell apart. A late addition to Garrison's witness list, New York accountant Charles Spiesel, testified that he had attended a 1963 party at which Ferrie, Shaw, and Oswald had discussed plans to kill Kennedy. Under cross-examination, however, Spiesel also revealed that his psychiatrist and the police were conspiring to interfere with his thought processes and that he fingerprinted his daughter each time she returned from college to confirm her identity.

Although many assassination researchers distanced themselves from Garrison after the trial, they benefited greatly from the new material his subpoena power had shaken loose—most notably the eight-millimeter film shot by Abraham Zapruder, shown publicly for the first time at the Shaw trial. For five years, Time-Life had jealously guarded Zapruder's film of the assassination, fighting Garrison's subpoena all the way to the Supreme Court before surrending the film. It was quickly bootlegged.

MISSISSIPPI BURNING

William H. Chafe

Freedom Summer

In Mississippi during the fall of 1963, the Council of Federated Organizations (COFO), a coalition of church and civil rights groups, sponsored the Freedom Vote to prove that blacks would cast ballots if given the chance. To help get out that vote, Bob Moses of the Student Nonviolent Coordinating Committee worked with Allard Lowenstein to bring in white student volunteers from Yale and Stanford who walked door to door in the black neighborhoods, spreading the word.

At a SNCC staff meeting a week after the election, Moses proposed the logical next step in his voter-registration efforts: the organization of a political party to challenge Mississippi's white regulars at the 1964 Democratic National Convention. Even COFO, however, lacked the money and manpower for such a task. The obvious solution was to invite more white volunteers to Mississippi, which would guarantee the attention of the press and also help fund-raising efforts.

In June, nearly one thousand volunteers—three-quarters of them white, nearly half female—showed up for a week-long training course at the Western College for Women in Oxford, Ohio. They were repeatedly warned of the dangers awaiting them in Mississippi (and depicted in *Mississippi Burning*). "There's not even a sharp line between living and dying," one SNCC trainer said, "it's just a thin fuzz."

IN THE HISTORY OF AMERICA SINCE WORLD War II, few events loom larger than the civil rights movement of the 1950s and 1960s. Seeking finally to implement the century-old promises of equality guaranteed by the Fourteenth and Fifteenth Amendments, the movement galvanized the nation as it created a new pantheon of heroes and heroines. Martin Luther King, Jr., became a household name—yet he was the product, not the cause, of a movement that was created for the most part by ordinary people.

It was the "local heroes" who made it all possible: Rosa Parks, the seamstress who refused to give up her seat to a white person on a Montgomery bus in 1955; the four black freshmen from North Carolina Agricultural and Technical College who sat down at a Woolworth's lunch counter to demand the same service granted to white people; the Freedom Riders who endured beatings and abuse to secure equal treatment in bus terminals; and the countless thousands of black Americans, joined by some whites, who risked their lives by registering to vote so they could end the iniquities of second-class citizenship and Jim Crow segregation.

Nowhere was this struggle more dramatic than in the state of Mississippi, a place that one activist called "as bad as—maybe worse than—South Africa." Between 1880 and 1940, nearly six hundred black people were lynched in Mississippi without a single person's being jailed for any one of the murders. In 1944, the Reverend Isaac Simmons of Amite County refused to sell a piece of land that a white person wanted to buy. After Simmons consulted a lawyer, he was ambushed on the road: As his son looked on, he was shot three times in the back and his tongue was cut out. None of the accused was found guilty. In 1955, the Reverend George Lee led a voter-registration rally in Belzoni. Later, as he drove along the main street of the town, white men in a convertible blew away his jaw and lower face. The governor refused to investigate, saying he never responded to NAACP requests.

Despite such systemic terror, black citizens continued to demand their rights. World War II veterans such as Amzie Moore, Medgar Evers, and Vernando Collier courageously went to local courthouses to insist on their right to vote. In retaliation, Mississippi's White Citizens Council arranged for local bankers to call in the mortgages of black citizens who sought to protest. Similarly, insurance policies were canceled, and other forms of credit cut off. Still, ten thousand blacks gathered in Mound Bayou in 1955 to declare their determination to vote.

The struggle for Mississippi reached a cusp during the summer of 1964, when nearly a thousand volunteers, most of them white, joined with

274

Fannie Lou Hamer

Fannie Lou Hamer was a sharecropper in Sunflower County, Mississippi, the youngest of twenty children. Growing up, she had never known that African Americans had the right to vote. In 1962, she attended a SNCC meeting at a church in Ruleville, where she learned of her right to register; immediately, she volunteered to exercise that right. "The only thing they could do to me was kill me," she said, "and it seemed like they'd been trying to do that a little bit at a time ever since I could remember." When Mrs. Hamer went to register at the courthouse, she was arrested and jailed. The next day her landlord told her to withdraw her request to vote or she would be forced off the land she farmed. She moved out, joined the SNCC staff, and became one of the most venerated and beloved freedom fighters in the state, known everywhere for her warmth of spirit and her ability to inspire with her speechmaking and singing.

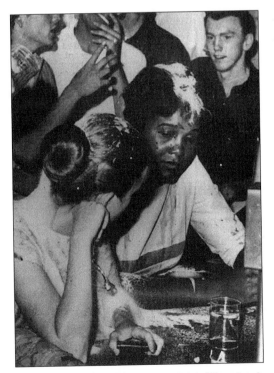

Anne Moody at a Jackson, Miss., lunch counter in 1963

Anne Moody

As a high school student in 1950s Mississippi, Anne Moody performed day work for several white families, learning through overheard conversations of the emergence of the White Citizens Councils and their determination to resist desegregation at all costs. The lynching of Emmett Till, a black teenager, for allegedly leering at a white woman crystallized her own determination to fight against racism. Moody was a brilliant student and a fine athlete. She learned about the NAACP from a brave schoolteacher. Insistent on not allowing her own life to be circumscribed by the racial status quo, she took jobs in New Orleans; went to college in Natchez, Mississippi; and soon joined a chapter of the Congress of Racial Equality in Canton, Mississippi. There she carried on her part of the struggle for voter registration and freedom. Her book about these years, *Coming of Age in Mississippi* (1968), has become a classic recounting of the horrors of white racism in Mississippi and the courage of those local people who went to war against it.

Goodman, Schwerner, and Chaney

Twenty-year-old volunteer Andrew Goodman left the Freedom Summer training center at Oxford, Ohio, on June 20, 1964, in the company of Mickey Schwerner, twenty-four, and James Chaney, twenty-one. Early the next morning, after a sixteen-hour drive, the three of them arrived in Meridian, Mississippi. Schwerner was, like Goodman, a white New Yorker; Chaney, a black Mississippian. Both Schwerner and Chaney were experienced field workers for the Congress of Racial Equality.

Later that afternoon, the three young men traveled in their blue Ford station wagon to Neshoba Country, where they visited a black church that had been burned; the church had lately been used as a Freedom School. On their way back, their car was stopped at about 3:00 P.M. by Deputy Sheriff Cecil Price. (Four black witnesses later testified that Price shot out the station wagon's right front tire.) Price later testified that he released Goodman, Schwerner, and Chaney about 10:30 P.M. after fining them twenty dollars for speeding. They were never seen alive again. (Although they are never mentioned by name, the three missing civil rights workers in *Mississippi Burning* are clearly Goodman, Schwerner, and Chaney.)

Because field workers were required to phone in at regular intervals, the CORE staff in Meridian knew by late afternoon that something was wrong. At 6:00 P.M., SNCC state headquarters in Jackson notified the FBI and the Mississippi Highway Patrol. For the next six weeks, while newspapers carried daily reports of the search, four hundred sailors from the Meridian naval air station joined FBI agents in dragging swamps and combing the countryside. They found a number of bodies belonging to long-missing lynching victims, but not those of the three civil rights workers. Finally, the offer of a twenty-five-thousand-dollar reward produced information that led to the discovery of their bodies in an earthen dam on August 4.

As a show of solidarity, the parents of the three young men asked that their sons be buried together. They soon learned, however, that Mississippi state law did not permit integrated cemeteries, so Chaney was buried alone. At Chaney's funeral, David Dennis of CORE said, "If you go back home and sit down and take what these white men in Mississippi are doing to us . . . if you take it and don't do something about it . . . then God damn your souls!"

black veterans of the civil rights movement to end the terror and secure justice in the nation's most racist state. They started Freedom Schools, established health clinics, and mobilized support for the Mississippi Freedom Democratic Party, seeking to build the foundation for a different kind of Mississippi—a multiracial democracy committed to equality and justice for all.

Because black registration threatened white control of the state's political machinery, white racists responded to Freedom Summer with total repression. They torched scores of black churches and systematically beat and arrested civil rights workers. Then in June, just as the Freedom Summer volunteers began to arrive, three movement activists, two whites and one black, disappeared after spending several hours in the Neshoba County jail on a trumped-up speeding charge. Six weeks later, the FBI found their bullet-riddled bodies buried in an earthen dam near Philadelphia, Mississippi.

Mississippi Burning represents one of Hollywood's few attempts to tell the story of what took place during the civil rights years. Using the murder of these three young men as its departure point, the film effectively and accurately depicts the reign of supremacist terror that permeated Mississippi's white community and enlisted its police chiefs, mayors, and prominent citizens. Understandably, perhaps, the filmmakers seem to believe they need the dramatic tension of the murder case to keep up audience interest in the story. Yet the story they tell is an atrocious distortion of history. As *Mississippi Burning* would have it, the only thing happening in that state during the summer of 1964 was, on the one hand, a fight between local white racists and, on the other, heroic FBI agents sent to the rescue of submissive, illiterate, quaking black people unable and unwilling to stand up for themselves.

The movie's two chief protagonists are both FBI men. Gene Hackman plays a former southern sheriff now working for the feds; he is folksy and sympathetic. Willem Dafoe is a young northern agent, Kennedyesque in his moralism and arrogance. The conflict between them is the real nub of the movie. Dafoe is a stick figure who utters platitudes of the "some things are worth dying for" sort. Early on, he puts his moral politics on display when he insists on sitting next to a young black man at a restaurant lunch counter (the young man is later beaten by the Klan). In contrast, Hackman is the ethnographer, making small talk with his fellow southerners and trying to show Dafoe—at one point actually described in the dialogue as a "Kennedy boy"—how a good white southern law officer goes about finding criminals. In this case, while Dafoe follows procedure, Hackman seduces the deputy sheriff's wife, his relationship with her producing the crucial information that Dafoe's investigative methods do not.

At one point, an FBI agent remarks that there "was a war [going on] long before we got here." But the only war we see is between white people. That, of course, is the problem. How can a movie about Freedom

Summer feature no black protagonists? In 1963, eighty-five thousand black Mississippians cast "freedom ballots" to show their determination and prove, contrary to white declarations, that they were quite serious about voting. A year later, despite the church burnings, arrests, and murders, Mississippi blacks met at local Freedom Schools all summer long. They voted for Freedom Democratic party delegates to represent them at the Democratic National Convention in Atlantic City and created an autonomous social movement. They showed they would not be terrorized into silence. Eventually, they prevailed.

But where are these activists in the film? The blacks in *Mississippi Burning* tremble in fear of whites, disband their conversations whenever whites approach, and retreat in mute submission. There is one brave black child who stands up, but no one else. The only anger expressed comes at the end of the film, when a black minister declares at the funeral of a black lynching victim that he is "sick and tired of going to the funerals of black men who have been murdered by white men." But where are the Fannie Lou Hamers, the Anne Moodys, the Amzie Moores,

> # "Mississippi is unreal when you're not there, and the rest of the country is unreal when you are."
>
> *Robert Moses*

and the other local people who heroically sustained and built the movement in defiance of white terror? In *Mississippi Burning*, black people are even more like stick figures than Willem Dafoe. They sing movement spirituals like "Precious Lord" (at the beginning) and "Walk On" (at the end), but otherwise they don't count.

Background Reading

Clayborne Carson, *In Struggle: The History of the Student Non-Violent Coordinating Committee* (Harvard University Press, 1984)

John Dittmer, *Local People: The Struggle for Civil Rights in Mississippi* (University of Illinois Press, 1994)

1988/USA/Color
DIRECTOR: Alan Parker; **PRODUCER:** Frederick Zollo, Robert E. Colesberry; **SCREENPLAY:** Chris Gerolmo; **STUDIO:** Orion; **VIDEO:** Orion; **RUNNING TIME:** 127 min.

The MFDP in Atlantic City

The MFDP

The goal of the Mississippi Freedom Democratic party was simple: to unseat the all-white party regulars (most of whom publicly supported the Republican candidate, Barry Goldwater) at the 1964 Democratic National Convention in Atlantic City. Having already been endorsed by the New York and Michigan delegations, the MFDP believed its prospects in a roll-call vote were good.

Lyndon Johnson, however, desperately wanted to avoid a floor fight that might upset southern delegates. With the vice-presidential nomination hanging in the balance, LBJ told Minnesota senator Hubert Humphrey to make the problem go away. Humphrey, in turn, had his protégé, Walter Mondale, offer the MFDP a deal: two at-large seats and the promise that all future delegations would be integrated. Martin Luther King, Jr., and other black leaders urged the MFDP to take the offer, but the delegates refused unanimously. "We didn't come all this way for no two seats when all of us is tired," MFDP vice-chairman Fannie Lou Hamer said.

Later...

On December 4, 1964, the FBI arrested twenty-one Neshoba County men (including Deputy Cecil Price) for the murders of Goodman, Schwerner, and Chaney. State charges were dropped when Mississippi governor Paul B. Johnson, Jr., refused to allow prosecution of the men because of inadequate evidence. The Justice Department then convened a federal grand jury that indicted eighteen of the twenty-one for conspiring to violate the civil rights workers' constitutional rights. District court judge William Harold Cox tried to reduce the charge to a misdemeanor; the Supreme Court reversed him.

When the verdict was finally handed down in 1967, the jury found seven of the defendants guilty, Price among them. They each received sentences of three to ten years in jail, Price serving forty-four months. It was the first time an all-white jury in Mississippi had convicted white defendants in a civil rights case.

WILLIAM H. CHAFE

MALCOLM X

Clayborne Carson

C A S T

Malcolm X   *(Denzel Washington)*
Betty Shabazz   *(Angela Bassett)*

Malcolm, 1940s

Malcolm's Memory of His Father

My father was a big, six-foot-four, very black man. He had only one eye. How he had lost the other one I have never known. He was from Reynolds, Georgia, where he had left school after the third or maybe fourth grade. . . . One of the reasons I've always felt that my father favored me was that to the best of my remembrance, it was only me that he sometimes took with him to the Garvey U.N.I.A. meetings which he held quietly in people's homes. . . . I noticed how differently they all acted, although sometimes they were the same people who jumped and shouted in church. But in these meetings both they and my father were more intense, more intelligent and down to earth. It made me feel the same way. . . . I remember how the meetings always closed with my father saying, several times, and the people chanting after him, "Up, you mighty race, you can accomplish what you will!"

From *The Autobiography of Malcolm X*

Near the beginning of Spike Lee's cinema biography, Malcolm X's father dies. As idealized in the film, Earl Little is a race leader, willing to brave white opposition to promote Marcus Garvey's Universal Negro Improvement Association. The film's flashbacks and narration by the Malcolm character leave no doubt that white racists murdered Little.

The Autobiography of Malcolm X, written with Alex Haley's assistance and published posthumously, paints a far less idealized portrait of Little. As remembered by his son, Little was an abusive husband and father who "savagely" beat his children, except for Malcolm. "I actually believe that as anti-white as my father was," Malcolm recalled, "he was subconsciously so afflicted with the white man's brainwashing of Negroes that he inclined to favor the light one." Only six at the time of his father's death in 1931, Malcolm remembered only "a vague commotion, the house filled up with people crying, saying bitterly that the white Black Legion had finally gotten him." Although the actual circumstances of Little's death remain ambiguous—contemporary police reports dismissed it as an accident, his insurance company suspected suicide—the *Autobiography* and the film have transformed an obscure event into a crucial part of a historical legend that blends personal memory with racial myth.

The film conveys neither the complexity nor the self-critical aspects of the *Autobiography*, which told Malcolm's story from the perspective of his final year. Throughout its more than three hours, Lee's film is resolutely respectful, glamorizing the truculence of Malcolm's Detroit Red period and the dogmatism of some of his speeches as a Muslim minister. As source documents, Lee used Malcolm's memoirs and public statements rather than the testimony of those who knew him. The resulting film is iconolatry rather than iconoclasm.

As a historian, I do not find it useful to quibble about inaccuracies, simplifications, invented characters, imagined dialogue, anachronisms, and various other improbabilities. To complain that Denzel Washington is not Malcolm X is to miss the point of the film and the book, which communicate a constructed image to a far larger audience than Malcolm ever reached during his lifetime. It is far more important to note the film's more serious limitations, particularly its failure to give adequate attention to Malcolm's evolving political ideas and activities during the last year of his life. Although these inadequacies derive from the *Autobiography*, which also focused on Malcolm's years as a petty criminal and then as a minister of the Nation of Islam, Lee further downplays those elements of Malcolm's narrative that indicated his capacity for rigorous self-criticism.

HISTORY

After his father's death in 1931, Malcolm watched his family fall apart. The strain of feeding and caring for seven children proved too much for Louise Little. Although she resisted as best she could pressure from social workers to place her children in foster homes, her psychological decline finally forced her admission to the Kalamazoo State Mental Hospital in December 1938.

At the time his mother was committed, Malcolm was living in a white juvenile home. When his half-sister Ella came to visit from Boston, where she lived, Malcolm thought she was "the first really proud black woman I had ever seen in my life." In 1940, when he was fifteen, Malcolm made his first trip to Boston. On his return to Michigan, he noticed and became annoyed by treatment he had previously shrugged off: "Where 'nigger' had slipped off my back before, wherever I heard it now, I stopped and looked at whoever said it. And they looked surprised that I did."

HOLLYWOOD

Denzel Washington

The transformation of *The Autobiography of Malcolm X* into Spike Lee's film took almost a quarter of a century. Some admirers of Malcolm argued that only a black writer and director could do justice to his story. James Baldwin, the most prominent African-American writer of the period, prepared the initial script, but his screenplay—later published as *One Day, When I Was Lost* (1972)—included a vast number of flashbacks and historical scenes that would have been prohibitively expensive to film. During the early 1970s, a white screenwriter, Arnold Perl, wrote another script, but the project lost favor in Hollywood as the nation's interest in black militancy waned. More than a decade later, Warner Brothers finally agreed to finance the film, and Lee was chosen to direct. (The announcement was made after Lee had publicly insisted that a black director should make *Malcolm X*.)

Elijah Muhammad

The Nation of Islam

Mecca-born silk peddler Wallace D. Fard emigrated to the United States sometime around 1930; a year later, he founded the Nation of Islam in Detroit. Fard taught his followers that blacks were members of a superior race descended from Muslims of Afro-Asia. He claimed that he was a messenger sent by Allah to save his lost people from the "white devils" who were making their lives miserable. Fard insisted that Christianity was a false religion used by whites to enslave blacks.

By 1934, the Black Muslim movement had grown to about eight thousand members. That year, Fard disappeared mysteriously and was succeeded by Elijah Poole, the thirty-seven-year-old son of a Baptist preacher. Poole had moved north from Georgia in 1923 and was living on relief in Detroit when he first met Fard. After becoming Fard's assistant minister, Poole took the name Elijah Muhammad. When he succeeded Fard, Muhammad added the title "Messenger of Allah to the Lost-Found Nation of Islam in the Wilderness of North America."

Because of dissent within the Detroit temple, Muhammad soon moved to Chicago, where he established Temple No. 2 and spread Fard's message that, in order to overcome racial discrimination, blacks must become independent of their white "slave masters." During World War II, Muhammad counseled his followers to refuse to fight for the United States. He was convicted of encouraging resistance to the draft and served three and a half years in prison. After his release in 1946, Muhammad began an intensive recruitment drive, especially in prisons, where the Black Muslim message of racial pride and economic independence had particular appeal. Several of Malcolm's siblings converted to the Nation of Islam during this period, and Malcolm was himself introduced to the faith while in prison by his brother Reginald. "The hardest test I ever faced in my life was praying," Malcolm later said. "You understand. My comprehending, my believing the teachings of Mr. Muhammad had only required my mind's saying to me, 'That's right!' or 'I never thought of that.' But bending my knees to pray—that *act*—well, that took me a week."

The film's most engaging scenes depict Malcolm's life as a hustler and later his speechmaking on behalf of the Nation of Islam. It largely ignores his activities outside the Nation. Instead of clarifying his mature political perspective, the film emphasizes his earlier cynicism, racial pessimism, and uncritical acceptance of Elijah Muhammad's teachings. The film treats Malcolm X's break with Muhammad as a son's disillusionment with a morally flawed surrogate father, but Malcolm left the Nation for political as well as personal reasons. The *Autobiography* makes it clear that before he learned of Muhammad's marital infidelities, Malcolm had already become dissatisfied with his leader's policy of nonengagement, which not only prevented members of the group from participating in civil rights protests but even forbade voting. Malcolm's sardonic verbal attacks on national black leaders—excerpts from which enliven the film—were harshly critical, but Malcolm's ties with militant civil rights activists actually became increasingly close late in his life.

As the southern black civil rights movement grew in scale during 1963, Malcolm recognized that the nonengagement policy was hurting his recruitment efforts in black communities. In the *Autobiography*, Malcolm admits his disappointment in the failure of the Nation of Islam to become involved in the expanding freedom struggle. "I felt that, wherever black people committed themselves, the Little Rocks and the Birminghams and other places, militantly disciplined Muslims should also be there—for all the world to see, and respect, and discuss. It could be heard

> ## "My first impression was how could a Black man talk about the government, white people, and act so bold, and not be shot at?"
>
> *Muhammad Ali*

increasingly in the Negro communities: 'Those Muslims *talk* tough, but they never *do* anything, unless somebody bothers Muslims.'"

This telling criticism of the Nation of Islam's stance regarding political action appears in the film, but Lee's misleading handling of it reflects his unwillingness to examine critically Malcolm's black nationalist rhetoric as a Muslim minister. In the film, the criticism precedes the only scene in which Malcolm and his fellow Muslims actually stand up to white authorities. Malcolm is shown demanding and getting hospital treatment for a member of the Nation, Brother Johnson (Johnson Hinton), who was beaten by New York City police in 1957. Although the incident confirms the notion that the Nation of Islam did not engage in militant action unless its members were threatened, Lee stages the event to suggest that the Nation was far more willing to challenge white authority than it was.

Malcolm initially defended Elijah Muhammad's nonengagement policy and fiercely attacked Martin Luther King, Jr.'s strategy of nonviolent resistance, but he later recognized that the Nation offered no real alternative to black activists who were facing vicious white racists in the South. It was easier to talk about armed self-defense in New York than to face Bull Connor's police dogs in Birmingham. Indeed, even though the film ignores this fact, Malcolm knew that the Nation of Islam was not above making deals with white people when such deals served its leaders' interests. Near the end of his life, Malcolm admitted that, even while criticizing civil rights activists for working with white liberals, he once, on Elijah Muhammad's orders, negotiated a mutual noninterference agreement with Ku Klux Klan leaders in Atlanta. Like Marcus Garvey's in the 1920s, Muhammad's insistence that all whites were devils made it possible for him to justify dealing with the worst of them.

Although the film depicts Malcolm's period of independence from the Nation mainly through scenes of foreboding, such as repeated threatening telephone calls, his final months consisted of much more than waiting for martyrdom. Among the many important episodes of Malcolm's last year that the film mentions only in passing, if at all, are:

- his brief meeting with Martin Luther King, Jr., at the U.S. Capitol;

- his crucial "The Ballot or the Bullet" speech delivered at a symposium sponsored by the Congress of Racial Equality;

- his attendance at a meeting of the Organization of African Unity and subsequent talks with leaders of Egypt, Tanzania, Nigeria, Ghana, Guinea, Kenya, and Uganda;

- his day-long October 1964 meeting in Nairobi with leaders of the Student Nonviolent Coordinating Committee and the resulting cooperation between SNCC and Malcolm's newly formed Organization of Afro-American Unity;

- the December 1964 appearance of Fannie Lou Hamer and other Mississippi civil rights activists as Malcolm's honored guests at an OAAU meeting in Harlem.

The film shows Malcolm watching televised scenes of black protest activities (including some that occurred after his death!) but remarkably does not mention his February 1965 trip to Selma, Alabama, where he addressed young protesters and expressed support for the voting rights struggle. While in Selma, he met with Coretta Scott King, whose husband was then in jail. Malcolm affirmed his desire to assist King's voting rights efforts, explaining that if whites knew that Malcolm was the alternative, "It might be easier for them to accept Martin's proposals." Malcolm's increasing political involvement was further indicated in the weeks

Writing the Autobiography

Alex Haley first began writing during his twenty-year tour of duty in the U.S. Coast Guard (1939–59)—to hold off the boredom of long voyages, he said. *The Autobiography of Malcolm X* (1965), based on his extensive interviews with Malcolm, was Haley's first major work:

One night, Malcolm X arrived nearly out on his feet from fatigue. For two hours, he paced the floor delivering a tirade against Negro leaders who were attacking Elijah Muhammad and himself. I don't know what gave me the inspiration to say once he paused for breath, "I wonder if you'd tell me something about your mother?"

Abruptly he quit pacing, and the look he shot at me made me sense that somehow the chance question had hit him. When I look back at it now, I believe I must have caught him so physically weak that his defenses were vulnerable.

Slowly, Malcolm began to talk, now walking in a tight circle. "She was always standing over the stove, trying to stretch whatever we had to eat. We stayed so hungry that we were dizzy. I remember the color of dresses she used to wear—they were a kind of faded-out gray. . . ." And he kept on talking until dawn, so tired that the big feet would often stumble in their pacing. . . . After that night he never again hesitated to tell me even the most intimate details of his personal life, over the next two years.

Malcolm sends "greetings from Kenya."

Abroad in 1964

During the last year of his life, Malcolm X made two trips to the Middle East and Africa. In the aftermath of his split from the Nation of Islam, he sought to build a new spiritual and political base from which to lead his followers. His first trip, in April 1964, began with the *hajj*, the annual Muslim pilgrimage to Mecca. In Mecca, Malcolm experienced a revolution in his system of beliefs: Witnessing men of all colors—brown, yellow, red, black, *and* white—worshiping together as brothers made him realize that not all whites were devils. Accepting that American racism was not a function of whiteness per se, Malcolm began to consider the possibility of a reconciliation between the races in the United States.

On the other hand, Malcolm was not quite ready to forgive white America. In fact, one purpose of his trips was to encourage the newly independent nations of Africa to push for UN condemnation of the United States for human rights abuses against its black citizens. Malcolm's internationalist, pan-African speeches were well received, and during the August 1964 meeting of the Organization of African Unity in Cairo, Malcolm was embraced as a legitimate ambassador of black America.

After visiting a number of heads of state—including Kwame Nkrumah of Ghana, Alhaji Isa Wali of Nigeria, and Prince Faysal of Saudi Arabia—Malcolm returned to the United States, bringing with him a new Islamic name to match his new beliefs: He would be El-Hajj Malik El-Shabazz.

before his assassination by the telegram he sent to the head of the American Nazi party: "I am no longer held in check from fighting white supremacists by Elijah Muhammad's separationist Black Muslim Movement, and if your present racist agitation of our people there in Alabama causes physical harm to Reverend King or any other Black Americans . . . you and your KKK friends will be met with maximum physical retaliation."

Malcolm's political militancy led to increasing governmental repression and escalating threats from members of the Nation of Islam. Lee's handling of the assassination reflects his overall failure to indicate why Malcolm's independent political course caused him to attract such deadly enemies. The film shows various members of the Nation of Islam preparing to kill Malcolm, while also hinting that white operatives were involved. Malcolm is shown being followed, presumably by CIA agents, while on his trip to Mecca and Africa. We see a bug in Malcolm's New York City hotel room. When Malcolm and his wife, Betty, discuss the many threats they have received, Malcolm speculates, "The more I keep thinking about the things that have been happening lately, I'm not at all sure it's solely the Muslims. I trained them, I know what they can and cannot do, and they can't do some of the stuff that's recently been going on."

> ## "I remember Malcolm literally crying out one night. He said, 'I'm trying to turn the corner, but they won't let me.'"
>
> *Alex Haley*

It is hardly revelatory for the film to suggest that the FBI and the CIA saw Malcolm as a threat, but speculation about government-sponsored conspiracy obscures the extent to which Malcolm's death resulted from a mentality that allowed some black people to define others as race traitors. Malcolm was a source as well as a victim of the Nation of Islam's often vicious rhetorical militancy. His former protégé, Louis X (later Farrakhan), declared in late 1964 that Malcolm was a Judas "worthy of death." Such self-righteous vilification created a climate that made Malcolm's death inevitable. Despite its reputation as an antiwhite group, the Nation of Islam directed nearly all of its violence against black people, particularly defectors. Malcolm's death was a precursor of the kind of internecine warfare that weakened the Black Power movement and increased its vulnerability to outside attack. Although Malcolm ultimately struggled to find "a common solution to a common problem," the film does not show him working in concert with other black political groups.

In the film, Malcolm never completely leaves behind the smug self-right-eousness of his years as a hustler and proselytizer. As a result, many young viewers may prefer to emulate the self-destructive rebelliousness of Malcolm's youth or the racist demagoguery of his years in the Nation of Islam rather than his mature statesmanship. Some may even mistake Farrakhan as Malcolm's modern-day counterpart.

Spike Lee frames Malcolm's life story with contemporary scenes: opening footage of Los Angeles police beating Rodney King and an epilogue showing Nelson Mandela, in front of a classroom filled with South African children, affirming Malcolm's call for liberation "by any means necessary." This iconic mixture gives his film a greater sense of political importance than it would otherwise have had, but its political message is nevertheless ambiguous. Lee's strongest images suggest the immutability of white racism (King's beating) rather than possibility of overcoming it (Mandela). His film's Malcolm ends his life resigned to his fate rather than displaying confidence in his hard-won political understanding. The film's Malcolm becomes, like the filmmaker himself, a social critic rather than a political insurgent. Malcolm helped to create his own myth during a period when fundamental political change seemed feasible. Spike Lee has revised Malcolm's myth for a time when political cynicism prevails. *Malcolm X* thus reflects the current tendency in African-American life to supplant politics with attitude—that is, to express diffuse racial resentment rather than to engage in collective action to achieve racial advancement.

Background Reading

Clayborne Carson, *Malcolm X: The FBI File* (Carroll & Graf, 1991)
Alex Haley, *The Autobiography of Malcolm X* (Grove, 1965)

1992/USA/Color
DIRECTOR: Spike Lee; PRODUCER: Marvin Worth, Spike Lee; SCREENPLAY: Arnold Perl, Spike Lee; STUDIO: Warner; VIDEO: Warner; RUNNING TIME: 201 min.

Later...

In the years since Malcolm X's assassination, his legacy has been pitted against that of Martin Luther King, Jr.—the black nationalist versus the integrationist, the proponent of liberation "by any means necessary" versus the advocate of Gandhian nonviolence. Contemporary followers have tended to divide themselves into mutually exclusive competing groups, inheriting either Malcolm's ideological legacy or Martin's—but never both. Devotees of Malcolm's rhetoric often ignore his own retrospective criticisms of his Nation of Islam demagoguery. Similarly, Martin's disciples often overstate the extent to which he controlled the mass struggles that brought him to public attention.

Not surprisingly, Malcolm's legacy has been affirmed most strongly by African Americans who share his cynicism about the future of black-white relations in the United States. During the 1970s and 1980s, black nationalists and rap artists injected Malcolm's name and image into African-American youth culture, preparing the way for Spike Lee's film. Despite the commercialization of "X" caps and other memorabilia, Malcolm remains a provocative icon.

In contrast to the grass-roots celebrations of Malcolm, Martin's legacy has been sustained by African Americans who continue to believe in the American dream. Since 1986, the federal government has given its stolid imprimatur to an official celebration of Martin's birth. Once a controversial protest leader, Martin has become the innocuous black equivalent of Washington and Lincoln.

In recent years, some African-American leaders and intellectuals have recognized that the two leaders were multifaceted, that they failed to achieve many of their objectives, and that they offered complementary rather than conflicting advice regarding problems that still confront African Americans. Three decades after Malcolm's death, his call for strong, militant, black-controlled institutions has been only partly realized, while the decline of the black family and the black community has left black Americans less able to achieve Martin's dream of racial equality. Within this context, Malcolm's tactical disagreements with Martin have come to mean little; it is their mutual commitment to politically effective black action that merits attention.

APOLLO 13

Andrew Chaikin

CAST

Jim Lovell	(Tom Hanks)
Fred Haise	(Bill Paxton)
Jack Swigert	(Kevin Bacon)
Gene Kranz	(Ed Harris)

Space shuttle astronauts during weightlessness training aboard NASA's KC-135.

Filming in Zero Gravity

Apollo 13 director Ron Howard was the first commercial filmmaker ever to work aboard NASA's converted KC-135 cargo plane, known as the Vomit Comet. This aircraft flies in a series of parabolic arcs designed to simulate the weightlessness of space. Each arc generates twenty-three seconds of weightlessness immediately followed by the onslaught of twice-normal gravity, after which the cycle repeats. On this roller-coaster ride, Howard's cast and crew faced some unusual challenges and hardships. Because of engine noise, none of the dialogue recorded on the plane could be used (it was overdubbed later). Also, motion sickness reared its head once or twice during the hundreds of parabolas logged by the *Apollo 13* team over several weeks of KC-135 flights. The Vomit Comet lived up to its name.

DURING MY EIGHT YEARS OF CONVERSATIONS with the men who went to the moon, it was inevitable that I would hear some surprises. Few, however, were as unanticipated as Jim Lovell's feelings about his ill-fated Apollo 13 mission in 1970. Unlike his crewman Fred Haise, who carried a lingering sense of disappointment about the flight's lost objectives, Lovell was remarkably upbeat when I interviewed him in 1988. Despite the fact that Apollo 13's near-disaster had robbed him of his only chance to land on the moon, an achievement that was to have culminated his long and successful spaceflight career, Lovell said that he did not regret the experience of commanding that mission. He was proud of the way he and his crew had coped with a seemingly unending series of crises during their four-day struggle to return to earth. Said Lovell flatly, "Apollo 13 was a test pilot's mission."

At the same time, Lovell was somewhat miffed that the astronauts' role in saving Apollo 13 hadn't received the recognition he felt it deserved. After the flight, most popular accounts stressed the truly heroic efforts of the earthbound flight controllers and engineers, who had labored around the clock to bring the astronauts home. But, as Lovell pointed out, it's one thing for an army of experts to devise procedures on earth; it's quite another for three tired, cold astronauts to implement those procedures for the first time in the depths of translunar space—knowing that a mistake could be deadly. "The real story of [Apollo 13]," Lovell said, "has never been told."

But telling the story of Apollo 13, or that of any other moon flight, is not an easy task. For one thing, the spacecraft and their missions were unbelievably complex; even after nearly a decade of research, I'm sure I don't fully comprehend them. Then there is the language problem: The astronauts' conversations with mission control were so laden with high-tech jargon that television anchormen constantly had to explain what was going on. It's a problem that doesn't go away for the writer or the filmmaker; the desire for accuracy is often at odds with the need for clarity. The astronauts themselves are often the source of the trouble. Their celebrated test-pilot cool, which helped get them to the moon, made their spoken words remarkably unrevealing, at least to the untrained ear. During the critical minutes before Apollo 11's touchdown on the moon, as Neil Armstrong hunted for a safe place to land, he looked out the window to see that the computer was steering the lunar module toward a giant crater ringed with boulders. The onboard voice recorder captured his only comment: "Pretty rocky area."

HISTORY

Even before the Apollo 13 mission, Jim Lovell was the world's most experienced astronaut. On three previous flights, he'd racked up 572 hours in space. In December 1965, Lovell spent two weeks in earth orbit with Frank Borman aboard Gemini 7, paving the way for Apollo's lunar journeys. In November 1966, Lovell returned to orbit as commander of Gemini 12, the final mission of the Gemini program. Then, in December 1968, came the flight that Lovell calls his most awe-inspiring: Apollo 8, the first circumlunar voyage. With Frank Borman and Bill Anders, Lovell circled the moon on Christmas Eve, looking back at a tiny and radiant earth, which Lovell called "a grand oasis in the big vastness of space."

HOLLYWOOD

An avowed space enthusiast, Tom Hanks leapt at the chance to play Jim Lovell. To prepare for the role, Hanks met with Lovell at the astronaut's Texas home and even went flying with him, an experience that convinced Hanks that Lovell had the right stuff. Hanks is also a huge fan of *2001: A Space Odyssey*, so much so that he named his production company after that film's lunar outpost, Clavius Base.

President Richard Nixon congratulates Jim Lovell at Hickham Air Force Base in Hawaii the day after Apollo 13's return to earth.

Apollo 13, We Have a Problem

After the release of *Apollo 13*, a cadre of self-proclaimed "NASA dweebs" produced a list of the film's historical inaccuracies, ranging from errors in the Saturn V rocket's paint job to the mislocation of certain lunar features. I noticed many of these, along with the script's understandable tendency to verbalize emotions that in reality went unspoken. I also recognized that Lovell's famous statement—"Houston, we've had a problem"—had been changed to "Houston, we have a problem," presumably to enhance its impact.

But there were three departures from fact that I found especially annoying: One was Lovell and Haise's apparent mistrust of replacement crewman Jack Swigert, played by Kevin Bacon. The real Swigert was an expert on the Apollo command module who literally wrote the book on emergency procedures. His last-minute inclusion on the flight did give Lovell and Haise some short-lived apprehension about whether Swigert would easily mesh with a new crew. But they never doubted his abilities.

Unnecessary dramatics also creep into the film when the astronauts fire the lunar module's engine to correct their homeward trajectory. On screen all hell breaks loose as the pilots struggle to keep their spacecraft from gyrating out of control. To be sure, the maneuver was unorthodox, especially the untried scheme of using the earth as a reference point for orientation. But the real firing went so smoothly that the craft never wobbled more than a fraction of a degree.

Finally, the film's lone representative of the Grumman Corporation, which built the lunar module, is portrayed as a doubter mostly worried about keeping his job. Nothing could have been further from the truth.

It's enough of a challenge to surmount these obstacles in print; on film, the task is even more daunting. For this reason, director Ron Howard was brave even to consider re-creating the flight of Apollo 13. Howard and his partner, Brian Grazer, were alerted to the mission's cinematic potential by Michael Bostick, a member of their staff at Imagine Films who happened to be the son of a former Apollo flight controller. Bostick had seen a treatment for a book about the flight called *Lost Moon*, which was being written by Jim Lovell and journalist Jeffrey Kluger. Apollo 13 held special attraction for Howard, he said later, because it had the arc of a story: a definite beginning (the first fifty-five hours, when everything was still going normally), a middle (the accident and its immediate aftermath), and an ending (the astronauts' homeward voyage). Like Lovell, Howard believed it was a story that should be told.

By the time *Apollo 13* opened in June 1995, a couple of months after the twenty-fifth anniversary of the real Apollo 13, I knew enough about the production to be excited by its release. I had visited the set and seen the extraordinary lengths to which Howard and his crew had gone to ensure accuracy. I was glad that *Apollo 13* was the first commercial film to employ real weightlessness, thanks to a NASA training aircraft affectionately known as the Vomit Comet. (Having been a passenger on a dozen Vomit Comet flights during the 1980s, I knew how evocative of spaceflight the experience could be.) I'd also met Tom Hanks, a died-in-the-wool space nut if there ever was one. Hanks, I had heard, had fought to keep the script from straying too far from NASA-ese verity.

But when I saw the film at a press screening, my reactions were strongly mixed. I enjoyed the film's period look

> ## "Apollo 13 was a test pilot's mission."
>
> *Jim Lovell*

(complete with sideburns and white lipstick) and the special effects, which benefited from the same type of computer-graphic magic that resurrected the dinosaurs of *Jurassic Park*. The re-creations of the Apollo spacecraft were superb. Best of all, of course, was the weightlessness. But I chafed at some of the uses of dramatic license. At the same time, I wondered how audiences would respond to lines like, "Houston, I'm switching over Quad C to Main A."

Apollo 13's galloping pace made me long for another film, Stanley Kubrick's *2001: A Space Odyssey*. Released in 1968, *2001* was the last space epic produced before the lunar missions began. To my mind, it was also the truest depiction of spaceflight ever put on film, partly because of its restraint. There were long stretches with no dialogue during which images of sunlit planets and spacecraft moving with celestial precision spoke for themselves. (Many of the Apollo astronauts saw *2001*. Bill Anders, one of Jim Lovell's crewmates on the Apollo 8 lunar-orbit mission in 1968, told me that one reason he felt disappointed when he saw the far side of the moon with his own eyes was that he thought it was less inspiring than the movie version.)

Of course, *Apollo 13* is an action film, and appropriately so. There was nothing slow-moving about Apollo 13's Saturn V launch or about the oxygen tank explosion that crippled its command module (named, not coincidentally, *Odyssey*). The hours after the accident were so intense that everyone involved, on earth and in space, lost track of time. But during the long ride back to earth, there was often little for the astronauts to do but endure, and I wished that the film had stopped to catch its breath with a few silent, contemplative moments.

Then I went to see *Apollo 13* again—not as an Apollo historian, but as a moviegoer—and I had a much better time. I realized that Howard had done a good job of navigating between story and history. There were moments, such as when Hanks's Lovell explains the upcoming flight to his young son Jeffrey, that powerfully conveyed the risks of the whole enterprise as well as the self-confident courage of the astronauts. Most of all, the film captured Apollo's mythic quality; for me, this was epitomized by the scene in which Lovell and his crew suit up on launch morning, like latter-day gladiators. And Howard was right to emphasize the parts played by Flight Director Gene Kranz and his mission controllers. The engineers' nerdy presence on the screen, not as extras but as heroes, communicated the determination and ingenuity that got human beings to the moon. It's one of the reasons Jim Lovell, like many other Apollo veterans I've questioned, praises *Apollo 13*. With a few departures, it tells the real story.

Astronaut Ed Mitchell, with Apollo 14's lunar "rickshaw," explores the moon's Fra Mauro highlands.

Later...

In the wake of Apollo 13, NASA fixed the design flaw that had caused the oxygen tank explosion, and on January 31, 1971, Apollo 14 astronauts Alan Shepard, Ed Mitchell, and Stu Roosa left earth to carry out the mission Jim Lovell's crew had been denied—an exploration of the moon's Fra Mauro highlands. In July 1971, Apollo 15's Dave Scott and Jim Irwin became the first astronauts to visit the mountains of the moon, bringing along a battery-powered Lunar Roving Vehicle for the most ambitious expedition yet. There would be two more lunar missions: Apollo 16 in April 1972 and Apollo 17 eight months later. After that, with space budgets tightening, NASA abandoned the moon to develop the earth-orbiting reusable space shuttle.

Background Reading

Andrew Chaikin, *A Man on the Moon: The Voyages of the Apollo Astronauts* (Viking, 1994)

Jim Lovell with Jeffrey Kluger, *Lost Moon: The Perilous Voyage of Apollo 13* (Houghton Mifflin, 1994)

1995/USA/Color
DIRECTOR: Ron Howard; PRODUCER: Brian Grazer; SCREENPLAY: William Broyles, Jr.; Al Reinert; STUDIO: Universal; VIDEO: MCA; RUNNING TIME: 140 min.

APOCALYPSE NOW

Frances FitzGerald

CAST

Col. Kurtz (Marlon Brando)
Lt. Col. Kilgore (Robert Duvall)
Capt. Willard (Martin Sheen)

OF ALL THE BIG-BUDGET HOLLYWOOD FILMS about the Vietnam War, *Apocalypse Now* is the one that has become a classic, thanks to the sheer brilliance of three or four scenes. Two decades after the movie was made, there was an Apocalypse Now bar in Ho Chi Minh City, and when the American invasion of Haiti began, journalists waiting for the U.S. helicopters to land hummed Wagner's "Ride of the Valkyries." Director Francis Ford Coppola did not set out to make the quintessential Vietnam War movie; he undertook the far more ambitious task of re-creating Joseph Conrad's *Heart of Darkness* against the backdrop of Vietnam. And though the film went awry and Coppola failed in his attempt, his failure is actually the perfect metaphor for the whole Vietnam experience.

Most of the brilliance of *Apocalypse Now* has to do with helicopters and napalm. The film opens with a shot of a wall of palm trees rising out of the ocean and the sound of a chopper's rotor blades. Struts move across the top of the picture frame and a helicopter passes through. With the *snick-snick-snick* of the rotors growing louder, the chopper looks like a huge, malevolent insect. To the sound of The Doors singing, "This is the end," the jungle suddenly erupts in flame. When I first saw these breathtaking pyrotechnics, I thought Coppola had seen the war in Vietnam and filmed what the TV cameras could only approximate.

From this moment on, however, *Apocalypse Now* seems to be two different films spliced together with an editing machine. One of them, unfortunately the shorter of the two, is a daring and stylish satire on the American army in Vietnam; the other is Coppola's misguided attempt to translate Conrad's novel into film.

As the tale unfolds, we see Captain Willard (Martin Sheen), a Special Forces officer, getting drunk on Rémy Martin in a Saigon hotel room, waiting for a mission and contemplating how great a warrior he is. This is serious, sweaty stuff. Just before he bleeds to death after cutting himself on a bottle, Willard is rescued by military police, who take him to Nha Trang. There, a general briefs him on his mission: Colonel Kurtz, an "outstanding officer," has murdered several South Vietnamese officers—perhaps double agents—and crossed the border into Cambodia with an army of Montagnards. The tribesmen, who treat Kurtz like a god, are killing people indiscriminately. The army suspects that Kurtz has become "unsound," so his command must be terminated "with extreme prejudice." However, the scene is confusing, for while the general and his aides are clearly comic figures, the mission, as it turns out, is a serious one.

In order to begin the boat journey that will take him upriver into Cambodia, Willard seeks the aid of an air cavalry battalion operating along

HISTORY

Air Cav soldiers at Firebase A-Luoi, Laos

The First Air Cavalry Division was the product of a new concept in air assault tactics pioneered during the early 1960s by Gen. Harry W.O. Kinnard. Based initially at An Khe, the First Cav became one of the most distinguished U.S. divisions in Vietnam, known for its effectiveness in combat and its high morale. Cav generals, including the division commander, piloted their own helicopters and spent many Sundays flying to hospitals across the country to visit their wounded. The First Cav was a division that professional soldiers wanted to join, and its almost company-size complement of information officers built up its good reputation among the press. Lt. Col. Kilgore is not based on any particular First Cav officer—which is not to say there weren't flamboyant, swashbuckling officers in Vietnam. Col. George S. Patton, Jr., of the Eleventh Armored Cavalry Regiment used to try to talk like his famous father. "Boys," he once said, "I don't have anything against the Vietnamese people personally, but I sure do like to see those arms and legs fly."

HOLLYWOOD

Robert Duvall as Lt. Col. Kilgore

Francis Ford Coppola started filming *Apocalypse Now* in the jungles of the Philippines in March 1976. After only one week's shooting, the director fired Harvey Keitel, who had been cast to play Captain Willard, and replaced him with Martin Sheen. Sheen had reservations about his health but thought he could endure the scheduled sixteen weeks of filming. In fact, a year later, the disaster-prone production was still stuck in the jungle. Four months into the principal photography, a typhoon hit, destroying most of the movie's elaborate sets and delaying the production for two months. The movie suffered yet another setback in March 1977 when Sheen suffered a massive heart attack. By the time the film was completed, Coppola, the cast, and the crew had all nearly reached the point of Kurtz's madness. As the director himself said at the 1979 Cannes Film Festival, "We were in the jungle, there were too many of us, we had access to too much money, too much equipment, and, little by little, we went insane."

Special Forces

The Special Forces, also known as the Green Berets because of their distinctive headgear, were elite army troops trained in unconventional warfare and counterinsurgency tactics. First sent to Vietnam in 1957 under the aegis of the CIA, they were much favored by President Kennedy, who thought they could meet the challenges of political and guerrilla warfare in Indochina. Although celebrated in film and song, the Green Berets never had much success in winning "the hearts and minds" of the Vietnamese. They operated in small teams along the Cambodian and Laotian borders, organizing Montagnard villagers to harass infiltration routes and specializing in intelligence collection and "black" cross-border operations.

While Coppola's Kurtz is essentially based on the Conrad character, some of his biography parallels that of Col. Robert B. Rheault, the straight-arrow Special Forces commander who was court-martialed by the army after some of his men were accused of killing a Vietnamese guide in 1969. There was solid evidence that the guide had betrayed Green Beret patrols to the North Vietnamese and that a CIA officer had sanctioned his murder. Still, the case was pursued, in part because of the animosity felt by Gen. Creighton W. Abrams, the top U.S. commander in Vietnam, toward the "elitist" Special Forces. The charges were later dropped, though Colonel Rheault's military career was ruined.

The Vietnam Oeuvre

Such antiwar movies as *Platoon* and *The Deer Hunter* were not the only films to get Vietnam wrong. *The Green Berets*, starring John Wayne, was a 1968 attempt to transpose World War II us-versus-them values to Vietnam. It showed an equal disregard for the country's geography—and even for basic astronomy. In the final scene, John Wayne—the kindly officer—walks along a Vietnamese beach at sunset with a native orphan he has befriended. The movie ends with the sun going down—a huge red ball—into the Pacific! (In Vietnam, the sun sets over land.) The one notable exception to this catalog of misrepresentation is *Go Tell the Spartans* (1978), based on the book *Incident at Muc Hoa* about a special forces team in the Mekong Delta. It is perhaps the best Vietnam War movie made to date.

the beaches of Central Vietnam, and what follows is a marvelously self-contained black comedy. The battalion's commander, Lieutenant Colonel Kilgore (Robert Duvall), is a fabulous caricature of the soldier's soldier, as well as the media's soldier, circa 1966. With Wagner bellowing from the loudspeakers of his Huey, Kilgore stages a sunrise assault on a Vietcong village. After much mayhem and carnage, the soldiers go surfing on perfect six-foot waves.

The patrol boat assigned to Colonel Willard is manned by a crew modeled on the post-1969 flaky army: They are skeptical and usually either doped out or wired. As the boat travels farther upriver and deeper into the jungle, Willard's journey becomes more and more surreal. The American bases he and the crew pass are lit like amusement parks; we see huge PXs and a USO show in which Playboy bunnies descend via helicopter and take off again with soldiers hanging on the skids; Jimi Hendrix blares from the trenches, flares drop, and combat-crazed soldiers fire at random into the threatening night. Gradually things turn seriously nasty, and when the last U.S. base is left behind the film loses its sense of humor *and* all relationship to the Vietnam War.

>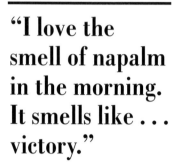
>
> "I love the smell of napalm in the morning. It smells like . . . victory."
>
> *Lieutenant Colonel Kilgore*

Eventually the boat pulls into a place that looks vaguely like Angkor Wat, with thousands of sweating natives, corpses all over the place, altars covered with skulls, and a lot of pink smoke or mist half-obscuring the scene. In the midst of this phantasmagoria, Kurtz (Marlon Brando) reads from T.S. Eliot's "The Hollow Men," with *The Golden Bough* at his side. He speaks unbearably slowly. "The horror, the horror," he repeats with portentous pauses. Clearly something is eating him, but it's hard to know what. In any case, lots of unspeakable things happen until Willard finally puts him out of his misery—and the credits put us out of ours.

Of course, anyone who has spent any time in Vietnam would feel uneasy about Willard's journey from the start and become more uncomfortable as time goes by. Kurtz is said to have gone into Cambodia with a Montagnard army, yet there are no Montagnards in Cambodia for the simple reason that there are no mountains to speak of there. Willard's journey, we are told, begins in Nha Trang, and Kilgore's battalion surfs a beach that is surely in Central Vietnam. But you can't get to Cambodia from Central Vietnam by river because there are mountains in between (rivers don't flow uphill). While you *can* get to Cambodia via the Mekong, that river passes through densely populated rice land, not jungle—and it doesn't get you anywhere near any Montagnard settlements or Angkor Wat.

Because *Apocalypse Now* is fiction (and in no way naturalistic), Coppola has the perfect right to invent geography and depict imaginary tribesmen who, it appears, make ritual sacrifices before breakfast. However, the film loses interest as it strays from the realities of Vietnam—and the more it strays, the worse it gets as fiction. This may be coincidence, but I think not, for fiction must have a credible landscape, even if that landscape is imaginary. The best scenes in the film are those in which Coppola has meticulously re-created Vietnam. When he starts to make up the geography, it's a sign of his more general retreat into abstraction and solipsism. The film gradually empties out and Kurtz, when we finally meet him, has nothing to say. He is merely a symbol: Colonel Thanatos, Mr. Death Wish. There is nobody home. So all we have is Marlon Brando's famous face, melodramatically lit, and mumbled quotations pointing back to Coppola's literary sources.

Curiously enough, the other ambitious Hollywood films about Vietnam suffer from this same solipsism. *Full Metal Jacket, The Deer Hunter, Platoon,* and *Casualties of War* are all morality plays or parables decked out in special effects and extravagant Technicolor gore. There are no idiosyncratic characters. Life is missing, and so is an attention to landscape, to detail. Oliver Stone's *Platoon* begins with an extraordinary, hyper-real evocation of jungle warfare, but then the film descends into facile mythmaking—and at the same time departs from its particular landscape. In *Full Metal Jacket,* Hue during the Tet offensive looks like a bombed-out Miami suburb. *Casualties of War* features huge railway bridges and trains, though the one railroad in Vietnam was built early in the century and had no trains running on it during the war. In *The Deer Hunter*—which, to my mind, is the most pretentious and awful of the lot—the Vietnamese speak Thai and play Russian roulette, and even the deer is clearly a prop.

Because these ambitious films all fail to take the reality of Vietnam into account, they remind us of the war itself. To most Americans, including those in positions of authority, Vietnam was an abstraction—a symbol, not a place—and the American troops who went there suffered as a result. Just like those who made the war, the filmmakers put extravagant resources to work and got almost nothing right. Although none of these is a gung-ho prowar movie, all of them treat Vietnam (and the Vietnamese) in such a clichéd way that they will soon seem as dated as World War II propaganda films.

Background Reading

Frances FitzGerald, *Fire in the Lake: The Vietnamese and the Americans in Vietnam* (Atlantic/Little, Brown, 1972)

Michael Herr, *Dispatches* (Knopf, 1977)

Neil Sheehan, *A Bright Shining Lie: John Paul Vann and America in Vietnam* (Random House, 1988)

1979/USA/Color
DIRECTOR: Francis Ford Coppola; PRODUCER: Francis Ford Coppola; SCREENPLAY: John Milius, Francis Ford Coppola; STUDIO: Zoetrope; VIDEO: Paramount; RUNNING TIME: 139 min.

Bombs Away

Coppola's re-creation of a Vietcong village is fairly accurate, but there couldn't have been any flag-flying Vietcong villages intact on the coast after 1965 because the Americans had complete control of the air and such a village would have been too easy a target. What *Apocalypse Now* and other fictional films about the Vietnam War do not tell us is that most of the damage the U.S. military inflicted on the enemy—and to the Vietnamese, Laotians, and Cambodians generally—was achieved by air and artillery strikes (that is, by technology rather than by individual soldiers in combat). The United States expended more ordnance in Vietnam than it did during all of World War II. Thus, in a sense, the Kurtz of Vietnam was not a soldier but rather the massive and often indiscriminate use of air and artillery power.

Brando and Coppola on the set

Later...

Apocalypse Now was the first movie produced by Francis Ford Coppola's independent studio, Zoetrope. The film's original budget was twelve million dollars, but the eventual cost exceeded thirty-one million, and the film's distributor, Universal, made Coppola personally liable for the financial shortfall at the box office. The movie was a huge critical success, but on its initial release it grossed only five million dollars, making Zoetrope's survival uncertain. Coppola had always intended his outfit to serve as an antidote to the mainstream Hollywood studio system; its aim was to produce films controlled by artists rather than by financiers. After *Apocalypse Now,* Coppola continued to pursue ambitious projects—including *Rumble Fish* (1983), *The Cotton Club* (1984), and *Gardens of Stone* (1987). All of these films were commercial flops, but it was the disastrous box office failure of his twenty-six-million-dollar musical, *One from the Heart,* that really crippled Zoetrope. The studio's spiraling debts finally forced Coppola to accept Paramount's offer to direct a third installment of his Godfather series. Zoetrope filed for Chapter 11 bankruptcy in 1990, just after Coppola began shooting *Godfather III* in Rome.

ALL THE PRESIDENT'S MEN

William E. Leuchtenburg

CAST

Carl Bernstein	*(Dustin Hoffman)*
Bob Woodward	*(Robert Redford)*
Harry Rosenfeld	*(Jack Warden)*
Howard Simmons	*(Martin Balsam)*
Deep Throat	*(Hal Holbrook)*
Ben Bradlee	*(Jason Robards)*

ALL THE PRESIDENT'S MEN IS A FILM THAT is ostensibly about politics but is actually about journalism. It opens on the night of June 17, 1972, with a re-creation of the break-in at the Watergate complex in Washington, D.C., and it ends with a series of staccato reports on the downfall of the Nixon administration. The remainder of the movie, though, focuses not on politicians and their illegal activities but on two "hungry" young *Washington Post* reporters—Bob Woodward and Carl Bernstein, sometimes known collectively as "Woodstein"—and their dogged investigation of government malefactors.

Although, as *New York Times* critic Vincent Canby once pointed out, "the dimensions and implications of the Watergate story obviously give it an emotional punch that might be lacking if, say, Bernstein and Woodward had been exposing corruption in the Junior League," the film takes us not to the Oval Office but to the newsroom; it concentrates our attention not on state papers but on typewriters and notepads.

To bring to the screen Woodward and Bernstein's prize-winning book about how they exposed the Watergate conspiracy, Warner Brothers took great pains to achieve authenticity. The company spent huge sums to create a facsimile of the *Washington Post* newsroom on two sound stages in Burbank, California. The producers ordered nearly two hundred desks from the same firm that supplied the newspaper and even had them painted with identical hues: 6 ½ PA Blue and 22 PE Green. The principal actors, particularly leads Robert Redford (Woodward) and Dustin Hoffman (Bernstein), spent months at the *Post* observing how the paper's reporters and editors behaved. The studio even arranged to have trash from the *Post* newsroom shipped to California to fill the wastebaskets on the set.

All this demonstrates that a film can be accurate without being true. Although it rarely invents facts or episodes, *All the President's Men* does misinterpret the events that culminated in Richard Nixon's August 1974 resignation. The film particularly strains credibility when it suggests that the reporters' lives were in danger. "*All the President's Men* . . . is steeped in . . . a paranoia as deep as that which I witnessed inside the embattled White House," complained one of those men, presidential counsel Charles W. Colson. " 'Woodstein' fear that they are being bugged and that their lives are threatened. Come, come now. There was not a shred of evidence that anything of the sort was going on."

Especially in the scenes that show editors debating the makeup of the next day's paper, *All the President's Men* succeeds brilliantly in providing

The Book

When Bob Woodward and Carl Bernstein sold their book proposal to Simon & Schuster, they pitched it as "the story behind the story." *All the President's Men*, published in June 1974, earned about a million dollars in royalties during its first year in print. Woodward used the money to buy a six-figure house in Georgetown and a new BMW to replace the aging Karmann-Ghia in which he and his partner crisscrossed Washington during their nocturnal investigations. Bernstein bought a cooperative apartment in a marginal northwest Washington neighborhood and filled its closets with expensive clothes ("which he wears badly," said one acquaintance quoted in *Time* magazine).

HISTORY

Carl Bernstein (left) and Bob Woodward

At the time of the Watergate break-in, Bob Woodward was twenty-nine years old; Carl Bernstein, twenty-eight. The son of a county judge in suburban Chicago, Woodward attended Yale on a naval ROTC scholarship and served a five-year tour of duty before taking a $115-a-week job as a reporter on the Montgomery County (Md.) *Sentinel*. He moved to the *Post* in September 1971. Bernstein was born in Washington, D.C., and attended public schools there. His parents, both leaders in the labor movement, were accused during the 1950s of being Communist party sympathizers, but their son had more of an interest in reporting the news than making it. By his own admission "a terrible student," Bernstein wanted only to work for a newspaper. He got his first job when he was just sixteen, as a copy boy for the now-defunct *Washington Star*.

HOLLYWOOD

Dustin Hoffman

Robert Redford

Robert Redford first contacted Woodward and Bernstein while they were still writing daily news stories about Watergate. He soon began to hang around with them, and the reporters credit him with influencing their work on the book. It was Redford, for example, who suggested that they write *All the President's Men* in the third person. The actor turned producer then paid them $450,000 for the film rights to the book and hired William Goldman to write a screenplay.

Goldman's work was both good and bad: He pared down the story into a simple narrative that could be filmed, but his dialogue emphasized the sort of coarse newsroom humor that *The Front Page* had turned into a cliché. Bernstein complained that the script read like a Henny Youngman joke book, and he spent some time rewriting it—without success. Apparently, Bernstein built his part up at the expense of Woodward and portrayed himself as a swinger. "Carl," Redford had to tell him, "Errol Flynn is dead."

Alexander Butterfield

The White House Tapes

July 16, 1973 During televised testimony before the Senate Watergate committee, Deputy White House Chief of Staff Alexander Butterfield reveals that President Nixon secretly recorded conversations held in the Oval Office.

July 23, 1973 Special prosecutor Archibald Cox subpoenas nine tapes relating to the cover-up.

October 12, 1973 A Court of Appeals ruling upholds federal district court judge John J. Sirica's order that Nixon comply with Cox's subpoena and turn over the nine tapes.

October 20, 1973 After Cox refuses to back down, Nixon orders Attorney General Elliot Richardson to fire him. Richardson and his deputy, William Ruckelshaus, resign rather than comply. Finally, Solicitor General Robert H. Bork agrees to carry out the order. The press calls it the Saturday Night Massacre.

November 21, 1973 J. Fred Buzhardt, special counsel to the president for the tapes, informs Judge Sirica that the tape of a crucial June 20, 1972, conversation between Haldeman and Nixon includes an 18½-minute gap, which Nixon secretary Rose Mary Woods claims she created when she pressed a wrong button.

April 29, 1974 Nixon announces that he will release transcripts of the subpoenaed tapes to the public. When the House Judiciary Committee compares these "edited" transcripts to the few tapes in its possession, it finds many suspicious discrepancies and omissions.

July 24, 1974 The Supreme Court rules unanimously that the president must turn over sixty-four tapes subpoenaed by Cox's replacement, Leon Jaworski. That night, Nixon lawyer James St. Clair announces live on network news programs that Nixon will comply.

August 5, 1974 President Nixon releases transcripts of three conversations that took place on June 23, 1972, six days after the break-in. They are the "smoking gun," proving his knowledge and direction of the cover-up. In an accompanying statement, he admits that these transcripts are "at variance with certain of my previous statements." Three days later, he resigns.

the public policy context of Watergate. Its use of television footage also gives the film a *cinema verité* quality. Yet despite its virtuosity, *All the President's Men* still conveys a highly misleading impression of how Nixon and his cronies met their fate. The film draws to a close in 1973 with the completion of the *Post*'s Watergate investigation—but, curiously, with Nixon, reelected to a second term, triumphant. It then tags on an awkward, though riveting, coda: a series of teletyped dispatches reporting the convictions of high-ranking government officials. These postscripts are no doubt intended to imply that the guilty have been brought to justice through the perseverance of the two intrepid young reporters.

This implication has one grievous shortcoming, however: It leaves out almost all the history of the Watergate affair. Sen. Sam Ervin, whose select committee held the first congressional Watergate hearings and discov-

> **"The irony of Watergate is that Richard Nixon made us all famous —the people he most despised."**
>
> *Ben Bradlee*

ered the existence of the White House tapes, never makes an appearance. Nor does Congressman Peter Rodino, chairman of the House Judiciary Committee that approved three articles of impeachment against Nixon; nor Archibald Cox, the special prosecutor fired in the Saturday Night Massacre; nor Cox's replacement, Leon Jaworski; nor the tough-minded federal district court judge, John J. Sirica, who made it clear that he would squeeze the burglars until they talked—and the president until he turned over the tapes.

Instead of acknowledging these contributions, *All the President's Men* leaves one to understand that the country has been saved, not by conscientious public servants but by the press—particularly by the movie's two heroes, who have been likened to Frank and Joe Hardy. This message— delivered clearly at the end of the film when the rat-a-tat-tat of the teleprinter drowns out the cannon salvos celebrating Nixon's second inauguration—supports the film's underlying lesson: The press is more powerful than the president—and it's a good thing, too.

The foreshortened version of history in *All the President's Men* over-simplifies and rearranges the relationship between political power and the press. By suggesting that Woodward and Bernstein directly caused Nixon's fall—and thus inflating the importance of the press—the film marginalizes the special prosecutors, the congressional committees, the courts, and even the White House, disregarding the fact that collective action (and not heroic individualism) drove Nixon from power.

In response to such criticism, the filmmakers could well offer two responses. First, they could point out that the persistent young journalists do deserve considerable credit for keeping the break-in story alive at a time when most of the nation was indifferent. (A Gallup poll one month before Nixon's November 1972 reelection showed that forty-eight percent of the public had never heard of Watergate.) Second, they could argue that a motion picture has no obligation to relate events that take place after its particular story has been told.

Yet *All the President's Men* does not merely tack on a mischievous ending. Director Alan J. Pakula deliberately chooses to employ a Manichean vision of the forces of Good and Evil, which he perceives as Light and Darkness. In this scheme, the heroic representatives of the media are identified with the huge newsroom where Truth makes its home bathed in eye-dazzling light. Meanwhile, the seat of government in Washington—that sunny city of broad boulevards, white edifices, and pink cherry blossoms—is seen in spooky darkness. When the reporters leave the bright, airy, healthy newsroom, Washington becomes a dismal and threatening place. As a result, one is given to understand that government is not to be trusted, that its officials are creatures of the night, and that all—*all* the president's men—are complicit in the evildoings.

As a paean to investigative journalism, *All the President's Men* may well have inspired other reporters to uncover corruption, which is surely a worthy end. However, the film also condones certain unworthy means: It justifies invasions of privacy that would outrage journalists were they perpetrated by public officials. "One result of the Woodstein triumphs, a result certain to be intensified by the movie," Nat Hentoff has written, "is that an increasing number of reporters . . . are not paying much, if any, attention to how they get a story, so long as they get it." Though earlier films romanticized the press, *All the President's Men* was the first motion picture to suggest that the press was more important than the subjects it covered. It is a milestone in the process of exalting the press while demonizing government, not to mention a significant moment in the elevation of the American journalist to mythical status.

Background Reading

Jonathan Schell, *The Time of Illusion* (Knopf, 1976)
Theodore H. White, *Breach of Faith* (Atheneum, 1975)

1976/USA/Color
DIRECTOR: Alan J. Pakula; PRODUCER: Walter Coblenz; SCREENPLAY: William Goldman; STUDIO: Wildwood; VIDEO: Warner; RUNNING TIME: 138 min.

WILLIAM E. LEUCHTENBURG

Deep Throat

Bob Woodward has never revealed the identity of his indispensable source inside the government, whom a *Washington Post* editor dubbed Deep Throat. Some have speculated that Deep Throat was a woman—perhaps the garrulous Martha Mitchell—or a composite of several people. In choosing Hal Holbrook for the part, the filmmakers personalize Deep Throat as one individual, a man. This decision may prove embarrassing when Woodward finally discloses his source's identity, though most guesses do target one man: Alexander Haig. The code-name Deep Throat refers to the source's stipulation that whatever was said was on "deep background." His confidences could neither be quoted nor even paraphrased. *Deep Throat* is, of course, also the title of a well-known pornographic film. "I think there's a great similarity between the movie business and the newspaper business," Carl Bernstein once said. "We're all voyeurs."

Later...

After the success of *All the President's Men*, Woodward and Bernstein collaborated on a sequel, a book entitled *The Final Days* (1976), about the termination of the Nixon presidency. Fifty-six men were convicted of Watergate-related offenses, but not Nixon. On September 8, 1974, he was pardoned by his handpicked successor, Gerald Ford, for all federal crimes he "committed or may have committed or taken part in" while president. Subsequently, the media, which had taken such pleasure in battering Nixon, began work on his resurrection. They worked so energetically, in fact, that when Nixon died in 1994, he was lauded as an Elder Statesman of the first order, one whose presence would sorely be missed.

After Nixon's resignation, Woodstein split up. Bob Woodward remained at the *Post*, where he became managing editor in 1983. His 1987 bestseller, *Veil*, included a secret hospital interview with ailing CIA director William Casey. In his second-greatest scoop, Woodward reported Casey's deathbed confession that he (not Oliver North) had masterminded the Iran-Contra affair. Carl Bernstein left the *Post* in 1977 for ABC News, where he worked for two years with Ted Koppel as the first *Nightline* field correspondent.

NIXON

CAST

Richard Nixon	*(Anthony Hopkins)*
Pat Nixon	*(Joan Allen)*
H. R. Haldeman	*(James Woods)*
John Ehrlichman	*(J. T. Walsh)*
Henry Kissinger	*(Paul Sorvino)*
Alexander Haig	*(Powers Boothe)*

Bob Woodward

Director Oliver Stone

History Into Film

It's not easy turning history into film. I have closely watched filmmakers translate two books I co-authored. I have some sympathy, having seen the process up close. *All the President's Men*, the book Carl Bernstein and I wrote about reporting the Watergate story, was made into a movie in 1976. The filmmakers were painstaking with the facts, but still there were compromises. Four key editors at the *Washington Post* supervised our Watergate reporting. In the movie version, they became three. Things said by one editor were put in the mouth of another for dramatic compression.

In one climactic scene, Benjamin C. Bradlee, the executive editor of the *Post*, played by Jason Robards, tells his reporters to pursue the story even though it looks as though Watergate is going to lead to Nixon himself: "Nothing is at stake except freedom of the press, free speech and possibly the future of the country." In fact, as the book version shows, Bradlee said that night, "What the hell do we do now?" It was the right question, because Watergate was unknown journalistic territory. But the real question didn't have dramatic punch.

THE AUTHENTIC IMAGES OF THE REAL Richard Nixon will be replayed for generations. Two videos will likely stand out: First, Nixon's famous 1952 Checkers speech, one of live television's rawest and most emotional moments, in which he successfully appealed to the public for his political survival and forced Dwight Eisenhower to keep him on the ticket as his running mate. Second, Nixon's 1974 farewell to the White House staff the day he resigned the presidency—another raw and emotional moment. In those twenty-two years between the pleading and the goodbye lies the heart of Nixon's political career.

Future viewers, who never had the real Nixon in their lives, will likely ask: How could such a man have been president? Even those of us who lived through Nixon's era have asked that question.

In Oliver Stone's *Nixon*, he and actor Anthony Hopkins, in the title role, attempt to find answers. But for all the power and superb spirit of this movie, they never reach the heights of the real Nixon of those speeches. Nixon himself later wrote of the Checkers speech: "Apparently my emotional nerve endings had been rubbed so raw by the events of the previous few days that I was able to convey the intensity of my feelings to the audience."

Raw, rubbed nerve endings were the theme of Nixon's life, and his story was of triumphs and failures on the epic scale. This is the moviemaker's dilemma: The actual facts of the rise and fall of Richard Nixon cannot be made more dramatic, no matter how they might be dressed up. But Stone has not made a history. As best I can tell, about half the movie is based on facts. The other half ranges from sound speculation to borderline slander.

What Stone undertakes is nothing less than a cinematic psychoanalysis of perhaps our most mysterious president. As with all psychoanalysis, the result is a mixture of fact, interpretation, and some fantasy.

A single question—Why?—pulses through *Nixon*. The movie Nixon (like the real Nixon) searches mercilessly for scapegoats—the East Coast, the Kennedys, the CIA. Hopkins, as Nixon, says "the press, the kids, the liberals—they're out there trying to figure out how to tear me down." But Stone and Hopkins show that Nixon did it to himself.

Why? In scene after scene, Stone shows Nixon searching for a qualified analyst, someone to explain him to himself. Desperately, Nixon auditions everyone around him on his psychic casting couch—from his wife, Pat, to his top aide, H. R. "Bob" Haldeman; from his mother, Hannah, to

HISTORY

Stone ends his film with an epilogue noting that Nixon lived for twenty years after his resignation, wrote six more books, traveled the world as an elder statesman, and was eulogized at his funeral by President Clinton and Senator Bob Dole.

But a stronger ending was available: On the final page of his thick 1978 autobiography, *RN*, Nixon tells of leaving the White House that August day in 1974. After delivering his raw and powerful farewell address, he gave his famous double-V salute and climbed into the presidential helicopter.

"The engines started," Nixon wrote. "The blades began to turn. The noise grew until it almost blotted out thought....There was no talk. There were no tears left. I leaned my head back against the seat and closed my eyes. I heard Pat saying to no one in particular, 'It's so sad. It's so sad.'"

HOLLYWOOD

Stone decided during preproduction not to use "mask" makeup on Hopkins. As he later explained, "I didn't want the audience to sit there and say, 'Wow, what a fantastic makeup job! He looks exactly like Nixon!' instead of concentrating on the character and story. We did experiment for several tests, and at great expense, with Nixonian prosthetics—the jowls and prominent nose—but you always risk the Madame Tussaud pitfall." In the end, Hopkins performed with just a hairpiece, Nixon-like upper teeth, brown contact lenses, and artificially prominent eyebrows.

Fact and Fiction

I've spent some hours trying to truth-squad the movie and its annotated script—which cites such sources as books, tapes, and testimony in 168 footnotes. Stone has the outline of Nixon's life about right. He sees the centrality of Watergate. The movie begins with the Watergate burglary in June 1972 as Nixon is seeking reelection as president, and it ends with Nixon's resignation. Most characters are at least partially true to life; the only totally concocted one is a rich Texas oilman, played by Larry Hagman.

Stone nicely portrays some of the complex reality of Nixon's key relationships with men—particularly with Henry Kissinger, and with his two chiefs of staff, Haldeman and Alexander Haig. Nixon's interactions with women in the film—particularly with his mother and with Pat—are wildly speculative, however, and among the least supported parts of the film. But Stone uses these invented scenes convincingly to show Nixon's deep isolation and his cold, needy, rocky love. They are high drama but very bad history.

In a manufactured confrontation near the end of the movie, Nixon and his wife get into a spat about the secret White House tape recordings. "No one will ever see those tapes," Nixon says. "Including you!"

"And what would I find out that I haven't known for years?" Pat replies in this fictitious conversation. "What makes it so damn sad is that you couldn't confide in any of us. You had to make a record...for the whole world."

"They were for me," Nixon says. "They're mine."

"No," Pat answers. "They're not yours. *They are you.*"

the nineteen-year-old woman he confronts during an antiwar protest, who tells him that even the president is not in control, that the system is an unmanageable "wild beast."

In the end, Nixon gets the analyst he deserved—Oliver Stone. Both manifest paranoia. Though Stone shows some tenderness and empathy, like a good shrink he is relentless. And his ultimate version of Nixon is, in many respects, at least as compelling as the truth.

To Stone's credit, the movie quite nicely lays out the whole range of illegal activities undertaken by Nixon's administration—bogus national security wiretaps, the payment of hush money to the Watergate conspirators, the break-in at the office of Daniel Ellsberg's psychiatrist in the truly bizarre effort to discredit the man who had leaked the Pentagon Papers in 1971.

But he places Watergate in an imaginary context of some deep-seated obstacle hampering Nixon. Stone hypothesizes that Nixon is racked with guilt over some vague, perhaps indirect, pre-presidential involvement in CIA plots to assassinate Cuban leader Fidel Castro; this fiasco, Stone suggests, in turn led to the 1963 assassination of John F. Kennedy. Thus, when Stone's Nixon is told that one of the Watergate operatives is a former CIA agent named E. Howard Hunt, he worries obsessively that the whole tale might become public. For Stone, this is a key motive for the Watergate coverup.

There is no convincing evidence of this. In reality, the core problem for Nixon during Watergate was not a sense of guilt. It was an absence of guilt. The voluminous Watergate record shows that Nixon had little or no regard for the law. The Watergate coverup became necessary because Nixon's administration had used government power—the FBI, the IRS, the CIA—illegally. Not in the distant Eisenhower era, but during his own presidency. Such conduct was widespread. It was habit. And when some of his operatives were caught in the Watergate burglary, they had to be silenced before they led to what Nixon attorney general John Mitchell later called the "White House horrors."

The mix of fact and fiction is intricate. The 126 scenes in Stone's film are themselves often a blizzard of fragments—phrases from the tapes, real dialogue, concocted dialogue, real news clips, Hopkins speaking real Nixon speeches, and so on. For those who know the story, Stone's version feels as if the script had been written on note cards that Stone dropped, then scooped up in random order, on his way into the studio to make his film.

But Stone is honest in his labeling. At the beginning, he issues a clear warning that scenes have been compressed and "hypothesized." So this is fiction. Stone has told us so.

Is it possible that Nixon's greatest corruption of office was using the presidency for his own radical psychoanalysis, to finish the business of his childhood and other real or perceived slights? Scene after scene in Stone's film turns on discussions or depictions of mother, father, death, childhood, hate, love, lies, secrets, power, darkness, sacrifice, tears, manhood. The stuff of psychiatry.

Nixon is shown cavorting with his past relentlessly, self-indulgently. And everyone plays the game. Unfortunately, it seems all too true.

After the assassinations of John and Robert Kennedy and the thousands of deaths in Vietnam, and after Nixon has won the presidency, Stone shows him reflecting aloud, "Who's helping us? Is it God? Or is it…Death?" It's a great line, but the annotated script gives no footnote. There is no reason to believe it was ever said. Yet it is plausible. Nixon could, conceivably, have seen God and history as servants in his own cause.

Or his line: "I feel too much sometimes." Again, I don't know any evidence that he said it. The line is right out of *Oprah*, but again it is powerfully plausible. Nixon felt his way through the presidency. He personalized everything, every event. "This is about me," Stone's Nixon tells Pat. "It's not the war. It's Nixon! They want to destroy Nixon!"

I have a good deal of sympathy for Nixon's two daughters and their husbands; they issued a statement shortly after the film's release charging that it includes scenes "calculated solely and maliciously to defame and degrade President and Mrs. Nixon's memories in the mind of the American public." But beyond their personal feelings, theirs is a magnificently Nixonian statement, one the old man would no doubt be proud of: Still and always, "they" want to destroy Nixon.

I believe Stone's emphatic denial that his intent was to defame and degrade. He has said he was trying to reexamine and understand. The energy, depth, and richness of his film prove that. But at the same time, Stone was unnecessarily sloppy and self-indulgent. There was no need to mix up history this badly, because his central theme converges with the facts.

Stone is saying, in dramatic terms, precisely what history has said and will say with increasing authority as more tapes are released, more books are published, and more testimony is sifted. The point is simple: America had the wrong person as president. Nixon was not suited to the office. It's not just the criminality, the insularity, the almost total absence of higher purpose. It was the sheer inadequacy of the man, who could not order his own life, much less the life of the country.

Background Reading

Carl Bernstein and Bob Woodward, *All the President's Men* (Simon & Schuster, 1974)
Carl Bernstein and Bob Woodward, *The Final Days* (Simon & Schuster, 1976)
Eric Hamburg, ed., *Nixon: An Oliver Stone Film* (Hyperion, 1995)

1995/USA/Color
DIRECTOR: Oliver Stone; PRODUCER: Clayton Townsend, Oliver Stone, Andrew G. Vajna; SCREENPLAY: Stephen J. Rivele, Christopher Wilkinson, Oliver Stone; STUDIO: Hollywood; VIDEO: Buena Vista; RUNNING TIME: 191 min.

1972 Nixon-Agnew campaign poster

Later…

Stone's is not the final version of Nixon, surely. There are reasons to hope for a better, fuller, *truer* version. Before Nixon found an analyst in Oliver Stone, he had his private Dictabelt machine. These weren't the famous White House tapes, but a more intimate private diary. Only a few of these Dictabelts made their way into the public record during Watergate, and Nixon used carefully selected excerpts from dozens more in preparing his memoirs.

According to Nixon's Watergate lawyer, the late J. Fred Buzhardt, Jr.—one of the few people who ever heard more than a few of these recordings—these evening monologues were "not meant for human ears." The machine was his psychiatrist, Buzhardt said once in an interview. "It was uninhibited. I'm embarrassed at the insights I have from those." Though he declined to give much detail, he said that Nixon on the Dictabelts was a true introvert who hated campaigning and public gatherings. His chosen work, politics, was the antithesis of his nature. Nixon lived a false life, Buzhardt said, creating an almost unbearable psychic strain.

"When a man does something like that to himself, [he] puts on an outer shell," Buzhardt said, and Nixon's shell made close relationships impossible. Nixon lived a submerged, artificial, and distant life.

There are about five hundred of these Dictabelts in the hands of Nixon's family. Whoever gets to study them—if anyone does—will likely make the next significant advance on the Nixon mystery.

THE EMPEROR'S LAST REVIEW: A ROUGH TREATMENT

Simon Schama

Scene: A bare room in semidarkness. Two short, stout, balding men are seen from behind watching the last triple-screen, tricolor-tinted frames of Napoleon. *One is wearing a shapeless sweater; the other is swathed in a bulky, shabby greatcoat that has evidently seen better days. As the lights come up and the camera finds them from the front, Fiscal (the sweater), in horn-rim glasses, looks brightly at Goodpart (the greatcoat), who sighs deeply, takes off small wire-rim spectacles, and rubs his eyes, revealing as he does so a disconcerting resemblance to both Rod Steiger and Marlon Brando.*

Fiscal: So, Goodpart, whatdya think, an outstanding spectacle, no? A must-see for the technical wizardry alone: Polyvision, Russian montage, crazy hand-held shots—really, you've got to call this film a revolution.

Goodpart: (wearily) It's a bloody mess, yes.

Fiscal: Uh, oh, did we have a tiny problem, then, with the way Albert Dieudonné portrayed you? The hat, all wrong was it?

Goodpart: Hah, *Dieudonné*, a fitting name for such presumption! He carried himself well, *quand même*; and he has a good head. But did no one tell him not to strut so? Great generals never strut. They stride. Now the great Talma, *there* was an actor.

Fiscal: Yes, yes, listen, what about that glare, though? Really *imperious*, no?

Goodpart: Bah, I never glared. I merely observed, looked. The strong paid attention; the cowardly slunk into their holes. Only that *salaud*, Talleyrand, dared smirk back as if he were enjoying a private joke, a lump of shit in silk hose.

Fiscal: Now hold on, Goodpart. Excuse me, this is supposed to be family viewing; we're talking civilization-renewing History here. But, er, what about Josephine, eh?

Goodpart: Who? Oh, the Creole hoyden. *Vraiment bizarre.* Where did your M. Gance find such a creature with her big moon face and barnyard haunches? Now Josephine, the traitorous slut, her bed was her bivouac, but she was never the *grosse poule*. She was slender, always, a sharp little nose, dangerous eyes. She smelled of jasmine and wickedness. This woman I saw through the *lanterne magique*, she was like a horse with a *coiffure*. And the faux-Napoleon, why does he grovel and mince about her skirts like an imbecile? Does he imagine that was the way I behaved? I took her like a general.

Fiscal: So I guess you didn't go for the Victims Ball sequence, huh? Myself I thought it was great, a society orgy to celebrate escape from the guillotine.

Goodpart: A risible farce, a miserable *bal des arts,* like *comment-dire*, a flapper-girl party? I saw better things in the brothels of the Palais-Royal . . . or would have done if I had not spent every waking hour saving France from the criminals who had thrown her into the mire.

Fiscal: Sure, right, so tell me, was there anything about this film you *did* like? I mean, you know, the word is, like, this is the classic of the silent screen.

Goodpart: Silence, what silence? As if enduring my history made into mummery were not enough, you had to inflict on me music of indescribable vulgarity from this M. Coppola. Was it for that I conquered Italy, to be strangled in musical macaroni? Better the silence of Ste-Hélène.

Fiscal: Well, I thought he gave the movie great bounce. So that's it, then, zilch?

Goodpart: No, *crapaud*, that's not "it." The boy. He was worthy. *Madame mère* would have wept.

Fiscal: Oh, the Russian kid actor, you in the snowball fight. He was all right, feisty, yeah.

Goodpart: He stood like I stood, defiant, *fier*; he fought like I fought, with his brain and his will; a still center in the middle of the *mêlée*. And those scenes at school at Brienne, *je vous avoue*, I was stirred. For a moment I believed your M. Gance understood the art of command; the thrill of holding fast to one's reason when everything else gallops to hell. But I know his secret. I see to the hearts of men. This Gance, *au fond*, he is like all the rest; he wants to be ME, to be the Napoleon of the film. Dressing up as the undergraduate murderer St-Just with his fatuous complacency and an earring like a gypsy, does he imagine I was deceived? No, I saw he thinks he commands an army, *pauvre type*; an army of cameramen and actors and makeup women; he thinks he can do things the mediocre said were impossible, to make a conquest. But, excuse-for-a-man, don't you see that I made laws and trampled kingdoms beneath the dust of my chargers while he reigns in the world of dreams and shadows? I gave the world the *Codes*; Gance gave the world the trapeze-mounted camera. I went to Russia. He invented Russian montage. But these are the emperors you wish for, are they not? Manipulators of folly? I dealt with democracy my way. By giving the *misérables* the chance to be men, to be soldiers such as the world had not seen since Alexander. What is the way of your kine-kings? To lull the people to sleep like dribbling infants, swaddled in make-believe—

Fiscal: Well, gee thanks, Goodpart, Sire. That's really fascinating and all and I'd love to hear more, but I'm afraid we're right out of—

Goodpart: (rising, putting on an old hat) SILENCE! INSOLENT WORM! YOU WILL HEAR ME! YOU WILL NOT MOVE UNTIL PERMITTED. *ENTENDU*?

Fiscal: (gesticulating desperate throat-cutting motion toward control room) Oh, right, sure, anything you say. . . .

Goodpart: (sitting again, with his hat on) What I do not comprehend of your world is the great store it sets by all this machinery of illusion. Oh, I suppose, of his sort, this M. Gance (his father was a *fabricant des lumières électriques, n'est-ce-pas?*) is a fine engineer, with all his flying contraptions and his visions like a drunkard with three pairs of eyes that could take in a panorama at a single glance. And the eyes of the eagle that, how to say, dissolved into mine—that I liked, and when my ruffians marched into Italy six abreast while my phantom galloped past on a white horse; yes, for a second I felt my cold blood warm in the darkness. But a genius? No, the scientists of the Institute, they were geniuses, my Lannes, my Desaix, even the painter David, they were geniuses. Gance is not even *chef de brigade*. He is what he is, a *romancier*.

Fiscal: (back to his normal voice, leaning toward Goodpart) But, well, I hate to bring this up, but didn't you like the PR boys, the image-makers? I mean, correct me if I'm wrong, but wasn't your alpine transportation a mule but in the picture opportunity there you are on that old white horse again, its front legs halfway over the Saint Bernard? Wasn't that the idea, to keep the little people hero-happy while you got on with the laws and wars and stuff with no arguments? So what did old Abel do so wrong that you wouldn't have made him duke of Livonia or something, huh?

Goodpart: So you're not a complete cretin after all? It's true. I believed France, the world, needed a Hero risen from the people to save them from the anarchy of revolution and the stupidity of kings. But you must understand one thing: The true hero is the enemy of fanaticism; whether priests or *idéologues*. In your century, the hero has been the fanatic himself. And what was Gance, with his nimbuses of light, turning me into some sort of ten-sou saint, what was he but the servant of lunatics to come; their obedient little wizard?

    Ecoute, all I wanted was to save France from the criminals and their whores. When Gance had me laughing bitterly at the desecration of the Rights of Man by the monsters of the Terror, he was right even though I was never there watching Robespierre. And, yes, to make the Convention into a great sea-storm with that camera of his lurching and plunging from crests to hollows, ah, that was *très bien aperçu*. The Revolution, what was it in the end but a *démence*, falling sickness. Yet, of all the mad lies he tells, none was so insolent as the notion I needed advice from the ghosts of the Jacobins, from Marat, *bon dieu* (and who told Artaud that eye-rolling is acting?). Me, being lectured by Robespierre and St-Just. A good joke, that.

Fiscal: So I guess this one will just get a split decision, huh? From me, a decided thumbs-up; from Goodpart here, a thumbs-down. Next week we'll be back to our usual format.

Goodpart: What is this thumbs . . . ? Oh I see, the Roman emperor in the circus. Well, you know there was one moment I stuck my thumb up, when your Gance freed me from the exile of the tomb and took me home; the dark hills and black shores of Corsica; the horses of my pursuers galloping under the livid sky. . . . That was something to see.

Fiscal: (relieved to see the on-camera lights are out at last, gets up, puts a hand on the ancient greatcoat) Hey, listen, Goodpart, it's just a movie, you know, and I'll tell you something now—don't take this wrong and start getting on your high horse again— you know, in our day you could have been a real contender, a star.

Goodpart: Star, star? But *imbecile*, don't you understand, I was the SUN. The powers revolved around me. I was their light, their force, their life. Where are you going? Come back, *j'ordonne—*

Fiscal: (making for the exit) Sorry, got to fly. Hey, I'll call you. What can I say, it's been a real *experience . . . a pleasure.*

Goodpart: (sighing again and slumping in his chair) That it never was.

ROLL TITLE, CREDITS.

1927/France/B&W
DIRECTOR: Abel Gance; **PRODUCER:** Abel Gance; **SCREENPLAY:** Abel Gance; **STUDIO:** Gaumont; **VIDEO:** MCA; **RUNNING TIME:** 235 min.

Mark Carnes: In this collection of essays, which covers about one hundred historical films, we see all sorts of "enhancements" of the historical record, including complete and utter fabrications that have no basis in fact. We see in some movies that Custer was a hero to the Indians or that Hoover's FBI was pro–civil rights. The license you have taken in your films is, at worst, let's say, in the middle range of this panoply of invention, yet you have been sharply criticized—by historians, in particular—after *JFK*, and also after *Nixon*. Do you care that historians have criticized your work? And has their criticism influenced the way you go about making your films?

Oliver Stone: I think many historians come at filmmakers with attitude and with hostility. It's as though history is their territory, and we don't belong. We just pervert the paradigm with emotion, sentimentality, and so on.

Carnes: But do you care what they say?

Stone: For some reason I do care. I went to school, I was educated, I loved history and current affairs, and I was good at them. Some part of me is still that schoolboy being graded by a professor. Of course, kids in school don't always agree with the professors. Yesterday I was visiting a college where some students told me their history professor had said there was no doubt that Lee Oswald had shot the president by himself. They also said that most of the class didn't believe him.

I think there's a sort of pomposity, a solemnity, that historians carry about with them. They feel they are in possession of the facts and the truth as though they were the chief priests in ancient Egypt caring for the sacred innards. You know, the prophecies belong to them. But from what I know about history—not only from my personal experience of it in France and Russia and America, in Vietnam and Asia, but also from reading—I know that many of these subjects are ambivalent.

Movies about history, in particular, are often hotly disputed. *Lawrence of Arabia*, which I saw as a young boy, was torn apart by the reviewers, who called it a camel opera. People said much of it never happened, that Lawrence was never at

the massacre of the Turks. But watching that film made me want to go back and read *The Seven Pillars of Wisdom* because the movie excited my interest. I think that's the only answer to people who say that movies brainwash young minds. Movies are just the first draft. They raise questions and inspire students to find out more.

Carnes: The brainwashing charge comes from those who say you're intentionally tricking viewers. Certainly your use of pseudodocumentary footage is sneaky. But your films nonetheless make clear the presence of an active, intervening director. You don't simply use a naturalistic style and pretend that your motionless camera is looking directly into the past.

Stone: My point is, what is the past? As we know from Mr. Kissinger's memoirs and those of other people, if you had five men in a room when an important decision was made, no two of them will agree later on what happened. They might agree on what time of day it was, or whether the blinds were drawn, but I don't think you can ever put together an objective viewpoint.

We all saw those "you are there" films when we were young and they were very boring. They generally showed history from an awestruck viewpoint. The Winston Churchills and the Alexanders and other greats of history would stand there and speak in long sentences. They were simply not believable. I think that our leaders—the Richard Nixons, the John Kennedys—are just like us, and I've tried to humanize them in my films.

We read most everything there was on Nixon: books from the left, from the right, from the center—the so-called center. And at the end of the day, not one of the historians who wrote those books—except possibly Fawn Brodie, whom I would call a psychohistorian—none of them tried to gain a deeper understanding of what the man was thinking and feeling, what kind of human being he was. Perhaps Brodie overstepped the bounds of contemporary historians when she theorized about Nixon's relationship with his mother, his father, and the two young brothers who died. But then you have Stephen Ambrose, who brings to his biography of Nixon a different point of view. The way Ambrose writes reveals an author who is proper but seems afraid to delve into the darker shadows of history, into the conspiracies in which Nixon may have been involved. What you get from Ambrose is a very clean Nixon, and I think he misses the point. I know Ambrose is very respected, and he's got all these prizes, but my point is that American historians today are too involved in the business of getting prizes. They want respectability, and they worry that if they go into the shadow areas that Fawn Brodie went into, they will lose the respect of their contemporaries. They might even lose their tenure or their ability to publish books.

So, in answer to your question, we as dramatists are undertaking a deconstruction of history, questioning some of the given realities. What you call "sneaky" is, to me, an ambivalent and shifting style that makes us aware that we *are* watching a movie and that reality itself is in question.

JFK was the beginning of a new era for me in terms of filmmaking because it's not just about a conspiracy to kill John Kennedy. It's not just about that. It's also about the way we look at our recent history, the way that we assume reality is what it seems to be. I think historians assume too much. My movies are made using a deconstructionist style. The film is looking at itself, conscious of itself. It moves from black and white to color. The angles are offbeat. Somebody says one thing in an external moment, but then the movie cuts to an internal moment and you see another expression wholly opposite to what is being said. Nixon may say one thing, but he feels another. Maybe I'll use one image. Maybe I'll use five. But I will make you aware that you are watching a movie, that I'm playing with your mind, and that there is no objective reality.

Carnes: Since you have made explicit that there is a dark side to your own background—

Stone: I know what you're going to say. You're going to say that I went to Vietnam, my parents were divorced, I come from a dysfunctional family, and that I bring my own dark view of America to my movies. Well, I think you can say that. You are welcome to say that—

Carnes: Well, you've said it, too.

Stone: I've never hidden that part of my life. But I think that if you look closely at Richard Nixon, you're going to find a very troubled individual. He was awkward, sweaty, tense, anguished in his expressions. Everyone says that, not just me. But where does Nixon's anguish come from? As a dramatist, and also as a historian, one has to push into the shadow areas—into the psychiatric areas, the relationship to mother and father and siblings—in order to understand why this man was so tortured. That is not being done by historians today. I don't see any new Brodies on the scene now. Instead, I see Ambrose, the sanitized man with no secrets, the Eisenhower historian.

Carnes: In *Nixon*, you show Richard as a little boy telling his mother that he wants to be her faithful dog, and it happens that the ten-year-old Nixon actually wrote that to his mother. You also show Kissinger and Nixon getting down on their knees to pray after Nixon decides to resign, and this also happens to be true. Historians—perhaps of the pompous variety, but also of any other sort—wonder why, when the reality is so wonderful, you still feel the need to enhance it. Why go beyond the known facts?

Stone: Because "the known facts" are often in dispute. The Warren Commission and Watergate are still clouded in mystery. "Reality," as you call it, *is* wonderful, but can you string together a movie of external "realities" without probing into the subterranean and unknown areas that make a human life fully rounded?

Look, a movie is supposed to be gripping. It's supposed to be exciting. It's supposed to be watchable. We are dealing with a dense body of information in *Nixon*, as we did in *JFK*. Dense. A huge amount of material is imparted, and you have to keep the audience involved, so you make it as gripping as you can—but not by distorting the "truth." The truth *is* elusive, so we must arrive at it from a combination of the conscious and unconscious lives of the individual.

Carnes: I don't think any historian who wants to talk about movies can complain about compression. You can't run a movie over several years—

Stone: Well, it bothers me all the time, because we have to make jumps. We don't have time to show the realistic decision-making process—which, by the way, is often uncertain. Decisions are often not made dramatically, as in our Vietnam War scene, but are, as we all know, the results of endless phone calls, rumors, gossip, backbiting, and so on.

Carnes: The problem for historians, much more so than the compression of events or characters, is that life is a churning sea of confusion, ambiguity, and personality. Good historians try to take that ambiguity and complexity and build something out of it that still has meaning. Yet movies, because they are so clean in their dramatic flow, necessarily do violence to the complexity that is the real world.

Stone: That certainly is a valid criticism, and you can say that life is more complex than any movie. But I think you have to be specific. Where have we gone wrong? Is our Nixon wrong? Dramatists look, as should historians, for patterns in the world. We've tried to relate Ellsberg to Hiss. We've tried to relate Watergate to Nixon's mother and father and the deaths of his two brothers. We've tried to relate his brothers' deaths and the survivor's guilt he felt to the deaths of the two Kennedys. I don't think that's ever been done before—I've never seen it in a history book—but these are patterns that we're looking for to bring together this three-hour movie.

We may be dead wrong on this, but we're groping for the elusive thread that brings to Nixon's life some sort of order. Obviously you're right about chaos. We all live with it, and I do believe in chaos. My own life is one of chaos. Yet I still see patterns in my life.

What I'd like to do now, though, is circle back to *JFK* and try to bring all this together in some way. I'm looking for a very difficult pattern in our history. What I see from 1963, with Kennedy's murder at high noon in Dallas, to 1974, with Nixon's removal, is a pattern. Call me wrong, but we have John Kennedy suspiciously killed, we have Robert Kennedy suspiciously killed, we have Martin Luther King suspiciously killed, and we have Nixon suspiciously "falling on his sword." These four men came from different political perspectives, but they were pushing the envelope, trying to lead America to new levels. We posit that, in some way, they pissed off what we call "the Beast," the Beast being a force (or forces) greater than the presidency. Now you must look at the Beast as metaphor, because that's the way it's intended. In his farewell address, President Eisenhower, the most conservative president, whom Stephen Ambrose worships, said we should beware the military-industrial complex. He went out of his way to make—

Carnes: I don't think Ike meant those people would be going after presidents with a rifle.

Stone: Don't say what he meant. He *said* it. He said, "Beware the military-industrial complex." And he said it in a way that was stunning because he just stopped in the middle of his speech and made a big point about it. He saw something coming. He saw the power of money— the power money would have over government, the power of multinational corporations. And through the years, that power has grown. We've seen a huge war in Vietnam that cost more than a hundred, perhaps two hundred, billion dollars, and now that the Cold War is over, there's no peace dividend. Instead, the military-industrial contracts just keep growing.

Carnes: O.K., Oliver, but it's one thing to say that the military-industrial complex has gained power and another to say it has gone out and pointed guns at people in the White House.

Stone: I think historians such as yourself had to have been there during the 1950s and 1960s to understand the true nature of those men. Kennedy, in looking at the movie *Seven Days in May*, explicitly said that a military dictatorship and the removal of a president could have happened here if he had screwed up one more time on Cuba.

But the Beast to me means more than the military-industrial complex. When Nixon said on the tapes "those Wall Street bastards!" he meant it. I think the power of the bond market and the stock market is enormous. Today, if a Clinton/Kennedy were to change the Federal Reserve board, or the way we issue our currency, he wouldn't have to be assassinated. The bond market would simply tremble, and that tremble would be felt around the world. And the media—which is ten times bigger today than it was in Kennedy's time—would echo and echo and echo this message of doom until the president backed down. A president today doesn't have to be assassinated. It's simply enough for the power of money and the media to prohibit him from making significant changes in the way things run. My point is that between 1963 and 1974, these four men all ran up against "the Beast" and were removed or killed as a consequence. In Nixon's case, it would be more accurate to say he fell on his sword to preserve the Beast.

Carnes: This is a question that Arthur Schlesinger gave me. He wrote, "*JFK* seemed to me preposterous in its contention that LBJ, the FBI, the

CIA, and the Joint Chiefs of Staff got together to murder Kennedy because he wanted to get out of Vietnam. Ask Oliver whether he *really* believes it happened this way, and if he has doubts, does he not feel some responsibility not to mislead the young?"

Stone: *JFK* is such a misunderstood movie. You should watch it again and pay attention to what is actually being said. Kevin Costner describes *possibilities*. He talks about the people and the organizations that hated change—and hated Kennedy, specifically, for making changes. In 1963, Kennedy changed enormously, and afterwards he was not the same man. I think Schlesinger would agree with me on that. Nineteen sixty-three was a watershed year, and the changes it brought in relations with the Soviet Union, Vietnam, and Cuba threatened groups of powerful people. What we say in the movie is that these groups were pissed off, these people were upset, because change threatened them. Nowhere do we say that they all sat down together in some conference room and plotted to knock off the president. I think that's ludicrous, because it's just too large a conspiracy. It wouldn't work.

What happened, I think, is that somewhere from one of these possibilities came the directive, the order, the need to kill Kennedy, and it was probably held to a very small group. ten or twenty people, a Julius Caesar–style murder. Now LBJ didn't say, "Yes, go kill Kennedy." We *never* say that in the movie. We say that LBJ had to know something more than he said he did, and we think he was involved in the process of covering up by appointing the Warren Commission and approving its report. Back channel, LBJ himself didn't believe the report, so why should we believe these fairy tales?

Anyone who reads history has to acknowledge the power of conspiracy. Alexander the Great's father, Philip of Macedon, was killed by a conspiracy that haunted Alexander throughout his life. Julius Caesar, Lincoln, popes left and right, kings—they have all been removed as the result of conspiracies. Why should American history be any different? Even Franklin Roosevelt was almost removed by a coup d'état. Historians seem to believe in this fairy-tale simplicity about America, that we are somehow free of conspiracy. I grew up under the biggest conspiracy of them all: My father convinced me, and Richard Nixon convinced me, that there was a monolithic Communist conspiracy out there involving Moscow and Beijing, that the Communists were going to invade America, and that they were already in the schools, perverting our minds.

Carnes: Of course our history has been filled with conspiracies, and historians have ferreted out many of them. But there's also an American fascination with conspiracies. Writing about the Red scares of the 1950s, Richard Hofstadter speculated that conspiracy theories are part and parcel of American life, that they have to do with the anxieties Americans feel in this society where status is uncertain and instability common. These little fits of conspiratorial fear that infect the body politic—

Stone: I find that so condescending. Hofstadter is trotted out every time. It's condescending because we've had so many conspiracies in America—Watergate and more recently Irangate, which has significant implications regarding the military-industrial complex. Our reporters are backing off stories because editors and the power of conservative media money are telling them to. But the American people, I hope, will stay turbulent and agitated enough to question their leaders, to question authority.

Carnes: I don't think there's much of a dispute that there has been a concentration of power, certainly during the 1980s and probably during the 1990s as well, a concentration of wealth and certainly a great expansion of the power of global corporations, but the explicit underlying issue in *JFK* and *Nixon* is that somehow these forces were harnessed to particular assassins. If these forces are as powerful as you say they are, why have they left you alone? I don't mean this purely facetiously. If you are blowing the whistle on them—

Stone: Assassination and coup d'état were methods used during the 1950s and 1960s in Cuba, the Congo, Iran, Indonesia, Guatemala, Vietnam, and elsewhere—much of this when Nixon was vice president. Now, in the 1980s and 1990s, people are assassinated metaphorically, in the media. There has been a significant onslaught in the political press against me and the things I have tried to say, implying that I'm making them up as I go along or that I have no credibility. That's the way you assassinate somebody's character. It happened very viciously to Martin Luther King, too, before he was killed.

Carnes: Certainly J. Edgar Hoover's conspiracy to assassinate King's *character* has been well documented, but that's not—

Stone: But at the time, if you had said that there was an FBI conspiracy against Martin Luther King, people would have thought you were crazy. Wasn't it Juvenal who said, "Who shall guard the guardians? Who shall guard the guardians?"

But there's one more thing I want to say about historians like Stephen Ambrose—

Carnes: Ambrose again?

Stone: He attacked us quite a lot when *Nixon* came out. He said that we had no right to put dialogue into a real person's mouth. Well, I don't think he understands that there's a genre called historical drama. The Greeks and Elizabethans had it. The films we're making are interpretive dramas. We don't know what Nixon actually said to Pat and what Nixon actually said to Kissinger. You read Kissinger, and he's fighting for his own place in history. You read Seymour Hersh and Walter Isaacson, and they tear Kissinger down.

You know, when Steve Spielberg made *Schindler's List*, he was praised everywhere in the world for it. But he created dialogue behind closed doors, and no one said a word. I'm told the original screenwriter quit after two years because he thought Schindler actually was a Nazi, and the movie, of course, makes him much more empathetic. The widow came out recently with highly negative comments about her husband's real motives.

I would say, however, that there's something inherently wrong with Ambrose's approach to history, because when you read his books, which we did and we learned something from them, you find an avoidance of the shadow areas in history. Ambrose particularly took us to task for suggesting that Nixon could have been involved in any way with the Kennedy assassination. I think if you are a serious historian you must ask yourself a few questions. Mr. Nixon mentions the Bay of Pigs and "the Cuban thing" about a dozen times on several of the Watergate tapes that have been released. On the June 20, 1972, tape, which has the famous eighteen-and-a-half-minute gap, "the Cuban thing" is mentioned again and again. Now why is that gap there? Mr. Ambrose doesn't even intuit an explanation. He's safely on the side of "fact." But the fact is that there is an erasure, a multiple erasure. That's also a "fact."

Isn't it the historian's duty to speculate about who might have made this erasure, and why, and what may have been on the tape? We did that in our movie, and we went back to the Bay of Pigs because five or six of the Watergate burglars were at the Bay of Pigs. That may just be coincidence, but if you go back into the past you find that Nixon was very involved with Cuba throughout his professional life, especially as vice president. He detested Castro and supervised operations against him from the White House. This is documented. He knew about the invasion, and so on. The only area of speculation is whether Mr. Nixon knew about the assassination attempts against Mr. Castro. If he did not, then it means the CIA was operating off the shelf during the 1950s, which is what Mr. Ambrose implies, trying to protect Eisenhower. He says that Eisenhower didn't really know about this stuff. Fine. But how does Ambrose know that? We don't know how he gets to that conclusion. And if the CIA is, in fact, practicing "black ops" in Guatemala and Iran and the Congo and bumping off Castro without the permission of the White House, that seems to me a far more dangerous situation than one in which the president knows and approves.

If the president knew, if you grant us that, then obviously the vice president, who was the hawk of the group, also knew. And if Nixon knew that Castro was a target of American paramilitary operations, then he must correspondingly have known, or had some intuition, that some element of this operation may have blown back and shot Mr. Kennedy. When we suggested this in *Nixon*, we were treated by Ambrose as though we were totally raving mad and making up stuff. But I'm just as shocked that responsible historians aren't asking these questions. Why are historians avoiding these dark areas of American history?

Stephen E. Ambrose is the author of *Eisenhower* (1983) and *D-Day: June 6, 1944* (1994). He teaches at the University of New Orleans, where he is Boyd Professor of History and the chairman of the National D-Day Museum Foundation.

Joyce Antler teaches American studies at Brandeis University and writes frequently on American Jewish culture and gender history. She is currently writing *Journey Home: The History of Twentieth-Century American Jewish Women and the Struggle for Identity.*

James Axtell is Kenan Professor of Humanities at the College of William and Mary. He is the prize-winning author of *The Invasion Within: The Contest of Cultures in Colonial North America* (1985) and other books on Indian-European relations in early America.

Paul Boyer is Merle Curti Professor of History at the University of Wisconsin–Madison. He is the author of a number of books on U.S. history, including *By the Bomb's Early Light: American Thought and Culture at the Dawn of the Atomic Age* (1994) and, most recently, *Promises to Keep: The United States Since World War II* (1995).

Alan Brinkley is Professor of History at Columbia University. He is the author of *Voices of Protest: Huey Long, Father Coughlin, and the Great Depression* (1982) and *The End of Reform: New Deal Liberalism in Recession and War* (1995).

Dee Brown is the author of *Bury My Heart at Wounded Knee* (1971). His most recent book is *When the Century Was Young* (1993).

David Cannadine is Moore Collegiate Professor of History at Columbia University. Among his books are *The Pleasures of the Past* (1989), *The Decline and Fall of the British Aristocracy* (1990), *G.M. Trevelyan: A Life in History* (1992), and *Aspects of Aristocracy: Grandeur and Decline in Modern Britain* (1994).

Mark C. Carnes teaches American history at Barnard College, Columbia University, where he chairs the history department. He is the author most recently of *Mapping America's Past* (1996).

Clayborne Carson is the director and senior editor of the Martin Luther King, Jr., Papers Project and a professor of history at Stanford University. He is the author of *In Struggle: SNCC and the Black Awakening of the 1960s* (1981) and *Malcolm X: The FBI File* (1991).

William H. Chafe is Alice Mary Baldwin Professor of History at Duke University. He is the author of *Civilities and Civil Rights: Greensboro, North Carolina, and the Black Struggle for Freedom* (1980) and *Never Stop Running: Allard Lowenstein and the Struggle to Save American Liberalism* (1993).

Andrew Chaikin is the author of *A Man on the Moon: The Voyages of the Apollo Astronauts* (1994) and is at work on a history of flight for the National Air and Space Museum.

George Chauncey is a professor of history at the University of Chicago. He is the author of *Gay New York: Gender, Urban Culture, and the Making of the Gay Male World, 1890–1940* (1994). He is currently writing *The Making of the Modern Gay World, 1935–1975.*

Catherine Clinton is the author of *Tara Revisited: Women, War, and the Plantation Legend* (1995), *The Plantation Mistress: Women's World in the Old South* (1982), and, with Nina Silber, *Divided Houses: Gender and the Civil War* (1992). She has also edited *Half Sisters of History: Southern Women and the American Past* (1994).

Nancy F. Cott is Stanley Woodward Professor of History and chair of the American Studies Program at Yale University, where she has taught women's history since 1975. Among her published works are *The Bonds of Womanhood: "Woman's Sphere" in New England, 1780–1835* (1977) and *The Grounding of Modern Feminism* (1987).

Robert Darnton is Professor of History at Princeton University. He is the author of *The Great Cat Massacre and Other Episodes in French Cultural History* (1984), *The Kiss of Lamourette: Reflections in Cultural History* (1990), and *The Forbidden Best-Sellers of Pre-Revolutionary France* (1995).

Marshall De Bruhl, author of *Sword of San Jacinto: A Life of Sam Houston* (1993) and co-editor of *The International Thesaurus of Quotations* (1995), has been a senior editor at several major publishers and editorial director of the *Dictionary of American Biography* and the *Dictionary of American History.* He is working on a book about the bombing of Dresden.

Greg Dening is Professor of History Emeritus at the University of Melbourne and a fellow of the Academy of Social Sciences of Australia. He is the author of a dozen books of history of an anthropological sort.

John Patrick Diggins is Distinguished Professor of History at the Graduate Center of the City University of New York. He is the author of *The Promise of Pragmatism: Modernism and the Crisis of Knowledge and Authority* (1994) and a forthcoming study of Max Weber.

Carolly Erickson, who grew up in Hollywood and loves movies, has been writing histories and biographies for nearly three decades. Her most recent book is *Great Catherine* (1994).

John Mack Faragher is a historian of the American frontier in the department of history at Yale University. He is the author most recently of *Daniel Boone: The Life and Legend of an American Pioneer* (1992) and is working on a new history of the French and Indian War.

Frances FitzGerald, a journalist who has written for many periodicals (notably *The New Yorker*), spent many months in Vietnam during the war. She is the author of, among other books, *Fire in the Lake: The Vietnamese and the Americans in Vietnam* (1972).

Thomas Fleming, historian and novelist, is the author of *1776: Year of Illusions* (1975) and *Liberty Tavern* (1976).

Eric Foner is DeWitt Clinton Professor of History at Columbia University. He is the author of *Reconstruction: America's Unfinished Revolution, 1863–1877* (1988), which won the Parkman and Bancroft prizes.

Antonia Fraser is the author of a series of historical biographies and studies of women in history—including *Mary Queen of Scots* (1969), winner of the James Tait Black Prize for Biography; *The Weaker Vessel: Woman's Lot in Seventeenth-Century England* (1984), winner of the Wolfson Award for History; and, most recently, *The Wives of Henry VIII* (1992).

Paul Fussell is Professor of English Literature Emeritus at the University of Pennsylvania. He is the author of numerous books on literary and cultural history, including *The Great War and Modern Memory* (1975) and *Wartime: Understanding and Behavior in the Second World War* (1989).

Peter Gay is Professor of History Emeritus at Yale University. He is the author of *Freud: A Life for Our Time* (1988) and *The Bourgeois Experience: Victoria to Freud* (three volumes, 1984-1993).

Carol Gluck is George Sansom Professor of Japanese History at Columbia University. She is the author of *Japan's Modern Myths: Ideology in the Late Meiji Period* (1985) and *Showa: The Japan of Hirohito* (1992).

Stephen Jay Gould is Alexander Agassiz Professor of Zoology at Harvard University. He is the author of *The Panda's Thumb* (1980), winner of the National Book Award, and *The Mismeasure of Man* (1981), winner of the National Book Critics Circle Award.

Michael Grant is the author of more than fifty books of classical history, including *Julius Caesar* (1969).

W.V. Harris is Professor of History at Columbia University. He is the author of *War and Imperialism in Republican Rome, 327–70 B.C.* (1979) and *Ancient Literacy* (1989).

Akira Iriye is Professor of History at Harvard University. Among his many works are *Across the Pacific: An Inner History of American–East Asian Relations* (1967), *China and Japan in the Global Setting* (1992), and *The Cambridge History of American Foreign Relations* (1993).

Kenneth T. Jackson teaches a seminar on military history at Columbia University, where he is Jacques Barzun Professor of History and the Social Sciences and chairman of the department of history.

Jacqueline Jones is Harry S. Truman Professor of American Civilization at Brandeis University. She is the author of *Labor of Love, Labor of Sorrow: Black Women, Work, and the Family from Slavery to the Present* (1985) and *The Dispossessed: America's Underclasses from the Civil War to the Present* (1992).

Alvin M. Josephy, Jr., a longtime member of the Society of American Historians and past president of the Western History Association, is well known for his many award-winning books on Indian and American Western history, including *The Civil War in the American West* (1991) and *500 Nations* (1994).

Stanley Karnow, author of *Vietnam: A History* (1983), was awarded the Pulitzer Prize for History in 1990 for *In Our Image: America's Empire in the Philippines* (1989).

John F. Kasson is Bowman and Gordon Gray Professor of History at the University of North Carolina at Chapel Hill. He is the author of *Civilizing the Machine: Technology and Republican Values in America, 1776–1900* (1976), *Amusing the Million: Coney Island at the Turn of the Century* (1978), and *Rudeness and Civility: Manners in Nineteenth-Century Urban America* (1990).

Gerda Lerner is Robinson-Edwards Professor of History Emerita at the University of Wisconsin-Madison. She is the author of eight books of women's history, including *The Creation of Patriarchy* (1986) and *The Creation of Feminist Consciousness* (1993).

William E. Leuchtenburg is William Rand Kenan, Jr., Professor of History at the University of North Carolina at Chapel Hill. He has served as president of the American Historical Association, the Organization of American Historians, and the Society of American Historians. His most recent book is *The Supreme Court Reborn: The Constitutional Revolution in the Age of Roosevelt* (1995).

Anthony Lewis is a columnist for the *New York Times* and the author of *Make No Law: The Sullivan Case and the First Amendment* (1991).

David Levering Lewis has written works of history in several fields, most recently *The Race to Fashoda: Colonialism and African Resistance* (1995) and *W.E.B. Du Bois: Biography of a Race, 1868–1919* (1993), which won the Bancroft and Parkman prizes and the Pulitzer Prize for Biography. He is Martin Luther King, Jr., University Professor at Rutgers University-New Brunswick.

Leon F. Litwack is A.F. and May T. Morrison Professor of History at the University of California at Berkeley. He is the author of *Been in the Storm So Long: The Aftermath of Slavery* (1979), winner of the Parkman Prize and the Pulitzer Prize for History.

J. Anthony Lukas won his second Pulitzer Prize for *Common Ground: A Turbulent Decade in the Lives of Three American Families* (1985). He is currently working on a book about the events surrounding the assassination of former Idaho governor Frank Steunenberg in 1905.

William Manchester is Professor of History Emeritus at Wesleyan University and a fellow of Yale College. His eighteen books have been translated into nineteen languages and Braille.

Richard Marius is the author of the biography *Thomas More* (1984), a finalist for the National Book Award. He has also published three novels, a biographical study of Martin Luther, and three textbooks on writing, and for years worked as an editor on the *Yale Edition of the Complete Works of St. Thomas More.*

James M. McPherson is George Henry Davis '86 Professor of American History at Princeton University. He is the author of several books on the Civil War era, and his *Battle Cry of Freedom: The Civil War Era* (1988) won the Pulitzer Prize for History.

Stephen Minta teaches at the University of York. He is the author of *Aguirre: The Re-creation of a Sixteenth-Century Journey Across South America* (1993) and is working on a book about Byron.

Mark E. Neely, Jr., is John Francis Bannon Professor of History and American Studies at St. Louis University. He is the author of *The Fate of Liberty: Abraham Lincoln and Civil Liberties* (1991).

Carla Rahn Phillips is Professor of History at the University of Minnesota. She specializes in early modern Europe, particularly Spain. Her publications include three books and numerous articles on Spain's economy, society, shipping, trade, and overseas exploration from 1500 to 1800, including *The Worlds of Christopher Columbus* (1992), co-authored with William D. Phillips, Jr.

William D. Phillips, Jr., is Professor of History at the University of Minnesota. He specializes in medieval and early modern Europe and Europe's connections with the wider world. He has written four books and numerous articles on Spain's economic and political development, slavery in the Mediterranean world, and European expansion overseas.

Richard Reeves is the author of *President Kennedy: Profile of Power* (1993).

Simon Schama is Old Dominion Foundation Professor of Humanities at Columbia University. His most recent book is *Landscape and Memory* (1995).

Arthur Schlesinger, Jr., has taught history at Harvard University and the City University of New York. He is the author of many books and has served as a film critic for *Show*, *Vogue*, and the *Saturday Review of Literature.*

Alan F. Segal is Professor of Religion at Barnard College, Columbia University. He is the author of *Rebecca's Children: Judaism and Christianity in the Roman World* (1986) and *Paul the Convert: The Apostolate and Apostasy of Saul the Pharisee* (1990).

Richard Slotkin is Olin Professor of American Studies at Wesleyan University. He is the author of an award-winning trilogy on the myth of the frontier in American history—*Regeneration Through Violence* (1973), *The Fatal Environment* (1985), and *Gunfighter Nation* (1992)—and two historical novels, *The Crater* (1980) and *The Return of Henry Starr* (1988).

Jonathan D. Spence teaches the history of modern China at Yale University. He is the author, most recently, of *God's Chinese Son: The Taiping Heavenly Kingdom of Hong Xiuquan* (1996).

Christine Stansell teaches American history and women's studies at Princeton University. She is the author of *City of Women: Sex and Class in New York, 1789–1860* (1986) and is writing a book about sex, radicalism, and the metropolitan intelligentsia in early twentieth-century America.

Gore Vidal is the author of many novels, including his multivolume fictional chronicle of American history: *Burr* (1973), *Lincoln* (1984), *1876* (1976), *Empire* (1987), *Hollywood* (1990), and *Washington, D.C.* (1967). His collections of essays include *United States: Essays, 1952–1992* (1993), winner of the National Book Award, and *Screening History* (1992).

Anthony F.C. Wallace is University Professor of Anthropology Emeritus at the University of Pennsylvania. His books on Native Americans include *The Death and Rebirth of the Seneca* (1970) and *The Long, Bitter Trail: Andrew Jackson and the Indians* (1993).

Geoffrey C. Ward is a biographer of Franklin Roosevelt and principal writer of *The Civil War* and other historical documentaries for PBS.

Richard White is Professor of History at the University of Washington. Among his published works are *The Middle Ground: Indians, Empires, and Republics in the Great Lakes Region, 1650–1815* (1991), winner of the Parkman Prize, and his most recent book, *The Organic Machine* (1995).

Tom Wicker, a retired columnist for the *New York Times*, is the author of a number of books and novels.

Sean Wilentz is Professor of History at Princeton University and an editor of *Dissent*. He is the author of *Chants Democratic: New York City and the Rise of the American Working Class, 1788–1850* (1984) and, with Paul E. Johnson, *The Kingdom of Matthias* (1994).

Bob Woodward, assistant managing editor of investigative news for the *Washington Post*, is the author of numerous best-selling books, including *The Choice* (1996).

Index

Credits

Text Permissions

Robert Darnton's essay on *Danton* was adapted from *The Kiss of Lamourette: Reflections in Cultural History* by Robert Darnton, reproduced with the permission of the author and W.W. Norton Co., Inc. Copyright © 1990 by Robert Darnton.

James McPherson's essay on *Glory* was adapted from an article originally published in *The New Republic*.

Stephen E. Ambrose's essay on *The Longest Day* was adapted from an article that appeared in the *Historical Journal of Film, Radio, and Television*, published by the Carfax Publishing Company, P.O. Box 2025, Dunnellon, Florida, 34430-2025.

Bob Woodward's essay on *Nixon* was adapted from an article originally published in the *Washington Post* © 1995. Reprinted with permission.

Photo Credits

The Bettmann Archive: 38, 40t, 44b, 45t, 46, 48t, 48b, 49t, 52, 54, 55t, 59, 60b, 64, 66, 67t, 69, 70t, 70b, 71b, 73, 74, 76, 78t, 82t, 85, 86t, 86b, 88, 92t, 95t, 98t, 104t, 104b, 106, 107m, 107b, 109, 110t, 111t, 116b, 117b, 120t, 121t, 122, 124b, 126, 128t, 129, 130, 131, 132b, 133t, 134, 142t, 143t, 145, 150, 154t, 155tl, 155tr, 156b, 161, 163t, 164, 166b, 167t, 170b, 172, 173, 174b, 175t, 175b, 176, 177t, 177b, 181, 183t, 191, 192t, 192b, 193t, 196, 197t, 199, 200b, 201t, 203, 204t, 204b, 205t, 207, 208b, 211, 217t, 218tl, 218b, 219, 220b, 221t, 221b, 223, 224t, 224b, 226, 227, 228t, 228b, 229t, 232, 233t, 233b, 234, 235, 236b, 237t, 239, 242, 243t, 244, 246b, 247t, 248, 249, 254b, 255t, 255b, 256, 257, 258b, 259t, 262t, 262b, 264, 265, 266t, 267l, 267m, 267r, 268, 270t, 270b, 271t, 271b, 272, 274b, 275t, 277, 278t, 279b, 280, 288, 289t, 290, 293t, 293bl, 293br, 294, 295, 297b

The Library of Congress: 53, 63, 65, 83t, 90b, 93t, 93b, 94b, 100, 112, 114, 136t, 136b, 137t, 142b, 146b, 147t, 148t, 162, 165, 166t, 169, 170t, 171t, 178t, 178b, 179t, 182, 184, 186, 187t, 188, 200t, 206, 209t, 212b, 213t, 215, 225t, 241, 245, 250, 251t, 252, 254t, 282

Michael Grant: 44t; Charles M. Pallardy: 61t; Jane Tyler: 75t; James Axtell: 78b, 79t, 80t, 80b, 81; Jack Hoffman: 91b; Abraham and Paula Rosman: 94t; Greg Dening: 98b, 99t, 101b; Marshall De Bruhl: 118; Pinkerton Security and Investigation Services: 144; Arizona Historical Society: 151t, 152; John Mack Faragher: 157b; Rockefeller Archive Center: 210; Sidney H. Radner Collection, Houdini Historical Center, Appleton, WI: 214; Museum of Modern Art: 240; Paul Boyer: 266b; Schomburg Center for Research in Black Culture: 275b, 278b, 279t

Still Credits

We appreciate the cooperation of all those companies that have licensed stills for our use. We are especially indebted to Catherine Craig of American Zoetrope, Marta Fischer of Cineplex Odeon, Anne Bernstein of Gaumont, Annie Auerbach and Scott Straw of MCA, Harris Dew of New Yorker Video, Linda Duchin of October Films, Larry McCallister of Paramount, Grahame Newman of Rank, Kathy Lendech of Turner Entertainment, Rebecca Herrera of Twentieth Century-Fox, and Robert Yampolsky.

American Zoetrope: *Apocalypse Now* (289b, 291)

Cineplex Odeon Corporation: *The Long Walk Home* (263b)

Gaumont: *The Passion of Joan of Arc* (55b), *Danton* (105b)

MCA: *Jurassic Park* (30), *Spartacus* (41b), *Anne of the Thousand Days* (67b), *The Scarlet Empress* (87b), *Law and Order* (160), *Freud* (171b), *All Quiet on the Western Front* (187b, 190mt), *The Front Page* (202b), *Shanghai Express* (209b), *Sullivan's Travels* (216b, 217b), *Apollo 13* (285b)
All MCA stills copyright © by Universal City Studios, Inc. Courtesy of MCA Publishing Rights, a Division of MCA Inc.

First Run Features: *Hester Street* (179b)

New Yorker Films: *Aguirre, the Wrath of God* (75b), *Rosa Luxemburg* (197b)

October Films: *Matewan* (205b)

Paramount: *The Ten Commandments* (37b), *1492: The Conquest of Paradise* (61b), *The Buccaneer* (111m, 111b), *The Molly Maguires* (143b), *Gunfight at the O.K. Corral* (157t), *Gallipoli* (183b), *Reds* (193b, 194), *Houdini* (213b), *Fat Man and Little Boy* (247b)
All Paramount stills courtesy of Paramount Pictures. Copyright © 1995 by Paramount Pictures. All Rights Reserved.

Rank: *Henry V* (49bl, 50)
Stills from the film *Henry V* by courtesy of The Rank Organisation Plc.

Samuel Goldwyn: *Henry V* (49br), *Black Robe* (79b)

Shochiku: *The Human Condition* (251b)

Turner: *Julius Caesar* (45b) © 1953 Turner Entertainment Co., *Mutiny on the Bounty* (99b, 101t, 103) © 1935 Turner Entertainment Co., *Mutiny on the Bounty* (102) © 1962 Turner Entertainment Co., *The Charge of the Light Brigade* (121b) © 1936 Turner Entertainment Co., *Gunga Din* (123) © 1939 RKO Pictures Inc. Used by Permission Turner Entertainment Co., *Abe Lincoln in Illinois* (125b) © 1940 RKO Pictures Inc. Used by Permission Turner Entertainment Co., *Gone with the Wind* (132t, 133b) © 1939 Turner Entertainment Co., *They Died with Their Boots On* (147b, 148b, 149) © 1941 Turner Entertainment Co., *Fort Apache* (151b) © 1948 RKO Pictures Inc. Used by Permission Turner Entertainment Co., *The Big Parade* (190t) © 1925 Turner Entertainment Co., *The Dawn Patrol* (190m), © 1938 Turner Entertainment Co., *The Fighting 69th* (190mb) © 1940 Turner Entertainment Co., *Tea and Sympathy* (258t, 259b) © 1956 Turner Entertainment Co.
All Rights Reserved.

Twentieth Century-Fox: *The Last of the Mohicans* (83b), *Drums along the Mohawk* (95b), *Young Mr. Lincoln* (125m), *My Darling Clementine* (155bl, 155br), *Frontier Marshall* (156t), *The Grapes of Wrath* (225b), *Tora! Tora! Tora!* (229b), *The Longest Day* (237b), *Patton* (243b)
All Twentieth Century-Fox stills courtesy of Twentieth Century-Fox. Copyright © 1995 by Twentieth Century-Fox. All Rights Reserved.